BRISTOL

TENNESSEE/VIRGINIA

A HISTORY — 1852-1900

V.N. (BUD) PHILLIPS

The Overmountain Press
JOHNSON CITY, TENNESSEE

ISBN 0-932807-63-1
Printed in the United States of America

2 3 4 5 6 7 8 9 0

PREFACE

Thirty-seven years ago there lived in Bristol several sons and daughters of her pioneer settlers and developers. Some of them had memories that went back to within a few years of the founding of the town, while others had clear recollections of what had been told them by their parents and other older persons. It was the author's privilege and good fortune to know and interview most of these venerable old citizens of Bristol. All of those interviewed shared freely their priceless knowledge; and several of them had old documents, letters, diaries, account books, newspapers and scrapbooks which they loaned or gave to the author. These also proved to be a rich source of local historical information. Within a few years those who had been interviewed had, one by one, passed away; and with them went a vast — indeed a staggering — amount of early Bristol history. But much of what they told will be shared with the reader in this book. This city owes a debt of gratitude to those sons and daughters of the pioneers, who so freely shared their memories of days that even then were long ago. For much of the data later uncovered by intensive documentary research could not have been woven together in logical order had it not been for the information which they supplied.

Through the passing years the author was fortunate to discover other very rich sources of heretofore unpublished local history. Then about three years ago a decision was made to write a new Bristol history. At that time an intensive research effort began which has included a careful study of numerous maps, deeds, tax and marriage records, minute books, census records, and old newspapers. Especially rewarding was a tedious and time-consuming search of tens of thousands of papers contained in a forty-eight year file (1852-1900) of Chancery and probate records. In all these sources the dead yet spoke. And it was pleasing to see the harmony that existed between that which was revealed by these official sources, and that which had been told by the sons and daughters of the pioneers. In many instances certain missing links were supplied by one source or the other. And along with this recent search of official records, the author again began interviewing older Bristol residents and was amply rewarded with much valuable information.

It is deeply regretted that a complete listing cannot here be made of the scores of local citizens, many of them now deceased, who contributed in some manner to the compiling of this history. However, special recognition is due several who were especially helpful in bringing this project to completion: Mrs. Ann Peake of the King College Library, who greatly aided in the production of the finished manuscript, and Dr. William J. Wade, head of the History Department of King College, who gave special assistance and encouragement as the original manuscript was written. Gratitude is also expressed to Sue Francisco and William A. Muller of the Bristol Public Library, who along with Oliver Taylor, Jr., of Tuscon, Arizona, David M. Cooper and Gary D. Rose of Bristol, Tennessee, did pre-publication reviews of the work. Mr. Rose did photography for inclusion in this volume, and Mr. Cooper did the art work and also supplied old photos. Others who shared old family photos include Mrs. Joseph A. Caldwell, Jr., Mrs. William Hepburn, Dr. and Mrs. Bennett Cowan, Miss Mary Preston Gray, Mrs. A. C. Crymble, Misses Nita and Will Baumgardner, Charles Henritze, Mrs. Frances Combs Thomas, Miss Mary Hedrick, Fred Worley, and Tim Buchanan. And through the years, priceless old photos have been given to the author by persons too numerous to mention. The author will ever be grateful to these and others who willingly and freely shared the treasures of their hands and the bounty of their knowledge that Bristol might have a comprehensive and exhaustive history.

The author holds a great amount of information that is not contained in this publication. Other works will follow. This is number one in a series of planned Bristol books. The readers may assist this effort by sharing pertinent information, papers, documents, or photos for possible future use. For the moment the reader is invited to take a slow journey through Bristol's formative years, to meet and know those pioneers who developed our city, and to relive many of those numerous events of which local history is made.

V. N. (Bud) Phillips
Pleasant Hill
214 Johnson Street
Bristol, Virginia 24201
703-466-6435
October 8, 1990

FOREWORD

It is appropriate to recall here the counsel of Sir Francis Bacon that "some books are to be tasted, others to be swallowed, and some few to be chewed and digested." Mr. V. N. Phillips' comprehensive study of the early history of Bristol belongs to the latter category; indeed, it is a volume to be read not merely once, but savored over again and again with increasing appreciation and delight.

This is in fact the most thorough and exhaustive study of Bristol ever attempted, and indeed, few metropolitan centers have been researched with such meticulous care and attention to detail. Mr. Phillips traces the origins of the municipality from its antecedent settlements and carries the story down to the closing decade of the nineteenth century. Through its pages the reader will find himself a guest in the spacious plantation home of Colonel James King, a pioneer settler whose iron furnace on Beaver Creek first brought industry to the valley. Then onto the scene strides Joseph Anderson, keen-eyed and intrepid businessman who foresaw commercial opportunities in the coming of the first railroad. And in company with Anderson the reader will trace the laying out of streets and lot lines across the rural meadow. With breathless anticipation we join a crowd of citizens in October 1856, waiting at the original depot as the headlights of the first train ever to enter Bristol broke through the darkness of the evening and signalled the coming of a new era and destiny. This is a book filled with vignettes of the past — a record of triumphs, of hopes, of perseverance in adversity, and of misfortune and disaster.

The work is the product of nearly four decades of interest and research on the part of the author. He has swept back the dust from countless court records and brought to life forgotten moments of our municipal past. He has interviewed and listened to the remembrances of scores of Bristolians, some of them now dead, who shared treasured family accounts that shed light on the lives of pioneers. Some have entrusted to his care precious family documents — diaries, journals, letters, and photographs — from which he has gleaned intimate glimpses of the town's first citizens. He has searched the surviving files of Bristol's newspapers, and from all of these sources Mr. Phillips has amassed a great trove of detail. His book is encyclopedic in coverage and will be read and consulted by all of its citizens interested in Bristol's origins. For genealogists and those whose family connections stretch back a century, his detailed cataloging of early inhabitants and families will be a boon to their research. Indeed, within its covers one will find the whole panorama of life in early Bristol — occupations, commercial ventures, housing, religion, schooling, social and cultural activities.

Bristol is fortunate that Mr. Phillips came into the life of this city two score years ago and that he decided to write its story while so many original sources and older witnesses remained, just waiting for the moment when his pen could breathe life and excitement into the dry bones of our past. The citizens of Bristol will be in his debt for many years to come.

William J. Wade
Chairman, History Department
King College
November 1990

PROLOGUE

Only four ancient and gnarled maples mark the site. They stand as silent sentinels over the place where stood "Holly Bend," the principal home and country seat of Col. James King. This is hallowed ground, not only for Bristol, but for all the great State of Tennessee. For here events transpired long ago that had a direct bearing on the founding of both Bristol and Memphis, now recognized as the gateways of the Volunteer State. Albeit nearly five hundred long miles separate them, they share a certain historic merging of fate here near the old maples.

Nearby, the peaceful Beaver Creek still winds its sinuous way among the low hills, sweeping around the great bend where once stood a beautiful holly grove. It quietly ripples over the rocks and ledges, sparkling under the effulgent sun, and graying under the somber skies of winter; its sights and sounds unchanged by the passing centuries. The days still steal gently over the high ridge beyond Cedar Creek and reluctantly fade beyond the knobs to the west, as regular and welcome as in those days when the old King homestead was in its full glory.

The opening of Sweet Potato Cave still yawns from a nearby hillside, but the abundant family provisions once stored there are no more. And that pathway beaten to it by the King servants has faded and become overgrown by the passing of nearly two hundred summers. The twin giant lilacs that once displayed their spring-heralding lavender boughs by the welcoming home gate have vanished. The shrill cry of the strutting, lordly peacocks has long faded from the dooryard. The blazing fire of the trailing red rose no longer brightens fresh spring days.

Old servants row, that stretched beyond the back gate and along which the wild plums grew, is no more. The neatly-constructed hewed log cabins, have long ago melted into the mother earth. Below the home gate and toward the spring, the sound of the joiner's hammer and saw no longer fills the carpenter's shop; it too has gone the way of all the buildings of the Holly Bend estate. A stark landfill now covers the free flowing, cool and refreshing spring and the stone house that long stood over it. The diverted water from Beaver Creek no longer races through the mill chute; the creak of the mammoth wheel is forever silent.

Back on the hill above the old home site where once great billowy clouds of pear and apple blossoms filled balmy spring breezes with spicy fragrance, now stand rows of granite and marble, mute testimony to the change that must come to all things, that indeed did come to Holly Bend. The great or-

Artist conception of the Col. James King home at Holly Bend on Beaver near Bristol, Tennessee. This drawing is based on a faded old photograph made about 1915. The original house was of log construction but was early covered with poplar siding. The house was demolished about 1925. Drawing by D.M. Cooper.

chard is gone, along with the many beehives that once were strewn beneath the waving flower- and fruit-laden boughs. The humming of the bees in a bountiful orchard, and the low tinkle of sheep bells that once sounded in the sloping pastures around it, have long given way to the noise of rushing traffic on a broad highway nearby.

The smoke of the iron furnaces no longer billows upwards, darkening the skies and drifting through the woods at the joining of Beaver and Steele Creeks above Holly Bend. The huge wafts of drifting smoke, like the clouds of two centuries ago, have floated upward and away, to be forever lost in the atmosphere. The once white-hot furnaces are forever cold.

And along with things material, the people are gone: old Master King, his beloved wife, his children, and his servants. They no longer stroll over the pleasant fields, nor linger under the fruited boughs of the orchard, nor tarry by the refreshing, swift waters of the Beaver. No longer are they drawn close around the blazing fireside as snow lies heavy on the East Tennessee hills. Neither can they rejoice to see spring gently spread its great mantle of flower-studded, soft green over the bleak yielding scenes of winter. They can no longer delight in the glad high days of fruitful summer, or again know the pleasant sadness of golden autumn. They were a long time passing, but one by one they were conquered by mortality. And Holly Bend went with them. But it was here; only the sad old maples mark the site.

The reader may go and see. From Bristol's State Street, turn southward on the Volunteer Parkway. Measure four and three-tenth miles. At that point, Phillipswood Drive turns squarely to the right. Enter and proceed 396 feet forward. The old King home was on the right, and just back of a yet remaining foundation of a later house.

These old maples standing by Phillipswood Drive, Bristol, Tennessee, mark the site of the Col. James King home, Holly Bend on Beaver.

TABLE OF CONTENTS

The only known likeness of Col. James King, taken from original portrait, which is said to have been painted by an itinerant artist named Jubal LeBlanc.

Chapter One
BEFORE BRISTOL

COLONEL JAMES KING

Col. James King, who played a vital role in the pre-development of Bristol and whose grandson-in-law founded it, was born October 12, 1752, in Londonderry, Ireland. Shortly before his voyage to America, he lived briefly in London, England. At the age of seventeen (1769) he came to the Colony of Virginia, living first near the eastern shore, but then moving inland to present Montgomery County. Soon after his arrival there he became an assistant to Capt. Daniel Smith and journeyed with him to southwestern Virginia where the two, along with others, surveyed several thousand acres of land. At that time (1773) the area was mostly wilderness.

After returning to Montgomery County, he took up residence in the Capt. Smith home. Largely because of the glowing recommendation of his host, he soon was continually engaged in surveying; and his reputation increased with the passing years.

By the time of the outbreak of the American Revolution, his love for his chosen land and its people had become so great that he readily took up arms in defense of the Colonies. He served as an Ensign and Lieutenant under General Daniel Morgan and later became a Colonel. For a time he was with the legendary General Francis Marion.

His faithful service to the Colonies was not without its suffering. He was captured at Guilford's Courthouse and imprisoned on a ship. Conditions during that imprisonment were so miserable that he was always reluctant to talk of the ordeal. He was wounded in the right leg at Eutaw Springs, the effects of which intermittently plagued him for the rest of his life.

Col. King had a fiery and severely independent disposition. Once during the Revolution, he resigned his rank rather than deliver to the quartermaster a fine mare he had taken from a British officer. Later he rejoined and was privileged to witness the surrender at Yorktown, an event he delighted to describe in vivid detail to those who shared his fireside at Holly Bend.

Near the Smith residence, where young James King boarded after his settlement in Montgomery County, Virginia, lived Thomas Goodson. Mr. Goodson and his wife, Sarah Riddle (Reddell) Goodson, had a large family, the oldest daughter of which was the beautiful and vivacious Ann. She was thirteen when King arrived in the neighborhood, but ere long the love stricken emigrant sought to marry her (such young brides were not uncommon in those days). However, the Goodsons would not consent to the match. After a few years the courtship resumed and eventually ended in an engagement, to which the parents agreed. But those were trying times and young James King had to be away for long stretches of time. Finally returning, eager for the planned wedding, he was devastated to learn that Ann had eloped with a neighbor lad, only a few days before. According to tales handed down through the Goodson and King families, King went into deep mourning and depression, ''as though for one dead.'' But there were always those to comfort the mourning. Shortly Ann's younger sister Sarah, then seventeen, voluntarily stepped forward and offered herself in the place of her sister. From what is said, no modern anti-depressant could have had such a quick and beneficial effect on the emotional condition of the jilted lover. In the glory of the golden autumn of 1782, James King and Sarah Goodson were married, standing under a heavily laden apple tree in the corner of the Goodson yard. This wedding, on October 15, 1782, was just three days past the groom's thirtieth birthday.

The young couple first settled on a portion of the Goodson farm. But apparently young James King kept remembering the Western Country, where he had surveyed several years before. No doubt it seemed to offer great opportunities for the industrious settler, and during those closing years of the eighteenth century, he began to buy up land on Beaver Creek, below present Bristol and circling out from where the old maples now stand. In time, through purchase and government grants, he would acquire several thousand acres, though not all of it was contiguous with his homeplace on Beaver.

He chose for a homesite a picturesque location near a pronounced bend of Beaver Creek. On the little bottom immediately to the right of the bend was a thick grove of holly trees; thus came the name, Holly Bend, which was finally applied to his grand country seat. Evidently someone had occupied the land before him, for it is known that the great apple and pear orchard was already in production at the time of the purchase. And there is strong indication that the ample, two-story log house was also standing at that time. It was to this Holly Bend location that Col. King moved his wife, shortly after their marriage.

SOJOURN IN FT. LOUDON AND KNOXVILLE

But Col. King did not long enjoy the solitude and peacefulness of the Holly Bend estate. In 1792 George Washington appointed him to command Ft.

Loudon, now Knoxville, Tennessee. He moved his family there and spent a productive period while in the service of his government. He helped to plan and survey Knoxville and profitably engaged in its early development. He donated the lot on which the First Methodist Church later stood. It is said that his daughter Sarah was the first child to be born in Knoxville. One of his greatest services was as a commissioner in the negotiation of the Treaty of Holston. Within a few years he was back on the Holly Bend estate below Bristol.

THE IRON WORKS

Before his move to Knoxville, Col. King had recognized the possibility of profitable iron production in the area where he had settled. He chose a site at the mouth of Steele Creek, some distance above his Holly Bend homestead, for the erection of his iron works. These iron works were among the first in Tennessee. To aid in this production, he bought a tract of land near present Kingsport, on which there was a rich bank of iron ore. Modern Orebank owes its name to this operation. In time he established a nailery at the boatyard of Christianville, now known as old Kingsport.

It is apparent that the iron works were being set up even as Col. King sojourned in Knoxville. However, the date of the beginning of actual production has not been precisely established. From very recent documentation the date was probably about 1794, some ten years later than what has long been believed. In time King set up another iron works in Shady Valley. He built a cabin near these works, in which he often spent several weeks at a time, overseeing the operation of the furnaces. The same was true of Orebank near Kingsport.

King's iron products were principally shipped by boat from what is now old Kingsport, Tennessee. A large caravan of heavy wagons was maintained for hauling these products from the furnaces to the shipping point. During the area farmers' off season (between laying by crops and harvest), some of them made extra money by hauling for Col. King. Only one name of that group is known. A certain John Worley left Holly Bend with a load of pig iron, July 31, 1816. Big Richard, King's personal body servant, remembered that on hauling days these neighboring farmers arrived long before daylight and were served a very ample breakfast of boiled beef or pork, with hot bread and butter. Leftovers from the breakfast were sent with the men for their lunch. The iron products, thus delivered to the boat dock some twenty-five miles from Holly Bend, were shipped all over the south. It is said that some of the cannonballs used in the War of 1812 were made at the mouth of Steele Creek above the King home.

By 1800 the master of Holly Bend was being called the "Iron King," whereas his cousin William King of Abingdon, who operated the salt works at Saltville, Virginia, was known as the "Salt King." On November 11, 1802, the Salt King and the Iron King bought lots in Christianville, or what is now known as old Kingsport. It has long been assumed that these lots, bought from Robert Christian, were to be used as sites for cottages in which the Kings and their workmen might shelter when seeing to shipping matters.

The iron works brought much wealth to Col. James King, as did other enterprises set up on the Holly Bend estate. One such enterprise was a furniture shop, presided over by a slave who had been brought from a tidewater plantation of eastern Virginia. The carpenter's shop, as it was known, stood between the main house and Beaver Creek, just above the large spring that long provided water for the plantation. In back of this shop was a room where coffins were stored. (Col. King made most of the coffins for the surrounding area.) This room was always locked, though it might just as well have been unlocked. For the old master had, for reasons that will shortly be revealed, made sure that the coffin room was haunted. At night there had been strange sounds — low moanings, screams, and heavy knockings. Not a servant would go near this coffin room at night, and they were also a bit leery of it in broad daylight. Even the chief furniture craftsman would not work in the shop alone, and all water had to be carried from the nearby spring before nightfall.

There were two coffins in this room that were of extra fine craftsmanship. Both were made of walnut and were said to be for Col. King and his wife. Actually, they were storage bins for the King gold. Thus, when a neighbor died, the master himself went into the coffin room to make the selection, making sure that the money bins were not touched.

It is apparent that James King served as banker for this area, at least in providing loans. But when a loan was granted, the grantee was always told that it would take a while for the money to be in hand and to return in a certain number days. Some dark night before the return of the grantee, Col. King would slip into the coffin room and count out the amount to be loaned. And if anyone saw the flickering candlelight while this was being done, it only added to the ghosty atmosphere of the feared room.

One winter day a young lawyer, an acquaintance of Col. King, arrived at Holly Bend. That night by a roaring fireside, the young gentleman told his host that he and some friends desired to buy a tract of promising land at the Chickasaw Bluffs along the Mississippi River in western Tennessee. The young friend had not the funds to join in the purchase and had come to King seeking a loan. Before his departure on the following morning, he had been promised a loan of twenty-five hundred dollars but was told that he would have to return in one week for it.

Again the ghosty light flickered in the coffin room, so feebly symbolic of that great galaxy of light that would someday light up Tennessee's western gateway. For the young man to whom the money was loaned was Andrew Jackson, who along with others made the purchase of Chickasaw Bluffs and founded the City of Memphis.

THE GREAT HOUSE THAT NEVER WAS

Even though Col. King suffered some severe reverses in those early years, even the loss of some of his real estate, his progress in acquiring wealth seems to have never faltered. By the early 1800s the coffins were filled to the brim with money. In those days he and his beloved Sarah began to think of a great house for the Holly Bend plantation. The substantial old log house, by then sided over and enlarged, had served long and well; but the time had come when a man of his standing seemed to need a better display of wealth. Not long before, he had served a term or two in the General Assembly of Tennessee and had been impressed by several grand country seats he had seen on his rides to and from the capital.

Up at the edge of the orchard was an ideal spot for his mansion. It was a commanding position with a magnificent view of the grand sweep of the Holly Bend of Beaver Creek. The site is said to have been a favorite resting place for Mrs. King, who often went there to sit under the fine apple trees and to "reflect on the beauty of the Holly Bend estate that peacefully spread around her."

By mid-December 1806, suitable clay had been found, and a brick kiln had been put into operation in anticipation of the construction of the new mansion. It was then that Col. King decided to go to Abingdon, Virginia, to study the house that had been erected there by his cousin William King. (This house still stands at 106 Court Street, Abingdon, Virginia.) He had planned to spend several days with the "Salt King," and to make drawings of the new house to use as a model in building his own.

A few nights before his departure for Abingdon, his wife began having a strange, recurring dream. It seems that she was again sitting under a large apple tree that stood on the proposed site of the mansion. But try as she would she could never arise to come down to her home again. There was a row of birds on a limb of the tree, and during the dream one would arise and fly away. Thus the number of birds decreased with each nightly occurrence of the dream. The Kings thought little of it, except the strangeness of its nightly recurrence. But an old slave cook, who was somewhat of a mystic and reputed interpreter of dreams, heard the dream and became greatly nervous and worried. She began the countdown on the birds. When the day came for the Colonel's departure, she ventured to beg him not to go, saying that he would have to return before his planned stay in Abingdon had ended. Unheeding this strange plea, Col. King rode away, doubtless with visions of his grand mansion before him.

On the morning of Saturday, December 20, 1806, Mrs. King came to breakfast cheerfully telling that perhaps her troubling dream would now cease since the last bird had flown away the night before. But this did not ease the cook's prolonged anxiety. At the news she became so nervous that she could hardly finish serving the morning meal and would not leave the side of her mistress except for short intervals. At mid-morning a neighbor, Mrs. O'Brian, came in for a visit. She and Mrs. King sat by the fireside, where the latter began talking of the great house that was soon to grace the orchard hill. It was noted that Mrs. King was especially cheerful and optimistic that day. In the midst of that conversation she suddenly leaned forward and fell from her chair dead. The last bird had flown away — her last day was gone. Sarah Goodson King was forty-one years old.

A rider was quickly sent for Col. King. Upon his arrival the old cook told him that the flying birds had been the numbering of days for the deceased, and that the fact that Mrs. King could not move from under the apple tree meant that she was to be buried there. And Mrs. King was buried under the great spreading apple tree, marking the beginning of what is now known as the Ordway Cemetery, though it was first called the Orchard Hill Cemetery, later King, then Trigg, and then took its present name around 1900.

The brick kiln was cooled, the seasoning timbers were used for other purposes, and Col. King never mentioned the proposed house again. In less than a year the old master of Holly Bend took a new bride. She was young Miss Margaret Richie, a cousin of some degree. It was not known where she lived, but according to the daughter of Big Richard, King made only one "courting trip" before he brought her to Holly Bend. She bore him three children, two of whom were twins. All died in infancy and were buried in the Orchard Hill (now Ordway) Cemetery, but no markers now exist. It is likely that the children were buried near the first Mrs. King. This second wife was living as late as November 23, 1827, but there is no definite information about her after that date. Big Richard's daughter thought that this Mrs. King remarried and "moved way off somewhere."

FINAL YEARS AT HOLLY BEND

After his second marriage Col. King was privileged to spend eighteen more years at his beloved Holly bend. For most of those years he showed a youthful vigor that was amazing for one his age. Big Richard had fond memories of how the old master worked right along side his slaves in the homeplace fields and in the operation of the iron works. He remembered that after apple harvest there would be a cider grinding, and then a night and day of "jollification" during which King would spread an extra big feast for all. Occasionally there was such a celebration when there was "burn-off" at the iron works. Even up to within five years of his death, the "Iron King" would take Big Richard and go down river with a shipment of iron. The latter recalled the uncertainties of the sometimes treacherous river on the way down, and the toil of the overland journey home. The old master delighted in these trips, in spite of the hardships, and was very grieved when the time came that he could no longer participate in them.

Two or three years before his death, Col. King became virtually unable to walk due to chronic gout. However, his interest continued unabated in the operation of his plantation. Every work day morning all hands had to gather at the doorway of his home, where orders were given for the various tasks. Occasionally several slaves were sent to nearby hills to cut charcoal wood for the iron furnaces. At such times a fine telescope that he had bought in London, England, came in handy. From the home yard he could watch the woodcutting activities. If a slave loafed on the job, the Colonel would surprise the offender by telling him exactly the time of the offense and just how committed. This supposed "divine" power put a fear in the servants that all but ended these unscheduled rest periods.

A few years before his death, Col. James King suddenly became religious. He began attending church services at the newly organized Presbyterian Church at Paperville, Tennessee. He may have been a member there. It is known that he contributed heavily to the building of the church, including numerous wagon loads of brick that had been made for his proposed mansion. Big Richard remembered that when there was to be a Sunday meeting at the new church, the household would be aroused early. There would be breakfast by candlelight, and then all, including the servants, would set off for Paperville, some six or so miles away.

During the last year of Col. King's life his chronic gout became almost unbearable. He learned of a doctor at Greeneville, Tennessee, who had a wide reputation for treating such cases. It was determined that he should go and spend some time there, hoping for at least a measure of relief. Big Richard recalled that three feather beds were placed, one atop the other, in a wagon or carriage for this trip. By that time this personal body slave, was "serving as legs" for his master as he put it — which meant that Big Richard carried Col. King whenever King needed to be moved.

At Greeneville, King and Big Richard were boarded by the doctor while treatment was given. Finally there was enough relief so that the homeward journey was started. The Holston River was crossed at what is now Bluff City, and very shortly beyond it (within sight) the old Colonel suddenly complained that the gout had moved to his chest. (No doubt it was a heart attack.) At the master's request, Big Richard stopped the carriage, lifted the sick man from it, and laid him in the shade of a huge beech tree that stood near the roadside. In moments the illustrious old master of Holly Bend was dead. The day was August 17, 1825. The ten-year-old daughter of Big Richard remembered her father's arrival at the front gate later that day, bearing his dead master home. In delight she ran out, hoping to be first to greet and welcome "old master King." She vividly remembered the shock that followed and the prolonged "mourning and wailing" that swept through the household.

The next morning Col. James King was buried beside his first wife underneath the big apple tree. It was long his request that his slaves be buried around him. The custom of the time was that there should be a separate cemetery for slaves. However, Col. King reasoned that they had worked with him in life and should rest with him in death. Several slaves were buried near him, but their graves are unmarked and' lost.

Though Holly Bend and the iron works continued to operate for a few years, under management of the two King sons, the glory had departed with the death of the old Colonel. On April 17, 1833, a large portion of the old estate, including the iron works, was sold to George Bushong. Mr. Bushong continued operation of the furnaces for several years.

THE KING CHILDREN

Only three children were reared to maturity by Col. James and Sarah Goodson King. The only daughter, Sarah King, who is connected historically with Knoxville, Tennessee, as noted earlier, married William Williams and lived on a large plantation near that city. In later years she donated this plantation to further the educational endeavors of the Methodist Church.

William King, one of the two sons, never married. He commanded a company in the Creek War, at the Battle of Horse Shoe Bend, and it is said that his gun was the first over the Indian breastworks there. This gun remained in the family for years, and was last known to have been owned by Col. Sam L. King of Bristol, Tennessee, a great nephew. Back home in Sullivan County, Tennessee, he became a prominent and beloved citizen. He is buried near his father in what is now the Ordway Cemetery, but his grave is unmarked.

Rev. James King, the second son, played a foundation role in the history of Bristol, as detailed in the following chapter.

William King, son of Col. James King and brother of Rev. James King. He helped drive the coach that transported Andrew Jackson to Washington for the latter's presidential inauguration.

Bibliography - Chapter One

Anderson, Melinda King. As told to Mrs. Herman Blackley. 1890-1908.

Anderson, Rhea. Interviews with Clora Eldridge. 1920.

Crymble, A. Carter. Notes and documents. Kingsport, Tennessee.

Eldridge, Clora, daughter of the body servant of Col. James King. Interviews with Hattie King Taylor. 1918.

Goodson, Samuel E. Information given to Joseph W. Owen, and preserved by Owen's daughter, Miss Revely Owen.

Jonesboro, Tennessee. Chancery Records.

Preston, Thomas W. Notes.

Sullivan County, Blountville, Tennessee. Deed Records.

Taylor, Hattie King. *The Iron King*. Unpublished manuscript. 1920.

Taylor, Oliver. *Historic Sullivan*. 1909.

Rev. James King who established Mountain View plantation on the site of present Bristol.

Chapter Two
JAMES KING AND THE SAPLING GROVE PURCHASE

James King, one of the two sons of Col. James King, was born at Holly Bend, February 11, 1791. He always signed as James King, Senior, which has caused some confusion among researchers. By the time he was twenty years old, he had become known for his marked hedonism — very much given to participation in the frolics of the area and often delighted in the golden cup. By that age he had engaged in a tempestuous romance with the beautiful Katie O'Brian, a neighbor girl, who persisted in her refusal of his proposals of marriage, as she did those of King's first cousin, Samuel E. Goodson.

WHIRLWIND ROMANCE LEADS TO SAPLING GROVE PURCHASE
In the golden autumn of 1811, young James King, still smarting from Katie O'Brian's refusal, delivered his sister, Sarah King, to a Moravian school at Salem, North Carolina. While there he met Miss Mourning Micajah Watkins, then sixteen years old. This fair young lady was the daughter of Mrs. Sarah Williams Watkins, widow of Micajah Watkins, of Halifax County, Virginia. The young lady's father had died just before her birth. The widow, then in mourning, gave her the unusual name of Mourning Micajah. Through the Williams side of the family, young Miss Watkins was related to George Washington. It may be mentioned here that the widow Watkins later married Joseph Chalmers and became the mother of a rather prominent and distinguished family of that name.

The pretty and sweet natured Mourning Micajah Watkins instantly captured the heart of young James King. Twenty-four hours had not passed until he proposed marriage to her. She evidently was much infatuated with the dashing and charming young man from the Western Country, for she immediately accepted his proposal. But Prince Charming then had to deal with her guardian. Instead of returning to Tennessee, James King and those with him journeyed on northeastward to Halifax County, Virginia. There he received a rather cool reception from stern old Henry Coleman, the young lady's guardian. Mr. Coleman was not greatly impressed with the young upstart from what he considered the backwoods, and doubtless thought him to be far from equal, socially and financially, to the young Watkins heiress. Of course, he did not know that the young man before him had been a brilliant student of Greeneville College in Tennessee, nor that his family wealth was great, nor that the Kings were accepted in the best circles of their area. Finally old Mr. Coleman laid down the stipulation that if King could prove that his estate equaled the girl's dowry, then permission to marry would be granted. He then dismissed young Mr. King, doubtless thinking that he would never see him again.

Somewhat frustrated but with strong determination, the ardent suitor quickly returned to Holly Bend on Beaver and apprised his father of the situation. The Irish in old Col. King flared. How dare anyone question his wealth and social standing. It is said that he spent weeks in assembling documents that would prove his affluence. These included letters showing that negotiations were underway with Isaac Shelby of Kentucky for the purchase of a large tract of land that would be used as a plantation for the young James King.

He had the family coach polished up and loaded a keg of gold in its baggage compartment (he would somehow make sure that Coleman saw this). With his coach and four matched horses, four outriders and uniformed attendants, and the striking Big Richard, his personal body servant, he was off during a cold late January for the Watkins estate in Halifax County, Virginia. In time, with a trumpeter heralding his coming, he arrived with a grand flourish before the Watkins gate.

Evidently, old Henry Coleman was favorably impressed, for on February 12, 1812, one day after James King's twenty-first birthday, he was married to his beloved Mourning Micajah Watkins, whom he, to the end, always addressed as "sweet Mourning." Soon thereafter the bride and groom rode the grand coach back to Holly Bend in Sullivan County, Tennessee. It is said that the young bride never looked back and that she never went back to the old Virginia plantation. For the first five years of their marriage, the happy young couple lived with Col. King at Holly Bend. Their first two children, Sarah and James, were born there.

PURCHASE OF THE SITE OF BRISTOL

Finally, in the late summer of 1814, negotiations with Isaac Shelby for the site on which the future Bristol would stand were successfully concluded. Shelby required that the money ($10,000.00) be in hard coin, and that it be delivered to him at his home in Frankfort, Kentucky. Again the candle flickered in the coffin room as old Col. King counted out and sacked the gold. Look well to that old walnut coffin: from it came the money that played such a vital role in the pre-history of both Bristol and Memphis — so far apart they are — but they both arose from the same coffin at Holly Bend on Beaver.

In early September 1814 a strange party left Holly Bend for the long trip to Frankfort: three horses and three men, old Col. King, young James King, and Big Richard, the trusted body servant. All were dressed in the worst of rags, several days growth of beard on their faces, and very worn shoes on their feet. They carried old hunting rifles (but you may be sure that dependable pistols were at hand also). There were two or three very heavy sacks, double sacks they were, with the outer one being very aged and torn, with grain or straw showing in the openings. This was one time Col. King did not wish to parade his wealth before the public. Slipping away hours before daylight, they were well beyond the area of recognition before sunrise. Those whom they met upon the road must have felt pity for the poor devils heading into the wilds of Kentucky, apparently so ill-prepared for making a new settlement there.

The trip was made in safety, and on September 26, 1814, Shelby made his deed to James King, Jr. (though he called himself Senior), for sixteen hundred acres of land lying mostly in Sullivan County, Tennessee, but with several acres being in Washington County, Virginia. This deed was made before Achilles Sneed, Clerk of the Kentucky Court of Appeals. The next day (September 27) Susanna Shelby, wife of Isaac, was examined privately before John Boyle, Chief Justice of Kentucky, and Presiding Judge of the Kentucky Court of Appeals. She swore that she entered willingly into the execution of the deed.

The horses that had borne the heavy sacks from Holly Bend to Frankfort were strained beyond use. Consequently Col. King had to purchase three fine horses for the return trip. And the party rode home more in keeping with their station in life, rather than as the road bums they had pretended to be on the outward journey. Big Richard remembered that they were royally entertained in various fine homes along the way, whereas going out they had often begged the privilege of camping in barns, when penniless travelers they were supposed to be! About six weeks after the deed was made in Frankfort, Kentucky, it was ordered recorded in Washington County, Virginia, by David Campbell, then Clerk of the Court, but who would later serve the Commonwealth as Governor.

CHOOSING A HOME SITE

The land then owned by the young James King contained the old wilderness refuge and trading post known as Ft. Shelby. The old fort had stood in an area roughly bounded by present Locust, Rose, Sixth and Seventh Streets. The gates to this fort would now be approximately at the southeast intersection of Seventh and Locust, and the old fort spring still seeps into the basement of the house on the northeast corner of Rose and Seventh.

When young King bought the tract, the old fort was in shambles, though the old Shelby home that had stood within it was in a rather solid condition. Around this fort had once spread out great cultivated fields. Where downtown Bristol is now located was known as the Beaver Dam bottom and was a choice field. Other fields were on Beaver west of the fort and on the low uplands along present Holston Avenue. In these fields Shelby had grown produce to feed the prodigious number of travelers who stopped at his frontier fort. But the plantation had been deserted for years and was fast reverting to nature. The fields were overgrown with brush and flourishing saplings, and little remained of the old rail fencing.

The first thing to be done by the new master of the place was to set the slaves to clearing the land and rebuilding the fences. According to Big Richard, only a small crop was raised the first year (1815), but by the next year the plantation was in near full production.

A GREAT HOUSE FOR HIS BRIDE

From the first, James King had planned a great house for this high-born wife. He first chose the site of the old Ft. Shelby for this planned mansion. One may venture that he would have built on the highest prominence of that location which would have been along Seventh between Locust and Cherry Streets (site of the Weaver Funeral Home). It would have been a fine site with sweeping views in all directions.

But old General Shelby had started a slave cemetery back of his fort walls, on what is now the southeast corner of Rose and Seventh Streets. Understandably, young Mourning Micajah Watkins King had a pronounced aversion to having a cemetery in the back or side yard, so this choice site was not used. Instead, a site was selected across Beaver and in Washington County, Virginia. This was on what was later Lancaster's Hill and later the area became known as Solar Hill. This too was a prime location with fine views, especially that of the Iron and Holston Mountains to the south. Indeed, for this reason the King estate took the name Mountain View.

Before work began on the great house, a fair sized log building was erected to house the King slaves who were to labor on the project. Later this building, which stood just to the southeast of the main house, was bricked over and a second story was added. The lower part was long used as an outside kitchen, while the upper room served as the overseer's quarters. This building stood until 1881 when John J. Lancaster erected the greater part of the present house which contained an inside kitchen. The presence of this early log building has given rise to a legend that a log room exists within the present

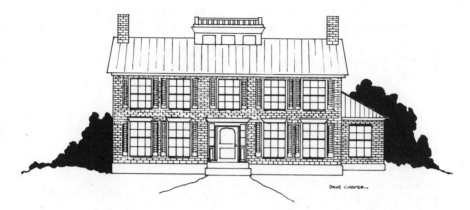

Artist conception of Mountain View, the home built by Rev. James King in 1816-1817. This grand home was erected on what was later called Lancaster's Hill and then Solar Hill. It overlooked what is now downtown Bristol. It later served as the first home of Sullins College. This sketch is based on a detailed description by Hattie King Taylor, a granddaughter of the builder. Sketch by D.M. Cooper.

house. Untrue as it is, from time to time it continues to be told and published.

The grand house that was built at what is now 54 King Street was of solid brick construction. The bricks were made in Flat Hollow near the present intersection of Oak View and Buckner Streets, where years later would be made the brick of which the first house in the new Town of Bristol was constructed. King's mansion was of the Federal style, a large two-over-two with broad central halls. The walls were straight-lined and austere, broken only by five windows across the long sides upstairs, and four downstairs with large central doorways of identical design in front and back. (The long sides faced east and west.) There were no porches. Huge built-in-the-wall chimneys stood at the north and south ends of the house, and a massive fireplace was located at the south end of the detached kitchen. There was a narrow, non-ornamental cornice under the roof line.

There were heavy shutters at each window, and it may be said that these were about the only ornamentation of the entire east and west (long) sides of the house. The grandeur of the King house was not in embellishment, but was rather in its enormity. Mrs. Hattie King Taylor, a granddaughter of James King, who as a young woman had been often in the house (then occupied by the T. C. Lancaster family), wrote that all rooms were large with high ceilings, and that the central halls were spacious. The latter were used more as rooms than as halls, especially downstairs where the space served as a reception area. The stairway featured some scroll work and a polished cherry rail. In the south parlor was a very beautiful mantel, made, it is said, by an Abingdon, Virginia, craftsman. This mantel and stairway seemed to have been the most elegant features in an otherwise plain interior. The fine mantel was saved and placed in the music room of the present house.

Mrs. Taylor also told that originally the house fronted westward toward the old King iron works road that wound up Baker's Creek (later called Little Creek) to join the Island Road back of the Susong farm. The east side later became the front when the stage road passed within a few yards of what had been the back (east) door. Soon after this change, a one-over-one brick guest house was erected in the northeast corner of the yard. A broad stone walkway leading from the front gate to the east door passed between this guest house and the detached kitchen. Around 1840 a lean-to room was added to the north end of the house to provide space for the Sapling Grove post office.

In the center of the long roof line was a crow's nest or widow's walk which was reached by a stairway from the attic. It is said that James King often used this high perch to keep watch on his servants laboring in his distant fields. He had inherited his father's fine telescope, and with it could tell who was laboring and who was loafing. The great width of the house and steep pitch of the roof had created an enormous attic space. Soon after the house was built, this space was made into a large ballroom. The Kings' annual Christmas ball there was a greatly anticipated event that drew folks from as far away as Abingdon and Jonesboro. Later the balls became a matter of religious conscience to the Rev. King and were discontinued.

Before this great hilltop setup stretched the well-cultivated fields and meadows of the plantation. There were fine bottoms along Beaver, a sheep pasture encircled the site of old Ft. Shelby, picturesque upland pastures stretched along present Holston Avenue, and open fields reached into the northern portion of what is now the Fairmount section of Bristol, Tennessee. One noted cornfield lay along Fifth Street, across Alabama and Edgemont, and over to Sixth Street. In time the area where is now located most of downtown Bristol was made into a lush meadow, where grazed King's prize herd of shorthorn cattle. Many referred to the area as King's Meadows. All in all it was a grand setup, of which even the discriminating old Henry Coleman (Mrs. King's former guardian) could have been proud.

Perhaps before going further it would be well to pursue the course of the King mansion to its final fate. In June 1853, the Rev. King and his family left the mansion and moved to a new home he had built on Beaver Creek near the present Melrose Street Bridge. The old house stood vacant for awhile, but was later rented to Drs. Hammer and Willoughby who kept a boarding house there. On July 8, 1858, King sold the house and sixty-five acres of surrounding land to David F. Scranton and Joseph Johnston then of Savannah, Georgia, for $16,325.00. On April 21, 1860, Johnston sold the mansion and its large four-acre yard to Valentine Keebler, early Bristol merchant, for $8,000.00. On September 14, 1864, Keebler sold the estate to Thomas C. Lancaster, local hotel keeper for $20,000.00 (highly inflated Confederate money). Mr. Lancaster died in September 1875. His widow, Julia A. Lancaster, and two maiden daughters continued to occupy the former King home. In 1881, John J. Lancaster, son of Thomas C. and Julia Lancaster, a wealthy banker of New York City, contracted with local builder John M. Crowell to erect a new brick house on the site, apparently as a gift for his mother and sisters. Newspaper items of the period tell of the construction of this new house and call it "highly ornamental to the town."

On November 18, 1881, Julia A. Lancaster (widow of Thomas C.) deeded the four acre tract that included the newly constructed house to her son, John J. Lancaster. However, this deed was later voided by certain court action.

The house that John J. Lancaster erected in 1881 certainly included the two-over-two section that then fronted on Cumberland Street, and now comprises the northern portion of the present Mitchell home. It is fortunate that a diagram of Lancaster's building, made soon after its construction, still exists, and shows the north portion of the present Mitchell home with its bay windows at the east and west ends. Court testimony given on December 19, 1890, reveals that the cost of Lancaster's house was around six thousand dollars.

It appears that John J. Lancaster left the old King house standing as a broad and long ell to his new building. It is possible that he may have allowed some outbuildings to remain on the lot.

On April 15, 1891, William F. Rhea, a local lawyer, bought the four-acre tract containing the buildings as heretofore described. He soon sold the property, with lot size considerably reduced, to H.E. McCoy, a local banker, for $3,800.00. In December 1891, Mr. Rhea made known his plans to build his mansion in what had been Lancaster's front yard, and nearer to Cumberland Street. Thus it was necessary for McCoy to plan a new entryway to his home, an entrance facing King Street. In December 1891, he employed Beane, Hoffmeister, and Arnold, architects with offices in Bristol, Tennessee, to plan a new addition to the existing structure. The McCoy project included renovation of the Lancaster portion of the house. It also appears that he had the south portion of the old King house demolished, along with the outbuildings.

McCoy's new addition included the front porch, hall, music room, upstairs hall, bedroom and bath of the present house. Mr. McCoy specified in his plans that the fine mantel from the demolished south parlor of the King house was to be placed in what is now the music room of the present Mitchell house, and that the mantel from the north parlor (then the kitchen) was to be placed in his upstairs bedroom.

H. E. McCoy died a few years after his addition was completed. On February 24, 1899, the house was bought by Joseph D. Mitchell. Mr. Mitchell had rented a room (present dining room) from Mrs. Lancaster when he arrived in Bristol in 1882. It is said that when spending his first night there he vowed that he would someday own the house. In 1903 he added the kitchen wing, thus bringing the building to its present form.

But, getting back to those early days on Mountain View plantation, it may be said that increasing prosperity marked them. The young master of Mountain View wisely developed and expanded his abundant resources. His fertile agricultural setup was well tended and managed, quickly becoming a paragon of efficiency and productivity, the envy of his scattered neighbors.

On March 1, 1818, Cyrus King became the first of the fast growing family to be born on the Mountain View estate. That same year James King went to Raleigh, North Carolina, and brought his newly widowed sister Sarah King Williams to live for a time in his home. She had married William Williams in April 1808, and the couple had lived for awhile on a farm at Strawberry Plains, Tennessee. Mr. Williams developed tuberculosis, and the couple began to travel for his health. He died in Raleigh in the summer of 1818. Mrs. Williams lived for a few years with her brother but later returned to Strawberry Plains.

At 10:00 A.M. on June 27, 1821, there was born at Mountain View a chubby little girl baby, who was named Melinda Williams King, the Williams being for her Aunt Sarah who then lived in the home. This girl would play a major role in the future events leading toward the establishment of present Bristol. And during those years events were occurring in the life of James King that would have a profound influence on the course of his future years. He was converted to the Christian faith and became a charter member of the Blountville Presbyterian Church. Later he would become a member at nearby Paperville. Then on Sunday, April 23, 1831, he was ordained to the gospel ministry. This ordination took place at the Presbyterian Church in Blountville, Tennessee. According to information handed down through the family, a heavy snow fell late that day, "making the journey back to Mountain View rather difficult." James King was widely known for his impartial hospitality. His home was always open to the humble and the great. Being within sight of and short distance from the Great Road, there was a near-steady stream of visitors to Mountain View. Though he never promoted his home as such, it finally became a tavern-in-fact for the stage line, though many — perhaps most — of the guests were of the non-paying variety.

But no guest was better known than Andrew Jackson, who on various occasions made the King mansion his stopping point for a three-day rest period on his trips to and from Washington. Of course, he usually stopped for each night at some stage road tavern, but there were four places where he came off the road for a three-day rest period, and Mountain View was one of them.

Jackson had been a close friend of the old Col. King and had continued strong ties with the surviving children. (He often stopped with Sarah King Williams at Strawberry Plains, Tennessee.) Melinda King Anderson remembered that the servants and family were always drilled to be at their best for the visits of the noted Jackson, but also fondly remembered that he was "common as an old shoe," and quickly made everyone around him at ease. She recalled that his favorite dish was a bowl of stewed turnips into which he crumbled corn bread. A special section of the turnip hole (place where turnips were covered with earth to preserve them through the winter) was reserved for what the servants called the Jackson turnips, evidently the best ones.

It was remembered that on one of these visits, Jackson and King became so engrossed in a discussion on religion, that candles had to be replaced before the two finally retired to bed. This discussion took place in the south parlor before the great mantel that is now in the music room of the Margaret Mitchell house at 54 King Street. According to King family members, Jackson always slept in the bedroom over the north parlor. Though there was no secret service in those days, Jackson, having many enemies, always had a body servant (actually a guard) who always slept on a trundle bed that was pulled from under the larger bed in which the President slept. During one of the Mountain View visits, a near tragedy occurred because of this situation. It seems that Jackson was not sleeping well (Had he eaten too many turnips or was he troubled by a pre-bedtime discussion of religion?), and consequently was toss-ing about in a restless slumber. Sometime during the night he rolled off the bed and onto the sleeping guard. The guard, thinking he was being attacked by an enemy who perchance had broken into the King home, grabbed his pistol and was ready to fire when he became aware that his "attacker" was President Jackson.

When Jackson was on the way to his inauguration, he was joined at Mountain View by William King, brother of Rev. James King, who helped escort the new President to Washington. On this occasion Rev. King called all the group into the south parlor, and there prayed long and earnestly for the country's new leader.

Another event of noted consequence during those early years was the establishment of the Sapling Grove post office. In the autumn of 1838, King and his twenty-year-old son Cyrus rode horseback to Washington, D.C., for the purpose of petitioning for a post office for the area. Their efforts were rewarded. On January 12, 1839, the office was established and James King was appointed postmaster. It is said that he committed most of the work of this office to the young Cyrus King. It was then that a small, one-story addition was added to the north end of the mansion. This was to house the new post office. According to stories handed down, some who came from a distance for mail spent a day or two at Mountain View, enjoying the hospitality of King and his wife. And one young man, who came for the family mail, was hired to work on the plantation and never returned home.

A YOUNG MERCHANT COMES COURTING

In the autumn of 1844, there was a special service of some type at the Blountville Presbyterian Church. The Rev. James King of Mountain View was called upon to speak at this service. Later he and members of his family were entertained at lunch in the home of Samuel Rhea, a prominent merchant of Blountville. Young Joseph Rhea Anderson, a nephew of Mr. Rhea, was then present. For some time he had been associated with his uncle in the mercantile and private banking business. He was a son of Isaac and Margaret Rhea Anderson and was born at the famous block house near Kingsport, Tennessee, October 25, 1819. Young Mr. Anderson was highly intelligent, markedly industrious, and ruggedly handsome.

All through the time that the Kings and the Rheas lunched and visited, Joseph Anderson could not keep his eyes off the beautiful Melinda King; and before the guests had departed he had her and Rev. King's permission to come calling. And call he did, week after week, month after month, and the romance blossomed softly in the coming spring. On June 3, 1845, Joseph Rhea Anderson and Melinda Williams King were married at Mountain View, standing before the elegant mantel in the south parlor. The guest house in the northeast corner of the King yard was their honeymoon cottage. The next day they rode back to Blountville in a new carriage that Anderson had bought for the occasion. Another stone had been laid in the foundation of the coming Bristol.

Prosperity was the continual lot of the happy young couple during the few years they would live in Blountville. Anderson was of a pronounced thrifty nature, and was doubtless thinking of what he would do with his fast accumulating wealth in the near future. And what he did with it should mean much to those who now live in and love the City of Bristol.

As the new son-in-law prospered in Blountville, there was growing excitement at Mountain View on Beaver. For years there had been talk of a proposed railway, which seemed to be certain to have its terminus somewhere on or near the King lands. Several surveys had been made, including one through nearby Paperville, one along the old Island Road toward Kingsport, and another directly into Mountain View plantation, or more specifically,

Joseph Rhea Anderson as a young man. This likeness of Bristol's founder was long worn in a locket, by his wife Melinda King Anderson.

the King's Meadows area of that plantation. If the railroad did have its terminal on the King lands, then conditions would be favorable for a town building there. This was James King's grand opportunity. He could have become the founder of both Bristol, Virginia, and Bristol, Tennessee, and likely would have given his town a different name. He, as did so many others along the proposed railroad, gave the required eighty-foot right-of-way, his ending at the state line. Then on June 18, 1848, he gave additional land, lying on either side of the already donated right of way, beginning at the state line, three hundred and seventy feet wide and extending northward for a distance of fifteen hundred feet, containing, according to his estimate, ten acres. This is the site of the present depot. His deed specified that the railroad company could not sell the land, could not use it for any other purpose, could not erect houses for servants or company agents thereon, and he retained the right to use any portion of said land not being used for railroad purposes. Later, for a consideration of two hundred and fifty dollars, he gave the right to build houses on the tract for use by company agents. At the same time, he was laying off a depot lot on the Tennessee side in anticipation of a railroad reaching that point from the south. But that was all; his vision ended. He would leave the honor of town founding to his new and highly regarded son-in-law, Joseph R. Anderson.

NEW SPIRITUAL PERCEPTION CHANGES LOCAL HISTORY

Soon after donating the depot lots, the Rev. James King, according to his own statement, "had a new spiritual perception that caused the vainness of wealth and fame to become acutely delineated." Along with his new awareness of the vanity of wealth and fame, came a "clear insight into the folly of worldly pursuits and pleasures." With this there seems to have been reborn in him a sense of guilt over the "transgressions of his youth." In those youthful days he had been fond of the dance, a fondness that extended well into those years after the building of the mansion on present Solar Hill. That mansion, because of its enormity, had a spacious attic. This he turned into a ballroom, and it was well used. But when his new spiritual insight came, he developed a great sense of guilt over the presence of this yet remaining symbol of "those worldly days and activities." Consequently, he began to make plans to leave "the hill, that he might put reminders of his former folly behind him." For the time it seems that he had lost all interest in materialism and intended to spend the rest of his days in spiritual contemplation.

There is indication that this new spiritual perception may have been brought about by years-long grief and depression suffered by the Rev. King because of the death of a son. This son, Lt. William King, was born at Holly Bend, December 10, 1815. He never married but remained with his father as a chief assistant in the administration of the King enterprises. He enlisted in the Mexican War and was in some of the principal battles of that conflict. In late June 1848 he set sail for home, but sickened on the journey and died July 2, 1848, two days before the vessel reached New Orleans. A yet extant letter of a companion tells of how Lt. King had appeared well the night before but was taken ill and died the next morning. This companion and others sought to gain permission to bring King's body home, but the chief officer, fearing transmission of disease, had the deceased buried at sea. The companion wrote that Lt. King was "unceremoniously lowered into the deep green waters of the Gulf," and deeply regretted that there was not "so much as a hymn or prayer." No doubt all this caused much deep and serious thought on the part of the Rev. James King.

But as the vision of an old man faded, that of a young man increased. In the thriving store at Blountville, young Joseph R. Anderson was dreaming. For years he had been acutely aware of the proposed railroad for the area, and knew that it would bring much opportunity for the enterprising. He did not intend to let such a golden opportunity pass.

On December 12, 1851, he bought the Andrew Susong farm, comprised of some two hundred acres of land. This acreage lay along present Common-wealth Avenue in the vicinity of the Valleydale packing plant. It bordered on the Island Road rail survey and would certainly be well situated if that route were used. It is said that he reasoned that even if the railroad did not use that route and perchance his father-in-law would not sell him King's Meadows, any city that might develop at the latter location would someday reach his land and be of great profit to him. For this possible city site he paid two thousand six hundred dollars cash. It may be mentioned here that his farm was a part of the vast Susong lands, and had passed to its former owner by the will of Jacob Susong in 1831. Though Anderson did not live to see it, Bristol did indeed reach to and beyond the Susong tract.

Bibliography - Chapter Two

Anderson, Melinda King. As told to her granddaughter, Mrs. Herman Blackley. 1890-1908.

Crymble, A. Carter. Notes and documents. Kingsport, Tennessee.

Eldridge, Clora. As told to Hattie King Taylor and Rhea Anderson.

Frankfort, Kentucky. Court Records. 1814.

Sullivan County, Tennessee. Deed Records. 1814-1854.

Taylor, Hattie King. *The Iron King*. Unpublished manuscript, 1920.

Washington County, Virginia. Deed Records. 1814-1854.

Joseph Rhea Anderson (1819-1888) founded the Town of Bristol in 1852. His Bristol was located in both Virginia and Tennessee.

Chapter Three
THE FOUNDING OF BRISTOL

It finally became certain that the survey to be used for the building of the Virginia and Tennessee Railroad would reach the King lands at about the crossing of Beaver Creek, and skirt on by the eastern edge of the meadows to the Tennessee line. Of course, Anderson realized that this was the place for the town. Consequently, in early 1852 he approached his father-in-law, Rev. James King, with a proposition to purchase a site for the envisioned city. It is said that he, at first, was refused for reasons unknown. (Perhaps his father-in-law did not want him to become overly concerned with fame and fortune.) However, in June 1852, Melinda King Anderson went to see her father. It is said that the two closeted themselves in the south parlor, where they talked for a good half day. What was said we will never know, but when the determined daughter emerged from that room, she had her father's firm promise that he would sell the King's Meadows to her husband. One may imagine that the prospering young merchant of Blountville smiled in deep satisfaction when his wife arrived home to tell him the good news.

On July 10, 1852, James King and his son-in-law Joseph R. Anderson sat down in the south parlor of the old King mansion, and there drew up and signed a contract for one hundred acres of the King plantation. (It is said that King always used the south parlor for business transactions.) The consideration was for ten thousand dollars, though this was later lowered to eight thousand because of reduced acreage. By the signing of this contract Anderson must have felt a great elation in that his town was virtually assured. It is certain that he lost no time in proceeding with plans for it.

NAMING THE TOWN

In Anderson's last account book for his Blountville store is a list of sales made on July 16, 1852. On the back of that page is a list of names that were under consideration for the town he planned to found upon the site he had just secured from his father-in-law. Following each name were marks that apparently had the value of one point each. Names under consideration were:

King's Meadows	11
Kingsland	111
Mountain View	1
Andersonville	11111
Paradise	111111
Bristol	1111111

Thus, our city missed being Paradise by only one point! Family tradition has it that this "heavenly" name was the choice of Mrs. Anderson. She had grown up near the site and considered her old home plantation as being a near paradise. Another possibility is that it may have been Anderson's first choice had his town developed on his first purchase in the area (Andrew Susong farm). The little valley in which this land was situated was long known as Paradise Valley. It may be that he intended to call the projected town there Paradise and carried the name over to the latter site. But Anderson was a practical man; and envisioning the development of a thriving industrial city, he chose the name of the great iron center in England. Thus, what was almost Paradise became the rather earthly Bristol.

THE SURVEY AND PROSPECTUS

Very soon after the signing of the contract with his father-in-law, Anderson hired his cousin Henry Anderson to survey and map the tract. On the morning of August 1, 1852, the staff, chain and compass were borne into the meadows, then still the domain of Rev. King's fine herd of shorthorn cattle, and the laying out of Bristol was begun. Henry Anderson was assisted in this project by Samuel Anderson, a brother of Joseph R. Anderson. The survey was finished on August 3, 1852.

Shortly thereafter, maps containing a prospectus were printed on the steam press of Wagner McGuigans at Number 4, Franklin Place, Philadelphia, Pennsylvania. These were delivered by stage to the Anderson store in Blountville, Tennessee. It was told by Melinda King Anderson that her husband spent most of the night following the delivery of these maps preparing and labeling them for distribution. They were rather expensive so were not produced in large quantities. Therefore, Anderson followed the plan of having them posted in public places, though a few are known to have been given to individuals. It is known that one was placed in the courthouse at Abingdon, Virginia, though over the objections of certain merchants there who feared competition. Others were displayed in Jonesboro and Rogersville, Tennessee. Anderson also had them placed in towns along the route of the approaching railroad. Apparently this was a wise move, for a study of early land sales indicates that an amazing number of early buyers came from along this route. This author knows of three copies of the map that are yet extant and there may well be others.

It was stated in the prospectus that each deed was to contain a clause forbidding the manufacture or sale of strong drink upon the conveyed property. But, for some unknown reason, this clause does not appear in a single Anderson deed.

A dream was coming true for Joseph R. Anderson. The town that he envisioned was planned, surveyed and mapped, and lots were offered for sale there in 1852. For all practical reasons and purposes, the founding of Bristol may so be dated.

But as a dream came true for Anderson, an era was ending for Rev. James King, long the master of Mountain View plantation. In the late summer of 1852, he commenced the building of a one-story brick house near his water mill on Beaver Creek. This house site was near the west bank of Beaver Creek, across from the junction of Ash Street with Sixth and Seventh Streets (often called Five Points). The mill, with its pond reaching almost to present Shelby Street, was nearby. The estate was first known as Mill Grove, but was later called English Grove after it became the property of King's daughter Margaret, who had married John G. English. Rev. King would soon leave the hill from whence he had so long looked out over his verdant meadows to the hills and majestic mountains beyond, and where shortly a thriving town would forever obliterate the peaceful pastoral scene in which he had often delighted.

THE TOWN OF BRISTOL

Perhaps it will be well here to delineate the Town of Bristol as it was originally laid out in the year 1852. Anderson's Bristol was situated both in Virginia and Tennessee. The northern boundary of the Virginia portion of the town laying west of the railway was along Beaver Creek, and the land line followed that creek around its bend and southward to the state line at present State Street. (The bed of that creek has been slightly changed since the making of that map.) On the east the west line of the depot lot given by Rev. James King formed the boundary of the larger portion of Bristol, Virginia. This depot lot completely cut the town in two. Beyond it was a four-acre portion of Bristol, lying in that area east of the site of the old freight depot (burned in 1987) and extending to the back of the First Baptist Church, the northern boundary thereof being roughly along present Buford Street. The state line formed the southern boundary of the Virginia portion of the town. Thus, it may be seen that the Bristol, Virginia, founded by Joseph

Anderson in 1852, included virtually all the downtown section of our city that lies north of the state line.

On the Tennessee side the Town of Bristol lay south of the state line from a point across from the end of present Virginia Street, roughly southward to Ash Street, then along Ash, passing south of the present Beecham plant to near Alabama Street, then angling northwestward to reach the state line near where Beaver Creek then crossed the proposed Main Street (now State) of the new town.

Perhaps for the sake of better acceptance of future statements, it will be well to mention here that the Town of Bristol as then planned did not include the King home on Solar Hill, nor the General Shelby home at the old fort site, nor the Isaac Baker home, said to have been about nine hundred feet north of the present Athens Steak House. It was founded upon lands that had formerly been open fields and pastures, its only mark of development being a small cemetery near what is now the intersection of Fifth and Shelby.

Pencil sketch of the first building erected in the Town of Bristol. This was the home and store of Joseph R. Anderson, built on the southwest corner of Main and Fourth (now State and Edgemont) in 1853. This building also housed Bristol's first post office and bank. Here, on Christmas Day 1853, was held the first religious service in Bristol; and here the first Sunday School in the town was taught, beginning in January, 1854. The first town election for Bristol, Tennessee, was held at the west door of this house on May 1, 1856, and the first meeting of the Town Council occurred here on November 18, 1856.

EARLY DEVELOPMENT

In early 1853 James Fields and William Rodefer of Abingdon, Virginia, began construction of the Joseph R. Anderson home. This brick house, erected on the southwest corner of what is now State and Edgemont (then Fourth and Main) was finished in September 1853. It was the first building in the Town of Bristol. All around it stretched open fields and meadows. From the corner of present Fifth to Beaver, and stretching back to the slope beyond Broad Street, was an immense field of corn, ripening to harvest.

On September 18, 1853, Joseph Anderson and his family arrived from Blountville by wagon to take up residence in their new home. Not a road led to it; the wagon had to be driven across the meadows to reach it. As long as Melinda King Anderson lived, she delighted to tell of this move and of being met at the Beaver crossing by the old King family dog. And when within sight of the house, she saw her aged father and mother standing by the front door to greet the first pioneer residents of the Town of Bristol. The Kings, with the aid of a servant or two, had prepared a bountiful supper for the road weary Anderson family.

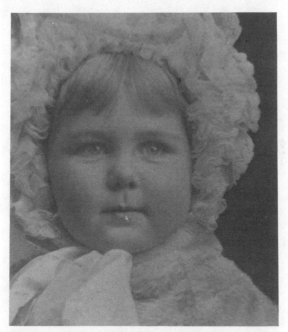

DAUGHTER OF PIONEER SETTLER: Mrs. Margaret Anderson Piper, pictured as a child, was the daughter of a true Bristol pioneer. Her father, John C. Anderson, was only three years old when his family moved into their home at what is now the southwest corner of State and Edgemont. Mrs. Piper died June 24, 1991.

All this may seem so long ago; so long that it may be difficult to relate those first pioneer settlers to anyone living today. But a little tired and hungry three-year-old pioneer who sat down to that bountiful supper on that late summer evening 136 years ago, yet has two living children. John C. Anderson, Little Johnnie they then called him, born 1850, later a prominent citizen of Bristol, and once its mayor, was the father of Mrs. Margaret Piper of this city, and Robert B. Anderson of Valdosta, Georgia. This daughter and son of a true Bristol pioneer are yet living links to the very first day of the settlement of Bristol, Virginia-Tennessee.

Anderson's home contained a room for a store in its west side. This store was stocked and ready for business by Christmas 1853. This was the first store in Bristol, and Joseph Anderson was the town's first merchant.

Isaac Anderson, son of Joseph R. and Melinda King Anderson, was the first child born in Bristol, Tennessee. He became a noted Presbyterian minister and gave to King College the site of the present campus.

THE BRISTOL POST OFFICE

A substantial boost for Anderson's town came when the Bristol Post Office was established on November 5, 1853. As before noted, the Sapling Grove Post Office had been established on January 12, 1839. (It was not within the bounds of the new town of Bristol.) James King had served as its postmaster until June 9, 1853. In that month the Kings left the old Mountain View mansion and moved to the new house at Mill Grove on Beaver Creek. Campbell Galliher, King's overseer, then became postmaster, moving the office to his home beyond what is now Commonwealth Avenue. He served until the Sapling Grove Post Office was discontinued on October 1, 1853. The new Bristol Post Office was kept in a booth, described as hardly larger than an oversized closet, in the southwest corner of Anderson's store. This post office served both Bristol, Tennessee, and Bristol, Virginia, adjoining Goodsonville, and the surrounding area. Thus the reader will note that the town's first post office was on the historic Anderson Corner, and Joseph R. Anderson was Bristol's first postmaster.

It may be of interest to the reader to know how the mail came to Bristol. In those early years most of the mail arrived by stagecoach. The stage did not come into what is now downtown Bristol, but ran across Solar Hill, along King's Alley and King Street. Though a passenger stop was made at the former King home, the mail for the Bristol Post Office was not delivered there. Instead, there was what was known as the mail stop. A servant of Joseph R. Anderson, one Nehemiah Strange, was always dispatched by Anderson to go to that point and make the mail exchange. (Often passengers alighted from the stage there and followed the "mail boy" to the new town.) This servant always carried a leather pouch (probably a former saddle bag) in which to transport the mail. Anderson later used the same pouch in his banking activities. That pouch, which long ago carried the dispatches of good news and sorrow, is now owned by this author and kept at his home, Pleasant Hill. Nothing kept Nehemiah Strange from making his rounds. This always (winter and summer) barefoot mail boy (He preferred it that way; Anderson could not persuade him to wear shoes.) kept his appointments at the mail stop, even though it might mean wading snow, swimming a flooding Beaver Creek, or walking through storm and rain. If a piece of mail appeared to be of great importance, Anderson might send Nehemiah to bear the letter to the recipient. It is known that a letter edged in black, then a sign of a death message, was carried by Nehemiah to the north side of Goodsonville, through a sleet storm. This faithful mail boy of the first days of Bristol died in 1897 and was buried in a little overgrown cemetery near Greeneville, Tennessee.

On July 27, 1858, John Keys became Bristol's second postmaster. He immediately moved the office to the Zimmerman property near the northeast corner of present Lee and State on the Virginia side. (Keys had married the widow of Dr. Zimmerman.) The office remained as Bristol, with Keys remaining as postmaster, until the name was changed to Goodson on February 15, 1859.

SALE OF FIRST LOTS — FIRST BUILDINGS

In early 1853 William Rodefer contracted to buy the choice lot on the northwest corner of what was then Main and Fourth, later Main and Front, and now State and Randall Expressway. (Most of this lot was taken by the Randall Expressway.) This lot was number 143 in the Bristol, Virginia, portion of Anderson's town. This contract between Anderson and Rodefer was the first real estate activity in Bristol. It must be mentioned that Rodefer did not follow through with this contract, and the lot later was sold to W. W. James of Blountville, Tennessee.

The second developmental activity involved the contracting for the sale of lots 154 and 153 in Bristol, Virginia, to Dr. B. F. Zimmerman in the latter half of 1853. Lot 154 was on the northeast corner of what is now Lee and State Streets (Signet Bank location), and included about half the frontage of the four hundred block of Main Street. The other lot lay behind it along present Lee Street. The deed for these lots was executed on July 11, 1854, well after the erection of Zimmerman's home.

It was also in 1853 that Anderson contracted the sale of lot 164, located in the Bristol, Virginia, portion of the town, to John H. Moore of Russell County, Virginia. This lot was located on the northwest corner of what is now State and Lee Streets. Moore was already building upon this lot when his deed was issued July 11, 1854.

The first lots sold in Bristol, Tennessee, were numbers 54, 55 and 56, and were conveyed to Montgomery Lynch and Edmond Winston, Jr. of Washington County, Tennessee. The deed is dated April 26, 1854, though they may have been under contract prior to that date. Lot 54 was on the northwest corner of what is now Olive and Beecham (old Fourth) Streets. The other two lots were just south of this intersection and are now covered by the Beecham plant. The second lot sale on the Tennessee side of the Town of Bristol was made to Dennis Noland of Sullivan County, Tennessee. Lot number 16 was conveyed to him on May 8, 1854. This lot is located just back of the old Interstate Hardware building and near the southeast corner of Third and State. Noland was soon to have a neighbor. On May 26, 1854, lot 17, just to the south of Noland's purchase, was sold to John G. Simpson of the same county. These lots fronted on the Tennessee Depot lot that had been reserved by Rev. James King and were considered to be prime locations.

Of course, the first building erected in the Town of Bristol, Virginia-Tennessee was the Anderson home on Fourth and Main (State and Randall Expressway). The second was the home of Dr. B. F. Zimmerman, built in 1853-54 in old Bristol, Virginia. As before noted, this house stood near the northeast corner of State and Lee Streets. The third building in the town was also in old Bristol, Virginia, and was on the northwest corner of State and Lee. This was the store and dwelling of John H. Moore. The second building to have been erected in Bristol, Tennessee, was probably the little school house built by James King which stood near the intersection of Fifth and Shelby.

FIRST RELIGIOUS SERVICE

The first religious service to be conducted in the Town of Bristol was on Christmas Day, 1853. On that occasion Rev. James King preached to a small assembly of area residents who had gathered in the parlor of the Joseph Anderson home. This assembly included the servants of Anderson and King and some from the Susong families. In recent years a descendant of Rev. King presented this author with the hymn book (psalter) that was used on that occasion. It is considered to be a priceless possession. Later Mrs. Anderson conducted Sunday School classes in the same parlor.

FIRST BANK

For years before he came to Bristol, Joseph R. Anderson had been associated with his Uncle Samuel Rhea in providing private banking services for Blountville and vicinity. It appears that from the beginning he was determined to do the same in his new Bristol. When his house was under construction he swore William Rodefer to masonic secrecy and then proceeded to instruct him how to build a salt bin that was to include a secret compartment for the storage of deposited funds. At the top there was indeed a bin for salt, the bottom of which was doubled and tightly fitted to prevent salt from falling through on the stored money. There were latches hidden underneath that would lower a box-like compartment. This was the repository for money. This secret place for money storage echoes the "coffin bank" of Anderson's grandfather-in-law, Col. James King. Strange as the "salt bin bank" may appear, it marked the beginning of banking services in the Town of Bristol (Virginia and Tennessee).

The exact date of the beginning of Anderson's banking services is not known, but in that he had his "vault" made at the same time as the building of his house, he probably did banking in the area from near the time his store was opened (late 1853). There is a paper extant, dated June 12, 1854, which mentions funds deposited with Joseph Anderson, Banker. The history of the

First National Bank, published on the occasion of the 60th anniversary of that institution, indicated that Anderson had engaged in private banking for thirteen years when that bank was established (1868).

Information coming from John C. Anderson, son of the first banker, indicates that when there was more money in the salt bin than was thought to be safe to keep, the surplus would be taken to Abingdon, Virginia, and deposited in a regular bank there. Joseph Anderson used the same leather pouch for the carrying of this money as was used by his servant, Nehemiah Strange, for the transportation of mail to and from the Bristol post office. The pouch was hidden in a bag of feed that Anderson carried on his horse. It may be noted by the reader that Bristol's first bank was on the historic Anderson corner, at what is now State and Edgemont Streets.

Allie Lin, daughter of John C. Anderson and grand- daughter of Joseph R. Anderson, seems to be intently listening in this childhood picture. Indeed as she grew up she did listen intently to the tales of her grandmother. Much of what she learned and retold is included in this book. She will be remembered by many Bristolians as Mrs. Herman Blackley.

THE DEED FOR THE TOWN

Though some development had already been done in the town, Anderson did not receive a deed for the site of Bristol until April 12, 1854. The deed for the Virginia portion of Bristol is a two-part deed, made necessary because James King's depot lot cut completely across what became the Bristol tract. A four-acre tract lay east of the depot and this is the first land conveyed in the deed. The remainder, which included most of what is now downtown Bristol, Virginia, was conveyed in the second portion of the deed. The contract made on July 10, 1852, for this purchase provided for fifty-two acres in the Virginia portion of the sale. For some unknown reason only thirty-two acres were conveyed to Anderson. This is why King deducted two thousand dollars from the purchase price. (The land had been valued at ten thousand dollars for the one-hundred-acre tract, situated in both Tennessee and Virginia.)

THE TOWN GROWS

The year 1854 brought a marked increase in the sale of Bristol lots. Other than those already mentioned, lots in Bristol, Tennessee, were sold to Alexander Lazenby, William Martin, William P. Carmack, S. B. Morgan, the Constitutional Presbyterian Church, and Alexander Morgan. Lazenby's lot is now covered by the back portion of the Interstate Hardware building near State and Third Streets. William Martin, who came here from Bedford County, Virginia, bought the lot on the southeast corner of Sixth and State, where so long stood the Bank of Bristol. William P. Carmack, a native of this area, bought lot 104, which was west of the intersection of present Sixth and State. S. B. Morgan bought two adjoining lots on Third Street, facing the Tennessee depot lot. The lot purchased by the Constitutional Presbyterian Church fronted on Fourth at the corner of Shelby. The deed was made to the trustees, namely Dr. B.F. Zimmerman, George Worley, Malhon Susong, William Cowan, and John G. King. Alexander Morgan, who came here from Bedford County, Virginia, bought two adjoining lots on Fourth Street near the corner of present Olive Street.

Those who bought lots in Bristol, Virginia, in 1854 were George M. Spencer, Alfred T. Wilson, and John W. Kneeland. Spencer's lot was on Fourth (later Front) across from the depot. Alfred T. Wilson, of Johnson County, Tennessee, bought property fronting on Main (State) between Virginia and Washington Streets. On this he built Bristol's first hotel. Kneeland, of Hawkins County, Tennessee, bought lots (140 and 150) situated back to back and fronting on Fourth and what is now Lee Street. Prices of these lots varied but averaged about one hundred dollars each.

In 1855 lots in Bristol, Tennessee, were sold to John N. Bosang, James Fields, James H. Dunn and Samuel Anderson. There is evidence that several others were contracted. John N. Bosang bought two lots on Fourth Street, a little south of where the Salvation Army thrift store is now located. James Fields, who had helped to build the home of the town's founder Joseph R. Anderson, bought four lots. Two of these lots fronted on Main, beginning at the west corner of present Fifth Street. The other two were directly in back of them and reached to present Shelby Street. This choice location cost Mr. Fields six hundred dollars. James H. Dunn's lot (47) was on Fourth Street, across from where Rutherford's Transfer and Storage Company is now located. Samuel Anderson, a brother of Joseph R. Anderson, bought lots fronting on Fourth Street, immediately south of his brother's home lot. These were just beyond the present offices of Gillenwater and Law and others (126 Edgemont).

Those who bought lots in Bristol, Virginia, in 1855 were Jesse Aydlotte, W. W. James, Alfred T. Wilson, Alexander W. Carmack, Fletcher C. Luken, and G. H. Mattox. Aydlotte of Smyth County, Virginia, bought lot 162, which is a short distance below the west corner of Lee and State Streets. W. W. James bought what was later known as James Corner. This was on the corner of what was then Fourth and Main and across from the depot lot. This is now State and Randall Expressway, but most of the lot was taken by the west lanes of this Expressway. This very choice location cost Mr. James the sum of six hundred dollars. Alfred T. Wilson bought the lot immediately in back of his hotel and store. Alexander W. Carmack bought a lot fronting on Main (State) Street in that section between the present Dominion Bank and the J. C. Penney Store. Fletcher C. Luken, of Campbell County, Virginia, bought a lot on the corner of what is now Virginia and Buford Streets (Virginia was then Second Street). G. H. Mattox, also of Campbell County, Virginia, bought lots 1 and 2. These lots fronted on both First and Second Streets (now Washington and Virginia) and were a short distance behind A. T. Wilson's hotel property.

By the end of 1855, the development of Anderson's town was well on its way. It was clear that his dream would be realized. The railroad was soon to arrive and it was correctly predicted that its coming would bring an acceleration in the growth of the new town. The point has now been reached where consideration must be given to Goodsonville, that was developing along side of old Bristol, Virginia.

TRIPLE DESTINY

On September 10, 1799, William Baker of Knox County, Tennessee, sold a 348-acre tract of land to John Goodson, this land being a portion of the old Sapling Grove tract that had formerly been owned by Isaac Baker, father of the seller. John Goodson's sister, Sarah Goodson, was the first wife of

Col. James King, and the mother of Rev. James King, who would later buy the site of Bristol that adjoined the Goodson lands. This 348-acre tract was later inherited by Col. Samuel Eason Goodson, only son of John Goodson and his wife, Sarah Wickham Goodson. Col. Goodson, born October 7, 1793, grew to manhood at his father's farm some two miles up Beaver Creek above what became Bristol. He was of average height, built a bit stocky, and had sandy red hair. Very early in life, probably in his late teens, he grew a goatee beard, which earned him the uncomplimentary nickname of "Goat" Goodson. This he highly resented, sometimes very near fought over it, but never shaved it as his only known photo shows. (This photo was made four days before his death.) He never married, but tried, unsuccessfully, to win the hand of one woman for nearly fifty years. (This lady was twice married during that period.)

His formal education was not extensive — most of it was by tutor — but he possessed a natural intelligence that sufficed where education failed. He was also gifted with the power of persuasive speech. By the time of his father's death in July 1829, Samuel Goodson was already managing the large family farm. After the death of his parents, he continued to live at the family home until he moved into the fast developing Bristol-Goodson in 1857.

In 1837 he entered politics and was elected to the House of Delegates. His first session was January 1 through April 9, 1838. He served until March 23, 1847. Then in 1849 he replaced John B. Floyd, who had been elected Governor, and served through the term ending August 17, 1849. John Goodson, father of Samuel, had served in the House of Delegates from Washington County, Virginia, in the session of 1817-18.

Col. Goodson always rode a horse to Richmond for the sessions. These sessions usually commenced on January 1st, which necessitated a ride during the dead of winter, often through bitter cold and snow. It is told that he had one of his servants make him a long, wraparound robe of sheepskin with which he almost completely covered himself (head and ears included) for these long, cold journeys. A story is told of how somewhere along his route, a lad saw him and then ran into the family cabin, greatly frightened, and blurted out that some kind of big furry beast was riding a horse along the road!

By the time it became certain that the railroad would pass through his lands, he was then — at least by the standards of that time — an old man. But old men do sometimes have visions. Knowing that the railroad would have its western terminus at the state line, he, like Anderson, realized the potential for town development. However, the Goodson lands did not reach the state line. The southern boundary of the 348-acre tract ran along Beaver Creek above King's Meadows, then reaching a point near the route of the proposed railroad, angled toward the state line but did not reach it until well behind the site of the present First Baptist Church. Between the Goodson lands and the state line (present State Street) lay lands belonging to Goodson's first cousin, Rev. James King; and this tract would be sold to Joseph R. Anderson for the development of the Virginia portion of the Town of Bristol. Also King owned the most likely site for a depot. Indeed, King had surveyed and given the site in 1848 (site of the present depot).

Where the railroad yard is now, Goodson had a choice cornfield, neatly kept and tended, as was the rest of his vast farmlands. From this fine field he deeded seven acres for what he called the depot lot, along with the required 80-foot right-of-way through all his land. This deed was not recorded and its existence would not be known had it not been mentioned in another deed of 1854. Whether Goodson had hoped to persuade the railroad to use his lot as a depot site is not known, but it seems between the time the first deed was made and October 1854, it became apparent that the depot would be built in Bristol, Virginia, just beyond the Goodson lands. This action by the railroad probably sounded the death knell for permanent recognition of Goodsonville or the later Goodson.

On October 17, 1854, Samuel Goodson made a new deed, cancelling the one he had previously made in which he had given seven acres of his choice cornfield to the railroad for a depot lot. In this new deed he included that seven acre tract but added four and one-tenth acres to it, for the consideration of one hundred and ten dollars per acre. The legal description of this tract states that it was situated in the County of Washington and adjoining the Town of Bristol. This joining was near where Beaver Creek now passes under the railroad.

GOODSONVILLE

Col. Samuel E. Goodson hired Edmond Winston to survey and map his development which he called Goodsonville. Mr. Winston later became the son-in-law of Robert Preston, the distinguished master of Walnut Grove plantation located four miles above Bristol. The date of this survey is not known, but was likely about 1852-53. It is well here to delineate the Town of Goodsonville. Most of the southern boundary of Goodsonville was marked by the meandering Beaver Creek and beyond the railroad by the first section of Buford Street. The west side of present Goodson Street formed its eastern limits. The western boundary was the west side of present Lee Street, while Mary Street was the northern limits of the town, though the map indicates that it was anticipated that the town would eventually move beyond that street. A few lots were located along Scott Street west of Lee.

It is clear that the depot lot was intended to be the core or center of the town. Indeed, a street skirting by it to the west was called Depot Street. One

Col. Samuel E. Goodson as he appeared four days before his death. This is the only known photograph of him. Col. Goodson founded Goodsonville, which adjoined the original Bristol, Virginia, cir. 1852-53.

cannot help but feel a twinge of sympathy for the old town builder who must have been severely disappointed when the depot was built in adjoining Bristol, Virginia. However, the eleven and one-tenth acre tract taken from Goodson's cornfield was used for a large portion of the rail yards, and the round house was built upon it.

DEVELOPMENT OF GOODSONVILLE

The first lot contracted for sale in Goodsonville was number 16, let to Isaac Booher in 1853, though the deed was not executed until October 3, 1854. This lot lay along Edmond and fronted on both Washington and Virginia Streets. The name J. Booker appears on this lot on the map of Goodsonville, but this must have been a later notation and the name may have been meant for Booher. On Christmas Day, 1854, Goodson gave a lot to Jane G. Wells, wife of Henry Wells. A stipulation of the deed was that she could not sell to her husband or his heirs. This lot was on Washington, across from the end of Camp Street (erroneously listed as Champ Street on Winston's map). It is said that this Jane Wells was a daughter of the lady whom Goodson tried to marry for nearly fifty years.

There were many buyers of lots in Goodsonville in 1855. Among them were Reuben Crabtree, Thomas Bibb, John N. Bosang, M. T. Morgan, J. W. Thomas, James H. Johnson, James C. Hayter, John R. Steptoe, Samuel Sells, and possibly others. In addition lots were conveyed to the Trustees of the Methodist Church and the Independent Order of Odd Fellows. The Methodist lot was on the northeast corner of Scott and Lee where now stands the John Wesley United Methodist Church. The Odd Fellow lot fronted on Scott Street, a little distance east of the Methodist site.

Undoubtedly other lots were under contract. It is known that S. B. Morgan and Company had plans for building on lots 23, 24 and 25 as early as October 22, 1854. This may have been the case with others. It is also evident that Col. Goodson did much building of rental property during those early years. Perhaps this was to give his town the boost he so greatly desired it to have. It appears that if Goodsonville had developed into a town, its business section would have been on Washington Street, just beyond where it connected with First Street in old Bristol, Virginia, and on beyond William(s) Street. Some of the capitalists of the area invested early in lots in that area of the town. Among them were John G. and James King, sons of the Rev. James King.

INCORPORATION

Incorporation does not make a town. Many exist without ever passing through this legal process but have much other official recognition. It was so with the triple towns at the terminus of the Virginia and Tennessee Railroad. All three towns were recognized on the tax and deed records of their respective counties. Bristol was recognized by the U. S. Postal Department, and also by the railroad in that the depot would bear that name. And there was some recognition on official court papers and other documents, as well as by private letters, diaries and newspapers of the period.

An article in an Abingdon, Virginia, newspaper dated 1856 describes Bristol as having about one hundred twenty houses, most of them brick, and about eight hundred citizens. Many feel that his estimate of the population was too high. It is very likely that the writer of this article included the three towns under the designation of Bristol. Be that as it may, it was clear that the time had come for local government. Joseph Anderson greatly desired to preserve the identity of his Bristol, Virginia, and he and others diligently tried to bring the towns together as one. But, of course, there was the matter of the state line. Had all of Anderson's development been in one state, there is little doubt that the entire Town of Bristol would have remained as one. As it was, a move developed to incorporate all the Virginia side as Goodson. A bitter controversy over the matter dragged on for weeks during the late fall of 1855.

Though there is no indication that Samuel Goodson took any part in the move to use his or his family name (it is not known which) for the town on the Virginia side, it is known that the highly esteemed old gentleman had many ardent supporters and faithful friends who opposed Anderson's plan to have a united town. Feelings were so high during this controversy that an actual fight or two took place over the matter. Ann Bachelor recalled how on a Sunday afternoon in December 1855, young Joseph William James, an ardent Anderson supporter, had called at the Bachelor home. While there, a supporter of the Goodson movement came by. Seeing James, he haughtily called out, "It's going to be Goodson or Hell." James, his temper flaring, called back, "I'd rather it would be Hell." Other words followed, during which James jumped over the picket fence that surrounded the Bachelor yard and soon had his foe engaged in what Ann Bachelor called "intensive battle."

It was this same Joseph William James, who two days after the citizens voted to incorporate the Virginia side as Goodson, had a large sign attached to the front of the family store proclaiming that the store was in Bristol, Virginia (James and Seneker-Bristol, Virginia). This sign remained for years afterwards and could clearly be seen from the depot and railroad.

On December 17, 1855, a citizens meeting was held in a little building that stood on the northwest corner of Cumberland and Fourth in Bristol, Virginia. (This site was later occupied by the St. Lawrence and later the General Shelby Hotel.) At the time the little building was occupied by a saloon, and it is said that the meeting was "well sparked" with strong drink. It has long been believed that Rev. James King presided at this meeting, but this is very doubtful. This writer once saw a letter dated December 25, 1855, and written by King, in which he expressed extreme disapproval of what the citizens had done and hoped that it might "yet be righted." Ann Bachelor wrote that "old man" (John N.) Bosang led the move to use the name of Goodson for the Virginia side, and that he "drove the horses" at the citizens meeting. Bosang, who owned Bristol's first saloon, detested Anderson, who was an ardent temperance leader. And there is strong indication that the feeling was mutual! At least there was financial support for the new town. V. Keebler, an early Bristol, Virginia, merchant, gave the first dollar for the operation of the local government.

Meanwhile, Bristol, Tennessee, was moving forward with plans to incorporate. The Tennessee state legislature passed an act of incorporation for the town on February 22, 1856. The sheriff of Sullivan County was directed to conduct an election in the town on May 1, 1856. Joseph R. Anderson was elected first mayor. The first aldermen were Lafayette Johnson, an early merchant who then lived on Third Street; E. P. Cawood, who managed Billy Butler's Famous Hotel on Main Street; Dr. Flavius L. Hartman, a very early physician of the town; and Thomas W. Farley, who later operated the Exchange Hotel. P. H. J. Crockett became the first of a long line of quickly changing constables.

The act for the Virginia side moved a little slower. It is said that William King Heiskell, one of the delegates representing Washington County, opposed the move and had to be persuaded by ex-Governor John B. Floyd, the other delegate, to give support to it. Incorporation of Goodson was finally granted on March 5, 1856. As incorporated, Goodson was a composite town made up of both Goodsonville and the original Bristol, Virginia, with perhaps a little territory added. Recently discovered documents among the court papers in Abingdon, Virginia, indicate that Austin M. Appling was the first mayor of Goodson. It is also indicated that he was followed (about 1861) by Rev. Philip Rohr, formerly of Abingdon, and that Rohr served until the town charter was amended in 1870. Valentine Keebler was the town clerk, being selected at the citizens meeting of December 17, 1855, and he served for many years. Among the earliest trustees were John N. Bosang and William H. Trammell. The same documents mentioned above also indicate that the early town records were mostly kept on scraps of paper that have apparently been lost. Books were not kept until the amending of the charter in 1870.

IDENTITY PROBLEM

From the beginning Goodson had an identity problem; the new name was never universally accepted or used. All through its thirty-four years or so of legal existence, it was popularly known as Bristol. Indeed, intensive research of recent years indicates that even Goodsonville before it had the same situation. Some official papers and contemporary writings of the period call it Bristol, as the same later did in relation to Goodson. Virtually all the writings in existence of those who visited or settled here during those first years (1852-56) refer to the entire town as Bristol, as do letters, legal agreements and other papers of the period.

After the incorporation many businesses kept right on giving their location as Bristol, Virginia. Some newspapers published on the Virginia side of town gave Bristol, Virginia, as their location. Numerous business cards and letterheads of the period did likewise. Contracts are extant which flatly give the location as Bristol, Virginia. All checked official papers of the Confederacy give the location as Bristol, Virginia. Even some deeds used the name several years after the incorporation of Goodson. The careful researcher can find hundreds of instances like those enumerated above. There are also numerous papers showing the double identity, such as Bristol-Goodson or Goodson-Bristol when locations were on the Virginia side of town. And occasionally one may find references to "Bristol, north of Main Street," or locations on the "Virginia side of Bristol." Goodson had a post office of the name only from February 15, 1859, until July 9, 1866. And from July 27, 1858, until February 15, 1859, the Bristol Post office was in Goodson. It is no wonder that confusion plagued the newly incorporated town!

To add to it all, the Virginia and Tennessee Railroad flatly refused to recognize Goodson and continued to give the depot location as Bristol, Virginia. The time tables and tickets bore this designation throughout the thirty-four years of Goodson's existence. The story is told of an old timer of this area who made a visit to northern Virginia. When he was ready to return home he asked for a ticket to Goodson, Virginia. The agent could find no such listing, but the puzzled customer persisted in his quest until a rather heated argument ensued. Finally in exasperation the old timer blurted out, "Well, jist give me a ticket to as fer as yore rails go!" This tale well illustrates the confusion that a double identity could and often did cause.

Indeed, the double identity caused endless problems and, for at least one Baltimore wholesaler, a bit of anxiety. In those early years most local merchants bought their goods in Baltimore, Philadelphia, or New York. There are numerous instances where wholesalers in these cities had to sue local merchants for their bills. One deposition in Chancery filed in the Abingdon, Virginia, courthouse illustrates how perplexing the double identity could be. Clearly in puzzlement the plantiff deposed that he had sold a bill of goods to a merchant who said he was doing business in a place called Goodson,

Virginia. The goods had been sent to Bristol, Virginia. Yet the man gave his address as Bristol, Tennessee! The poor wholesaler was perhaps one of many who thought he had been "taken" by this triple location business. The confusion continued until 1890 when the town took the name that Joseph R. Anderson had given his Virginia development in 1852, and by which the Virginia side had always been popularly known. It is interesting that the local depot agent C.E. Finch offered the resolution to incorporate as Bristol, in that his employer had been troubled with the double identity situation since 1856. Again the depot and the town had the same name.

Bibliography - Chapter Three

Abingdon Virginian (newspaper). Early 1850s.

Anderson, Joseph R. Notes, cir. 1880.

Anderson, Melinda King (Mrs. Joseph R.). Material related to her granddaughter, Mrs. Herman Blackley, 1890-1908.

Goodson, Col. Samuel Eason. As told to Joseph W. Owen, and preserved by Miss Revely Owen.

Johnson, L. F. Notes (unpublished), cir. 1893.

King, John G. Material related to his daughter, Hattie King Taylor.

Palmer, Joseph B. Diary (unpublished), 1855-1876.

Rhea, Samuel, uncle of Joseph R. Anderson. Notes, 1852-1857.

Sullivan County, Tennessee. Deed Records, 1850s.

Washington County, Virginia. Deed Records, 1850s.

Washington County, Virginia. Tax Records, 1850s.

Chapter Four
BRISTOL 1856-1871

Truly 1856 was a very eventful year for Bristol-Goodson. First there was the incorporation, then the virtual sell-out of lots and land on the Virginia side, plans for a new town, and the long-awaited coming of the Virginia and Tennessee Railroad. John H. Moore, the first merchant on the Virginia side of Bristol, had a cousin, Albion K. Moore, who was engaged in developmental activities in Savannah, Chatham County, Georgia. Seeing that Bristol was on the move, he wrote this cousin, apprising him of what appeared to be great opportunity for such activities in the new town. In April 1856 A. K. Moore arrived here, stayed for a few days with his cousin, then moved into the Columbia Hotel for the remainder of his exploratory visit. Apparently he was very impressed with the prospects for development here, later predicting that Bristol would become the hub of a great trading area.

Moore lost no time in beginning negotiations with Joseph R. Anderson, Samuel Goodson and Rev. James King, for the purchase of town lots and adjoining land. Another far-seeing individual was dreaming dreams and having visions of a thriving city at the terminus of the Virginia and Tennessee Railroad. He confided to a newly made local friend that though a little developing was going on in Bristol-Goodson, it was too slow for him. And once he was in control, he would "shoot the steam" to local growth. Indeed, he hoped to create a new town, perhaps absorbing the former into it. On July 10, 1856, he contracted with Samuel Goodson for the purchase of fifty-one and one-half acres of land, the consideration of which was thirty-eight hundred dollars. This land included a portion of old Goodsonville, along with acreage west of Lee Street and bordering on the old stage road (approximately present Oak View Street). From Anderson, Moore bought fifty-six lots situated in old Bristol, Virginia, roughly bounded by present Lee Street, Beaver Creek on the north and west and Winston's Alley on the south. The agreement for this sale was made the day following the contract for the purchase of the Goodson lands.

A. K. Moore then made a trip down to Mill Grove on Beaver and there conferred at length with Rev. James King. When he came away he had the much coveted option to buy sixty-seven acres of the old Mountain View estate,

This drawing of a very early Bristol home was made from an old, very faded photograph. The house was erected on Third Street, likely in the late 1850s. For years it was occupied by the Robertson family. Drawing by D.M. Cooper.

including the former King mansion. This land extended westward from Beaver Creek toward present Commonwealth Avenue and was bounded on the south by Main Street (State) and on the north and west by the Susong lands. This included the present Solar Hill section of Bristol, Virginia, and a small portion along the lower part of the three hundred block of present Moore Street.

But there was more land needed to round out Moore's purchase, that being a tract bordered by the Stage Road (Oakview Street) on the east, Park Street on the west, and what is now Euclid Avenue on the north. For weeks Moore diligently tried to buy this needed area from its owner, Mahlon Susong. If this could be obtained he would have an auspicious layout for his new Mooresburg or Mooresville, which he once privately predicted would eclipse "puny Goodson" to the east and south of his land. Apparently he had hopes that this "puny" town might be absorbed into his own. Though not saying a positive no, Susong held out for an exorbitant price, which Moore did not readily agree to pay.

In addition to land and lots bought from Anderson, Goodson, and King, A. K. Moore also bought scattered lots over the town. His position was enviable. He not only owned choice lots in Bristol-Goodson but fine tracts of land adjoining the town on the north and west sides. There is also indication that he tried to buy land from James King east of present Second Street and south of East State Street into the present Fairmount section of Bristol. But Rev. King had reserved this as a plantation for his son James and thus was not willing to sell. On September 2, 1856, Anderson made a conditional deed for his sale to Moore. (This was later turned over to Scranton and Johnston.) The purchase price of four thousand two hundred dollars was not fully paid until after Anderson's death (1888). It appears that in the intensive push to realize his dream of town building, Moore had over-extended himself. By October 1856 it became apparent that he was in severe financial difficulty. The firm of Scranton and Johnston (Daniel T. Scranton and Joseph Johnston) of Savannah, Georgia, had advanced him large sums of money on his purchases, creating an obligation that he was not able to meet.

November 3, 1856, was a dark day for A. K. Moore; it was then that he turned over to Scranton and Johnston all deeds, contracts and options on his Bristol-Goodson and vicinity holdings. For all this he was allowed three thousand five hundred dollars on his indebtedness. (His contracted purchases here amounted to several times that amount. The King option amounted to over sixteen thousand dollars.) This ended his hopes and plans for Mooresburg or Mooresville. As this writer walks about this city, the realization often comes to him that here in this little valley of the Beaver, many great hopes have been crushed as well as many fully realized, including many of his own. But Moore, the dreamer, did not slip away in despair. He remained in Bristol-Goodson, having a comfortable but unpretentious home on the northwest corner of Moore and Cumberland Streets, where he lived the remaining few years left to him. For a short time he edited and published *The News,* Bristol's third newspaper, in the smokehouse behind this home. He tried in vain to have Cumberland Street made into a new Main Street of the town. This would have led from the depot to his dwelling.

In time he became the agent and representative for Joseph Johnston. (This was after Scranton dropped out of the firm.) Perhaps it is well to note here that Scranton and Johnston followed through with the purchase of the contracted land. Not much was done with it until the greater portion of it was sold to the Town of Goodson in 1871. According to those who knew him, Moore was well educated, of marked intelligence, and usually easy going, but behind it all he had an impetuous nature that occasionally brought him into violent or near-violent confrontation with those with whom he disagreed. One noted example of this was when William King Heiskell, high sheriff of Washington County, Virginia, came to collect taxes owed by Moore's employer, Mr. Joseph Johnston.

It seems that for the year 1861, Mr. Johnston owed $101.25 on his property in and adjoining the Town of Goodson. (Johnston was still a resident of Savannah, Georgia, at the time.) Heiskell rode into Bristol-Goodson and presented Mr. Moore with the tickets. Moore claimed there was an error and asked Heiskell to change the bill. Sheriff Heiskell was not empowered to do this and tried to explain his position to Moore. The effort was fruitless, but several times later Heiskell again called on Moore for payment. These calls extended into 1862, during which there were what Heiskell called "angry meetings" with Moore. In the court case that later resulted over the matter, Heiskell described one of these meetings:

> In September [1862] I went to Mr. Moore's residence in Bristol [corner of Moore and Cumberland Streets], again asking him for the taxes. He refused to pay. We had a very angry quarrel, so much so that I thought would end fatally to one or both of us [it is said that each had a hand on a gun in his coat pocket]. But it cooled.

Moore died before the matter was settled. L. F. Johnson became an agent for Joseph Johnston and it was he who finally had to face the matter in Washington County Court.

Moore's fiery, impetuous nature finally resulted in his tragic death. In those early years there lived in Bristol-Goodson a young woman who was considered a "high-classed prostitute." She catered only to the prominent men of the town. She apparently considered Mr. Moore to be in the prominent class. In April 1863 a Capt. Lucas of Kentucky was staying at the Famous (later Thomas House) Hotel that stood on the site of the present Paramount Theatre. It seems that he too was quickly elevated to the prominent class by this prostitute. It also seems that Moore highly resented the favored position of Lucas. Moore's temper finally flared so much that he stormed into the Famous Hotel with pistol in hand. He kicked in the door of the Captain's room, shouting insults along with his frenzied action. The Captain was apparently napping but quickly arose with pistol blazing. Moore was killed but not before he had put three bullet holes through the headboard of the Captain's bed. This bed was soon given to a maid who then worked in the hotel. In 1954 it was still owned by her daughter who was yet living here, and has been viewed several times by this author.

Capt. Lucas hurriedly left town within an hour after the incident. Perhaps he feared the enraged friends of Moore. The dream of A. K. Moore was never realized but he had the consolation prize of a well known street of the town being named for him, one which remains today.

COMING OF THE RAILROADS

The Town of Bristol had been planned in anticipation of the coming of the railroads. Surprisingly, the town had experienced considerable growth long before the arrival of the first train. But while the young town expanded, the Virginia and Tennessee Railroad was slowly pushing toward it. Right-of-way clearing and preliminary grading had entered the town in late 1855. In September or October of that year, several tents for workmen are known to have been set up just below the present Janie Hammitt Home. An old gentleman living here in 1953 told of his father peddling corn and pumpkins to these workmen. And as the work moved on toward the state line, there was growing excitement among the local citizens.

An impromptu railroad celebration took place here on September 24, 1856. A. T. Wilson, who operated Bristol's first hotel, stood watching the rail-laying crew as they labored below his location on the corner of Washington and Main (State) Street. Realizing that the laying of the last rail was imminent, he hastened to the gong that then hung on Fourth (Front) Street and summoned the town. (This gong was largely used as a fire warning.) A large crowd came running and the announcement was made of the approaching historic moment. The workmen were surrounded by a large assembly as the last rail was spiked in place. There was a loud cheer but no speeches or presentations. An old timer reported that J. R. Anderson turned and walked silently back down Main Street with tears streaming from his eyes. He knew that the town he had founded was secure. John N. Bosang then led the foreman and workers to his nearby saloon for free drinks.

It was planned that the first run of a passenger train into Bristol would be on October 1, 1856. On September 24, 1856, John Robin McDaniel, the president of the Virginia and Tennessee Railroad, issued the notice and invitation for this excursion. The cost of the round trip was to be five dollars, but about half of those who made the trip received complimentary tickets from McDaniel. The trip to Bristol would consume the first day. There was to be entertainment the second day, and the return trip would be on the third day. Meanwhile, plans were being made and executed in Bristol for the big event. R. T. LeGard erected a "triumphal arch" over the railroad just east of the newly built brick depot. (The depot had been erected by James Fields, beginning in 1855.) Timbers for the erection of this arch had been bought from Morgan's saw mill, which was then located at Washington and William(s) Street. It is told that LeGard carried much of this material on his back from the mill to the site of the arch. And across Fourth (Front) Street, James Fields was busy building a dance floor and speakers' stand on a vacant lot adjoining the Magnolia Hotel property on the east.

At 6:30 A.M., October 1, 1856, two passenger trains left Lynchburg, one pulled by the "Washington" and the other by the "John Robin McDaniel." Engines were named instead of numbered at that time. The lead train, the Washington, had William Goodson Lindsey as engineer. It was a slow trip. The trains were heavily loaded and there were grades that could barely be made. Stops had to be made for fuel (wood) and a lunch stop was part of the schedule. There was a grand inspection stop at Wytheville, and of course speed left something to be desired. A passenger later related that somewhere along the line a mounted rider was able to keep up with the train for some distance. A late supper stop was made at Abingdon, Virginia, where a great throng of people had gathered to view the trains. But that "viewing" had to be done in the dark.

At the Bristol depot a large crowd waited in the autumn chill, ears straining to hear the first faint sound of a whistle. Several climbed atop the new depot, hoping to be first to catch a glimpse of the headlights of the expected trains. It appeared that every available lamp and candle in town had been lit for the occasion. Shortly after dark bonfires were lit on the hills around the town. By far the largest one was on Virginia Hill about where the Robinson mortuary is now located. That afternoon the arch had been covered with evergreens. Ann Bachelor recalled helping her foster father, Lewis Bachelor, haul these from Round Hill, just below the west end of what is now the East Hill Cemetery.

A few minutes before 9:00 P.M., someone atop the depot shouted down to the waiting crowds that a whistle had been heard. In minutes the crowd could hear the "joyful sound." And those atop the depot soon saw the faint headlight of the first train as it came into what would now be the upper end of the rail yards. By then the trains were blowing almost incessantly; indeed the back train blew so much that its steam power was greatly weakened, forcing a brief pause to "catch its breath." Thus, Lindsey's Washington was ahead of the other by some distance when it finally rolled through the arch and stopped at the rail's end on the state line. In a sense it was homecoming for Lindsey. He soon bought property here, became a prominent businessman, and died here in 1898. Lindsey is buried in the East Hill Cemetery. A local street, which ended in front of his fine Euclid Avenue home, was named for him. It is known that several others on those trains decided to settle in the growing town at the end of the Virginia and Tennessee rails.

But there was a problem. It is said that there were eight hundred persons on the trains. At that time there were only three hotels, which jointly had perhaps forty rooms. Ann Bachelor remembered that virtually every home in town opened to the weary travelers. The hotels slept three and four to the bed. Some were taken far into the surrounding country by hospitable hosts, and still many were forced to sleep in the train coaches.

Ann Bachelor remembered that the next morning, a bright and mild October day, saw the visitors fan out all over town and into the fields and pastures surrounding it, viewing out the land, many with thoughts and plans for settlement here. At noon a fine barbecue was served to the crowd. This was

Ann Bachelor as she appeared in about 1900 as the grand dame of a fine Georgia plantation. She grew up in early Bristol and her memoirs were priceless in the preparation of this history.

spread at railside just north of the depot. The oratory began at the conclusion of this feast and continued for possibly four hours. Among the speakers was Bristol's own Rev. James King, who gave a moving review of the town site from the time he first saw it. After the speeches a tour was made of the new depot, the proposed railroad yard and the unfinished roundhouse. Then there was more feasting and fellowship, concluding with a lively dance over by the Magnolia Hotel. Caesar Susong, a servant of the Susong family, masterfully played the fiddle for this dance. He never tired as long as there were those willing to dance, and some were willing to well into the wee hours of morning.

The trains loaded and left Bristol at daybreak on October 3, 1856. A few single men did not board the returning trains but stayed to take roots in Bristol, and other passengers would soon return. Facilities for turning the engines had not then been completed. Thus the trains had to be backed to Saltville Junction at Glade Springs before the change could be made. Passenger service did not begin immediately. A little time elapsed before the next train was seen in Bristol, but an era had begun that continues to this day.

At that time Bristol was the end of the line, but the rails of the East Tennessee and Virginia Railroad were headed toward the town. The building of a depot on the Tennessee side of town was commenced in 1857, in the vacant area just south of the state line, between Third Street and the tracks. The road was not finished until 1858. It was Greeneville that then held the big celebration on May 20, 1858, with excursion trains running from Bristol and Knoxville. Many Bristolians attended the event, leaving the new depot early on the appointed day. Among them was Joseph R. Anderson, who had done much to see that the railroad was finished. He gave a brief address during the festivities in Greeneville.

NEW BRISTOL

It seems that by 1861 the new spiritual perception of Rev. James King may have dimmed a bit. He still owned the land south of Main (State) Street and west of Beaver Creek, and the Town of Bristol was steadily moving toward it. By then it was apparent that Anderson's vision had been well justified; a city was in the making. King then decided to ''get back on the bandwagon.'' He planned a New Bristol along West Main Street beyond Seventh Street — extending southward toward his Mill Grove property and extending westward to the low hills (along the present Volunteer Parkway). One of the first sales in New Bristol was made to William Briscoe of Sullivan County, Tennessee, on April 20, 1861. However, it appears from Briscoe's deed that a Samuel Phillips had previously purchased a lot in King's development. Mr. Briscoe was one of the town's early master builders.

It may have been that the advent of the Civil War stopped King's development. And of course the old and highly honored Rev. King was in his declining years and health was failing. Likely he could not and did not promote it as he would have done in former days. The dream of a New Bristol soon ended. At about the time of the planning of New Bristol, Rev. James King decided to move into the Town of Bristol-Goodson. He bought from Thomas Johnston a brick English cottage that stood on the lot at the northeast corner of Moore and Main (State) Streets. This cottage stood near the back of the lot with a shrub- and flower-filled front yard. Old-timers called this yard the most beautiful spot in early downtown Bristol. The front entry was in the form of a trellis over which a climbing white rose grew. A "descendant" of that rose still brightens the back yard at Pleasant Hill, home of this author.

It was in this pleasant location that Rev. James King spent his final years. Ann Bachelor recalled that almost daily the beloved old patriarch strolled forth from the cottage, gold headed cane in hand, to visit friends and relatives along the streets. Sometimes he walked all the way to his former home on Lancaster's Hill (later a part of Solar Hill). There he might sit for hours looking out over his former plantation, then dotted by the buildings of a fast growing town. He once remarked to a member of the Lancaster family that where the English cottage stood (his current home) was the site of his winter feed lot during the high years of the operation of Mountain View plantation. Small wonder that the flowers grew so well there. But Rev. King did not simply idle away his last years. All the while he was still dealing in town real estate. The King Block on Front Street was one result of his final development efforts.

It seems that Rev. King was not the only old man who was having dreams of a new town. John N. Bosang, who was among the earliest settlers of Bristol (he came in 1854), greatly desired to leave a lasting memorial in the area he had chosen as home. On November 13, 1862, he bought ten acres of land for that purpose from Rev. James King. This land was situated along the south side of the state line, west of what is now the Volunteer Parkway. (The extension of West Main Street later formed the northern boundary.) On this was laid out Bosangville. In derision, several of Bosang's enemies (and he had many) called it the "ten acre town." Bosang's town site cost him two thousand dollars. Apparently there was not much, if any, development in this new town until well after the War. It is known that Eliza J. Aydlotte bought Lot 8 in Bosangville, on September 3, 1868. This lot fronted on Main Street. (Apparently Main had been extended to that area by that date.)

One of the selling points used by John N. Bosang for his new development was that "from its well situated heights one may look down into adjoining Bristol and to the hills and mountains beyond." But with splendid view and all, Bosangville was finally absorbed into the sprawling Bristol. Bosang's hoped for memorial did not even survive as an additional name in the growing town. And only by chance did this writer learn that it ever existed.

THE LONG PAUSE 1861-1865

The tragic Civil War caused a long pause in the rapid development of Bristol. The burning fires of progress had to be banked (though certainly not completely extinguished) until the country's worst nightmare could end. But as President Lincoln had said during the War's darkest hours, "This, too, must pass," so did Bristol's long trial end. And with that end came new vision, new strength, and new goals. The building of a city on King's Meadows would continue.

PROGRESS REPORT

By the early autumn after the close of the War, business prospects were again favorable, and some building was once more being planned. The September 29, 1865, edition of *The News* carried an article under the heading, "Looking Up," that gave an optimistic picture of the progress in the new town:

We are pleased to see business generally looking up. At present we have some twenty stores and business houses which are thronged during the day with customers and from the wagons on the streets we presume that a good deal of trade is coming from the back counties. Some of our businessmen are advertising and several more have promised to as soon as they receive their fall and winter stocks. We trust they will do so, for it speaks well of their enterprise and thrift of a town to see the business community offering enducements (sic) through their press, to their customers and the public generally. Our mechanics also seem to be busy. This is a good omen; for nothing speaks better for a town or adds more to its prosperity.

The same paper reported that a new school was ready to open in the town. The newspaper had plans for a semi- or tri-weekly publication. J. R. Anderson had just received a stock of new fall goods, the saloons had loaded up for the winter season, and several ads offered local and nearby real estate for sale. The paper also noted that the churches of the town were on the forward move again. The long pause had turned to future progress.

NEW LEADERS FOR THE TOWN

Soon after the close of the Civil War there came to Bristol many men of outstanding intelligence and leadership ability. Some of these had already gained a degree of prominence and wealth in the areas from whence they came. Among them were several ex-Confederate officers, broken in fortune, but rich in determination and patience. They came from Abingdon; Blountville; Scott County, Virginia; Carter County, Tennessee; and numerous other places. It has always been a source of profound amazement to this author how so many came here with virtually nothing but the worn clothes upon their war-weary backs, yet in a very short time they were among the wealthiest of the town. They sought and found, they knocked and doors were opened to them. Yet they only asked for the opportunity of earnest endeavor. In time many of their names were among the best known and highest honored in town. They lived in honor and renown and died mourned by their fellow citizens, and the town was better for their having lived and labored in it.

THE OLD MUST DIE

Those first few years following the close of the war saw the passing of three of Bristol's best known citizens. First was Mourning Micajah Watkins King, wife of Rev. James King. The stress of the war years had been hard on "Sweet Little Mourning" as she was called by her husband. During that conflict her health had broken and numerous ailments with resultant increasing weakness had been her lot from then on. She was sleeping peacefully at about 2:00 the afternoon of July 24, 1866, as her husband (fan in hand) sat by her bedside. She suddenly awoke and asked him, "Is it ready?" He, knowing what she meant, replied that it was. She dropped back to sleep and a few minutes later, "simply quit breathing," as he later expressed it.

The "it" of which Mrs. King inquired was the family tomb. It seems that she harbored a life-long fear of burial and had requested that an above-ground tomb be built. Rev. King hired John Aiken, a local builder, to construct the tomb on the bank of Beaver Creek near the north corner of the home yard at Mill Grove (later English Grove). The stone for its construction was quarried from the hills back of present Ninth Street. It was finished the day before the death of Mrs. King, and she was the first to be placed in it. This pioneer mother was nearly three months past her 70th birthday.

Rev. King was left with two orphans in his household: Joseph Chalmers King and his sister Charlotte Louise (called Chassie). Their two sisters, Alice Margaret and Mary Francis, who had also been taken into the home, had married before the passing of Mrs. King. They were the children of Cyrus King, son of James and Mourning M. King. Alice was the first wife of Capt. Joseph W. Owen, and Mary Francis had married Joe S. Hill.

In July 1867 Rev. King went to visit his daughter and son-in-law, John G. and Margaret King English, who then lived at Egypt, Monroe County, Mississippi. He died suddenly a few days after his arrival there. His body was placed in a cherry coffin and returned to Bristol by train. L. F. Johnson remembered the large crowd that waited at the depot for the arrival of this

train. It was more than two hours late, arriving at sundown. He remembered
that several strong men of the town carried the coffin on their shoulders to
the King home at Main and Moore. By King's previous request, the funeral
was held in the front yard of this home, the coffin being placed under a
spreading apple tree that stood near the front gate. (One old citizen said east
of that gate.) He was placed in the family tomb at the old Beaver Creek home.
Over sixty years ago this tomb began to deteriorate, after having been flooded
several times by the nearby creek. It was then that the bodies were moved
to East Hill Cemetery. Some of the cut stones from this tomb are in the front
doorsteps of the J. E. Baumgardner home on Prospect Avenue, Bristol,
Virginia.

**The old King vault at English Grove on Beaver.
Finished shortly before the death of Mrs. James King
(1866), it served as a tomb for Mrs. King, Rev. James
King, and others of his family. The bodies were moved
to East Hill Cemetery in the 1920s and the vault was
demolished.**

On March 16, 1867, Rev. King had written his will, using dark brown ink and a pale blue paper so popular at that time. This seven-page will was witnessed by Robert A. Wood, Audley Anderson (a brother of the town's founder), John Keys (who had been second postmaster of Bristol), and E.B. McClanahan, prominent citizen of Bristol-Goodson. King wisely signed every page of this document. Much of the real estate passed by this will would affect the future development of Bristol. The Mill Grove property on Beaver Creek was willed to his son-in-law, John G. English, and thus became English Grove. Land farther down Beaver was willed to the orphans of his son, Cyrus King. The land east of Beaver Creek to present Fifth Street and extending southward to beyond Stine Street, as well as five hundred acres in the knobs, was willed to his son John Goodson King. This son also got the hay scales. Joseph Anderson, a son-in-law, received the land along Ice or Whittaker Branch, and King's compass and chain. The large tract of land extending eastward from Second Street and south of Main (State) and well into the Fairmount section was willed to the children of James King, III (sometimes called James King, Jr.). These children also received the Shady Valley lands. It is believed that James King, III was then living, creating a mystery as to why the land was given to the children.

At the time of his death, Rev. King's orphaned granddaughter Charlotte (Chassie) King was still living in his home. To her he willed this home and its contents, as well as all his real estate on the Virginia side of town. She later became the bride of Dr. A.M. Carter, who was a direct descendant of Governor John Sevier. While yet a very young woman, Chassie King Carter developed tuberculosis. The family then moved to what was later known as the Bunting home (formerly Jones-Lancaster-Coleman house) in the 300 block of Moore Street. Dr. Carter feared that the dampness of the Beaver Creek bottoms would aggravate the disease and that moving to a higher location would be beneficial to his suffering wife. She died soon after this move. Only one of her three children survived — Maude, who became the mother of the late A. Carter Crymble of Kingsport, Tennessee. He kindly supplied the author with much of this information on the King family. Dr. Carter soon married Nannie Zimmerman, a daughter of the town's first physician. The property at the corner of Moore and State Streets, where King's English cottage with its colorful dooryard once stood, still remains in the family.

When Samuel E. Goodson was a child, he often played under a huge beechnut tree standing in the corner of the yard of the old John Goodson home on Beaver Creek. This home was about two miles above Bristol. Later he and the family slaves cooled themselves there after laboring in the home fields. After he became an old man and before his move to Bristol in 1857, he spent many hours sitting under this tree. In late 1857, desiring to be nearer his development projects in Bristol-Goodson, he moved into town, living first in the Magnolia Hotel and later in the Lancaster House Hotel, where his room was number 8.

During the Civil War, he fled town barely ahead of Stoneman's raiders. He prepared himself a bed in a freight car, and his train had hardly cleared the town when the raiders arrived and tore up the tracks. He spent the remainder of the war in Richmond and other places. One of the first things he did upon arrival back in Bristol-Goodson was to send workmen to cut the huge beech tree in the old family yard, having it sawed into lumber at Hoffman's mill, located near the Goodson farm. This lumber was stored in a barn at the old Goodson homestead. In 1869 he had a portion of the lumber brought into town, and G.H. Mattox made a coffin of it. By then Goodson had moved in with the Joseph W. Owen family on Mary Street. He had the coffin placed in his bedroom at this home, and there it remained until his death. It is said that Mrs. Owen was a little shaken by this reminder of mortality in her home, so she covered it with a blanket and stacked quilts on it.

Samuel Goodson died on January 31, 1870. He had made his home with the Owens family since 1866. (For more on his death see the chapter entitled "Mortality/Cemeteries.") Col. Goodson had made his will on December 16, 1869. This will was apparently written by the law firm of York and Fulkerson. The partners in this firm, U.L. York and A. Fulkerson, signed as witnesses. In this will he gave all his real estate to Joseph W. Owen, over whom he was once guardian. James Owen, a brother of Joseph, was given five thousand dollars. A widow Rust was given twelve hundred dollars, a portion of which was to be used to buy a home for her. Other relatives were given lesser amounts, including a two hundred fifty dollar bequest to Mrs. Elizabeth King, wife of James King, III. Goodson specifically directed that all cash bequests be paid in United States currency. Goodson also forgave the debts of James Fields and Henry A. Wells, and kindly remembered his former slaves, Ed Stoffle and wife, by giving each of them fifty dollars, plus two horses, an old wagon, gearing and farming equipment, which apparently Stoffle was already using. Goodson had already given his household furniture to J.W. Owen, but still had a small amount of personal property, most of which remained on the old home farm. On February 28, 1870, the court appointed John Keys, Roland T. Legard and Hugh M. Millard to appraise this property. Their report follows:

Bay horse	$100.00	1 Buggy	$45.00
Roan horse	40.00	2 Hay forks	1.00
Plow and harness	7.00	1 Bull Tongue plow	1.00
Lot of bacon		1 Lot of old iron	2.00
(about 800 lbs @ .14	112.00	1 Large iron band	1.00

Two planes & foot adz	3.00	2 Sacks of plaster	2.50
1 Old oven	.50	2 Hoes & mattock	.50
1 White cow & calf	30.00	1 Set harness	25.00
1 Roan cow	30.00	1 Harrow	2.00
1 Black cow	16.00		
1 Two horse wagon	30.00	TOTAL	$485.50

Court records in Abingdon, Virginia, show that Goodson's estate took several years to settle. Several lots he had sold were not paid for at the time of his death, and it appears that the administrators had to resort to court action to collect on some of them.

Eighty-three long years had passed since the death of Col. Goodson, when this writer arrived in Bristol. An elderly lady who lived here at that time had a fond memory of him. As a five-year-old girl, she had once stood with her mother at the edge of a muddy street, crying to be carried across to keep from getting her new shoes muddy. The mother, holding a baby in one arm and a two-year old child in the other, could offer no help to the little girl. Col. Goodson stood nearby, conversing with a friend, and when he saw the little girl's dilemma he walked over, lifted her to his shoulder, and delivered her to the other side of the street, clean shoes and all. Memories such as these, shared with this author so many years ago, were his real inspiration for writing this book.

ENLARGING THE BORDERS

Even before the Civil War there were those in Bristol who were casting aspiring glances toward Solar and Virginia Hills. They seemed to be the logical areas for future development. Indeed, there had been some development on the eastern portion of Virginia Hill, upon lots that had been laid out as part of Goodsonville. However, with the exception of the old King mansion and its grounds, most of Solar Hill remained as pasture land with a wooded area near the present railroad cut on the north side and back toward the Susong lands. There was a grove of large oaks on what is now the northwest corner of Solar and Cumberland. Just why this grove was left in the midst of a pasture is not known. Some say there were a few graves there. What is more plausible is the belief of certain King descendants that their ancestor left these oaks as shade for his stock. He is known to have had a propensity for doing things of that nature, being ever concerned for the comfort of his livestock. Huge trees had been left here and there over King's Meadows for the same reason. One of them, a big sycamore standing near the middle of the six hundred block of State Street, was used as a starting point for town boundaries in the incorporation of 1856. Another, a giant cherry tree standing near the depot, was used as a state line marker. It is known that the town residents used to cut firewood in the wooded area of Solar Hill.

The hills offered natural advantages. They were high, well drained, and, for those with an eye toward beauty, they offered splendid views of the town as well as the hills and mountains beyond. Too, the Beaver Flats (now downtown Bristol) were considered to be unhealthy because of the extreme dampness. This dampness was sometimes called "sickly vapors" by the old settlers. Thus, those seeking more salubrious residential areas were looking toward the hills. Of course, the expansion of the town southward was blocked by the King farm lands. Various farms blocked westward growth. To the northeast toward present Fairmount, that portion of the King lands that had been set aside as a home farm for James King, III and on which he then lived, halted expansion in that direction. Yet the hills were owned by Joseph Johnston, a capitalist, of Savannah, Georgia (later of Philadelphia, Pennsylvania). From the time he had bought the deeds and options on these areas from A.K. Moore in late 1856, he had shown little interest in their development, though he had sold small tracts from time to time; however, it is evident that he saw the value of holding on to them, because he paid Daniel T. Scranton a considerable amount for the latter's interest in the acreage. There was the interruption of the war and the period of struggle immediately thereafter, during which little expansion or development was done. But even during that period, there were a few men with great foresight who were looking to the hills. Then came the solar eclipse of 1869, and those who looked out from Bristol's hills into the depths of the universe were somewhat symbolic of those who, a short time later, would have an unlimited vision of an expanded Bristol itself.

THE SOLAR ECLIPSE, 1869

To observe the great solar eclipse of August 7, 1869, astronomers were sent from Washington, D.C., to various locations in the United States and to some foreign points. Bristol was chosen as one of the observation points, along with such other diverse places as Hannibal, Missouri; Mt. Vernon, Indiana; Alton, Illinois; Oakland Station, Kentucky; and White Top Mountain in southwest Virginia. On the day of the eclipse, Mr. F.W. (Aid) Bardwell and his assistant, Mr. Thomas Davidson, arrived in Bristol by train. They were told that another party had set up on Lancaster Hill (later Solar Hill) and were then directed to the site. Near the intersection of present Cumberland and Solar Streets, General Cutts and his Coast Survey party had a rather elaborate platform built atop solid brick pillars. I.C. Fowler, writing in the *Bristol News* two years later, used these pillars as a landmark when informing his readers of the beginning point of Solar Street. It appears that Bardwell and Davidson went a little farther up the ridge to set up their observation point. Tradition has it that this point was on or near the vacant lot between

203 and 213 Solar, the present Woody and Rayburn homes. In writing of the matter, Bardwell states:

> The point selected was on the brow of a hill moderately elevated above the surrounding country, with an extended view of the western horizon.... The set-up was at a distance of the station of the other parties, and far enough from the public highway to be free from the intrusions of idle visitors.

Bardwell wrote of experiencing some anxiety in the early part of the day because of an overcast sky. However, he noted that the skies brightened by noon and became completely clear as the critical hour approached.

Bardwell observed as Davidson counted the seconds. The total eclipse commenced at one minute sixteen seconds past six o'clock and continued for two minutes and thirty seconds. Evidently it was awesome from Bardwell's station, and it appears to have been even more so from White Top Mountain, where Brigadier General A.J. Meyer and Colonel W. Winthrop of the U.S. Army had established their station.

At the same time many amateur astronomers were watching the skies. Letters had been sent to postmasters across the land asking them to encourage observers to send in reports of the eclipse. At the same time newspapers were asked to publish instructions for these amateur observers. Mr. Charles Coale of Abingdon, Virginia, won high commendation for his accurate observations. And all across the nation, Western Union wired the results of official stations free of charge.

But as scientific eyes fearlessly watched the heavens, there was anxiety to the point of panic among those of a more superstitious nature. One lady, who lived on upper Washington Street, was gathering eggs in her hen house when the untimely darkness settled in. She was found later, still in the hen house, frozen in fear and clutching a squashed egg in one hand. It took some doing to convince her that the world really had not ended. Elsewhere, an old fellow on Second Street called his family to prayer as he awaited the judgment to fall upon the earth. And others, thinking the end of the world had come, fled to the woods, screaming as they went.

Near town someone died during the darkness. The officiating minister at the funeral profited on the situation by saying that the heavens had wept in darkness at the passing of an old "saint." (The author must add that his own great-great grandfather, Eley Boggs of Letcher County, Kentucky, also lay dying when the strange darkness spread across the surrounding hills. However, folks there ascribed a slightly different interpretation of the fearful event, being convinced that it portended everlasting perdition for their aged neighbor.) Today we have Solar Hill and Solar Street to remind us of the observations that were made there in 1869.

THE JOHNSTON LAND SALE

At the beginning of the 1870s, virtually all the residences in Bristol were located on the Beaver Flats. Main Street (now State) had numerous dwellings interspersed among the stores and other business establishments. Shelby and Broad were residential streets. Cumberland on the Virginia side, while having a few businesses, was mostly residential, as was the rest of the King's Meadow in that area. Homes stretched up along East Main (State) to present Goodson Street on the Virginia side and to Second Street on the Tennessee side. Beyond Second Street the cultivated fields of James King, III began. According to one old-timer, "When the wind was jist right ye could hear Marion Gose (plowman for King) cussin' his mules plum down town, when he wuz plowin' rat square where Pennsylvania Avenue is now."

One house had been built high on the hill beyond Pennsylvania Avenue, but it was not within the town limits. (It still stands at 122 East State Street.) The cemetery was then "up in the woods," far beyond town. There were a few homes on the eastern part of Virginia Hill (Lee, Russell, Spencer Street area) and perhaps a few on Virginia and Goodson Streets across the tracks to the north. These areas were a part of the old Goodsonville that, along with the old Bristol, Virginia, became a part of the composite Town of Goodson in 1856. Some of the finer residences in town stood along Third and Fourth Streets. The town was largely residential along Main (State) beyond Seventh Street, and about played out before reaching the area of present Commonwealth Avenue. Beyond on both sides of the state line stretched fields and pastures with a farmhouse here and there. Cornfields crowded the town beyond Broad Street and west of College Street (now Fifth). Just beyond and to the west of the railroad overpass across Piedmont Avenue, and to the west of Oak View Street, stretched open farm lands. Great fields of wheat and corn grew in the vicinity of Highland, Fairmount and Euclid and westward toward present Commonwealth Avenue.

The Beaver Flats (now downtown Bristol) were becoming rather crowded, and expanding businesses were almost constantly demolishing residences to make way for new commercial buildings. Too, many of the first Bristol homes were small and had been constructed of poorly burned brick. By 1870 many of them were already deteriorating, and records show that one or two actually collapsed. The time had come when many of the town's citizens, their wealth increasing, were looking for places to build finer and larger homes. The hills presented the most logical answer to their needs.

ALMOST A PRIVATE DEVELOPMENT

W. W. James was not one to let a money-making opportunity pass. Neither was his newly acquired son-in-law, Capt. J. H. Wood. In 1870 the two made a trip to Philadelphia to consult with Joseph Johnston concerning the purchase of his Bristol-Goodson lands. (Johnston had moved to that city from Savannah, Georgia.) Johnston agreed to sell the land, resulting in plans by James and Wood to make the purchase and use it for private development. However, at about that time Mr. James encountered severe financial difficulties, and J. H. Wood had not yet amassed his fortune. Consequently, another Bristol dream failed. However, it was J. H. Wood who headed the move to have the town of Goodson make the purchase and then offer the lots at public sale. His efforts continued into 1871, when negotiations were begun with Johnston to sell the land to the town on a long term payment plan. As the negotiations drew to a successful conclusion, Joseph Johnston made a trip to Bristol to consummate the deal. According to an old newspaper report, Mr. Johnston stayed at the Virginia House Hotel and endeared himself to the town fathers by his kind and reasonable dealings with them. Joseph Palmer, writing in his diary, described Johnston as being of rather tall and large build, having an Abe Lincoln style beard and always dressing formally, including a silk top hat which added to his stature. Palmer went on to comment that Johnston always stood as straight as a "poplar sapling," and walked about with "awesome dignity." But some added that this "transplanted southern aristocrat" had a kind and easygoing disposition and was very careful of his statements. He sold his very valuable lands in Bristol for the generous price of $24,937.50, with ten years to pay. J.H. Wood, a practicing lawyer, drew up the agreement and terms and drafted the deed, which Johnston apparently carried back to Philadelphia, where it was later signed and notarized, well after the voters of the town had given their approval to the move.

The General Assembly of Virginia had amended the charter of Goodson on March 14, 1871, granting, among other things, the right to purchase the Johnston lands, but with the restriction that the action would have to be approved by three-fifths of the voters of the town. The election during which the issue would be presented to the public was set for Tuesday, May 9, 1871. During the meeting of the Common Council (as the City Council was then called) on May 2, 1871, Dr. C. T. Pepper moved that William H. Trammel, John N. Bosang, and John Keys be appointed to serve as judges during that election. These noted citizens later received two dollars each for their services. On election day, one hundred and twenty-two men of Goodson went to the mayor's office on Lee Street and bravely called out their vote. (This was before the secret ballot was used in Bristol.) One hundred and one voted in favor of the purchase, while twenty-one voted against it. The requirement of the amended charter had been met; the Johnston lands could be bought.

During the Common Council meeting of May 29, 1871, Mr. S. L. Saul moved that five hundred stakes be obtained for the marking of the lots for the coming land sale. Other records show that these stakes were supplied by G. H. Mattox, a local undertaker and furniture maker, at three cents each. During the same meeting a committee was appointed to oversee laying off the lots. This committee consisted of Mayor I. C. Fowler, John H. Winston and Capt. Joseph W. Owen. Prof. Thomas D. Walthall was hired to survey and map the lots and streets, and on June 20, 1871, he reported that he had completed the survey and had prepared a map of the same. Prof. J. H. Winston then moved to allow Walthall sixty-five dollars for his services; the motion carried. Then Winston moved that a committee with the power needed to hire assistance be formed to stake and number the lots. Mayor Fowler promptly appointed J. H. Winston, G. H. DeVault and T. J. Millard to this committee, and the task was soon completed.

By this date the sale was being heavily advertised, both publicly and privately. Many of the leading citizens of the town contacted friends of means in other places, hoping to interest them in moving to Bristol-Goodson. It appears that their efforts were successful. Ads were placed in several area papers, as well as in papers in Lynchburg, Virginia, from where a good many settlers had already come. The known papers that carried advertisements for the sale and their charges for that service were:

Bristol Courier	$20.00
Jonesboro Patriot	5.00
Jonesboro Flag	5.00
Lynchburg Republican	15.00
Lynchburg News	12.50

In addition the *Bristol News* carried paid advertisements and printed the needed forms, bonds and coupons. The charge for it all was ninety dollars. Oddly, there is no record of any Abingdon, Virginia, newspaper having carried any advertisements whatsoever for this sale.

On June 21, 1871, it was decided to have S. L. Saul and J. W. Owen see to the selling of hay on the Johnston land. Within two days they had sold it to J. W. Thomas for sixty-five dollars and had granted him the right to pasture two or three cows. (Included was the restriction that no pasturing be done during wet weather and the requirement that Thomas was to keep up the fences.) It is likely that the cows Mr. Thomas wished to pasture were those used to provide milk for his Thomas House Hotel, since the practice at that time was for local hotels to have cows of their own for that purpose.

By late June the Common Council had chosen James F. Saul to be the auctioneer for the coming sale of lots. He was to be paid five dollars per day for his services. The Council also granted permission for a snack vendor to set up on Cumberland Street for the benefit of the expected sale-day crowd. On June 27, 1871, the Council set up a committee to assess the lots and directed that no lot be valued at less than one hundred twenty-five dollars. This committee consisted of Major Zachariah L. Burson, W. W. James and Rev. David Sullins.

I. C. Fowler, then Mayor of Goodson, was also editor of the *Bristol News*. Not only had he sold advertising space to the Council, but his paper had carried a great deal of free advertising. In June 1871 his paper carried the following notice:

GREAT SALE OF TOWN LOTS
The Council of Goodson has fixed upon the 5th day of July for the sale of the lots just purchased from Joseph Johnston. They will probably aggregate fifty acres, and will be sold to the highest bidder at auction. Purchasers will be required to pay a small amount down in cash, and on the remainder they will have an accommodation of one, two, three, four, and five years. These lots are very beautiful and the soil is of excellent quality; very many of them incomparably desirable, commanding a view of the entire town and much of the vicinity.... It may be well to remark that these lands are bisected by the Cumberland Gap Railway [survey] which will be completed in two years or less. [Alas, Fowler's optimism was not rewarded; the C.G.R. was never finished.] The sale will be continued from day to day, until completed.

Editor Fowler was emphatic in his belief that the time was ripe for expansion. He mentioned that over seventy houses had been built in Bristol during the past year, and estimated the population of the town (both Bristol-Goodson, Virginia, and Bristol, Tennessee) to be two thousand people. He projected that within five years the population would be ten thousand! But he was overly optimistic: fifteen years later, the town had barely reached five thousand.

As sale day neared, there was growing uneasiness among the town fathers. Not that they feared that the sale would be unsuccessful; indeed, some worried that there would not be enough lots to fill the demand. The main cause of anxiety among nearly all of them was that the promised deed had not arrived. The reasons for this delay are uncertain, but the most plausible explanation — and this is supported by information handed down from those who lived at the time — is that Mary Johnston, wife of the seller, was reluctant to let such valuable land go. She hesitated in signing the deed, but finally, in late June, J. H. Wood hurried to Philadelphia to look into the matter. He later said that Mrs. Johnston softened when he told her that a choice street in the new development had been named as a memorial for her husband, and upon hearing this, she signed the deed on June 29, 1871, before Joseph Brobston, Notary of Philadelphia County, Pennsylvania. Lawyer Wood arrived back in Bristol on July 2, bearing the long-sought document, and the town fathers doubtlessly slept a little easier that night.

The sale was scheduled to begin at 8:30 A.M., July 5, 1871. Several days prior to this date, prospective buyers began arriving. There was a constant stream of outsiders as well as local citizens going to the hills to examine the staked-out, numbered lots. Many of these potential buyers, both local and out-of-town, took their wives and children along with them to help in choosing a spot for their future home. Hopes and aspirations were unquestionably high as they trod the ground where their dreams might play out; and it is likely that some looked out and exulted in the grand view to be had. The day and night before the sale brought an even greater influx of interested and curious parties. The hotels became packed, the restaurants did great business, and at least two saloons stayed open through the night. The area had rarely seen the like of it.

The town was in the grip of a sweltering heat wave, causing many of those who could not sleep in the stuffy rooms of the local hotels to stay up most of the night. An old-timer recalled that many of them congregated around the depot, talking and planning the big day ahead. Long before the starting hour, a Mr. Everitt was setting up his snack table under a huge elm that stood about where the Episcopal Church is now located, and a steady stream of townsmen and visitors was winding toward the starting point. Just about everyone in town, including many of the women, turned out for the noted event. Stores were left in the care of clerks, and offices were closed as the town's leading citizens sought to witness what they hoped would be the beginning of Bristol's big boom.

It was decided that because David Sullins knew the lots and terms of the sale, he should sell the first two or three, warming up for the selected auctioneer. The lot chosen was that at the southwest corner of King and Sullins. It was a choice building lot, commanding a grand, sweeping view of the King's Meadows and Beaver Flats, as well as the ascending farm land to the west and the picturesque, pastoral scenes along and above present Holston Avenue. It is said that twenty or more men were interested in this site, and thus bidding went on at great length, with Rev. Sullins expertly guiding and encouraging the proceedings. Finally Nathan Dodd prevailed and obtained the choice lot for three hundred dollars. After another sale or two, the committee, with the approval of auctioneer James F. Saul, asked Sullins to go on with the sale. He consented and about that time J. H. Wood offered him the use of his horse, Prince. Prince was somewhat of a historic horse, and perhaps it was fitting that he should again figure in a historic event. He had been taken to Maryland in his younger days for the purpose of transporting Capt. Wood back to his Virginia home, Wood having been released from a Union prison and too weak to make the long journey on foot. (Prince Street was named for this horse.) Sullins rode the horse on through the day, preceded by two lads who "flagged" the lots. Those placing the flags were Frank Winston and a Pepper youth. Each received three dollars and a quarter for working through the sale.

The day was a "scorcher", making business good for two enterprising boys. Editor Fowler soon published the following note in the *Bristol News* concerning their venture:

> Masters Willie and Henry Thomas will accept our thanks for their courtesy in furnishing us with ice cold lemonade during the scorching hours of the great land sale on Wednesday.

> Their energy is worthy of the imitation of our grown men, and we predict for them the success and regard to which they have some claims by way of inheritance.

Alas, poor Willie had not time to succeed. About eight years later he, then being about twenty-one years old, fell in a pool of his own blood, shed by the hand of a murderer. The tragedy occurred in downtown Bristol-Goodson.

Among the memories of old pioneers of Bristol is the recollection that the boys only had a half dozen or so tin cups with which to serve their thirsty customers. Of course, there was no way to wash these between servings. It is told that one rather fastidious lady in the crowd made quite a fuss because the preceding customer had left tobacco stains on and in the cup. The lemonade cart was pulled by two goats. The cart and goats had been borrowed from the sons of Dr. J. J. Ensor. The lemonade sold for five cents a cup, and it is told that some customers consumed a quarter's worth before relinquishing the cup to the next awaiting person.

At noon the hungry crowd fled to the snack table that had been set up by Mr. Everitt. There was food enough for only a fraction of the crowd. So David Sullins declared an extra hour for the noon recess to enable the unfed to hasten into town to eat.

The sale continued until near sunset and resumed on Thursday, July 6th. It ended about noon that day. On this second day of sales several lots that had not sold the previous day were again offered for sale. A few of them sold. Among these was a very choice lot on Johnston (Johnson) Street. It was the middle lot of the first block, west side, and would now encompass 110 and 116 Johnson Street. Mayor I. C. Fowler suggested that this lot be turned over to Rev. David Sullins at a token price, in appreciation of his

expert conducting of the sale. The crowd agreed and the lot was turned over
to Sullins for fifty dollars, with the cost being paid by W.W. James. It was
a bargain; the lots on either side of it had brought over three hundred dollars
each.

Later Fowler suggested that the town give Sullins a lot (presumably another
lot) in recognition of his services. In his *Bristol News*, published the day
after the close of the sale, appeared an item concerning this matter:

> The Rev. David Sullins consented to be the auctioneer on Wednesday
> last. It was a happy hit, he is a high souled, high toned gentleman and
> gave dignity to the occasion, inspired confidence, and humored the
> crowd. His services were of very great value, and as recognition on
> the part of the people, we suggest that the Council make him a present
> of a lot. If the people are consulted, it will be unanimous.

The outcome of this plea is not known.

In spite of all efforts, sixteen lots remained unsold, though some of them
were well situated. The lots, along with the reserved five and three-tenth
acres of Meadow Square (this was in downtown Bristol-Goodson), were
evaluated at ten thousand twenty-five dollars. (The square was valued at
seventy-five hundred dollars.) Thus, the value of the unsold lots added to
thirty-one thousand two hundred forty-three dollars in actual sales, totaled
to forty-one thousand two hundred sixty-eight dollars, causing the Council
to claim a profit of approximately sixteen thousand dollars on the Johnston
land purchase and sale.

Though each lot was to be valued at no less than one hundred twenty-five
dollars, and bidding was supposed to start at that point, it is apparent that
in actual practice, lots went for whatever could be had for them. It appears
that the great bargain of the day was claimed by J. S. Jefferson, who bought
three lots at fifteen dollars each. Thirteen other lots sold for less than one
hundred dollars each. The highest price at which a single lot sold was six
hundred and five dollars that was paid by a Mr. McCormack for the lot at
the southwest corner of Scott and Johnston. While this may be a surprise
to those familiar with the area today, it must be remembered that this was
expected to be railroad frontage, and it was believed that Scott would soon
be among the elite sections of the town. In those days railroad frontage was
much desired for residential building.

The second highest lot was number 32, now encompassing 210, 214, and
220 Johnson Street, which went to R. E. Moore for five hundred and ninety-
five dollars. It was soon taken over by Capt. J. H. Wood, who built his
"Pleasant Hill" in the center of it. This is now the home of this author.

On the evening of July 6, 1871, a few hours after the sale closed, the Common Council voted to deposit the receipts in the Exchange Bank of Goodson, that had been founded only a short time before the sale. There was not much to deposit; most of the sales had been made on credit, with very small down payments. Each buyer was issued and signed a bond, at the bottom of which were several coupons. These coupons were to be detached as payments were made. The writer is privileged to own a few of these original bonds, and has seen several more. Alas, many of them remain "unpicked." Default in payment was appallingly common over the next several years. Numerous lawsuits were instigated over payment failures, and Fowler's paper contained many pleas for the buyers to come forth and settle accounts. Even the town, having made agreement with Johnston to make full payment in ten years — that is by 1881 — did not fully pay up until 1882.

It is apparent that some bought for speculative purposes. Lot resales and swaps began almost immediately — some say on the very day of the sale. As one looks over the list of buyers and then checks tax and deed records later, it is clear that very few who bought the lots actually built upon them. It is interesting to note that some built, even before they had deeds to the property. Apparently, they had great confidence that the financial obligations could be met. It was so with J. H. Wood, who built this author's home. It was finished in the spring of 1873, long before he had paid for the lot.

Before the sale was over, at least one buyer had started his building. On the morning of the second day of sales (July 6, 1871), W. W. James sent building materials and local contractors Briscoe and Caldwell to commence erection of a house on the lot he had purchased on Sullins Street the previous day. And Mr. G. M. Whitten was not far behind him. Mr. Whitten had purchased the lot on the northeast corner of Sycamore and Solar, apparently from John H. Winston, who had bought it on the first day of the land sale. Within a week of the sale, Mr. Whitten had Andrew Fillinger erecting the brick walls of his home. I. C. Fowler noted in the *Bristol News* that James and Whitten were racing to see which of them could claim the distinction of having completed the first building on the Johnston Purchase tract. James won by a few days, when his house was completed on September 11, 1871, slightly over two months after the sale was held. The James house was demolished years ago, but the Whitten home still stands at 203 Solar, and is now the oldest structure on that street, and among the oldest in this city. It is now the home of the Dave Woody family.

I. C. Fowler, the ever optimistic editor of the *Bristol News,* believed that the great response experienced during the land sale was portentous of a great boom and a glowing future for his town. He commented that the quality of buyers indicated that much building of a substantial nature was certain to come. However, it does not appear that the Council wholly agreed with this statement concerning the quality of the buyers. It appears that some got carried away at the sale, as often happens on such occasions, and bid on property with little possibility of paying for it. So it was that on August 15, 1871, the Council directed a Mr. Harmeling to notify parties that had been deemed insolvent that their claims had been forfeited.

THE GRAND INVITATION

During the height of elation over the success of the sale, Fowler wrote his famous invitation to the world. It was published as an editorial in the *Bristol News*, and was taken up by friendly papers over the area. Waxing a bit eloquent, he wrote:

COME

Any one doubting the future growth of Bristol would have had those doubts removed by attending the sale on Wednesday last. It seems to be a settled fact that we are to have a population of ten thousand within the next five years. Building has ever been active in town and an impetus will hence forward be given it that has been unfelt and unknown theretofore. As a point for manufacturing Bristol has advantages over any of the older cities along the line. There is a vast fortune awaiting the men, who will with energy and perseverance, commence the manufacture of improved agricultural implements at this point. Woolen and cotton goods will yield a handsome profit and a thousand articles could be made here upon which we now pay tribute to New England. We buy our threshing machines at Schenectady, New York, our shellers from Massachusetts, cutters from Connecticut, reapers and mowers from Ohio and New York, while stoves are bought from Baltimore and New York. The Cumberland Gap road will open a wide field to us and furnish the finest coal, iron and timber known to the continent. Who will step forward and reap the rich harvest sown upon this great highway by nature's bountiful hand, and which even the roaming buffalo had instinct to discover, and Daniel Boone the sense and hardihood to follow up?

To the stranger from whatever land and whatever clime, we say come; we have a home for you and a work to do. To the Irishman we say come, we have railroads to build and ditches to dig; to the Scotchman we say come, we have mountain slopes for you to tend and craggy heights to be reclaimed; to the Englishman we say come, we have green fields to graze and beef to roast; to the German we say come, we have fields to till and bogs to be reclaimed; to the Italian we say come, we have vineyards to grow and fruits to gather; to the manufacturer we say come, we have power in every mountain to rent and a market around the family hearthstone; to the mechanic we say come, we have mills to build and houses to erect; to the miner we say come and dig where nature's seedman broke the lapstring and spilled the richest treasures given him to sow; to the wayworn traveler, sick of life and tired of an endless path we say come and drink at our mineral fountains, breathe the pure air of our mountain homes, and rest thy weary limbs beneath the cool shades of our beautiful trees, whatever thy lot in life, whether prince or peasant, in the silken bower of thy ancestral home, or the humble cottage where poverty wars against thee and thy loved ones, we have a home for thee, and a work to do.

They may have come, but all of Johnston's tract was not settled immediately. Nearly twenty years later there were only scattered homes on Solar Hill and the same situation existed on Virginia Hill. There were only four houses on all the west side of Solar Street as late as 1890, and about the same number on the east side of the same street. Johnson Street had only eleven buildings along its entire length. But let another fifteen years pass and the situation would dramatically change.

On September 12, 1871, the town treasurer reported that he had collected only a little more than three thousand dollars on the land sale, and deposited the same in the designated bank. At the same time the Council voted to have Professor Walthall make a copy of the Johnston Purchase map and send to Mr. Joseph Johnston at Philadelphia. We can only imagine that it pleased the old gentleman to see that broad streets and spacious lots had been laid out in his former hay field and pastures.

MOVING SOUTHWARD
Before the ink was dry on the contracts of the Johnston land, John G. King was offering to take down the fences around his corn and wheat fields and allow the town to move southward. In 1867 he had inherited from his father, Rev. James King, a vast tract of land that included the area now traversed by Alabama Street, Edgemont Avenue, Sixth and Seventh Streets, and Fifth Street south of Anderson Park, and the several streets running across these thoroughfares. In the July 7, 1871, edition of the *Bristol News* there appeared an ad placed by King, offering two hundred one-fourth-acre lots at from one to two hundred dollars each. This ad notes that nearly all these lots were beautifully situated for residences and convenient to the business center. These were to be sold on liberal terms, especially to those who desired to build immediately. Those interested were asked to contact King's attorney, D. F. Bailey, of Bristol-Goodson, Virginia. It is known that a few lots were sold soon after this offer. The committee to lay off these lots was composed of

David Sullins, L. F. Johnson, John Slack, I. C. Fowler, and E. B. McClanahan. King reserved the right to name all streets, though he gave notice that he was open to suggestions. Some of these streets were extensions of those already in existence.

Meanwhile, on September 1, 1871, King College joined the "land rush" tide that was sweeping Bristol by offering twenty-five or thirty surplus lots on a tract of land adjoining its campus. It was mentioned that some of these fronted on or lay along the railroad (a prime selling point in those days). These lots were sold at private sale and brought the college much needed money.

At the time of the college offering, John G. King announced there would be no more private sales of his lots. Instead he planned a big auction in November that year (1871). In the same issue of the *Bristol News* that carried King's announcement, Editor Fowler, again bubbling with optimism, wrote:

BLOUNTVILLE COMING

We are glad to find that every lawyer and every official — at least all the good ones — at Blountville contemplate purchasing lots in Bristol at the November sale. We will welcome these gentlemen to our young city, but we will thank them just to bring the courthouse along with them, as it will be sometime before our street cars reach it where it now is. In the meantime Bristol grows and building after building goes up.

On November 10, 1871, it was announced that Rev. David Sullins, who so ably had conducted the Johnston Land Sale, would do the auctioneering for King. A selling point stressed by the owner was that lots should be bought before the advent of the Cumberland Gap Railroad, which would most certainly drive up land prices in Bristol. The sale was set for November 15.

It was hot coffee, rather than ice cold lemonade, that was needed on that sale day. The skies were dark, the wind was sharp and there were light snow flurries. Nevertheless, a large crowd assembled early, including some of the more hardy women of the town. John G. King made a little speech at the opening, during which he waved a hand toward the recently stripped corn stalks, and declared that the last crops had been raised in the sweeping fields around him. "Where now the denuded corn stalks stand shall many of the town's finest residences rise," he had said. A very old citizen of the town thirty-five years ago could almost quote King's speech word for word, and was not hard to persuade to do so. True, many of the town's finer residences did eventually stand over the leveled corn rows, but corn growing was not totally through in the area. Nearly thirty years later a large field of corn flourished along the west side of Alabama Street in the five hundred block.

The second day of the sale saw bright sunshine and much warmer temperatures. The sale ended as the sun set that day, but the sun was rising on the development of South Bristol. The least expensive lot was sold to James Wilson for fifty dollars. The highest price brought by a single lot was two hundred fifty dollars. The highest grouping of lots (three) went to L. H. Rogan for seven hundred twenty-five dollars. Col. J. P. Snapp of Blountville bought the grove containing the old slave cemetery (lots 175-79) for six hundred and fifty dollars. A few weeks later a news item states that Col. Snapp was having the bodies removed from his lots. Building began almost immediately. Mr. J. S. Bingley, who had bought lot 142 for one hundred and forty dollars, was the first to start construction after the sale. His house was under way by December 8, 1871.

As the year drew to a close, editor Fowler gave this glowing report to the town:

A Citizen of our town, noted for the accuracy of his observation and the usual exactness of his judgment, estimates that not less than four hundred persons have been added to the population of Bristol-Goodson within the last ninety days. Under the circumstances this is a very remarkable fact.

Bristol had entered the 1870s at full steam ahead and the trend was to continue through the decade and beyond.

Bibliography - Chapter Four

Anderson, Rhea. Notes, 1930-1939.

Bachelor, Ann. Memoirs (unpublished), 1935-1937.

Bristol News, newspaper. Various issues, 1857-1872.

Johnson, L. F. Notes, 1893.

Palmer, Joseph B. Diary (unpublished), 1855-1876.

Phillips, V. N. (Bud). Interviews with several older Bristol citizens, 1953-1956.

Sullivan County, Tennessee. Chancery Court Records.

Sullivan County, Tennessee. Deed Records.

Taylor, Hattie King. Papers (unpublished). 1927.

Washington County, Virginia. Chancery Court Records.

Washington County, Virginia. Deed Records.

Washington County, Virginia. Tax Records.

Chapter Five
BRISTOL 1872-1900

The great success of the Johnston Land Sale, followed swiftly by the sale of a portion of the land of John G. King, caused others who owned land adjoining Bristol to think seriously of real estate development. It was clear that selling lots was far more profitable than growing hay and grain crops. Among those who owned land that was highly subject to become profitable by the expansion of the town was the legendary Major Zachariah L. Burson.

SPREADING WESTWARD
Soon after arriving in Bristol in the late 1860s, Major Burson had bought some choice tracts of land. One of these tracts straddled the state line along what is now West State Street, some distance beyond present Morrison Boulevard. In March 1872 Burson had this tract divided into two hundred lots, several of which fronted on Main (State) Street in both Virginia and Tennessee. The April 12, 1872, edition of the *Bristol News* carried an advertisement for the sale of these unimproved lots, along with seven dwelling houses. The lots were to be auctioned on May 22, 1872, to the highest bidder and on terms of fifteen percent down and the balance in five equal installments, payable annually. Burson's ad stated that complete maps of the new development could be had at the Main Street office of his son, John E. Burson. Editor Fowler commented on the sale:

> The advertisement of Mr. Burson will convince our readers that the month of May will be an important one for Bristol. On the 22nd of May that gentleman will place on the market seven houses and lots, some of which are located in Virginia, and others in Tennessee, and two hundred unimproved lots. After work shall have been inaugurated upon the Kentucky road, property will advance very rapidly, and those wishing to invest would do well to take time by the forelock.

The seven houses mentioned in connection with this sale had been built by Burson as rental property. He had intended to build dozens more, but finally decided that it would be best to sell unimproved lots.

May 22nd was dark and stormy, but many prospective buyers braved the threatening weather to bid on the Burson lots. However, sales were disap-

pointing. The town was not quite ready for a fast jump westward. Consequently, prices were not to Burson's liking. He had advertised that the sale
would continue day by day until all lots were sold, but he stopped sales at
mid-afternoon of the first day. However, through the years immediately ahead,
sales increased in that area, much to the satisfaction of Mr. Burson. In time
he offered more of the tract for sale, including what he called the celebrated
Williams property, a grand estate containing a fourteen-room brick mansion.

STRENGTHENING THE HEART

And while growth was spreading into the adjoining farm lands, Bristol was
growing stronger in the heart of the business district. The same paper that
carried Burson's ad carried that of Henry Rosenheim, early Bristol merchant,
for an unimproved lot on Main Street, immediately west of Seneker and
Brother. The Electrolux Co. now stands on this lot (505 State Street). At
the same time Rosenheim offered his former garden spot, fronting one hundred
eighty feet on Fifth Street. This garden lay at the back of what is now the
First National Bank building. This is a story often repeated during that period,
with gardens, potato patches, stables, and horse lots giving way for the erection
of downtown business buildings.

The same edition of the newspaper that carried Burson and Rosenheim's
offerings also contained the following advertisement:

RARE OPPORTUNITY
BUSINESS LOTS FOR SALE
IN BRISTOL
ON WEDNESDAY, MAY 1ST, 1872

The Common Council of the Town of Goodson (Virginia half of Bristol)
having a view of the approaching work on the Cumberland Gap Railroad,
determined to throw on the market on the first day of May, about thirty
positions for business and a number of lots suitable for residences. These
lots lie within a single square of [from] Main and Front Streets, and
in the direction of the new railroad junction. The number of foreign
applicants for these localities has become so great, and the desire to
obtain them so general, that it is deemed proper to withhold them no
longer from the market; and they will on the 1st day of May next, be
offered for sale to the highest bidder, upon the terms of the sale of July
last, to wit: 15 percent of the purchase money down, the remainder
in one, two, three, four and five years, with interest at six percent,
payable semi-annually. The Cumberland Gap Railroad will very soon
be let to contract and finished with great rapidity, and the present opportunity to acquire property in our rising young city is one that is not

likely to occur again. For further particulars address, I. C. Fowler, Mayor.

If James L. Saul, Auctioneer, had been disappointed at not having been allowed to proceed with the Johnston sale, he may have been somewhat soothed by being chosen to sell this downtown property. The sale, held as scheduled, was a tremendous success and helped to extend the town north-ward toward Beaver Creek and the southern boundary of old Goodsonville. While Bristol was expanding outward, it was also growing stronger at the heart. And while Bristol grew, those in the building trades were alert and seeking opportunity. A news item of the period exemplified this:

Returned to Bristol: Messrs. Stokes and Pusey have returned to Bristol, and will undertake the erection or repair of buildings on favorable terms. They are well known as architects of very superior skill and ability.

Home of John C. Anderson, son of Bristol's founder, Joseph R. Anderson. This photo was made in 1875. The home stood on East Main (State) Street, across from the parking lot of the First Baptist Church. The corn patch at the left covers the site of Bristol's first hotel (the Columbia built in old Bristol, Virginia, in 1854-55). In the extreme upper left may be seen the front of the Baptist Church.

In early 1873 editor Fowler happily reported to his readers that over one hundred buildings had been added to the town in 1872. He went on to say that most of them were of brick. At the same time he urged those in the building trades to move to the booming town, giving assurance that there would be work for all.

MEADOW SQUARE

On the Virginia side it had long been planned to leave a central, block-sized public square. This would have been bounded by Cumberland on the south, Sycamore on the north, Moore on the west and Lee on the east. It was hoped that in time the Washington County courthouse would become the central feature of this area; or if not, a fine city hall might be built there. The name was to be Meadow Square, so called because it was located in the better part of King's Meadows.

But as building boomed on that side of Bristol, a few with an eye for fast money began to cast covetous eyes toward the grand square. Lots carved from it would certainly bring top dollar. So it was that a move developed to have the town divide the square into lots and offer the same for commercial development. A petition was circulated asking for this sale. With seventy-five names thereon it was presented to the Common Council of Goodson on December 1, 1874. At that time the council consisted of Mayor I. C. Fowler, G. H. Devault, Dr. H. T. Berry, Dr. C. T. Pepper, Prof. J. H. Winston, David A. Wheeler and S. L. Saul. This Council agreed to the sale. On January 8, 1875, the Council appointed E. B. Faidley and a Mr. Jordon to hold a public election on the matter on the 12th of that month. Faidley and Jordon were paid two dollars each for their services.

On January 12, 1875, sixty-six voters went to the mayor's office to call out their votes. Fifty-six voted for the sale and ten voted against it. It is said that when the results were announced, Capt. J. H. Wood, who always had an eye for beauty, commented that it was the biggest mistake the town ever made. Perhaps he had longed to look down from his home on Solar Hill to view a green, park-like square in the midst of the town below.

For some reason the town did not immediately proceed with the sale. It was not until October 26, 1875, that Dr. C. T. Pepper was appointed to correspond with certain newspapers concerning private sale of the land. At the same time it was agreed to appoint a committee of four — two from the council and two private citizens — to evaluate the lots in Meadow Square. David A. Wheeler and J. W. Owen represented the Council, while I. C. Fowler and Major Zack Burson were to represent the citizenry. (By that time John F. Terry had become mayor, and Capt. J. W. Owen had been elected to the Council.) On November 9, it was ordered that the lots be advertised in the *Lynchburg Virginian*. Then on December 7, 1875, Prof. Winston moved that the Mayor be authorized to "sell the lots in the Meadow," reserving lots five through eight for public use. At the same time it was decreed that all buildings to be erected on the Meadow lots be of brick.

The winter passed and on April 4, 1876, the private sale idea was dropped and a public auction was planned for the following May 10th. It was stipulated that no lot could be sold below evaluation. On May 2, 1876, the Council met to make final plans for the sale. At that time the Council consisted of Mayor John F. Terry, S. L. Saul, David A. Wheeler, J. H. Winston, Dr. C. T. Pepper and George Hammitt. This Council voted to deduct twenty-five percent from the evaluation of the lots. At the same time a petition, signed by fifty-five citizens and asking for postponement of the sale, was presented to the Council but did not prevail. This move for postponement was headed by Capt. J. H. Wood.

The sale was held as planned with all lots being quickly bought at handsome prices by prospective builders and speculators. By May 16th following the sale, Major Burson was before the Council asking that the lots he had bought in the Meadow be exchanged for property nearer his residence on Virginia Hill. His request was granted on July 11th. And lot 5, which had originally been reserved for public use, was sold to John Oyler on August 17, 1876, for one thousand dollars. What would have been a green, tree-shaded park in the heart of Bristol-Goodson, soon resounded to the sound of the brick mason's trowel and the carpenter's hammer. What could have been a place of restful beauty to this day was sacrificed to raw commercialism.

JOHNSTON SQUARE

In June 1876 Mr. Joseph Johnston of Philadelphia offered to sell what was called the Mosby lot "to be used in connection with the rest of the grove (Mosby's Grove) as a public square." Col. Mosby had contracted for this land when he lived in Bristol-Goodson, but never paid for it. It embraced the site where now stands the office building of Bristol Steel, along and across Piedmont Avenue and Scott Street. Apparently the intention was for a public park, rather than a place for a courthouse, or around which commercial development might take place. Indeed, Capt. J. H. Wood envisioned fine homes occupying choice spots around what he hoped would be called Johnston Square or Park, as a fitting tribute to one who had been very kind to Bristol. The Common Council proposed to put the issue to a vote and to offer Johnston five hundred dollars for the property. What happened a little later is not clear, but on August 1, 1876, the Council voted to rescind the call for an election on the matter. Apparently this action ended the movement for Johnston Square. And on the slope where Capt. Wood hoped that grand homes might arise, developed one of the most notorious slums (Burson's Grove or sometimes called Burson's Row) ever known in this city. A little later the area was briefly used for a Methodist camp meeting ground.

MOVING SOUTHEASTWARD

A large farm began on the east side of Second Street and stretched along the south side of Main (State) toward East Hill Cemetery (then known as the City Cemetery). Until 1876, corn grew in the middle of what is now Pennsylvania Avenue and in the area bordering it. This was the plantation of James King, III (sometimes called James King, Jr.). His home stood on the west side of Second Street, near the foot of High View Hill. It was actually about half way between Second and Third Streets, causing some to give its location as being on the latter street. (This home stood until sometime after 1953.) James King died in 1875. His widow, Elizabeth R. Buchanan King, was left with three unmarried children: William R. King, Micajah Watkins King (female) and John B. King. As was the lot of so many widows in those days, Mrs. King soon found herself in severe financial straights. It was the distress of this widow that allowed the town to move southeastward, across Lynwood plantation toward Fairmount Forest. On October 30, 1876, Mrs. Elizabeth Buchanan King filed suit in Chancery Court at Blountville, Tennessee, asking that a portion of the farm be sold. She stated that the land was poor and the yield so scanty that the family could not be clothed, fed and educated with the proceeds from it. She further plead that the land could not be profitably rented. The court granted her request.

That section of Lynwood that was laid off for sale was actually only a part of the large acreage owned by the heirs of James King. Their holdings included most of the original Fairmount Forest (Fairmount) area of this city. The platted portion extended only to present McDowell Street on the south and almost to the cemetery on the east. The Lynwood sale was set for April 26, 1877, and advertised in the *Bristol Courier*.

Times were not propitious for real estate sales. Though all lots offered were sold, the prices were disappointing. Major A. D. Reynolds was able to buy thirteen lots for only four hundred and thirteen dollars. Marion L. Blackley, a local lawyer, bought eleven lots for only two hundred eighty-six dollars. However, he paid over three hundred dollars for the choice lot where now stands Kay's Ice Cream (State and Pennsylvania). W. P. Brewer, an early merchant, bought three lots at thirty-one dollars each. John B. Keller bought a good house site for thirty-six dollars. While Nelson Clay's house site was not quite as nice as that of Keller's, he got it for eighteen dollars! All this caused lawyer Byron G. McDowell (for whom McDowell Street was named), who was guardian of the King children, to grumble that it might have been more profitable to have continued growing corn on the land.

This sale started the town moving southeastward. Several years later when the youngest King heir became of legal age, the forested part of Lynwood (Fairmount) was sold, and thus began the development of one of the better sections of our city.

As the end of the 1870s neared, optimistic editor Fowler penned a bright note for his *Bristol News*:

> Improvement has broken out like Yellow fever or Chicken Pox in our town. This season will find more houses in position than any previous one. Mr. W. T. Hayter has purchased the store property he now occupies from Fulton, Sparger and Byrd and will at once commence the erection of a splendid new store house 100 feet by 30, beside the present. In 90 days he will have his new goods in it. William H. Smith has the brick work and James Oney the woodwork. On the Goodson side, Messrs. J. P. Farris, Z. L. Burson and John M. Crowell will erect a block of brick stores, 3 in number near the creek. Messrs. Smith and Crowell have the brick work. Mrs. Pepper and Dr. C. T. Pepper will soon erect another brick store one door west of J. A. Dickey and Company's drug store. Mr. W. W. Davis will put up a new brick building adjoining the Thomas House on Main Street. Mr. W. W. James has his new block nearly completed and it looks well.
>
> May 20, 1879

In 1880 the population of Bristol-Goodson, Virginia, was 1,562 residents. The population of Bristol, Tennessee, was then 1,647, making a total of 3,209 for the double town. This was quite an increase from that day in September 1853 when J. R. Anderson and his family, numbering eight souls (including three slaves), became the first residents of Bristol, Virginia-Tennessee.

TOWARD MATURITY

The town was now nearly thirty years old. In all aspects of its existence it was growing toward maturity. Streets had been somewhat improved, though mud and dust was still the norm. Its schools were on firmer footing. Government was more efficient. Most of the less-stable businesses had given way to more reliable and lasting firms. Manufacturing was increasing; the population was not quite as transient as it had been during the first decades, with more affluent industrialists and businessmen being attracted to the fast growing town.

For the greater part of the 1880s, there was not the building boom and town expansion as had been witnessed during the past decade, but there was

Marked prosperity was the constant lot of Bristol's founder, Joseph R. Anderson. In 1881 he erected the first unit (left foreground) of his noted Anderson Block (400 block of State Street, Tennessee side). Due to damage from the tornado of June 1893, a portion of this block was lowered to two stories.

what may be termed a filling-up time. That is, lots in and near downtown were being built upon, while many of those quickly sold during the big expansions of the 1870s were unused, and many were overgrown with weeds and brush. And those who built during this filling-up time were erecting larger and better structures. Some of those early businessmen of Bristol, who had been patiently operating over the years, had by then amassed considerable fortunes and were ready to use a portion of their wealth to erect more substantial business houses and grander mansions as their private residences. Indicative of this change in the face of Bristol is this item from the *Bristol News*, dated October 18, 1881:

> The new Anderson store is ready for the finishing touches. Its cornices are of galvanized iron. It now presents the finest front in Southwest Virginia or upper East Tennessee.

Anderson's first store had been a twelve by sixteen foot room in his home. Later he had erected and moved his store into a two-story brick building on Fourth Street across from the backyard of his residence. There he had remained until he built the three-story brick building at 410 Main Street. Uncle Will Smith had gone all out to make this building the crowning effort of his building career.

TOWN FOUNDER'S LAST HOME: In 1881, Joseph R. Anderson built this fine Victorian home at 516 Anderson Street. He died there seven years later. It last served as Bristol's Y.W.C.A., before being demolished in the late 1960s.

At about the same time Anderson had his new mansion built at 516 Anderson Street. This site had long been used as a second garden by the Anderson family. (The early garden back of the Main and Fourth Street home had all but been crowded out by business buildings.) When the foundation trenches were being dug for this home, a cache of gold was unearthed. It was thought that the treasure had been buried there during the Civil War.

Improvements such as Anderson's were repeated by many others during those golden years of the century's eighth decade. But aggrandizement often means the loss of the old, the honored, the beautiful in the path of progress. Such was the case in Bristol during the 1880s. Then many of the town's familiar landmarks, some having existed since near the beginning of the town, were torn down for better replacements. Many an early home perished at this time, as did many of the downtown buildings. However, some old buildings were merely given new faces, and some received new faces again in later years; so it is likely that a few old inner brick walls yet remain of those first Bristol buildings.

Also in the 1880s many of the town's first pioneer settlers passed from this earthly scene. Among them were John N. Bosang, a resident of the town

The widow and children of Bristol's founder, Joseph R. Anderson, posed for this photo soon after Mr. Anderson's death (1888). Pictured with the widow (foreground) left to right are James King Anderson (known as Major—never married), Rev. Issac Anderson, John Campbell Anderson, and Margaret Anderson Caldwell.

since 1854; Mrs. John Ackin, whose husband had been one of the town's
first builders; and U. L. York, who had practiced law here since just after
the close of the Civil War. Then on May 18, 1888, the end came to Joseph
R. Anderson, the town's founder and first resident. It is interesting to note
that Anderson was attended in his final illness by the mulatto, illegitimate
son of his bitterest enemy, John N. Bosang. This male nurse was as dedicated
to Anderson as his sire had been against him. And while many of the town's
true pioneers left us in the 1880s, and even more would pass in the 1890s,
some lingered until two decades or so after the turn of the century.

NEW HOPE

If there had been a bit of languishing through most of the 1880s, new hope
stirred strongly near the end of that decade. General John D. Imboden, who
long lived at the Virginia House Hotel, proved that almost unlimited coal
deposits existed in southwestern Virginia. About the same time, what appeared
to be great iron ore deposits were also discovered in the area. Imboden set
about promoting these great resources and encouraged the building of a railroad
through the promising area. And the lumber interests were rapidly expanding.
All this caused many a capitalist here and elsewhere to gear up for the great
boom. Bristol appeared to be in for a great future with an expected tremendous
increase in population. It would be the new Pittsburgh or the new Birmingham.

To further support the great hope, it appeared that Bristol was to be the
crossroads of two or three projected railroads. The most promising of these
was the great northwest-southeast route that would terminate at Cincinnati,
Ohio, and Wilmington, North Carolina. Bristol was already on the northeast-
southwest corridor. To have these great lines cross and connect at Bristol
was a developer's fondest dream. If that were not enough, the Danville and
East Tennessee Railroad was being surveyed into the optimistic town. And
there were plans for a Nashville and Bristol Railway that would originate
at Nashville, Tennessee, and reach Bristol by way of Kingsport and
Blountville. There was even talk of a railroad from Savannah, Georgia, to
Pittsburgh, Pennsylvania, by way of Bristol. Optimists predicted that within
a few decades, Bristol would be the largest city in the south. And well it
might have been had all plans materialized. This very hopeful outlook caused
land prices to soar in and around the town. Land and development companies
sprang up almost overnight. Outside investors took note and began to arrive
in town with checkbooks ready.

INSTANT CITIZENSHIP

The urge to adjust to the new boom caused a sordid episode in the history
of Bristol-Goodson, Virginia. It appears that this skeleton in the closet has

never before been rattled and might well have remained unrevealed had not this writer gone through thousands of old court papers that are stored in the basement of the courthouse in Abingdon, Virginia. (Nearly three years were consumed in this search.) And desiring to unflinchingly tell all like it was, he cannot honestly "keep the closet locked."

The Danville and East Tennessee Railroad needed financial help. It would be much to the advantage of Bristol-Goodson to render such assistance. But to issue bonds meant that city status would have to be gained, and that meant the need for a population of five thousand or more citizens; and any careful observer could easily deduce that the town just did not have that many residents. Nevertheless, on December 16, 1889, the Common Council of Goodson resolved that two competent persons be employed to take a census of the town (Bristol-Goodson, Virginia), the cost of which was not to exceed forty dollars. Two men were employed for this task—one of them a member of the Council and the other a prominent local lawyer—both of whose names were more or less household words in the town at that time. These men were instructed, apparently by the Council or some other interested "authority," that article VI, Section 14 of the Virginia Constitution should not be taken as meaning actual residents of a town, but to go out on the premise that it simply meant people. And the two census takers went after people! It mattered not that they might be visitors from New York or mountaineers from toward Shady Valley; they were quickly listed on the enumerators' book. And many simply alighting from the train for a quick lunch or dinner suddenly found themselves citizens of the town. There were later accusations that many resting in the East Hill Cemetery had had their citizenships renewed.

On January 7, 1890, the enumerators reported to the Council that the ordered census had been started in December 1889 and finished on January 4, 1890. The two went on to report that "after carefully and accurately taking the census," it was found that the population was five thousand, three hundred eighty-two. There must have been some suppressed smiles among those who heard of this "careful and accurate census!" And no doubt, many righteous eyebrows were raised by it.

At the same sitting of the Council, it was voted to change the name of Goodson to Bristol, and to apply for a charter as an incorporated city. Immediately, contact was made with E. S. Kendrick and James Crow, representatives from Washington County, Virginia, to proceed with the proper action in Richmond.

The city's name change from Goodson to Bristol was of no great surprise and was the natural and right course to take. From the beginning the developments on the Virginia side had popularly been known as Bristol, the name that Joseph Anderson had given his Virginia town in 1852. The depot had always remained under the Bristol name and the post office for both towns, with the exception of a few years, bore that designation from near the founding. The time had come when it would be of great advantage to have the double town under one name. To have called both cities Goodson would have only added to the already stifling confusion caused by the double identity.

It is well that Samuel Goodson, the founder of Goodsonville which adjoined the original Bristol, Virginia, did not live to see that change. It is said that he was always troubled and frustrated by the fact that even though the Virginia side was incorporated as Goodson in 1856, still the change had been far from totally accepted by its residents, who persisted in using the name that Anderson had given his Virginia development in 1852. Sadly, Anderson lived only a short time longer; he died on May 18, 1888. He too had been troubled and frustrated that his development on the Virginia side had all come under the name of Goodson. Doubtless he would have rejoiced to see the return of the Virginia side to his chosen name. It is tragic that both these early Bristol pioneers had to die in regret and frustration.

The charter for Bristol, Virginia, was granted on February 12, 1890, then amended on the following March 5th, limiting the issuance of railroad bonds to seventy-five thousand dollars. By then the move was under way to issue bonds in that amount to the Danville and East Tennessee Railway. This action was put to a vote of the citizens on April 10, 1890. The issue was approved.

But there were several prominent citizens of Bristol who were keenly aware of the increased taxation soon to be imposed on property owners. Too, they had not been blind to the thinly veiled chicanery that had brought about the incorporation of the city. Consequently, in February 1891, a suit was filed to halt the issuance of the bonds. Plaintiffs named in the suit were E. S. Godsey, John B. Keller, Edward Stanley, Matthew Powers, John Powers, Jr., James Powers, Edward Powers, Major Z. L. Burson, George Cooke, Col. Abram Fulkerson, Samuel V. Fulkerson, A. Luttrell, A. H. Blanchard, John Powers, Sr., Jere Bunting, Sr. and Jere Bunting, Jr. and Col. D. F. Bailey. Of this group A. H. Blanchard, Col. Fulkerson and Col. Bailey were leading lawyers of Bristol, Virginia, and they, along with Page and Hurt, filed the suit.

Matthew Powers had been employed to take the U.S. Census of 1890 for Bristol. He testified that he was motivated to take an accurate census in that he was paid two cents per head for every resident listed. He further stated that he had advertised in local newspapers for missed residents and that none appeared. His count was two thousand, nine hundred and fifty-one. Of this number the census bureau voided forty-nine, making an official count of two thousand nine hundred two. On March 13, 1891, Col. Fulkerson received from Albert Childs, acting superintendent of the U. S. Census Bureau, an official paper certifying that the actual population of Bristol, Virginia, was as stated above. Almost a century later when Fulkerson's old desk was emptied and the contents given to this author, that certificate, still complete with its red ribbons and shiny seal, was found among his papers.

The judge refused to rule on the census matter, much to the bitter disappointment of many Bristol citizens. However, the suit did point out the almost certainty that a city status and incorporation had been obtained by fraud. Ten years later (1900) the city was still short of the five thousand mark by nearly five hundred citizens. Bristol-Goodson lost at least one bona fide citizen because of the deceptive census. Frank T. Blanchard was so righteously indignant over the matter that he publicly vowed that he would not dwell in a town that had winked at such underhanded doings. In time he made good on his vow by building and moving into the fine brick home that yet stands on the southeast corner of Taylor and Maryland in Bristol, Tennessee. Some of his former neighbors on the Virginia side of town, thinking Mr. Blanchard posed a "holier than thou attitude," soon dubbed his new home the holy house, a name it bore for several years.

ENLARGING THE BORDERS

The optimism generated by the prospect that Bristol might become a great rail center with increased industry resulting in the organization of numerous land and development companies. Wooded areas and farmland adjoining the town were quickly bought up and platted into lots and streets, quickly followed by brochures and booklets offering home sites for sale.

Among the giants of these organizations was the Bristol Land and Improvement Company, which was established in the late 1880s by Major A. D. Reynolds, his brother R. J. Reynolds and Col. J. M. Barker. This company sought to develop what is now known as the Fairmount section of Bristol, Tennessee. Local developers had long been looking toward this choice property, which extended southeastward from the town. It was the southern portion of Lynwood, the plantation of James King, III. But the land was cleared and cultivated only to about where Taylor Street is now located. Beyond was the great Fairmount forest, consisting of a thick growth of virgin timber. A road led through it toward Holston Valley. (This road was known as Holston Pike.) Travelers dreaded to pass through it at night because several robberies and a murder or two had occurred there. And after the murders a dreadful ghost was reputed to terrorize late travelers.

This area was long estate property. After the youngest son of James King, III reached legal age, A. D. Reynolds, working through lawyer Byron G. McDowell, who had been guardian of the King children, was able to obtain an option on the choice property. At the same time, others were making a strong bid for it. It is said that Reynolds was successful because he promised to rename an already existing street for McDowell, assuring him that this would be his (McDowell's) lasting memorial. It is interesting to note that Reynolds sacrificed one of his own memorials for this purpose; what had been Reynolds Street became McDowell.

In time a stock company was organized under the name of Bristol Land and Improvement Company, with Major A. D. Reynolds as president and Albert Parlett as secretary and treasurer. Directors were R. J. Reynolds, General Thomas Ewing, and Hal H. Haynes. General Thomas Ewing, a former congressman of Ohio but then from New York, had been allowed to purchase a one-fourth interest in the company because it was felt that his influence would be great in bringing in big capital. He was then president of the Danville and Atlantic and Danville and East Tennessee Railroads.

One of the first improvements by this company was the erection of the fabulous Fairmount Hotel. This magnificent edifice was erected on a low hill that was encompassed by Spruce and Cypress Streets, and Carolina and Kentucky Avenues, its park-like yard being two square blocks in extent. This hotel was opened in July 1889 when most of the Fairmount section was still a dense forest. Beginning about midway of the hotel lot and extending two blocks southward was reserved for Fairmount Forest Park. For years it was left in its pristine condition. Some distance south of this park was the noted ten acre lake, where prospective buyers were encouraged to fish, swim and boat, in order "to get the feel of the new development." This lake was located between Georgia and Virginia Avenues, and Lakeside on the north and Beechwood on the south, the site of the present Food City shopping center. Hack service was provided by the hotel for transportation to and from this lake.

The Bristol Belt Line Railway, in which the company owned a controlling interest, soon extended its lines to this hotel. First development of the area mainly took place along this line. By mid-1890 four miles of streets had been graded in Fairmount and five more were graded soon thereafter. As a display of faith in the new development, R. J. Reynolds erected a large and grand home at the edge of the hotel property. It has been said, though not verified, that this house occupied the northwest corner of Spruce and Carolina, at what is now numbered 423 Spruce. (H. W. Powers later built there.) Members of the Reynolds family, including the mother of R. J. and A. D., occupied this home for a few years. Major A. D. Reynolds planned his mansion for the northeast corner of Spruce and Carolina. Plans had been drawn for this house by 1890, though it was not built until a short time later. It appears that the developers of Fairmount intended to make an elite residential section around the hotel grounds.

Though building began in Fairmount in the late 1880s along Pennsylvania Avenue and around the hotel, progress in other parts of the development was slow. By 1900 there still were numerous unsold lots, many of which were covered with timber and brush. Indeed, some streets had only a house or two along their entire lengths.

OTHER TENNESSEE LAND COMPANIES

Just beyond the area reserved for Fairmount Forest Park was the land of the Fairmount Land Company. The noted Fairmount Lake was within this property. Mr. Samuel L. King, a son of John G. King and grandson of Rev. James King, was president of this organization. Just beyond Fairmount Lake was the property of the Lakeside Land and Improvement Company. This development bordered on both sides of the East Tennessee, Virginia and Georgia Railroad. It was expected that an elite residential section would develop upon the lands of this company, because of the railroad and lake frontage, and because of the grand view afforded by the location. Mr. Leroy H. Fields of Norfolk, Virginia, was president of this land company, while local merchant A. S. Gump was vice president, and W. G. Sheen was secretary and general manager. Though there were great expectations for the development in that area, five years later there was only one house within its boundaries, and that was an old farm house that had been standing when the company had laid off its land.

The Southwest Bristol Land Company owned 420 acres of land adjoining the properties of the Lakeside and Fairmount Land Companies. This development also had the benefit of railroad frontage and close proximity to the streetcar line, Fairmount Lake and hotel. It boasted a company stock of three hundred thousand dollars and was headed by the prominent John R. Pace of Danville, Virginia, with local real estate agent G. P. Cannon as vice president. H. G. Peters, local lawyer, was the secretary and L. D. Yarnell was company attorney. The list of directors for this well financed company included Col. N. M. Taylor (a prominent Bristol lawyer) and Dr. James A. Dickey. Non-resident directors were Dr. B. D. Downey of Roanoke, Virginia; T. L. Massie of Pulaski, Virginia; Silas Shelbourne of Richmond, Virginia; M. L. T. David of Norfolk, Virginia; and Col. E. C. Manning of Washington, D.C. Soon after the organization of this company (around 1890) negotiations were begun for the establishment of a college and sanitarium upon its lands, but these hoped for institutions were never built.

The property of the Pioneer Land Company, containing 334 acres, began near the old Mill Grove (English Grove) site on Beaver Creek (near present Melrose Street) and extended for one and a half miles down the stream. The Bristol, Elizabethton and North Carolina Railroad passed through this land, greatly increasing its value. The company offered strong inducements to industrial plants that would locate in that section. A free site was early given to the Pioneer Steel and Rolling Mill Company. This company, projected to employ from two to three hundred men, was under construction in 1890. Judge Martin B. Wood, who then lived at 124 Solar Street, was president of the Pioneer Land Company. John I. Cox was secretary, and the directors were W. A. Sparger, Major A. D. Reynolds, Judge William F. Rhea, John H. Caldwell and Hal H. Haynes. Capital stock was in the amount of five hundred thousand dollars, a portion of which was retained in the treasury for the encouragement of industries.

By 1890 it was clear that the town would begin to push into the fields and pastures that extended west of Bristol, Tennessee, which then ended along Beaver Creek. J. H. Caldwell, son-in-law of Joseph R. Anderson, opened a small development extending from the west bank of this creek to just beyond Tenth Street and northward to the alley south of Anderson Street. It was in this area that he originally planned to build his "Windsor Castle," thus came the name for Windsor Avenue. Just beyond Caldwell's development and extending on to Thirteenth Street on the west and from about Hill to Anderson on the south and north was land owned by the Southwest Bristol Improvement Company. Within this section was a small area known as Somerville. Some referred to the whole as the Blountville Addition, so called because so many residents of that town had bought lots there. The Tennessee Investment Company had land on the high knobs behind present Holston Avenue. This was the area which G. W. Bagby had viewed in the 1870s from the tower of King College and predicted that the Bristol elite would eventually build there. Though this company was in existence by 1890, no known development was done in that part of the knobs until well after 1900. But it does appear that there was expectation that Bristol would eventually spread into the hills and knobs. Around 1890, large tracts in that area were owned by Dr. William Dulaney, William H. Smith (a Bristol builder) and Col. John G. English. Col. English had inherited much of this land from his father-in-law, Rev. James King.

For more westward expansion the West Bristol Land Company planned a development beyond Thirteenth Street and reaching to Eighteenth, with Hill Street on the south and West Main (State) on the north. The influence of out-of-town developers is indicated by such street names as Knoxville, Danville and Farmville, clustering around a grand Richmond Avenue. These names were not used in the final development. To serve those with a flair for unique homesites, the Bristol Heights Company, composed of capitalists of Richmond, Danville and Bristol, was organized about 1890. Their tract consisted of one hundred acres, located in the high knobs off the end of

Eighteenth Street and south of Windsor Avenue. The region was described as being made up of high hills and noble table lands from which one might view a cyclorama of unsurpassing interest and never ending enchantment. This was to be the Lookout Mountain of Bristol. An incline railway was to be built to the top of these heights. Their literature claimed "in addition to the health-giving altitude and fresh air, there is a sense of exultation and restfulness on the hills, never felt in the lowlands," and ended with a bit of poetry:

"On these grand heights were e'en toils echoes cease,
There is a region of unbroken peace."

Yes, and the Heights largely remained the peaceful abode of squirrels, rabbits and the singing birds for many years thereafter. Clifton Heights was a later designation of this area.

THE IRONWOOD BUBBLE

Perhaps the grandest plan of any of the numerous land companies of the 1890s was that of the South Bristol Industrial Land Company. This company was put together by such leading figures of the time as John H. Caldwell (who was its president), Ben L. Dulaney, Hal H. Haynes, C. H. Slack, Major A. D. Reynolds, Col. J. M. Barker, C. E. Finch, and John C. Anderson. The company was capitalized at two million dollars, eight hundred thousand of which had been sold by 1891. Four hundred thousand had been set aside for improvements, and eight hundred thousand had been reserved to aid manufacturing industries. Free sites were offered for factory locations. Further, the company offered to donate a portion of the eight hundred thousand dollar fund to every manufacturer who located on the land. The amount was to be prorated according to the number of workmen and wages paid.

The lands of this company, consisting of four thousand three hundred acres, began about two and one half miles down Beaver from the Main Street of the town, and extended for three miles along the stream. Most of this land was a part of the old Col. James King estate, and included a farm that had formerly belonged to him. This farm, known as Ironwood, encompassed the old iron works site at the mouth of Steele Creek.

The Bristol, Elizabethton and North Carolina Railway was projected to run through the whole of this tract, thereby increasing its desirability and enhancing land values. But what was first planned as what might be called Bristol's first industrial park soon was scrapped for the idea of an entire new city; Ironwood City it would be called, the center of which would be slightly above what is now Hill's Shopping Center. A sulphur spring was on the property, which was said to have medicinal properties equal to the great Greenbrier White Sulphur Spring. A fine hotel similar to the existing Fairmount was planned. A street car would run from this hotel to another spring on the property where a bath house would be built. The Bristol Belt Line Railway (street car system) would extend a line down Beaver to connect the cities with twice-per-hour fast transportation. But Ironwood City only reached the paper stage. Perhaps its developers were too busy with their enterprises in Bristol proper. Too, the railroad, which was to be only a link in the line from Wilmington, North Carolina, to Cincinnati, Ohio, remained isolated; its connections to the Atlantic Ocean and Ohio Valley were never built. Only the Ordway Furniture Factory finally stood as a reminder of what might have been. The Woodlawn addition situated beyond Ash Street (then English) and between College and Southside was the last push south before the turn of the century.

The developing craze also hit Bristol, Virginia, in the late 1880s and early to mid 1890s. The giant of the Virginia developments was that of the Bristol Land Company (not to be confused with the Bristol Land and Improvement Company). The land of this company was roughly west of Oak View Street, north of Scott Street, over to Commonwealth and northward to just beyond Glenway, with a twenty-six acre reserve beyond the Sullins College campus. This area included Euclid Avenue, which was to be the principal business center of the new Bristol. Euclid was then called New Main Street. J. E. Nader surveyed this section in early 1890. Then in May 1890 a second addition was laid off by the same surveyor. This addition extended westward from Commonwealth and some distance north of West Main (State Street) to beyond Randolph Street. Some streets from the first addition were extended into this section. There were other named streets, such as Floyd, Fair, Gunning, Short Lane, Lee Place and Susong. But the failure to become the great envisioned rail center and little development of the iron industry meant very slow development of this section of the town. As late as 1920 there were cornfields along portions of Euclid Avenue, and cattle contentedly grazed in the upland pastures between Euclid and Glenway.

The Fairview Land Company, the Virginia portion of the Bristol Land and Improvement Company, had land north of Mary Street, between Fairview and Washington and beyond Danville to the north. This area was surveyed by C. S. Davis on March 5, 1890, and dedicated on August 5th the same year. On March 4, 1897, this addition was enlarged to include Buchanan and Bluff Streets, and then became known as Fairview Hill. It appears that Fairview Land Company also owned the lowlands along Beaver Creek and toward Norfolk Avenue. A spur of the railroad had been extended into this little valley, and it was meant to become an industrial development. Too, the projected Danville and East Tennessee Railway would have passed through this valley, thereby increasing its potential and value.

A. S. Gump was not only a successful local Jewish merchant, but he also did a small amount of city developing. In June 1890 he dedicated Gump's Addition to Bristol, Virginia. This lay along both sides of Russell Street from Lester to Buchanan. Though this was a small development, in time many nice homes were built within its limits.

Capt. J. H. Wood's addition to Bristol was dedicated June 9, 1890. This expansion was up Moore Street beyond Mary, from Oak View on the west to beyond Moore on the east, and ending near Virginia Intermont. This land was surveyed by Capt. Robert Gray. During this survey Capt. Gray sat down under a large tree at the highest point of the tract to have his lunch. The site so impressed him that he determined then and there that he someday would build his home upon that spot. This dream was realized in 1900. His home still stands and is occupied by his daughter, Miss Mary Preston Gray, who was recently recognized by the Bristol Preservation Society as having the record for Bristol's longest occupancy (since 1900). Beyond Wood's addition and reaching to Randall Street and over to upper Euclid was the Oak View addition. This was done at about the same time as that of Capt. Wood. Neither this nor the Wood addition had much development until well after 1900.

The year 1891 saw the quick formation of other land companies. Among them was the Twin City Land and Improvement Company. The survey and map of this development was made by Aaron Ward Morris in 1891, but there was no dedication until July 25, 1895. This addition to Bristol, Virginia, included New Hampshire, Vermont, Montpelier, Concord and the east side of Massachusetts Avenue.

Hobson's addition to Bristol, Virginia, was dedicated February 10, 1891. This included an area north of Buford Street from Hobson's Grove and around Cemetery Hill. Streets within it include Lottie, Lynn, Second Taylor and Haddon. This area was replatted by Col. J. M. Barker after 1900. Portions of this area north of the cemetery were heavily covered with dense brush and high grass. It was noted for its abundance of snakes. When the first survey was made in the late summer of 1890, fifty-seven snakes, including several copperheads, were killed.

The Mountain View addition to Bristol was platted and lots were sold at auction in 1891. This was the former Lancaster tract on Solar Hill, extending from behind the present home of Margaret Mitchell at 54 King Street, along Cumberland to Scranton, and over to what is now Sullins Street (at first Spruce). This sale was ordered by the courts to make a settlement of the estate of Thomas C. Lancaster who had died in 1875. There was a later replat of this addition by William F. Rhea.

One rather strange platting of lots was known locally as Jett's big fan. In

August 1892 John W. Jett, a local businessman, had laid out on the high ground immediately to the south of Highland Avenue and between Prince and Pearl Streets a small fan-like development, with lots eighty-eight feet on the front and slanting back as ribs of a fan to points from nothing to ten feet in width. It is apparent that this big fan development was intended to appeal to the elite who might wish to build fine homes overlooking the nearby valley and toward the mountains beyond. But for some reason Jett's big fan soon fanned out!

It was almost at the turn of the century that Major A. D. Reynolds dedicated what he called Cecil's addition to Bristol. This development took in most of present Norfolk Avenue. It finally became a popular building area, but not until well after 1900.

THE BRISTOL OF THE 1890s

As the end of the century neared, the two Bristols had a combined population of just under ten thousand. (The 1900 population is given as 4,579 in Bristol, Virginia, and 5,271 in Bristol, Tennessee.) This was a remarkable growth for what had been but an oversized village in the mid-1850s. It may come as a surprise to many readers to learn that most of the better Bristol homes of the late 1890s had electric power, as erratic as it may have been. Oil lamps were still kept at hand. And perhaps one-half to three-fourths of the homes had running water. For most, the cost of lights and water ran less than two dollars per month. There were no meters then; both power and water came at a fixed monthly or yearly rate. And if one thinks that the tie-on fee and resulting controversy is new, search the records. The issue was hotly debated by the citizens and officials of early Bristol. During the same period over half of the homes had telephones.

The closing of the century saw better and faster rail service. The town then had greatly improved schools and bigger and better churches. Business and industry were flourishing. The quality and effectiveness of professional services offered in Bristol drew clients and patients from far and near.

By this period the first three blocks of Main Street west of the railroad had become solidly commercial with one possible exception. A house that may have been used as a residence still stood about midway through the 600 block on the Virginia side. The old Anderson home (first building in Bristol) still stood on the southwest corner of Fourth and Main, but it had been turned into a grocery store and bakery. A cottage still stood about where the old H. P. King building is now located, but it was then being used as a confectionery. The 700 block on the Virginia side was a mixture of commercial buildings and homes, and contained one large church (Main Street Methodist), and a former residence that had become a notorious brothel (The Black Shawl).

Looking west on Main (State) Street, from the railroad, cir. 1895. The famous Nickels House is the first building on the left. The noted James corner is on the right. The first building erected in Bristol, the Anderson home, may be seen on the left and just beyond the Nickels House.

The Tennessee side of the 700 block contained more business houses than did the Virginia side, but a large part of the first half of the block was mostly vacant.

The Virginia side of the 800 block was largely residential, with the exception of Burson's Church, the warehouse of the Farmer's Protective Union, and two general stores, one of which was on the corner of Main and Scranton. Several stores were in the first half of the 800 block on the Tennessee side, but from the alley to Ninth Street was all residential.

Shelby and Broad Streets were virtually all residential. There was a flourishing cornfield just below the old Tennessee post office, and a large wheat field extended from the corner of Seventh and Broad back toward Eighth Street. There were many residences along Cumberland and Sycamore Streets, as well as Moore and Lee in that section which later become a portion of downtown Bristol (south and east of Beaver Creek).

Fourth and Fifth Streets were two of the most densely populated streets of the town, with houses extending to well beyond the old King College Campus. Alabama Street had several houses, and Chalmers (later called Woodlawn and now Edgemont) had nine houses from Anderson to Garland Avenue. A large lot on this street contained the Black school. Sixth and Seventh Streets had only scattered residences. Present Holston Avenue had not a house. Indeed, it was in the midst of an upland pasture. Along Windsor Avenue the town all but ended at Eleventh Street. No houses stood on Anderson beyond Twelfth Street, and there were very few in the two blocks before Twelfth. The last house on Broad was at Thirteenth Street. Just beyond the end of Thirteenth was the old English ore bank. There were only two houses on Shelby beyond Twelfth, the last being at Fourteenth Street. Most of West State was residential beyond present Commonwealth Avenue, being fairly well filled in to Twelfth Street.

Dr. William Dulaney had a large and fine home on the Virginia side across from the mouth of Twelfth Street. He had ten small rent houses behind his home. These small houses were identical, causing a little flurry of excitement late one dark night. Thomas Shane, who rented one of these houses, worked in the rail yards until midnight. His neighbor, Paschal Logan, often visited the numerous saloons in town, usually coming home in a "feeling no pain" condition. Those were the days when few people locked their doors at night. Mrs. Tom Shane retired early as usual, only slightly awaking to hear her 'husband' come in about the usual time and slip into bed. All went well for perhaps an hour when suddenly the 'husband' raised up and bellowed out, "Damn to Hell, Harriet, lay a little stiller, I can't sleep fer yore kickin' about." Her name wasn't Harriet but her neighbor's name was (wife of the drunk); and Tom Shane, a devout Baptist, didn't curse. The sudden realization caused a leaping exit from the bed and house by Mrs. Shane, who had to summon several sleeping neighbors to carry Paschal Logan from her bed. Her son, an aged Bristol citizen when this writer arrived in town (1953), used to double in laughter when he told this incident. And he always added, "Maw always locked the door after that."

Beyond the Dulaney place was a large tract of land that was owned by Z. L. Burson. Commonwealth had not a single house from Goode Street to the Benhams Road (across from the Valleydale plant). There was one small house in Furnace Bottom to the west of Commonwealth, but there was not a single house along all west Euclid Avenue or the streets along it, with the exception of the old Susong home that stood above where Revco Drug is now located in Little Creek Shopping Center. All that area was field and pasture land.

Houses were scattered over Solar Hill, but many—perhaps most—lots were unimproved. The west side of Solar Street above Cumberland had only one dwelling, the present Canter home (124 Solar Street). The second block had only three buildings, and these were clustered together near Scott Street. Perhaps five houses stood along the east side of Solar. Johnston (Johnson) Street, being a little closer to town, had a few more homes, but most of them were in the first block north of Cumberland.

There was only one house on Fairmount. Four were on the corners around Highland Avenue and Park Street, and there were four on Euclid Avenue. No houses were on the streets between Euclid and Glenway, except a farmhouse that is now numbered 816 Prince Street. Scott Street then had some of the better Bristol homes. North of Scott a few houses stood along Moore, Lee, Russell, Spencer and Edmond Streets. (This area was then known as Virginia Hill.) Mary Street, which was virtually the end of the town, had twenty-three houses along its length from Wood Street eastward, and these were about evenly divided along its north and south sides. North of this street and especially beyond Clinton Avenue were vast pastures. Cattle grazed in front of what is now Virginia Intermont College.

Railroad Street, later called Spencer and now the Randall Expressway, had twenty-two houses from Scott Street to near what is now the Janie Hammitt Home. Across the railroad yards, Washington, Virginia, Goodson, Edmond, Williams, Buford, and Winston Streets were graded, and some homes had been built, but many lots remained unimproved. East Main (State) Street beyond the railroad was virtually all residential. Development ended near the cemetery.

Pennsylvania Avenue to Maple Street had twenty-two houses on its west side but only five on the east. There were only three houses on Taylor Street, one on Carolina, four on Maryland, two or three on Georgia and none on

Florida Avenue. The cross streets of the Fairmount section contained only a very few buildings.

That's the way Bristol was in the closing years of the 19th century. But things would change within a few years. Soon there would be a great filling in of lots close to the center of the city and further extensions made into the surrounding country, a trend which continues to this day.

A CHILD OF THE FORMATIVE YEARS YET LIVES: Miss Mary Preston Gray, born August 2, 1896, and pictured here as a child, contributed much information and encouragement to the writing of this history. [Editor's note: Miss Gray died February 3, 1992, as this book was going to press.]

Bibliography - Chapter Five

Anderson, Melinda King. As told to her granddaughter, Mrs. Herman Blackley.

Anderson, Rhea. Notes, 1930s.

Baist, G. E. Map of Bristol, 1891. Copies owned by Tim Buchanan and Herbert Hayes of Bristol, Virginia.

Bristol News, newspaper. Various issues of the period.

Bristol Land and Improvement Company. Publications, Cir. 1890.

Bristol, Virginia. Development Maps.

Bristol, Tennessee. Development Maps.

Insurance Maps for Bristol, Virginia, and Bristol, Tennessee, 1889 and 1893.

Johnson, L. F. Notes, 1893.

Phillips, V. N. (Bud). Interviews with several older Bristol Citizens, 1953-1956.

Sullivan County, Tennessee. Chancery Court Records.

Sullivan County, Tennessee. Deed Records.

Sullivan County, Tennessee. Tax Records.

Taylor, Hattie King. Writings (unpublished). 1920s.

Washington County, Virginia. Chancery Court Records.

Washington County, Virginia. Deed Records.

Washington County, Virginia. Tax Records.

Chapter Six
LOCAL GOVERNMENT

BRISTOL, VIRGINIA

Originally two towns were planned and laid out on what is now the Virginia side of Bristol. In 1852 Bristol, Virginia, was mapped for Joseph Anderson; and Goodsonville was mapped about the same time for Samuel Goodson. When the time came for local government, the composite town of Goodson was incorporated on March 5, 1856. It was then directed that an election be held on April 5, 1856, for the purpose of electing officers for the new town. James Fields, local builder; James N. Bosang, saloon keeper; and A. T. Wilson, hotel operator and merchant, were commissioned to hold the election (any two of them could act).

Unfortunately, no records can be found of the results of that election. Ann Bachelor mentions in her notes that the votes were called out on the porch of Langhorne's Tavern (hotel) and that one man (whom she does not name) was severely wounded (stabbed) in a drunken fight that broke out during the time the votes were being called. From old papers recently discovered in the courthouse at Abingdon, Virginia, it appears that Austin M. Appling was elected the first mayor. Mr. Appling was a local merchant, having operated for some time what was popularly known as the Yellow House Store. There is strong indication that John N. Bosang was among the first councilmen, and that a little later W. H. Trammell also served in that capacity. All the records of the first fourteen years or so of the operation of local government were kept on whatever scraps of paper that might have been at hand. As far as can be determined, those papers have been scattered and lost. One early story goes that these papers were in the store house of R. T. Lancaster when it burned. It is known that the council often met there. There is no way of verifying this claim.

Although records of the early government of the town were lost, from other sources it may be determined that Philip Rohr was the second mayor. Rohr had early moved to Bristol from Abingdon, Virginia, where he had long engaged in the merchandising business. His Abingdon home, built in 1845, still stands at 133 Main Street. Old Chancery records show that Valentine Keebler was the first recorder-treasurer and that he so served for many years. It is known that Philip Rohr was still mayor in the early 1860s and that serving with him as aldermen were J. N. Bosang, J. E. Pepper, John Johnston and W. H. Trammell. John N. Bosang, John Keys, and W. S. Minor are known

Col. John N. Bosang and his wife posed for this picture in G.B. Smith's studio about 1879. Col. Bosang operated Bristol's first saloon and was also an early town councilman.

to have been among the aldermen just before the new charter of 1870 was issued.

On June 17, 1870, the town charter was amended. This act permitted local government to consist of a mayor, recorder, sergeant and five councilmen. It also directed that an election be held on July 2 (one record gives the date as July 12) that year to elect the officials of the town. It is of interest to note that John N. Bosang, who had helped conduct the election of 1856, was one of those selected to conduct that of 1870. The others selected for this purpose were former Bristol and Goodson postmaster John Keys and local builder Jesse H. Pepper.

Isaac Chapman Fowler, a native of Tazewell County, Virginia, was elected first mayor under the new charter. He was editor of the *Bristol News*. Thomas J. Millard became the recorder and John L. Ligon (or Liggon) became the sergeant. The first aldermen under the new charter were Prof. John H. Winston, president; Samuel L. Saul, an early merchant; Charles T. Pepper,

M.D.; George DeVault; and Capt. Joseph W. Owen. On March 14, 1871, the town charter was amended again to enlarge the Council to seven members. In those days this governing body was called the Common Council. The first meeting of the newly elected Council was held on July 27, 1870. At first these meetings were held in various places, usually a store room, office, or hotel; but on August 5, 1870, a room was rented from Mayor Fowler at sixty dollars for eight months. In 1872 this space became both a meeting room and office for the mayor, and the rent was increased to one hundred twenty dollars per year.

In 1871 the mayor's salary was sixty-one dollars per year. It was jokingly told that the extra dollar was compensation for cleaning the cuspidors (spittoons) in the meeting room. In those days of heavy tobacco chewing and snuff dipping, the one dollar was likely well earned! The mayor's salary was increased to one hundred dollars in 1872. By 1891 the salary had been increased to two hundred fifty dollars plus ten percent of all fines collected.

In 1871 the city recorder-treasurer was receiving fifty dollars per year; it increased to seventy-five dollars in 1872. The town sergeant began at thirty dollars in 1871; it increased to seventy dollars in 1872. In addition the sergeant received an extra five dollars every six months.

Captain John F. Terry, who first tried for mayor in 1872 (Fowler defeated him by 65 votes), was elected in 1875. He served eleven years, and then was defeated by A. F. Miles on May 14, 1886, by only three votes. Beware all who ride a high tide of political popularity; such tides have a way of suddenly receding. Poor Terry tried for a come-back in 1889 and received only one vote!

Political interest must have been at a high level in 1872; twenty-three citizens ran for council seats that year! Philip Rohr, who early had served as mayor for several years, received only three votes. Several others received only one vote each. An indication of the increase of the population of the town is that the number of voters increased from 72 in 1879 to 175 in 1882, and to 358 in 1889.

One of the first acts of the council elected in 1870 was to appoint a committee on safety to watch over the town regarding fire and other dangers. This committee was instructed to confer with the aldermen of Bristol, Tennessee, regarding cooperation in the matter. Some of the early buildings of Bristol had been put up quickly of highly inflammable materials causing the ever-present threat of devastating fires. Thus, it was natural for great concern to be shown in this area. A later ordinance decreed that a frame building of over a certain height could not be erected unless all property owners in the block agreed to the plan. And finally, the erection of any frame building was forbidden without approval by the Council.

In 1871 the town ordered a fire engine. There is indication that a better engine and other fire fighting equipment were purchased in 1881. The town's first welfare system was set up on October 24, 1870, when the Common Council decreed that the corporation should be responsible for the support of its poor. The mayor was to hear all applications and then pass his findings on to a committee, which at first was composed of J. H. Winston and Samuel L. Saul. This committee had the power to approve the application and then draw upon the recorder for necessary funds. As a part of this program, Dr. J. A. Templeton was retained to doctor the needy of the town at $1.25 per visit. Thirty years later (1900) Dr. J. T. Williams contracted to doctor paupers for $150.00 per year.

The first person approved for welfare aid in Goodson was a Mr. Coley, who was granted fifty cents per week to be paid monthly. The second was a Mrs. Echols who applied on November 4, 1871. On November 9 she was allowed seventy-five cents per week and was released from paying taxes. This Mrs. Echols had been a home nurse and was greatly beloved in the town. At the time of application she was dying of cancer.

An early grant of the welfare program was five dollars to Mattox and Trammell for burying the child of Anna Ward. Later records mention a coffin for a pauper at three dollars; and on May 27, 1872, the legendary undertaker H. A. Bickley was allowed four dollars for providing a coffin and funeral for an indigent.

The Common Council passed a blue law on October 7, 1870, which required that all the town's ordinary businesses must close at midnight on Saturday and not open again for twenty-four hours. John N. Bosang, who operated a saloon, is said to have stood before his business with watch in hand so that at exactly midnight on Sunday he could throw open his doors to the railroad trade.

As now, sometimes dangers had to be tragically dramatized before remedial steps were taken. The Mary Street crossing of the railroad was always hazardous. That street was a connecting link between the old stage road and the main pike leading to Paperville and was heavily traveled. In June 1871 a young mother was riding a horse from her home near Paperville to visit her relatives who lived on Virginia Hill. She carried her baby in her arms. Before she reached the railroad, a storm broke, causing her to be unaware of a train approaching in the heavy rain. Apparently she urged the horse forward and into the path of the train. Mother, child, and horse were killed. Soon a petition was circulated among the citizens of the town asking that a bridge be erected over the tracks. This petition was presented to the Common Council on July 18, 1871. It was favorably received. An agreement was reached with the railroad to furnish labor while the town would furnish the materials. It may be of interest to know that the nails which were purchased from John A. James for that project cost $4.99.

In at least one retrogressive act, the council in 1871 voted to cancel the lamplighter's contract, thus allowing the town to go back into darkness. It was agreed that any of the lamps on Main Street might be used by store owners if such persons would become responsible for the upkeep "of said lamps and oil therefor." According to what was told the author by persons who had lived during that time, not many took advantage of the offer to use the lamps. The streets remained in darkness for years. In 1881 editor Fowler, writing in the *Bristol News*, lamented this fact and expressed the belief that the time was past due when the town should make arrangements to light the streets on nights when there was no full moon. Perhaps his urging was effective. There is record that John Templin was paid $7.50 per month for his services as lamp lighter in 1885. Two years later a Mr. Thomas was paid $8.33 per month for the same service.

No doubt the citizens rejoiced in 1871 when the tax rate, which had been thirty-five cents per hundred evaluation, was reduced to twenty-five cents. On September 11, 1872, the privilege tax fees were set. A sampling of privilege fees is listed below:

Liquor merchants (saloons)	$50.00
Liquor stores	25.00
Bankers	20.00
Peddlers	$1.00 to 25.00
Merchants	10.00
Fortune tellers	5.00
Book agents (Bibles and hymnals exempted)	5.00
Auctioneers	5.00
Restaurants without bar	15.00
Restaurants with bar	30.00
Lawyers	10.00
Doctors	5.00
Dentists	5.00
Photographers	10.00
Circuses	20.00 per day, plus $2.50 for each stand.

Very early there was frequent talk of building a city hall for the town. A site for such a building was reserved when the Meadow Square land was sold in the mid-1870s. Around 1880 a substantial, two-story brick building was erected upon this site, which was on the north side of Cumberland, between Lee and Water Streets. Space in this new city hall or courthouse was to be assigned by the mayor. The building stood until well after 1900.

Though the Council had bought more chairs than needed for its members in 1870 (Twelve chairs at nine dollars per dozen had been bought from Col. I. B. Dunn in August that year.), there is little indication of public attendance of the meetings of that body until 1897, when a rule was made and was to be rigidly enforced that no one could address the Council without permission. Old timers told that just prior to the making of that rule, local citizens sometimes called out their comments and advice and even heckled the Council members "without warning."

As the end of the century neared, the burden of local government grew heavier, largely because of a swelling population and the resultant problems created thereby. Perhaps the mentioning of one of those problems before closing this chapter may be of interest to the reader. Virtually every residence had one or more milk cows in the back lot, and nearly all those cows wore bells. The clanging of those bells created a din hard to imagine by those who live today. And old bossy did not always choose to graze during daylight hours. Thus, a loud bell might sound at 3:00 A.M. or whenever. So, in 1895 the town fathers passed an ordinance that forbade the use of cowbells in the town. Some refused to obey at first, but this was a law with a built-in alarm.

In the early days of Bristol virtually every home had one or more milk cows. The din of their ringing bells during the wee hours of the morning caused the city fathers to pass an ordinance that "Bossy's bell had to go."

When and where a cowbell sounded, it gave notice that the law was being broken, and the constable might be expected shortly. Soon a sound so familiar to the pioneer settlers of Bristol was silenced forever. But isn't that the duty of governments — to be concerned and offer remedy for every problem of the people?

Councilmen who served Bristol-Goodson, Virginia, in the 1870s were

George Harmeling	Major Z.L. Burson
Peter C. Archer	W.W. James
David Sullins	W.G. Lindsey
Dr. H. T. Berry	J.S. Good
David A. Wheeler	Charles C. Campbell
George W. Hammitt	J.M. Trammell
Martin Fleenor	

Councilmen who served in the 1880s were

Jesse A. Buckner	Augustus S. McNeil
E. H. Seneker	Charles E. Finch
Dr. Jere Bunting	John W. Jett
H. E. Graves	H.B. Echols
M. R. Kerby	A.A. Hobson
A. B. Echols	J.M. Trammell
John R. Dickey	W.C. Carrington
E. S. Kendrick	W.A. Rader
Frank Winston	W.P. Hamilton
John A. Smith	Samuel McCrary

Councilmen who served in the 1890s were

W. H. Fillinger	M. T. Crowell
S. W. Frizzell	E. D. Pendleton
George Wolfe	Robert F. Wagner
George Harmeling	H. E. McCoy
J. W. Walker	J. T. LeSuer
C. L. Bunting	Rives Walker
W. E. Reynolds	M. T. Devault
J. G. Owen	Joseph Combs
P. A. Pepper	W. T. Senter
Charles Patterson	Charles Harmeling
Jere Bunting, Sr.	William Pitzer
N. T. Dulaney	E. B. Faidley
Samuel Millard	Dr. W. T. Delaney
George A. Blackmore	Charles F. Gauthier
W. S. Trammell	C. W. Hanna

J. D. Mitchell	H. G. Peters
James McCrary	J. W. Mort
E. T. Jones	H. E. Jones
G. C. Fuquas	_____? Parrish
J. D. Huddle	

In 1900 the Council consisted of Charles F. Gauthier, Mayor; G. C. Fuqua, president; H. E. Jones; E. T. Jones; C. W. Hanna; W. T. Senter; James McCrary; and J. D. Huddle.

Those who served Bristol-Goodson, Virginia, as mayor during the period 1870-1900 were

Isaac Chapman Fowler	1871-1875
Capt. John F. Terry	1875-1886
A. F. Miles	1886-1889
W. A. Rader	1889-1894
J. H. Winston, Jr.	1894-1898
Charles F. Gauthier	1898-1902

Those who served Bristol-Goodson, Virginia, as town sergeants during the period 1870-1900 were

J. L. Ligon	1871-1872
David A. Wheeler	1872-1874
W. H. Trammell	1874-1875
R. T. Hamlet	1875-1877
John B. Keller	1877-1881
David A. Wheeler	1881-1884
Charles Worley	1884-1887
W. P. Hughes	1887-1888
Charles Worley	1888-1890
W. J. Cox	1890-1892
Justin King	1892-1894
Luther Rush	(dates indefinite)

Those who served Bristol-Goodson, Virginia, as recorder-treasurer during the period 1870-1890 were

T. J. Millard	1870-1876
M. T. DeVault	1876-1878
G. G. Hickman	1878-1884
James Byrne	1884-1885
A. F. Miles	1885-1886
G. G. Hickman	1886-1887
John D. Witt	1887-1888
J. W. Mort	1888-1890

In 1890 the recorder became known as the clerk. The treasurer then became a separate office. Those who served as clerk after this change were

J. H. Winston, Jr.	1890-1894
J. A. Stone	1894-1896
G. H. Reed	1896-1897
Henri Doriot	1897-1900

Those who served as treasurer during the period 1890-1900 were

C. C. Minor	1890
J. L. C. Smith	1890-1896
J. W. Owen	1896-1904

Those who served Bristol, Virginia as judges of the Corporation Court, during the period 1890-1900 were William F. Rhea (1890-1896) and William S. Stuart (1896-1904). Those who served as commonwealth attorneys during the same period were William S. Hamilton (1890-1894), Preston Lewis Gray (1894-1896), and John S. Ashworth (1896-1904). Those who served as clerks of the Corporation Court during this period were J. H. Winston, Jr. (1890-1894), Isaac Sharett (1894-1896), James A. Stone (1896-1898), and W. H. Price, Jr. (1898-1902). Commissioners of the Revenue during this period were J. W. Mort (1890-1896) and J. W. Frizzell (1896-1900).

LOCAL GOVERNMENT — BRISTOL, TENNESSEE

The town charter for Bristol, Tennessee, granted February 22, 1856, required that the sheriff of Sullivan County hold an election in the town on May 1 that year for the purpose of electing a mayor and other governing officials. The election was duly held at the front door of the store of Joseph R. Anderson, where qualified townsmen came and called out their choices. According to one who lived in the town at that time, probably not more than twenty men voted. The records of the local government for Bristol, Tennessee, begin on November 18, 1856, when the officials of the newly incorporated town met in the parlor of Joseph R. Anderson's home on the southwest corner of Main and Fourth Streets (now State and Edgemont). According to a granddaughter of Anderson, the meeting was set for early candlelight (dusk) and came to early adjournment when a heavy snow began to fall. Joseph R. Anderson, who had founded Bristol in 1852, presided as the town's first mayor. James W. Morgan, formerly of Bedford County, Virginia, was elected first recorder. Though there likely were others, E. P. Cawood, local hotel keeper, is the only alderman named in the minutes of that first meeting.

At this first meeting several laws and ordinances were adopted and fifty copies of the same were ordered to be printed on fool's cap paper. An appropriation was made for the purchase of record books, paper, quills and ink for the recorder, treasurer and constable. Joseph R. Anderson became the first treasurer. It appears that later the offices of treasurer and recorder were combined. An indication of how little official business there was for the town in those early days is the fact that there was not another meeting of mayor and aldermen until May 15, 1857. At that meeting Joseph R. Anderson was paid $17.65 for work on streets and bridges. As far as can be determined, this was the first money ever spent by Bristol, Tennessee. James W. Morgan has the honor of having received the town's second payment — $6.38 on July 10, 1857. The main concern of the very earliest years of local government here seems to have been street improvement and bridge building. To do this, money had to be borrowed from individuals and repayment seems to have been rather difficult. That funds were short is no surprise; the first tax rate was only ten cents per hundred dollars of valuation!

Before long the town fathers were taking steps to raise more revenue. On July 10, 1857, a system of retail licenses was set up and fees established. Merchants having less than five-hundred dollars in stock were charged five dollars. Those having stock valued between five-hundred and two-thousand dollars were charged seven dollars and fifty cents, and those with stock valued at over two-thousand were charged twenty-five dollars. Free, black males were required to pay one dollar per year for residency rights, and their poll tax was set at one dollar and fifty cents.

On November 18, 1858, real estate taxes were doubled from ten to twenty cents per hundred of valuation. At the same time the poll tax was doubled from one to two dollars. For every male dog a fifty cent tax was to be paid, and for a second dog the fee went to one dollar. All female dogs were taxed at two dollars each. A horse or mule cost the owner twenty-five cents in taxes. Hogs running loose were taxed at twenty-five cents each. And one who had a wagon or cart for hire must pay two dollars. Occasionally a citizen earned tax credit by improving the street in front of his property.

By 1860 the real estate tax had doubled again. Horses were then being taxed at fifty cents per head, and a one-horse vehicle was charged at one dollar and fifty cents. A two-horse vehicle was charged at two dollars and fifty cents, while a four-horse carriage or wagon was taxed at four dollars. At that time a merchant with stock of under two-thousand dollars paid a tax of ten dollars. Those with stock up to five-thousand paid fifteen dollars. A ten thousand dollar stock was charged at twenty dollars and all over that amount paid twenty-five dollars. The tax rate climbed throughout the remainder of the century. Indeed, when it reached fifty cents on the hundred (January 4, 1870), there was a near tax revolt of the local citizens!

In 1860 the mayor and aldermen approved Bristol's first storm sewer. It was made of boards forming a hollow square and during heavy rains it drained, a pond that formed near the southeast corner of Fourth and Main (now State and Edgemont). This wooden "pipe" came down Main Street to near the present corner of State and Lee, then turned northward for a short distance where it emptied into an open ditch that flowed into Beaver Creek.

On June 6, 1860, an ordinance was passed that was good news to many while very vexing to others. It was decreed that any hog running loose in the streets was a public nuisance and any citizen might lawfully remove the same. You may be sure that many a hog was removed and taken to the smoke house of some provident householder! The same law applied to dogs.

During the Civil War the meetings of the mayor and aldermen gradually decreased in frequency as the war dragged on. Near the end of the war, there were hardly any meetings at all. But after the end of that conflict, a fairly regular schedule was soon resumed.

In those early years there was no regular meeting place for the board. Anderson's banking room was a popular point of assembly. Rosenheim's store often served the same purpose. Some meetings were held in the Exchange Hotel (later Nickels House). The Campbell and Thomas Drug Store often hosted many meetings, as did the Martin Brothers Store on the southeast corner of what is now State and Sixth. After about 1870 most of the meetings were held in Conway Hall, which stood in the first block of Fifth Street.

In September 1869 the very dignified E. B. McClanahan was stiffly walking down Main Street near Martin's store. Some boys were busily engaged in a game of marbles near the sidewalk. A flipped marble landed under a foot of Mr. McClanahan who also flipped right backward into a mudhole while his tall silk top hat rolled under the wheels of a passing carriage and was ruined. Now this old town aristocrat had influence at "city hall." And wouldn't one just know it, at the next meeting of the board (September 17, 1869) an ordinance appeared on the city books making it illegal to play marbles on the streets of Bristol! As an additional precaution, it was also decreed that balls could not be thrown on the sidewalks.

That the town fathers were becoming aware of the need for better fire protection is shown by action taken on November 29, 1873, toward securing fire fighting equipment. Great advancement along this line was made in the immediate years following that action.

Being a city official in those days was not without times of embarrassment. On December 6, 1873, a Sullivan County Grand Jury indicted the mayor and aldermen for failing to keep up the road leading to the East Hill Cemetery. Immediate action was taken to have the street committee look into the situation.

As the population of the town increased, the demands on the town officials became greater and greater. However, there were always local citizens who could fill the need well. It is heartening to see how those who served through the remainder of the century worked as diligently as those before them to take advantage of the many opportunities to improve and expand a town that was fast becoming a city.

Mayors who served Bristol, Tennessee, during the period 1856-1900 were (dates when available)

Joseph R. Anderson	1856-1859
L. F. Johnson	Elected 1859
Joseph R. Anderson	1866 (served one month)
A. J. Campbell	February 1866
Jacob R. Crumley	1867-1870
E. B. McClanahan	May 1870
Thomas L. Nelms	Elected May 6, 1872
G. B. Smith	1873
Dr. James A. Dickey	1878-1885
J. W. Norvell	1885-1889
John H. Caldwell	1889-1891
Dr. Samuel W. Rhea, D.D.S.	1891-1893
John C. Anderson	Sworn in by W. A. Ray, June 12, 1893

Those known to have served in the office of recorder during the period 1852-1900 were

James W. Morgan	1856
Samuel R. Anderson	1857
J. H. Martin	1858
George C. Pile	1860
Charles R. Vance	1861
Joseph R. Anderson	1863
Charles R. Vance	1866
John Slack	1866
L. F. Johnson	1870
J. A. Burrow	1885
T. J. Burrow	1896

Aldermen known to have served Bristol in the earliest year (1856-1860) were

E. P. Caywood
W. P. Carmack
J. W. Morgan
Samuel R. Anderson
Dr. Flavius Hartman

Jesse Aydlotte
Thomas W. Farley
T. P. Reed
J. H. Martin
L. F. Johnson
Eli Marsh
T. B. Pickering
Dr. William Hammer
J. Austin Sperry
Henry Rosenheim
Paris Pepper

The 1860s saw many of the earliest aldermen continuing to serve with others being added from time to time. Those known to have served during the 1860s were

Thomas W. Farley	James King, Jr. (III)
George C. Pile	W. P. Brewer
Henry Rosenheim	Charles Barker
Joseph R. Anderson	J. M. Robinson
Charles R. Vance	David Ensor
L. H. Stokes	J. P. Hammer
L. A. Womack	Thomas Johnston
Walter H. Nickels	John Slack
J. W. Thomas	W. L. Martin
Jacob Hamilton	Robert Martin
E. W. Ellis	W. W. Neal
W. H. Robinson	

Many new names appear in the 1870s, yet at least one name (L. F. Johnson) still remains from the earliest days. Those who came to the Board of Aldermen in the 1870s were

I. A. Nickels	Audley Anderson
John G. Pepper	W. B. Melvin
John Crowell	W. N. Keller
L. F. Johnson	John H. Seneker
David F. Bailey	Thomas F. Wood
T. L. Nelms	J. D. Robertson
G. B. Smith	J. M. Barker

Aldermen known to have served during the 1880s include

J. D. Thomas	W. T. Sullivan
John H. Caldwell	John Slack
G. B. Smith	Joe Pile

Major A. D. Reynolds   S. G. Lamer
J. C. Maide   John C. Anderson
John P. Steffner   Co. N. M. Taylor
W. A. Ray   Dr. M. M. Butler
A. P. Moore   John Hennessee
W. H. Smith   George T. Hammer
Dr. Samuel Rhea   James Bondurant
George C. Pile   Dr. James A. Dickey

As far as can be determined, no one who served in the earliest years was still in the city government by the last decade of the century. Those who served in the 1890s were

Robert Pile   J. W. Waynick (or Warnick)
John I. Cox   Dr. N. H. Reeve
J. A. Faw   Thomas P. Godsey
S. T. Graves   Dr. J. F. Hicks
J. P. Rader   J. B. Baumgardner
D. N. Bufford   H. W. Powers
Jeremiah Bunting, Jr.   George T. Hammer
A. Riley   Joe D. Taylor
E. A. Warren   S. R. Ferguson
W. W. Davis   Anson King

In the late winter of 1892, the town issued bonds in the amount of $48,000 for the purpose of building a city hall (known as the courthouse), a public market house, and other improvements. The market house was wrecked by the tornado of June 5, 1893, but the sturdy brick courthouse located near the northwest corner of Broad and Eighth Streets stood until recent years.

Bibliography - Chapter Six

Anderson, Joseph R. Manuscript. cir. 1880.

Anderson, Melinda King. As told to Mrs. Herman Blackley, 1890-1908.

Anderson, Rhea. Notes, 1930-1939.

Bristol News, newspaper. Various issues 1857-1881.

Bristol-Goodson, Virginia. City Council Minute Books.

Bristol, Tennessee. City Council Minute Books.

Johnson, L. F. Notes, 1893.

Phillips, V. N. (Bud). Interviews with several older Bristol citizens, 1953-1956.

Washington County, Virginia. Chancery Records, 1852-1900.

Washington County, Virginia. County Court Minute Books, 1852-1900.

Chapter Seven
STREETS OF THE CITY

In 1852 the streets of Bristol were only rows of oak stakes rising slightly above the lush, waving grass of the King Meadows. These stakes, made in the carpenter shop of Campbell Galliher, were set in place by aides of Henry Anderson when he surveyed the Town of Bristol, Virginia-Tennessee, on August 1st, 2nd and 3rd, 1852. Each stake was topped by a wisp of linen cloth which, when blowing in gentle breezes, resembled a field of open cotton bolls ready for harvest (so described by an early Southern visitor). These stakes and flags not only marked the streets of the new town, but also identified individual lots fronting on them. The numbers of such lots were marked on the corner stakes. And at the corner of each street was a four inch board, set upright, upon which was written the street name. This was to aid prospective buyers in locating properties. Some of these stakes and boards were still in place as late as 1860.

The first surveyed streets of Bristol presented a hodge-podge of numbered thoroughfares with little rhyme or reason, all centered around Main Street, which lay all in Tennessee but bordered on the Virginia line. It was necessary to place Main Street all in Tennessee because the Virginia and Tennessee Railroad Company would not permit its tracks to be crossed. When first surveyed, Main Street extended from a point just back of the present First Baptist Church to the crossing of Beaver Creek, which was then between present Moore and Piedmont on the Virginia side and Sixth and Seventh on the Tennessee side. (The channel was later changed.) Fourth Street ran parallel with the railroad from about present Ash Street, through Bristol, Tennessee, crossed the state line, and ran completely through old Bristol, Virginia, to a point near Beaver Creek. The Virginia portion later became Front Street. There were only four other streets in Bristol, Tennessee. Sixth Street followed the route of present Fifth to present Ash Street. It was crossed by Fifth Street which is now Olive Street. East of the railroad there was First Street, which soon became Third Street. It turned sharply west at the end of the Tennessee depot lot, reached a point near the railroad, then turned southward to follow the tracks to near present Ash Street. Along its southern side it was intersected by a short Third Street which also ran southward to near Ash.

In old Bristol, Virginia, there was an Eighth Street that followed the line of present Lee. Between present Cumberland and the old route of Sycamore

Street and extending westward to Beaver Creek, was Seventh Street. East of and parallel to the railroad was the Virginia portion of First Street, extending to about present Buford, where it became Washington Street in adjoining Goodsonville. One block east and parallel to First was Second Street, which is now named Virginia and was then so named beyond the Goodsonville line.

On both sides of the state line in the original Town of Bristol, there were numerous lots, not fronting on or reached by any planned street. Thus, it soon became necessary to create new streets. Shelby and Cumberland were the first to be laid out for this purpose.

STREET DEVELOPMENT

The first streets to take on any semblance of even deeply rutted roadways were Main and Fourth. Fourth became a favorite site of early development because it was near the railroad and also ran parallel with it. First Street east of the tracks followed closely behind Fourth Street in early and rapid development, for the same reason. (It soon became Third Street.) Business firms wanted to locate near the tracks for obvious reasons, while it was somewhat of a status symbol to have residences in view of passing trains. Fourth Street saw so much development in those early years that it was often referred to as Main Street. This unofficial, but commonly used designation, even found its way into a few deeds made during the formative years.

Main Street was a connector to the old stage road near present Volunteer Parkway. For that reason it was much in use, especially by the Blountville-Sullivan County trade. The very first years of Bristol saw much development in the first two blocks of Main, west of Fourth Street. Traffic was then hampered by a troublesome, muddy, and steep-banked crossing of Beaver Creek, near present Seventh and Piedmont Streets. This caused much agitation for a bridge at that point, both by local citizens and incoming trade.

At a meeting of the City Council of Bristol, Tennessee, May 15, 1857, it was ordered that a bridge be built over the troublesome crossing. The committee appointed to oversee the project consisted of Joseph R. Anderson, William P. Carmack and J. W. Morgan. Specifications called for a rather substantial structure for that early time.

The bridge was to have rock abutments, twenty-four feet wide, two feet thick, and seven feet high. There were to be wings of the same thickness, beginning at the same heights, but sloping back for at least fifteen feet to the terminus. These abutments were to be spanned by seven sawed sills, eight by fourteen inches and thirty-two feet long. These were to be covered by two-inch oak planks, two feet wide. This was Bristol's first bridge. It was not long until a similar structure was erected over Little Beaver Creek (or

Baker's Creek) near the present plant of the Paty Lumber Company.

FIRST SIDEWALKS

On October 1, 1857, the City Council of Bristol, Tennessee, ordered that all Main Street merchants build sidewalks in front of their establishments. To be made of brick, they were to be seven feet wide and six inches above the street level. Merchants of the Virginia side of Main Street cooperated by building similar sidewalks at the same time. About this time residents along Third Street volunteered to build brick sidewalks three feet wide. Thus, the first residential sidewalk in our city was along what was then considered the best address in town.

EARLY STREET LAWS

In the first few years of Bristol's existence, it became necessary to make laws relating to the use of its streets. One of the first and one said to be very necessary in those days was a law forbidding any person to relieve himself on the streets within the public gaze. An early case concerning such a violation questioned what distance constituted the public gaze. The "gaze" was determined as being fifty steps, or one hundred and fifty feet. Violation of this law brought a fine of one dollar or five days in jail. On May 20, 1858, a law was passed forbidding the leaving of a dead carcass on the street or throwing one in a well. The penalty was a little heavier here: five dollars or twenty days in jail.

Then was made the law (same date) that those who fed stock or stood wagons on the sidewalks were to be fined one dollar or to be jailed five days. The first person to be tried for this latter offense was Isaac Shelby (not the son of General Shelby), whose case was heard on December 3, 1858. He was fully pardoned with no fine or jail term.

Other laws followed in quick succession. A horse was not to be ridden through the streets at more than a fast walk. And there was to be no racing of wagons, buggies, surreys, or carriages on Bristol streets. (There was only one carriage in all lower Washington County or Sullivan County at that time and it belonged to the aging Rev. James King.) Alas, Pleasant Biggs gained the distinction of being Bristol's first "hot-rodder" (or shall we say hot hoofer) when he had a violent argument with his wife. He jumped in his buggy, left her standing in front of Anderson's store, and raced furiously down Main Street. Pleasant Biggs did not find life so pleasant for the next ten days, for such was his sentence to the Blountville jail. (Bristol then had no jail.)

As the town grew. it became necessary for the town fathers to enact an ordinance that no lewd woman should be seen on the streets after early candlelight (dusk). One local editor asked the pointed question in his publication, "and what of lewd men?" Apparently he was not beset by the double standard!

Early it was decreed that any citizen allowing a slut dog to run loose in the streets would be fined one dollar or spend five days in jail. A like fine or sentence might face the person who allowed any dog to run loose without a collar. The collar was evidence that the dog tax (one dollar for first dog, fifty cents for each additional dog owned) had been paid. It was not forbidden that hogs be allowed to run loose in the streets in those earliest years (later laws did forbid such), but owners must pay twenty cents per head for the privilege. (How a hog showed that his "roaming fee" had been paid is not known.)

MUD AND DUST

In those first years of Bristol all streets were either mud or dust. During hot, dry times the dust arose in clouds as horsemen and wagons passed through the thoroughfares of the growing town. It was virtually impossible to keep store stocks clean. The women of the town fretted because white washings soon turned yellow. Pedestrians were choked as they passed along the sidewalks. Then when rains, snows, and freezes came, the streets became endless mud holes and puddles. Wagons sometimes sank up to the axles, horses bogged down, and pedestrians searched for safe crossings which were few and far between. Thoughtful merchants placed stepping stones across the street near their stores. It is known that some used split logs for the same purpose. But, alas, both stones and logs often became slippery. Many a shopper or town visitor lost his or her dignity and clean attire by suddenly "sailing" into a sea of seemingly bottomless mud.

One enterprising merchant, E. H. Seneker, was granted the right to erect an overhead walkway which swung from cables and extended from near the front of his store across the state line to the Tennessee side of Main Street. Seneker's bridge quickly became the most popular Main Street crossing in town. The overhead bridge from the depot to the Virginia House Hotel (Front Street) was built for the same purpose, as well as for the convenience of those train passengers who wished to have a meal there.

MACADAMIZING MAIN STREET

Macadamizing, a process developed by John Loudon (1756-1836), consists of compacting a layer of small broken stone into a solid mass on a convex well-drained roadbed. J. W. Morgan, one of the early city fathers, had seen this done on roadways near his old home in Bedford County, Virginia, and suggested that such might be a solution to the endless mud and dust of Bristol's Main Street.

On June 1, 1858, the council "ordered a committee to locate a grade of Main Street, so as to be macadamized," from Dr. Hammer's (present site of Interstate Hardware Building) to the "west end at the big sycamore." The committee consisted of J. W. Morgan, Thomas Reed, Thomas Farley, and John H. Martin. Later L. F. Johnson and Joseph R. Anderson were ordered to write the specifications for this work.

Until then there had been no crossing of the railroad on Main Street. The tracks were elevated at that point with moderately high embankments on both sides. Just east of the tracks was a pond, sometimes called Hammer's pond, that had been filled in by August 1857, after Dr. Flavius Hartman had taken up donations for that purpose. Those persons who needed to go to homes or business houses had to go to a bumpy crossing near the end of present Olive Street or to a point just beyond the end of the old depot. Most pedestrians favored the latter route. There was a wagon crossing at the end of Camp Street. So, before Main Street could be macadamized, the railroad crossing had to be graded.

In July 1858 it was determined that a grade of three degrees and twenty feet wide over the railroad would cost two hundred dollars. The council asked the railroad company to pay for the grading, but the railroad refused. In time the crossing was built at a $465.80 expense to the town.

By January 1859 preliminary grading of Main Street in preparation for macadamizing had been completed. The work was done by a Mr. Crumley and a Mr. Godsey. It was then that the project was opened for bidding with specifications that the rock fill be nine inches deep in the middle, sloping to six inches at the curb. Bids came slowly so that by April 1859 it was felt that an ad should be placed in the *Bristol News* for the purpose of stimulating interest among prospective contractors. In time John Hennesey made the successful bid. (It was this Mr. Hennesey who built the grade over the railroad.)

Before the surfacing of Main Street was completed, extensions had been made to Mr. Andrew J. Blair's property to the east (back of First Baptist Church) and to a point well beyond the Beaver Creek bridge. The original width of sixty feet had been reduced to twenty feet.

The work was completed by August 16, 1859, at a total cost of $2,931.67. At that time the town was in rather dire financial straits, so that it was necessary for individuals and firms to make loans to the corporation. Those loaning three hundred dollars each were L. F. Johnson, Joseph R. Anderson, James King, Sr., Stern and Rosenheim, and W. J. Betterton and Company. Keebler and Pepper loaned two hundred dollars.

At a final settlement two or three months later, the town was still short by several hundred dollars. Therefore, additional loans had to be sought with

J. A. Sperry and Samuel R. Anderson (brother of J. R. Anderson) doing the soliciting.

For a time the nightmare of mud and dust was only an unpleasant memory. Ladies of the town had whiter washes, and there was less dusting to do in the stores. Seneker's bridge fell into disrepair, because one could then cross the street about anywhere without the peril of bottomless mud holes. But crushed rock has a way of eventually working its way downward, and washing soil soon covers and increases in depth. There was little or no repair during the war years and the period immediately thereafter. By 1870 Main and other town streets were about back to the conditions that existed at the beginning.

There was little, if any, improvement throughout the remainder of the century. Block and brick would not come until after 1900, and that is beyond the scope of this book.

THE STREETS OF GOODSONVILLE

It has been noted that all the original streets except one in the Town of Bristol, Virginia-Tennessee, were numbered. It is interesting to note that all the streets in adjoining Goodsonville were named. When Col. Samuel E. Goodson engaged Capt. Edmond Winston to survey the proposed town, he gave him the privilege of naming all the streets except one. Col. Goodson had long been an admirer of early Virginia Governor Henry Lee, who was in that office when Goodson was born. He wanted to honor this early governor by naming a street for him.

There were but ten streets in the original plan of Goodsonville. These were Mary, Edmond (or Edmund), Depot (later Spencer), Scott, Lee, Russell, Camp (erroneously written as Champ on the original plat map), William (popularly called Williams), Virginia, and Washington.

It is apparent that Washington was meant to be the principal or main street of this development. It connected to First Street in old Bristol, Virginia, and thus was well suited for the purpose. There appears to have been some business activity along the lower (southern) portion of this street in the earliest days, but it was never extensive. However, a business district was expected to develop there, and some of the area's leading capitalists bought lots in what might one day become the downtown section of Goodsonville. But it soon became evident that most of the business interest was moving toward Fourth and Main Streets in Bristol, Virginia-Tennessee.

As in neighboring Bristol, many of the planned streets in Goodsonville remained only lines on paper for many years after the proposed town was surveyed. And for the remainder of the century, the existing streets continued as narrow, muddy, or dusty roadways.

CREATING NEW STREETS

When old Bristol, Virginia, and adjoining Goodsonville were put together to form the composite Town of Goodson (1856), the borders were enlarged a little and a few new streets were created. In this new area were King, West, and Scranton. At this writing King is only one block long, but in 1856 it extended across present Solar Hill along what is now King's Alley, across present Piedmont, and on to connect with Edmond Street. This was actually the route of the old stage road. West Street began on West Main (State) near the present Paty Lumber Company and angled toward Solar Hill. Scranton formed the beginning of present Commonwealth Avenue. There was a First Street, forming the beginning of what is now Piedmont, and a Second Street which is now Goode.

Within the limits of old Bristol, Virginia, were created Moore, Water, and an extension of Lee Street. In the area of old Goodsonville were formed Buford (which ran along the old dividing line between the original Bristol, Virginia and Goodsonville), Spencer Street (then ending at Russell) and Shelby. This latter so-called street was more of an alley that lay between and parallel with Lee and Russell Streets. Church Alley, which came nearer to being a street than did Shelby, lay between and parallel with Scott and Spencer Streets.

The next significant creation of streets came in 1871, when the Johnston lands were divided into lots and sold. Most of these new streets were formed on Solar Hill. About the same time and on the Tennessee side of town, John G. King opened a new subdivision which contained several new streets, such as King (now Sixth), Alabama, Rose, Cherry, Locust, and others.

As the century moved on, more additions were made to the original towns, and many new streets were formed. But many—perhaps most—of these remained as lines on paper until well up toward the turn of the century. Still others, planned on paper, never came into existence at all.

NAMING THE STREETS

Naming the streets in Bristol, Tennessee, was no problem—at least at the beginning—they were simply numbered. The first named street in that side of town, other than Main, was Shelby. Shelby came into existence shortly before the Civil War because of sheer necessity. Lots joined along the line it followed; but until it was opened, there was no access to them. It was named because it first terminated at the old Shelby burying ground. (It was not cut through to Fourth until well after 1890.) Broad Street, also a street of necessity, was named not because of its width (as we well know today), but because a surveyor, noting that it crossed what was known locally as the Broad Bottom, suggested that name. Bank Street began as a yard-wide trail laid out by W. W. Davis so that he might have passage from his Main Street store to his home which stood on Shelby Street. For years it was called Davis Alley, but later became Bank Street because a bank long operated on the southwest corner of its intersection with Main (State) Street. The bank building still stands.

Present Anderson Street, while planned in 1852, was not then named or numbered. It was first called Lee Street for the noted Civil War General. Later it was called, albeit briefly, Royal Street, because much of the town's "royalty" built along it. Then it became Anderson for Joseph R. Anderson, who built a fine home on it in 1881. The name was a compromise as will later be explained. What is now Sixth Street was named King Street when that area was subdivided. This was for John G. King, who then owned the land. Seventh Street was first called Bridge Street because it started from Main near the Beaver Creek bridge. Eighth was at first Mill Street because it led to the King Mill near present Melrose Street (later English and finally Wood's Mill).

Locust Street now has its third name. It was first called Barn Street because the old King sheep barn stood by it. Later it was called Ensor Street for David J. Ensor, the town's second druggist, who built the oldest portion of what is now the Weaver Funeral Home. For many years his was the only house on the street. Cherry Street took its name for a huge tree that stood near it, and under which King's sheep used to rest. There was an old slave cemetery at the southwest corner of what is now Rose Street. Supposedly, Mrs. James King planted an old-fashioned climbing rose at the grave of the old cook for the King family. By the time that area was developed, this rose had covered much of the cemetery fence and ground around it. Thus came the name Rose Street.

What is now Edgemont was first Chalmers Street, named for Cyrus Chalmers English, who was a favorite nephew of John G. King, the developer of that area. In the early 1870s John G. English sold to T. F. Wood, ancestor of Bristol attorney Bernard Via, a large acreage including the old English Mill (formerly King Mill) located near the end of Ash Street. Mr. Wood built a fine home near the site of the present Edgemont Towers. This estate was known as Woodlawn. In time, the name of Chalmers Street was changed to Woodlawn, its name when this writer moved to Bristol in 1953.

Alabama Street took its name from Alabama Cane, a servant girl of John G. King. Fifth Street was first Sixth Street, but was changed as the town developed. In those years it was graded only to present Shelby Street, where it ended at the gate of the Shelby Cemetery. Many of the town fathers envisioned a grand avenue leading to and by the fast growing King College, then located on the site of the present Beecham plant. The vision was so great that a move commenced to relocate the cemetery in the name of progress.

This was bitterly opposed by Joseph R. Anderson and others related to the King family who had buried several of the clan there. A lengthy law suit resulted. During the furor, I. C. Fowler, editor of the *Bristol News,* suggested, rather facetiously perhaps, that a compromise solution might be the boring of a tunnel beneath the disputed cemetery. He added that it might be fitting for the old hero (Shelby) to rest high above the avenue traffic. Anderson and his allies dropped the suit, thus allowing the cemetery to be moved. Fifth Street was then advanced to well beyond the college. It was called College Avenue (often called College Street). In time it reverted back to Fifth.

Across the tracks Pennsylvania was originally called First Street, but received its present name when Fairmount was developed. It was the principal lead-in street from that section. McDowell Street, at first called Reynolds, was named for Byron G. McDowell, a prominent Bristol, Tennessee, attorney. Taylor was named for Nathaniel M. Taylor, one of the city's very early lawyers. Both McDowell and Taylor were highly favored lawyers by the developers of Fairmount and were rewarded with street names.

When Fairmount Forest (the Forest was later dropped) was planned by J. M. Barker, Abram D. Reynolds, and R. J. Reynolds, they agreed that Mrs. A. D. Reynolds and Mrs. J. M. Barker would have the privilege of naming the streets. The two at first thought of some rather pretentious names but failed to agree completely, allowing time to slip away until the map makers were being delayed, thus holding up the entire project. At the same time, Mrs. Reynolds received an urgent call to go to Giles County, Virginia, where a loved one lay dying. Just hours before train time, she and Mrs. Barker sat down and agreed to name the streets running north and south for states of their particular liking, and the cross streets for favorite trees. To harmonize the proceedings, each lady alternately chose a street name. Their hasty choices now designate the Fairmount thoroughfares.

On the Virginia side the streets have equally fascinating name origins. The shortest street in Bristol appropriately named Short Street, was once a private driveway. About 1860 James Buford bought several acres lying between Goodson Street and the East Hill Cemetery. He soon built a large house on the site of the present Athens Steak House. Large oaks surrounded the place and thus he called his estate Oak Grove. It was later Campbell's Grove and finally Hobson's Grove. Buford prepared a driveway from Main Street leading to his home. It was rather pretentious for early Bristol because it was lined with flowering shrubs, and at the entrance there were two brick pillars topped by metal urns. Before too long, present Buford Street was brought through and eliminated the need for the grand driveway. Today Buford's driveway is Short Street.

Williams Street (originally William Street) was named for the deceased younger brother of J. W. Morgan, early Bristol industrialist. Winston Street led to the nursery of J. H. Winston, early King College professor and businessman. Camp Street was so named because Edmond Winston and his helpers camped there on their first night of surveying Goodsonville. This camp was made under the low spreading limbs of a giant beechnut tree which then stood near the western end of the street. Washington Street took its name from the county in which it was located. Virginia Street was named for the Commonwealth. Goodson was first called Broad Street, and the section beyond Mary retained that name for several years. It was called Broad because, for some unknown reason, it was surveyed a little wider than other streets in that area. Lottie Street was named for the wife of one of the surveying crew. Taylor took the name of a popular Tennessee governor; but because there was a Taylor on the Tennessee side, it long bore the name Second Taylor.

West of the railroad one comes to Front Street (now part of the Randall Expressway), so called because it fronted on the depot lot. It was originally Fourth Street when it was in the old Bristol, Virginia. That portion of Sycamore across the flat (old King's Meadow) was first Beaver Street.

Cumberland was named because of a rather unique situation. It was long hoped and planned that a railroad would be built through to Cumberland Gap. It was first planned that this railway would branch from the Virginia and Tennessee Railroad at Abingdon. Plans were made to have it originate in Bristol as the town developed. Before the Civil War, several meetings were held in Bristol to consider this venture. Most of these were in the home of Albion K. Moore, who then lived on what is now the northwest corner of Moore and Cumberland (where later stood the Hotel Bristol). Several came by train from various places to attend this meeting. To aid them in finding his home, Moore had a sign painted pointing down what was then barely a lane through corn patches and meadows. On the sign was inscribed "Cumberland Meeting". It was only natural that the path leading to the Cumberland meeting should become Cumberland Street.

In the beginning, there was a trail leading from A.M. Appling's home and store (which stood on Cumberland near Lee) to a garden near the banks of Beaver Creek. One day Mrs. Appling sent her husband to this garden for a bucket of onions. Upon arriving there he found the garden covered in muddy water from the flooding creek. In disgust he scooped up a pail full of the turbid water and returned with it to the house. Placing this pail on the back stoop, he stated that the onions had turned to muddy water. This became quite a joke among the local citizenry. When development started along the old garden trail, what might have been more appropriately called Garden Street became Water Street.

Moore Street was named for A. K. Moore. Although formerly of Savannah, Georgia, he became an early developer here. What is now Piedmont went through at least six names. It began as First Street, then was briefly known as James, for early merchant W. W. James. (This was before the present James Street took its name.) Then it became Wood's Alley, so named for Capt. J. H. Wood, and later became Wood Street for the same reason. Then when old Beaver Street became a part of Sycamore, old Wood Street was briefly called Beaver. Finally, it became Piedmont.

Scott Street, though named early for General Winfield Scott, was for years popularly known as Jesse's Road, because it was more or less a road leading to Jesse Aydlotte's cottage which stood on the southeast corner of Scott and Moore. Spencer Street took its name from George Spencer, who has the distinction of having bought a choice lot on it then, accidentally building his home on an adjoining lot that he did not own. Edmond Street was named for Edmond Winston who surveyed the original Goodsonville. It was once renamed Terry for early mayor John F. Terry, but it did not bear this designation long. Russell Street was named for Andrew Russell, longtime clerk of Washington County, Virginia. (Edmond Winston, who surveyed Goodsonville, thought Mr. Russell should be memorialized by a street name in the new town.)

Mary Street, which was the limits of old Goodsonville, was named for Mary Preston Winston, sweetheart and later the wife of Capt. Edmond Winston, the surveyor. A daughter of Dr. Robert F. Preston, Mary was born and reared in the old Walnut Grove house which still stands near Lee Highway in Bristol, Virginia. By popular usage Mary Street was once called Goodson Street. Beyond Mary is Clinton Avenue, named for Major Henry Clinton Wood. His brother, Capt. J. H. Wood, developed that section and put his brother's name on one of the streets. Buckner was named for J. A. Buckner, an early merchant of Bristol.

Before the Johnston land sale of July 4-5, 1871, a local committee made up of David C. Sullins, I. C. Fowler, W. W. James, and perhaps one or two others was designated to lay off and name the streets for this addition. Joseph Johnston, from whom the land was bought, had been very kind to the city in matters concerning this purchase. Thus it was felt that he should be memorialized with a street name. So it was that Johnston was the first street laid off in the Solar Hill section. Unfortunately, by common usage, it is now known as Johnson Street. Solar was named for the solar observatory that had been set up to monitor the great eclipse of August 1869. Most of the committee wanted to name it Sullins, in honor of the Rev. David Sullins, but for some reason he preferred that the street near the college bear his name. Johnston and Solar early became popular with the elite of the town, and both were often called silk stocking row or blue stocking row. There are a few old timers yet living who refer to the area as "snob hill," a designation it gained early when the town's wealthy began to build their palatial homes on these two choice streets.

King Street, already in existence when the 1871 development began, was so named because it ran by Rev. James King's home. Oak Street was cut through a grove of oak trees that stood near the old school building, thus the name. James Street took its name from W. W. James who owned much property in the area and who finally built a fine brick house near its merger with Johnston Street.

Thomas C. Lancaster, an early hotel keeper here, bought the old King mansion and several acres back of it. This area was long called Lancaster's Hill. Lancaster Street was named for this early Bristolian. Lancaster's lawn was large, consisting of four acres or so. The passage near the western edge of this large yard was often referred to as the road west of the lawn. Today, we have West Lawn Street.

Across the railroad cut, there's Park Street, so called because it led to the City park near what later became the campus of Sullins College. Lindsey Street was so called because it led to the estate of W. G. Lindsey at what is now 711 Euclid Avenue. Highland Avenue was a natural for a street that so sharply ascended up from Piedmont Avenue. It is not known how the names of several other streets in that area of the city were chosen.

West of Beaver Creek is Holston Avenue. The area was at one time a vast highland pasture, offering a splendid view of the Holston Mountain. It was still pasture when the street was laid out, so Holston was a fitting selection. Orchard Street took its name from seven old apple trees that stood near where the Lyle Burrow home was later located. Haynes Street was named for Judge Hal H. Haynes; Reynolds was named for Major A. D. Reynolds. Hill was not so named because of its location, but for an early land owner in that section. John H. Caldwell planned to build a fine mansion near present Tenth and Windsor. Some who had seen the plans jokingly said it would rival Windsor Castle in grandeur. Later, Caldwell was content to remodel and enlarge the old David Ensor home into a fine Greek revival house (present Weaver Funeral Home). Windsor Avenue is a reminder of his grand aspirations.

LOST STREETS

There were some streets planned that were never developed and some streets that were but are no more. And, as often mentioned in this chapter, there have been several name changes, as well as proposed names that never were adopted. A broad Mineral Avenue was planned to run west of and parallel with Commonwealth, but its only existence was on paper. A grand Richmond Avenue was proposed to leave West Main (State) near the intersection

of Twelfth Street and angle toward the knobs. Susong Avenue was planned
for slightly east of Morrison Boulevard. Here and there over town, there
were others that died "a-borning."

The first block ·or so of old Woodlawn (formerly Chalmers) was called
New Street. A one block street skirting the north side of Anderson Park was
Franklin or Frankland (both names were used). There were two Railroad
Streets in Bristol. One ran from Woodlawn across Alabama and on to Fourth
Street beyond King College. The other ran west of and parallel with the
railroad beyond Edmond Street on the Virginia side. It was later called Spencer
Street and is now replaced by the Randall Expressway. All that remains of
the Railroad Street on the Tennessee side is a small portion of an alley. That
part of Ash Street from the railroad overpass west was once English Street,
so called because it led to the old John G. English home and mill on Beaver
Creek.

What is now an alley running from Cherry to Shelby, and between Sixth
and Seventh Streets, was once Brooks Street. Caldwell Street is now an alley
between Sixth and Seventh and lies parallel to Locust and Anderson. The
alley running from the site of the present post office to Seventh Street was
meant to be Crumley Street. And on the Virginia side, Winston's alley, running through from Piedmont to Lee, was once more of a street than an alley.
Sycamore has borne its name twice. Originally Sycamore, it became Terry
Street for a time, then Sycamore again.

On a low hill between the southern ends of Second and Third Streets was
once a fine estate house called Highview. In time it was demolished, and
a short street developed there called High or Second High Street. In contrast
to the fine mansion that once occupied the hilltop, this street was lined with
the very humblest of homes. The street and cottages no longer exist.

STREET NAMES THAT ALMOST WERE

What is now Broad Street was originally intended to be named in honor
of the Martin brothers who early had established a thriving mercantile business
on the southeast corner of what is now State and Sixth. But both brothers,
being modest men, opposed the move. It is said that one of them stated that
if it took a street to memorialize him, then he didn't have much worth
memorializing.

At the tragic death of President James Garfield a move started to change
the name of Cumberland Street to Garfield Avenue. For a time this movement was rather strong; however, as the emotions of the period cooled, so
did the move to change the street name, and Cumberland yet remains. Talk
urging the change of Main Street to Anderson Avenue began at the funeral
of the town's founder (May 20, 1888). My informant of long ago, who was

present at Anderson's funeral, stated that the first mention of this possibility was by Col. N. M. Taylor, an early and prominent Bristol attorney. The town became sharply divided on the issue. A compromise was finally reached whereby old Lee or Royal Street was given the founder's name, which it bears today.

When the street now known as Edgemont was first laid out, it was planned as Field Street since it ran through one of John G. King's choice corn fields. However, King finally decided on Chalmers, which name it bore for several years. The late J. Hoge Reynolds used to say that originally Carolina Avenue was planned to be the grand divider of Fairmount and was to be given the somewhat pretentious name of Forest Park Boulevard. Apparently the name was passed over when Mrs. Barker and Mrs. Reynolds hastily chose names for that section of the city. A few years after Fairmount began its development, friends of Col. J. M. Barker sought to change Virginia Avenue to Barker Avenue, but this, too, came to naught. And when Congressman William F. Rhea was at the height of his popularity, a petition was circulated to rename Front Street in his honor. Unfortunately for Rhea, a political enemy had extensive property holdings on this street, and his somewhat pronounced objection squelched the move. There was a similar situation when an effort was made in 1882 to rename Fourth beyond its junction with Anderson (then Lee) to Dixon Street. This would have honored William Dixon, who early set up a thriving iron foundry on Fourth Street and also had his residence near this foundry.

THE FIRST STREET NUMBERS

The January 21, 1873, edition of the *Bristol News* carried the following item:

> Our citizens will be glad to learn that Mr. James (W. W.) by designating his new stand as No. 4 (Main Street) means to commence the long needed building numbers of our town. He will begin at the corner and number the doors of his entire block.

This was the beginning of Bristol's street numbering program. However, another decade passed before there was much uniformity in this improvement effort. The much used method of identifying locations by their proximity to better known landmarks continued for many years.

THE FIRST STREET MARKERS

To A. T. M. Provence, an early monument dealer, belongs the honor of having erected the town's first street marker. The marble works of Mr. Provence was located at the southeast corner of Second and Main Streets. Perhaps to relieve the boredom of a somewhat slow business, he one day picked up a scrap of marble and chiseled the words Second Street onto it. He set this at the corner of his lot. Bristol street marking began in 1869. A few others in the area made street markers, following the example of Provence. Instead of using marble though, most had to content themselves with wood or metal. However, decades would pass before there was a city-wide system of street marking. One very early marker, made of metal with punched holes forming the letters, is yet extant and has been viewed by this author.

STREET LIGHTING

Though a few street lights were erected in the late 1860s, they soon fell into disuse; and as late as 1881 there was not a single street light in Bristol. Some merchants had outside oil lamps at the front of their stores, but these were usually extinguished when business closed at 8:00 or 9:00 P.M. There were hanging lights along the depot platform, but these were used only at train time. Wood's famous over-the-street bridge from the depot to his Virginia House Hotel had two oil lamps mounted on the bridge rail, but these were only in use when passengers were expected to cross over from the depot.

Otherwise the streets of early Bristol were dark as pitch and fearsome to most who had to travel about at night. Robbery and muggings were not infrequent, and some of the more respectable men of the town complained that lewd women lurked in virtually every doorway. Most citizens rejoiced when a full of the moon came, for the town seemed to be just a little safer.

In the mid-1880s both sides of town put up a few oil street lights. These were confined to the heart of the business section. The residential areas still remained in darkness. At the very first, the oil lamps were not used at all during a full moon. One old timer remarked that the moon gave a better light than "those on the pole." These primitive lights were mounted on poles, perhaps eight feet tall. The poles were painted a very dark green. The old lamplighter on the Tennessee side was J. P. Rader, who nightly replenished the oil, trimmed the wicks, and lit the lamps. An aged citizen, who remembered those days, once said that seldom did any of these burn completely through the night, and many had sputtered out by midnight. Steve Allen, a man of color, was the lamplighter on the Virginia side, at least for a short while. Those who followed him were John Templin and a Mr. Thomas. Oil for these lamps cost about six cents per gallon.

By 1891 Bristol, Virginia, had its own power plant, located on the north bank of Beaver Creek, a short distance below the present Randall Expressway crossing. A little later Bristol, Tennessee, was able to secure electric power from the trolley system plant.

The first electric street lights in Bristol were of the carbon arc type, and the carbon had to be replaced daily. They were a few degrees brighter than the old oil lamps. Soon came the enclosed carbon lamp, which with luck might last one week without replacement. But while downtown Bristol was a little lighter and a little safer, the residential areas would remain dark at night for several more years. And the full moon was still very welcome in those areas of town.

MOVABLE MAIN STREET

Though Main Street (State) remains as Anderson had it planned in 1852, it has often been threatened. There have been several times when other streets came close to being Main. Initially, the development along Fourth was greater than down Main. At that time it was preferred that both business houses and homes face the railroad. For that reason, Fourth was for a time the principal business street. Some called it Main, and it is even named on some early deeds as such. Whether inadvertently or by design is not known.

Albion K. Moore, an early developer and very influential citizen of the earliest years of Bristol, conducted a spirited campaign to have Cumberland become the main street of the town. His reasoning was that future years would see the building of a great Union Depot for Bristol, and that its main door

The streets of Bristol were not always pleasant. This snow scene was made in 1888. In it may be seen the two first houses erected in the town; the Anderson house on the left and the Dr. Zimmerman house on the right.

would be at the head of this street. Thus passengers exiting might be greatly impressed by looking directly down a thriving business thoroughfare. He even offered to personally pay for the macadamizing of the street and to lay stone sidewalks. Though Cumberland did for awhile rival Main in business activity, the name was never changed.

In the late 1880s much expected development along Scranton Street (now Commonwealth) set off a move to have it made the Main Street of Bristol. And with this came plans to route a railroad track down the middle of old Main (State), so that freight could be hauled to a new industrial section that was fast developing to the west of Scranton Street. The thought of long, heavy freight trains rolling down Main sent shivers up the spines of merchants, many of whom put their establishments up for sale, and bought property on the planned new Main. Though the merchants' fears proved groundless, Scranton did come close to becoming the principal business street.

Then came the most grandiose plan of all. Along with the Bristol Iron and Steel Company, the Bristol Land Company was organized. It was thought that the iron industry as promoted by the former company would create what was hoped to be the largest iron city in the south. It would be the new Birmingham, or better. Consequently, this company made plans to build a new Bristol. A vast amount of land lying mostly to the northwest of the old town was bought. It was then that Euclid Avenue was laid out to be the new Main Street around which the city would be built. Laid out in grand fashion, it was broad with an island in the center. A fine depot was planned to stand just south of the present Euclid Avenue railroad crossing and near Commonwealth. Another would be built on the Norfolk and Western Railroad at the foot of Euclid Avenue extension. A trolley was to take passengers up the rather steep incline and over into the new Bristol.

About midway of this great Main Street would be built a fine Bristol Hotel (originally planned for near the later site of Sullins College). Indeed, the foundation of this hotel was laid, but the building was never finished.

It was projected that by 1900, the population of Bristol would be near the one hundred thousand mark, and some optimists thought this projection was too conservative. With such a population, city planners thought it would be easy to win an election to move the Washington County Courthouse to Bristol. W. G. Lindsey owned a large lot facing what was to be this new Main Street. He offered that lot as a site for the new county courthouse. This large courtyard would reach to the corner of Main and Piedmont and was thought to be a splendid location for such an important building.

With an eye to impressive beauty, the Bristol Land Company offered a choice lot near the intersection of Chester and Euclid to any local church that would erect an edifice with a spire at least one hundred and fifty feet high. This, the planners opined, would be a "showy" ornament to the city and could be viewed from far, especially when approaching the city from the west or southern side.

But alas, the iron ore in the area was not of the quality or quantity to support such a grand scheme. The bubble burst rather hard, with tidal waves engendered thereby that almost swamped several promoters. This Bristol Land Company plan was the last major threat to old Main Street. Today, it remains where Anderson planned it in 1852.

Bibliography - Chapter Seven

Anderson, Joseph R. Map of Bristol, Virginia-Tennessee. 1852.

Anderson, Rhea. Research notes, 1930s. (Mr. Anderson had planned to write a history of Bristol.)

Bachelor, Ann. Memoirs (unpublished), 1855-1870 (written 1935-1937).

Bristol News, newspaper. Various issues, 1857-1881.

Goodson, Samuel. Map of Goodsonville, Virginia. Undated, but likely 1852-1853.

Johnson, L. F. Notes.

Owen, Joseph W. Notes, preserved by his daughter Miss Revely Owen. (Mr. Owen had received much of his information from Col. Samuel E. Goodson.)

Phillips, V. N. (Bud). Interviews with and information supplied by many older Bristol citizens, 1953-1956.

Wood, J. H., Capt. Manuscript (unpublished). 1888.

Chapter Eight
THE BUILDERS OF BRISTOL

"WORKMAN THAT NEEDETH NOT TO BE ASHAMED"
Plans may be made and materials assembled, but without builders there can be no buildings, and without buildings there is no city. The builders of Bristol were numerous. They came from near and far and possessed of various skills, but it may be said of many of them, perhaps of most of them, that they were workmen who needed not to be ashamed. Some of them remained day laborers, while others became contractors and developers. A few amassed modest fortunes. (The two tallest monuments — usually a sign of wealth — in East Hill Cemetery mark the graves of two of Bristol's early builders.) And some of them became outstanding citizens and civic leaders.

THE VERY EARLIEST BUILDERS
In early 1853 Bristol's founder, Joseph R. Anderson, rode horseback to Abingdon, Virginia, where he viewed a house that had a few years before been erected by James Fields and William Rodefer. This was the Philip Rohr house and still stands on Main near Pecan Street. While there he contracted with Rodefer and Fields to build him a similar house in his new Town of Bristol, Tennessee-Virginia. The construction of Anderson's house began soon after that trip. Thus William Rodefer and James Fields were the first to take up saw and hammer in the new town, and the house that they erected on the southwest corner of Main and Fourth (now State and Edgemont) was Bristol's first building.

Not to be overlooked is the brick-burner for Rodefer and Fields; he was Timothy Campbell, of the line of the slaves of Governor David Campbell. He, too, was a skilled workman in his trade. He set up his brick-burning operation near a red clay bank just below the Flat Hollow Cemetery (near the corner of present Buckner and Oak View Streets). And the smoke that rolled upward from his furnace was prophetic of the numerous smokestacks that would someday belch forth their cloudy symbols of industrial progress over a fast-growing town.

The late Ed Faidley used to tell a story handed down to him by his father, who had been hired as a helper for Tim Campbell. The two had loaded the wagon with brick and were proceeding through the old King Meadow toward the construction site when their usually uneventful delivery trip became a little exciting. At that time James King had not removed his herd of shorthorn Herefords from the meadow. The herd bull was evidently not in good humor that day and began a hostile charge toward the intruders. Old Tim and his helper just about unloaded the wagon defending themselves with sailing bricks. Finally, a well-aimed missile "addled" the angry bull, allowing the two men and what remained of their cargo to escape. Scattered bricks could be found in the meadow for years afterward.

From Mr. Faidley came the bit of information that while work progressed on the Anderson house, these first builders and workmen camped in the old King washhouse near the washing spring (near present Piedmont and Sycamore). While Rodefer worked on the Anderson house, he was eyeing the choice lot across the street in old Bristol, Virginia, and on the corner of what was then Fourth and Main (later Front and Main). On May 4, 1853, he contracted to buy that lot. This was the first real estate transaction in Bristol, Tennessee-Virginia. However, Rodefer did not fulfill his contract. The same lot was soon sold to W. W. James of Blountville. This lot brought the highest price of any location in the old Town of Bristol. It brought six hundred dollars, while others were bringing only one hundred twenty-five.

A few days after the land contract between Rodefer and Anderson, Dr. Benjamin Frederick Zimmerman, who was reared on Steele Creek near Bristol, but who was then living in Abingdon, contracted to buy the lot next to Rodefer, at the corner of Main and Eighth Streets (now State and Lee). As soon as Rodefer and Fields had finished the Anderson house, they commenced Zimmerman's dwelling and detached office. But the severely cold and snowy winter of 1853-54 halted work on this project. It was not finished until May of 1854. This was the first house erected in old Bristol, Virginia.

Rodefer and Fields also built the first Virginia House Hotel building (1855) and are known to have built the Presbyterian Church in 1857. Though James Fields maintained his residency in Abingdon, Virginia, by May 1867 he had erected a small cottage on his Main Street property for his local home while working in Bristol. Before the trains arrived here in the fall of 1856, this Mr. Fields had built the first depot in Bristol, Virginia.

Another very early builder in Bristol was Jesse Aydlotte, who in 1854 moved to the city from near Marion, Smyth County, Virginia. He lived briefly in one of J. R. Anderson's rent houses on Fourth Street, then moved to a cottage that stood on the southeast corner of Scott and Moore Streets. It was in this cottage that Aydlotte and others organized what is now the State Street Methodist Church.

Jesse Aydlotte was a master carpenter, much in demand for fine finish work. Over the next twenty years he built some of the finer homes and business houses in the fast-growing town. With one or two helpers (paid by himself), Aydlotte built the Methodist Church at Scott and Lee without charge to the

**Jesse Aydlotte, a very early builder of Bristol, was one of the
founders of the State Street Methodist Church.**

congregation. He always said that this was his gift to the town in which he
had chosen to live.

His last work was the repairing of the famous over-street walkway from
the depot to the Virginia House Hotel (Front Street). He was in failing health
at the time (autumn 1874) but tried to help his crew finish the job. An aged
son of one of his workmen once told me how the almost-blind master carpenter
bent three nails in a row because he could not see how to hit them straight.
He slowly laid down his hammer, told his workmen that his lifework was
done, turned and weeping as he went, walked slowly toward his nearby home.
He died in June 1875 and is buried in East Hill Cemetery.

George W. Blackley, a master carpenter and cabinetmaker of Albermarle
County, Virginia, moved with his family to Bristol around 1855. His services were soon much in demand, not only in erecting homes for the influx
of settlers, but in making fine furniture for these homes. He is known to
have made several pieces of furniture from the old state line cherry tree that

stood near the depot. At least one of these pieces is yet in a Bristol home.

To George Blackley belongs the honor of having been chosen to build the first bridge in the Town of Bristol. This solidly constructed bridge spanned Beaver Creek near present Piedmont and State Streets. It was finished around Christmastime, 1857. About thirteen years later he built his own home, which still stands at 122 East State Street. The fine fanlight over the front door was hand crafted by him. Mr. Blackley died here February 14, 1888, and is buried in East Hill Cemetery. Many of his descendants have become prominent citizens of Bristol.

The G.W. Blackley homeplace at 122 East State Street is among the oldest houses in this city. It was built by Mr. Blackley, a master carpenter and cabinet maker, about 1870.

Also in the 1850s came Barnard Campbell, whose works were numerous throughout the town. J. H. LeGard began working here about the same time. He was a much-in-demand builder. Soon after the close of the war, it was LeGard who was selected to rebuild the depot and express office. Both had been burned during Federal raids on the town. Campbell and LeGard remained in Bristol for several years.

In mid-1854, when John H. Moore built his store on the northwest corner of what is now Lee and State Streets, he brought in a carpenter and former neighbor of his in Russell County, Virginia, Andrew Fillinger. This fine builder is said to have returned to Bristol in the very late 1850s. He became one of the more noted of Bristol's early builders, working on for several years, he then moved back to Russell County, only to return later. (See section of this chapter entitled "Pride of Workmanship".)

LATER BUILDERS

Just after the close of the Civil War, new expansions began in the towns of Bristol and Goodson. This created a need for builders and building materials. The need was soon well met. One very noted builder who arrived here around 1867 was William H. Smith. In time he was affectionately called Uncle Will by many of the local citizens. Uncle Will was born near Blountville, Tennessee, March 3, 1830, and came to the new Town of Bristol at the urging of Joseph R. Anderson, a long-time friend. He was a brick mason by trade but was also capable of general carpentry. Soon after his arrival, he entered the field of general contracting, but still did much of the brickwork himself. According to old timers yet living here thirty-five years ago, even when he was not doing the actual work himself, he was right behind his workmen, making sure that every brick was properly placed.

About the time he entered the field of general contracting (possibly 1870), he set up his own brick plant. This was located a little east of the intersection of present Shelby Street and the Volunteer Parkway. There he nearly always had from two to three hundred thousand bricks on hand for immediate use and so advertised in newspapers of the period.

Several of Smith's buildings yet stand. In the summer of 1871 he erected on the southeast corner of Cherry and Seventh Streets a fine home for Dr. J. J. Ensor. This is the present Sesco Building. A story handed down illustrates how builders secured their work. It is said that Dr. Ensor gave a housewarming soon after he moved into his new home. Among the guests were Capt. and Mrs. J. H. Wood. They liked what they saw and then and there engaged Mr. Smith to build them a similar house during the coming year. Thus Pleasant Hill, the home of this author, was built by Smith in 1872. In 1875 Uncle Will built a house for John G. Pepper, who died before it was finished. It was later known as the Billy Wood house. Today it is the office of Dr. J. L. McCord. And downtown there are old walls, long covered by remodelings and new fronts, that were put up by this noted early builder.

Over the years Uncle Will Smith landed several large contracts. He built the huge Pepper and Jordon Woolen Mill in 1874. In 1875 he erected the enlarged, three-story store building of Col. J. M. Barker. Shortly thereafter he built the enormous James Livery Stable. During the same period he erected Burson's famous church, the finest in town up to that time. When bids were called for on the new depot (1881), which included specifications for three hundred feet of passenger sheds "to contain fancy and eye pleasing trim," Smith was the first bidder. That same year he built Anderson's new three-story business house in the four-hundred block of Main Street.

In time Uncle Will became rather prosperous. Occasionally he bought town lots. Then during slack periods he built residences and business houses upon them. These he either rented or sold for good profits. He then began to make loans to the extent that some referred to him as the walking bank. Sometimes, like all those in the loan field, he made a bad loan. But usually his extensions of credit made him a good interest income. It was always expected that he would erect a fine mansion for himself and family, and indeed he had made plans for one. But failing to secure the site he wanted, said to be where the old Tennessee post office is now located, his plans were never executed. In the latter part of the century he built several brick houses in the nine-hundred block of Shelby Street, known locally as Smith's row. He finally moved into one of these from his old home that was located on Main Street in downtown Bristol.

In the very last years of his life, Uncle Will Smith decided to build a grand family monument in East Hill Cemetery. By then his plant was producing a fine grade of brick aa well as ornamental trim. He had a mammoth big stone shaped and set at his chosen location. Upon this he built a towering brick monument, well decorated with his ornamental trim work. Though then old and feeble, he insisted on being taken to the cemetery daily so that he might sit nearby and direct his workmen. He would tell them that he wanted it to stand a hundred years. Here eighty-nine years later, it still stands and is easily seen as one travels up East State Street. Thus, the largest and tallest monument in East Hill Cemetery is to one of the builders of the town. After this monument was finished, Smith spent many hours sitting on his porch, looking across the town he had helped to build, to view his fine monument, standing high on Round Hill nearly a mile away. Uncle Will Smith died April 15, 1901, and was buried at the towering monument in East Hill Cemetery.

Another team of very noted builders of early Bristol was the Crowell brothers, John MacGregor, David and Madison. Madison did not long stay with the team, and before many years went by, John and David were working independently. These brothers were the sons of Joseph and Mary Crowell and before moving to Bristol are known to have resided in Washington County, Virginia, and may have been natives of that county. They seem to have arrived here around 1860. By April 1875 John Crowell had set up his brickworks. His plant and storage sheds were located on the slope of the hill, just behind the intersection of Piedmont and State (then Main and First). He often advertised that he had at least a quarter of a million bricks on hand.

One of the first big undertakings by John Crowell was the building of the Presbyterian Female Institute near the southwest corner of Shelby and Fifth Streets. He commenced the erection of this two-story thirty-by fifty-foot brick structure in August of 1872 and pledged to have it finished by November. Probably the best known example of his work that is yet standing is the Margaret Mitchell home at 54 King Street. He built the north half of this fine house in the late summer and autumn of 1881. I. C. Fowler, editor of the *Bristol News*, commented in the November 22, 1881, issue of his paper, that Crowell had put up the finest brick walls yet seen in the town. In addition to his construction work, by January 1875 John Crowell had opened a stove and tinware shop on Main Street. And in April of 1879 he offered himself for the mayorship "of Bristol-Goodson, Virginia."

As did Uncle Will Smith, John Crowell not only built for others but did some development of his own. On lower Main Street he owned three adjoining lots. In April 1879 he offered to give the outside lots to any person who would agree to erect thereon a two-story brick building within a specified period of time. Both lots were quickly taken. When the two brick buildings were finished, he immediately erected a front and back wall on the middle lot, added a roof, and some inside walls and had for himself a rather inexpensive downtown building for rent. A clever man was John Crowell.

Crowell built his own home near the northeast corner of Main (State) and Goodson Streets. It was later occupied by a prominent early lawyer of Bristol, Mr. D. F. Bailey. Mr. Crowell, who was born February 20, 1835, died at his home December 28, 1900. And it may be noted that again one of Bristol's builders has one of the largest monuments in East Hill Cemetery. Building, then as now, was a rather lucrative trade.

Another team of early builders was Mr. William H. Briscoe and Mr. William A. Caldwell, who operated under the name of Briscoe and Caldwell. Their reputation was such that when Col. J. M. Barker and Mr. R. A. Ayers planned Bristol's first three-story building (1870), this team was chosen as the builders. And for several years Briscoe and Caldwell continued to build fine homes and business houses in the fast-growing town.

William Shelton, a master brick layer, began his work in Bristol at about the same time as did Briscoe and Caldwell. He usually worked under the regular contractors, seldom ever taking a complete building job. It is said that Shelton was especially skillful in adding on to existing buildings, usually with very pleasing results. And this was often done in old Bristol, as prosperity created the need for larger business houses and more commodious homes.

Andrew Fillinger of Russell County, Virginia, first came to Bristol in 1854 to work on the store of John H. Moore. When that job was completed, he returned to his home. Several years later (perhaps in the late 1850s) he moved to Bristol. In time he formed a partnership with a Mr. Hubbard and the two built some notable local structures. In the early 1870s Fillinger and Hubbard built the three-story Reynolds Hall on Fourth Street. This was their first three-story building and the second such structure in the town. A little later they built the matching wing at King College. (This was a duplicate of the original college building with a space left between for a connecting section.) Then a little later they finished the connecting section containing the tower. Shortly after this, Fillinger returned to Russell County, where he settled for a year or so at Hansonville.

Mr. D. F. Carrier, who built many fine farm houses in the Holston Valley section near Bristol, sometimes took contracts for new houses in town. In 1873 he built the fine Crumley home that long stood at the corner of Seventh and Broad Streets. Over the years he built several homes in Bristol. One yet standing that is attributed to him is the present Landmark Realty office at 332 Seventh Street.

Often brick layers laid the walls and other workmen finished the buildings. Such was the case in 1872 when the *Bristol News* office was built on Lee Street, just behind what is now 501 State Street. A Mr. Hoss and Mr. Goode did the brickwork. A carpenter by the name of James C. Haynes did the woodwork. A house yet standing at 409 Fifth Street, and now popularly called the "Pink House," had its walls laid in 1881 by Mr. James P. Lewis. The carpentry was done by James Oney. Mr. Lewis was a town constable who sometimes worked at various other trades. It may be noted that he long lived in a small house that stood just north of the Pink House. He had lost a much-adored little girl to a plague in the 1870s, and was ever after a depressed and sad man. To ease his mental agony he often worked through the night. It is said that he actually laid much of the brick in the Pink House during the bright, moonlit nights. So expert at his trade was he, that no one could tell what bricks had been laid at night. This sad builder is buried in East Hill Cemetery near his little girl and John Crowell, for whom he had often worked. The upper shaft of his monument has fallen to the ground.

Some builders were also architects and planners. Such were Stokes and Pusey, who maintained offices on Lee Street in Goodson. Their work commenced in the mid-1870s about the same time Walter P. Tinsley of Bristol, Tennessee, offered the same type of services. Another architect, whose name has not been determined, charged Joseph R. Anderson, seventy-five dollars for planning the Anderson Store that was built at 410 Main Street in the summer of 1881.

A. C. Bruce, a prominent architect of Knoxville, Tennessee, was advertising for work in the Bristol papers in the 1870s. It is known that he designed Dr. J. F. Hicks' very fine home that long stood at 18 Fourth Street (where later stood the Bristol, Tennessee, Fire Department building). Henri Doriot was also a practicing architect and designed many fine buildings.

Largely though, Bristol builders did not use the services of architects or planners. Most often an employer simply told a workman what he wanted put up, and plans, if used at all, consisted of only a few simple lines often crudely drawn on cheap paper. (The author has some examples of such plans.) Very often an employer simply instructed his workmen to erect a building like one executed for a neighbor, friend or acquaintance. This seems to have been the most popular form of planning. Uncle Ed Faidley said he once saw John N. Bosang, an early Bristol resident, draw a "house pattern" in the dust of Moore Street as John Crowell looked on. From that dusty design a suitable house was erected. It should be mentioned, though, that detailed contracts were often drawn up between employers and workmen and that disputes over breeches of these contracts were frequent.

Along with the actual builders were the related workmen. In June 1871 William B. Snapp offered his services as a house, sign, and ornamental painter. About the same time E. D. Rader advertised that he did window glazing, paper hanging, and house painting. In those days most carpenters had special tools for the making of windows and doors, but the glass had to be glazed in by local tradesmen. Mr. Rader's ability as a glazer was well known in the new town. He boldly advertised that he had been employed by such notables of Bristol as J. R. Anderson, Dr. W. N. Vance, J. Wheeler Thomas, I. C. Fowler, John Slack, and the law firm of York and Fulkerson.

J. H. Swan, from London, England, came to Bristol around 1875. He soon married Sallie B. Hopkins and settled down in his work as house, sign, and ornamental painter, as well as an expert in paperhanging and wall tinting. He also did some building. In time he became a highly respected citizen, served long as a justice of the peace and notary public, and operated a very successful paint and wallpaper store at 23 Sixth Street.

It may have been noticed by the careful reader that these early house painters offered ornamental painting. It should be remembered that they were operating in an era of high Victorian trim work, commonly known as "gingerbread" ornamentation. To neatly paint this fancy trim work, often in contrasting colors, was an art in itself, thus prompting the specific advertisement for this type of painting.

An early team of plasterers was made up of J. T. and G. W. Jordon, who worked in Bristol as early as the mid-1860s. They were experts in the trade, going so far as to offer ornamental plasterwork. There were a few homes in early Bristol elaborate enough to require the latter type of service. Among them was the very fine home of Dr. J. F. Hicks that was erected on Fourth

Street in the 1870s. This team did most of the plasterwork in the first three decades of the town's existence.

BUILDERS AFTER 1875

There is some evidence that Thomas L. Nelms was working as a carpenter in Bristol as early as 1867, but his first known job was in the mid-1870s. He was known as the "singing carpenter" because there was hardly a moment in his working day that his voice was not lifted in song. And his selections ranged all the way from the ribald to the most solemn of hymns. He once walked off a job because his employer insisted that he quit singing and concentrate on the duties at hand. Nelms always claimed that he couldn't work unless he was singing.

In the 1880s James and Samuel McCrary began building in Goodson and Bristol. These brothers were sons of Samuel and Lydia Lewis McCrary of old Ruthton, Tennessee (near Bristol Caverns). Soon after arriving in Bristol, they began operating a planing mill near the corner of Goodson and Williams Streets. This mill was then water powered. In the years that followed, these brothers did considerable developing on both sides of the state line. To James belongs the honor of building the first split-level house in Bristol, his own home, that yet stands on the southeast corner of Goodson Street and Danville Avenue.

James McCrary was noted as a master stairway builder, being often called to distant points for that purpose. One of his out-of-town jobs was the fine stairway in the beautiful Hunter home in Elizabethton, Tennessee. This stairway was built of quartered sycamore that had been prepared at the McCrary mill in Bristol.

The McCrary brothers built the elegant Reynolds home that long stood on the northeast corner of Spruce and Carolina. This house was noted for its fancy Victorian trim, which was all made by James McCrary. John McCrary, a brother of James and Samuel, may have worked in the building trades with them but apparently was never in the partnership. James died in 1913, but Samuel lived for another decade. He built his grand home cir. 1910. It yet stands at 609 Taylor Street. Over a period of several years, Mr. McCrary hand picked and stored every piece of lumber that went into the building of his home. The McCrary brothers had a sister who married a Mr. Riley Stone. Their sons, James and Riley, entered the building trades in the very late 1800s and continued for several years. These brothers finally built two of the finer homes of this city: James at 900 Park Street, and Riley at 812 Holston Avenue.

Also very late in the last century, Robert F. Wagner began building in Bristol, mostly on the Virginia side of town. In time he became a prominent developer. Older homes yet standing that are known to have been built by him include the twin houses at 523 and 525 Goodson Street and the old Crymble home at 225 Solar Street. The present home of Dawn and Adrian White at 823 Euclid Avenue was also erected by this prolific builder as his own home, but before his death he had built and moved to the present Martin home at 701 Euclid Avenue.

Other carpenters known to have been working in Bristol during the fourth quarter of the last century are listed below. Though little is known of them, it must be remembered that they, too, helped build the city.

Samuel D. Black	Sam D. Kelsey	James R. Rod
Matthew Bridgemon	Leander M. Kesner	James D. Rodefer
William S. Bunn	Milton D. Kingsolver	John Sherwood
Columbus Carmack	William T. Layman	William I. Smith
William Cowan	John Logan	Peter T. Snyder
John B. Crowell	George A. McCary	James E. South
Newton Crowell	George P. McCrary	Charles Spraker
William H. Cullup	William McKamey	James R. Spraker
George W. Davis	Bacchus McLead	John H. Stump
James A. Dotson	Taylor Meade	Arthur Tate
Campbell C. Eads	James Moorfield	John B. Templin
George English	Charles Oney	George B. Tumblin
G. B. Graham	George W. Pippin	Samuel A. Wagner
John W. Jones	William Poore	John E. Wilson
John B. Keller	Walter Read	

Along with the carpenters, bricklayers were also helping to build Bristol. No doubt some of their walls and chimneys stand today. Those known to have been practicing their trade in the last quarter of the 1800s are listed below:

John Cross	Thomas R. Edwards	James Smith
Samuel Cross	Bud Jefferson	Homer Webb
Isaac Crowell	George W. Owens	Edward B. Williams
James M. Echols	Michael Slagle	

While many, perhaps most, carpenters did roofing along with their regular construction jobs, there were a few persons who specialized in that trade. They were commonly called tinners. Those known to have been such specialists include:

William S. Bare	William J. Blaicher	_____ Sheets
John W. Blaicher	S. W. C. Hudgens	

Other plasterers, other than those noted, who are known to have been working in Bristol before 1900 include:

John W. Bolton	Nathaniel Thomas	Charles Williams
George P. Brown		

Other painters working in Bristol before 1900 include:

James Baker	Augustus W. Edwards	William Snapp
Frank Carlton	Alexander Pope	Thomas C. Summer
George Carlton	Robert Pope	
Franklin Davis	Robert D. Pope	

Up to 1900, plumbers were rare in our city. Three known to have been in that slowly developing trade were:

Robert L. Blevins	Ed Faidley	Fred Hayes

PRIDE OF WORKMANSHIP

Most of the builders of Bristol took a fierce pride in their workmanship. Competition was very strong. Shoddy workmanship did not have to be tolerated. To build a reputation as a master carpenter or bricklayer meant steady and gainful employment. Then as now, some workers did not receive due credit for their notable accomplishments, while others tried to glory in the accomplishments of better craftsmen. In 1881 one William P. Hulse did some fine trim work on the new store of prince merchant, W. W. James, located on Front Street. Later he felt compelled to write a letter to the *Bristol News* criticizing another local carpenter and trim mill operator for claiming credit for the superb work. He explained that only the fancy trim work had been supplied by this carpenter and that even it had been turned out by Tobe Wood, an ex-slave and shop foreman.

The case of Andrew Fillinger can demonstrate just how devastating loss of reputation could be, both materially and emotionally. Fillinger was a very skillful builder and had shortly before finished work on Reynolds Hall when he was called to build the connecting unit between the twin buildings at King College. He had employed new help and found it necessary to leave them working alone while he attended to other matters. Shortly after this project was finished, a ceiling suddenly collapsed in a classroom that only minutes before had been emptied by a class. Of course Fillinger, though not having actually done the shoddy work, received the blame for it. He closeted himself at home for several days, never venturing outside in daylight. Then one night he gave most of his possessions to a neighbor, loaded a few bare necessities into his wagon, and just before dawn left Bristol for Russell County. He lived for a year or so at Hansonville, where he resumed work. The saintly old

Dr. J. A. Templeton finally persuaded this master builder to return and resume his work in Bristol.

It should not be assumed by the reader that all the worthy builders of our city have been mentioned here. No doubt there were many others. Some worked only briefly, whereas others came and stayed a lifetime. They are due much honor, for without them there would not have been a city.

MATERIALS FOR THE BUILDERS

An item in the *Abingdon Democrat* of October 11, 1856, states that Bristol contained about one hundred and twenty buildings and that most of them were built of brick. Indeed, brick was the most common building material in those days. The first house erected in Bristol, Virginia-Tennessee, the home of Joseph R. Anderson, was made of this material. Brick was cheap for there was plenty of suitable clay in the area for its manufacture. But even brick buildings require some wood. It is said that the wood for the Anderson home was hauled from a mill on Steele Creek, but as the new town grew, it was apparent that a lumber mill was needed in Bristol.

The Morgans, men of skill in the making of lumber, came to Bristol in the year 1854. Before leaving their native Bedford County, they drew up Articles of Agreement for their new lumber mill. The original is now in the possession of this author. The opening paragraph reads:

> Articles of agreement and partnership made, entered into and agreed upon, between Samuel B. Morgan, Alexander Morgan, James W. Morgan, and Madison T. Morgan, the 22nd day of October, 1854. Witness that the said partners have entered into a partnership for the purpose of milling, sawing, and making lumber with a steam engine and saw mill in Bristol, Washington County, Virginia.

This mill, the first industry in Bristol, was set up on lots near the corner of Williams and Washington Streets. The careful reader will immediately notice that the location is in Goodsonville, even though its contract states Bristol, Washington County, Virginia. These were the days when old Bristol, Virginia, was in existence and joined Goodsonville a short distance south of this mill site. And Goodsonville, never having a strong identity, was popularly called Bristol.

About the time the Morgans began the operation of this mill, Elisha Hoffman set up a water-powered lumber mill on Beaver Creek, some two or three miles upstream from the town. Thus, it may be said that Hoffman's mill and Morgan's mill supplied most of the lumber for the building of pre-Civil War Bristol. Ann Bachelor tells of the friendly rivalry between these mills. There were often price wars, with lumber costs dropping to nearly nothing. She recalled that her foster father built their first home with lumber from Hoffman's mill at two dollars per thousand feet, and that included delivery!

Initially, brick for new buildings was largely made on or near the site by individual brick burners. After W. H. (Uncle Will) Smith began work in the late 1860s, he set up the first large commercial brick making operation. John Crowell had followed suit by 1875. Old-timers used to tell that when these plants fired up and before the fires simmered to white heat, the town became filled with dense smoke. The late Myrtle Faidley stated that before her mother would put out a washing to dry, she would send a son or daughter (often Myrtle herself) to see if Uncle Will or Mr. John intended to fire up that day. If so, the washing would be delayed, for careful housewives in those days did not want their sheets blackened by soot and smoke. This seems to have been Bristol's first air pollution problem.

Building became so brisk in the 1870s that I. C. Fowler placed a notice in the *Bristol News* that an unlimited number of brick burners and layers were needed. He virtually guaranteed that all of the trade who cared to come to the fast developing town would be quickly employed. In 1877 Fowler announced that a new brick-making machine had been acquired by Thomas D. Walthall and J. W. Johnston that would turn out two thousand to thirty-five hundred brick per hour.

In the 1870s a sawmill was set up on Waterloo Farm about two miles below Bristol on Beaver Creek. It long supplied planking and timbers for Bristol builders. At about the same time, Charles C. Campbell set up a water-powered sawmill on Beaver Creek, just above the present Goodson Street Bridge and near his Campbell Grove estate (site of Athens Steak House). In or around 1881, this mill was acquired by A. A. Hobson, who soon was turning out fine hardwood lumber for interior trim work and furniture.

G. H. Mattox, who had very early set up his undertaking and cabinet-making business on the Virginia side of town, began (possible by 1874) turning out fancy exterior trim work. H. A. Bickley, another early undertaker, did likewise but on a smaller scale than Mattox.

For the most part, early carpenters did the making of their own doors and windows. However, demand became so great and urgent that by 1876 a door and sash making plant had been established by Major A. D. Reynolds. His plant was located on Williams Street, near Goodson. Later in the century, the McCrary brothers, James and Samuel, were turning out custom millwork at or near the same location. In the same area was later established the Bristol Door and Lumber Company. It was first known as Buffman Mills for the Buffmans who came here from Boston, Massachusetts. Also from Boston was W. O. Came, who later took over operation of this plant.

L. M. Winchester established in the 1870s what was probably the first general building supply company in Bristol. It stood on the site of Bristol's first hotel and restaurant, the area between Virginia and Washington Streets and facing Main (State). His advertisements offered "every imaginable building need."

The first shingle mill was set up by Jesse Aydlotte in 1856. It was water powered and was located near the present Moore Street bridge over Beaver Creek. His only known advertisement (March 1857) bore the slogan "I cover Bristol" and also stated that he did not make shingles during the light of the moon because it was then generally believed that shingles or shakes made during such times would curl upward. C. Harmeling was offering shingles and lumber by 1871, and long continued to do so. Strangely, most paint supplies and window glass was sold by the local drugstores. Most ads for such stores during those early years listed such materials. An ad for Pepper Brothers Drug Store, operated by J. G. and C. T. Pepper, both medical doctors, lists paints, oils, varnishes, and varnish brushes. Drugstores also seem to have been the principal sources of wallpaper.

In the late 1860s William Dixon and a Mr. Smith set up an iron foundry on Fourth Street in the general vicinity of the present S. P. Rutherford Company building. They not only made fancy ornamental fences to surround early Bristol homes, but through the 1870s and 1880s, also made fine iron mantels, some of which were hand decorated by a local artist. While these were never commonly used (they were rather expensive), a few may yet remain in Bristol homes.

Plumbing supplies were not needed locally until very late in the century. There was a path and a "back room" for most Bristol homes, and water was carried in by the pail from wells or from springs. Even when public water lines were supplied to the town in the 1880s, very few residents had inside water. For several years most were content to have one faucet in the yard. Even that was considered to be a great improvement.

Mr. Fred Hayes, a native of England who was working in Bristol in the late 1880s, was one of the city's first plumbers. He installed the first bathrooms in the town in the Hotel Fairmount about 1889. In short order, bathrooms were installed in the J. R. Dickey residence on East Main and in the H. E. McCoy house at 54 King Street, now the home of Margaret Mitchell. After this the need for plumbers and plumbing supplies increased steadily. Most of the supplies were shipped in from Philadelphia or Baltimore and were handled by local hardware stores and some general stores. W. W. James, the early prince merchant, had one of the more complete stocks of such supplies in his store at Front and Main (now State and Randall Expressway).

BUILDING COSTS

This chapter could not be considered complete unless information were given on the building costs of early Bristol. According to the Rhea papers, the first building erected in the Town of Bristol, that being the home of J. R. Anderson, cost eight hundred and thirty-seven dollars. Unfortunately no breakdown of the costs is given except that the cost of Timothy Campbell, the brick burner, was fifty cents per day, paid to his master. From the estate papers of Dr. B. F. Zimmerman, who built a much more elaborate brick home, the first in Bristol, Virginia, the cost was fourteen hundred and twenty-six dollars. This amount included his brick, two-room office, which stood in his yard near the corner of present Lee and State Streets.

The earliest bill for lumber that this author could locate was that of Mastin J. Ayers, who had purchased from Morgan-Thomas and Company on November 29, 1856, nineteen hundred and thirty-five feet of finished first grade lumber for twenty-nine dollars and two cents. J. M. Fields, one of the two first builders in Bristol, did work for Mastin J. Ayers in the fall of 1856, and spring of 1857. This author has his bill. It reads as follows:

Laying foundation of house	$36.00
Building chimney	52.00
Two teams one half day	2.50
310 yards plastering @ $.30	93.00
Laying 3 hearths	2.00
Total	$185.00

Ann Bachelor remembered that during one of Hoffman and Morgan's lumber price wars her father bought enough lumber to build a neat cottage for thirty-two dollars and that the carpenter's cost was about twice that amount.

During the Civil War, both the costs of materials and labor skyrocketed. Brick went to the unheard of price of five cents each, about five times their prewar cost. A bill is extant for Hoffman's lumber at eighty-two dollars per thousand feet. It must be remembered that these prices were in highly inflated Confederate money. But soon after the war, both materials and labor dropped back to about their prewar figures.

A receipt dated December 8, 1865, shows that one Richard Morrison received one dollar and fifty cents a day (probably ten or twelve hours) for cleaning old brick. Another receipt dated Feb. 22, 1856, shows that J. L. Heffner received fifty dollars for the complete job of painting the new Bristol Express Office. But paint then remained high compared to its prewar cost. From J. R. Anderson's store came two gallons of paint for the new express office at a total cost of $5.75. And the guttering, parts and labor, for the same office brought J. N. Hammit $22.25.

In 1870 the large, three-story, two-unit store building erected by Col. J. M. Barker and Rufus A. Ayers cost slightly over three thousand dollars. This building was of brick and measured sixty feet long by thirty-eight feet wide, with a dividing wall and cross walls. For decades the custom was that brick would be laid for its cost, that is, a brick that cost a penny would be laid for a penny. Barker and Ayers big store building contained one hundred and twenty-eight thousand, nine hundred and twelve brick. By the mid 1880s, brick costs had risen little.

When Uncle Will Smith built the home of Dr. J. J. Ensor (now Sesco) at the corner of Cherry and Seventh in 1871, his total bill for materials and labor came to fifteen hundred and thirty-nine dollars. A year later he built Pleasant Hill, the home of this author, for thirteen hundred and forty-two dollars.

But even in those days of cheap labor and materials, building could be expensive if a little grandeur and massive proportions were desired. When Major Z. L. Burson built his famous Bristol Baptist Church on Main Street in Bristol-Goodson, Virginia, in 1872, his bill was a staggering $8,266.34. This was more than double the cost of the most expensive church in town up to that time. And for those interested in detail, the walls in this church contained two hundred seventy-two thousand and forty bricks.

In July of 1879 J. B. Wagner spent twenty-two days repairing the large fairgrounds building. His bill for labor was fifty dollars. His materials bill amounted to fifty-five dollars. In 1889 J. D. Oney built a small house on Buchanan Street for one Elbert Taylor. His mechanics lien dated December 28, 1889, gives the costs:

Lumber for said house	$125.00
Shingles and brick for same	25.00
Tin work and plastering	44.00
Carpenter's work in building and erecting said house	56.00
Three pair of blinds	5.40
Total	$255.40

At about the same time this carpenter built a smaller house on the same street for Robert Smith. His bill for materials and labor came to the grand total of $128.00!

In 1887 Dr. A. M. Carter erected a two-unit, two-story brick business building on the northeast corner of Moore and Main (State) Streets. This was in the front yard of what had been the last home of Rev. James King. An old lady who was yet living in 1954, told of how an immense rose bush that had long marked the front gate of this yard had to be cut to make way for this new building. She had been fortunate enough to secure a sprout of that bush, and the result is an annual grand display of fragrant blooms at 214 Johnson Street. The building still stands and is home to The Merry-Go-Round and Ryland's Jewelry. It cost a grand total of two thousand, two hundred dollars!

On May 7, 1888, William T. Graham signed a contract to improve and enlarge the home of Mrs. Bettie Davis on Scott Street, just to the east of the present John Wesley United Methodist Church. The Davis home was a sixteen- by nineteen-foot one-story building with a detached kitchen in back. The contract called for a second story to be added to the old part, and a hall below and above at the end containing a nice stairway. Beyond that was to be a sixteen- by nineteen-foot new addition of two stories. In the front was to be added a five-and-a-half by sixteen-foot two-story portico, and at the back a six- by twenty-eight-foot one-story porch was to be added. A new chimney was called for, and the removing of the old and the addition of a new chimney in the old part was specified. W. T. Graham was to furnish all materials and labor. The total charge was to be $547.00!

But even at that price Mrs. Davis had difficulties paying the bill. On September 6, 1888, W. T. Graham assigned the contract to his brother G. B. Graham, and on February 6, 1889, the latter filed his mechanic's lien for the $116.75 balance due. Lengthy litigation followed, but in the end Mrs. Davis and her children retained the remodeled and enlarged home. This house was demolished long ago, but the home of William T. Graham, the carpenter, still stands at 945 Anderson Street.

The 1890s brought increased costs to Bristol builders, but prices were still surprisingly low. The account book for the McCrary brothers who operated a building supply at 8 Williams Street reveals these 1892 prices:

13 brackets and 16 scrolls	
(fancy Victorian trim)	$6.60
36 brackets	2.60
For dressing 110 feet of lumber	.40
150 feet 4″ crown mold	3.00
8 window pulleys	.30
90 joists $2 \times 10 \times 12$, and 20	
joists $2 \times 10 \times 16$	26.76
11 joists $2 \times 10 \times 18$	3.63
1 door	2.00
2 doors $2'8'' \times 6'8''$	3.20
10 brackets for Abingdon church	7.50
For turning 9 columns	6.75

2 gallons of paint	3.55
3250 old brick	16.25
2000 feet of sheeting	4.00
10 squares of slate roofing	100.00

As a comparison of prices now and then, the 150 feet of crown molding (item 4 above) that then sold for $3.00, in 1989 retailed for $118.00!

It may be mentioned that by the 1890s Bristolians were building much finer and more elaborate houses, but even so a truly grand house could still be erected for from three to four thousand dollars. The Queen Anne style fifteen-room house that yet stands at 518 Alabama Street was built in 1898 by Rev. and Mrs. Joseph McFerrin for three thousand, two hundred and thirty-one dollars. The very fine old Reynolds house that long stood on the northeast corner of Spruce and Carolina, built about 1890, only cost a little over five thousand dollars. And even during this period, a modest cottage could still be built for less than one thousand dollars.

Bristolians, then as now, hoped, planned, labored, and saved for homes. They delighted in occupying them. They lived, loved, labored, rejoiced, sorrowed, grew old, and died in them. And many of us are fortunate enough to enjoy the fruits of their labor.

Bibliography - Chapter Eight

Bachelor, Ann. Memoirs (unpublished), 1855-1870.

Bristol News, newspaper. Various issues, 1857-1881.

Bristol, Virginia-Tennessee. *City Directory, 1896-1897.*

Owen, Joseph W., Capt. As told to his daughter Revely Owen.

Phillips, V. N. (Bud). Interviews with numerous aged citizens of Bristol, 1953-1956.

Sullivan County, Tennessee. Chancery Records.

U.S. Census Records, 1860-1880. Washington, D.C.: Government Printing Office.

Washington County, Virginia. Chancery Records.

Wood, J. H., Capt. Manuscript (unpublished), 1888.

P.A.J. Crockett, "Mr. Law" in early Bristol, Tennessee. He was the town's first constable.

Chapter Nine
LAW AND ORDER

It is generally expected that a railroad terminus town or a border town will be heavily given to vice and lawlessness. Bristol was both a border town and a railroad terminus, and every indication is that from the beginning it fully lived up to the expectation. Very early it developed the reputation of being a wide open, wild and wooly, crime infested, vice-ridden railroad center. And in that like attracts like, it soon became a mecca for those who were given to such a manner of life.

At first the three developments—Bristol, Tennessee; Bristol, Virginia; and Goodsonville, Virginia—were under the legal jurisdiction of their respective counties: Sullivan County, Tennessee, and Washington County, Virginia. The few court papers that can be located for that era indicate that the end of the Virginia and Tennessee Railroad was the beginning of a pocket of crime and that the situation was causing problems for the county law enforcement officers. This was also a galling turn of events for Joseph R. Anderson, who had hoped that the town he had founded would, as he once expressed it to a friend, "become an assembly of upright and progressive citizens." But it seems that many of the citizens were not always upright, literally speaking. An old indictment found in loose papers at Abingdon, Virginia, tells of five men who were arrested for having been down in the street fighting in front of Bosang's Saloon in the village of Bristol, Virginia. (This is the only paper the author has found that calls Bristol a village.) Another paper tells of one Jasper Bellamy who had fallen to the street in a drunken stupor near the store of John H. Moore (present corner of Lee and State Streets). When incorporation came to both sides of the state line in early 1856, the towns came under limited local rule, with constables or sergeants being the principal peacekeepers. High crimes were still under county jurisdiction.

That the town fathers were well aware of local conditions and the difficult time ahead is shown by a statement recorded in the minutes of the first meeting of the Town Council of Bristol, Tennessee, on November 18, 1856.

We adopted a series of laws and ordinances for the protection of the citizens of said town, against the vices which all such towns, especially new ones, are addicted to.

P. A. J. Crockett was the first constable of Bristol, Tennessee. He served through a difficult time; he was succeeded by Thomas P. Reed on April 10,

1858. A little over three months later Mr. Reed resigned and was replaced by William A. Irvin. Slightly over two months later Irvin resigned, and P. A. J. Crockett became constable again, but only for about four months. The job was then turned over to Peter Kesner on January 24, 1859. On April 7, 1959, Eli Marsh was appointed to serve out the unexpired term of Mr. Kesner. It is known that at some time during those early years, Mr. Thomas W. Farley and J. Austin Sperry briefly served as law enforcement officers. According to information handed down, the general lawless condition of the town with its resultant constant threat to life and limb, coupled with frequent criticism by a fearful and insecure citizenry, caused this great turnover in the "justice department."

Others known to have served as constables during the earlier years of Bristol, Tennessee, were E. D. Rader, who served through most of the Civil War period; D. F. Bailey, a returned Confederate veteran who took the office in 1866 (he later served as a street commissioner), J. W. Meek, J. C. Hammer, and John W. Emmert.

On Saturday, November 9, 1861, Charles Robertson Vance offered a resolution to establish a night watch or police. On the first Monday in each month, the town constable was to appoint sixty-three persons who lived within the corporate limits of Bristol, Tennessee, to be on stand-by call to serve whenever the said constable thought it necessary. This may have been a measure to cope with added dangers during the Civil War period.

Perhaps it should be noted that the "justice department" was not above scandal in those days. An early constable resigned because of a morals charge that was leveled against him by the foster parents of a teenaged girl. However, the town must have been rather forgiving: within a short time he was elected to the office of alderman. Much later, a constable saw a chance to make a few extra dollars. An ordinance had been passed stipulating that any livestock found wandering in the streets would be impounded and that one dollar must be paid to the constable in order to obtain release. (The constable was allowed to keep the dollar as compensation for his trouble.) This particular constable went about the darkened streets opening lot gates and allowing livestock to escape. He immediately impounded the livestock and another dollar was his! In time he was caught, but disgrace seems to have been his only punishment. But in this case the town was not so forgiving. Eight years later he ran for another office and received only three votes.

Fines for petty offenses were nominal but frequently imposed, and they composed a great part of the early revenues of the town. The first fine recorded in Bristol, Tennessee, was assessed against Mr. P. Vance on December 3, 1857. The offense was not named. The same day Isaac Shelby (not the famous Governor of Kentucky) was fined for feeding his horse in the street. On June

1, 1858, a Mr. Womack was fined for fighting; and J. H. Martin (prominent local merchant and banker) was fined one dollar for leading his horse on a sidewalk. On November 11, 1858, W. W. James was fined for allowing two of his customers to feed horses in front of his store.

Certainly, not all the lawlessness of early Bristol-Goodson was chargeable to the street ruffians of the time. There was also what might be termed "white collar" crime. One such offense was fence moving. Nearly all occupied lots had some fencing upon them. If a lot next door had out-of-town owners, it was not uncommon for the adjoining owner to "ease his fence" well beyond his legal lines, thus enlarging his property at the loss of the other. If this encroachment came from both sides of an unoccupied lot, as it often did, an absentee owner might return to find that he only had space enough left for an alley, if indeed that much! The local fine for this illegal enlargement of property was one dollar or five days in jail.

Another white collar crime was sign displacement, theft, or destruction. Sometimes during the night, signs were taken from buildings, then hidden or destroyed. (Many were thrown into Beaver Creek.) Thus prospective customers might have difficulty in locating the stores they sought. Often, in a form of jest, signs were removed and attached to totally unrelated business houses. Thus, one morning back in 1858, young Jimmy Yoste arrived early at his blacksmith shop on Fourth Street in Bristol, Tennessee, to find that his place was identified as W. W. James & Company, Merchants, Bristol, Virginia. The fine for sign displacing or theft was the same as for fence moving.

FIRST BRISTOL, TENNESSEE JAIL

With local government and law enforcement came the need for a town jail. On June 24, 1859, Eli Marsh was chosen to see the county about a lockup for Bristol, Tennessee. Up to that time it had been the practice to use the county jail at Blountville for the keeping of Bristol criminals, and this prac- tice long continued for serious offenders. It was not until December 7, 1860, that bids were received for the construction of a local lockup. For some unstated reason, the bid of J. E. Pepper of $147.00 was rejected. W. J. Betterton was appointed to receive further bids. On February 7, 1861, the bid of Peter M. Kesner of $105.00 was accepted, and he was then author- ized to commence the jail at once. The site close to the old Shelby burying ground was chosen on the recommendation of Joseph R. Anderson, who thought that it might be of "great benefit to transgressors to reflect upon their crimes so close to this evidence of mortality and judgement." The site was rather isolated at that time, and lonely nights spent within easy sight of the tombs and markers of that old burying ground may have had a chilling effect on the more superstitious of the prisoners. This jail is described as having been made of eight- by eight-inch timbers laid one upon the other and spiked together with only open cutouts of one timber for windows. (It was rather airy in winter and stifling hot in summer.) The only sanitary facility was a cast iron potty. One prisoner is known to have escaped by throwing this potty into the face of the constable and then quickly fleeing. The jail thus described was ready for occupancy by June 7, 1861. For an unexplained reason, Kesner was paid fifteen dollars more than his bid for this construction. For the new jail J. R. Anderson donated a hasp and lock valued at seventy-five cents.

In late June 1871 John M. Crowell was hired to move the jail to a location on Fifth Street, near the present Masonic Lodge building. In 1873 it was moved a few feet north of that location. On September 2, 1871, a chain gang law was passed, whereby prisoners might work out their fines or be of use doing public works during their jail terms. Much needed street work was accomplished in this manner. One of the first projects on which the chain gang was used was a regrading of the road leading up to the City Cemetery (now East Hill Cemetery).

The office of constable was finally replaced by a regular police force. That was in operation before 1890. Early policemen were Chal Caldwell, George Jones, Sam Hammer, Sam Slack, and Bill Sullivan. Caldwell was head of the department for several years.

NEW COURT FOR BRISTOL, TENNESSEE

An item in the June 6, 1879, edition of the *Bristol News* describes the opening of the new court for Bristol, Tennessee:

> Judge Smith yesterday formally opened the new Chancery Court at Conway Hall (Fifth Street), in the presence of some 18 members of the bar and quite a crowd of spectators. Mr. E. A. Warren filed his bond as Clerk and Master with Messrs. John Slack, W. D. McCroskey, Judge Butler, W. W. Davis, I. A. Nickels, and J. R. Anderson as securities. Chancellor Smith then formally declared the court opened for the transaction of business. Mr. D. F. Bailey then asked that Mr. W. F. Rhea be allowed to qualify, and that gentleman had the honor of being the subject of the first official act ever done in the Bristol Chancery Court. The bench was then vacated to allow Judge Butler and Col. Gregg to discuss the Tennessee state debt.

The new court was a great convenience to the residents of Bristol. Much to the credit of the town fathers, it should be noted that in those early days whenever a new law was passed, it was published in a local newspaper. Often a notation followed asking that the educated read it to the illiterate. In the words of Mayor Anderson, this was done "that no one remain ignorant of the law."

LAW AND ORDER IN BRISTOL-GOODSON, VIRGINIA

Because the records of the first fourteen years of city government on the Virginia side of Bristol are lost, little can be learned of law enforcement for that period, but William L. Rice may have served as the first town sergeant. And there is some indication that A. K. Moore, Austin M. Appling, and Philip Rohr may have served in the same capacity. Further, an old record states that Campbell Galliher was elected town constable in 1861.

According to information handed down, the Virginia side of town was more lawless than was the Tennessee side. This may be why the Washington County Court felt compelled to appoint deputies to patrol the town, beginning in 1858. Those appointed were Hardy Pool, J. F. H. Ledbetter, John Hammitt, James Williams, Joseph Barnes, Samuel Booker (local merchant), John C. Carner, Edward Johnson, Lucian Johnson, and Robert B.. Moore. On his third night of patrol duty, Joseph Barnes of this group was forced to shoot and kill a desperado who was hiding in the railroad yard near the present Mary Street Bridge. The outlaw had shot Barnes through the left arm before he (the outlaw) was mortally wounded.

More lawlessness on the Virginia side may be accounted for in part by the fact that most of the lawbreakers seem to have clustered around the depot, railroad yards and shops, and the two or more saloons that were in that vicinity. Too, Samuel Goodson had built a number of rent houses in his Goodson-ville, some of which rented for small sums, and this tended to draw a rougher element to that section.

When the local government was reorganized in 1870, one of the first acts of the Common Council was to appoint a committee on police to superintend matters connected to the police department. This committee, appointed in Philip Rohr's store on July 29, 1870, consisted of Samuel L. Saul and Joseph W. Owen. On October 24, 1870, John Templin was appointed as temporary policeman for the town. Other sources reveal that there was an unusual amount of crime that autumn that made extra help necessary.

The first elected sergeant after the reorganization of the local government was John L. Ligon. He resigned on June 27, 1871, and William Trammell was appointed in his place. Trammell resigned May 20, 1872, and D. A. Wheeler began his term. Wheeler was bonded by A. Luttrell and J. W. Owen. One of the duties that fell upon Wheeler in 1874 was an order by the mayor to shoot Lewis Bachelor's dog if found loose upon the streets. The dog was found near the Bachelor home on lower Main Street. As Wheeler prepared to fire upon the dog, he was fired upon by the legendary Rosetta Bachelor, who had perceived the situation as she watched from an open window. (She always carried two loaded pistols under her ample skirts.) Rather than to engage in a shoot-out with a woman, Wheeler turned and fled. The resultant "disgrace" and ribbing that became his lot for having been put to flight by a woman caused him to give up his post and leave town for a short time. Strangely, the warrant issued for the arrest of Mrs. Bachelor was never served. A notation that she could not be found was made several times on the paper. Yet, she boldly walked the streets every day while the "diligent search" was being made for her. Perhaps the rumor that she had "enlarged her arsenal" had something to do with this "futile search" by the town authorities.

Wheeler was replaced by William H. Trammell, who was paid $179.00 for a year of service. R. T. Hamlet became the next sergeant. He was followed by the noted John B. Keller, "the whipping man," who served from 1877 to August 31, 1880. He resigned because of another disgrace of sorts, as we shall shortly see. Then D. A. Wheeler took the office again. This time there was no confrontation with Rosetta Bachelor! He served until 1884, when Charles Worley took the office. W. P. Hughes took the office in 1887 and served only one year, when the office was again assumed by Charles Worley. Those who served through the remainder of the century were W. J. Cox, 1890-1892; Justin King, 1892-1894; John H. Gose, 1894-1898; and Luther Rush, 1900.

Through those early years the mayor served as local judge for minor cases. (Serious crimes were still tried at Abingdon, Virginia.) The mayor levied fines for some petty crimes and prescribed the whipping post for others. The whipping post, a strong stake hewed of locust, stood in a little triangle formed by Lee, Water, and Cumberland Streets. (A service station stood on the site some forty years ago.) It was the duty of the town sergeant to tie the prisoner there and "lay on the whip," the number of lashes being set by the mayor, the number increasing with the seriousness of the crime. An amused crowd nearly always assembled for the spectacle and often loudly called out the lashes in unison with the sergeant. An old paper exists showing that R. T. Hamlet was paid fifty cents for whipping Henry H_____ on February 24, 1877. Another paper shows that John B. Keller was paid the same amount for whipping Alexander W_____ on December 11, 1879. The charge in both cases was petit larceny. Fifty cents appears to have been the going price for administering the lashes as prescribed by his honor, the mayor of Bristol-Goodson, Virginia. Because of his skill in using the whip, John B. Keller became known as the "whipping man." His most memorable case was that of Chief Mockingbird. The chief arrived in town from no one knew where in 1880. It was rumored that he was a brother of the notorious Pocahontas

Hale, who operated the town's largest brothel. He always went wrapped in a very large blanket, greasy though it was. He never gave his name but was called Chief Mockingbird because of his almost constant mimicking of that versatile bird. He was an enormous man, standing a good six and one-half feet and, though not fat, was very heavily built. It was soon rumored that he was lifting merchandise from local stores and hiding the loot under the blanket which he constantly wore. Alas, one day he was caught in the store of J. M. Barker with a ham under his covering. Mayor Terry ordered twenty-one lashes. The word quickly spread (indeed, time was allowed for it to spread) and when the whipping man arrived at the triangle, a large crowd had circled around that noted place of punishment. All were amazed to see the seeming meekness of the prisoner as he was led forth and tied to the post. Keller raised the leather whip and at the enthusiastic call of the crowd administered lash one. Chief Mockingbird then gave a mighty lunge and heave, and the post, which Keller had boasted could not be dislodged by an elephant, was jerked from the ground. (Heavy rains the night before might have helped in the matter.) With a well aimed kick to the stomach, the prisoner sent Keller sprawling backwards. Chief Mockingbird (minus his constant whistling) then tore through the crowd, the post swinging left and right at the end of the rope behind him. That post flattened many of the crowd, "like a whirlwind in a corn field," as Daddy Thomas expressed it thirty-seven years ago. Fleet as a chased deer the chief raced through town and disappeared toward the knobs. He was never seen in Bristol again. Having been "disgraced" by such a dramatic and public loss of a prisoner, Keller resigned his office.

An old paper turned in for collection by R. T. Hamlett in February 1877 gives an indication of the costs of law enforcement during that period:

To R. T. Hamlett, Sergeant of Bristol-Goodson, Virginia
For arresting Henry H_____, charged with petit larceny $1.00
Summoning one witness 20
Whipping said Henry H_____ 50
For arresting Edward T_____, for assault with intent to kill . 1.00
Summoning three witnesses 60
Conveying said Edward T_____ to jail and returning
   (Abingdon and back); 30 miles 3.00
Expense of prisoner 60
   Total $6.90

Another paper turned in by Hamlett shows that the railroad was not always used in transporting prisoners to Abingdon. In the case of Mrs. E. M. H. C_____, lunatic (insane), a wagon was hired at a cost of $2.50. It was stated that the presence of a lunatic on the train would "cause excitement among the passengers."

At a meeting of the Common Council on October 3, 1871, a motion was made by Dr. C. T. Pepper to establish a chain gang. The motion was favorably received and acted upon. As on the Tennessee side of town, the chain gang was used largely in the repair and improvement of streets and bridges. It was still in operation as late as June 1890. At that time prisoners over sixteen years of age could work out fines at twenty-five cents per day.

It is very apparent that even in those days when law enforcement was largely the responsibility of the sergeant or constable, as he was often called, the town also had a police force. In 1872 G. W. Hammitt was sworn in as a special policeman to serve under the local agent of the A. M. and O. Railroad (later Norfolk and Western). At that time a great many crimes occurred in the vicinity of the local depot and rail yards. Night crimes reached a peak around 1880. Thus, on March 2 that year the mayor was authorized to employ two extra policemen to patrol the town at night. They were to be paid seventy-five cents each for the twelve-hour shift. Those known to have been serving on the police force in 1890 were John H. Gose, Isaac Sharett, W. J. (Jim) Cox, and J. B. Cummings. W. B. Kilgore and H. S. Price were added to the force in 1893. In 1890 police pay was thirty dollars per month. In 1891 Chief Isaac Sharett was receiving forty-five dollars per month. Pay for the regular force had reached forty dollars per month by that date, and remained at that level as late as 1896. G. W. Wolfe served as chief sometime in the 1890s, and W. B. Kilgore had become chief by 1898.

Then as now, law enforcement officers sometimes became the center of scandal. There lived on Russell Street a young couple, the husband of which was a fireman on the railroad. He returned from work one night to find the town sergeant emerging from the back door of his home. There ensued a violent confrontation during which the husband was beaten senseless by the club-wielding sergeant. Though the sergeant claimed that the husband was resisting arrest, a Washington County grand jury apparently did not believe him. He was indicted for felonious assault with intent to kill. Though he was not convicted, the resultant disgrace and anger of an enraged citizenry caused him to leave Bristol. He left his family behind, and neither they nor any one else ever heard from him again.

THE FIRST BRISTOL-GOODSON JAIL

At first the town maintained a holding room (jail of sorts) in the Virginia House Hotel. Prisoners were locked in that room until the mayor could dispose of their cases. Later such a room was maintained in the Magnolia Hotel. The latter is described as being a windowless pantry, very dark and stuffy. Serious offenders were held only until the next train left for Abingdon. An old Bristol resident remembered seeing a felon being taken from this room and led across the street to the depot. Two heavily armed guards were at his side. It may be mentioned here that before the trains ran to Bristol, at least one murderer was taken to Abingdon on foot, tied with ropes between two guards. Ann Bachelor describes this event in her memoirs.

At a meeting of the Common Council on July 29, 1870, the committee on police (J. W. Owen and S. L. Saul) was instructed to see about building a jail. Then on August 20, 1870, S. L. Saul and Dr. C. T. Pepper were appointed to draw up specifications and determine the cost of such a building. On the following August 27th, it was reported that two bids had been received, one from William Templin and another from the partnership of Archer and Carmack (probably Peter C. Archer and William Carmack). The bid of Archer and Carmack was accepted. The town was to supply the materials, and the Council would superintend the work.

This first Bristol-Goodson jail was erected on the east side of the five hundred block of Washington Street (approximately 513 Washington). It was built of roughly cut stone with two small windows. These windows were formed by leaving out building stones of such small size that prisoners could not squeeze through the openings, or so it was supposed. The door was made of heavy timbers and secured by a lock and hasp costing $1.25 (purchased from W. W. James & Company). The roof was flat, made by laying six-by-six timbers side by side then tarring over them. Tar or not, it leaked like a sieve! On November 28, 1870, Archer and Carmack received thirty-five dollars for the erection of this "leaky" jail.

The first prisoner housed in this jail escaped during the first night. Apparently he had squeezed through one of the small windows. Another who later tried the same method was not so lucky. The sergeant arrived with breakfast for the inmate and found him half way through the window, seemingly stuck fast. It took considerable effort on the part of several citizens to free him. Soon after that the windows were reduced in size by bricking around them.

By October 3, 1871, the new jail was ready for repairs. Being in a rather isolated locality, it was an easy mark for friends of the imprisoned. These friends had knocked out the brickwork around the windows and further enlarged the windows by knocking out stones around them; had chopped a hole in the roof; and had battered down the door with a crow bar. It was stipulated by the Council that at the time of the repairs, the jail was to be made more secure for the keeping of lawbreakers. At that time the windows were barred, and an iron door was installed. Even so, no chances were taken when an important prisoner was within. Once a murderer had to be held there for ten days because the Abingdon jail was full. Two special policemen were hired to stand guard "during all the hours of darkness." For this service the two had fifteen dollars to split between them at the end of their ten nights of service. The guards were brothers, Samuel and William Penley.

For years the town sergeant was allowed forty cents per day for the feeding of prisoners, but efforts were constantly made to economize. Once the town was able to buy the produce of a cabbage patch for a pittance. It was noted that this had reduced the cost of feeding prisoners for several weeks to fifteen cents per day. One may but image that a lot of boiled cabbage was put through the feed slot of the local jail. Doctors were paid one or two dollars for visits to prisoners. In one case where Dr. R. F. Preston was called in to determine if Mrs. Eliza B_____ suffered from insanity, the charge was five dollars.

This first jail served until about 1880 or perhaps a year or two later. Then a concrete block building was erected on Water Street for that purpose. It, too, was rather primitive. In the 1890s the town lost a law suit brought by a prisoner who had nearly frozen to death in this second jail. His compensation was around six hundred dollars. Until 1881 the mayor's office continued to serve as the center of justice for Bristol-Goodson. At that time a brick courthouse was erected, and thereafter local court was held there. It was the mayor's duty to assign the offices in this new building. For the first time, the town sergeant and police had a permanent headquarters.

NEW COURT

For years Bristolians had complained of having to go to Abingdon to transact legal business. Thus, there was great relief and satisfaction when at the new incorporation in 1890, provision was made for a corporation court. The first session of this court was held on March 3, 1890, with William F. Rhea, presiding. J. H. Winston, Jr., became the first clerk. W. S. Hamilton, a local lawyer was appointed the first commonwealth attorney. C. C. Minor, who had long been a school teacher and later a druggist, became the first treasurer. Charles Worley was first sergeant, and the first commissioner of the revenue was J. W. Mort, who owned a local gun shop. Though Bristol then had its own court, many cases continued to be tried in Abingdon. This was true as late as 1900.

EARLY BRISTOL CRIME

The first known theft in the Town of Bristol occurred in a very unusual manner. John H. Moore, the first merchant in Bristol, Virginia, had a little wareroom in the back of his store in which there was a barrel of molasses. Early one morning Moore came to his store and found the barrel empty, but there was no sign of forced entry. He was greatly puzzled by this until he passed by on the outside and saw a large pool of molasses under the wareroom floor. It seems that some time during the night, a thief who had apparently noted the position of the barrel, had crawled under the floor and bored a hole straight up into it. He had drained a pail full of the sweet syrup, and then the rest had been wasted on the ground. Jesse Aydlotte, who had been deputized to serve as a peace officer in the town, was immediately put on the case. His task was not too hard. The thief had used a leaky pail and here and there on the dusty streets were gobs of molasses. He followed the trail to a little shack owned by Samuel Goodson and into which a man with a large family had recently moved. When Aydlotte entered the humble home, he found a starving bunch of children wolfing down what molasses had remained in the leaky pail. It was then that justice turned into mercy. Instead of arresting the man, Aydlotte hired him to work on a house he was constructing on Main Street. In time the desperate father learned the carpentry trade and became a highly respected citizen of the town. Descendants still live here, some of them being rather wealthy and influential Bristol citizens.

On through the forty and more years that remained of the nineteenth century, thefts were almost a daily occurrence. Indictment papers, court records, newspapers, and other sources tell the story. From an old indictment paper is learned that:

Eugene G_____ on the 24th day of May, 1871, in said county (Washington) and town (Bristol-Goodson) did between the hours of eight and eleven o'clock in the night time of that day, feloniously and burglariously break and enter into the dwelling house of one Col. J. M. Barker, with intent of taking unlawfully the money and property of the said Barker, and then and there did steal, take, and carry away three U. S. dollar notes and currency of the value of ten dollars, three ten-dollar notes, four five-dollar notes, and five dollars in silver coin, did take and carry away against the peace and dignity of the Commonwealth of Virginia.

On St. Patrick's day, 1871, thieves broke into the brick smokehouse of Col. John G. King and took over five hundred pounds of bacon. King offered a hundred dollar reward for the arrest and conviction of the responsible parties. A few days later some of the bacon was found hidden under a feather bed in the home of one Sam M_____, who had been sleeping on his loot! It seems that smokehouses were often the target of local thieves. The *Bristol News* of February 23, 1875, tells that on the previous night, the smokehouse of E. H. Seneker was entered and robbed of four pieces of bacon and a half can of lard. It is also mentioned that Mr. Audley Anderson (brother of Joseph R. Anderson) had recently met with a similar loss.

Some Bristol thieves were certainly soft of step and feather fingered. On

August 5, 1879, one entered a room in the Virginia House Hotel, where local telegraph operator R. B. Short was sleeping, and took $120.00 from a wallet which the unwary victim had under his pillow. The same thief then went to the room where hotel manager John G. Wood was deep in slumber and took $28.00 from his pants which hung on his bed post. On June 2, 1881, Mr. Noah Artrip, a merchant on the Clinch River seven miles north of Lebanon, Virginia, was relieved of $325.00 while he was sleeping in his wagon in Winston's warehouse yard. The thief cleanly cut the victim's pocket and several inches of his pants.

On the list of thieving goes: from the ordinary theft of an apple from J. A. Buckner's store to the very unusual case of the theft of stud service. The latter was wrought by Sam F_____, who slipped his mare into the lot with the prize stallion, Jupiter, owned by Smith Green. Mr. Green was away attending camp meeting, but unfortunately for Sam, a neighbor was at home and reported the incident. This 1887 case was dismissed because it could not be definitely proved that the mare's colt was sired by Jupiter.

The first known murder in the Town of Bristol involved an unknown victim and an unknown assailant. And the only date is that it was in blackberry time, 1857. Ann Bachelor was picking blackberries in a thicket near the railroad across from the east end of Scott Street, and she was the only witness to the murder. Two bitterly arguing men came walking along the grade. The argument turned into a savage fight, with one finally stabbing the other to death. By the time Ann ran back into town with the frightful news, the murderer had escaped and was never found. The unknown victim was buried in the old Shelby or Oak Grove Cemetery and presumably was moved to East Hill Cemetery in 1871.

While not as common as thefts, murders occasionally occurred through the remainder of the century. On June 7, 1881, Joshua (Bunch) Shipley was mortally wounded in Mosby's Grove (to the left of Piedmont, just north of Scott Street). Editor Fowler described his wounds thus:

> Shipley was found weltering in a pool of blood. He was shot under the right eye, the ball entering near his nose, and ranging slightly below the brain. His head was terribly cut and bruised with sharp limestone rocks taken from the Narrow Gage cut (along Scott near the end of Solar Street). His skull was fractured in four places... a tremendous scuffle had taken place.

It was later learned that several men had been involved in the Shipley murder. Whiskey and lewd women often played a role in the local murders as shown by a news item of the 1870s:

About half past ten o'clock on Sunday evening last a couple of pistol shots were heard in our still sabbath atmosphere. The event was immediately known to but few, the generality of the citizens being in bed... William Moore, a young man who had been clerking in Mr. Thomas Curtin's store, had shot and instantly killed Bob Quails, a switchman in the Tennessee yard. The few who were attracted to the spot found Quails groaning in the street, but unable to speak, and he died in a few minutes after he fell. The prime cause of the difficulty was whiskey and its immediate cause a lewd woman. After some words in the street, Moore had gone into a miserable and depraved brothel kept by one Keszia, a woman whose character should be sufficient to cause her ejectment from any tenement in town. Quails demanded admission and being refused, threatened to shoot into the door. Moore then escaped by the rear door and went around to the front where Quails was and demanded the cause of his following him. More words ensured and Moore fired on him twice, one ball taking effect in his left side, below the ribs and ranging upward passing out under the right shoulder. Moore escaped in the darkness, and is still at large. Quails was killed at almost the identical locality of the shooting of poor Pat Ryan in 1866.

One of the most sensational murders ever to occur in Bristol, and one which almost resulted in the immediate execution of the murderer by an enraged citizenry, happened just before Christmas, 1879. W. T. (Dug) Thomas was one of the most popular young men of the town. He was employed as a clerk in the J. M. Barker Store and showed much promise of becoming a fine merchant. A young lawyer of the town came in one day and told Thomas that Mr. Barker had said it would be all right for him to have a box of collars on credit. He was allowed to take the collars (cost of twenty-five cents). Later Mr. Barker returned to the store and when informed of the transaction, replied that he had not approved the credit sale, as the young lawyer had claimed. An evening or two later the lawyer again came into the store and was confronted by both Barker and Thomas about the matter. In anger the lawyer drew a knife and slit the throat of Dug Thomas. Young Thomas, trying vainly to stop the spurting blood with his fingers, ran to the nearby Dickey Drug Store and cried out, "My God, I am ruined," and fell to the floor where he died within minutes. The murderer fled to the southern part of town but was soon found. By then an enraged crowd had gathered and was planning to storm the little jail and hang the prisoner. Already rope had been measured and cut for the purpose. Finally, Rev. George A. Caldwell and lawyer U. L. York managed to quiet the crowd long enough to dissuade them from an immediate hanging. Eleven years later, this young lawyer was elected to high office in Bristol, Virginia.

The first known robbery to occur in the Town of Bristol might be called an inside job. W. L. and J. H. Martin had set up a private banking service in their store that stood at what is now the southeast corner of Sixth and State. (They were the second bankers in town.) Like Joseph Anderson, when a sizeable amount of money accumulated in their banking room, they took it to a regular bank in Abingdon. An old couple living east of town (it is thought that they were Rutherfords) had saved a large amount of gold and had been persuaded by the Martin brothers to bring it in early on a certain morning before a planned trip to Abingdon. The couple arrived in a wagon with their gold in a bucket. The wife remained in the wagon while the husband carried in the treasure. A young man had been hired to clerk in the store, and when he saw the great wealth being carried passed him, something must have clicked in his mind. Perhaps he realized that before him was more money than he could accumulate in a lifetime, that this was his grand opportunity for a life of ease and luxury. Whatever he thought, he grabbed a pistol from under the counter and robbed the old gentleman of his life savings and then turned upon his employers and robbed them of what money was in the store. He raced out the front door with pistol in one hand, the bucket of gold in the other. Alas, going out the front was his big mistake. The old lady saw and instantly perceived what had happened. She jumped from the wagon upon him; her very ample weight knocking him to the ground. In seconds both Martin brothers and the old gentleman were upon him also. Seemingly not interested in further proceedings of justice, the old couple grabbed their gold, jumped into the wagon and headed toward home, probably vowing never to deal with bankers again! Strangely, the Martins did not prosecute the young clerk. It is said that they told him if he would immediately leave town and never return, nothing further would be done. He did not even go by home on his way out of town. About forty years later a man of apparent wealth came here from Louisiana and spent several days looking around town. Many thought he was the store clerk bank robber of 1856.

Over the years there were numerous robberies in Bristol. Crime reached a peak around 1880. Robbery was then so common that virtually all store clerks and bank employees were armed to the teeth. J. A. Buckner, an early merchant, was robbed twice on his way from his store to his home. Afterwards he carried two wallets: one for the robbers (empty) and another very concealed one in which was his money. Court records at Abingdon, Virginia, and Blountville, Tennessee, are replete with indictments for armed robberies that occurred in the twin towns.

The first of many cases of rape that have occurred in Bristol happened in May 1856. A local merchant hired a young girl from the country (near present Wallace, Virginia) to stay in his home and help care for his ailing wife and two or three young children. One Sunday afternoon he asked the girl to go with him to the store to bring home a supply of groceries. The rape occurred while the two were in the store. However, the merchant was acquitted of the charge. His wife soon died. About a year later a traveling preacher conducted a protracted meeting (revival) at Wallace (then called Goforth's Mill or simply Goforth's). A strange doctrine preached by this evangelist was that the first man with whom a woman had sexual contact was fore-ordained to be her husband. He convinced the girl, then seventeen years of age, that she would be sinning if she did not adhere to that belief and act accordingly. She returned to Bristol and flatly offered to marry her rapist. The merchant agreed and the two reared a fine family. A few descendants of this couple yet live in Bristol.

Thirty-three years later a rape occurred near a trail that led through a pasture near the present campus of Virginia Intermont College. The indictment of the rapist is typical of many that are among the loose court papers at Abingdon, Virginia:

> That on the 12th day of June in the year 1889, the said Tom H_____ did in and upon the body of one Leah H. J_____, a female over the age of twelve years, that is of eighteen years, did make an assault, and with force did then and there, feloniously ravish and carnally know the body of the said Leah H. J_____, by raising her dress and doing other acts toward commission of the crime of rape.

The crimes through the first forty-eight years of Bristol's existence include about every violation of the law that can be named, from the common to the bizarre. There was Marshall C_____, who in 1867 was indicted for placing timbers and stones on the railroad, "thus endangering the lives and health of diverse people," as the court papers put it. James M_____ was arrested because he would not assist an officer in the apprehension of a felon. Henry W_____ gambled and faced the charge of cheating at cards. His only consolation was that he had won ten dollars! "Big" John K_____ paid dearly for shooting down Main (State) Street, "just to see the people run." The Washington County court, sitting in 1875, did not think the matter should be taken lightly. Another Bristolian, Jimmy H_____ shot under the feet of dancers "to see them get lively." He faced the same court that did not think *his* action funny either. The indictments in both cases state that the pistols were loaded with gunpowder and leaden bullets. Such was the exacting languages used in the indictments of the time.

Charles C_____ paid a heavy fine in 1877 for making loud, unholy and indecent sounds during a worship service in the Bristol Baptist Church. A local politician "got the book" for enticing an unqualified citizen to vote.

David L_____ was one of many local men who were taken to court for selling liquor without a license, and charges of liquor sales on the sabbath and to minors are numerous. J. G_____ found himself before the judge for poisoning his mother- in-law's horse (mothers-in-law beware!). Jonathan W_____ became angry with a local minister because the latter's efforts had converted the mistress of the former. He tried to set fire to the church with oil and sawdust. The charge of arson separated him from his mistress, converted or not. The easy way to obtain a mess of fish was tried by Lee S_____. His indictment reads:

> That the said Lee S_____ did on the tenth day of June, in the year 1881, place dynamite in the upper reaches of Campbell's mill pond on Beaver Creek, for the purpose of killing fish by the unlawful use of explosives, and did kill a great number of fish and created a frightening situation for the neighborhood.

The lawbreaker's easy mess of fish cost him three months in jail. And the list could go on. Carrying concealed weapons was a very common offense in those days. Forgery, assault and battery, cruelty to animals, seducement, operating houses of ill fame, lewd conduct, public swearing and profanity were among the crimes. Name it; it has been done in Bristol.

One interesting insight gained by a study of old court papers is that women were very often involved in crime. Maye A_____ and Julia J_____ along with several men were indicted in 1888 for entering the store of C. B. James and carrying away his goods and chattels. Martha C_____ pulled an armed holdup at the Thomas House Hotel in 1889. In 1891 Ellen S_____ set fire to the home of her husband's mistress, then assaulted the mistress as she fled from the burning house, "doing her great injury," so states the charge. But Ellen S_____ could not hold a light to Sally B_____ who on the 4th day of October 1894 "did severely wound Jacob J_____, Miriah B_____, and Louthia J_____ (wife of Jacob) by assault upon the bodies of the said afore mentioned parties, with a club, that is an apple butter paddle, and further did mortally wound the dog of the said Jacob J_____ (had the dog come to the defense of his master) and further by a kick to the groin of Jacob J_____ did further wound and cause distressful injury to him." And if all that were not enough, the indictment goes on to state that the said Sally B_____ "did with intent to inflict injury and suffering, throw hot apple butter on the backs of the afore named Miriah B_____ and Louthia J_____." (One wonders how Jacob escaped this part of the assault.) Apparently this was an apple butter making that was not so pleasant! It is doubtful that Sally B_____ had apple butter in her diet where she had to stay for several months.

Sometimes there were very major and very minor charges on the same indictment. In 1871 one Jane Y_____ killed her husband by severing his head from his body by the use of a sharp axe (yes, the indictment does give the condition of the axe). She tossed the severed head into a neighbor's well. The grand jury charged her with murder. She was also indicted for polluting the water supply of Hannah Webb.

MECCA FOR FUGITIVES

Over the years Bristol became a mecca for fugitives from the law. Court papers of the period tell of frequent arrests of outlaws from other places who had taken refuge here. Typical is the case of one George E_____ of Lee County, Virginia, who there, along with others, had entered a home on Mathis Creek in the wee hours of the night, shot off their guns, raped a daughter of the family, and carried away valuable property. The governor of Virginia offered a fifty dollar reward for the capture of the lawbreakers. George E_____, leader of the group, fled to Bristol. Constable E. Van Huss came to Bristol and spent several days searching for the fugitive. The constable learned that he was binding wheat for Col. John G. King, on King's farm near King's Spring, south of Bristol. Van Huss found the sought outlaw playing cards with others on the railroad tracks near the King farm. He managed to get the drop on him and forced his card playing companions to apply the handcuffs. The prisoner was marched at gunpoint up the railroad tracks to the Virginia Hotel. (A holding room was still maintained there at that time, 1881, for the convenience of law officers who needed to transport prisoners by train.) Editor Fowler remarked that George E_____ was only twenty-one years old, but looked twenty-five or thirty, and that he was physically "a wild cat and a notorious character." Fowler tells of another fugitive who, while being taken to a passenger train for transportation to Abingdon, broke loose from law officers and could not be apprehended until a shot in the leg stopped him.

BOND JUMPERS

Then as now, bondsmen often came to grief because prisoners freed on bond often took their temporary freedom as a time of flight. F. C. M_____, who had once served as a law officer in Bristol, Tennessee, had two serious charges against him at Blountville, Tennessee. He had been bonded by D. J. Ensor, local druggist. Mr. M_____ jumped bond and left the state. However, sometime later he returned and was immediately arrested at the request of his bondsman. A young man was hired to guard the Bristol jail (then on Fifth Street) until the prisoner could be moved to Blountville. Sometime during the night the young guard became sleepy and stole away

to his nearby home for a nap. During his absence Mr. M_____ escaped
and was never captured. It was thought that he went to Texas. This 1873
incident was typical of many such happenings in early Bristol.

NEAR DUEL

Something a little different in the line of crime almost occurred here on
October 6, 1881. Judge George W. Ward and William T. Mitchell were
publishers of the *Abingdon Virginian* at Abingdon, Virginia. Daniel Trigg,
Esquire, was one of the editors of the *Abingdon Standard*. Though the Civil
War had been over sixteen years, the Funders and Readjusters were still going
strong. On September 29, 1881, an article appeared in the *Abingdon Virginian*
in which was said:

> The wind this week of the Standard is no doubt comforting to the shorn
> lambs of the Burbon-Funder fold; for it is filled with lies. It should
> temper its sheet with a gentle gale of truth.

Of course, Editor Trigg was furious. Shortly he challenged Judge Ward
to a duel. It was decided to meet in Bristol, Tennessee. About noon on October 6th, both parties arrived at the Nickels House Hotel. William Mitchell
was with Judge Ward, and Mr. Trigg was accompanied by Captain Litchfield
and several others. Shortly, Mayor John F. Terry received a telegram from
Abingdon asking that the parties be arrested. Officers Guntner and Sullivan
arrived at the Nickels House just as Ward and Mitchell emerged from a back
door and started toward a buggy. Ward was arrested, but Mitchell was allowed
to escape. Meanwhile, Trigg and his party had escaped and had driven to
the chosen dueling ground. The place chosen was on the George Cowan farm
and would be near where the Akard Funeral home is now located. When
word reached Trigg's party that Judge Ward had been arrested by Tennessee
authorities, a crossing was made into Virginia, where all were soon arrested
by John B. Keller. Judge Ward was delivered into Virginia and was rearrested
by Keller. Thus was foiled what might have been a sensational duel in Bristol.
Indeed, a great many Bristolians who had heard of the planned duel had hastened toward the spot and were disappointed that "the show" was stopped. Such
is the bloodthirstiness of man.

ARMS FOR DEFENSE

It has been said by several who lived here when Bristol was little more
than a typical railroad and border town, that it was a rare gentleman who
did not go "armed to the teeth." The trend began when many former Confederate officers and soldiers settled in Bristol soon after the end of the Civil
War. Their enemies were numerous. Life, limb, and property were in near

constant jeopardy. This caused a vigilance that became a part of daily life. Then, as the next three decades became the most lawless in Bristol's history, the gun-carrying mania spread to the general population until "arms were as common as hats." Along with his pills and powders, the doctor's bag was likely to contain a pistol. In court the judge, jury, lawyers and most of the spectators bore arms. Virtually all merchants kept a weapon within easy reach. (E. H. Seneker kept several scattered about his large store.) Joseph Anderson was the only known town banker who did not carry at least two pistols on his person. His philosophy was that "they who live by the sword shall die by the sword."

Old Major Zack Burson, a Baptist minister, always had two fine pistols on his person and slept with one under his pillow. When walking home from his store, early merchant J. A. Buckner always had one of his pistols in his hand and sometimes fired a shot or two to let would-be outlaws know that he was armed. W. W. James, who came to his store before daylight and left long after dark, sometimes carried pistols in both hands, though there is no report that he followed Buckner's plan of serving notice to bandits along the way. Even the beloved Rev. George A. Caldwell carried a weapon for at least the first ten years he was pastor of the First Presbyterian Church. It is said that when his home was being built on the southwest corner of Sixth and Anderson Streets, the workmen laid their guns upon the rising walls in readiness for possible attack by Caldwell's former war enemies.

At Pleasant Hill, home of this author, a stump of a peg may be felt under the wallpaper to the right of the front door. Old Capt. Wood used to hang his pistol there in case an enemy came calling. Perhaps the best armed man in town was old Col. John N. Bosang, who is said to have felt insecure if he did not carry at least three fine pistols and a knife or two. His home was virtually an armed fortress containing numerous rifles, shotguns, a sword, two or three daggers, and his ever handy pistols.

And even females were not totally out of the "arms race." The legendary Rosetta Bachelor wore loose and heavily pleated skirts to conceal the two pistols that she always carried. Evidently these were kept in some type of pockets or holsters, for when she sat down upon the front pew (always the front pew) at the Presbyterian Church, there could be heard two distinct thuds as the weapons came hard against wood. She was always somewhat of an embarrassment to this church, but there is no record of any attempt to dismiss her. Pocahontas Hale, madam of the Black Shawl, was also known to be a bearer of arms. Madam Henrique, who once taught at the Bristol Institute, carried a tiny pistol at all times. And the genteel, dignified Mrs. L. F. (Harriet) Johnson could hit a bull'e-eye at thirty paces, and was thought to be armed until Bristol became "more civilized." Doubtless there were others of the female gender who felt that preparedness was the best defense against attack.

Bibliography - Chapter Nine

Anderson, Rhea. Manuscript (unpublished), 1930.

Bristol News, newspaper. Various issues, 1857-1881.

Bristol-Goodson, Virginia. City Council Minutes, 1870-1900.

Bristol, Tennessee. City Council Minutes, 1856-1900.

Johnson, L. F. Notes, 1893.

Phillips, V. N. (Bud). Interviews with several older Bristol citizens, 1953-1956.

Taylor, Hattie King. Notes.

Washington County, Virginia. Circuit Court Records, 1852-1900.

Washington County, Virginia. Minutes of the County Court, 1852-1900.

Chapter Ten
ROADS - TRANSPORTATION
- COMMUNICATION

When the Town of Bristol, Virginia-Tennessee, was planned by Joseph R. Anderson in 1852, there was not a single public road leading directly into or across the site. That portion of the King plantation upon which the new town was laid out was then all fields, meadows or woods. The old stage road passed nearby but nowhere came within the original boundaries of the town. At some distance was the Island Road, which had long played a major role in what became the Bristol area. At an even greater distance was the Jonesboro Road, passing through Paperville, which was the oldest village in the immediate vicinity. A connecting road led from Paperville to and along the upper (northern) boundary of Goodsonville, passed down Mary Street (this was not a part of the original Bristol, Virginia), crossed the old stage road at about the present intersection of Oak View and Mary, and then angled northwestward. It then turned westward a short distance above present Euclid Avenue, passed by the old Susong home at the site of the Little Creek Shopping Center, and then followed the valley by Belle Meadows Baptist Church to the junction with Island Road.

The old stage road came through Flat Gap behind Virginia Intermont College and down Flat Hollow along present Oak View Street. It ascended Solar Hill along what is now King's Alley (former King Street), passed directly behind Pleasant Hill (home of this author), and on to the stage stop at the old King Mansion, at what is now 54 King Street. (A little later there was a mail stop at the Sycamore Trail crossing, now Sycamore Street.) From the King place the road swung around the high curve (now the corner of Sullins and King Streets) from which there was a splendid view of the meadows and fields of the King plantation (Mountain View) and the majestic mountains beyond. From the curve the road passed down or near present Sullins Street to the Little or Baker's Creek Valley. A crossing of this creek was made between present State and Shelby Streets. The route angled into and followed what became Shelby Street to a point near 14th Street, where it made a slow angle into what is now Broad Street and roughly passed along the present route of that street toward Steele Creek Park and on toward Blountville. An "ancient road" came up Beaver Creek, passed west of the Shelby

Fort site and joined the stage road near present Shelby Street. This was the road that connected the old estate of Col. James King (Holly Bend) with the Mountain View estate of his son, the Rev. James King. Later a portion of this road was rerouted to enter Bristol along Sixth Street and was commonly known as the Sulphur Springs Road. The road leading from King's iron works at the mouth of Steele Creek to Paperville came up Cedar Creek, passing near King's Spring, well south of the future town of Bristol. Later an important road would lead from Bristol along Fifth Street (formerly College Avenue) to and across the Iron Works or Cedar Valley Road to join the old Jonesboro Road and thence to what is now Bluff City.

Those who built the first house in Bristol (Anderson's at present State and Edgemont) had to haul the building materials across open meadows to reach the construction site. And when Joseph Anderson moved to his new home in September 1853, there still were no roads or graded streets in his proposed town. Soon after Anderson's arrival in Bristol he had Main Street graded, and with the permission of his father-in-law, Rev. James King, he had a road graded from the street's end at Beaver Creek (7th and State) along what is now State Street to join with the old stage road near present Commonwealth. Even so, it was not unobstructed at first; two gates had to be opened to clear the King fields for another year or so. Shortly the road leading out along Fifth Street, as mentioned above, was graded and became known as the Union (Bluff City) Pike. About the same time a short road was sighted from the northwest corner of Bristol, Virginia, across the corner of old Goodsonville to connect with the stage road in Flat Hollow.

Even though the connection to the old stage road opened up a way to Abingdon, there were still those who thought that a new and better road was needed. In 1855 William L. Rice laid the case before the County Court. Subsequently a committee was appointed to view and mark out the most suitable route. This road left the Jonesboro stage route three miles west of Abingdon and came into Bristol-Goodson on the west side of the railroad into Depot and Russell Streets, finally entering Fourth (later Front Street and now Randall Expressway). On May 16, 1876, the court was petitioned to change the road to the east side of the railroad to enter Bristol along Washington Street. The petition to do so was granted.

About 1857 a grade was made from the east end of Main Street up the slope by the present East Hill Cemetery to make connection with the road that ran from Paperville to the Island Road. Very early the Holston Valley Pike was established, leaving Bristol along what is now Pennsylvania Avenue and running through the dense Fairmount Forest on the Linnwood plantation. This proved to be a very profitable move for Bristol merchants, in that it opened up a large and prosperous trade area, whose business had previously been largely given to Abingdon.

Another important "established" road, that is, one deliberately planned, was the Lebanon Pike. Early Bristol businessmen knew the importance of easy travel from Russell County to their town. Therefore a diligent effort was made to find the shortest and best route between the two points. The old survey, now stored among the loose court papers in Abingdon, Virginia, shows that the Lebanon Pike followed what is now Highway 19 through the Moccasin Gap to Holston, Virginia. Then following what is officially Garrett Creek but locally known as the Possum Hollow, it entered Rich Valley on the Garrett lands and thence by way of Black Hollow and Maple Grove to Wallace and Walnut Grove into Bristol. Those who drive the Possum Hollow section of this road now must realize what an undertaking it was for those driving wagons and teams.

When a degree of normalcy returned to the land after the Civil War, Joseph R. Anderson sought to organize the Bristol and Kendrick Creek Turnpike Company. The organization was perfected in February 1868, and chartered by the State of Tennessee on Wednesday, March 4, the same year. Joseph R. Anderson was the first secretary, and William Mullinix was the first treasurer. The books were opened to receive subscriptions at a meeting at the Blountville courthouse on Monday, April 6, 1868. Present to transact the business were William Mullinix, Joseph R. Anderson, John G. King, John Spurgeon, Jesse Childers, and Rolla P. Scott. The subscription that day was as follows:

SUBSCRIBER	SHARES	AMOUNT
Joseph R. Anderson	16	$400.00
John G. King	5	125.00
William Mullinix	4	100.00
William Perry	4	100.00
John Spurgeon	4	100.00
Gideon Cate	2	50.00
Andrew F. Coin	2	50.00
John L. Rhea	2	50.00
Jesse Childers	1	25.00

This subscription of one thousand dollars was enlarged that same day (April 6, 1868) by Sullivan County's purchase of 200 shares for five thousand dollars.

On Tuesday, April 14, 1868, William Mullinix, Joseph R. Anderson, John G. King, Gideon Cate, John L. Rhea, Jesse Childers, and William Perry were elected directors of the organization. On motion of Joseph R. Anderson, William Mullinix was elected president. Anderson then became the permanent secretary and treasurer. At that time Thomas D. Walthall was hired as chief surveyor and engineer. Specifications called for the road to be eighteen feet wide on hills and twenty-two feet wide in the lowlands. It was to run from Bristol by way of Blountville and Childress Ferry and terminate on Kendrick Creek with the Jonesboro and Reedy Creek Road. Most of the county subscription was paid in scrip to workmen in amounts ranging from fifty cents to three dollars. This united effort between a private company and Sullivan County provided better transportation for a large trade area.

The earliest Bristol merchants had to depend upon freight haulers for early store stocks. One of the earliest of these was Isaac Steffner. Another was Henry Bloomfield. Both had left Bristol by 1860, Steffner to settle near Sweetwater, Tennessee, and Bloomfield to settle near what is now Sikeston, Missouri. In the spring of 1855 Lewis Bachelor set up a local draying service but also did some long-distance hauling. These early freighters went to whatever point the railroad had reached to get their wares. In 1854 the railroad, which had been pushing westward from Lynchburg since 1850, reached Emory, Virginia. It was from there that most of the stock for the earliest merchants in Bristol was hauled. From old records it has been learned that freight charges from Emory amounted to about fifty cents per hundred pounds.

Once when Henry Bloomfield was on a freight haul from Emory, he had an unforgettable experience. Late at night he was nearing Bristol, driving along Beaver Creek at what is now Mumpower Park. A bandit stepped from the dense brush and stopped the team. Brandishing a gun, he demanded that Bloomfield surrender his weapon (a pistol) and hand over his money. Fearing for his life, the freight hauler quickly complied. The robber paused briefly, as if in deep thought, then handing the gun back to Bloomfield, he said, "Here, you'd better keep this. You might run into another robber before you get into Bristol." Having so said, he sprang back into the brush.

The noted Zack Burson, who operated an extensive freight service throughout several states, also delivered goods in those earliest days of Bristol, where he settled after the Civil War. But in spite of horses, wagons and stage coaches, there were some who arrived by the most primitive method of travel, walking. The noted David F. Bailey, later a great lawyer and politician, walked into Bristol just before the Civil War. The same Bailey always went barefoot around his home and sometimes would forget and come downtown without his shoes. Some called him "Barefoot" Bailey. In the summer of 1858 a young couple, having been reduced to dire poverty in their hometown of Lebanon, Russell County, Virginia, walked to Bristol. The husband pushed a wheelbarrow that bore the bare necessities; the wife carried a babe in arms, and behind her trailed a six-year-old girl (two children had died in Russell County). In Bristol, they offered all they had—their labor. In time they became moderately prosperous. Another man walked to Bristol from Whitesburg, Kentucky, went to work for Joseph Anderson, slept in back of Anderson's store, and in time had a store of his own. The growing Bristol offered hope to the enterprising. Many would come even if it meant walking every step of the way. And there were always those who, if they could manage it, stole free rides on the freight cars. A young man rode into Bristol in this manner in 1859. He has prosperous and respectable descendants who are well known in Bristol today.

When the Virginia and Tennessee Railway finally reached Bristol in 1856 the need for wagon freight was virtually ended. It was then that freight haulers from farther down in Tennessee began to come to Bristol for supplies, as others had gone to Emory in former days. Indeed, a few of these merchants came with their wagons, saw what was happening on the border, and permanently settled in Bristol. John Kneeland was one of the first to do so.

But surprisingly, the coming of trains to Bristol did not immediately end the stage service. However, most of the business from that time was beyond Bristol, toward Blountville, Kingsport and Rogersville. It appears that the service ended near the beginning of the Civil War. However, soon after the war, Henry Nave, who had been a stage driver in the earlier years, secured one of the old coaches that had long been in storage in Abingdon and started service from Bristol to Estillville (Gate City) by way of Blountville and Kingsport. Later he added a freight service. Both services were operating as late as 1879 and may have continued for some time afterwards. An old gentleman living here thirty-seven years ago once told this author that as a youth he had ridden Nave's stagecoach to old Kingsport. He recalled that there had been heavy rains the night before, causing the road up Eaton's Ridge to be hard to trasverse. About halfway up, all passengers had to alight and help push the coach through the deep mud. It is of interest to note that Bristol-Goodson, Virginia, had a stagecoach tax as late as 1872.

Mention has been made in another chapter of the town's first "taxi" service as offered by Rosetta Bachelor. Later, J. C. Conway, of Conway Hall fame, offered the same type of service. His "taxi" was a hack. He later added a surrey. A. M. Keys was driving for him in the early 1880s. The charge then was one dollar for the first hour and fifty cents for each hour thereafter. A special was a trip to the fairground and back for twenty-five cents. Conway's taxi service continued for several years.

THE RAILROADS

Of course the coming of the Virginia and Tennessee railroad in 1856 gave the town and area its biggest boost in the matter of transportation. And the completion of this railroad greatly aided the matter of bringing in materials

Mrs. William G. Lindsey (formerly Rebecca Josephine Templin) is pictured above with her grandson, Charles Herman Dixon. Her husband was at the throttle of the first train into Bristol, October 1, 1856.

to finish the East Tennessee and Virginia railway, which would enter Bristol from the southwest. The latter railroad came near to losing its charter but was saved by thirty of the wealthiest men who lived along or near the proposed route. This group, later called the Immortal Thirty, included Joseph Anderson of Bristol and his uncle Samuel Rhea of Blountville. When the connection was finally made in early 1858, the eastern seaboard was at last linked to the Mississippi valley. This northeast to southwest route became a very important supply line during the Civil War. The East Tennessee and Virginia merged with the East Tennessee and Georgia on February 24, 1869, and became the East Tennessee, Virginia and Georgia Railroad. It became a part of the Southern Railways system on August 1, 1894.

Rail service in those early days left much to be desired. Riding in the cars over rough tracks was but a little more comfortable than the lurching of stage coaches over rocky roads. Heavy smoke from the woodburning engines poured through the open coach windows in summer (cinders would later become a greater hazard). When stopped for long periods of time, as often happened, the coaches became stifling hot. In winter those nearest the coach stoves roasted while those farthest away shivered and froze. The first train from Lynchburg (204 miles) took fifteen hours to make the trip, and speed did not greatly increase for several years. From Knoxville to Bristol then required nine hours. By 1869 the traveling time from Lynchburg to Bristol had been cut to twelve and one-half hours. Traveling time between Bristol and Knoxville had been reduced to seven and one-half hours. Twelve years later (1881), passenger trains made it to Knoxville in a little over five hours, and the Lynchburg run only required about nine hours. Four years later nearly an hour had been cut from the latter run, but the trip to Knoxville required about the same time as it had in 1881.

From the beginning the trains ran on through the night, but speed had to be greatly reduced because of poor head lighting. The coaches were poorly lighted by oil lamps, left burning all night for safety's sake. The seats were about as rigid and straight as church pews. Rare was the person who could sleep while seated on them. No meals were served on the trains. Bristol was one of the meal stops where passengers might alight and have a hasty repast. Twenty-eight minutes was the allotted time for the Bristol meal stop. Hotel help had the meal spread and waiting when the train arrived. One toothless man bitterly complained that he could take little nourishment in that short a time. And a hotel manager complained that often passengers "fled his dining room" hurrying to make a train and forgetting to pay. Thereafter he stood by the door collecting as the passengers came in.

Bristol was not only a lunch stop, but for several years it had the unsavory reputation of being the "mosquito stop." West of the depot was an area known as frog level. This swampy area served as a harboring place for swarms of mosquitos. When open-windowed trains stopped during summer months, many of these tormenting creatures flew into the coaches. Once there they stayed, much to the discomfort of weary travelers. Many a mosquito took free passage to Knoxville or Lynchburg. The situation did not ease until frog level was drained, filled in, and covered with buildings.

For years there was no through passenger service. Those who came in on either the Virginia and Tennessee or the East Tennessee and Virginia had to alight and walk across the state line to one or the other of the depots. In cold, snowy, or rainy weather this was a real inconvenience. This situation did not change until some time in the 1870s. Fare on the Virginia and Tennessee Railway was four cents per mile in 1869. On the East Tennessee and

Virginia the fare was five cents per mile. Wood to fire the engines was usually stacked at local depots, but occasionally there were pickup points far out in the country. Often, bored male passengers alighted to help load the wood. In the early days there was a large wood yard immediately east of the Bristol depot.

Early freight trains were limited to fifteen cars. Movement was very slow. In 1869 twenty-five hours were required for the trip from Bristol to Lynchburg. In 1870 the Virginia and Tennessee Railroad merged with the Southside line and came under the control of General Mahone. The name then became the Atlantic, Mississippi and Ohio. Soon after Mahone took control some noted improvements were made. One of the first of these was the addition of what was then called the Pullman Palace Car. The first Pullman was brought into Bristol on Friday, April 12, 1872. As was the case at major points along the line, the car was put on display for one hour, during which time many townsmen passed through and noted the grand features of the new traveling luxury. Editor Fowler wrote of it in glowing terms:

> The Pullman Palace Car is worthy of enrollment among the prime luxuries of the nineteenth century. Our great air line thoroughfare is now amply stocked with these elegant appliances of travel, which without change to the traveler run through from Lynchburg to Mobile and will doubtless soon run to New Orleans.... The new cars are superb, being elegantly furnished, is [sic] spacious and roomy, and affords the traveler that which has heretofore been the exclusive province of home, repose. It is heated by steam pipes, uniformly at all points. Aside from the shaded lamps near the roof, each berth or pair of seats is furnished with a lamp, which, when desired, can be concealed, or exposed by elevating or dropping a heavy plate French mirror. The saloons and facilities for ablutions are models of mechanical perfection. To secure the exclusion of heat, cold, dampness, and dust, the windows are double.

Fowler mentioned in the same article that the roadbed was being improved with new ballast and rails, which would make for a much smoother ride. He also praised the passenger train conductors, calling them urbane and efficient gentlemen.

Another improvement which made for railroad safety was the addition of the air brake. The first passenger train of the AM&O to be so equipped came into Bristol on Tuesday, March 11, 1873. Editor Fowler wrote of the event in the next issue of his *Bristol News:*

> The new air brake is now in experimental use on one of the local passenger trains. On seeing the rapid approach of the train on the down grade to our passenger exchange, one would think that the engineer

meant to stop about a half mile beyond, but quick as thought almost, it stops at the desired spot. Capt. Jacques expresses himself as much pleased with the brake, which is the invention of Messrs. Westinghouse and Company of Schenectady, New York, a firm which has become famous for its superb threshers.

The improvement of the coupling mechanism was another great advancement in the field of railroad safety. In the early 1870s a passenger train headed for Bristol had the last coach break loose and roll backward down an incline, finally leaving the track and plunging into a deep ravine. Several were severely injured and three were killed, including a Bristol resident. This resident was a close friend of George Pile, local businessman and mechanical genius. Deeply troubled by the loss of this friend, Pile set to work to design a much better railroad coupler. His invention became widely used on the railroads of the nation.

It may be here mentioned that in those days railroad accidents were far too common and tragic. One that received much notoriety was the head-on collision of two freight trains near Piney Flats, Tennessee, on December 19, 1874. The *Bristol News* gave details of the accident:

> Last Saturday morning the up and the down freight trains collided seventeen miles west of Bristol and three miles east of Carter depot. But for the heroic action of a little girl who heard both trains approaching from opposite directions the result would have been much more dreadful. Comprehending the situation with wonderful precision, she gathered a red shawl and came very near being killed in her effort to stop the up train which was only able to slack its speed to about eight miles per hour, when it was met by the down train, and both engines leaped into the air and fell backward, killing J. Crouse, who lived near Union Depot (Bluff City), and was riding in the cab, endeavoring to reach Knoxville in quest of employment. And also (killed was) William Wyatt of this town, but formerly of Emory, Virginia. The latter was firing for fireman William Henderson who had been injured in one foot and was along in order to direct Wyatt as his substitute. Henderson was a good deal bruised up, but not seriously injured, and Mr. C. C. Trainham of this town, the engineer of the down train, had a leg broken and is otherwise bruised but will recover. Captain Ryland, conductor of the down train, was slightly injured, as were conductor Dooley, Engineer Staub and others, who owing to the brave little girl's warning were enabled to leap from the train. Both of the killed and Mr. Trainham were on the down train. Two car loads of goods and one car containing salt were burned and both the trains and both engines badly damaged.

The brave little girl, who came of a poor family, was later brought to Bristol and given a good education at Sullins College at the expense of several local citizens.

Under General Mahone, the AM&O instituted an express service that was of great benefit to local commerce. From near the beginning of rail service to Bristol, express shipments had been handled by a private firm known as the Southern Express Company. Before the Civil War this company had built a brick express station near the northern end of the depot passenger shed. Mahone set up what he called the Local Express which was a part of the railroad service. It was as fast as had been the service of the Southern Express Company and cut shipping rates by about one half. The old rate of $1.25 per hundred pounds from Bristol to Lynchburg was reduced to sixty-five cents. The same weight to New York had formerly cost $4.00 and was then cut to $2.10. The Local Express began to serve Bristol in July 1872.

In 1876 the AM&O went into receivership. About that time fire destroyed the Lynchburg roundhouse. In 1877 the line was bought by E. L. Clark and Company. Old newspaper articles indicate that the Louisville and Nashville Railroad Company owned the line for a brief period soon thereafter. It was then that a campaign was waged to have a near-cut line from Nashville to Bristol. By 1881 the line had become the Norfolk and Western.

THE BRISTOL DEPOTS

Both sides of Bristol had depots before the railroads were completed. That at Bristol-Goodson, Virginia, had been completed well before the arrival of the first train. (J. M. Fields was the builder.) The depot on the Tennessee side was started in 1857 and was completed just before the arrival of the first train in 1858. Both these depots were burned by Stoneman's raiders on December 14, 1864. According to old reports both railroads were using freight cars as depots at the conclusion of the war.

The depot on the Virginia side was rebuilt in late 1865 and early 1866. It is not known if the Tennessee depot was immediately rebuilt. However in March 1872 it was announced that the East Tennessee and Virginia Railroad planned to build a new depot and engine house in Bristol. Apparently this depot served until a union depot of sorts was established on the Virginia side of town. It is known that the Tennessee depot was still standing as late as March 29, 1881.

The year 1881 brought great improvement in local railroad facilities. Indicative of this was an advertisement that appeared in the *Bristol News* of Tuesday, May 24, 1881:

Sealed proposals will be received up until 12 o'clock noon on Wednesday the 1st of June at the office of the Supt. of Road Department of the Norfolk and Western Railroad at Petersburg for building a brick freight depot and office for the Norfolk and Western Railroad Company at Bristol. Plans and specifications can be seen after Thursday, the 26th of May, on application at the Company's Store House in Lynchburg, or of C. E. Finch, Depot Agent, Bristol. The company reserves the right to refuse any or all proposals.

It is known that William H. Smith and John M. Crowell, two leading builders, bid on this project, but the author has found no record as to who was successful. Progress was reported in the August 16, 1881, issue of the *Bristol News:*

The Norfolk and Western is pushing the local improvements steadily. The large stone culvert is nearly complete and brick are being delivered on the spot for the new depot. Captain Hunter was in town last Saturday and located the basement which will soon be excavated. The passenger shed begins to look well with its new tin roof. It is 326 feet long with platforms the entire length, and platforms on Front Street for the Narrow Gauge connection. The eaves and sides are being made quite ornamental, with projecting entrances.

It is known that John Powers did the excavating for this project and that his work had started by August 23, 1881. Local agent C. E. Finch estimated that the project would be completed by January 1, 1882. Powers may have had the contract for painting the passenger shed roof, a job done in August 1881. On September 4, 1881, while Powers was excavating the site, one of his horses broke through the roof of a cave and fell several feet into the opening. It was a great task to bring the animal out. This cave was said to be near the northeast corner of the new depot. Apparently the depot erected in 1881 served until the present building was erected soon after the turn of the century. The freight depot, erected at the same time and later added to and remodeled, burned in December 1987.

The Norfolk and Western also enlarged its switch yard in 1881. All lots between the railroad and Washington Street were bought at that time. These lots cost the railroad around three hundred each, with the exception of Kirby's Tanyard, which brought fifteen hundred. This purchase gave room for three more tracks to be added to the yard.

An early station agent was William Philip Brewer, who was serving in that capacity before 1861. In 1865 W. S. Minor was agent at a salary of $36.52 per month. By 1881 the station had come under agent Charles E. Finch, who was a son-in-law of L. F. Johnson, an early settler and merchant of Bristol. Mr. Finch served for at least ten years. He was also a member of the Common Council of Goodson, and it was his resolution that caused the name change in 1890. At some point during those early years, probably in the late 1870s, S. Y. B. Williams was the local ticket agent. Perhaps it may be well to mention that at various times Bristol had other depots. One was built on Scott Street, on the north side of the first block below the present Randall Expressway. This was to serve what was originally the South Atlantic and Ohio Railway. Another was erected for the Bristol, Elizabethton, and North Carolina Railroad. It stood immediately west of Commonwealth Avenue, a short distance north of present State Street.

OTHER RAILROADS

Several years before the Civil War there was an effort to establish a railroad leading from Abingdon, Virginia, to Cumberland Gap, Kentucky. Later the move shifted to make Bristol, Virginia, the starting point. The Virginia and Kentucky Railroad was chartered for this purpose. The advent of the Civil War delayed the plan for several years. Indeed, it appears that work did not resume until July 1872. However, due to a lack of financial support, work ceased when only a few miles of the route had been graded. About three years later several Bristolians sought to revive the railroad. The first meeting to organize for the purpose was held in the store of W. W. James on October 27, 1875. Then on March 27, 1876, the Virginia General Assembly granted the rights and privileges of the old Virginia and Kentucky Railroad to what was to be known as the Bristol Coal and Iron Narrow Gauge Railway. This company became commonly known as the Narrow Gauge or simply the N.G. Railway. The original stockholders of this company and number of shares held are as follows:

Scott County, Va.	250
Town of Bristol-Goodson	50
Henry C. Wood	4
J. H. Wood	2
W. W. James	2
J. R. Hill	2
Martin B. Wood	2
Joel Kaylor (Mendota)	5
R. A. Ayers	2
S. R. Ferguson	1
David F. Bailey	1
C. J. Cocke	1
D. A. Wheeler	1
S. P. McConnell	1
R. S. Payne	1
John F. Terry	1

Abram Fulkerson	1
Isaac A. Nickels	1
I. C. Fowler	1
Col. J. M. Barker	1
Thomas E. Bibb	1
Dr. J. F. Hicks	1
H. W. Holdway	1
E. H. Quillen	1
Fugate and Gibson	1
E. B. Hilton	1
Patrick Hagan	1
W. D. Jones	1
J. H. Winston	1
John G. Wood	1
Rev. David Sullins	1
C. H. Lewis	1

Shares in the Narrow Gauge Railway were valued at $20.00 each. Henry Clinton Wood was elected first president of this company. He was a native of Scott County, Virginia, and a prominent businessman and politician. In 1879 he was elected state senator by a large majority. He was commonly known as Clint Wood, and the two names put together is the source of the name for Clintwood, Virginia. He later moved to Bristol, where he successfully engaged in various business pursuits. The vice-president was W. W. James, Bristol merchant. Col. J. M. Barker was the first secretary and treasurer. He later resigned and became a director. John F. Terry then replaced Col. Barker. In August 1879 W. W. James turned the first shovel of dirt on construction of the Narrow Gauge road. This was done at a point near the present intersection of Scott Street and Randall Expressway. Virtually the entire town turned out for the event. There were speeches by I. C. Fowler and Col. R. M. Wiley, followed by free lemonade and watermelon for all.

A great boon to the proposed road was free prison labor. On July 22, 1879, Major Henry C. Wood arrived back in Bristol from Richmond with thirty-five prisoners and guards. Work had not then commenced on the road, so that it was necessary to set up camp in Mosby Grove (to the west of Piedmont and north of Scott Street). L. F. Johnson wrote of seeing the motley crew marched from the depot down Scott to this location. He tells of the great fear that settled over the town because of this prison camp. Doors were barred at night, citizens slept with guns within easy reach, and children were cautioned not to go near the camp. Hardly any one ventured forth to walk in darkness. About the only local citizens glad to have the camp were local merchants, who stood to gain by the sale of supplies for the prisoners. Almost daily "Tub" Wicks, a trustee and the camp cook, came downtown with his cart and tub to gather up foodstuffs for his "kitchen."

The state allowed thirty-five cents per day for the feeding of prisoners, but Wood hoped to cut the cost to ten cents. Each prisoner was allowed one ounce of coffee and one ounce of sugar each day. When they later camped near present Benhams, they purchased enough cornmeal to realize Major Wood's hope for a ten-cent food cost. The prisoners moved on with the road, and the further from Bristol they were, the easier town residents breathed. It is known that one of their camps was at Phillips, near Mendota, Virginia.

Though the deep dark forests that lay along a great portion of the route must have tempted many a prisoner to flee, there is record of only one who tried it. Of course, one strong deterrent to escape attempts was the law that a prisoner so doing would have his time doubled. But poor Frank Thomas, who had been sent up from Lynchburg for having "carved" a fellow mortal with a razor, could not squelch the urge. While work was being done near Benhams, he played sick, stole a pair of overalls, and fled into the woods. He was later spotted in Bristol—which didn't help local nerves any—but again eluded capture and fled toward Shady Valley. He was never recaptured.

Thomas E. Bibb and Chalmers King were the first civil engineers on this route. King died soon after work started and was replaced by J. H. McCue. One great outside promoter and financial backer of the N. G. Railway was General John D. Imboden. He had become aware of the vast coal deposits in southwestern Virginia and hoped to engage in their profitable development. In Bristol he took up near-permanent residence in the Virginia Hotel, later moving his family in with him. He planned a great Imboden City for the center of the coal fields. It was well surveyed and mapped, and Martin B. Wood became chief agent for the development. On at least one occasion, Wood set up a room in the Virginia House to display his maps and sign up buyers for the lots. He pleaded with local citizens to hurry as choice lots were going fast. But like so many planned cities, the choice lots remained a wilderness. There was long a small coal camp known as Imboden.

A long-range plan of Imboden's was to make the N. G. a link in a great trunk line extending from Wilmington, North Carolina, to Cincinnati, Ohio. Much surveying was done for the possible routes. One of these passed about mid-block between Edmond and Spencer Streets, crossed the AM&O tracks, and swung around to Campbell's Grove (site of Athens Steak House), then angled southwestward, but keeping north of the Tennessee tracks, and on into the country. Then it roughly followed Weaver Pike for some distance then angled to cross the Holston River just below Rockhold's Methodist Church, then up Dry Branch and on toward Elizabethton. This line was located by Capt. T. D. Walthall, who did much surveying in very early Bristol. Out along the northwestern portion of the proposed line, plans were being made for the coming boom. Joel Kaylor, a wealthy citizen from Phillips, gave a lot in the village of Mendota for a depot. Others were depending on increased land values because of proximity to the line. Many gladly gave the right-of-way, while others delighted in the money received in payment for passage through farms. Capt. J. H. Wood, who built Pleasant Hill, home of this writer, spent much time along the route negotiating for paid or free passage.

But the best laid plans of men often lead to disappointment. Because of a lack of financial backing, work had to cease on the Narrow Gauge about 1882. Bushes and blackberry vines covered much of the newly graded roadbed. And where cars should have rolled along steel rails, local residents rode their horses or walked, making the roadbed a trail and bridle path.

Then came the flamboyant Dr. J. M. Bailey, who, with the backing of Boston capitalists, revived interest in completing the road. In the hope that a connection could still be made between Wilmington, North Carolina, and Cincinnati, Ohio, the name was changed to the South Atlantic and Ohio Railroad. Before the autumn of 1887 the company had completed and put into operation about thirty-eight miles of track. Work continued until the track from Bristol to Big Stone Gap, Virginia, was opened for operation on May 1, 1890. Not long afterwards the line was extended to Appalachia to connect with the Louisville & Nashville. In 1899 the South Atlantic and Ohio was acquired by George L. Carter, who changed the name to the Virginia and Southwestern. This railroad was incorporated February 21, 1899.

In January 1887 Joseph R. Anderson appeared before the Mayor and Alderman of Bristol, Tennessee, asking for support of the proposed Bristol and South Atlantic Railroad. This line would pass through Elizabethton into North Carolina and angle southeastward to Wilmington. The route had been surveyed to the eastern seaboard by General Imboden several years before Anderson's request. It is said that the death of Anderson in 1888 caused the languishing of the plans for this line. Then on April 25, 1889, the Bristol, Elizabethton and North Carolina Railway was incorporated by Major A. D. Reynolds and Associates. Twenty-two miles of trackage had been completed by December 31, 1892, by the Unaka Construction Company. The line was sold by foreclosure on June 6, 1895, to A. H. Winterstein, whose deed is dated June 14th that year. A little later it was taken over by Ben L. Dulaney and F. M. Leonard. The railroad operated under the same name until it was sold to the Virginia and Southwestern on February 23, 1899.

Had all the railroads been built that were planned to originate, terminate, or pass through Bristol, a map of the area would resemble a cobweb! Mention has been made of the Danville and East Tennessee. Had this line been built it would have entered Bristol along Vermont Avenue, crossed Mary

Street just west of Beaver Creek, passed down Beaver, crossed Williams Street, curved around the base of the hill near Second Taylor Street, passed directly behind the Athens Steak House (old Campbell's Grove), and then joined the Norfolk and Western at the mouth of Buford Street. Another proposed but never built road was from Nashville and Lebanon, Tennessee, by way of Rogersville, Kingsport, and Blountville to Bristol. This line would have entered Bristol along Euclid Avenue to join the South Atlantic and Ohio near the end of Fairmount. Editor Fowler highly favored this road, writing that it would avoid the galling need to go all the way to Chattanooga in order to reach Nashville.

EARLY RAILROAD COSTS

In 1879 the average cost of a railroad engine was $3,700.00. A passenger coach cost $1,200.00. Freight cars sold for approximately $500.00. A mile of track averaged $2,346.00, but the cost could greatly vary. The first two miles of the Narrow Gauge Railroad cost only $1,500.50. This was mostly due to the cheap convict labor, but it did include the cost of tools and the salaries of the engineers. It was estimated that the total cost of the twenty-eight miles to Estillville (Gate City) would be $46,039.76. Crossties, numbering some sixty thousand for this portion of the road, were made by R. P. Smith and Son and cost about eighteen cents each. Smith worked 65 hands at eighty cents per day on this project but charged thirty cents a day for rations. On March 15, 1881, he gave notice that he had as many hands as he needed.

RAILROAD FEVER SPAWNS DRIVE FOR NEW COUNTY

When it finally became certain that the South Atlantic and Ohio Railroad was going to be built, there was a move toward development of the town of Mendota. Some of the leading citizens of the area went a step further and reasoned why not have a new county for that area with Mendota as the county seat. Several names were suggested for this proposed county, among them Kaylor, Barker, Clinch, Pleasant and Mountain. By petition a vote was set on the question for the first Monday in November 1887. The vote was 3,306 against the measure to only 413 for it. Bristol-Goodson cast nine votes for the new county but 509 votes against it. The measure was put before the voters again in 1889 but was defeated by an even greater number. The last effort to form this county was made in 1893, but the voters turned it down by six to one.

THE BRISTOL STREETCAR SYSTEM

On September 18, 1853, Joseph R. Anderson and family had arrived in the planned development of Bristol, Virginia-Tennessee, by wagon and riding over fields and meadow where not a single street or road existed. On Tuesday night, July 24, 1888, less than thirty-five years later, the streetcar system opened where so soon before had only been those fields, meadows and woods. Indeed, Bristol had experienced a remarkable growth.

The real impetus behind the organization of the Bristol Street Car Company was the proposed development of the Fairmount Forest section of Bristol, Tennessee. Most of this section was far from downtown, and this situation created a need for public transportation. Too, there was strong talk of spreading westward along Windsor Avenue and vicinity, which would also require a measure of the same service. The Bristol Street Car Company was organized on November 2, 1886, at a meeting in the room of F. S. Sampson at the Nickels House Hotel. The organizers were Col. J. M. Barker, who became the first president of the company, Major A. D. Reynolds, who was the first secretary and treasurer, and F. S. Sampson, who was general superintendent of the project. The company received its charter from the State of Tennessee on December 1, 1886. On Monday, January 10, 1887, this company applied to the Board of Mayor and Aldermen of Bristol, Tennessee, for a

By the late 1880s travel was improving in Bristol. Here is pictured the town's first street car.

franchise. One week later this franchise was granted. One day after the granting of this franchise, the company advertised for bids on construction of the line. For a time the effort stalled. But in April 1888 application was made for the privilege of electric trolleys, when and if desired. The city stipulated that the company must maintain that portion of the street enclosed by the rails and two feet on either side thereof. It was further required that the fare could not exceed five cents. By May 16, 1888, the line survey was being made from State (Main) Street to the Fairmount section. The tracks were of thirty pound rail and were first laid from the proposed site of the Hotel Fairmount over to Pennsylvania Avenue and along that avenue and down Main to Ninth Street.

The stables were located on the northeast corner of Pennsylvania and Ash Street. The first streetcar was pulled by two horses, and the first run was made on Tuesday night, July 24, 1888. The rides were free, and of course the cars were filled. A small band played on one of the cars.

Capitalists on the Virginia side had not been idle. Long before the first run was made in Bristol, Tennessee, the Bristol-Goodson Street Railway Company had been organized. The move was led by Dr. John M. Bailey, who became first president of the resultant company. W. D. Jones was first vice-president, William G. Sheen was first secretary, and W. W. James was the treasurer. The board of directors was made up of Charles James, J. H. Brittain and J. J. McSpiden. By a special drive, forty thousand dollars had been raised in one day for the promotion of the project. By May 26, 1888, rails and other supplies had been ordered and car sheds had been let to contract. The projection was that cars would be rolling on the Virginia side by November 1888. By July 15, 1888, the Virginia company had ordered two summer cars, grading was virtually completed, and service was expected to begin soon. It seems that the furthest projected point for this line at the time was the veneer factory and the railroad car works, near the present intersection of Euclid and Commonwealth. It appears that the Virginia operation was later taken over by the Bristol Belt Line Railway.

In August 1888 the Tennessee company was planning a steam-powered line to Sulphur Springs, four miles down Beaver Creek, but this line was never built. By late 1889 or early 1890 streetcar service had stopped in Bristol, Tennessee. Perhaps the fact that the line had grossed only $700.00 for the year 1889 caused the shutdown.

In early 1890 a charter was granted to the Bristol Belt Line Railway. This company was organized by James Strong, who became its first president; Ben L. Dulaney, who became first vice president; and S. M. Vance, who was the first general superintendent. The firm was capitalized at two hundred and fifty thousand dollars. It was granted a fifty-year franchise for the use of electric trolleys. Work on this line began in October 1890, but due to a hard winter was not finished until well into 1891. In the spring of 1891 this company agreed to supply electric power to the town from newly installed dynamos. When opened, the Bristol Belt Line Railway pulled its streetcars with a small steam engine. On November 1, 1891, at 2:20 P.M., the first electrically powered run was made. The new streetcar company used the route of its predecessor (along Poplar from the Fairmount Hotel area, north on Pennsylvania to Main, and west on Main to Ninth) but extended the route along Main to Seventeenth Street, then south to Windsor Avenue. Less than two weeks after the first electrically powered run, the company announced plans to extend the line to Blountville, Tennessee, and a little later the plan was enlarged to include service to Kingsport. But these grand plans never materialized. On the night of December 19, 1891, the car barn burned, destroying all the rolling stock. Kack Overstreet, the elderly keeper of the barn, was later found dead within the hoops of an oil barrel. It was later determined that another employee had killed Mr. Overstreet, stuffed his body into the barrel, and then set fire to the barn. The murderer-arsonist was tried, convicted, and given life imprisonment. Because of the car loss, service was discontinued for nearly one month, and resumed on January 17, 1892.

Tragedy struck again on May 13, 1892, when one of the cars was hit by a South Atlantic and Ohio freight train on present Commonwealth Avenue. Two passengers were injured, and the conductor, Alfred Parrott, was killed. By mid-1894 the company again had plans for service to Sulphur Springs on Beaver. The plan then was to use the tracks of the Bristol and Elizabethton Railroad. But again the plan was scrapped. At first the lines closed down during the hardest winter months, usually resuming full service by April 1, each year. However, business had increased to the point that all-winter service was announced to begin in 1897. But because the employees' wages were cut by twenty percent, a strike resulted and winter service was again abandoned. It was during that time that the company began to take up the heavy rails on Euclid Avenue and lay them down Main Street. It seems that an agreement had been reached with the Norfolk and Western whereby a connection of the upgraded line would be made to the freight yard. Thus the N & W could bring heavy cars through the downtown section of Bristol to reach the iron furnaces that were located west of Commonwealth. The furor that resulted over the removal of the tracks from Euclid Avenue resulted in the revoking of the Bristol Belt Line's franchise for the Virginia side of Bristol. This ended service in Bristol, Virginia, for a time (service for that city had been suspended temporarily in 1896).

On Valentine's Day 1899 fire again destroyed the storage building of the streetcar line. It was then that property was purchased on the corner of Shelby and Commerce Street (Pap's Alley). Immediately construction began on an enlarged car barn and power station. This was completed in two months, at which time service was resumed.

It was also in 1899 that a new line was built to King's Spring south of Bristol. This line followed Fourth to Anderson and then out Alabama Street. King's Spring was a popular resort at the time, and it was thought that there would be high patronage of this extension. It was later noted that the line was a total failure. However, the company, aware of the likely increase in settlement of South Bristol, continued to hold on to the franchise.

One short extension of the streetcar line was made from the Fairmount Hotel on Spruce Street to the Holston Valley Railway station on Georgia Avenue near Lakeside. The Holston Valley, a common carrier railroad had been incorporated on September 10, 1892, mainly for the purpose of hauling logs from the mountains beyond the South Fork of the Holston River to the A. F. Willey Lumber Mill. A little later a resort was developed on Big Creek, to which Bristolians often traveled during the hot summer months. This created a need for passenger service which was soon instituted by the Holston Valley line. The streetcar line extension was a great convenience for local residents.

COMMUNICATION

No doubt when the first few cottages dotted the area that is now the oldest portion of Bristol, the only communication between the town's residents had to be personal, that is, by face to face conversation or by written messages that were hand delivered. Community gatherings—most often of a religious nature—meant a time of news sharing, message sending, and announcement making. It has been told this writer that ministers of the period often made secular announcements from the pulpit, much to the dismay of some of the "holier members." The early newspapers did much to disseminate important information in the community.

One early railroad conductor, a Capt. Thomas Gilreath, had a propensity to gather up news along the line and to loudly proclaim it from a coach door of his stopped train. Consequently, a large crowd always gathered when Capt. Tom was expected. Among the crowd was always the local newspaper editor, who got much copy for his paper in that manner.

Very early—at least by late 1855 or early 1856—a heavy gong was hung on Fourth Street (later Front) near the Virginia House Hotel (later the Magnolia Hotel). A mallet was kept hanging by it. When an alarm needed to be sounded, or when the townsmen needed to be assembled to hear important news, the mallet was strongly applied, and there was a deep booming, throbbing, sound that could be heard all over the Town of Bristol and adjoining Goodsonville. This gong was later moved to a location near the intersection of present Fifth and Shelby Streets and was used to within the early 1880s, when Hobson's mill whistle became the town alarm. A series of blasts from that whistle appraised the town of danger or called for an assembly to hear important news. An old timer told of how a half-drunk night watchman once greatly frightened Bristol residents by jarring loose at about 2:00 A.M. There was no danger to the town, but much danger to the watchman when several men of the town seized him and dunked him in Beaver Creek until he was nearly drowned. Years before, a never-caught prankster had awakened the town by hammering the gong.

In the very early years of the town there were two or three youths who were known as runners. When urgent messages needed to be carried, a nickel, dime or rarely a quarter would be pressed into eager hands and away these youths would go at full speed, sometimes for short distances in town and occasionally for long distances into the surrounding country. One of these was Isaac _____ (the informant could not remember the lad's last name), who lived in the home of John N. Bosang. Another, whose name is lost, met a sudden death while on a mission for Dr. F. L. Hartman. Dr. Hartman had been called to Paperville to see a seriously ill patient. He found that he did not have a certain medicine with him that he felt the patient desperately needed. He hastened back to Bristol, placed the potent drug in the hands of the runner, and bade him go at top speed to Paperville. The lad apparently ran every step of the way and, having made his delivery, started back to town. Along the way he came by a home where a watermelon was being cut and was invited to have some. He filled himself with cool melon and then, preparing to leave, fell dead at the front gate. Sudden death of one so young was very rare in those days, and its occurrence cast a spirit of solemnity over the town for days. Soon thereafter the local Methodist minister preached an hour long sermon on the uncertainty of life and received many converts at its conclusion. One older runner was Nehemiah Strange, a servant of Joseph R. Anderson. Though he was not as fleet of foot as the younger lads, he could, as L. F. Johnson, expressed it, go at "a pretty good gallop."

An old loose paper in the court files at Abingdon, Virginia, mentions that a debtor's sale had been "well shouted." This would have presented quite a mystery had not there been former knowledge of a common custom in early Bristol of shouting out announcements, notices, and sometimes news. The person so doing was commonly called the town shouter. As in the case of runners, the shouters were paid by the person who needed such services. The custom was that the shouter walk through the town, stop at eighteen-step intervals, and shout out the notice, announcement or important news. If the announcement concerned a public entertainment, the shouter might be induced to make a strong appeal for attendance if an extra nickel or dime had been pressed into his hand.

Debtor's sales were common, and it is said that the publicly shouting out of the debtor's name served as a strong incentive for the payment of overdue bills. Hugh Timmons, a young man who boarded at the Nickels House Hotel was an early shouter, as was the pioneer settler John N. Bosang. It is said that Bosang had a booming voice that could clearly be heard a long block away. And there was at least one lady shouter. Rosetta Bachelor delighted in what she called a "high job" for several years. Mrs. Bachelor livened up her notices and announcements with bits of juicy gossip. Indeed, she was more of a news carrier than a notice giver. But being horrified by the least moral transgression, she sometimes found herself in trouble for having not only publicly proclaimed the baser side of someone's nature, but having rendered a personal opinion thereon. There was the time when between announcements she shouted out that "Canzada L_____ is with her third child and never yet been married. Girls like her ought to be moved out of town.' Canzada's mother took offense and tried a little fighting with Rosetta but came out the loser. It is known that there were town shouters as late as 1877.

The telegraph wires reached Bristol at a very early date. At first these were exclusively for railway use. However, there are known cases of emergency when the railroad allowed individuals the use of the wires. But within a few years of the founding of the town, there was a public telegraph office here. One of its first locations was in a small room near the east end of the Nickels House Hotel. The operator slept in the room with his equipment and often received important or urgent messages during the night. At such times he rousted out "Legs" Hicks, who also lived in the hotel, to deliver the message. This practice continued for years. When John G. English, son-in-law of Rev. James King, died at Egypt, Mississippi, in 1887, the telegram telling of his death did not arrive in Bristol until in the wee hours of the morning. But Legs Hicks hastened through the darkened streets to bear the sad news to the English relatives here. At one time the telegraph office (called room in those days) was in a small room just off the lobby of the Virginia House Hotel and later in the century was in a former storeroom on Front Street.

In late 1882 or possibly very early 1883, Capt. J. H. Wood made a business trip to Baltimore, Maryland. While there he saw a demonstration of a contraption that was fast catching the fancy of the land - the telephone. It immediately dawned upon him that the amazing instrument would be of great benefit to him. Mrs. Wood had been ill for some time, causing him to make two or three trips daily from his office back to his home to see about her. With the telephone he could communicate without the time-consuming trips. He bought the makings of two and sufficient wire by which they could be connected. Capt. Wood had a young brother-in-law, W. W. James, Jr., who was rather mechanically inclined. This young Mr. James assembled the instruments and installed them, one in the bedroom of Mrs. Wood at 214 Johnson Street, and the other in Capt. Wood's office at number 1 Lee Street. The connecting line was strung along through trees and from building to building to make the connection between the two telephones. The room in which Bristol's first telephone was installed is now the dining room at Pleasant Hill, home of this author.

From information handed down, the ailing Mrs. Wood did not have much rest for months after this telephone was installed. The curious came often to talk and listen "through the wire." But Capt. Wood was very obliging, often opening his office on Sunday afternoons so that folks might converse between the two locations.

Others soon followed suit. It is thought that George B. Smith had the second set of telephones in Bristol, one in his home and one in his photography studio. And this store-to-home connection was the general rule for the first two or three years of telephone service in Bristol. In late 1886 several local families instituted the first party-line system. There were numerous connections on one line with no chance of private conversation. An alarm (ring) brought all subscribers to the phone if they desired, and most desired! If urgent news was on tap, the caller often "called the roll" (that is inquired if all were listening) before giving the news.

On at least one occasion this party-line system caused a law suit for malicious slander. Rosetta Bachelor, always aware of the real or supposed moral delinquency of Bristol residents, was once talking to a friend when she glanced out a window and saw a neighbor girl passing by. Suddenly incensed by this "symbol of sin," she blurted out, "There goes the old street tramp to do two bit jobs in Maye Worden's house tonight." Maye Worden operated a house of ill fame on James Row. It so happened that a sister of this girl was on the line. Shortly a suit was filed, charging Mrs. Bachelor with malicious slander and seeking five thousand dollars compensation. The suit was dismissed on first hearing largely because it was widely known that the girl was indeed one of Maye Worden's "helpers." And obscene calls were not unknown in those days. In 1888 one Henry H_____ was heavily fined and sentenced to one month in jail for using a telephone to make an indecent proposal to a young widow of his acquaintance.

The Union Messenger Company was the first telephone company to operate in Bristol. It was organized by Hal H. Haynes, J. I. Cox (later governor of Tennessee), George T. Hammer, W. D. Haynes, and John H. Caldwell, and was incorporated on July 19, 1887. Service was started in Bristol in October 1887, and by the following January the lines had reached Blountville.

By 1891 another well-organized telephone company was operating in Bristol.

The East Tennessee Telephone Company then had headquarters at 18 Lee Street. It was long headed by Harvey Turner. By 1894 the Bristol Telephone Company was a strong competitor. William Fowler was one of its earliest managers. And it may come as a surprise that by 1900 over half of the Bristol homes had telephone service. By then there was connection to other nearby towns, though one had to go through three operators to reach Abingdon— one in Bristol, one in Wallace, and the last in Montgomery's Switch (now Wyndale).

The beginning of the Bristol post office has been covered in another chapter. It was long the communication center of the town. During the time that this office was known as Goodson (February 15, 1859, to July 9, 1866), John Keys served as postmaster. It must be here noted that on June 16, 1865, William Cunningham was appointed postmaster for Bristol, Sullivan County, Tennessee, this being over one year before the Goodson post office was discontinued. This may indicate that there were post offices on both sides of the state line during that period. Elkanah D. Rader was appointed Bristol postmaster on December 11, 1866. On January 25, 1867, the office was moved back to the Virginia side of town, but apparently the name remained as Bristol. In less than four months (May 25, 1867), the office was moved back into Tennessee, and John Slack was appointed postmaster. It is said that President Andrew Johnson took a personal hand in having the post office moved back to the Tennessee side of town.

In July 1873 the office was moved into a larger building on Fourth Street. At that time twenty lock boxes were installed. This was during the administration of postmaster Elkanah A. Milliard. Mr. Milliard seems to have delegated most of the postal duties to deputies. Even Joseph R. Anderson, the town's founder and first postmaster, served as deputy until 1873, when he retired and was replaced by Bruce Spurgeon. Due to ill health, Mr. Spurgeon resigned on June 29, 1875. It was then that William P. Brewer took active charge of the post office (as a deputy). Editor Fowler in writing of this change highly commended Mr. Brewer:

> Mr. W. P. Brewer has taken active charge of the postoffice, and we must say no better selection could have been made. "P" as he is called is accurate, patient, and accommodating. Hereafter he will open the Sunday mails at 5:00 P.M. and 8:30 P.M., but if anyone should be looking for anything important by the morning mail, he can be found at his residence and will wait on them. That is good enough.

An old-timer remembered Mr. Brewer sitting on a bench in front of the Fourth Street building, patiently reading and explaining a business letter to an old citizen who could not read or write. And in this case kind old "P" picked up the pen and wrote a reply to his patron's correspondent. Such was the personalized service of the office in those days.

In 1879 a town vote was held on the proposition to move the post office to the Knights of Honor building on Fifth Street. The move was approved by a vote of 330 to 91. The office opened in its new location on July 16, 1879. The lock boxes from the Memphis, Tennessee, post office were moved to Bristol and installed soon after this move.

In the mid-1880s the office was moved into the former Joseph Anderson home on the southwest corner of Main and Fourth. There it was housed in the very room where it had started in 1853. Later a move was made to the corner of Shelby and Sixth Streets.

Postmasters who served during the period covered by this history (1852-1900) are listed below with dates of appointment:

Joseph R. Anderson	November 5, 1853
John Keys	July 27, 1858
William E. Cunningham	June 16, 1865
Elkanah D. Rader	December 11, 1866
John Slack	May 22, 1867
M. W. N. Willoughby	April 2, 1869
Elkanah A. Milliard	June 29, 1870
William Mullinix	May 4, 1881
John Slack	May 11, 1885
William P. Roller	September 6, 1889
George T. Hammer	February 4, 1890
A. C. Harkleroad	April 11, 1894
Eli A. Warren	March 16, 1898

Bibliography - Chapter Ten

Anderson, Joseph. Manuscript, cir. 1880.

Anderson, Melinda King. As told to her granddaughter, Mrs. Herman Blackley.

Anderson, Rhea. Notes, 1930-1939.

Bachelor, Ann. Memoirs (unpublished), 1935-1937.

Bristol News, newspaper. Various issues, 1857-1881.

Bristol, Tennessee. Deed Records.

Developmental maps, 1890 and later.

James, Mrs. King. Information given to author.

Maps discovered in deed books Abingdon, Virginia and Bristol, Tennessee.

Norfolk and Western Railway Archives.

Phillips, V. N. (Bud). Interviews with several older Bristol citizens.

Road petitions found among loose papers, Courthouse, Abingdon, Virginia.

Sullivan County, Tennessee. Deed Records.

U. S. Office of the Postmaster General. Washington, D.C.

Washington County, Virginia. Chancery Records.

Washington County, Virginia. County Court, Minutes, 1852-1900.

Washington County, Virginia. Deed Records, 1852-1900

Chapter Eleven
EARLY BRISTOL
NEWSPAPERS

Wherever there are people, there is news. Whenever there is enough news, there is the need for a newspaper. And the need of a newspaper to round out the expected type of businesses in a new and growing town is essential. It was thus in early Bristol. In February 1855, Joseph R. Anderson began correspondence with Mr. R. F. Walker, a publisher of Richmond, Virginia, concerning the feasibility of starting a newspaper here. In April that year Mr. Walker sent one of his assistants, Mr. G. W. Bagby, to "view out the land." The writings of Bagby, concerning this visit to Bristol, Virginia-Tennessee, are priceless to the annals of early local history.

Bagby writes of changing stages at midnight in Abingdon, Virginia, and of the ride through darkness to the new Bristol, arriving in the wee hours toward dawn. And he mentions that the town was as dark as the surrounding country. Not a light showed anywhere, until a faint candle flickered in the hall of the old King house on what later became known as Solar Hill. The house was then serving as an inn, operated by Drs. Hammer and Willoughby (Rev. James King had left it nearly two years prior to Bagby's arrival).

After breakfast at the inn, Bagby headed for the newly opened Virginia House Hotel (later the Magnolia Hotel). He had to remove his shoes to wade Beaver Creek, and then plodded across a wet meadow to reach his desired hostelry. He arrived just as the hotel cows were being driven from a pasture along Beaver Creek to a stable near the hotel where they could be milked. Later that morning he was directed to the residence of Joseph R. Anderson, where he found the noted town builder directing the finishing work on a banking room that was being added to the back of his store. Bagby described the room as about the size of a one-horse stable. This was about the time that Anderson outgrew the "salt bin bank" and enlarged his financial services. There followed a day or two of negotiations, during which Anderson offered a free lot, number 125, in Bristol, Tennessee, for the erection of a newspaper office and home for the editor. This lot fronted on Fourth Street on the south side of present Shelby, and was near the site of the First Presbyterian Church. But Walker had told his agent that the paper must be located in Bristol, Virginia (this was before the Virginia side of town became Goodson). Thus, Anderson then offered lot 152 which was located directly behind the present Signet Bank and fronting on present Lee Street (then Eighth Street).

It may be well to mention here that any advertising done by local business firms had to be carried by the papers in Jonesboro, Tennessee, or Abingdon, Virginia. Competition must have been keen and desperate, for the editor of one of those papers sent Bagby a threat of bodily harm should he persist in his plans to set up a newspaper in Bristol, Virginia. Bagby noted that he had rather be back in Richmond with his sweet wife than to be fighting "barbaric editors at the edge of civilization." He seems to have taken the next stage home. The reader may be interested to know that Mr. Bagby did return here about 1877 for a brief visit. While here he viewed the growing town from the tower of the King College building, then located on Fifth Street. Looking westward he viewed the hills back of present Holston Avenue and correctly foresaw that in time, many of the town's elite would build their homes there. He may not have been a fearless editor, but at least he was an accurate seer.

Undaunted in his efforts to have a paper established here, Anderson again took up correspondence with publisher Walker, offering not only to give a lot but to erect a suitable building thereon, which was to be paid for at twenty-five dollars per year, interest free. Walker agreed and in September 1855 sent one Thomas Whaley here to operate Bristol's first newspaper. For his generosity Anderson asked the privilege of naming the publication. This was granted and Anderson chose the name *The Bristol Press*.

There was some delay in the erection of the "Press" building, so it was still unfinished when Whaley arrived here in late September 1855. Mr. Whaley boarded with Joseph Anderson while he awaited the completion of the promised building, and for the arrival of his printing equipment from Richmond, Virginia. According to Ann Bachelor, this equipment was brought here by freight wagons, owned by Z. L. Burson. The building still being unfinished, the press was set up in a corner of the store room of Joseph Anderson. It was in this room that the first edition of *The Bristol Press* was printed in early October 1855. The following two or three editions were also published there. Ann Bachelor thought that these first editions numbered about one hundred copies each and that they consisted of one page, printed front and back.

In late October 1855 the press building was finished. Lewis Bachelor, foster father of Ann, moved the equipment from the Anderson store to the new location. The building had been erected by Jesse Aydlotte, a master carpenter, with materials furnished by Morgan Brothers of Bristol, Virginia (their location was actually in adjoining Goodsonville, but the Morgans always used the popular designation of the Virginia side of town). This building is described as being of board and batten construction, long and narrow, with a fireplace in the side of the front office and press room, and a fireplace in the narrow end of the room in back. Whaley lived in this back one-room apartment. The night of November 6, 1855, was bitterly cold. Keeping a roaring fire in the fireplace, editor Whaley had worked until very late in the press room. Soon after he retired to his room, the front of the building was found to be in flames. All was lost, including a newly printed, but undistributed edition of *The Bristol Press*. From an old Chancery case it has been learned that this edition carried a two column ad by John H. Moore, Merchant, and a notice of J. R. Anderson's enlarged banking services.

Whaley soon returned to Richmond and his departure signaled the end of all efforts to revive *The Bristol Press*. But apparently the ashes of the old Press building were hardly cold until J. Rothwell Brixey arrived in town with plans for the establishment of a newspaper. The place of Brixey's nativity is unknown, but it is certain that he had lived for sometime in Jonesboro, Tennessee, where he had worked with the town's newspaper. Likely he had heard of the tragic end of *The Bristol Press* and had decided that it would be an opportune time to begin publishing operations here. He rented a building on Washington Street in the area known as Goodsonville, and announced his plans to begin publication of the *Bristol Visitor*. There then occurred one of the strangest episodes in the history of newspaper publishing. One of the rival editors in either Jonesboro or Abingdon resented a competitor in Bristol so much that a vigorous effort was made to stop him. Somehow this rival editor managed to hold up the shipment of Brixey's press (some say by bad reflection on the latter's credit). But Brixey had promised to have an edition of his paper out on a certain date, and had sold advertising for this first run. Not to be out done, he and his family and a hired person or two, took the newsprint sheets and by hand wrote the news and drew the display advertisements. The *Visitor* visited on time (December 20, 1855)! This newspaper continued to be handwritten until a few weeks later when the equipment was finally obtained. In February 1954 this writer had the privilege of seeing one of these strange, handwritten newspapers. It was then owned by an old gentleman living on Spencer Street. This venerable old citizen also had a printed copy of the *Visitor*, dated March 12, 1856. It is recalled and from notes made, that this paper carried unusual illustrations on its heading. On the one side of the title was a man speaking through a mouth piece. On the other was the image of an old lady, listening intently through an ear trumpet. The location was given as Bristol, Washington County, Virginia. In less than a month the old gentleman who owned these priceless papers died. It was later learned that his family, having no interest in such things, had burned them along with other historic documents and papers. Alas, the tragedy is often repeated!

Brixey's publishing venture soon floundered financially and was over by mid-1856 or before. There are no known copies of Bristol's second newspaper. Brixey tried operating a store for a few months, but this too soon failed. He then moved on to parts unknown.

In the interval between the failure of the *Bristol Visitor* and the setting up of the next newspaper there were numerous pleas and efforts to bring a publisher to the fast growing town. Of course the lack of a paper here meant good business for the papers in nearby towns. Ann Bachelor recalled that weekly, representatives of newspapers in Jonesboro and Abingdon could be seen in town soliciting both news and advertising. And she recalled that once two of these agents had a rolling fight in the street (apparently competition was razor sharp) in front of Rosenheim's store, and that they finally rolled into a deep mud hole. This ended the battle, but two very muddy and angry agents left town vowing revenge upon one another.

It was not until February 10, 1857, that citizens from both sides of the state line met in the home of John Keys (old Dr. Zimmerman house — Signet Bank location) and there finalized plans for the founding of a stock company for the purpose of establishing another newspaper here. The plans came to fruition in May and A. K. Moore, who had been made editor, and M. Comann immediately left for Philadelphia to purchase the press. Ann Bachelor remembered riding in the freight wagon with her father as he transported the press from the depot to Moore's property on the northwest corner of Moore and Cumberland Streets. The press was set up in the former smokehouse at the Moore place, and this humble edifice served as both office and press room for Bristol's third newspaper.

It has been erroneously stated that this newspaper was called the *Bristol News*. At first it was simply *The News*. A very early edition (probably the first) bears this name, and gives the location as Bristol, Virginia-Tennessee. Between the two word title the paper bore the seals of Virginia and Tennessee, with smoking trains added to the bottom of each. Beneath this heading were the words: "An independent paper, devoted to news, internal improvements, agriculture, and the mechanical arts." Moore served as editor until early 1858, when he was replaced by J. Austin Sperry. Sperry moved the paper at first to the basement of the Exchange building (later Exchange and Nickels House Hotel) on the southeast corner of Main and Fourth (now State and Randall Expressway). After a brief period, it was moved a short way up Fourth Street to a building owned by J. R. Anderson. This location was about half way between what is now State and Shelby Streets, and on the east side of present Randall Expressway, with back to the railroad.

This building is described by Ann Bachelor as consisting of two rooms downstairs and one upstairs that only covered half of the first floor and was at the back side. The first floor back room contained the press and a stairway led from this room to the one-room living quarters of Sperry, located on the second floor. The downstairs front room was more-or-less the news office, but was also the room where Sperry taught his private school. Young Miss Bachelor attended that school. Later she hired-in to help Sperry fold and address his papers.

Sperry became a highly respected and beloved citizen of the new Bristol, notwithstanding an early involvement in a morals scandal. About 1859 *The News* briefly became the *Tennessee-Virginia News*. By June 1860 it had become the *Bristol News*. The paper ceased publication in 1862, when Sperry moved to Knoxville, Tennessee, to edit the *Knoxville Register*. After the Federal occupation of that city, he moved the *Register* to Bristol, and again occupied the building on Fourth Street. It was while thus situated that he was captured by the Federals and taken back to Knoxville as a prisoner of war.

In the winter of 1862, Martin L. Comann and W. W. Neal purchased the equipment of the *Abingdon Democrat*, and moved it to Bristol on a flat car of the railroad. The first issue of their paper, *The Southern Advocate*, is dated March 27, 1862. Neal, a minister, served as editor of this newspaper, which professed to be dedicated to news, religion, temperance, agriculture, and the interests of the south generally. The paper failed in the late winter of 1863, largely due to the financial troubles of its owners. The last known issue was March 12, 1863. In February 1873 Reverend W. W. Neal, who was then living in Kentucky, returned to Bristol to sell his home, which was located on Fifth Street, across from the First Presbyterian Church.

On March 6, 1863, about one week before the demise of the *Southern Advocate*, the first issue of the *Bristol Gazette* was published. This newspaper, founded by Martin L. Comann and J. W. Dickey, was housed in a portion of the Virginia House Hotel on Front Street, in Goodson (then popularly known as Bristol — thus the name, *Bristol Gazette*). About one year later this paper became the *State Line Gazette* and was owned by Comann and W. L. Rice. It is said that it was financed by money which Rice had received from the sale of some of his land. W. W. Langhorne, an early Bristol lawyer, assisted in the publication of the paper. At first the *State Line Gazette* was published in the same location as its predecessor. But those were trying, war times, and newspapers were prime targets of raiding Federals. In mid-1864, the paper was moved to a barn on the Mahlon Susong farm (along present Euclid Avenue). While there, an issue or two was printed on the back of wallpaper, which had been bought from Mrs. M. M. Bailey for six of Comann's chickens. Such was the need for food and paper in those days. Thus the readers might say that the tragic news of the times had a rosy background. At least one issue of this paper was printed on a roll of brown wrapping paper from L. F. Johnson's store. A copy of this issue was owned by an old couple at Paperville, Tennessee, some thirty-five years ago. After the end of the War, the *State Line Gazette* was moved to a little building on East Main (State) Street. The last known issue was dated March 20, 1867. The equipment was stored in the basement of the Nickels House Hotel for six years or so until it was bought by Major Z. L. Burson and moved to a little building in the back corner of his yard, 332 Moore Street, for purposes to be told later.

In the summer of 1865 John Slack, a native of McMinn County, Tennessee, but who had been residing in Jonesboro, Tennessee, as half owner of *The Express,* put together his meager resources and moved to Bristol. Soon thereafter he hauled in equipment from Independence, Virginia and began publishing *The News.* Some say this was a reviving of the former Bristol paper of the same name. What is likely the first edition of this paper is dated September 29, 1865. Though the main heading is *The News,* in a small block at the left are the words, "The Bristol News." This is followed by the statement, "The News will be published every Friday morning." In the fall of 1866 this paper was leased to D. F. Bailey, who became a noted lawyer here. Bailey was assisted by a Mr. Ramey. On August 7, 1868, the paper was sold to I. C. and Elbert Fowler, brothers and natives of Tazewell, Virginia, who had recently arrived in Bristol. From that point the main heading was given as *The Bristol News.* The paper office was then moved to Goodson (it was there by February 19, 1869). In the early 1870s, it was moved into the new "News" building, which stood on Lee Street, north of the present Signet Bank. Though in Goodson the location was always listed on the paper heading as Bristol, Virginia-Tennessee.

The era of the Fowler editorship will never be forgotten. His paper prospered and became more and more popular with the passing years. Fowler was frank, courageous, impartial, often facetious, and possessed a gift of satire and wittiness that often infuriated some while delighting others. He was of a high moral character, intelligent and shrewd in business affairs. Once when a certain postmaster was replaced, Fowler candidly commented that the citizens were better off because of it. When J. R. Anderson's old barn was torn down, Fowler wrote that the town now looked much better. Writing of a murder that occurred in the back door of a local house of ill fame, the fearless editor of *The News* printed the names of the ladies who operated the place, and he commented that they were not fit to dwell in a decent society and should be vanquished from the town. When Jonesboro, Tennessee, celebrated its 100th anniversary, there was a request from that town for articles one hundred years old or older to be put on display there. Fowler wrote that some of the butter that was being sold on the streets of

I.C. FOWLER HOUSE: The home of the noted Bristol newspaper editor, I.C. Fowler, yet stands at 417 Spencer Street, Bristol, Virginia. This house was built in 1867-1868, and is said to be the oldest structure in Bristol that still retains its original integrity. It was recently donated by Sid Oakley to the Bristol-Goodson Preservationists for use as a museum and research center.

Bristol ought to be displayed among the other ancient relics!

Soon after locating in Bristol, he bought land from Joseph Johnston and built his home. This home still stands on Spencer Street. He and his wife were noted for their grand entertainments in this old home.

While in Bristol, Fowler served three consecutive terms in the legislature. There he served with distinction and honor and was much respected by other members of the governmental body who elected him speaker of the house. In 1884 he received an appointment as clerk of the U.S. Court at Abingdon, Virginia. He then turned his paper over to A. C. Smith, a long time employee. Smith continued the weekly paper until 1890, when it became a daily. At that time his son, Samuel Smith, was associated with the paper. *The Bristol News* continued until well after 1900.

Isaac Chapman Fowler, its former long-time editor and publisher, died at his home in Abingdon at 5:00 A.M. on Saturday, April 29, 1905. His body was returned to Bristol and buried in the East Hill Cemetery. His Abingdon home still stands on Main Street and was long the home of Mrs. Ada Carson.

About 1867 a paper known as the *Goodson Gazette* was published for a short time. It may have been a successor of the *State Line Gazette*. Meanwhile, John Slack was not idle. After selling the *Bristol News,* he went to Greeneville and served as editor of Andrew Johnson's personal paper, *The Union.* After one year there, he returned to Bristol in 1869 and was elected to the state legislature. In October of 1870 he established the *Bristol Courier,* a weekly newspaper, published in Bristol, Tennessee. This paper was sold to William Burrow in 1876, but only remained in his ownership for one year, when it was sold back to Slack. This became a daily in 1880, but for only three weeks. When Charles Slack took over the operation of the paper in 1888, it again became a daily. The first issue was dated September 15, 1888. In 1885 President Cleveland appointed John Slack to the Bristol postmastership, a position he held until his death in 1900. The John Slack home long stood at 536 Anderson Street.

In 1898 Slack's *Daily Courier* was sold to the *Daily Times* which had been launched in 1896 by Ben L. Dulaney and John H. Caldwell. Caldwell was a son-in-law of Bristol's founder, Joseph R. Anderson. The combined papers became the *Times Courier.* Charles Slack continued to publish the *Weekly Courier.* A Mr. John A. Faw was long associated with the *Daily Times* as editor and publisher. In 1897 he was living at 544 Alabama Street with his wife, Flora E. Faw and children, Annie, Julian H., and William J. Faw. A Lizzie Underwood, who in some manner was associated with the same paper, long lived (boarded) at 628 Fourth Street.

In September 1898 James A. Stone and John W. Price established the *Daily Tribune* with Herschel Dove as associate editor. This newspaper was formed to promote the campaign of William F. Rhea for Congress. In December 1898 it combined with the *Times Courier* to form the *Tribune-Times Courier.* At the time of the forming of this paper, Stone was boarding at the Hotel Hamilton, while Price, who was both an M.D. and a lawyer, was living at the St. Lawrence Hotel. Later this combined paper was bought by a company and again became the *Daily Courier.* This was the forerunner of the present *Bristol Herald Courier.*

In 1870 David F. Bailey, then a young, unmarried lawyer, and Col. N. M. Taylor, another early Bristol lawyer, established the very short lived *Beaver Bubble.* But like the *Mississippi Bubble,* it soon burst and floated away with the tide of time. Not a known copy exists, though this editor has been told that a Bailey descendant has one "somewhere among her old papers." In 1873 a Rev. Kincannon and Professor B. G. Manard began publication of the *Monthly Messenger.* This was a church and school journal for Baptists. The cost was fifty cents per year.

In 1873 Rev. W. C. Baldwin of Glade Springs, Virginia, came to Bristol to pastor the Bristol Baptist Church, often called Burson's Baptist Church, that stood on lower Main Street in Goodson. He took over as pastor of this church on the first Sunday in April 1873 (his first sermon was entitled, "The Reciprocal Duties of Pastor and Flock"). Being a writer of acknowledged ability, he also intended to publish a religious journal. Burson had long had a set of printing equipment stored in an outbuilding of his home yard at 342 Moore Street. This was brought back into operation and for a year or so printed *The Clarion Call*. But then Burson got into a controversy with several of the town fathers. He then hired Baldwin to become editor and publisher of a newspaper to promote the Burson side of the feud. This short-lived paper

Lucas (Luke) Dixon long served Bristol in the newspaper field. He later moved to Asheville, North Carolina.

was called the *Bristol Banner,* and was filled with more argument than news. But Burson had the money to put his views across. His publishing ceased with the departure of Rev. Baldwin.

About 1876 William Burrow began the publication of *The Souvenir,* a monthly literary magazine. Then in December 1879 William and T. J. Burrow began publication of the *Bristol Reporter.* The *Daily Argus* was published for a few months in 1880 by John Barnes and Z. T. Hammer.

In 1877 a stock company was formed at Jonesboro, Tennessee for the purpose of financing a newspaper to support the Democratic party. Among the numerous stockholders were C. J. Lyle, L. C. People, George W. St. John, A. B. Cummings, R. H. Dungan, and Frederick Devault, all prominent and substantial citizens of Washington County, Tennessee. Shares were ten dollars each. R. H. Dungan, who owned a stave, treenail and lumber business at Jonesboro, was the largest shareholder. The initial equipment for this paper was purchased second hand in Knoxville, Tennessee. It later proved to be much damaged, the job press having once been thrown from the second story of a burning building. Nevertheless, the *Jonesborough Journal* soon came into being with John S. Hayes as editor. It does not appear that the paper had much success. The value of the stock soon fell to fifty cents on the dollar. In 1883 R. A. Kinsloe began to buy up the stock and some was outright given to him on promise that he would take over and edit the failing paper. He later claimed, during heated court action over the matter, that he bought the equipment of *The Journal* in June 1883. At that time C. J. Lyle was president of the stock company with A. S. Deadrick as secretary. Though John S. Hayes had a lease lasting until January 1, 1885, he agreed to turn over the full management and editorship to Kinsloe. The equipment at that time was valued at around two thousand dollars. Kinsloe claimed that he lost over a thousand dollars during the next two years of operation.

About the first of April 1885, Kinsloe broke up housekeeping and spent the next several days with R. H. Dungan. About mid-April he loaded up the equipment and shipped it to the Bristol, Virginia, depot. Within a few days he had rented a building in Goodson, and there the short-lived *Goodson Democrat* was born. Meanwhile he had moved his family into a house on Virginia Hill that he had rented from Major Z. L. Burson. All went well for awhile. The paper seemed to prosper. It was well prepared, properly edited, heavily patronized by advertisers, and widely circulated.

In the late summer of 1885, a heated political campaign developed in which the prominent Col. Abram Fulkerson was the principal candidate. Several local democrats felt that Fulkerson was not the kind of democrat they desired and charged that he had obtained the party's nomination by fraud. As a consequence, they leased the *Goodson Democrat* from Kinsloe and began supporting independent candidates.

News of this action soon reached Jonesboro. In early October 1885 a suit was filed in Washington County, Virginia, by several of the stockholders of the Jonesboro Journal Stock Company, charging that Kinsloe had obtained much of the stock on promise to keep the paper in Jonesboro and never to support an independent or Republican candidate. It was further charged that Kinsloe had no right to move the equipment to Bristol-Goodson, and that he did so without the knowledge or permission of the stock company. The plaintiffs also sought an injunction to prohibit Kinsloe from further using the equipment to print the paper. This injunction was granted on October 8, 1885.

Kinsloe replied that he had given notice of his plans to move to Bristol-Goodson in several papers besides his own; that Dungan, with whom he has spent the last few days of his time in Jonesboro, knew full well of his plans; and that George W. St. John, one of the stockholders, was in town the day of the move and saw the equipment being loaded on the train. St. John later claimed that he had hired Charles E. Dosser, a prominent Jonesboro attorney, to prevent the removal of the property, but that Dosser was away in Memphis attending a Knights of Honor convention when the removal took place. Kinsloe expressed his wonderment as to why there had been no opposition from Jonesboro until the political controversy arose in Bristol. An impressive development in the case was that two or more of the stockholders filed affidavits that their names had been used in the filing of the suit without their knowledge or consent. Kinsloe introduced a very amicable letter from one of these to prove the claim. And the noted William P. Brownlow of Jonesboro testified for the defendant, stating that he well knew that Kinsloe had given notice of the move.

It appears that those who had leased the paper did print two or three issues after the court injunction (the injunction was against Kinsloe, not the lessors). The paper then supported Dr. William White as independent candidate for senator and John A. Buchanan and Robert H. Gray, independent candidates for the house of delegates. Under these endorsements is printed the following notice:

> This paper has been leased by a number of Democrats who are opposed to all forms of Bossism, and is edited and published by a committee appointed by them.

It is known that among the lessors of the paper was "Hell" John Burson, a noted local lawyer. Of the publishing committee only one is known, Cyrus W. Byrd, whose stay in Bristol was brief. In the closing weeks of the paper's existence, R. A. Kinsloe published his last statement to the town:

I am the victim of a deliberate and willful scheme, originated by demagogues and political hucksters, with the basest political motives, and designed for the purpose of suppressing free speech, and the direct interference with the freedom of the press.

Last week my connection with the Democrat ceased. I resign the trust to a committee of independents who are responsible gentlemen, and I hope will not abuse the power placed in their hands. After the present lease expires — which will be the first week in November — the equipment of the Goodson Democrat will be for sale. The undersigned has had all he wants of Virginia politics.

If the equipment is not sold, it will be moved; at least that is the intention now.

In conclusion, for myself, and in behalf of my family, I thank the citizens of Goodson-Bristol for any favors extended, and only regret the circumstances which compel me to give up an enterprise which started with such flattering prospects.

Very respectfully,
R. A. Kinsloe

And so the *Goodson Democrat* died a tragic death; a casualty of a political squabble. In early November 1885 Kinsloe and his family sold all their belongings and, with only a trunk or two and a suitcase, boarded a southbound train. Their destination is not known, and it is said that the disappointed editor was never seen in Bristol again. He was originally from Pennsylvania and may have eventually returned to that state. There are two known copies of the *Goodson Democrat*. One is dated July 24, 1885; the other October 16, 1885. Both are owned by this author.

NEWSPAPER COSTS

A little information is available concerning the financial picture of newspapers in those early Bristol years. In September 1865 *The News* advertised its subscription rates as three dollars per year, two dollars for six months, and one dollar for three months. In clubs of five, the cost was twelve fifty per year, and a club of ten might be had for twenty dollars.

By October 19, 1866, *The News* had changed its subscription rates to two dollars per year (payable in advance), and lowered its club rates to five for eight seventy-five, or ten for fifteen dollars. Ordinary advertising cost one dollar per square (ten lines or less) for each insertion. Transient advertising had to be paid in advance. Obituaries and communications to promote private ends went at the regular advertising rates. Ongoing advertising cost three dollars per month per square, and on up to fifteen dollars for one year. One-half column ran from ten dollars for one month to thirty-five dollars for one year. One-half double column ran from twelve fifty for one month to fifty dollars per year. By the above date *The News* had changed its location line from Bristol, Tennessee, to Bristol, Virginia-Tennessee.

In February 1869 *The Bristol News,* Bristol Virginia-Tennessee, gave its subscription rates as two fifty per year, or one fifty for six months. To clubs of ten or more, the rate was two dollars per year. One could then insert a five or more line ad at twenty-five cents per line per month, or one dollar per line for one year. Obituary notices of over four lines were charged at the regular advertising rate. An interesting notice in the *Bristol News* of February 19, 1869, is that the paper could be had for the duration of the current political campaign for fifty cents, payable in advance. The *Bristol News* was then offering job printing. In 1871 a year's subscription to the *Courier* cost two dollars, or only one twenty-five if paid in advance! One square (ten lines) in the *Courier* cost one dollar per insertion. At that time printers were paid at the rate of one dollar per day, while an apprentice earned only one dollar per week.

In 1872 the *Bristol News* offered subscriptions at two dollars per year, or one dollar in clubs of ten. At the same time this paper offered job printing at New York prices. Aiken and Company of Union (Bluff City), Tennessee, was then authorized to take subscriptions for the *News.* Griffin and Hoffman, Newspaper Advertising Agents, No. 4 South Street, Baltimore, Maryland, were authorized to take orders for advertising. George P. Rowell and Company, 40 and 41 Park Row, New York, did the same in that city.

When Major Zack Burson founded the short-lived *Bristol Banner* in 1873, he offered free subscriptions to all the "Godly and upright" citizens of the town. How it was determined who had a valid claim to that classification is not known. He also offered advertising at half the common rates.

By 1879 the *Bristol News* had lowered its subscription to one fifty per year, or only one dollar if paid in advance. The advertising rates for a one year run then stood at ten dollars for the first inch and four dollars for each additional inch. What we would now call classified then cost ten cents per line for transient advertisers or five cents per line for the local trade. Political announcements cost five dollars for candidates for congress, the legislature, or county offices. Those seeking town or township offices paid only two dollars.

The July 24, 1885, edition of the *Goodson Democrat* gave its subscription rate as one dollar per year. The same edition advertised that job printing was available. Unfortunately, no advertising rates were given. This edition does reveal that W. S. Hamilton, a local lawyer, was then serving as associate editor and that Jeff L. Duff was local editor.

The Bristol Courier of Friday, April 22, 1892, gives its weekly subscription at one dollar per year. The cost of the daily was fifteen cents per week, fifty cents per month, or six dollars per year. Its advertising rates ran from one inch, one week, for a dollar, to one column for a year at three hundred dollars. In the weekly, one could have one inch for a month at one dollar. It is likely that these prices did not vary much through the remainder of the century.

A PRINTER'S SALARY AND ECONOMIC LIFE

Albert C. Smith, who long was the printer for the *Bristol News*, and who later owned and edited that newspaper, kept careful accounts of his income and expenses. He noted in an extant account book that he commenced work for I. C. and Elbert Fowler on August 1, 1868, at the rate of forty dollars per month. The arrangement was that he receive his room and board (apparently valued at ten dollars per month) and thirty dollars for the first three months. It further appears that Fowler paid Smith's bills and then gave him what portion of the forty dollars remained. His first month's bills list tobacco at twenty cents, watch repair at one fifty, a box of collars for twenty-five cents, and a hat for four dollars. Among other things the second month's expenses included a wash bowl and pitcher at one fifty, chairs (unknown number) for two twenty-five, and a subscription for sidewalk work of one fifty. In November 1868 a half bushel of apples cost him twenty-five cents and twenty-seven pounds of beef cost him two thirty-five. It may be noted that an equal amount of bacon cost him double that amount. By December he apparently had set up housekeeping, his rent being ten dollars per month. That month he paid fifty cents for a bottle of Dr. Pepper's Bitters (a concoction made locally by Dr. J. G. Pepper). In the cold January of 1869 he paid one dollar for a load of wood. His groceries for that month amounted to nine dollars and twenty-three cents! This included four dozen eggs for sixty cents. In February 1869, the landlord raised his rent to twelve fifty per month. He apparently moved soon after this rent increase. In March his rent is listed at five dollars and eighty-eight cents. And it appears that the family celebrated spring with a chicken feast. He bought six chickens for one dollar and twenty cents. From this book we learn that he sowed turnips in September 1869, the seed costing him ten cents. But that month saw one of his biggest expenditures. He bought his wife a sewing machine that cost thirty dollars, plus two fifteen for shipping charges. Alas, in December, his expenses were above his salary by three dollars and nineteen cents. Maybe he over indulged for Christmas and those were the days before Master Charge! Perhaps January 1870 was a bit cold; on the 22nd of that month he paid E. H. Seneker nine dollars for four pairs of blankets.

On occasion Smith was able to draw a little overtime. In November 1870 he was paid four dollars for five nights of extra work putting out an order of pamphlets. This extra shift ran from five until eight P.M. By August 1871 his economic lot had improved. He was then being paid fifty dollars per month, and had moved into a fifteen-dollar-per-month house. Where before he had been buying flour in as little as six pound lots, he now was ordering one hundred pounds at a time. He even splurged one dollar on a lottery ticket in November that year.

As one goes on through this account until its end (October 1883), it is clear that Smith's faithful service was paying off. By then his wages had greatly increased, and it is clear that his general economic condition had improved.

PRINTING COSTS

From the Smith account book and other sources, one may gain an insight into the job printing costs of those days. In November 1870 two hundred pamphlets were printed and bound by Smith for three dollars and fifty cents. In December he charged the Town of Goodson, thirteen dollars for three hundred, eighteen-page booklets on the town ordinances (this writer now owns one of those booklets). In May 1872 one thousand tracts cost five dollars.

The account of J. R. Anderson, Merchant-Banker, for 1882, is very revealing of the printing costs of that period:

500 Circulars	2.50
2000 Notes	5.00
1500 Envelopes	3.20
500 Circulars	3.50
6000 Deposit Tickets	6.00
2500 Envelopes	6.25
2000 Postcards	2.50
500 Tracts	2.50
4000 Bank of Bristol	4.00
100 Circulars	1.50

Other old records show that there was not a great increase in printing costs through the remainder of the century.

Bibliography - Chapter Eleven

Anderson, Melinda King. As told to her granddaughter, Mrs. Herman Blackley.

Bachelor, Ann. Memoirs (unpublished).

Bagby, G. W. Various writings.

Bristol News, newspaper. Various issues, 1857-1881.

Fowler, Isaac C. Notes (unpublished), 1880.

Loving, Robert S. Double Destiny; the Story of Bristol, Tennessee-Virginia. Bristol, Tenn.: King Printing Co., 1955.

Phillips, V. N. (Bud). Interviews with numerous older Bristol citizens, 1953-1956.

Smith, A. C. Papers, unpublished, 1898.

Washington County, Virginia. Chancery Records, 1852-1900.

Chapter Twelve
BRISTOL BUSINESS AND INDUSTRY 1853-1900

The first business establishment in the new Town of Bristol, Virginia-Tennessee, was a general store owned and operated by Joseph R. Anderson. It was housed in the west room of his home that stood on the southwest corner of Fourth and Main (now State and Edgemont). This room, measuring twelve by sixteen feet, had a front door opening onto Main Street and a door that led into the residential part of the house. Anderson's store was open for business by Christmas 1853. An old lady who was still living in Bristol, Tennessee, in 1954 used to tell of how her grandfather, a Mr. Rutherford, who lived immediately east of what is now the East Hill Cemetery, walked through a heavily falling snow to buy Christmas "tricks" at Anderson's new store. She thought her grandfather was Anderson's first customer and that the trek through the snow had been made on Christmas Eve 1853.

She further recalled that her grandfather always said that he traded this first Bristol merchant side meat for the "tricks." And she never forgot how her grandfather said that Anderson's house then stood in a vast field or meadow with not another house or building in sight. About 1858 Mr. Anderson moved his store into a large two-story brick building he erected on Fourth Street (now Edgemont Avenue) across from the backyard of his home. His mercantile business remained there until late October 1881, when he moved into a large, three-story brick building that he had erected at 410 Main Street (State). By then he was devoting most of his time to banking, leaving the store in the hands of his son John Campbell Anderson and his nephew Arron B. Carr. But until his very last days, he always maintained an interest in the store that he had founded in 1853. His last day's work was helping balance the accounts of Anderson & Carr, as the store was then known. While poring over the store's accounts during the afternoon of May 10, 1888, he became ill and was taken home where he sat long on his shady porch. Finally, being put to bed by his wife and a man servant, he remarked that he would never rise from it. He was right. He died eight days later (May 18, 1888). He had lived to see a thriving town grow up around that lone store which had stood in the midst of a snow-covered field when Mr. Rutherford had come for his Christmas "tricks" in 1853.

In the autumn of 1853, John H. Moore of Russell County, Virginia, contracted for the choice lot on what would become the southwest corner of State and Lee (then Main and Eighth). Mr. Moore did not receive a deed for this lot until July 11, 1854 (likely at the completion of payment), but by then his new store building was almost ready for occupancy. His was the first mercantile business in old Bristol, Virginia. (This was before all the Virginia side of town became Goodson). Mr. Moore built his home, described by Joseph B. Palmer as being a neat cottage, immediately behind and attached to the store. He greatly prospered in his new venture, but desiring to move back to Russell County, sold out to his cousin A. K. Moore on October 23, 1856, for the sum of two thousand dollars.

Bristol's third merchant was Alfred T. Wilson of Johnson County, Tennessee, who bought lots 6 and 7 from Joseph R. Anderson on July 11, 1854. Lot 7 fronted on Main (State) Street and extended from Washington to Virginia Street (then First and Second Streets) and lot 6 was located directly in back of it. These valuable lots were sold to Wilson for one hundred and seventy-five dollars. On October 10, 1855, Wilson paid Anderson seventy-five dollars for lot 5, which adjoined lot 6 on the north.

Wilson had his store ready to open by mid-September 1854, and the hotel he had erected in connection therewith was opened soon afterwards. He had missed being Bristol, Virginia's, first merchant by about one month. (Moore's store had opened in mid-August 1854.) An early partner of Wilson was a Mr. Smith, but his interest in the firm seems to have been of short duration. Later, L. W. Loyd became associated with A. T. Wilson in the firm of Wilson and Loyd. Wilson's mercantile business flourished, so that by the summer of 1856, he had decided to leave the operation of his hotel to others. On September 13, 1856, he entered into a partnership with J. H. and E. G. Everett (or Everitt), recently of North Carolina, for the purpose of forming the firm of Everett-Wilson and Company, which would operate the hotel and boarding house. Each partner was to supply five hundred dollars as capital funds. The Everetts soon opened Bristol's first restaurant in connection with this hotel. (The hotel had maintained a kitchen and dining room prior to that time.) By then the Virginia House Hotel on Fourth (Front) Street was taking most of the trade, thus causing the Columbia (Everett and Wilson's establishment) to languish. After six month's operation the books showed that J. H. Everett's profit had only amounted to $83.25, E. G. Everett's profit was $17.62, and that of Wilson amounted to only $55.06. About that time J. H. Everett disappeared (at least for a time), and Wilson filed for court action to dissolve the partnership and sell the furnishings of the hotel.

Wilson's petition was granted and the furnishings were sold soon thereafter. Then on January 15, 1858, Wilson and his wife, Ellen H. Wilson, signed a deed conveying the property to Gardner Grant of Washington County, Virginia, for the sum of three thousand dollars, one thousand of which was paid down and the remainder was to be paid in two years. Wilson retained the right to use the portion of the property that housed the Wilson and Loyd store, rent free until September 15, 1858. By the date of the property sale, the hotel part had become Wilson's Virginia House Hotel. Gardner enjoyed moderate success, but lost all to a tragic fire in October 1859. Being very distraught by this occurrence, he left town the next morning, not knowing where he was headed. He finally reached Missouri, where he lived for a few years, but later returned to Washington County, Virginia.

When it became clear that Grant would not finish payment, Wilson, who by then was living on a farm three miles west of Blountville, made an effort to reclaim and resell the lot. At about that time Dr. R. S. Jackson of Russell County, Virginia, drove into town with his sole possessions: a Jersey spring wagon, a team and harness, and a Negro woman (slave) and her two-month-old child. He too had suffered a fire and had set forth in the world to seek a new fortune. Hoping to make a new start, he soon traded all his possessions, valued at one thousand dollars, to A. T. Wilson, for the Bristol lot where had stood the town's third store and first hotel. At the time of this trade, only the old smokehouse and a stable stood on the lot. Jackson soon rented this smokehouse as a home to J. D. Hoover for three dollars per month. (Both the stable and smokehouse, then unoccupied, were torn down and used for fire wood in the nearby Confederate hospital during the Civil War.)

The day the trade was made, Wilson claimed his possessions and drove to his Sullivan County farm where, as he testified later, he found the Negro woman, Alice, to be unsound. It seems that she had three fingers of her left hand drawn almost to the palm thereof (why this had not been seen at the time of the trade defies explanation). A dispute with Dr. Jackson ensued and was finally settled by arbitration before Matt Haynes, L. F. Johnson, and John G. King, at a meeting in the Exchange Hotel (later Nickels House) in Bristol. Dr. Jackson was required to pay Wilson some two hundred dollars to equalize the trade.

As the Civil War approached, Jackson, a hot-headed secessionist, sought to find a more favorable location for the promotion of his often-called radical ideas. Consequently, he moved to Georgia — first to Cuthbert, Randolph County, and from there to Atlanta in Fulton County, where he bought a home near the depot. He lost all when Sherman burned this city during the Civil War. Before leaving Bristol, he had sold the old hotel and store location to Joseph Combs of Russell County, Virginia, for one thousand dollars. (The deed was made on April 1, 1861.) A. T. Wilson soon filed suit, claiming that Jackson had not paid all his obligations to him, and sought to have the property sold so that he might gain his due. The war caused a delay of such matters for several years. The suit was not settled until around 1880. Such were the trials of Bristol's third merchant and first hotel keeper. It is known that Wilson finally moved to Bluff City, Tennessee (then called Union). In 1871 the Negro woman whom he had accepted in payment for his Bristol property was living at Carter's Depot, Tennessee, and apparently had married a Carr.

Even as Bristol's third merchant moved to the Blountville area, so did the fourth merchant hail from that section. W. W. James (his given names may have been William Walter) came from a long line of merchants. "It's in our blood," he used to say, and his outstanding success was proof that the trait was well developed. He was a son of Amos James, who finally moved to west Tennessee and made good in that area. A brother of W. W. James was an outstanding merchant of Memphis, Tennessee. Mr. James was twice married. His first wife is unknown, but his second wife was Mary Jones, a daughter of S. C. Jones, who lived in the extreme reaches of southwest Virginia (perhaps Lee County). This second wife bore several sons, all of whom were at one time virtually lined up side by side in downtown Bristol as competing merchants.

W. W. James began his merchandising career in Blountville, Tennessee, around 1845. A competing merchant there was Joseph R. Anderson. With him James formed a warm and helpful friendship, which grew stronger with the passing years. Anderson founded Bristol, Virginia-Tennessee, in 1852, and soon thereafter it became evident that the new town would flourish. On June 12, 1855, W. W. James bought what was then thought to be the best business location in Bristol, the northwest corner of Fourth and Main (later Front and Main and finally State and the Randall Expressway). For this choice site he paid six hundred dollars, which was the highest price paid for any early Bristol business lot. Soon after the purchase of this lot, James erected a store building and formed a partnership with E. H. Seneker. However, Mr. James did not move to Bristol at that time. For several years he continued as a merchant in Blountville, while James and Seneker in Bristol was operated by the firm's partner and young Joseph William James, who perhaps was a nephew of W. W. James. E. H. Seneker soon withdrew from the firm and set up his own store in the building that had been erected by Bristol, Virginia's, first merchant, John H. Moore (northwest corner of Lee and State). W. W. James moved to Bristol the night following the burning of his store during the Battle of Blountville, Civil War. In time he became the leading merchant on the Virginia side of town. He long was at the forefront of the civic leaders of Bristol, helped to form the second bank of Bristol, Virginia, did much real estate developing, and strongly supported the building of area

In 1855 J. William James, at the age of 18, began management of the W.W. James store in Bristol, Virginia. He was
a close relative, possibly a nephew, of Mr. James.

railroads. He played a leading role in the establishment of Sullins College,
so much so that it was almost called James College. His first Bristol home
was at the north side of his store. Later (1871) he built on Sullins Street and
finally erected a large brick home on what became James Street (at first
Johnston Street). This house was directly across the street from the present
annex of the Episcopal Church. He died in this home in 1901, having out-
lived most of his children. He is buried in East Hill Cemetery.

OTHER PRE-CIVIL WAR MERCHANTS

Other mercantile firms known to have operated in Bristol prior to the Civil
War were those of Nunley & Fuqua; Booker & Trammell; Henry Rosenheim;
Martin Brothers (who operated on the southeast corner of what is now State
and Sixth); Joseph W. Jones; Keebler & Simpson (which firm was composed
of Valentine Keebler and John G. Simpson); L. F. Johnson, who opened

his store in 1859; Raine & Megginson (also opened in 1859 but soon became Raine & Jamison); Gugginheimers; and Wingfield & Campbell (a firm composed of G. A. Wingfield and Nathan Campbell, both of Bedford County, Virginia).

It may puzzle the careful reader as to how so many firms could flourish in a town so small. Of course these stores did not depend wholly upon the local citizenry for support. There was a vast trade area around the new town which provided most of the patronage for these early stores.

And what would it have cost you to have shopped in these first mercantile houses? This type of information is scarce, but the author is fortunate to own receipts from James & Seneker and Keebler & Simpson. The James & Seneker receipt, headed Bristol, Virginia, March 7, 1857, lists the following articles:

1 sack flour	$3.00
20 lbs. sugar	3.00
Cording for bed	.50
2 pr. shoes	2.50
1 pr. boots (men's)	1.62
12 yards calico	1.25
1 wooden bucket	.35
10 lbs. butter	1.80
1 mirror 18×12	1.30
1 overcoat	3.50
3 doz. eggs	.36
109 lb. pork	6.54

On September 19, 1856, Keebler & Simpson sold M. J. Ayers the following bill of goods:

1 horse collar	$1.00
100 lb. flour	3.04
30 tallow candles	.25
1 gal. molasses	1.24
1 cap	.47
Ginger	.12
10 lb. nails	.90
1 spool cotton thread & 10 needles	.90
1 soap dish	.19
1 ladies hat	.57
50 lb. corn meal	1.25

And on January 10, 1857, Joseph R. Anderson, Merchant, charged the same Mr. Ayers as above eighteen cents for twenty envelopes and eighty-seven cents for a pair of gloves.

FIRST BANKING

In another section of this book, it has been well explained that Joseph R. Anderson was the town's first banker. The second banking business conducted in the town was also of a private nature, being done by W. L. Martin. His banking room was located in the back of his store that stood on the southeast corner of what is now State and Sixth Streets. Here occurred Bristol's first bank robbery (see chapter entitled Law and Order).

In 1857 several gentlemen residing on the Virginia side of Bristol-Goodson decided that it was time that a new bank be established in their part of the fast-growing town. Although this was to be a Virginia bank, a few residents of Tennessee signed the petition. The move for this bank was led by A. M. Appling (then mayor), John P. Megginson, and Valentine Keebler, the latter two being prominent merchants. The petition reads as follows:

Goodson, December 16, 1857

Messrs. Rice and Grant
Reps. Washington Co., Va.
At Richmond

Gentlemen:

We, the subscribers would most respectively petition the legislature (through you) for a charter for an Independent Bank to be located in this place; and to be titled, The Bank of Southwestern Virginia. We would further petition a precinct also be established at this point, as a larger number of voters would be greatly accommodated.

W. F. Moon	John P. Megginson
A. M. Appling	James A. Appling
George C. Langhorne	John F. Terry
William Clark	John Hill
James Fields	Wm. A. Irvin
John G. King	M. Burlingame
Robert F. Bibb	Thomas Bibb
James M. Morgan	V. Keebler
James W. Robinson	John P. Hammer
J. H. Pepper	Elijah Hall Seneker
George Pepper	Samuel E. Cox
_____ Taylor	Wm. H. Medley
A. K. Moore	

The voting precinct was not established, but there is evidence that the Bank of Southwestern Virginia did operate for a brief time in Bristol.

DRUGSTORES

In 1856 Dr. Richard M. Coleman opened Bristol's first drugstore. David J. Ensor had the second drugstore, followed closely by the firm of Thomas & Campbell (Dr. A. S. Campbell and a Mr. Thomas). For more on this matter see the chapter entitled The Healers.

SALOONS

In late 1855 John N. Bosang opened Bristol's first saloon. On July 31 of that year, he bought lot 80 in Goodsonville for eighty dollars. This triangular lot was located at the southeast corner of Edmund and Russell Streets, near the present First Christian Church. His first saloon was in a rented building that stood on the later site of the General Shelby Hotel (Front and Cumberland), but sometime afterward he moved to the site of the present Dominion Bank (Moore and State). In early 1856 Bosang had competition when Walter's Saloon opened on Fourth Street (later Front). This business was located at about the corner of the parking lot that is now in front of the Bristol, Virginia, police station.

Though J. R. Anderson had stated that he would put a clause in every deed forbidding the manufacture or sale of liquor upon the lots, this restriction was not written into any land transfer that he later made. Thus, the town was hardly begun until strong drink was being sold on both sides of the state line. It is known that the Columbia (later Wilson's Virginia House) Hotel had a bar, as did the Exchange Hotel (later Nickels House). In time saloon keeping became a major business in the new town.

FIRST BLACKSMITH SHOP

Bristol would not only be boosted by the railroad, but its lifeblood would come from the surrounding country, which was largely agricultural at the time. Consequently, there were many horses, mules, wagons, buggies, and all types of farm implements. The need for a blacksmith was one of the first to make itself known in the new town. In early 1855 an eloping couple led to the establishment of the first "smithy" shop in Bristol. Young James N. Yoste, then 21, from he never told where, being in love with Rebecca, whose last name was never known and who was then only sixteen, had been refused the privilege of marrying his beloved. Consequently, the two had eloped and arrived in Bristol late one rainy winter afternoon. They were taken in by the kindly widow, Martha Buchanan Zimmerman. Joseph R. Anderson, learning of the young man's trade, built the town's first blacksmith shop next to the lot where later stood his Fourth Street store. The business was a success from the opening day. Young Yoste proved his worth beyond all expectations, soon gaining a reputation that brought work from far and wide. The flash of his forge and the ring of his hammer were familiar to the settlers of early downtown Bristol. A local gentleman once showed me a cow bell that had been made by "Jimmy" Yoste, Bristol's first blacksmith. Anderson became so fond of the young man that he had set up in business that he soon built a small cottage further up Fourth, which he rented to the happy couple for virtually nothing.

FIRST TAILOR SHOP

The first shop of this type was opened in the Famous Hotel (later Thomas House) about 1858 by Mrs. Elizabeth J. Vance. Her husband, David Vance, had become disabled to the point that he could no longer work and provide for their family of three children. Fortunately, she had already learned the trade of a tailor and had established somewhat of a reputation as such. Uncle Billy Butler, who had recently opened the Famous Hotel and knew of the plight of the family, gave her the use of a front room for her tailoring shop and allowed the family to live in two adjoining rooms. By the time the oldest daughter was ten years old, she was helping earn the family lodging by cleaning the hotel rooms and working in the dining room. And young Melissa S. Vance, when fourteen, was the only witness to the murder of A. K. Moore, which occurred in a room of this hotel in 1863. Mrs. Vance became a noted tailor of early Bristol, finally building a home "by the strength of her needle."

Others known to have been engaged in this trade included Mrs. Indiana Lethridge, who with her sister Angeline (Bristol's first lady teacher) maintained a home and shop on Main Street. And included in this household was the bright-eyed Julia, daughter of Angeline, and somewhat of a child prodigy who could play beautiful music on the piano when only seven years old. Mrs. Elizabeth Steel also made her living by the needle and thereby supported her three young boys, David, William, and Henry. A widow, Elizabeth Lathim, was another noted plyer of the needle in early Bristol, as was Mrs. Bettie Robison, who began her career at the age of fifteen and by age twenty was making men's suits that were the talk of the town.

FIRST BAKERY

Samuel H. Buckalien and his wife Oratta opened Bristol's first bakery in 1858. It was located on Fourth Street in a small building owned by J. R. Anderson. The Buckaliens were from Baltimore, Maryland.

DRAYING

Lewis Bachelor, his wife Rosetta, and a foster daughter, Ann, arrived in Bristol from Fredricksburg, Virginia, in late April 1855. Both Lewis and Rosetta were natives of Germany. They possessed little more than a determination to survive in their new surroundings when they arrived. It has been said that the key to success is to find a need and fill it well. Lewis Bachelor saw a need and made plans to fill it. It was fortunate for him that Jesse Blevins soon arrived from Smyth County with an extra wagon and team that he bought for his move and that he proposed to sell soon after he was well settled. Lewis Bachelor paid down all he had on Blevins' surplus property and made a note for the balance. And with that wagon and team he began Bristol's first freight service.

Rosetta Bachelor, a giant of a woman and "stout as an ox," pitched right in and helped with the operation as did the thirteen-year-old foster daughter. And if Lewis happened to pick up extra work at various odd jobs, Rosetta took complete charge of the draying operation. Ann Bachelor relates in her memoirs how the three were often up at 3:00 A.M. to begin the work of the day, especially after the railroad reached Bristol in 1856, and that the work often ended several hours after darkness had come to the town. She also recalled that hauling a load of supplies from the depot to local merchants might bring a dollar and that small jobs were often done for a quarter. In about a year there was need for another wagon. It was bought, and this put Rosetta in complete charge of one half the operation.

The ever alert Rosetta Bachelor, perceiving that people needed transporting as much as freight needed hauling, dipped into the profits in 1857 and bought a fine buggy. The Bachelors hired a free man of color to take over the second wagon, freeing Rosetta to begin what might be called Bristol's first taxi service. She never missed an incoming train, usually finding a traveler or two who needed rides. Often there were those who wanted to go far into the surrounding country. They were obliged, but at a handsome charge. Ladies of the town often criticized the enterprising Rosetta for what they called a vulgar and unlady-like occupation, but the dollars were rolling in and that meant more to Rosetta than acceptance into local society. Others said it was a mighty dangerous operation for a woman, hauling strange men "through the wilderness," as she often did. Perhaps they did not know that somewhere within the folds of her ample skirts two or three loaded pistols were always secreted, and that under the driver's seat was a double edged knife with a foot long blade, and an iron club, both of which had been made for her by local blacksmith, Jimmy Yoste. And anyone knowing the strength and temperament of Rosetta Bachelor (and even a stranger would know this after one encounter with her) would not likely raise her ire again, especially when she had such an arsenal at hand.

From this humble beginning the Bachelors attained a degree of wealth that was the envy of the town. In time they owned valuable business property and built one of the finer brick homes on lower Main Street. And if their gold, which she buried, could be found today, its current value would be staggering. Others who were in the draying business in Bristol before the Civil War include Jacob Lanter and Sparrell Asque. Using her fist, not the iron club, Rosetta Bachelor once knocked Asque flat in the street because she thought he had "horned a job away from her."

COMMISSION HOUSES

The receiving, selling, and shipping of area produce was a profitable business in early Bristol. For this purpose Joseph R. Anderson built a grain exchange at the corner of Fourth and Main. This building, erected in 1858, later became the Exchange Hotel and finally was the famous Nickels House. Another commission house belonged to L. F. Johnson and Son, opening in 1859. Commissions received on abundant area produce contributed much to the fortunes of these enterprising merchants.

THE FINER ARTS

Strangely, for a young, wild and wooly border town, Bristol boasted two silversmiths in its early years. One was Joseph Bunn, who, with his wife Amanda, lived in a small cottage on Fourth Street belonging to Joseph Anderson. His shop was in this cottage. The other was A. S. Jones of whom nothing further is known. And it appears that young Richard More, a single man, set up Bristol's first photography studio in 1859. He operated in a room of the Langhorne Tavern on Fourth (later Front) Street.

FIRST BRISTOL INDUSTRIES

On his original map of Bristol, Joseph Anderson extolled the potential of Beaver Creek as a power-providing stream. At that time much of the hope of an industrial future for his town seemed to be based on the promise of this creek. However the first industry to locate in the town did not use this power source. On October 24, 1854, Samuel B. Morgan, Alexander Morgan, James W. Morgan, and Madison T. Morgan, all of Bedford County, Virginia, signed an agreement forming a partnership "for the purpose of milling, sawing, and making lumber with a steam engine, in Bristol, in the county of Washington, State of Virginia." This mill was set up near the southwest corner of Washington and Williams Street in May or June of 1855. Ann Bachelor recalled seeing the equipment for this mill being brought to the site, pulled by several oxen. (The railroad had not yet arrived.) She also recalled a

humorous incident that happened soon after the mill began operation. It seems
that some Bristol residents had never seen a steam engine in operation, so
they gathered up near the mill to watch the proceedings. The head sawyer
was a big, burly Irishman named O'Leary. Glancing about at the crowd he
thought of a way to have a little excitement. He released a valve on the boiler
causing a shrieking, hissing jet of steam to shoot upward. "Saints above save
us," he screamed as he lunged forward in pretended fright. "She's gonna
blow up." And the wild, screeching, yelling, stampede of the crowd was
on. Some fell over logs and lumber piles in the frenzied flight. But finally,
looking back, some of the crowd saw that the big Irishman was rolling in
the sawdust, nearly hysterical with laughter. Ann Bachelor thought it was
John Bosang, who, recognizing the hoax, returned and whipped the Irishman
with a board. It is said that O'Leary, the head sawyer, left town before
nightfall. This first Bristol industry supplied much of the lumber that went
into the earliest structures in town.

The second Bristol industry, which opened in the summer of 1855, harnessed
the waters of Beaver Creek for its power source. This was a shingle mill
set up by Jesse Aydlotte and located near the present Moore Street Bridge.
Virtually every building in the new town was covered with the products of
this mill.

On June 6, 1855, G. H. Mattox of Bedford County, Virginia, bought lots
1 and 2 from Joseph Anderson. These lots reached from present Washington
to Virginia Street with one fronting on what is now Buford Street. Here Mattox
set up his woodworking plant (actually cabinet shop). It was powered by oxen
on a tread wheel. Much later he went to steam power. In this shop was made
much of the fine furniture that graced early Bristol homes. He was Bristol's
first undertaker, making the coffins in his shop.

About 1856 a pottery works was set up in the six hundred block of Main
(State) Street. This was known as the Virginia and Tennessee Pottery Works
and the products were marked with VATE. The clay for this pottery was
obtained in Flat Hollow near the old slave burying ground (see chapter entitled Mortality/Cemeteries). Ann Bachelor could not remember the name
of the old gentleman who was the master potter and owner of the works but
thought that he died during the Civil War and that the pottery ceased operation at that time.

In the late 1850s, probably 1859, a Mr. Simon, who had a wagon and carriage factory at Abingdon, opened a branch of his works here. The factory
stood north of Main (State) above the Beaver Creek bridge, and part of this
factory extended over the creek bed. It is said that the wagon works survived the war and operated for some time afterward. It took a good deal of
meat to supply a growing town. Consequently, a slaughter house was estab-

lished around 1858 near the railroad on the Fourth Street side and across that street (now Edgemont) from the east end of Shelby. Several people were employed there. It seems that the operator had the habit of disposing of the offal by pitching it through holes in the floor, into a ditch by the railroad, or simply out the back door toward Fourth Street. The stench revolted the town. The city council of Bristol, Tennessee, found it necessary to send a committee to reckon with the owner about the matter. It seems that businesses and homes were having to keep windows and doors closed in the heat of summer because of the foul odor, and their owners were raising quite a "stink" with the council.

When twenty-one years old, William Briscoe decided to seek his fortune in the new town of Bristol. He had learned brick making at Abingdon; and sensing that such would be possible in Bristol, he rented land on Main (Virginia side) and in the first block beyond Beaver Creek. There he set up Bristol's first brickyard. The town was growing and most builders were using brick, thus his business was a success from the start. Mr. Briscoe later went into building but continued to manufacture brick.

The noted Peppers of Wythe County, Virginia, came to Bristol by 1857. Two of these enterprising new residents set up the town's first tannery near the present intersection of Piedmont and State, probably the northeast corner thereof. It operated through most of the ensuing decade. So was Bristol business and industry up to the beginning of the Civil War.

THE GREAT INTERRUPTION

The Civil War brought a great slowdown in Bristol business and industry. Other than the general distress of the country, access to eastern markets was cut off. Bristol stores had greatly depended upon Baltimore, Philadelphia, and New York wholesalers for supplies. Now, all these locations were considered as being on "foreign" soil. As the war dragged on, local stocks dwindled and prices soared. A perplexing problem long after the war was that local merchants had sold goods on credit at highly inflated prices (determined by Confederate money) and then, if ever collected, payments were based on current standards, which meant just pennies on the dollar. Also, it must be noted that eastern wholesalers had not been able to collect debts made just before the outbreak of the war and were a bit reluctant to extend further credit. Yet, some local merchants, among them Joseph R. Anderson and W. W. James, paid old prewar debts once communication with their former suppliers was resumed.

BUSINESS AS USUAL

It is truly amazing, viewed in the light of an economy in chaos, how quickly it was business as usual for Bristol stores and industries. A report in the September 29, 1865, edition of the *Bristol News* paints a glowing picture of flourishing business activity in the town. It seems that Joseph R. Anderson was then the leading merchant. His ad in the paper just mentioned gives a glimpse of the prices of those immediate postwar months:

Coffee	lb.	.50
Bacon	lb.	.20
Butter	lb.	.15
Cheese	lb.	.10
Country jeans cloth	yd.	.75
Flour	barrel	12.00
Salt	sack	4.00
Iron	lb.	.07
Vinegar	gal.	.25
Lard	gal.	.20

At the same time Anderson offered to pay $2.75 per bushel for wheat, forty cents per bushel for oats, and forty to fifty cents per bushel for corn. His ad mentioned that he had just returned from New York, Philadelphia and Baltimore, which indicates he had reestablished contact with his suppliers and that public transportation was then available. Records indicate that there were about twenty stores in town at the close of the war and that within months most of them were just about doing business as usual.

During this period it is known that R. F. Betterton was operating a produce commission house near the depot (Virginia) as was the firm of Johnson-Brewer & Company (L. F. Johnson and W. P. Brewer). Wilbar & Johnston offered such delicacies as sugar crackers (cookies?), raisins, French kisses, lemons, and soda water. (Did Bristolians then drink "pop?") Of course, there was no refrigeration then, but this store did offer pickled oysters! E. W. Ellis, basement of the Nickels House, had fresh coffee, the finest sugar in town, and was expecting Cheshire cheese. Adjoining Ellis was J. W. Reese and Company offering toys, candies, books, and fireworks. It may be mentioned here that the Nickels House basement was a choice business location. The west end of this building was high above the ground, offering a walk-in basement where several choice business rooms were always filled. In the same basement during this period was the Exchange Saloon, operated by Luttrell and Gillham (operators of the hotel) who offered free cigars with the drinks and assured the public that good order would be kept.

Rosetta Bachelor's taxi service seems to have never halted throughout the war, and she had added another buggy and a surrey by late 1865 and employed drivers for the same. (It is said that the surrey was reserved for special outings.)

And the taxi business not only made her much money, but it aided greatly in her news gathering "service." By then Rosetta had the reputation of being the carrier of news, usually bad, for the town. She was a near-fanatical religionist and super moralist; thus any activity of a lewd or shady character immediately received "front page coverage."

For a time during those postwar years, W. W. James, the prince merchant on the Virginia side, had added partners, John M. and W. D. Jones, brothers of his second wife, and the store was then known as James and Jones. In 1866 L. H. Rogan announced that his store was reestablished in the King block in Goodson and that merchandise was coming in from Baltimore. D. J. Ensor and Pepper Brothers (Drs. C. T. and J. G.) were the leading druggists during the five-year period following the close of the Civil War. And during that time (probably 1866) Hill and Miner opened a barber shop in the basement of the Walker House Hotel on Fourth Street. This shop was marked by the sign of the diamond pole. Williams and King were leading realtors and had much property, both city and rural, to offer the public. By October 1866 Bristol had its first jewelry store, Jones and Caldwell (A. S. Jones and H. C. Caldwell). Later this firm became H. C. Caldwell, Jeweler. Mr. Caldwell came to Bristol from New Orleans, Louisiana. This very capable jeweler died young (early 1870s) and is buried in the historic East Hill Cemetery. W. E. Cunningham & Company set up a confectionery here in about 1866.

By 1869 Mrs. Betty Gallaway had opened her exclusive millinery store. This came as a great relief to the ladies of the town, who before had been forced to buy personal articles of clothing in regular stores, though virtually all merchants could round up a female to wait on the ladies at such times. Some merchants were known to have kept a lady waiting while they sent home for their wives to come to the store for such purposes. There were women in the town who would not so much as buy a hat or dress without a lady clerk.

By the late 1860s, perhaps before, stoves, both cooking and heating, were plentiful on the markets here. One of the larger dealers was William N. Keller. Later W. P. Brewer was a leader in this field. And by late 1869 J. D. Robertson had set up his store in the 500 block of Main (State) Street, Tennessee side, where he offered "the finest, syrup, sugar, coffee and tea in town." J. S. Bingley's Corner Store, a leader at the time, offered everything from an orange to a ton of coal! The closing year of the decade (1860s) found Elijah Hall Seneker enlarging his store and stock at the noted Seneker's Corner (now Lee and State). He stressed that he could sell merchandise at nearly pre-war prices. By the closing year of the 1860s, George and H. Harmeling had set up a store in Bristol that sold everything from a hay rake to shaving mugs. At about the same time I. B. Dunn and Company opened a very large store which contained "1,000 things too tedious to mention." The ladies might breathe easier now, for H. C. Caldwell had put in a line of the Wilcox and Gibbs sewing machine, and his shop then housed a fine tailor, a Mr. William G. Stratton. And no less a person than I. C. Fowler became the agent for Worsley's perfumed soap for laundry and toilet. A new drugstore opened in the autumn of 1869. It was founded by Dr. Jere Bunting. This store became an institution in the town. In those early days he offered such diverse things as pure drugs, paints, tooth brushes and stationery. He would sell you five hundred sheets of fine paper for a quarter!

THE BIG TWENTY

The twenty-year period, 1870-1890, brought a tremendous increase in both business and industry. About the beginning of this period, Thomas C. Lancaster set up the largest commission house at the time on Front Street. Dr. H. T. Berry and William Burrow added to their wealth by opening a large mercantile establishment on the Virginia side of town. E. H. Seneker had prospered to the point that he erected a fine new brick building on Seneker's corner in 1872. A sign of the prosperity of the times was the organization in 1871 of the Exchange Bank of Goodson, which opened for business on May 15 that year with E. H. Seneker as president and W. W. James as cashier. The first board of directors was made up of J. H. Wood, W. W. Davis, John Keys, Jesse A. Buckner, J. H. Pepper, Col. N. M. Taylor and J. W. Owen. This bank was located on Front Street next door to the James store. Shares were valued at one hundred dollars each. This gave the town two major banks, Anderson's long private banking services had been organized into the First National Bank in 1868. John M. Crowell, long a builder in the town, set up a Main Street store and tin shop in 1875. At the same time Col. J. M. "Jeems" Barker erected a three-story brick store building in the 500 block of Main Street (Virginia side). Barker had started work as a clerk with E. H. Seneker, living in the Seneker home at the time, and had advanced to his own business. Strangely, his first business, sure to give Seneker competition (it stood only two or three doors west), was financed by this kind old Bristol merchant. At that time business property was selling for about ten dollars per front foot. Six years later it was bringing forty-five dollars per front foot.

In the mid-1870s S. R. Ferguson, formerly of Portsmouth, Virginia, opened a giant hardware store in Bristol. The noted Doriot's of Wytheville had arrived by that time and were offering fine jewelry to the town. Arch Pickens, formerly of London, England, was their chief competitor. He erected a huge thermometer and clock in front of his store which stood midway of the 400 block of Main Street, Virginia side. These were consulted hundreds of times daily by passing throngs. Pickens kept the first daily weather records in Bristol. His old home still stands at 409 Fifth Street, now the home of Mr. and Mr. Floyd L. Whitehead. Kuhnerts Bakery was opened in the mid-1870s and, along with baked goods, offered oysters served in any style. This business was on Front Street about a block north of Main. Joel Galliher's livery stable offered horse boarding at seventy-five cents per day. And you could heat your home with fuel from the Brush Mountain Coal Company, operated by W. B. Payne and Son. Cornelius A. Gray would cut and dress your hair at his shop on Front Street, one door south of Bunting and Pepper. Butler & Wolfe would sell you about anything for cash and would pay instant cash for produce. About every store then in town did a lot of barter trade, but this store sold for cash only. Among other articles, they sold cigars for two to twenty-five cents. E. J. Coman would make you a suit at his fashionable tailor shop on Main Street and gather the news at the same time. (He was a correspondent for the *Bristol News* and had once published a paper here.) During this period John A. James offered coffee at twenty-five cents per pound at his store at No. 1, James block (his was the first numbered store in town). If you had a yearn to read or write, King and Hill offered the works in their book and stationery store in the 400 block of Main Street, Tennessee side. This store could also order a Steiff piano for you. J. Bamberger & Company boasted that their clothes were the finest in town. Jesse A. Buckner was then considered a top merchant (Buckner Street was named for him). And those who died might be buried by the legendary H. A. Bickley, who could sell a casket for you and furniture to your mourners.

The late 1870s saw two more millinery shops in town, one by Miss Addie Gatchell, mid-400 block of Main Street, Tennessee side (about where Buntings later stood), and Mrs. E. J. Frost, also on Main Street. At the same time Mrs. Betty Gallaway, Bristol's first milliner, was pleading with the public to come forth and pay debts owed her. In this period (late 1870s) one could buy the finest in high Victorian furniture at G. C. Gallaway's Bristol Furniture House. He also had a hearse and would tend to the burying of the dead. Shoes could then be bought in a shop in the Nickels House Hotel basement. S. W. C. Hudgens, said to be a champion "cusser," offered tinware and roofing materials and services to the local home owners. D. J. Ensor had prospered to the point that a much larger drug store was needed. A. S. McNeil of Tazewell County, Virginia, arrived in 1879 to open a furniture and undertaking business in a building he rented from W. W. James on Main Street. About ten years later he built the three-story brick structure that now houses William King Clothiers and Goodman Jewelry. Yarbrough & Wood (C. B. Yarbrough, John G. and William M. (Uncle Billy) Wood) had a first-class store mid-400 block, Main Street, Tennessee side. And John W. Jett had enlarged his building to include a general store. Jett's old home still stands at 213 Solar Street.

The new decade, 1880, began with Williams & Keebler's erecting a huge general mercantile store on Main Street. A year later Joseph R. Anderson erected what was said to be the finest store building in East Tennessee or Southwest Virginia at 410 Main Street. This three-story brick building also housed the Masonic Lodge and the law offices of Haynes & Curtin. The building was thirty by one hundred feet. Insurance on these buildings and others could be arranged through I. C. Fowler or W. P. Brewer and others. G. M. Whitten offered all manner of farm implements, seeds, and feeds. He was located on Main Street, Bristol, Tennessee. A. S. Gump was then one of the most prominent merchants in town. He advertised as Gump, The Clothier.

On through the 1880s it may be found that W. T. Hayter had one of the larger stores in town (Tennessee side). Jeff L. Duff, merchant, was sole local distributor for Harpers Bazaar patterns and offered to fill orders by mail for country merchants. He was located at 103 Main Street. J. W. Mort found it necessary to move to larger quarters for his gun shop. He also carried a general line of sporting goods. He would make or duplicate keys. J. M. "Jeems" Barker had greatly enlarged his business. He offered rifle powder at five dollars per keg and blasting powder at two seventy-five for the same amount. C. L. Sevier, a direct descendant of Governor John Sevier, offered in his hardware store the Webster wagon and Chattanooga chilled plows. He also sold guns and once had a clerk quit because a gun he had sold had been used in a brutal murder.

In the 1880s one could buy saddles and such at the Bristol Saddle and Harness Emporium on Fifth Street, operated by M. F. DeArmond. S. J. James (son of the prince merchant W. W. James) asked that the public come to his store before buying anything; he would not be undersold and would match the prices of anyone in town. Those who wanted fine dinnerware could go to Dogett's China Company. Their stock was getting fuller and brighter. It was in the 1880s that Edward W. King came to the front among local merchants. A native of Piney Flats, Tennessee, New Bethel area, he had come to Bristol in the 1870s and began merchandising around 1878. In time he went into the wholesale business of which he made a great success. Soon after 1900 he erected the grand mansion that still adorns the southwest corner of Anderson and Seventh. His brother Henry P. King founded a store in 1889 that was long an institution in this city. For years he maintained a grand country home, The Oaks, near Wallace, Virginia. Another brother, Landon C. King, founded the overall factory that still bears his name. Other businesses known to have been operating in the 1880s include Hedrick & Cody, E. A. Burson,

Merchant (son of the legendary Z. L. Burson), J. W. and L. Hill, Norvell
& McDowell, Pendleton's Jewelry, W. F. Cooper, Jewelry, and William-
son & Minor, Druggist. The thirsty and pleasure loving could visit the Nickel
Plate Saloon, Bristol's most lavish drinking place operated by Isaac A. Nickels.
The hungry might go to Everett's Tip Top Cafe on Front Street, W. G. Lind-
sey's Oyster Restaurant in the Nickels House, or Kuhnerts Eureka Dining
Hall. And in connection with eating, Dr. S. W. Rhea offered the best set
of false teeth for fifteen dollars!

EARLY BRISTOL STORE DISPLAYS ITS WARES: The store pictured above was
operated by David Jenkins Hart and a Mr. Hicks in the late 1800s. It was located in
the 500 block of State Street (then Main).

The 1890s presented a time of new businesses, to be sure, but was more
noted for its strengthening of old firms and the weeding out of the weaker
ones. It was during this time that the Dominion Bank came into being with
H. E. McCoy as president; W. F. Rhea, vice president; H. E. Jones, cashier;
and J. M. Barker, 2nd vice-president. Others who were prominently identified with this bank include William Pitzer, J. B. Richmond, John Keys,
W. A. Sparger and E. C. Manning. Another new bank at that time was called
Bristol Title Bank and Trust Company and was located at the corner of Fifth
and Main. Its president was William McGeorge, Jr., and John H. Caldwell

was vice president. The Holston Building and Loan Association was in business during this last decade of the century. It claimed to be paying twenty-five percent interest. Its president was Major A. D. Reynolds and the treasurer was John C. Anderson.

Care to send flowers? Richardson Brothers offered hothouse plants, cut flowers and floral designs. C. P. Cannon, Realtor, would provide a lot and build a home complete for one-fourth down and easy monthly payments. The Bristol Land and Improvement Company would deduct one hundred dollars from the price of a lot if the buyer could show his readiness to erect a house at once. At W. B. Pemberton's 800 block, Main Street, Virginia side, one could buy everything from beans to coffins. Other firms of this decade included T. E. A. Sweet (you guessed it, they called him Tea Sweet and often Sweet Tea), tin shop; O. O. White, Tailor and Merchant; Hill & Travis, agents for unusual building materials, No. 7, Pile Block; Stark & Cochran, Druggist; Bristol Hardware Company, 509 Main Street; The Bee Hive, general merchandise; Pitzer's Department Store, one of the largest in town; and Model Clothing House. Also J. H. Everett and Sons had added a private dining room for ladies at their Tip Top Restaurant, and a first class saloon for gentlemen only. J. Wesley Davis then operated the City Barber Shop at the corner of Fourth and Main (basement of the Nickels House). Firms that yet exist from that period include Minor's Drugs, Pendleton's Jewelry, the Mitchell-Powers Hardware Company and Bunting's Drug Store.

It is well to mention that through all the period covered by this chapter, street peddling was big business in the Town of Bristol-Goodson. Farmers from near and far brought produce of all descriptions to sell on the streets of Bristol. Some simply parked a wagon and sold in place, while others carried their wares from door to door, both downtown and in the residential areas. Editor Fowler once wrote of his annoyance at having to look up from his writing to answer persons who had called at the door asking if he wanted apples, honey or what have you. He once wrote of the editor of the *Courier* having bought butter from a little boy who had claimed it was very fresh. He wondered how a boy so small could tell so big a story and ventured to predict that the lad would someday be a great writer of fiction. He went on to surmise that "the boy had been sharper on the sell than had been the editor on the smell!"

But the lad's story was mild compared to that of a back country woman who appeared in town one cold, blustery day carrying a lone chicken under her arm. Stopping at stores that sold groceries she would ask if she might have a little meal in return for the chicken. It was the last chicken on the place she said, and her three children would miss the eggs; they had been managing to have an egg each perhaps on Sunday, but now meal must be had. Likely true to her expectation, the kind old merchants of Bristol would not take the last chicken from a poor widow, but did give her a little meal and not a few other articles of food. It appears that before the day passed she had received enough meal to last a good while and still had her chicken. That chicken must have been hardy, for it was said that the same woman tried the trick several years later.

It was recommended that a market house be built on the Virginia side of town and that all peddlers be required to confine their selling to its stalls, at a fee of course. This was never built, but in the early 1890s such a place was built on the Tennessee side, where now stands the old post office building. It was soon destroyed by a tornado, much to the delight of the ever-present street peddlers.

One favorite parking place for the over mountain peddlers from extreme east Tennessee and western North Carolina was along Shelby Street between Eighth and Ninth Streets. This became known as Apple Row for one of the chief articles of produce sold there. A mule and horse trading barn was set up about where the bus station is now located and many a peddler drove a different team home because of the trades made there. And the section along Ninth between Shelby and Broad became a red-light district catering to the out-of-town trade. The story goes that many a peck of apples was bartered for lewd purposes in that section.

BUSINESS SIGNS

Virtually all Bristol businesses displayed signs, but not all prospective customers could read them. Many, perhaps most, of those who passed through the streets of the town could not recognize one letter. For that reason several enterprising merchants displayed an emblem or some other means of identifying their locations. Austin M. Appling, who early had a store in the original Bristol, Virginia, painted his building a bright yellow for this purpose. For years it was known as the yellow house and is so designated on old deeds and records. I. B. Dunn & Company painted the store front a "heavy" red; and if that were not enough, a red flag was displayed along with it! The blue store, owned by Rufus Ayers was so known because of its identifying color. And up Fourth Street was a building known as the spotted house because it was painted deep green with red spots. One business place was identified by its flat roof (most stores still had the standard gabled roof).

Pepper's Drug Store displayed a large red mortar over the door, while the drug business of Bunting & Dickey was marked by a golden eagle. A boot cut from wood hung over the entry of G. W. Frost's shoe business on Main Street. A giant pair of wooden scissors marked a local tailor shop. A rifle cut from wood, with a wooden pistol hanging beneath, pointed to J.

W. Mort's gun and sporting goods store. Yarbrough & Wood simply displayed a red flag. And Pocahontas Hale, noted madam of the Black Shawl, the most "prosperous" house of ill fame in town, was not to be outdone. While most of such houses in town had only a single red shaded light burning in a front window (that was sign enough), Madam Hale had an artist paint a life size figure of a beautiful woman (fully clothed, of course) smiling and pointing to the front door of her (Hale's) notorious place of business.

"Strings" Lewis Whitten, who made a small fortune on Bristol's dead and injured chickens. Sweet Molly's sandwiches pleased many a railroad passenger.

"Sweet" Molly Whitten, wife of "Strings" Lewis Whitten. Most of her adult years were spent in processing Bristol's rejected chickens.

NO SIGN NEEDED

But there were some enterprising souls here who did not need signs. Indeed they operated without buildings, yet even Horatio Alger would have been proud of their success stories. One of these was "Strings" Lewis Whitten, so called because he always pulled his trouser legs to his knees and tied them with strings. With muddy streets and unbridged creeks and branches over the town at that time, perhaps such action was well warranted. Strings lived off East Main (State) Street with his wife whom he and everyone else called "Sweet Molly." Late every day Strings made the rounds of all local stores where chickens were taken in barter. His booming call of "got any chickens today" meant had the merchant culled out any dead, injured or defective fowls from the day's take. If so, Strings would take them. The dead ones free and the others for about a dime each. That night he and "Sweet Molly" butchered, cleaned and cooked and made dozens of chicken sandwiches seasoned to perfection with their secret herb mix. Next day he boarded every stopped passenger train, ambled down the aisles calling out, "Sweet Molly's sandwiches, folks, jist a nickel, jist a nickel will do." His reputation spread until regular passengers looked forward to the Bristol stop and a feast on Sweet Molly's very tasty productions. They would never know of course, that some of those sandwiches had to have a little extra herb mix to mask the rancid taste of some chickens that had been dead too long. But once a regular passenger, having heard rumors of the meat source of these sand-wiches, asked the vendor point blank if his offerings were made of dead chicken. Quick as a wink, Strings Lewis Whitten quipped back, "Why, shore 'nuff sir, I ain't never been able to get a live chicken to lay still on a piece of bread yet!"

And Strings and Molly saved and wisely invested those nickels. In a few years they were able to buy a house on Clinton Avenue, where they con-tinued to make chicken sandwiches by the score. In October 1886, Strings, loaded with sandwiches, took hold of the hand rail by a passenger coach door and started to pull himself up. He faltered and staggered backward and, gasp-ing, crumpled to the platform dead.

Some say it was about 1870 while others say it was just shortly after the war that "Aunt" Annie Goforth, a recently freed slave, set up her shade tree laundry on the south bank of Beaver Creek at about the present Randall Expressway crossing. Old-timers told that her "plant equipment" consisted of two or three tubs, a cast iron boiling pot, and a rub board and water pail that had been given her by W. P. Brewer, an early tinware dealer here. All this was scattered about under a spreading sycamore that stood between the creek and the pasture where the milk cows of the Virginia Hotel grazed. And, oh yes, there was one battered chair in which she sat just once per day, usually in mid-afternoon, to smoke her little stone pipe. She made her own soap, often going from door to door to ask for old meat scraps for this purpose.

Laboring in humid summer heat and often while standing in winter's snow, she always kept the lines that were strung up and down Beaver loaded with the town's laundry. If anyone ventured to offer sympathy for her hard lot in life, she would just smile and say, "hit's a sight better than digging in them rocky old hills on North Fork" (River). She always kindly blest those who passed by, "the Lawd bless you sah," or "the Lawd bless you honey," was heard by many a passing citizen. And if, as often happened, downpours drenched the clothes on her line (she always took refuge under a huge piece of oil cloth at such times even in severe thunderstorms), unperturbed, she would just smile and calmly say, ''No matter; the sun'll come out again. Hit always does!'' This author has often thought of those words when times have been a little dark.

Like Strings Whitten, Aunt Annie saved her nickels, dimes and quarters. A house was bought, then another, and another. She started keeping boarders in the largest house, walking a half mile one way every noon to ''feed my people,'' as she always expressed it. When she ''retired'' at eighty-four, she owned more than a dozen rent houses and lived on the revenue from them for another twelve years. When her aged daughter told this writer much of this over thirty years ago, she still had a cherished possession — an old wooden bucket in which she, as a child, had carried countless buckets of water from Beaver to her mother's pots and tubs.

COMPETITION

Not all trade dollars stayed in Bristol. The citizens were under constant bombardment from distant advertisers who loaded the columns of local newspapers with their offerings from grand pianos to teeth saving toothpicks, formulas, nostrums, magic potions, sure-cure pills for cancer to impotency (then called seminal weakness), to cures for baldness; all these and more were constantly dangled before an often unwary public. Some were outright frauds. One advertiser offered a sure way to take three pounds of butter from a gallon of milk, only one dollar postpaid. When the near magic formula came to many a local and area household, it was even more generous than expected, for it offered three ways. The formula read:

> If three pounds of butter have fallen or been placed in a gallon of milk, you may recover it with your hands (please wash first), use various types of tongs, or pour the milk out!

It is doubtful if anyone tried it, but all knew it would work.

In those days many a local woman was burdened (and often killed) by excessive child bearing. Some freshened in hope when an ad appeared in a local paper offering a sure remedy for the prevention of further enlargement of one's family. (''Pregnancy'' would have then been considered a vulgar word.) It assured the reader that the remedy required no dangerous pills or harmful devices and could be had for just two dollars. Off went many an order. After the advertiser waited awhile to receive as many orders as possible from the town, he produced the sure-fire, guaranteed never to fail remedy: ''Dear Madam: To prevent further enlargement of your family carefully make sure that you have no physical contact whatever with your husband or any other man. If possible keep at least a yard's distance between you and all males at all times. Do this, and your worries are over!'' It would work, wouldn't it? In 1955 an old gentleman living on McDowell Street showed this writer a yellowed and torn copy of this remedy and remarked that, "Maw must have not used it for I was born several years after she received it!"

Early Bristolians were plagued by mosquitos. Thus, many sent for an advertised method — no powders, sprays or other harmful chemicals — to kill the pests and absolutely warranted to work. Indeed it would work! The method consisted of two small wooden blocks. The instructions said, "Put them between these blocks and mash hell out of them!"

POSTWAR BRISTOL INDUSTRY

Industry was a bit slow in coming to Bristol during the first five years after the close of the war. Town leaders were still looking to the Beaver (a much stronger stream than now) to entice industrialists to the town. Indeed, it was with the expectation that Johnston and Scranton of Savannah, Georgia, would put in much machinery on this creek that Anderson had sold a great portion of the original Bristol, Virginia, in 1856. The war had stopped all these plans, and for some reason Beaver was not much used as a power source until the 1870s.

H. A. Bickley of Wise County, Virginia, came here during the later part of the Civil War. Soon after peace was made, he began manufacturing furniture and coffins at his location near the present First Christian Church. His specialty (other than coffins) was bedsteads and bureaus.

In 1866 William Dixon, a native of Lunenburg County, Virginia, but who had lived a few years in Montgomery County, Alabama, being advised to seek a high elevation for his health, came to Bristol. He and his wife Elizabeth Charles Lucas bought a strip of land along Fourth Street, where the S. P. Rutherford Transfer and Storage Company now is located. This lot was to include his home, a rent house and an iron foundry. He took in a partner, a Mr. Smith from Marion, Virginia, and formed the firm of Dixon & Smith. His iron foundry prospered, becoming one of the important industries of the post-war period. One noted product of this foundry was wrought iron fencing, which, in time, surrounded many a Bristol home and cemetery lot. The fences varied in class from common to the most elegant. The superb wrought iron door of the King tomb on Beaver was one of the early products of this foundry. Mr. Dixon spent the remainder of his life in Bristol and is buried in the East Hill Cemetery. He was the great grandfather of the noted local historian, Mr. Charles Henritze, who has supplied much information for this book.

Around 1870 Mr. Charles C. Campbell set up a water-powered saw mill on Beaver near what is now the Goodson Street bridge and in back of his home, Campbell Grove. This industry supplied much of the lumber for local

William Dixon came to Bristol soon after the Civil War and founded the Dixon-Smith Iron Works. His ornamental iron fences surrounded many Bristol homes and cemetery lots.

building through the 1870s. About 1875 he had a flouring mill installed. Someone later complained that there had been a bit of sawdust in the morning biscuits. Campbell publicly vowed to correct the matter at once and promised flour as white and pure as a rose. Thus was born his famous White Rose Flour, that was long sold in the area. Mr. Campbell's establishment was known as Bristol Mills.

In the late 1860s or perhaps around 1870, two large brick plants were set up here: one by William H. (Uncle Will) Smith near the intersection of Shelby and Ninth; and the other by John Crowell above the northwest corner of present Piedmont and State Streets. While a great part of the output was used locally, both plants shipped to distant points. Smith later made ornamental trim for brick buildings, examples of which may yet be seen on his monument in East Hill Cemetery.

Charles P. Feldburg was operating a thriving mattress factory on Main (State) Street near the Beaver Creek bridge through the 1870s. He boasted that more people in southwest Virginia and east Tennessee slept on a Feldburg mattress than any other brand.

G. W. Frost & Company manufactured shoes and boots at a corner of Sixth and Main (thought to be the southwest corner). In the mid-1870s he employed fifteen hands, later doubling the number. His Frost Proof Boot was sold all over the south. He often traveled to Boston, Massachusetts, to buy supplies for the factory. At one time this firm was in the Hurt building on the Virginia side of Main Street.

For several years, beginning in the early 1870s, the Common Sense Bee Hive was manufactured in Bristol, Tennessee. The factory was owned by G. W. C. Gillespie, formerly of Union (Bluff City), Tennessee. His products were sold by agents traveling throughout the south. For several decades beginning around 1871, the Bristol tobacco industry flourished. J. H. Winston had the first auction house. The first tobacco sold in Bristol was handled by this house, which was located on the Virginia side of town. This sale took place in the fall of 1871, and was conducted by Rev. David Sullins. In 1872 the noted Major Abram D. Reynolds moved to Bristol from Patrick County, Virginia. He soon erected the first of three large buildings that stood side by side on Fourth Street, with backs to the railroad. Here Reynolds began the manufacture of twist and plug tobacco. Among his brands were Tennessee Leaf, Double Thick, Premium, May Queen, Geranium Rose, and Tennessee-Virginia Plug Cut. Smoking tobacco was sold under most of these brands. The association of prominent figures with tobacco seems to have been a subtle form of advertising even then. Tennessee-Virginia Plug Cut carried likenesses of Jefferson and Jackson on the package. Two Bristolians, John B. Childres and John H. Hager, were prominently associated with Reynolds in his tobacco works. Another Bristol tobacco firm was Critz & Reynolds, operating in a building at the side of the A. D. Reynolds Factory. It was owned by a brother and brother-in-law of Major Reynolds.

H. E. Graves with a Mr. Conway owned a tobacco warehouse on Cumberland Street. Major Z. L. Burson built a tobacco warehouse on West Main (State) in the early 1880s.

It is little known that Joseph R. Anderson, Bristol's founder, was once heavily involved in the tobacco processing business. He and his nephew, A. B. Carr, were partners with T. H. Penn in the firm of T. H. Penn and Company, with a large building on Fourth Street. By 1881 the company employed seventy-five workers. The firm operated both a warehouse and processing plant. Principal brand names were Contentment and Southern Gentleman. Mr. Penn rented the former home of Joseph Anderson when the latter moved to his Anderson Street mansion in 1881. The Penn firm ceased operations before 1900.

About 1870 Mr. W. G. Taylor, formerly of Blountville, set up a large tannery on Beaver Creek, below Shelby Street. Associated with him was a close relative, Mr. George C. Pile. Here Mr. Pile perfected a method whereby the time of the tanning process was cut by two-thirds. This process, patented in 1872, was eventually used in tanneries all over the world. Products from Taylor's tanning operation were marketed nationwide. A son of this early tanner was Oliver Taylor, Sr., who wrote the still widely read book, *Historic Sullivan.*

On December 1, 1871, Professor J. H. Winston bought eight acres from J. W. Owen, situated to the east of Goodson Street, north of Campbell's Mill, and south of Mary Street. Here Prof. Winston laid out Winston's Nurseries, that for years supplied fine stock to a wide area. Several agents worked southwest Virginia, east Tennessee, and east Kentucky. Here was developed the once popular Charlotte apple.

Around 1870 Mr. C. H. Lewis arrived from Danville, Virginia. He had long been engaged in the manufacture of textiles in that city. He set up the Bristol Woolen Mills (water-powered) at the southern end of what is now Mumpower Park, across Beaver from the Janie Hammitt Home. Among other services one might have custom spinning done at this mill at the rate of fifteen cents per pound. The mill provided employment for several Bristolians. In 1874 the firm of Jordon & Pepper employed Uncle Will Smith to build a woolen mill on Beaver Creek, a short distance below Main Street. The mill employed women and girls, as did a cotton mill erected by Thomas C. Lancaster a little further down Beaver Creek (between present Broad and Windsor). Both mills were water powered.

In 1876 Col. J. M. Barker, a Mr. Bibb (probably Robert or Thomas) and Dr. J. F. Hicks organized the Virginia Marble Works and set up a processing yard on the western slope of Solar Hill near Scranton Street. A vein of unusually deep red marble with lighter and contrasting shades of the same color was leased from Joel Kaylor, who had a large spread of land near Mendota, Virginia. The marble was hauled by wagon from the Kaylor lands (The railroad had not yet been built through that area.) and processed at the local yard. It was made into ornamental building marble, for both interior and exterior use. (Red would never have been then accepted for grave markers, which had to be of white or gray.) At one time this yard employed about twenty-five hands, one of whom was the late Ed Faidley, who through a daughter, supplied much information for this book.

Bristol, Tennessee, almost landed what might broadly be called an industry, at least a setup that would have ensured a big payroll here, perhaps to this day. In 1873 the state sought to build a new insane asylum for the eastern part of the state. Bristol was one of the favored locations. John G. King of Bristol was chosen as one of three commissioners to select the site. One of the requirements by the state was that the favored town provide three hundred acres of land for the institution's grounds and farmland. The state planned to spend seventy-five thousand dollars on the erection of buildings, and wise old editor Fowler commented in the *Bristol News* that such an expenditure here would be a great boon to the town. John G. King offered to sell the necessary land from his vast holdings just south of town, offering to give the ten acres necessary for the actual building site, which would have been at the end of Alabama Street. But the town procrastinated until the institution went elsewhere.

Brown Brothers Carriage Factory seems to have had its beginning in the mid or late 1870s. The factory and yards once stretched from Lee to Moore along Sycamore. The factory not only made their own designs but would custom make for individual customers. One of the strangest ever made was the design by General Imboden, prominent coal developer. In 1879 Imboden had the factory make for him a cart that had two wheels in front and tapered to one behind. The reason is not known.

The enterprising Doriots set up two unusual factories in Bristol in the late 1870s (likely 1879). One was a watch factory, which was housed in a small building near the north end of West Street. The other was a pencil factory, which occupied a small building on the southwest corner of Moore and Scott. At about the same time a Mr. Jordon set up a cigar factory near the north end of Solar Street on Solar Hill. The "factory" was actually a portion of his home, but he did employ several hands during peak production. His brand was Jordon's Mellow Gold.

In April 1879 A. S. McNeil, who had just moved from Tazewell County, Virginia, bought a half interest in the furniture business being operated on Lee Street by the pioneer industrialist, G. H. Mattox. At that time the plant was enlarged and several hands were employed. The plant sold furniture over a wide three- or four-state area.

In 1881 A. A. Hobson, formerly of Richmond, Virginia, later of Montgomery County, Virginia, and then of Johnson City, Tennessee, bought what had been the Campbell grove property (site of the present Athens Steak House on Buford Street) and the mill which stood in back of the grove. Mr. Hobson greatly enlarged the mill and began to buy and process choice hardwoods of the area. In time he was supplying fine hardwood trim for the homes of the nation, sometimes working as many as fifty hands. In 1884 Major A. D. Reynolds established the Bristol Bone Meal Company, buying bones by the wagon load and processing them into a special fertilizer. He later offered a prize for the finest produce "sparked" by this fertilizer.

In the early 1880s (indication is that it was 1881) a Mr. Phillips of Delaware set up a fruit drying plant in Bristol. He bought fruit by the "ton," employed several ladies to prepare it, and dried it on huge steel sheets spread out over a portion of the Winston nursery lot. His brand "Sun Dried Fruit" enjoyed a wide market. He also had ovens for the purpose, but mainly his fruit was indeed sun dried.

Around 1890 the Bristol Iron and Steel Company set up its plant in what became known as Furnace Bottom, lying to the west of Commonwealth near Euclid. The plant was supposed to signal the beginning of the new Pittsburgh of the South. It operated for a long time and gave a tremendous boost to the local economy. Folks used to gather on Solar Hill to watch the great flash of light when the slag was dumped at the plant. This was an awesome sight at night.

The area along Williams Street toward Norfolk seems to have been an early industrial park of sorts. In the 1890s the McCrary brothers, James and Samuel, operated a planing and millwork plant in this area. A box factory was also in the area at that time, as well as a cannery. It was in this area that John Buffman of Boston, Massachusetts, built Buffman Mills around 1889. This later became what is now known as Bristol Door and Lumber Company. Mr. Buffman and his wife, Sarah A. Buffman, built the home that still stands at 700 Pennsylvania Avenue, now occupied by Mae N. Rogers and Evelyn Werner.

In the 1890s there was a brickyard, planing mill, foundry, and terra cotta works in an industrial area about where the Melrose Street bridge is located now and extending for some distance down Beaver Creek and along the railroad.

WORKING CONDITIONS

Working in a business or factory in those days meant heavy toil from 6:00 A.M. until 6:00 P.M. and sometimes later in the stores. Wages were low; fifteen dollars per month was average for a store clerk, and less than a dollar per day for factory hands. There were no coffee breaks and only a short time for lunch. Most factories had work-call bells, with some later adding steam whistles where such was the power source. The slightest infraction might get one fired, with a dozen waiting to fill the vacancy. Just taking too long for a necessary trip to the toilet (outside privies) was considered a cause for instant dismissal. And there were no pension or profit sharing plans.

The plants and store buildings were stifling hot in summer and numbing cold in winter. Yet as bad as working conditions were, and as meager as the monetary reward was, many area men, and not a few women, felt that was better than laboring on the farm with little if any cash return, and so flocked into Bristol to join the labor force. And not a few saved their hard earned pennies and later became store and plant owners. One notable example of this was Col. J. M. Barker, who for several years clerked for E. H. Seneker. He finally set up his own store with a little financial backing by his former employer. In time he became one of the wealthiest citizens of Bristol.

It should not be assumed by the reader that this chapter contains a complete listing of Bristol businesses and industries of this period. There were many others that are not listed here. This is merely a sampling with an emphasis on those that have heretofore been but little, if at all, publicized.

Bibliography - Chapter Twelve

Anderson, Joseph R. Manuscript, cir. 1880.

Anderson, Rhea. Notes, 1930-1939.

Bachelor, Ann. Memoirs (unpublished), 1935-1937.

Bristol News, newspaper. Various issues, 1857-1881.

Developmental maps, cir. 1890

Johnson, L. F. Notes, 1893.

Loving, Robert S. *Double Destiny; the Story of Bristol, Tennessee-Virginia.* Bristol, Tennessee: King Printing Company, 1955.

Phillips, V. N. (Bud). Interviews with various older citizens, 1953-1956.

Sullivan County, Tennessee. Chancery Court Records.

Sullivan County, Tennessee. Deed and Tax Records.

Washington County, Virginia. Chancery Court Records.

Washington County, Virginia. Deed and Tax Records.

Chapter Thirteen
EARLY BRISTOL HOTELS

One of the first needs in a developing town is good hotels. Incoming prospective buyers and developers must have good accommodations, and the quality of such often is the source of the first impression, whether favorable or unfavorable, of a place of possible settlement. This was so in the Town of Bristol. In the earliest days, Joseph R. Anderson often kept travelers and prospective settlers in his home at Main and Fourth (now State and Edgemont Streets). Indeed, the upper east room of this house was set aside for that purpose. One early traveler remembered that there were four beds in that room, so closely crowded that one could almost go from one to the other without setting foot upon the floor. This traveler also stated that sometimes this room was so full that occasionally a late arriver might have to sleep on a saddle blanket in a nearby barn.

By 1855 Doctors John P. Hammer and W. A. M. Willoughby were keeping roomers in the Rev. James King house at 54 King Street, but this was not in the town limits of old Bristol, Virginia, so it cannot be said to have been the first hotel here. At that time the old King home was still the stage stop for the area. Thus, many travelers coming to Bristol spent their first night there and came into town the next day. However, it is known that some alighted from the stage at the mail stop (present intersection of King's Alley and Sycamore Street) and followed Anderson's mail boy, Nehemiah Strange, either to Anderson's home or later to the first Bristol hotel.

But the town was hardly a village when its first hotel was erected. On July 11, 1854, Joseph R. Anderson issued a deed to Alfred T. Wilson of Johnson County, Tennessee, for lots 6 and 7 in Bristol, Virginia. Lot 7 fronted on Main (State) Street, between Washington and Virginia Streets. Other sources state that the contract for the sale of these lots had been made in late 1853 and that Wilson's store building was under construction at the time the deed was made. It is said that Anderson persuaded Wilson to add a hotel to his store building. He realized that that would be a great improvement in the town he was trying to build. Wilson built his hotel over the west side of his store. It was named the Columbia Hotel and opened to travelers in October of 1854. Perhaps one year later a Mr. Everett opened a restaurant in Wilson's building. Thus Bristol's first hotel and first restaurant were located on what is now a parking lot in front of the First Baptist Church.

In late April 1855, Lewis and Rosetta Bachelor and their foster daughter

Ann arrived by stage in Bristol, Virginia. Their first few days here were spent at the Columbia Hotel. The best description that can be had of this establishment was written by Ann Bachelor some eighty years later. A portion of her manuscript is quoted here:

> Arriving tired, dirty, and hungry, we were directed to the Columbia Hotel, that was under the care of a Mr. Wilson and his kind, but overworked and always tired wife. It was located up an incline above where the roadbed of the coming railway was being prepared. We had to skirt around the end of a marshy pond to reach our desired haven. There was a store and by it, or perhaps on it, was a two-story affair. It was very narrow. Strange that upstairs all the rooms were on one side, the village side, [west side] and the hall formed the rest of the upstairs. There was an outside stairway at the back of the hall that led down to a yard and a path that led through a briar thicket to a back house [privy]. With shudders I recall that the well was near this back house, indeed hard by it. The water tasted no good, and I heard complaining that there were wiggle tails in it.
>
> Our supper was ample but very plain. I recall there was tender boiled meat and perhaps beans and potatoes; it has been so long now and hard to recall. Through the time we were there the diet hardly changed, except once or twice we had the finest butter milk which a man brought from somewhere in the country. Meals were in a room back of the store.
>
> There were wash bowls in our rooms and a convenience pot. The toweling was of so coarse a material as to be nearly of no avail. The beds were of shredded shucks that did indeed rattle at every movement so as to cause one to dream often, and create bad dreams.
>
> Far in that first night I woke suddenly because of loud talking in the hall. A horseman had arrived and cared not for the sleep of others. Long before day, there was much talking and walking about as travelers prepared to journey along.
>
> We stayed there several days and longed for old Fredricksburg, but papa allowed we would have to settle in the new town. I think he paid around a dollar a day for our room and board. It was our first place in the west. [At least it was west of Eastern Virginia, from whence the Bachelors had come!]
>
> I was sad about four years later [1859] when I watched it burn. I recall the frantic efforts to save furnishing but to little avail.

The partnership with the Everetts did not prove to be amicable, which caused Wilson to file a plea in Chancery to have the partnership dissolved and to sell the contents of the hotel and restaurant. The petition was granted and on September 30, 1857, H. C. Gibbons, Receiver, conducted the court-ordered sale.

The cheapest item sold was the meal sifter, which went to D. Clark for one cent! The kitchen table, around which many a diner had sat, went for fifty cents. Three sets of pitchers and bowls were sold for three and a half dollars. The establishment must have had the niceties of curtains — two sets sold for twenty-two cents. J. N. Bosang, Bristol's first saloon keeper got the remaining ten gallons of brandy for fifteen dollars. And the last bacon in the smokehouse went to W. L. Rice for three and a half dollars.

By that time a Mr. Lloyd had become associated with Wilson, and the two bought back many of the furnishings. They continued to operate the hotel for something over a year after this sale. During that period the establishment became known as Wilson's Virginia House Hotel. It was sold to Gardner Grant on January 15, 1858. Bristol's first hotel burned during breakfast time, October 23, 1859. Ann Bachelor places the time as being about daybreak. Apparently the fire was caused by a cat, perhaps a cat and mouse. The cook had gone into a pantry off the kitchen and had set a candle on a low shelf while she searched for some needed article. She returned to the kitchen without the candle. The family cat soon jumped upon the shelf, likely in pursuit of a mouse, and knocked the candle into a box of very rich pine kindling. This resulted in the burning of the store and hotel. It was never rebuilt.

From overwhelming evidence it appears that Bristol's second hotel was built much earlier than formerly believed and indicated. Perhaps it is well to mention here that there were buildings in early Bristol, Virginia, that did not show up on the tax records of Washington County until several years later. In one notable case a building known to have been erected in 1856-57 did not appear on the tax records until after the Civil War. Another building was continually listed on the wrong lot. Therefore, those records, while a good guide to early building in this city, are certainly not infallible. Be that as it may, it is known that the firm of Peck-Langhorne and Handford, that had long been engaged in hotel building and operating in upstate Virginia, built the first Virginia House Hotel here in early 1855. (G. W. Bagby, editor and journalist, wrote that this hotel was in operation in April 1855.) Though officially named the Virginia House, the hotel was popularly known as Langhorne's Tavern.

It appears that this new hotel offered finer accommodations than had formerly been available in the new town. And it soon became the accepted social center for those of the local citizens who felt such inclinations. This author owns an old letter of invitation that was issued to an area resident to attend a party at this hotel. It reads as follows:

The pleasure of your company is solicited
at a party to be given at the
Virginia House on Friday the 25th instant,
at 4 o'clock P.M.
Bristol, Virginia, January 18, 1856

T. E. Bibbs	*Dr. T. A. Harris*
S. R. Anderson	*R. C. Hanger*
James King, Jr.	*T. W. Hughes*
W. L. Hardon	*A. A. Moore*

Managers

It is known that this hotel was still standing at the coming of the first train to Bristol (October 1, 1856). Soon thereafter it either burned or was demolished. In 1857 John Langhorne built a much nicer hotel on the same site which he named the Magnolia. In keeping with the name several magnolia trees were set around this building. These were destroyed when it burned sometime later. Jesse Aydlotte was the contractor who erected the Magnolia and from his contract we have a good description of the building. It was of frame construction and contained fourteen bedrooms. (The first building had only ten.) There was to be a wide central hall (fourteen feet) with a "fitting" stairway. To the north of the hall was to be a large "gathering" room and to the south was to be a "great" dining room. Both these public rooms were to have double-wide fireplaces. How comforting the roaring fires must have been to those cold and weary travelers of long ago. Across the front there was to be a double veranda with "pleasing and fancy trim."

A visitor to this hotel in 1857 told of how milk cows were kept in a pasture located north of the building and reaching to Beaver Creek. This would include the present site of the Bristol, Virginia, police station and jail. Early every morning a hotel servant was sent to milk those cows so that fresh milk (still warm from the cow) might be on the breakfast table. G. W. Bagby also mentioned that there were hotel cows in the same pasture when he was a guest at the Virginia House in 1855. And Bristol residents still persisted in calling the grand Magnolia, Langhorne's Tavern.

On May 9, 1858, the late train brought from Lynchburg a family that would play a noted role in the new town's development. This family, obviously of much refinement and wealth, registered at the Magnolia as Mr. and Mrs. T. C. Lancaster and family, and a married son as R. T. Lancaster, wife and children. The coming of this family was fortunate for the owners and guests of the Magnolia, as we shall shortly see.

Ordinarily at 1:00 A.M. the hotel would have been in darkness with all guests and owners fast asleep. But on that early morning of May 10, 1858, there were oil lamps burning in an upstairs room, one or two in the halls, and the porch lamp had been lit in anticipation of the coming of Dr. Flavius Hartman, for whom a messenger had been hastily sent. The wife of R. T. Lancaster had gone into labor even, though the birth of her expected child was not due for two more months.

Dr. Hartman had barely arrived and set to his task when a fire was discovered in an unoccupied attic guest room, called the pauper's room because it was rented for a few cents per day. The laboring mother was quickly removed to the home of A. M. Appling, that stood a short distance back on Cumberland Street. Her baby died before daybreak and was buried in what is now East Hill Cemetery. And as she was giving birth to this baby, the Magnolia was burning to the ground. But had it not been for her premature labor, it is likely that many of the sleeping guests would have perished in this tragic fire.

The Lancasters decided to settle in the new town. Before another year had passed, Tom C. Lancaster had bought the lot where had stood the Magnolia and had erected a much finer hotel called the Lancaster House. During the Civil War this hotel was closed. It reopened soon after the end of that conflict as the Virginia House, and under the management of John G. Wood, formerly of Scott County, Virginia. He was one of the five prominent Wood brothers who settled here. Later he and his brother-in-law Isaac A. Nickels, who long operated the famous Nickels House, bought the Virginia House with the exception of one share held by a daughter of R. T. Lancaster. More will be said of this hotel later in this chapter.

BRISTOL'S THIRD HOTEL

Bristol's third hotel opened in 1858. It stood on the site of the present Paramount Theatre, and was built by Fields and Rodefer for William F. Butler, who had bought the lot perhaps two years before. At first, it was known as the Famous, and was operated by Mr. Butler and his family. The Butlers owned much land on Steele and Reedy creeks, which they let out to tenants after opening the hotel in Bristol. The Famous Hotel was a plain but comfortable building and soon had its share of guests. However, it was some distance from the depot and this proved to be a drawback, especially in securing a share of incoming visitors on late trains. To overcome this, young Matthew Moore Butler, who would later be a beloved physician of the town, was sent to meet night trains and escort guests through the pitch dark streets of Bristol to the Famous Hotel. In front of this hotel was a raised brick platform, a sort of roofless porch, that was elevated above the new town sidewalks by six inches or so. One dark night young Mr. Butler, perhaps engaged in distracting conversation with some interesting guest, tripped on this raised platform and landed full-weight upon his chin. This fall injured his neck to the extent that he ever afterwards suffered with reoccurring bouts of pain and stiffness, often becoming so afflicted that he would turn his head only with the greatest of difficulty. For a brief period the Famous Hotel became known as the Bristol Hotel. Then it was taken over by J. Wheeler Thomas and became the noted Thomas House. In the early 1870s it was rented to Dr. H. Q. A. Boyer, who briefly used it for a hospital. Later it was taken over by James Thomas, son of J. Wheeler Thomas. The Thomas House operated until around 1900.

FOURTH HOTEL WAS FORMERLY A WAREHOUSE
In 1858 Joseph R. Anderson erected a huge brick warehouse on Main and Fourth Streets and bordering on the railroad to the east. This was to be used as a grain commission house and did briefly serve that purpose. Ann Bachelor relates how children delighted in playing among the barrels and sacks that often filled the loading ramp leading to the tracks. About a year after the erection of this warehouse, Anderson decided that guests were more profitable than grain. Almost nightly the local hotels were filled to capacity, with late comers sometimes having to find lodging in private homes. Old papers show that on June 5, 1859, he contracted with Jesse Aydlotte to remodel the warehouse into a hotel. The work was duly executed, and Bristol had its fourth hotel, at first called the Exchange, but later becoming the Nickels House. This new hotel opened on Christmas day 1859.

When the new hotel was completed, J. R. Anderson leased it to Thomas W. Farley for a rent of $722.47 per year. For the first year's rent Farley gave a note to Anderson, due September 18, 1860, and secured by a Deed of Trust on the furnishings of the hotel (these furnishings were evidently supplied and owned by Farley), with Gideon Burkhart as trustee. It may be remembered that Mr. Burkhart was Bristol's first lawyer. This deed lists these furnishings and gives us a good picture of how early Bristol hotel rooms supplied the comforts and necessities of home to the travelers of that bygone era. The listing follows:

15 French beds
15 Mattresses
30 Pair of bed blankets
16 New quilts
Bed furniture for 15 beds
15 Feather bolsters
30 Feather pillows
15 Wash stands with bowls and pitchers
15 Small tables
15 Mirrors

15 White chamber pots
148 Yards of ingrain wool carpet
40 Yards of oil cloth
25 Oil wind curtains
25 Damask curtains
10 Feather beds and ticks
220 Pounds of feathers
36 Windsor chairs

From this listing one may deduce that the Exchange Hotel had fifteen guest rooms. Each room was furnished with a double bed, a table, mirror, wash stand, a bowl and pitcher set, two or more Windsor chairs, and the necessary chamber pot. There was a bolster (bed wide pillow) topped by two single pillows, and two blankets for each bed. And it appears that only ten of these beds boasted the luxury of feather beds. Perhaps these rooms rented for a little more, or maybe some guests did not care for such cozy softness.

Tom Farley operated the Exchange Hotel for about two years. In 1862 it was leased to L. A. Womack. About a year later it became a Confederate hospital. The occupation by this hospital virtually ruined all the earlier fine furnishings and also did much damage to the building. Then on February 12, 1864, it was sold to Isaac A. Nickels, who hailed from the Nickelsville section of Scott County, Virginia. The selling price was twenty thousand dollars in Confederate notes. As times worsened, W. H. Nickels, the father of Isaac, gave Anderson three thousand bushels of salt as payment on the debt. Later, the Federals burned the valuable salt. I. A. Nickels spent the next two or so years trying to refurnish and repair the badly damaged building. At this time he finished the ample basement on the west end (the first floor was far off the ground there), providing several office rooms and a large store room. Several early Bristol lawyers rented space in this basement area, including Vance and Wood, M. L. Blackley, and "Big" Bill Clarkson. The hotel reopened as the Nickels House in late 1866.

Nickels and his family lived in a suite of rooms on the first floor. It was in this suite that the first Mrs. Nickels suddenly died on May 24, 1873. By 1872 Nickels had added a general store to his enterprises, which he had set up in the raised basement of his hotel. At the same time, William Rencher had opened his famous barber shop there. About the same time Nickels set up a saloon adjoining his grocery store. It was known as the Nickels House Bar, and must have vexed the bone dry soul of J. R. Anderson, who lived just across the street!

In 1875 Isaac Nickels leased out his hotel and moved to Montgomery, Alabama, where he opened a restaurant near the depot. But life in the steaming hot humid deep south was not for the mountain man. He soon returned north and reassumed operation of the Nickels House. All through those early years he had maintained a three-eighths interest in the Virginia House, then being operated by his brother-in-law John Godsey Wood. Later he opened the Nickel Plate Saloon in the same block with this hotel. For the most part it was under the management of his son "Angel" George Nickels. Probably the most famous person ever to register at the Nickels House Hotel was Horace Greeley, who spent October 3rd and 4th, 1872, in the so-called parlor room (said to be the best room). The parlor room was actually two rooms, a parlor with adjoining bedroom.

On January 1, 1879, Nickels rented his hotel to W. G. Lindsey, who had brought the first train into Bristol in 1856. Lindsey was to assume operation on April 1st. To celebrate his leasing of the hotel, Nickels threw a big feast for thirty or so of his close friends. The New Year's evening (1879) feast was held in his private suite and before a roaring fireplace. There, after a blessing by Nickels' brother-in-law, Rev. C. B. Yarbrough, the guests partook of an assortment of oysters, wild turkey, wild geese, pheasants, quails, prairie chicken and rabbits. And Capt. Lindsey, furnished Siberian crabapple wine. I. C. Fowler described the event in the *Bristol News* and stated that Mr. Nickels was one of the most generous and liberal men ever to live in the city.

During the spring of 1879 and before the hotel was turned over to W. G. Lindsey, Nickels did extensive remodeling and repairing of the building. Up until then the structure was rather plain and austere, having been built in warehouse style. To fancy things up a bit, a double steamboat veranda was added all across the front (Main Street) side. With its lacy trim work, a new image was given to the plain old Nickels house.

The feasting was not over. When Lindsey took charge, he threw a public banquet to which he invited the town. It was described as the largest supper ever spread in the area. And Lindsey later confided to a friend that it took two years to pay for it. Lindsey later opened an "oyster restaurant" in the Nickels House. After a few years of operation by Lindsey, the hotel was turned back to Nickels. About 1890 he leased it to A. H. Burroughs, the noted marrying parson. It was early in the Burroughs years that a single inside toilet was installed. Up to that time the hotel had been served by a double three-holer privy, located in back of the building and on the embankment of the railroad. And horrors, it was high above the hotel well; the second deepest and best well in town (Dr. Zimmerman's was first). According to a former servant of this hotel (she was 95 in 1953) that outhouse was so located that one peering out the small, square air hole at head level might conclude that an approaching train was heading straight at the shaky little building. At night a train swinging around that nearby curve cast its headlight straight into that little window, thus intensifying the illusion. More than one guest is known to have quickly "abdicated the throne" and jumped from the privy with clothes not quite arranged for street appearances.

A. H. Burroughs' operation of the Nickels House Hotel is highlighted by the numerous weddings he performed there. Many an eloping couple was "captured" at the depot by the "Marrying Parson," conducted to the hotel, married, and then shown to the bridal suite (actually only one room) situated at the end of the downstairs hall. The servant, before referred to, recalled that one special item in the bridal room was a beautiful bowl and pitcher decorated in a wild rose pattern. The other rooms had to make out with plain white sets. She had been given the bridal set, and it, though badly cracked, adorned the jelly cabinet in the kitchen of her High Street home when she was interviewed by this author in 1953.

Isaac A. Nickels died in the early 1890s and is buried near the highest point in the East Hill Cemetery. The graves of his wife and "Angel" George are near his. Burroughs operated the hotel until it was sold and demolished about 1898.

THE SHORT-LIVED, BUT LONG-REMEMBERED WALKER HOUSE

The only other known pre-Civil War hotel in Bristol was the notorious Walker House. This hostelry of very unusual design stood on Fourth Street in Bristol, Tennessee. Most sources say it was on the railroad side of Fourth, about half way through the first block south of Main (State) Street. One very unusual feature of this building was that all rooms opened onto porches. There were no halls. On both the east and west sides of this hotel were double-decker steamboat-style porches. The rooms were back to back and each had its own private entry from the east or west porch. The style itself created suspicion in the minds of the more censorious of the town. And the censors became a little more incensed when a well-known madam from Lynchburg, known for some strange reason as the "skinned horse," leased the hotel. She brought with her a staff of "maids" whose hands did not seem to be reddened by scrubbing or washing. The hotel seemed to enjoy a thriving business, but a few guests were heard to complain that there were knocks on doors at all hours. Too, no lights were ever kept burning on the darkened porches (most hotels of that period maintained oil porch lights). And there were reports that gambling was being carried on there. The Walker House operated full blast through Civil War years. It seemed to be a favorite shelter for members of the military who might be stopping in town for short stays. And all the while it seemed that the establishment required the help of numerous cooks and maids, many of whom were then being recruited from the local and area citizenry.

But the war had been hard on the owner of the building. At the close of that conflict he was in financial ruin and could not recover. In very late 1866 the Walker House went on the block. It was quickly bought by a wealthy merchant, whose righteous soul must have been long vexed by the suspected "den of iniquity" that had been within view of his back door. He immediately evicted the "skinned horse" and her many "cooks and maids." And before the ink was hardly dry on his check, he began the dismantling of the building. The materials served to erect three small rent houses a little further up Fourth Street. The saga of the notorious Walker House had ended.

Shortly after the Civil War there was an establishment known as the Central Hotel that stood somewhere near the depot. It does not appear that it operated very long. No further information has been found concerning this early Bristol hotel.

BRISTOL HOTELS 1875-1900

Of the five hotels established in Bristol before the Civil War, three were still operating in 1875, namely the Virginia House, Thomas House, and Nickels House. All were doing well as the first decade after the close of the Civil War drew to an end. About 1870 John G. Wood, who had been managing the Virginia House Hotel, bought it in partnership with his brother-in-law Isaac A. Nickels.

It was at that time that the building was renovated and the famous bridge built from the depot platform, over Fourth (later Front) Street, to the hotel. This was for the convenience of travelers who had to alight from the train and eat meals in local hotels.

At that time the Virginia House was the most imposing structure in town. It was rather large, of the Greek Revival style, complete with columned portico in front. About 1876 (perhaps early 1877), Wood added a third floor and raised the grand portico accordingly. This portico was triple decked with Chippendale railing. This railing may not have been in keeping with the Greek style, but at least it was fancy and was described as very showy.

John G. Wood did not neglect the inside of his hotel. All public areas and the guest rooms were hung with fine papers, an expensive luxury for that time. Three grades of sample rooms were set up on the ground floor, so that prospective guests might see what they were getting before registering at the hotel. A grand suite of rooms was set up at the head of the stairs for the wealthy and distinguished. The author has old papers showing that a bedroom set bought for this suite cost $520.00. It must have been truly grand for at that time what was considered a very fine set could be bought for less than one hundred dollars. This suite also boasted fine carpeting and velvet draperies.

The most expert cooks were hired and the menu enlarged, so that the Virginia House soon had the reputation of being the finest eating place between Lynchburg and Knoxville. At that time the social life of Bristol centered at this hotel. For an unknown reason, Wood and Nickels leased the Virginia House to James Thomas, of the Thomas House, for about two years in the early 1870s, but by 1875 Wood had moved back in and resumed operation.

FAMOUS GUESTS AT THE VIRGINIA HOUSE

A news item of June 22, 1875, mentions that Senator Andrew Johnson was at the Virginia House that day. And there had been several occasions when the expresident had been a guest there. A year or two later Jefferson Davis occupied the grand suite at the head of the stairs for two days. I. C. Fowler of the *Bristol News* interviewed the ex-Confederate President during his stop in Bristol and remarked that Davis was more cheerful than he had expected to find him.

In late January 1879 General W. T. Sherman had Sunday dinner at the Virginia House. His train had been due in Bristol at 11:00 P.M., Saturday, but had been delayed by a slide near Big Spring in Montgomery County (Kettle Hollow). Somehow news later reached Bristol that while stranded there, the general had gotten off the train and asked an old resident what was raised around there. The saucy old resident quickly replied that when there was a damned yankee around more hell was usually raised than anything else. The general was said to have quickly "tucked his feathers and sought refuge in the train."

On March 8, 1879, there walked across the overhead bridge none other than the President of the United States, Rutherford B. Hayes. With him were his wife and daughter and others, including General Grant and Nellie and Charles Grant. The President and family got the grand suite at the head of the stairs, which was always later referred to as the Hayes suite. Alas, Grant and party had to take the next best. But about a year later Grant came through Bristol alone and that time spent one night in the Hayes suite.

THE WOODS' FAMOUS CHRISTMAS PARTIES

It is said that there was no equal to Mrs. Wood when it came to serving as hostess on any occasion. One annual event that was still remembered and talked of by a few very old people some thirty-six years ago, was the Woods' annual Christmas party for the children. An item from the January 11, 1881, edition of the *Bristol News* describes such a party:

Mr. and Mrs. J. G. Wood of the Virginia House gave the little people one of the handsomest Christmas parties ever given in Bristol. The table was splendidly furnished by Mrs. Wood, who has no superior as a

hostess. The ample hall of the Virginia House afforded the finest pro-
menades for the children who enjoyed the social feast immensely and
will carry through life the kindest memories of Mr. and Mrs. Wood.

And a teary-eyed old lady did speak of the Woods with kindest memories
as she was interviewed by this author in October 1953.

WOES IN LATER YEARS

It seems that the financial woes of John G. Wood began about 1884. Perhaps
in trying to maintain the grandest hotel in all southwest Virginia or east Tennessee, he had overextended his credit. About that time creditors began "to
come out of the woodwork" demanding payment. There had been a bout
with the same trouble in the 1870's, even to the point of a commissioner's
sale, but Wood had managed to retain ownership and prosper on through
several good years. But the crisis of the early 1880s was more severe. General
Imboden, a noted developer of the southwest Virginia coal and iron resources,
and for many years a resident of the Virginia House, tried to arrange a solution that sounds so familiar now, namely, debt consolidation. But failing to
arrange a loan for that purpose, the best he could do was to write a long
letter extolling the honesty of Wood and stating that he knew that Wood was
trying hard to pay his creditors.

During that financial crisis the Virginia House was leased to S. A. Vick,
who was its proprietor, beginning August 1, 1885. Mr. C. Harmeling was
then serving as chief clerk. The terms of this lease called for fifteen hundred
dollars per year rent. J. G. Wood and family were to maintain a suite in
the hotel, the cost of which (fifty dollars per month) was to be deducted from
the rent. And J. G. Wood, aristocrat that he was, demanded that he be allowed
to occupy the Hayes suite. A kindly S. A. Vick granted his request. The
lease ran for one year with option to renew for four years, but that at sixteen
hundred per year.

One note of interest on the economics of the time is that, when Wood gave
up the hotel on lease, he had five hogs fattening in a pen near the back door
(nice odor for the kitchen) and that he sold these hogs to one Morton, a butcher,
for sixty dollars.

In 1886 after involved chancery proceedings, a court-appointed commissioner sold the Virginia House at public auction. It was bought by Col. J.
M. Barker for $8,000.00. However Wood, still living in hope, offered an
upset bid of $9,000.00, which the court accepted. One interesting item on
prices of the time from this transaction reveals that insurance on the hotel
cost eighteen dollars per month.

During the hectic times that followed, Wood finally made a Deed of Trust
to secure his upset bid. This deed, dated January 8, 1887, gives one some

knowledge of the hotel furnishings and other interesting data. It appears that there were twenty-five rooms, all well furnished, with many having nice marble topped furniture. Alas, poor Wood was not able to meet the conditions of the deed, so that on October 8, 1887, the hotel was sold by Col. Abram Fulkerson, trustee. The successful bidder was W. P. Hamilton, who paid nineteen thousand one hundred dollars for Bristol's finest hotel. In 1889 Hamilton contracted with J. J. Adams to renovate the existing building and to make a large addition thereto. The work was finished on December 20, 1889, and the bill came to $2,094.91 1/2. The name Virginia House was dropped and the establishment became know as the Hotel Hamilton. It remained as such until well after 1900.

WOOD'S LAST STAND

Even though Wood's beloved Virginia House was lost, innkeeping was in his soul and he would not rest. He had moved into the Speer House Hotel soon after his former stand was sold. The Speer House had been in operation as early as 1881 and possibly for sometime before that date. Wood and his family lived there for several months while he made plans for another setup. A choice lot located at the northwest corner of Front and Cumberland became available to him. On it stood a somewhat run-down building that had formerly housed Bosang's Saloon. This was demolished and in its place arose one of the most Victorian buildings ever erected in this city. Designed by Walter P. Tinsley of Bristol, Tennessee, and built by Hamilton and Wagner, the building was a full three stories with several rooms finished in the attic. There were numerous second and third story balconies. Stained glass and lacy trim work marked it clearly as being done in the high Victorian style. But for its size, it very much resembled the grand Hotel Fairmount that was soon to be built by Reynolds and Barker. Indeed, for years it was often called the little Fairmount. In spite of its magnificently grandeur, this building took only $7,564.23 of the $11,000.00 that had been Wood's share of the sale of the Virginia House. Wood's last stand, the grand Palace Hotel, opened on Thanksgiving Day 1888. To celebrate, a great turkey dinner was prepared, with Wood inviting all his friends.

It may be mentioned here that it took an act of the town council before Wood was allowed to build this hotel. There was then a town ordinance that forbade the building of any wooden structure over ten feet in height. Doubtless, this was a fire preventive measure. But the Palace was designed as a frame building. On May 23, 1888, John G. Wood applied to the town council for a waiver. It was granted on June 5, 1888, and it is said that construction began the next morning. With his reputation as an incomparable host, and the renewal of his excellent food offerings, Wood soon had a very well-

This grand Victorian structure, first housing the Palace Hotel (later St. Lawrence) long occupied the northwest corner of front and Cumberland Streets. It was built by the noted hotel keeper, John Godsey Wood.

patronized house.

At first the hotel made do with furniture that had formerly been used in a Lynchburg hotel. But having a new hotel and used furniture went against the grain of John G. Wood's aristocratic soul. On July 4, 1889, he leased enough furniture to furnish eighteen rooms from the prestigious firm of R. Rothschild and Sons of Cincinnati, Ohio. It may be noted that payments of this lease were to be made through H. E. McCoy and Company, Bankers, forerunner of the present Dominion Bank of Bristol, Virginia. These furnishings included fine sets for the bedrooms and elaborate, velvet-covered sofas and side chairs for the parlor.

But Mr. Wood was growing older and his health was failing. Even before the opening of the Palace, he was sorely plagued with worsening gout, so much so that he could no longer ascend the stairway to the family suite. Back of the reception counter he had built a little bedroom, probably for the night clerk. The doorway of this room had been made narrow in order to make room for certain fixtures of the hotel lobby. But Wood managed to squeeze his then 350-pound frame through it. He then came down with week-long sieges of sickness, and he was forced to stay in bed most of the time. Later he became able to sit in his chair again, and from it he directed the activities of the hotel. But his appetite waned not with his failing health, for he ate more and more of the rich foods he loved so well, and grew fatter and fatter; so much so that he became a prisoner of himself. For the remainder of his life he never left, indeed, could not leave, that little room again; the door was too narrow, or shall it be said that he was too big. In time he outgrew his clothes and was reduced to sitting all day in a straight sided night shirt. Even so he gladly received visitors and guests who cared to come in through the little door that was now too narrow for his passage. An old-timer living here in 1954, remembered seeing him sitting on a chair that could not be seen because of his ample bulk, dressed in a clean, pale green night shirt. He remembered that Wood was still jolly and talkative, but would not tolerate comments or questions concerning his size. Some wanted to bring in scales and weigh him, but he would not hear to it. One daring local newspaper editor ventured to comment in late 1889 that he believed Mr. Wood had reached the five-fifty mark.

John Godsey Wood, the Prince of Bristol innkeepers, died in his little room on January 21, 1890. To remove his body, the door had to be removed and the opening widened by a local carpenter, William Graham. But that did not end the problem. H. A. Bickley, the local undertaker did not have a large enough casket for Wood's body. He worked through the night to prepare one of suitable size. Then it could not be gotten into his hearse. A local drayman hauled the body to the East Hill Cemetery in an open wagon. Even so, Bickley did not fail to do his grand strut through a light snow as the solemn procession moved slowly up East Main Street.

Soon after the death of John G. Wood, his family turned the hotel over to others and moved to a neat Victorian house at 27 James Street. By 1896 the Palace had become the St. Lawrence Hotel and was being operated by Joseph P. Davis. The St. Lawrence operated to well within the present century and was a favorite stopping place for many travelers and was home to several permanent boarders. Many readers will remember the General Shelby Hotel that long occupied the site of the St. Lawrence (formerly the Palace Hotel).

On April 21, 1882, John N. Bosang, one of the first settlers of Bristol, sold to Edward Stanley a piece of property situated just to the north of the Virginia House lot. This lot, number 80 in the plan of Goodson, reached to the old bed of Beaver Creek and included a part of the old Virginia House cow pasture. The price of the lot, $1,500.00, would indicate that there was probably then a building of some type located upon it. A little later Stanley erected a sizeable hotel on this lot. It was at first called the Stanley House. He and his wife Jennie Stanley operated this hotel for several years. It was numbered 150 Front Street (Front is now the Randall Expressway). Later this hotel became the Arlington House or Arlington Hotel. Then later it became the Bristol Inn, and remained in business until after 1900.

In the 1880s there was built on the southeast corner of Goode and King Streets an almost square, two-story frame building which long housed the Commercial Hotel. From all indications it was indeed ''commercial.'' Very dim lights flickered in the hallways, but a bright red light was kept burning in a front window. Like the Walker House years before, the Commercial seemed to have need for a great many cooks and maids. The court records at Abingdon, Virginia, are replete with indictments of these ''cooks and maids,'' and in many cases their ''visitors'' names are also given. The hotel closed before 1900.

Some think that the Hotel Tip Top (later the Colonial) that long graced the northwest corner of Front and Main (State) Streets was built about 1898. If so it would come within the scope of this book. It is the opinion of this author that it was built in 1901. But at least it was once a part of old hotel row, and served until around 1960.

No work on the hotels of Bristol would be complete without mention of the queen of them all, the famous Fairmount. However, since so much has already been published about it, only a little space will be given to it in this book. This rambling, high Victorian structure was built on a rounded knoll near the corner of Spruce and Carolina, in the midst of extensive, park-like grounds. To the south was the large Fairmount Forest, later the grounds of the Fairmount School. It was a favorite place for walks and picnics. Just beyond present Lakeview Street in an area now occupied by a shopping center and fronting on Virginia Avenue was the Fairmount Lake.

Construction of the large Fairmount Hotel began in August 1888 and was finished in the late spring or early summer of 1889. It was built by Hamilton and Wagner for Major A. D. Reynolds, Col. J. M. Barker, and R. J. Reynolds. It is said to have had the first bathrooms in Bristol. For years the social life of the city centered at the Fairmount. Doubtless many a romance blossomed there, but perhaps none so fast as that of a young engineer, who went stag to a dance there about 1892. His brother, later a lawyer here, took a fair young lady of the town to this dance. During the evening the young engineer asked his brother's date for a dance. And they danced on and on and on. He fell instantly in love with her, some how managed to take her to a moon-bathed veranda, and there proposed marriage, perhaps three hours after he had first met her. The girl, who later said that she adored him the moment they met, accepted his proposal on the spot. Their first child, ninety-two years old in 1989, resides in Bristol and is a treasured friend of this author. The Fairmount burned about 1901. In 1903 Col. J. M. Barker erected a grand house on the site. In 1989 the house was owned by Albert Bowers, who carefully restored it.

And there was the plan for a grand hotel that never was. In connection with the development of the Euclid Avenue area, it was at first planned that a great Hotel Bristol would adorn the heights where the Sullins College campus is located now. Later the plan was to build it in the 800 block of Euclid just above the present home of Mark and Faith Dillow Espisito. The foundation was actually started at this site and reached about head high when the plan was discarded. The cut stone of the foundation was later used in the foundation of The Towers, the fine home of H. E. Graves and in the present Espisito home.

LODGING COSTS

Information concerning the cost of lodging in early Bristol hotels is somewhat scarce, but based on what material is available, it may be said that it was very inexpensive. When the family of Lewis Bachelor stayed at the Columbia in Bristol, Virginia in 1855, the room and board for three people cost something like one dollar per day. When Joseph B. Palmer spent a night at the Virginia House in 1855, he noted in his diary that his lodging had cost fifty cents and breakfast was fifteen cents, and he added that it was not very tasty!

Near the end of the Civil War the cost of everything was tremendously inflated. A Confederate officer, who spent a night at the Famous (later Thomas House), complained that his bill was ten dollars. But he was lucky. About the same time the Lancaster House (formerly and later the Virginia House) was charging twelve fifty for the same type accommodation. But the War had hardly ended when costs dropped quickly back to 1850s level, or even lower.

When Capt. J. H. Wood married in 1868, he took his bride to live at the Virginia House, until a home could be had. Room and board for the two came to twenty-two fifty per month. During the mid and late 1870s, General Imboden had room and board at the same hotel for seventeen dollars per month, and he lived in one of the better rooms. A train traveler of about 1876 noted that he had a fine meal at the Virginia House for thirty cents. When President Hayes stayed a night at the Virginia House in 1879, the best suite, later called the Hayes suite, was renting at two fifty per night per person. This means that the presidential family, three in number, paid seven fifty for the night's lodging.

When John G. Wood leased the Virginia House in the mid 1880s to S. A. Vick, he took room and board for his family as part of the rent. This room and board for four people was set at fifty dollars per month, and that included occupancy of the Hayes suite. Old papers show that a gentleman staying at the Nickels House, during the time that it was operated by A. H. Burroughs (1890s) was paying four dollars per week for room and board. It was stated that a room without board could then be had for three dollars per week. A little later, as shown by an advertisement, the Nickels House offered a breakfast of ham, eggs, coffee, biscuits and butter for twenty-five cents.

FAREWELL TO THE HOTELS

The hotel was one of the most important establishments in early Bristol. And they, several in number, were here, offering shelter, rest, and food to weary travelers and home for those away from home. Many a person, including this writer, first "dropped anchor" in one of them, and there rested before the labor of finding and establishing a permanent dwelling. And enjoying grander rooms later, never forgot that first place of shelter in a strange city. But they are gone; not one remains with us.

Bibliography - Chapter Thirteen

Anderson, Joseph R. Writings, cir. 1880.

Anderson, Melinda King. As told to her granddaughter, Mrs. Herman Blackley.

Anderson, Rhea. Notes, 1930-1939.

Bachelor, Ann. Memoirs (unpublished), 1935-1937.

Bagby, G. W., journalist. Various writings.

Bristol News, newspaper. Various issues, 1857-1881.

Palmer, Joseph B. Diary, 1855-1876.

Phillips, V. N. (Bud). Interviews with several older Bristol citizens, 1953-1956.

Sullivan County, Tennessee. Deed and Tax Records.

Taylor, Hattie King. Writings (unpublished), 1927.

Washington County, Virginia. Chancery Court Records.

Washington County, Virginia. Deed and Tax Records.

Chapter Fourteen
WATER RIGHTS

Where there are people, there must be a water supply. And as a concentration of people develops, the problem of finding a sufficient and suitable source of water usually becomes greater. Such was the case in early Bristol. True, the water table under the great meadow upon which Bristol developed was very near the surface, but that was part of the problem. The water at that shallow depth was easy to reach but was not of pure quality or pleasant taste.

When Joseph R. Anderson had his home built in 1853, he had a well dug at the edge of the back porch. According to an old notation, it was scarcely twenty feet deep. This well supplied drinking water, though of not so pleasant taste, but was not sufficient for other purposes. This necessitated placing rain barrels at the corners of both back porches. This later brought a tragedy to the Anderson family (see chapter on mortality). Though countless wells were later put down in the developing town, those interested in firsts may note that Anderson's, on the lot of the southwest corner of Main and Fourth (now State and Edgemont), was the first well in the Town of Bristol, Virginia-Tennessee.

The second well was put down on the Dr. Zimmerman property which included the lot where the Signet Bank now stands at Lee and State Streets. Its site may be roughly approximated as being a few feet east of the back door of this bank. This well was put down to a depth of around fifty feet and for years was considered the best water source in town. Zimmerman's order for a payment of $12.50 to be made to the well digger, one Tobe Matthews, and drawn on Joseph Anderson, Banker, is the first indication of banking activities in the Town of Bristol. This order, now in the Zimmerman estate papers, is dated June 19, 1854. The widow Zimmerman (the doctor died in late 1854) was very generous with her fine water supply, allowing many to use water from her well. Ann Bachelor tells that her family carried water from Zimmerman's until a well could be dug on their lot. And she notes that many other early settlers did likewise.

The well long considered to be the second best in town was the one put down behind the old grain commission house when Joseph R. Anderson made a hotel of this warehouse in 1859. This hotel stood on Main Street between Fourth Street and the railroad (now between Edgemont and the railroad). The well was located in back of this building and near the railroad embankment. It was also perilously close to and below the hotel's outside toilet facilities. But because Anderson was by then aware that shallow wells did not produce good water, this well was dug to about the depth of the Zimmerman well. And polluted or not, its water was more pleasing to the taste than most of the wells in the new town. This well served the hotel and other renters in the hotel building until the late 1880s.

As business houses and residences were erected in the new town, more wells went down, and most of them in lazy fashion, that is, when the shaft reached water the digging ceased. From all accounts water from these wells had a taste something like a mixture of burnt bread and rotten leaves. Of course they were in swampy ground, and being so shallow and open, the wells were often contaminated with surface water. The taste was so unpleasant that some of the very earliest settlers chose to drink and use water from the then clear and supposedly uncontaminated Beaver Creek. Even then the purity of that stream was questionable. Typhoid often ravaged the town, and Beaver Creek was likely to blame. But even long after it was realized that this stream was unfit for drinking, it was used for washing and other purposes. Indeed, Bristol's first laundry was set up on the banks of this creek at a location which would now be just back of the Bristol, Virginia, Police Department (see chapter entitled Bristol Business and Industry).

As the town grew, the flats became a virtual pin cushion of well shafts and an increasing number of cisterns. Some early residents realized that cisterns might be a little safer than shallow wells, so this means of obtainig a water supply was very common by the beginning of the Civil War.

BRISTOL SPRINGS

There were a few springs located within the limits of the original Town of Bristol, Virginia-Tennessee. Building sites containing these much desired water sources commanded a much higher price from the very beginning. One flowed from the foot of the bank in front of the depot site. Anderson at first planned to build his home on Front Street, across from this spring. Later, perhaps realizing that the prized water source was on railroad property, or perhaps for commercial reasons, he chose the Fourth and Main location. It was just as well, for this spring suddenly dried up when a well was being dug at the Columbia Hotel on East Main (State) Street; evidently the stream had been tapped.

There was a small and more or less wet-weather spring at the side of Fourth, just across from Anderson's home. It was of little consequence except that it formed a little pond that sometimes overflowed into the street and created muddy conditions for travelers. Another small spring had formed a pond, sometimes called Hammer's Pond, that lay across the present State Street and just to the east of the railroad.

There was a big spring just west of the old Shelby burying ground near the corner of Fifth and Shelby Streets. The location is now under the new post office. It was used by the school and church that were early located near that cemetery, and several town residents carried their drinking water from it. However, many had an aversion to this water, for the gushing stream seemed to come from under the cemetery. Commercial development destroyed what some people called the Shelby Spring.

Though not within the town limits of old Bristol, Virginia, but close enough to be of some consequence were two large springs that flowed from the base of Solar Hill. One of these was on the site of the present Boswell Insurance Agency building, Piedmont Avenue, Bristol, Virginia. It was known as the Old King Spring to distinguish it from the King Spring located near Fifth and Stine Street. It was the source of water for the King home located high on the hill above it. A hewed log springhouse was located just below it and remained for years after the beginning of Bristol. Up about where the drive-in station for Charter Federal is now situated was another spring. Actually it was a larger stream than the Old King Spring, but the water was not as good. The Kings had erected a good-sized wash house just below it and it was here that servants did the family laundry. Thus, this water source was called the Washing Spring or the Sycamore Spring, because a huge tree of that species stood just above and leaned over it. This old log wash house was later used briefly as a school room. These two springs were near enough to the new town that some of the early residents carried water from them.

There were perhaps two or three other springs within the town limits. One of these bubbled up near the bank of Beaver Creek close to the northwest corner of Cumberland and Moore, and was the water source for the home of A. K. Moore, for whom Moore Street is named. Those fortunate enough to have springs on their property soon found themselves overrun by neighbors who, with or without permission, took water from them. This problem became so great that a few were known to have built shelters over these springs and secured them behind locked doors. Such was finally done to the Old King Spring, after Sullins College was built on the hill just behind the present Bristol Public Library. The college and one or two homes had keys to this choice water source. A former student, still living in 1953, told how fifteen or twenty girls used to be chosen daily by the house mother to bring up the night water. Late in the day these girls took buckets and wound their way down a well-beaten path to the cool, clear, gushing spring. The kitchen at the college and the student rooms were thus supplied with water. The bright-eyed, silver-haired old lady who long ago told this to the author was quick to add that the girls were well chaperoned on these treks from the safety of their "convent" on the hill out into the dangers of the world. A teacher walked ahead and another guarded the rear of the dutiful procession. And she told of times when the beloved old Dr. David Sullins served as a guard for the water brigade.

PROFITING ON A PLIGHT

There were a few who profited from Bristol's plight. Hugh Siler did a thriving business hauling little kegs of water from the large or lower King Spring, which still provides a delightful pool in DeFriece Park near Stine and Fifth streets. He sold the water at ten cents per keg, but one had to provide a vessel with which to receive the water from the keg.

After John G. King inherited the property, he charged Siler three cents for each keg of water, thus cutting the hauler's share to seven cents. Ann Bachelor remembered seeing the water wagon moving slowly along the street as old Hugh called out, "Good tastin' and fittin' water to drink frum the big spring! Jist ten cents, jist ten cents!" Some days, especially in hot, dry weather, he might make seven or eight trips to the big spring.

While water from the big spring might have been cool and good "tastin," its purity is doubtful. It is the opinion of this author that the spring is merely a portion of Ice or Whittaker Branch having gone underground and emerging again. Be that as it may, it later served as the water supply for Bristol, Tennessee. However, it was later tested and found to be contaminated. But water from the big spring (King's Spring) doubtlessly quenched the thirst of many a Bristol pioneer.

By bringing spring or country well water into town for sale on the streets, a few nearby farmers made a little extra money after crops were laid by. One of these water peddlers is remembered as an old but spry grandmother, who made many trips into Bristol from her Steele Creek home with four one-gallon jugs of water. She had sewed special pouches for these jugs, one for each shoulder, and each with a filled jug in front and one behind. She had a well-known and supposedly mineral or medicinal spring, causing her water to command high prices. Her water was more or less auctioned; that is, as she entered town, folks gathered around her and began making offers for her "burdens," as she called her filled jugs. Sometimes a gallon sold for as much as a quarter—this when Hugh Siler's five-gallon kegs were bringing only a dime! Often she left town with smiles and perhaps a dollar in coins jingling in her apron pocket. She always apologized to unsuccessful bidders, stating that it would be tomorrow before she could return to town. "I jist can't make two trips in a day," she would say. Her spring still flows in a little cove out on Steele Creek.

WATER POLLUTION

Polluted water was a problem for Bristol from very near the beginning. Many of the early wells were almost certainly polluted with surface water, and it seems that the early settlers had a propensity for building their outside toilets very near the water wells, in many cases on slopes above them! And those fortunate enough to have springs, sometimes were careless about contamination of their water supply. It is known that one of these spring owners had a chicken house on the slope above the spring.

Beaver Creek, said to have been sparkling clear at the coming of the very first settlers, soon became polluted with the town's refuse. Loose running hogs wallowed in it; it was the most common watering place for the animals of the town; stock lots were built by the side of it and sometimes across it. Then the inevitable privies or outside toilets began to be erected on its banks. Any branch or ditch emptying into it was likely to bring some of the garbage of the town. When the first Virginia House Hotel was built, the back porch was extended to a nearby drainage ditch so that the cooks could have a covered path to the garbage dumping place. And of course, this ditch carried the garbage into the nearby Beaver Creek. The hotel privy was also built over this ditch for easy sewage disposal. Indeed, here and there over town, wherever there was a branch or drainage ditch, beams might be laid across the stream and the privy built thereon.

In the 1870s I. C. Fowler, editor of the *Bristol News,* openly advised that the proposed farmer's market shed be built on the banks of Beaver Creek so that sewage disposal might be easy. The shed was never built.

By the time Bristol was two decades old, the beautiful and once sparkling clear Beaver Creek was virtually an open sewer. Yet the men and boys and sometimes girls of the town continued to swim in it. And the open air laundry on its banks near Front Street still continued to operate, though the laundress was once heard to say that it seemed that the water needed washing! And at some brush-screened, secluded portion of Beaver, and there were many such places even within the town's limits, men of the town might take towel and soap and there take their Saturday evening bath, and that in the water that the old laundress said needed washing! For the first two decades of its existence, the Virginia House Hotel is known to have maintained such a bathing area below the Moore Street crossing. The male guests were guided there by a porter, who then stood guard at the narrow trail leading into the brush-screened area.

TEMPLETON'S TASTE TEST

Even in those early days many, perhaps most, of the Bristol residents realized that most of the local water sources were unhealthy and often feared

Dr. James A. (Tasty Jim) Templeton, an early Bristol physician. He caused many Bristol wells to be dug a little deeper.

the water that they had to drink. The saintly old Dr. J. A. Templeton had a reputation of being an expert water taster. He was often called upon to "tongue test" water supplies to see if he might detect an unusual amount of badness. He often was called to well-digging operations for this purpose. If he expressed an opinion that the found water was "too tasty," the shaft was usually sunk deeper. His charge for water tasting was fifty cents, later raised to one dollar. His oft used expression that the water was "too tasty" earned him a nickname that he highly resented. If one wanted to see his usually pious expression turn into that of contorted anger, all one had to do was call him "Tasty" Jim Templeton. No doubt many local wells were pronounced too tasty by this beloved old early Bristol physician.

WATER RIGHTS AND WATER FIGHTS

That there would be trouble over early Bristol water sources was virtually inevitable. In some instances three or more families used water from the same well or spring. Such an arrangement was often conducive to feuding. It is known that in one situation of this type, a well was filled with rotten pumpkins as one user took his spite on another. And over the years there were other similar incidents.

At least one feud developed because two wells had been dug too close to each other. J. G. Pepper had a fairly good well in the side yard of his drugstore and home, that stood in the 500 block of State Street. But because "Tasty" Jim Templeton (may his saintly soul not be troubled by the use of his disliked nickname) pronounced it a bit too tasty, Pepper decided to have it dug a little deeper. While this was being done, the well digger had to quickly ascend the pole in order to escape a flood of water that suddenly rushed through a break in the well's west wall. But while Pepper and his well digger rejoiced over the great stream of water, there went up a wail from a servant of the Famous Hotel that the well there had suddenly gone dry. The well for the Famous Hotel was just over the dividing fence, perhaps twenty feet away. It was a very shallow well and apparently its water had drained through an underground opening into the deeper well at Pepper's. Though J. G. Pepper had a very flourishing well, Bill Butler of the Famous was left with a house full of guests and no water. A lawsuit was almost filed over this, but the parties finally compromised by filling the old wells and sinking a new one on the line between the two business establishments. It is said that a fine stream of clear, cool water was reached in the new well, and that Dr. Templeton pronounced it extra safe. Both contending parties were made happy over their fine new water source, hostilities ceased, and the two remained friends for life. The compromise well was still in use when the public water works were put in and remained so for a few years afterwards.

Another water dispute did not end so amicably. When Lewis and Rosetta Bachelor, two of the very earliest settlers of Bristol, moved to the 800 block of Main (State) Street, they prepared a very good cistern at the back of their new building. A neighbor who lived on adjoining property had a daughter whose morals were somewhat suspect. Now the ever suspicious and verbose Rosetta Bachelor began to spread tales concerning the wayward daughter.

In addition and as a means of retaliation against what she thought was blatant moral transgression, she forbade the neighbors to carry water from her cistern as she had formerly allowed them to do.

Within days the angry neighbors thought up a way of getting even. Somewhere the man of the house found a dead and decaying dog. And in the dead of night he threw it into the Bachelor cistern. The first water drawn for the morning coffee was indeed tasty and contained a bit of dog hair. Ann Bachelor, Rosetta's foster daughter, describes quiet vividly in her memoirs what followed:

> Mama went into a rage and threw the water across the back porch. She then jumped into the house and took from under her pillow the ancient pistol that she always kept there. Papa was frightened and kept calling out, "remember the commandments Rosey, 'member the commandments." But mama was in the yard and saw the man (neighbor next door) in his yard chopping fire wood. She fired and it knocked the hat from his head. He looked around and I guess he saw the pure devil that was in mama's expression at such times (I recall it well). And the old pistol still smoked greatly in her hand. I guess it was lucky for the man that the gun was a single shot. Like a fleeing deer he jumped the opposite fence (he had thrown the ax at her first as a reflex action I think) and was gone.
>
> Later that man stated that he was past Steele Creek before he regained his mind. Mama had reloaded and a thunderous report told us she had fired again but I know not what at for the man was gone.
>
> Neighbors intervened and helped clean the cistern, but it was an uneasy truce between mama and him. He would never step into the yard in daylight. He took his wife and erring daughter and left for I know not where, within two or three weeks.

It is known that Rosetta forced her weak and timid husband to talk to the city councilmen. And soon after this incident, a law was passed forbidding the throwing of dead carcasses into a well, cistern or spring. The fine was twenty dollars (an enormous sum for those days) and twenty days in jail. But such a penalty was far better and safer than facing Rosetta Bachelor's ancient cap and ball pistol.

THE WATER WITCH

All through those early years many of those who desired to dig wells consulted the local water witch. She was Pocahontas Hale, probably the tallest woman who ever lived in Bristol. Standing six feet four inches, she stood and walked as straight as a steel poker, except when she was "witching."

Then she doubled almost to the ground and appeared to be listening as well as tightly gripping her witch stick. She was mostly Indian but also claimed to be part French. No one knew where she came from; she just more or less appeared from nowhere in the very early days of pioneer settlement and remained in Bristol for the rest of her life. Besides being a water witch, she was a fortune teller, seer, and the madam of a notorious house of ill fame.

For witching, Pocahontas Hale used a peach limb that had to have grown more than six feet above ground. And before it became effective, it had to have been cut from the tree for more than twenty-four hours. Another requirement was that it must have been placed under her bed the night before. The actual witching consisted in the stick's being held tightly in her hands as she walked slowly over the area where a well was desired. When the stick turned over in her hands, she stopped and marked the spot. Then holding the stick lightly, she counted the number of times it bobbed up and down. Each bob meant five feet to water. Old-timers said she never failed. Her reputation was such that settlers from miles around came to seek her assistance. The late Bob Carmack used to tell of seeing her ''witching'' in the village of Paperville, and he had knowledge that she had been taken much further into the country for such purposes.

Pocahontas Hale, the water witch, died in 1889 and was buried in the Flat Hollow Cemetery, corner of Oak View and Buckner Streets. When that cemetery was moved, she was placed in the Citizen's Cemetery at the end of Piedmont and rests there in an unmarked grave.

NO CHANGE

For well over three decades after the founding of the city, the water situation continued virtually unchanged, except that cisterns became more and more popular. But for every home, school, church, or business, it was either well, cistern, or spring, or cooperative water source by the same means. And as the population increased so did the ever-present pollution. These polluted water sources were the cause of much sickness and death. Typhoid and other plagues were a constant threat; sickness, suffering, and death were ever present.

As water sources became more a suspect in the causes of these plagues, many became fearful of their own water supplies. No one could live without water, and yet many did not live because of it. The late Ed Faidley used to tell of seeing a young mother carrying large water pails past his childhood home on West Street. It seems that over a period of two or three years this mother had lost her husband and three children to typhoid fever. Then dreadfully afraid that she would lose her remaining two children, she walked daily, through heat or storm, to a reputedly pure spring somewhere near the pre-

Col. Samuel L. King devoted a great part of life to bringing more and better water to the town. He was a grandson
of Rev. James King.

sent Valleydale Packing Company lot to secure safe water. She must have
been successful, for both her children lived to be over ninety and were close
friends of this author. But Bristolians would not always be satisfied with
shallow wells and often-dry cisterns. And the hope that pure, clear, sparkling hill country water was so nearby was always a tantalizing prospect. Neither
could much desired industrial development proceed without a sufficient water
supply.

As early as March 1880, a move was afoot to build a public waterworks.
Three leading Bristol citizens — Joseph R. Anderson, W. W. James, and
Dr. J. F. Hicks — tentatively formed a company and made plans for a dam
on Beaver Creek. The dam was to be located about one mile above Campbell's mill (located near Goodson Street). One of the common objections to
this first effort for a public waterworks was that the streets would be torn

up and made muddy by the installation of water pipes. The plan was soon dropped. But the need for a public water system would not long be denied. On May 20, 1887, the Bristol-Goodson Water Company was incorporated by the Commonwealth of Virginia. On October 14 that same year, two individuals, Samuel L. King and Joseph W. Owen, bought the water rights of Ezekiel and Martha E. Rutter's farm. This farm was located about three miles northwest of Bristol-Goodson. (This right was conveyed to the Bristol-Goodson Water Company on July 22, 1889.) The Bristol-Goodson Water Company was incorporated in Tennessee on January 5, 1888. Incorporators were: S. Lawrence French, H. W. Bates, John M. Bailey, Dr. J. F. Hicks, R. M. Page, John R. Dickey, George A. Blackmore, J. R. Wood, Rufus A. Ayers, William F. Rhea, Francis Preston and Major A. D. Reynolds. Later that year Bristol, Tennessee, contracted with private capital to build a public waterworks. The most likely source of water for this town was the noted King Spring, which still flows from under a hill north of the intersection of Fifth and Stine Streets. It was from this spring that the first public water supply of the Town of Bristol, Tennessee, was obtained. In April 1888 the water of this spring was tested and found to contain only 34/100th grain of organic matter to the gallon. A steam-powered pumping system, having a capacity of sixty thousand gallons per hour, was installed and a water tower was erected on Fifth Street, north of the present intersection of that street and College Avenue. The waterworks on the Tennessee side of town remained under the control of the heirs of John G. King until April 4, 1898, when the company was reorganized and rebonded and sold to Samuel L. King, a son of the afore mentioned John G. King. This one-heir takeover was financed by Charles S. Hinchman of Philadelphia, Pennsylvania. Sam L. King became the president of the new company, with R. L. Blevins as superintendent. Offices were located on Sixth Street near Main (State) Street.

Meanwhile Bristol-Goodson, Virginia, had bought the Moore farm northwest of town for $17,500.00 and on it had drilled a well to the depth of 1264 feet. But when it was pumped, all the adjacent wells and springs went dry, creating endless troubles for the town. A water committee was formed in 1888 with E. S. Kendrick as chairman. This committee soon began negotiations with the Glamorgan Company of Lynchburg, Virginia, to construct a more suitable waterworks system. On December 4, 1888, the Town of Bristol-Goodson entered into a contract with the Glamorgan Company to build a rock dam and reservoir on Moore's, or Mumpower's, Creek about three and one-fourth miles northwest of the town. Further to lay pipes from the dam to the town, the first five hundred feet to be of ten-inch pipe, the next ten thousand feet to be of eight-inch pipe, and the remainder to be of six-inch pipe. It was required that the pipes withstand a pressure of three hundred

pounds per square inch. Within the town the company was to lay nine thousand, five hundred feet of four-inch pipe in the streets designated by the water
committee. The company was also to install forty double-nozzle fire hydrants
at locations choosen by the water committee. Sufficient pressure was to be
maintained to throw a stream of water over any house in the highest location
in the town.

The construction of the Bristol-Goodson water system was to begin on or
before March 1, 1889, and was to be completed by the following first day
of June. For all this the Glamorgan Company was to receive the sum of
$23,560.00. If dam or pipes developed leaks within thirty days, repairs were
to be made without cost to the town. To pay the cost of the construction of
the waterworks, the town issued thirty-four-year bonds, payable through the
People's National Bank of Lynchburg, Virginia.

Members of the Common Council of Bristol-Goodson, Virginia, at the time
this contract was made, were William A. Rader, a local lawyer; E. H. Seneker,
a prominent merchant; W. P. Hamilton, hotel keeper; Samuel McCrary,
building contractor; E. S. Kendrick, politician; and W. G. Lindsey, who
had brought the first train into Bristol in 1856. On February 21, 1889, this
Council voted to hire Charles Jones to make a waterworks map of the town,
showing all streets and alleys, location and size of pipes, and grades of the
town for streets and sewers. Jones was to receive three dollars per day with
an allowance of one dollar per day for an assistant, and provision for two
laborers at seventy-five cents per day. If the work exceeded three months,
Jones' pay was to be cut in half.

At about this time it was realized that a master plumber was needed to
superintend the installation of the water system. Mr. Fred Hayes, who had
been trained in the trade in his native England but who then was residing
in Philadelphia, Pennsylvania, was contacted and soon moved to Bristol. His
very satisfactory work for the city earned for him a fine reputatiuon so that
he was called upon for private jobs. The plumbing firm that he then founded
still exists.

On September 9, 1889, John R. Dickey, who had recently become a member
of the Common Council, offered a resolution that all tapping of the water
line must be by permit only and that the work must be done by a licensed
plumber, with all costs borne by the applicant. Those who applied before
October 1, 1889, would get free pipe and fixtures for the tie-in. On November
7, 1889, Hiriam A. Bickley, another new councilman, made a motion that
all churches were to have free water. His motion carried.

But it soon became apparent that all was not well with the waterworks system
on the Virginia side of town. There were times, perhaps two or three days
at a time, when there was no water at all. Sometimes the available water

was muddy. A local ice company was accused of making yellow (muddy) ice, and the railroad company complained of having to delay trains because there was insufficient water for the boilers. On October 16, 1891, the City of Bristol, Virginia, filed a suit against William Mumpower, charging that the latter, who owned a mill just above the reservoir, was completely closing off the stream for days at a time in order to gain a head of water for his milling operation. W. S. Hamilton, attorney for the city, went on to charge that when the water was finally released, it stirred up the mud in the mill-race and thus polluted Bristol's water supply. A. H. Blanchard and Col. Abram Fulkerson, attorneys for Mumpower, contended that the mill was in existence when the reservoir was constructed and should take priority over the reservoir. The water committee under E. S. Kendrick sought to solve the problem by adding four feet to the existing reservoir walls. The unusually dry summer that followed proved that this was not a sufficient remedy.

As the lawsuit dragged on, witnesses claimed that Mumpower was feeding hogs along the stream below his mill and that he had boasted that he would give Bristol a diet of hog dung until the city bought his land. It was further claimed that several privies were located along the stream and that cattle and other stock were adding to the pollution. It is known that John E. Burson and E. H. Seneker were sent by the city to consult with Mumpower concerning the purchase of his land, but apparently no agreement was reached in the matter. Even though the court issued an injunction in November 1891, forbidding Mumpower from completely closing off the water supply, public outrage at the awful pollution of the town's water by then had reached the point that local officials were already looking elsewhere for new water sources. In time the pure, clear water of the Preston Spring, located above Wallace, Virginia, was brought into Bristol. The abandoned reservoir of Bristol's first public water supply may yet be seen at the side of the Benham's road.

WATER RATES

At first there were no water meters. Water was sold to the consumer on a yearly contract. Six dollars per year was the beginning rate on the Virginia side of town, and this charge remained in effect for the first five years of service. Later, a system was worked out whereby the home rates were fixed by the number of rooms. The rates for 1896 were as follows:

Stores, offices, banks, churches $6.00
Drugstores . . . . 6 - 12.00
    (The higher rate was for drugstores with refreshment fountains.)
Houses
    less than four rooms 4.00
    four rooms 5.50

(Each additional room, $1.00)
Water closets
    private 4.00
    public 12.00
Urinals
    private 3.00
    public 6.00
Restaurants . . . . .12 - 16.00
Bakeries 5.00
Saloons . . . . .10 - 15.00
Barbers, per chair 4.00
Smith's Shop, per fire 3.00
Horse and carriage 2.00
Street sprinkler 4.00
Irrigation of lawn, $1.00 per thousand square feet
Boarding house, regular room charge plus .75 per boarder
Bath, $4.00, plus $1.00 if supplied with hot water.

It was noted that the same charge applied even if baths were not taken during the winter months!

Evidently a few meters were in use by 1896. Measured water cost twenty-five cents per thousand gallon. All water customers had to pay quarterly and in advance.

Bibliography - Chapter Fourteen

Anderson, Rhea. Notes, 1930-1939.

Bachelor, Ann. Memoirs (unpublished), 1935-1937.

Bristol-Goodson, Virginia. City Council Minutes, 1880-1900.

Bristol, Tennessee. City Council Minutes, 1880-1900.

Johnson, L. F. Notes, 1893.

King, Samuel L., Col. Writings. (Now owned by Tim Buchanan, Bristol, Virginia.)

Palmer, Joseph B. Diary, 1855-1876.

Phillips, V. N. (Bud). Interviews with numerous Bristol citizens, 1953-1956.

Sullivan County, Tennessee. Deed Books, 1880-1900.

Taylor, Hattie King. Paper (unpublished), 1930.

Washington County, Virginia. Chancery Court Records, 1852-1900.

Washington County, Virginia. Deed Books, 1880-1900.

Chapter Fifteen
FROM LABOR TO REFRESHMENT

RECREATION AND ENTERTAINMENT IN EARLY BRISTOL

Was it all work and no play in early Bristol? No, far from it. Even though work was generally hard and the hours were long (fourteen hours per day, six days per week was not uncommon), most citizens found time to leaven their burdensome toils with the pursuit of the lighter pleasures of life. Even some of the older folks became as little children again, briefly though it may have been, when there was a little time and opportunity to play.

Ann Bachelor wrote of how the children of the town used to rush up to Fifth Street hill after spring and summer rains to dam up the wagon ruts and form little lakes or pretend mill ponds. And she mentioned that among the children were often those in their late teens or even early twenties, who joined heartily in the fun. Another form of recreation enjoyed back in the 1850's and much later was fishing in Beaver Creek. This stream was then very clear and unpolluted and had a much greater flow of water than now. Many fish thrived in it.

Ann Bachelor also remembered the many exciting footraces in the big meadow north of Cumberland Street. The participants were mainly young men and boys, but sometimes older men took part in these races. One of the best racers was J. Austin Sperry, who once edited the *Bristol News* and taught a private school. He was then in his thirties but often outran those who were much younger. It was remembered that old man Austin M. Appling, early merchant and long-time mayor of Goodson, was once enticed into a race. Midway across the meadow he slipped and did a cartwheeling fall. He arose and walked stiffly to his nearby store. Though the fall did more damage to his honor's dignity than to his body, he would never enter the races again.

A huge old tree stood at the edge of the hill directly east of what is now 214 Johnson Street. A rambling grapevine had climbed high into the upper limbs of this giant tree. Someone had cut the vine near the ground, thus making a fine swing. Men, boys, and not a few girls often assembled there on lazy Sunday afternoons or long summer evenings for a thrilling swing far out over the hill's edge and high above the Beaver Creek valley. One day a very fat young man took his turn at the swing. When he zoomed "far out in space" the vine suddenly tore loose from the limbs above, causing "big boy" to plunge into the brush near the bottom of the hill. It was soon known that he was not severely injured, for he jumped up shaking a fist at the crowd at the top of the hill and profanely swearing, dared anyone to laugh at him. An informant of long ago said that "big boy" died on the battlefield at Gettysburg.

Men and boys often stripped off all their clothing and made good use of the old swimming hole near the present Leisure Towers building on Piedmont. Heavy brush along the creek shielded the nude swimmers from the public gaze, or so it was thought. Once two young maidens of the town sought to do a little peeping through the dense brush. All was well until one of them ventured too close and promptly fell into the water, only a few feet from the much startled swimmers. It is said that not one of them volunteered to help her out. Indeed, they were scrambling to the brush on the far side of the creek. But the girl survived. Daddy Thomas told who she was and to whom she was finally married. The matter will be left to rest; descendants still live in Bristol.

Tug-of-war was another very popular game that was often played in the big meadow. Sometimes as many as twenty people of all ages and including some of the more fun-loving women and girls of the town, pulled against a like number on the opposite end of the rope. Often there was such an even distribution of strength that the rope snapped before either team had been pulled across the line. At such times there was what Rosetta Bachelor, the town's super moralist, called a vulgar pile up and entanglement of the contenders.

On the shady side there were several in town who enjoyed cockfighting. At that time the highest portion of what is now East Hill Cemetery was heavily wooded. It was there that most of the "sport" was carried on. The area, previously known as Round Hill, became known as Rooster Hill. Several fights took place there after a few burials had been made at the location. After there was a conviction or two for desecrating a cemetery, the cock fighters moved into the dense woods in what is now the Fairmount section of town.

Sledding down cemetery hill was a favorite wintertime sport for the boys and young men of the town. They also sledded down Sycamore trail that followed what is now Sycamore Street across Solar Hill. More than one unfortunate lad lost control of his sled and wound up in the icy waters of Beaver Creek. And that section of Solar Hill was a favorite place for snowball fights. According to one who lived during that time, there were occasions when the fights became a little rough and ended in the "real thing."

Another popular winter sport was ice skating on the several millponds that were scattered along Beaver Creek. One of the most popular of these was the pond above the English Mill (formerly King's Mill and later Wood's Mill). This pond extended up Beaver from just above the Melrose Street bridge almost to Anderson Street. During hard freezes this pond was often resorted to by the fun-loving of Bristol. I. C. Fowler of the *Bristol News* noted in his paper of January 4, 1879, that on the previous night and under a bright full moon, a great number had regaled themselves by skating on the English pond. He noted that some were sliding on sleds and chairs and the beginners provided great entertainment. Another popular pond was that of Bristol Mills (C. C. Campbell) that stretched up Beaver from a dam just above the Goodson Street bridge. One very cold Sunday afternoon, a young lad went skating there against the stern admonition of his super-religious mother, who warned him that he would go to hell for desecrating the sabbath. Fortunately, when the ice broke under him that day, he was near enough to the edge of the pond that he only fell into waist deep icy water. He was soon thawed out by a roaring fire at nearly Campbell's Grove. Later he told of how his mother said to him, "Son, you sure just about went to hell today!" Then his father whipped him for smarting back, "If it was hell it was a lot cooler than I ever imagined!"

Public places of recreation came very early to Bristol. In 1859 David P., John S., and Edward H. Jamison owned and operated Jamison's Bowling Saloon on Fourth Street (later Front) near the depot. In 1861 John T. Megginson operated a Tin Pin Alley along with a liquor store. This too was near the depot and old court records mention that another such place was operating nearby. It should be noted that the Common Council of Goodson (popularly known as Bristol) once passed an ordinance prohibiting the operation of bowling alleys within the town. It was claimed that such places had "become the mecca of the vile and wicked, and that from them all sorts of crime and vice was being fostered upon the citizens."

The following item appeared in the *Bristol News* dated September 18, 1873.

Mr. C. D. Charles has established a skating rink at Reynolds Hall (Fourth Street). The very best citizens of the town are patrons. This is elegant exercise and is beneficial to both sexes.

Perhaps old John Bosang (then sixty-six years old) thought it would be beneficial to him. He eagerly tried the "elegant exercise." Later, obviously stiff and bruised, he regaled the Main Street bench sitters by telling of his first and last skating experience. It seems that one foot had gone northeast and the other southwest, and it was where the rest of him went that caused the pain!

Soon after the Civil War, professional entertainers began to appear on the local scene. In October 1866 Stone-Rosston-and-Murray's Circus performed in the Virginia Hotel cow pasture, about where the Bristol, Virginia, jail now stands. This circus was very large for the time, having some 180 performers and employees. Most circuses then traveled by rail, but this one traveled the roads. The management thought this good advertising, as the caravan created great interest in small towns and villages through which it passed on the way to larger towns where a setup was to be made. The hotel cows were moved to another pasture to make room for the circus. When they were moved back, they went wild, running and jumping about over the pasture and were extremely nervous for days. It was believed that the remaining scent of the wild animals that had been displayed there caused this upset. The hotel would never allow another circus to use the pasture, but the area was known as circus bottom for years afterwards.

Many lone entertainers wandered into town from time to time. One of these, calling himself Professor Dare, "acted the fool," as editor Fowler expressed it, by walking a tight rope, stretched fifty feet above Main (State) Street. Fowler, who did not appreciate this daredevil's act, commented that more people lost a day's work over the show than the poor fellow's future life could atone for. Alas, not much future life was left for Professor Dare. During the rope walker's next performance (perhaps in Greeneville or Knoxville, Tennessee), he slipped and fell to his death.

Lecturers, especially if the topic was sensational, provided much entertainment and instruction for the early residents of the town. At first Conway Hall on Fifth Street was the usual meeting place. Later, Reynolds Hall on Fourth Street served the same purpose, and finally Harmeling's Opera House was the most frequently used. In April 1879 the town folks flocked to Conway Hall to hear the boy orator Eddie Hawkins of Madison County, North Carolina. Though only six and one-half years old, he could hold an audience spellbound for hours with his fluent, golden oratory. His subject was "The Coming Populist Revolution in America." Old lawyer J. H. Wood made notes on that speech that are now in the hands of this author. Admission to little Eddie's lecture was fifteen cents for reserved seats, with back seats going for five and ten cents. It is told that the child used part of his earnings to buy toys to carry back to his North Carolina home.

One speaker who drew a great crowd to Reynolds Hall was a Professor Davenport. Speaking in September 1878, he held forth for two hours on his theory that the Mountain Empire would be "gloriously tropical" by the year 1890. His theory was presented in glowing terms and with what seemed to be convincing evidence. "These lovely hills around your town will be crowned with stately palm trees, bananas will grow in your back yards, orange and grapefruit groves will cover your pastures and pineapple fields will fill your valleys. The Royal Poinciana tree will line your streets, the hibiscus will eclipse your roses, and the flamingo will reflect its pink feathers in the clear waters of the Beaver.'' Such were the grand promises made by the eloquent Professor Davenport. When an unusually mild winter followed this lecture, many Bristolians had their hopes strengthened. Alas, no backyard in Bristol yet yields bananas nor do stately palms crown the surrounding hills. But apparently the professor made enough money to do the next best thing. By 1895 he was living just south of Palm Beach, Florida.

But not all lecturers were so well received as Professor Davenport. Before Rev. Kenton of New York could finish his address supporting the doctrine of reincarnation, he was shouted down by a fundamentalist audience and advised to leave town on the next train. (Bristolians of 1882 were not ready to hear anything that conflicted with their religious beliefs.) And to add insult to injury, a local hotel keeper would not refund the Reverend's room fee. Rev. Kenton left in the wee hours of the night vowing that he would never waste time on such a town again, a pronouncement that saddened no local citizen.

Summer picnics were always popular. King's Spring near Fifth and Stine Streets was one of the favorite local grounds. Many a watermelon cooled in the clear flowing waters, as eager Bristolians awaited a grand feast. An old newspaper, dated 1875, tells of a King-Anderson family gathering there at which time a great spread of food was made under the nearby oak trees. The account mentions that some relatives had come the day before and had made overnight camp near the spring.

In July 1879 the pupils and friends of the Bristol Baptist Sunday School chartered a special train to take the group to Preston's spring, some six miles east of town, for a day of picnicking. There lemonade was made and served free to the crowd. Thomas F. Wood was in charge of the eight-hour-long event. After feasting and frolicking around the spring under the big oak, the crowd was called to order and there were speeches (hopefully short) by Mr. Wood, I. C. Fowler, A. H. Blanchard, and Rev. C. B. Yarbrough. The special train brought the happy but tired group back to Bristol at 7:00 P.M. The outing cost fifty dollars, a rather significant amount in those days.

Local fraternal organizations often put on entertainments, usually as fund raisers. This notice which appeared in the *Bristol News,* February 23, 1875, is typical of the period:

> Another theatrical entertainment by the Knights of Pythias will be given next Thursday evening. Only twenty-five cents admission is to be charged. As it is one of the best yet given in Bristol, a crowded house may be expected.

School entertainments, usually given as closing exercises, nearly always drew standing room only crowds. Whether the programs were by preparatory classes or for college graduations, there was always much oratory, with local judges to award prizes. A few medals were awarded in the names of certain local businessmen. One of these was the Joseph R. Anderson medal given for outstanding orations by Bristol-Goodson Male Academy graduates.

Dancing was a year-round favorite form of recreation among early Bristolians. However, the town was sharply divided on the issue. There were many who hotly contended that the dance was of the devil and the doorway to moral downfall. Further, that hell spoke from the fiddle. Some local churches forbade dancing under penalty of expulsion, but still there were always a few rebellious members ''who jumped the traces'' when they heard the sound of fiddle and banjo. Among these was old Major Zack Burson. Though a strong Baptist, he loved the sound of the fiddle and was not above doing a jig now and then. He owned a warehouse on Moore Street, which when empty, he allowed to be used for public dances. He was usually in attendance and when the fiddling got lively, he might be seen to the side somewhere ''cutting a few steps.'' He would never dance with a partner; his was a solitary joy.

Some dances were held in private homes, but then as now, an irate neighbor often complained of the noise and sent for the town sergeant. Rarely, local saloons had small areas for dancing, but because few ladies, even of the shadier type, would go near these establishments, partners were extremely limited.

Of course there were always the more formal dances at the better hotels. Some of these frolics were dignified by being called balls. The Virginia House on Front Street seems to have been the favorite place for such activities until it was eclipsed by the Fairmount around 1890. The most ''worldly'' of the dance spots seems to have been a dance floor (open air variety) that was erected in Flat Hollow, near the present intersection of Mary and Piedmont. It was frequented by the rednecks of the town along with girls and women of questionable character. Moonshine flowed freely there and drunken brawls were common. And the super-moralists of the town were concerned that it was at the edge of a large expanse of bushes. Indeed, one rather wealthy moralist bought the site to rid the town of what he called ''a place of open sin.'' But the ''sinners'' simply bought more plank and moved their playground to the backside of Furnace Bottom.

By far the most popular fiddler in those days was Caesar Susong, a former servant of the Susong family, of Little Creek (sometimes called Baker's Creek). A close second was Tom Faidley. Then there was a lady fiddler, Nora Cross, who lived toward Blountville, but who spent several summers in Bristol, fiddling for various dances. She always went barefoot, but with one of those feet could "rattle the window panes" while patting to her own music.

Home entertaining was always in vogue. Invitations to suppers flew back and forth among friends and relatives. Weddings, birthdays, or wedding anniversaries were considered to be times for great feasting and partying. Often there was visiting for two or three hours, then a large feast that might last until well after midnight. Sometimes these events were celebrated in local hotels, the Virginia House and the Nickels House being favorite places for them. After parlor organs became common, many a Sunday afternoon was spent by gathered neighbors, singing hymns or ballads. Only a few people could play these instruments. Some of the more elite of the town owned pianos, which were then status symbols. Even in that time of cheap prices, pianos were rather expensive.

In the 1870s a Border Fair Association was organized. This association sponsored a yearly fair on grounds to the north of West Main (State) Street, across from the end of 17th Street. It was a typical fair with displays of livestock, fruit, vegetables, baked goods, and home-sewn garments. Prizes or medals were hotly contested. It was a much anticipated annual event, attended by throngs from far and near. Finally, beset by internal problems and a devastating law suit, the association disbanded and with it went the annual fair.

Though now Bristolians may entertain themselves by reading in the local library, it was not always thus. But as early as September 1875, editor Fowler was crusading for a local reading room (library). Unfortunately his crusade did not succeed. Fowler mentioned that Jonesboro had set the area an example in this matter, and urged that leading citizens of Bristol take the lead and establish a similar library. Before the century ended, the local Y.M.C.A. had a small reading room, but a public library was still several years in the future.

By the late 1880s it was clear that a larger opera house or local assembly hall was needed. Charles Harmeling, who then operated a saloon on the northwest corner of Front and Cumberland, decided that the building and operation of such a place would be profitable. In 1889 he built a combination business and opera house on the Virginia side of the 500 block of Main (State) Street (517 Main Street). This was a two-story building with a central stairway of wide proportions. Business rooms were on the ground floor on either side of the stairway. Harmeling moved his saloon to one of these rooms. Upstairs were offices in front of a dividing hall behind which was a grand auditorium which had a seating capacity of one thousand. The house opened on January 2, 1890, with a program by the Boston Quintette Club, forerunner of the noted Boston Symphony Orchestra. This was strictly a black tie affair with a then restrictive price of five dollars per seat. The elite and would-be-elite of the town tried to outdo one another in a never-before-matched display of finery. From Abingdon, Virginia, and Greeneville, Tennessee came special trains bearing many of the cultured and refined citizens of those old towns. It is said that in the audience on opening night was the governor of Tennessee and John Fox, Jr., who later became a noted author. Sullivan County native Oliver Taylor was at first assistant manager and then manager of the opera house. His original play, ''The Moonshiner,'' was presented there, and others may have followed. Harmeling's Opera House served as a cultural center for Bristol a quarter of a century or more, but only during the cooler months. It was closed during summer months because of oppressive heat in the second-story auditorium.

Because the opera house had to be closed during the summer months when many people sought entertainment, Oliver Taylor, Sr., decided to build Clifton Heights Theatre and park. This resort was located in the high knobs, south of the then outer reaches of Windsor Avenue (near 19th Street). The theater was built to the natural contour of the hill and could seat seven hundred persons. Near it was a dance pavilion, picnic tables and refreshment stand. A streetcar track ran far up the hill, and from where it ended short flights of stairs led upward and over to the theater. Sheltered benches were placed between the flights of stairs from which a splendid view of the town might be had. Numerous plays were presented in this theater, including Taylor's own version of Rip Van Winkle. Clifton Heights took its name from a place of the same designation in Bristol, England. The theater, erected about 1897, burned soon after 1900.

There was always the sand lot variety of ball games in early Bristol, and many local men and boys frequently participated in the sport. A favorite site for some of these early games was a field situated north of Second Street, just beyond where Hurt's Supermarket is now located. Another site was a large lot near the present intersection of Shelby Street and the Volunteer Parkway. And the area laid off by Joseph Anderson for a playground (present Anderson Park) was also used for this purpose. It appears that Bristol had an organized baseball team by 1885. Charles R. Vance, a local lawyer, was its manager. It is remembered that he appeared on the ball field in full dress, including a high collar and tie and his ever-present derby hat. Known players on this team were Meigs Dulaney, Jack Winston, Bert McDowell, Hugh Gookin, Dave Frizzell, Will Sheen, Will Palmer (son of Bristol's second lawyer), George Kuhnert and James Carrico.

The first basketball team in Bristol was organized about 1890 in the old Y.M.C.A. building that stood on the west side of the first block of Fifth Street. King College had a football team by 1897. And if all these forms of entertainment and recreation were not available to local citizens, or if they were not suitable to specific tastes or likes, one might go ghost hunting or spook sniffing to find a diversion or relief from day-to-day bland existence and heavy toil. And this was often done by the braver souls of Bristol. Often groups went to an old abandoned house that stood on Spencer Street, hoping to communicate with a knocking spirit. But several of these groups are known to have fled when the spirit cooperated! A strange light was said to move around over an old abandoned pasture that lay along what is now Solar and Johnson Streets. But when the curious got within a few feet of this light, it would suddenly sink into the earth. And Col. J. M. Barker had non-buying customers when word got out that a young clerk who had been murdered at his store door was making sudden appearances in the shadowy areas of Barker's establishment. What she actually saw no one knows, but a local matron once threw down her egg basket and ran screaming from the store, never to return. Apparently she was not one to be entertained by ghosts! Barker finally moved his business because of this store's ghosty reputation. These are only some of the ways that early Bristolians were called from labor to refreshment.

Bibliography - Chapter Fifteen

Anderson, Melinda King. As told to her granddaughter, Mrs. Herman Blackley.

Bachelor, Ann. Memoirs (unpublished), 1935-1937.

Bristol News, newspaper. Various issues, 1857-1881.

Phillips, V. N. (Bud). Interviews with numerous Bristol citizens, 1953-1956.

Washington County, Virginia. Chancery Court Records, 1855-1900.

Chapter Sixteen
TEMPLES OF THE TIME

THE EARLY CHURCHES OF BRISTOL, VIRGINIA-TENNESSEE

The first Christian service in the town of Bristol, Virginia-Tennessee was conducted in the parlor of Joseph R. Anderson's new home which stood on the southwest corner of Main and Fourth (now State and Edgemont). This service began shortly before noon on Christmas Day 1853. The Rev. James King led the group of perhaps twenty-five persons, including several slaves of the King, Anderson and Susong families, in singing number 23 from the *Presbyterian Psalter*. (The Psalter used in that service is now owned by this author.) After the singing of this Psalm, Rev. King spoke briefly on the text, "Behold, I make all things new" (Revelation 21:5).

Soon after this first Bristol service the Andersons began a Sabbath School in their home. Mrs. King taught the children in the parlor, and Mr. Anderson taught older scholars in the dining room. Occasionally, the Rev. King preached to the combined classes and others who came especially for preaching services. Thus, it may be noted that Christian worship began in the new town on historic Anderson corner in downtown Bristol.

It soon became apparent that these early religious gatherings were outgrowing the Anderson home. Thus in March 1854, Rev. James King hired John Aiken to erect a framed church and school building on a portion of the Shelby graveyard lot. The location of this building was a short distance west of what became the southwest corner of Fifth and Shelby Streets. The site is now covered by the U. S. Post Office. In her memoirs Ann Bachelor estimated that the building measured perhaps sixteen by twenty-four feet. She described it as being 'well white washed' and had only one window to each long side and one in the south end, directly opposite the north (front) door. One of the huge cemetery oaks spread heavily over the southeast corner of this building, providing cool summer shade. In winter things were a bit different. Old-timers told of how worshippers often sat wrapped in blankets with feet upon hot rocks in the unheated building. Rev. King preached twice each month in this building. By late 1854, and perhaps before, this was being called the Presbyterian Church at Bristol. Ann Bachelor, whose first attendance at this church was in May 1855, remembered that a narrow trail wound upward from Main Street to the little white chapel near the grove of giant oaks. On meeting days many local and area citizens, some walking, some mounted on horseback, could be seen winding up this trail.

In anticipation of the expected need for a larger and better situated building, Joseph R. Anderson, on September 4, 1854, deeded lot 126 in the plan of Bristol to the trustees of the Constitutional Presbyterian Church. These trustees were Dr. B. F. Zimmerman (who died a short time later), George L. Worley, Mahlon Susong, William Cowan and John G. King. This lot, then valued at $150.00, was on Fourth Street and on what later became the southwest corner of that street and Shelby (that portion of Shelby was not cut through until around 1890). However, this lot was not used until 1857.

Meanwhile, Rev. King, realizing the need for a larger place of worship, built a new school and church building on what became the southwest corner of Fifth and Shelby, where later stood the Presbyterian Female Institute. And in much later years the Redeemer Lutheran Church was erected on the same site. At the time, this new King building was on the graveyard lot. Shelby's grave was almost against the southeast corner of this structure. The old building was then sold to Dr. Flavius Hartman who immediately sold it to others. It was soon remodeled as a residence and so served for many years. King's new building also housed the Sons of Temperance. After the new Presbyterian Church building was erected in 1857, the old became known as Temperance Hall. Several years later it was rolled to the lot immediately in back of its first location and was made into a residence. Soon after this it became the home of G. B. Smith, a noted local photographer. It stood until the 1950s or later. In 1857 a new building was erected on Anderson's gift lot. It was a rather large structure and faced Fourth Street. Rodefer and Fields erected this structure at a cost of four thousand dollars, most of which was paid by Joseph Anderson and Rev. James King. The Presbyterian Church of Bristol met here, beginning in the autumn of 1857, and it was here that formal organization of what is now the First Presbyterian Church took place on September 5, 1858. This was done by New River Presbytery. The Rev. Andrew Blackburn became the stated supply pastor at a salary of $325.00 per year. The first ruling elders were Alexander Susong, Alfred Carmack, George L. Worley, E. H. Seneker and Joseph R. Anderson. E. H. Seneker was made the first treasurer and Joseph R. Anderson became the first clerk. There were no deacons until February 1860, when Samuel R. Anderson (brother of Joseph R.) and John Keys were chosen to serve in that capacity.

Rev. James King soon became pastor, finally being assisted by Rev. D. H. Rogan. Other pastors who served throughout the remainder of the century were J. M. Hoffmeister, I. D. Robinson, George A. Caldwell, Dr. William R. Laird and Dr. W. O. Cochrane. Of these, George A. Caldwell served the longest tenure, 1865-1892.

The building erected in 1857 and renovated at least once, served well until the early 1880s. That a new building was planned is shown by this article

Rev. G. A. Caldwell, long served as pastor of the First Presbyterian Church. Several of his descendants still reside in Bristol.

which appeared in the *Bristol News* on June 21, 1881:

> The members of the First Presbyterian Church are going right ahead in their efforts to raise funds for a new church. A meeting was held last Thursday night at which designs were exhibited and a partial report made by the committee. The design is beautiful. The spire is to be 120 feet from its base to top. It (the church) will have a width of about 60 feet and a depth of 100 feet. The cost when completed will be eight to ten thousand dollars, and will be one of the most handsome and ornamental buildings of the kind in east Tennessee or southwest Virginia. The committee have already raised $7,500.00. The building will be an ornament to the town. We give a partial list of the committee as follows: J. M. Barker (Chairman), Col. Charles R. Vance, W. W. Davis, S. Y. B. Williams and J. B. Childers.

The church was built and, with occassional remodeling, served for another seventy-five years or so. The new church fronted on Fifth Street. For some time a residence stood between it and what became Shelby Street. Later a portion of the educational unit of the church was added where the residence had once stood.

Not all early Bristol ministers were poor. In 1870, Rev. George A. Caldwell built this grand house on the southwest corner of Anderson and Seventh Streets. It was then considered to be the finest home in town.

FIRST CHRISTIAN CHURCH

Before the first depot on the Virginia side of Bristol was finished, Rev. Samuel Millard sought and was granted permission to preach in the passenger room of this building. Rev. Millard's first sermon in that location was in late September 1854. Millard's preaching services were well attended and from them came the move to organize the Christian Baptist Church. In 1855 Col. Samuel E. Goodson gave a lot as a building site for the anticipated church. This lot fronted on what was then called Depot Street, later called Spencer, and now the Randall Expressway. The present First Christian Church occupies this lot. A brick building of modest size was started in the spring of 1855. The brick for this building was made in Flat Hollow at the same clay source

Rev. Samuel Millard was one of the first to preach in the new Town of Bristol. He founded what is now the First Christian Church.

where those for the J. R. Anderson home had been burned in 1853. The building was more or less on the Federal style and had a well designed and executed belfry over the front door.

John Worley, who then lived in what is now the Ed and Linda Stout home on King Mill Pike, gave one thousand dollars toward the erection of this building, then gave another two hundred to finish paying the bill when it was completed.

On July 19, 1856, as lightning flashed and thunder rolled outside, the church was officially organized with S. H. Millard, Alfred Millard and Col. Joel N. Barker as the first elders. An eldership was offered to John Worley, who turned it down fearing that because of his large gift, folks would say that he had bought a position of power. One of the first acts of these elders was to order a strong picket fence erected around the church building to keep out wandering livestock, especially swine that were "creating a foul nuisance upon the place."

The church flourished from the beginning. Twenty years after its founding, it had a membership of around 150. It may be of interest to know that the generous John Worley left his home to Rev. Millard, with certain requirements to be met by the latter. The Millard family occupied the former Worley home for several years, but later lost it through certain court action.

The identity of at least one person who attended those first depot meetings is known. In old court papers in Abingdon, Virginia, is record of a fine of two dollars imposed upon Rosetta Bachelor for disturbing public worship and an injunction against further attendance of the Christian Baptist services upon complaint of S. H. Millard and others. From other sources it has been learned this amazon of a woman, a "dyed in the wool" Presbyterian from her youth, had risen up during an especially strong doctrinal sermon of Millard's, strode forward and seized the startled preacher by the coat collars. Red-faced with righteous indignation, she bellowed into his face, "now old squint eyes, you've made your fool claims, now prove them by chapter and verse!" Though the never-to-be-matched Rosetta Bachelor was enjoined from further attendance at the depot meetings, she often "waylaid" Rev. Millard, seeking further argument. But in spite of Rosetta and much other opposition, the Christian Baptist continued to move forward and in time became the First Christian Church.

STATE STREET METHODIST

Seeing the grandeur of the present plant of the State Street Methodist Church, it is hard to imagine that it all began in a small room of a humble cottage that once stood on the southeast corner of Moore and Scott Streets. In 1854 Jesse Aydlotte, a master carpenter, arrived in the new town of Bristol. He soon settled in the little cottage before mentioned. It was then reached by a muddy road that had been named Scott Street but for years was popularly known as Jesse's Lane or Road. Mr. Aydlotte was a very devout, old-style, sanctified, shouting Methodist. Hardly was he settled in his new home until he began having cottage prayer meetings. These were well attended and were rather of a fervent and highly joyous nature. According to Ann Bachelor her foster mother, who had "disturbed" the Christian Baptist meetings, quit attending these prayer sessions because a young lady whose "morals were suspect" had been "overcome with holy joy" and had put on quite a scene for the assembled worshippers.

It soon became apparent that a church would form from these meetings. Thus, on January 15, 1855, Col. Samuel E. Goodson gave lot 103 in his plan of Goodsonville for the purpose of erecting thereon a Methodist meeting house. This lot was located at the northeast corner of Lee and Scott Streets. Trustees named in this deed were W. F. (Uncle Billy) Butler, Jesse Aydlotte, John Fleming, John Moore, Daniel W. Crumley, William W. James, Fleming Crumley, Hardy Pool and William H. Snodgrass.

In 1856 the Rev. George W. Miles of the Blountville Circuit designated the home of Jesse Aydlotte as a preaching point. Soon after this action, a Methodist Society of nineteen members was officially organized. Meetings continued in the Aydlotte home, and there plans were made for the erection of a new house of worship. Aydlotte offered to give his services as a master carpenter, and James Fields was chosen to assist him in the execution of this project. Elisha Hoffman, who had a sawmill about two miles up Beaver Creek pledged most of the lumber for the proposed building. It should be noted that he was not then or ever was a member of this church. The Rev. John Boring was pastor at that time.

Actual erection of the building began in September 1857 and was finished in the spring of 1858. One old citizen of Bristol estimated that this building was perhaps twenty by thirty-five feet in size. It had only one large room. A small bell tower was over the front door. This one entry faced south, overlooking what was to become the present downtown Bristol, Virginia. Then, a swampy area along the present Lee Street and known as Frog Level was the principal view from the front of this little chapel on the rise above Scott Street. The Rev. Josiah Torbett was the pastor when the congregation moved to its new location. In 1860 this group was granted the status of a station church.

Among the several pastors who served the Bristol Methodist Church in those early years was the prominent minister and educator Rev. David Sullins, for whom Sullins College was named. During his pastorship a site on the northwest corner of James and Main was bought from Joseph Johnston of

Philadelphia, Pennsylvania. The deed for this site is dated June 26, 1869, and stipulates that the price was $250.00. In 1875 John Crowell, whose brick yard was a few yards northeast of this site, erected the walls of the new church building. The carpentry work was completed in 1876. This new building was a large, one-story structure, with a soaring tower in front. Costing around eight thousand dollars, it was one of the most expensive buildings of the town at that time. It then became known as the Main Street Methodist Church and so remained until Main was renamed State Street in 1901.

From 1856 the church enjoyed a steady growth so that by 1900 there were nearly eight hundred names on its membership rolls. Pastors who served in the little chapel overlooking Frog Level were:

Josiah Torbett
William Robeson
T. K. Catlett
P. S. Sutton
A. D. Stewart
John A. Waggs
W. E. Munsey
W. H. Bates
C. T. Carroll
David Sullins
H. W. Bays
G. Taylor
David Sullins (Second term)
R. H. Parker

Pastors who served in the new building on Main Street were:

J. Tyler Frazier
E. W. Moore
R. H. Parker
D. Atkins
H. W. Bays
J. H. Keith
R. N. Price
George D. French
Frank Richardson
D. Vance Price
J. H. Keith (Second term)
C. O. Jones
W. S. Neighbors

It is remembered that the Main Street Church followed the old-style seating arrangements, at least to a point. Men sat on the left and women on the right, but married couples were permitted to sit in the center section. Rosetta Bachelor, who lived nearby, and who sometimes attended revivals in the new church, liked the arrangement and tried in vain to have the session of the Presbyterian congregation, of which she was a member, adopt the same plan. Her argument was that such seating helped to keep one's thoughts more spiritually centered during worship services. The Main Street building stood until 1902, when it was demolished to make way for a much finer structure.

FIRST BAPTIST

In 1858 the Rev. William Cate of Jonesboro, Tennessee, began preaching once per month in Temperance Hall, which stood on what was later the southwest corner of Fifth and Shelby Streets. (It was then in Shelby Cemetery.) Interest grew so that in the spring of 1859 a Baptist church was organized with seven charter members. Among them were W. J. Betterton, W. P. Hamilton and Mrs. Mary Coleman. It is also likely that M. W. Weathers, A. Edwards, J. W. Wingfield and James Stuart were among these first members.

Soon after this group organized in Temperance Hall, plans were made to secure a building site. Joseph R. Anderson had a choice lot on what is now the northeast corner of Virginia and State Streets (then First and Main) on which he had long hoped that some building of importance might be erected. On April 22, 1859, he deeded this lot to M. W. Weathers, W. J. Betterton, J. W. Wingfield and James Stuart, trustees of the Baptist Church of Bristol, Virginia. Anderson donated one hundred dollars of the one hundred fifty dollar valuation of this lot.

It appears that the congregation continued to meet in old Temperance Hall for two or three more years and seems to have had no pastor until 1862, when the Rev. J. D. Chambers came to the new church. But even without a regular minister the membership had increased from twenty-eight white members in 1860 to about forty when Rev. Chambers took charge of the congregation. In addition there was almost an equal number of black members, many of whom were slaves or former slaves of the King family.

A church building was begun soon after the arrival of Rev. Chambers, and he did much of the actual labor in its erection, occasionally calling on Jesse Aydlotte to assist in "tedious" portions of the work. William Briscoe donated brick for the foundation and chimney of the frame building. This building faced Main (State) Street. At first it contained only one large room, but a few years later two rooms were added to the back. In 1873 the building was insured for three thousand dollars.

A new building was erected in 1886-87. Old records show that Samuel and James McCrary did a portion of this new construction. The total cost was $3,651.70, and insurance was taken in the amount of $3,500.00. It was a much more imposing building than the first had been, having a tall and ornate bell tower and other eye-pleasing features. This building served until well after 1900.

The church was called at various times Bristol Missionary Baptist, Bristol Baptist, Goodson Baptist, finally becoming First Baptist in 1895. Its membership had increased to around four hundred by 1900. Known pastors of the period 1862-1900 were:

J. D. Chambers	1862-63
M. B. Whorton	864-65
J. T. Kincannon	1872-73
_____ Lloyd	1874-75
B. G. Manard	1877-79
W. W. Worley	1879-80
W. A. Clark	1880-81
J. T. Kincannon	1881-84 (Second term)
R. D. Haymore	1885-90
C. S. Williams	1891-96
Dr. M. E. Broadus	1896-1900

In those years this church was very strict as to the conduct of its members. Church trials were frequent, with many members disciplined or excluded from the membership. One very unusual practice was a monthly "accusation" meeting, during which members might expose the "known sins" of their fellow members. Some common accusations were for lying, fighting, drinking of ardent spirits, dancing, swearing, stealing and speaking ill of one another or the pastor, the latter being grounds for immediate dismissal. One member was severely reprimanded and put on probation because he rented a building to a saloon keeper. These accusation meetings may have done something for the purity of the church, but according to old-timers they did not much help in the realm of Christian love and fellowship.

G. A. Wingfield, an early member of the congregation, was almost dismissed because a super-religious sister accused him of profane swearing. In those days there were many mill dams along Beaver Creek. One of the largest of these was at C. C. Campbell's lumber and flouring mill just above the present bridge on Goodson Street. One day Wingfield stood by this mill discussing with Mr. Campbell the qualities of Beaver for such purposes. The sister had come to buy flour and stood near the conversing gentlemen. Finally, Wingfield declared that the Beaver was the best dam creek he ever saw, meaning that it was good for damming up for power purposes. The horrified sister took the opportunity in the next accusation meeting to tell of Mr. Wingfield's "great transgression." It took a great deal of earnest explanation on the part of the accused brother to prevent his dismissal from the church. Even so, he received a stern warning from the pastor to avoid language that would even sound evil.

This open airing of sin appeared to be unwise to Dr. J. F. Hicks who finally persuaded the church to have these accusations presented only to a committee headed by the pastor. In 1885 a vigilance committee was set up to look after the morals of the church. Members of this committee were W. F. Cooper, a local jeweler; John R. Dickey, druggist and drug manufacturer; Thomas F. Wood, local miller and merchant; and A. K. Brown. How long this committee guarded the morals of the church is not known.

EMANUEL EPISCOPAL CHURCH — "Strange songs in a strange land"

Several of the early Bristol pioneers were Episcopalians from central and eastern Virginia. For years they had no church here. A few of them, including Thomas C. Lancaster, early hotel keeper, tried going to the services of other denominations. It is remembered that Mr. Lancaster once remarked to a fellow townsman that nothing in these churches seemed familiar. "We have strange songs in a strange land." No doubt his sentiment was echoed by others who long hoped for the establishment of an Episcopal church here. The onset of the Civil War with its resultant unrest and constant insecurity only intensified the desire of these people to have the comfort and refreshment of their own faith.

In late 1861 C. W. Yates and family, refugees from Baltimore, Maryland, arrived in the still young town of Bristol. At about the same time two brothers, W. B. and R. A. Williams, arrived here on a government assignment. These new arrivals, all Episcopalians, sought out others of the same faith, and along with Dr. L. M. Hall, a local dentist, led a move to establish a local church. The Academy building on Virginia Street (just north of the present First Baptist Church) was secured as a meeting place. It was there on January 26, 1862, that the Emanuel Episcopal Church was organized with sixteen charter members. Those first members were:

Mr. and Mrs. Albion K. Moore
Mr. and Mrs. C. W. Yates
Mr. and Mrs. W. B. Williams
Dr. and Mrs. L. M. Hall
Mr. and Mrs. R. W. Broadnax
Thomas C. Lancaster
R. A. Williams

W. L. Martin
M. W. Hutchinson
Miss Sallie Lancaster
Miss Mittie Lancaster

The Rev. Mr. Mowbray, a refined, very dignified, and well-educated English gentleman of Chattanooga, Tennessee, conducted the first services of the new church.

Hardly had the new church been organized when the building was taken over by the government as a military hospital. Just a few feet away stood the very new building of the Baptist Church. (It had been finished in late May before the June takeover by the government.) The new Episcopal Church was allowed to use this building for their services. The Episcopal service was at 9:00 A.M., thus clearing the building for the Baptists who met two hours later. Old-timers have told this writer that some of the Baptists came for the early service and that it was not unusual for the Episcopalians to stay for the latter. In early Bristol the ecumenical spirit was stronger than one would have supposed. And the Christian Baptists on Virginia Hill allowed the Episcopalians to use the larger sanctuary of that church for special events.

The Rev. James King, a Presbyterian minister, gave a lot to Emanuel Episcopal Church soon after it was organized. This gift was made in 1863. Later, when a more suitable lot was found, the gift lot was sold for $400.00, and this was applied to the price of the new site. This site was on the southeast corner of Cumberland and Moore, owned by Joseph Johnston, and valued at $500.00. Mr. Johnston donated one hundred dollars of the purchaser price thus making an even trade for the church. The war was on, so nothing was done toward building until after 1865. All through those years the group worshipped in the Baptist meeting house. After the close of the war, a building committee was set up. It consisted of I. C. Fowler, editor of the *Bristol News;* Col. Abram Fulkerson, a very prominent lawyer; and R. A. Williams. In February 1869 a new frame building, large enough to seat 150 people was completed. The total cost was $1,005.38. This building was consecrated in October 1872 by Rt. Rev. John Johns. This building served an ever-increasing congregation for around fifty years. Rectors who served this church for the period 1862-1900 were:

Rev. Mr. Mowbray	1862
Rev. Charles P. Rodifer	1862
Rev. E. H. Ingle	1864-66
Rev. L. B. Wharton	
Rev. E. C. Penick	
Rev. Pendleton Brooks	1871-77

Rev. John McNabb   1877-79
Rev. James Funston   1884
Rev. Mr. Sikes
Rev. Mr. Charley   1889
Rev. John Lloyd   1893
Rev. Robert Carter
Rev. John Scott Meredith
Rev. E. W. Towson
Rev. Thomas S. Russell

It may be of interest to note that the Rev. Russell, who was the last minister to serve before the turn of the century, received fifty dollars per month for his services until his marriage. His pay was then raised to seventy-five dollars per month.

POSTWAR REPORT

In the September 29, 1865, edition of the *Bristol News* appeared an article reporting the condition and progress of the local churches. Mr. John Slack, editor, wrote:

We are forcibly impressed with the idea that the churches in this place bid fair for great religious success and interest in the future, especially when we take into consideration the able, talented, and zealous ministers in charge. The Presbyterian Church has been fortunate in having secured the services of Rev. George A. Caldwell, who is not only acceptable to his own large congregation, but beloved by all denominations, and to the community at large. To his exertions in a great measure is attributable the revival that closed recently, resulting in near one hundred conversions — many accessions to his own and other churches in this place, changing much the morals of the community.

The Methodist Church has received the appointment of Rev. W. E. Munsey to her pastorship, who delivered his introductory sermon on the last sabbath. It was but another able and powerful effort for which he is proverbial. This church may consider herself complimented in the assignment by the conference of so able and talented a minister to her charge.

The Baptist Church, as yet, has no pastor, but efforts are being made to secure a minister whose abilities will be commensurate to so important a charge. She has a large and intelligent membership.

The Episcopal membership is one of much interest and intelligence, presided over by Rev. Mr. Ingles, a young man of much merit and ability. The worship of this church is conducted in the Baptist Church for the present; but we are gratified to learn that a church is in anticipation of construction, and that as soon as the present financial embarrassment is removed from the country, a church equal to the demands of its members will at once be constructed. The future is full of interest and promise to this church.

The Christian Baptists have services in their own church under the pastoral care of Rev. Sam Millard, who is a zealous and working minister, much devoted to the good of the church and community. He is said to have a large and intelligent membership.

The three former churches (Presbyterians, Methodist, and Baptists) have large and interesting Sabbath Schools, which is ominous of a growing and prosperous condition of the churches.

We argue for these churches. We are more than pleased to see such a great religious interest manifested among the people, in whose midst we have cast our lot. We can but look forward to the period when our churches shall be second to none in the country, and from whose bowers shall emanate an influence that shall form a powerful bulwark in the sustenance of peace and quiet in the land, as well as to the evangelization of the human family.

POSTWAR CHURCHES

LEE STREET BAPTIST CHURCH
By the summer of 1865 the black membership of the Bristol Baptist Church about equalled that of the whites. It was then that forty-two of these black members sought and were granted letters of dismissal to form their own church. This action was not of malice, bitterness or strife; and not all the black members lettered out at this time. A few — some say four or five — remained with the whites; and several black people, who were not members, continued to worship with the whites for several years. It is also known that on special occasions, such as revivals, baptisms, etc., the whites and blacks often came together again.

For some time the black Baptists met in the homes of the members. Finally they were able to obtain the services of Rev. Lewis Parks, formerly of Atlanta, Georgia, as their first pastor. During his tenure the old Brush School house was erected in northeast Bristol. This building, measuring eighteen by thirty-two feet, served both as a school and as a house of worship for the black Baptists. During those early days this church was often called the Anglo African Baptist Church of Bristol, Virginia.

Shortly the church broke into two factions, each claiming to be the original church. The Rev. T. P. Smith, formerly of Campbell County, Virginia, presided over one group, while the Rev. Parks pastored the other. During Rev. Smith's ministry a lot was obtained on Solar Hill for a building site. This lot was near (but not on) the southwest corner of Solar and Scott, possibly about where the John Heffernan family now resides. A building was started there but while yet under construction was destroyed by a violent wind storm. The lot was then exchanged for another site located near the junction of King (present Oak View) and Mary Streets. Though not yet united, it seems that Rev. Parks did most of the carpentry on the building that was erected on this latter site. The building measured some thirty by sixty feet and had lofty ceilings.

About this time (1873) a Rev. Walker of Salem, Virginia, arrived in town and began preaching in a private home. He attracted much of the black Baptist congregation, but no third organization resulted. It may have been about this time that the warring factions decided to burn the old records and start over. Such a move was reported by I. C. Fowler in the *Bristol News* in June 1874. In July that year a Rev. Spiller of Lynchburg, Virginia, became the new pastor. The new minister began his work in an unfinished church building that had only planks supported by stacks of rock and brick for pews. His ministry, which reached through the winter and into early spring of 1876, was very effective. The building was finished and many persons brought into the membership. Rev. Spiller was followed by Rev. A. B. Cross of Richmond, Virginia, who served until 1881. He was followed by Rev. J. C. Richardson of Knoxville, Tennessee, who served until 1886.

During the tenure of Rev. Richardson, a church building was erected on Sycamore Street near downtown Bristol-Goodson. After Richardson resigned in the fall of 1886, Rev. Taylor Persinger of Roanoke, Virginia, was called to fill his place. He soon sickened and had to end his service to the congregation only a few months after his arrival here. The Rev. J. W. Payne of Roanoke then served as pastor for about two years. It was then that the group secured the services of the Rev. C. H. Johnson, D.D., of Lynchburg, Virginia, who began his local ministry in January 1890. At the time Dr. Johnson began his ministry the church had 139 members and a Sabbath School with about forty-five scholars, housed in a thirty by sixty building, which was valued at eight hundred dollars. The bell was mounted on a pole in the front yard of the unpainted building. Within five years Dr. Johnson had added around a hundred members to the rolls and had made numerous improvements to the building, including a bell tower.

Even so, the building soon proved to be inadequate to meet the needs of a fast-growing congregation. In spite of the then (1896) depressed condition of the economy, the group bought a lot from J. L. C. Smith for two thousand dollars, paying only two hundred fifty down. The lot was located on the corner of Lee and Sycamore Streets. Almost immediately the church went further and bought an adjoining lot from the Border Star Lodge of Odd Fellows for six hundred fifty dollars. Though not finished before 1900, where the scope of this book ends, a new twenty thousand dollar building was eventually finished to house what then became the Lee Street Baptist Church.

JOHN WESLEY UNITED METHODIST CHURCH

In 1865 when Samuel Johnson, Sr., his wife Liddie, and children Samuel, Jr. and Matilda arrived in Bristol from Pulaski, Virginia, they were very disappointed to find that there was no black Methodist Church in the young town. They soon were having Methodist services in their home and in the home of a neighbor, Mr. Buckner Brown. The Sunday School for this group was held in the home of Mrs. Isabell Jefferson. In 1870 the Rev. Martin Spriddle of the Washington Conference formally organized this group into the first Negro Methodist Church in Bristol. It appears that for a time this church shared a building on Burson Hill with a Baptist group. Some called this the Union Church. Shortly the building collapsed during a violent wind storm. The Methodist group then moved to a building on Sullins Hill (near Sullins College — King, Sullins, James Street area). Then, under the leadership of the Rev. L. W. Coates, a larger building was secured on Johnson Street (some say a portion of this building stood until 1929). But soon more space was needed. It was then that their new pastor, the Rev. James Scott, arranged for the purchase of the building recently vacated by what became Main Street Methodist Church (now State Street Methodist). This building, located on the northeast corner of Scott and Lee, overlooking Frog Level, was bought for $2,200.00. But a severe blow came to the struggling church when shortly after this purchase the building was condemned. Some say that it had been greatly weakened in the same storm that had destroyed the Union Church.

Undaunted, the members launched a new building campaign, with Robert Smith and a Mr. Hamilton giving two hundred dollars as the first contribution. The Rev. James Guthrie and the Rev. Owen Hypshire of the Washington Conference came to the aid of the church and secured help from the Board of Church Extension. In time a new building was completed. It contained one large room over a full basement and had a vestibule at the front, over which there was a modest belfry. This building served until the present structure was erected.

But the financial woes of this church had not ended. Around 1880 heavy indebtedness resulted in a chancery suit, the end of which was an order to sell the church property. Big-hearted I. C. Fowler, of the *Bristol News*, came to the rescue by running an appeal in his paper for his fellow townsmen to contribute funds to save this church. He strongly emphasized that just fifty dollars would be sufficient. As usual, the golden hearted Bristolians reached into their pockets. From a ten-dollar gift from the prince merchant W. W. James to a quarter, meekly presented to Fowler by a poor servant lady, the gifts came in and added up. In the August 23, 1881, edition of the *Bristol News* appeared the following statement:

Editor News:

Please allow me a small space in your valuable paper to express our heart-felt gratitude to the generous public for their liberal contributions to enable us to retain a house of worship in your midst. Language cannot describe the thanks we bestow upon you for the aid realized. The cloud truly has been great, but God has raised it. The sun has risen and the three lights cheer us. The church is from under the hammer — the deed is secured. Truly we will remember you at the throne of grace. Ever yours in bonds of fraternity.

Rev. J. H. Burley, Pastor

Samuel Johnson	M. V. Shepherd
John Logan	David Jefferson
Barnett Smith	Charles Scott
Isaac Harper	Henry Gibson
Samuel Johnson, Jr.	

Board of Trustees

Among the earliest members of this church were Martin and Maggie Shepherd, Buckner Brown, Samuel and Liddie Johnson, Samuel Johnson, Jr., Matilda Johnson, David and Isabell Jefferson, John and Rachel Logans, Myrtle Johnson Peters, Moses Brooks, Jane Black, Julia Brooks, Barnie Smith, Robert Burdine, "Grandma" Boyd, Ella Boyd, Ester Hendricks and Rachel Thomas. Martin V. Shepherd (1843-1911) was an early lay leader in this church. He and his wife Margaret (1849-1928) were the parents of Marcellus Shepherd (June 7, 1868-February 22, 1902) who was the first black lawyer in Bristol. These three early Bristolians are buried near the highest point of the Citizens Cemetery. The site is overgrown in briars and brush and the main shaft of their marker has fallen to the ground.

The earliest ministers of this church include:

The Rev. Robert Wheeler
The Rev. L. W. Coates
The Rev. James Scott

The Rev. John Bean
The Rev. William Rider
The Rev. W. H. Pleasants
The Rev. Diggs
The Rev. R. D. Richardson
The Rev. I. R. Hill
The Rev. E. T. Wright
The Rev. W. T. Marley (1896-97)
The Rev. W. T. Anderson

SAINT ANNE'S CATHOLIC CHURCH

In early Bristol Catholic families and individuals were even fewer than Episcopalians. Yet those who were here strongly desired to have a church of their own faith. It was the O'Shea family who arranged for the Rev. Father Bois (formerly DeBois) to begin Catholic services in Bristol. Father Bois arrived here in November 1869 and lived with the O'Shea family while making preparations to formally organize a church. The organization of St. Anne's was done in 1870. First parishioners of this church included the Harmelings (George, Charles G., Herman and Henry), Charles (Bud) Byrnes, John Delaney, Michael Riordan, John Powers (other members of the Powers family also attended this church), Anthony Deprato, Henry Welch, James Dalton and the O'Shea family. John N. Bosang, though not a Catholic and said to not have been a member of any church, often attended services at St. Anne's.

In late 1870 a church building was begun on a lot fronting on what was then Depot Street (later called Spencer). This site was donated by Samuel E. Goodson. Andrew Fillinger did most of the carpentry work on the new church, charging only half price for his labor. The building was finished in the late spring of 1871. This building still stands, now the chapel of Robinson Mortuary, and is one of the oldest structures in this city.

About a decade after the founding of this church, a burial ground was secured which is now at the west side of the present building on Euclid Avenue. At that time the site was far out in the country and was in a wooded area. A winding, rough, muddy road led up to it from the old stage route (present Oak View Street). Several of those listed heretofore as the first parishioners are buried there.

BURSON'S CHURCH

Major Zachariah Lyles Burson, one of Bristol's most colorful characters and among its wealthiest citizens, came to the new town shortly after the Civil War. He was an ordained Baptist minister and soon joined the local church of his faith. One of the strict rules of the church at that time was that anyone who spoke ill of the pastor was subject to immediate dismissal. Soon after Rev. J. T. Kincannon became the pastor, he and Burson had several severe disagreements — partly over doctrine and partly over manner of life. Major Burson did not believe in closed communion, which was strictly practiced by the Bristol Baptist Church. Too, he was fond of the dance and of a few other practices thought to be "of the Devil" at that time.

During an "accusation meeting" in October 1871, a brother arose and charged that he had heard Burson say that the pastor (Rev. Kincannon) was a narrow-minded, deluded, bigot and needed "straightening out." The brother further charged that it was common knowledge that Burson had attended several dances at the Virginia House Hotel and had been seen to "cut a jig" while Caesar Susong fiddled for him. The accused member did not deny a word of the charge. He remarked that he felt he hadn't said enough to fully express his true feelings about Rev. Kincannon. He further added that when Caesar Susong fiddled "Fire On the Mountain," a popular dance tune at that time, that any Baptist preacher would have to pat a foot, "even if he was on the way to the sacrament (communion) meeting!" Independent, fiery, plain-spoken old Zack Burson added that he'd talk when he pleased, about whom he would, and he'd danced lots and would dance again! Need it be added that Burson was instantly dismissed from the fellowship of the Bristol Baptist Church.

On January 10, 1872, the Rev. Alfred H. Burroughs and George Ambrose were dismissed for "identifying with Major Burson." Rev. Burroughs, who was then the principal of what was known as the Bristol High School, went on to become the legendary "Marrying Parson." He did work with Burson for a short time, but being no longer connected with Bristol High School, he needed a new source of income. He borrowed money from Major Burson to set up a draying business. This field was a bit overcrowded at the time so that he did not much profit from his new occupation. Consequently he fell behind in repayment of the debt, a lawsuit followed, and that ended his work in the new church.

Soon after Major Burson was dismissed from what is now First Baptist Church, he began holding services in his home on Moore Street. There he organized what at first was known as the Missionary Baptist Church. By March 1, 1872, the services of this new church were being held in the Episcopal chapel at 3:00 P.M. on Sunday and at 7:00 P.M. on Thursday. About two months later the group moved to a small dwelling house that stood on the Virginia side of the 800 block of Main (State) Street. This house set far back from the street with a large, level lot in front. On a bright Sunday morning in May 1872, Burson looked out over this lot from the door of the little cottage and remarked to a friend that he would soon build Bristol's finest church building on the site.

On May 24, 1872, Major Burson entered into a contract with "Uncle" Will Smith to erect the building upon this choice fifty-five by one hundred sixty foot lot. Smith contracted to do the brickwork at nine dollars per thousand, a dollar less than his usual price. Specifications called for a four-foot foundation wall, upon which the main walls were to be erected to the height of nineteen feet. There was to be a vestibule fifteen feet square, topped by a forty-six foot tower. The contract required that all brick be hand burnt and that the best sand to be found in the country be used in the mortar. It was estimated that the walls would contain two hundred twenty-five thousand brick. Smith was to be paid two hundred dollars in cash, three hundred dollars in store trade, and the balance within eighteen months. John B. Keller was to do the carpentry work.

Though the contract specified that construction was to be completed by November 15, 1872, several delays drew the work into the following year. The *Bristol News* of March 18, 1873, carried a description of the nearly completed building:

> The new church on West Main Street is one of the most elegant and substantial buildings ever erected in Bristol. It is 45 x 80 (contract says 45 x 70) and has a very handsome tower. In front are three rooms, affording great convenience to a congregation in approaching or leaving the church, and in the upper portion of the tower is an excellent room for a library or study. A good stairway leads to the top of the tower which affords quite a good view of the town. The entire building is of brick and the carpenter's work has been done by John B. Keller, who deserves particular notice for the skill and ability he has displayed. The building will soon be ready for the plasterer and painter and will cost some $8,000.00. The brick work was done by Mr. William Smith and is a good job. The greater part of the expense has been borne by Elder Z. L. Burson.

Painting started on the exterior of the building soon after this news item was published. A young painter had arrived in town from Chattanooga, Tennessee. He had hoped to find work enough here to make the town his home. Burson's church was his first job. About two hours after he commenced work on the high steeple, he slipped and fell to the roof below and then rolled off into the yard, landing on a pile of rejected brick. His fall was witnessed by several onlookers who had gathered to watch the high painting project. The young man was very severely injured. It was remembered that he was taken into the home of Dr. J. A. Templeton where he was cared for until able to ride home on three feather beds that had been stacked in the baggage

car of a passenger train. As a side note of interest, it may be well to record
that these feather beds were given by Major Burson, Rosetta Bachelor and
Dr. Templeton. It is said that Burson had great difficulty hiring another painter
to finish the work.

The first service in this church was held on Easter Sunday, 1873. The opening sermon was by Major Burson, who used the text, ''What Hath God
Wrought.'' Some of his former Baptist brethren remarked that the work was
wrought by the pride and wealth of Burson, without any divine assistance!
The massive, heavily carved, solid walnut pulpit that had been made in
Philadelphia, arrived two days before this opening service. No doubt it was
the finest ever had by a Bristol church, even to this time. Its center portion
was supported upon the outstretched wings of a large angel. On either side
were cherubim, one holding an uplifted trumpet, the other a lyre or harp.
At the feet of the middle angel was a scroll on which was inscribed, ''Make
a joyful noise unto the Lord all ye lands.'' When this pulpit arrived at the
freight depot, it was unpacked and hauled down Main Street by drayman
Lewis Bachelor. L. F. Johnson later wrote that Bachelor could hardly drive
along the street because of the crowds that gathered around his wagon to

**BURSON'S BELL STILL RINGS: The bell purchased by Major Z.L. Burson in the
early 1870s, and which the town did indeed think would ring forevermore, still announces
the hour of worship in Bristol's Calvary Baptist Church. Tim Buchanan is the current
bell ringer.**

view the unusual masterpiece of the carver's art.

Burson also ordered a fine bell for his church tower, but it did not arrive in time for the opening service. The order was placed with the Mennelly Bell Foundry of West Troy, New York in early 1873, but shipment was not made until the following autumn. On November 11, 1873, the *Bristol News* carried an item entitled, "Hanging the Bell." It read:

> The large bell for the Baptist Church on West Main Street was put in position on last Friday (Nov. 7). It weighs 1,050 pounds and cost $530.00. Upon it is inscribed in Roman letters: "This bell donated by Z. L. Burson in the year 1873. To the holiness of the Lord, free." It is by far the largest and finest one in (this) country, and it was quite a difficult matter to get it into position in the tall tower of the church.

Hardly was this bell in place when a myth made the rounds concerning the inscription. Burson had been dismissed from the Baptist Church because of his troubles with Pastor Kincannon, and a man named Byrd (or Bird) had been involved. Thus, the myth went that the inscription read: "Birds may twitter, and cannons may roar, but Burson's bell will ring forevermore." And soon after it was installed the town folk indeed thought it would ring forevermore! Burson announced a special Thanksgiving Day service to be held at 11:00 A.M. in the new church. This was also to be the day that the bell would be used for the first time. Burson lined up his ringers, including a lady or two, who by taking turns, kept the thunderous bell ringing continuously, "without missing a lick," from 8:00 A.M. until the beginning of the service. It is certain that no one in Bristol was able to sleep late on that Thanksgiving morning! And though forevermore has not passed, the bell still peals out its call to worship every Sunday morning. It is now in the belfry of the Calvary Baptist Church in Bristol, Tennessee.

But though Burson's great wealth had been able to build the finest church in town, money could not buy what he most needed — a congregation. Attendance was very weak from the beginning. And it seems that most of the membership came from the poorer part of the local citizenry. Burson paid the pastors, among them W. C. Baldwin (probably the first pastor), a Mr. Talbot, who boarded with John B. Keller, and later a Rev. A. M. Stewart, a young man from Texas. Rev. Stewart was boarded free in the Burson home. He soon became discouraged and "without warning or farewells, quietly stole away." At that time the church only had five or six attending members, and perhaps a few more who were unable to support the services. Burson once remarked that the membership needed financial help instead of being able to help support a minister. The trustees in 1881 were George P. Pepper (a Presbyterian), James Orendorf, Paris Pepper and J. H. Ross. The latter was

quickly voted out when he and Burson had a severe dispute. By this date
the church was known as the Bristol Baptist Church. At about that time,
Burson, hoping to draw a crowd, announced that he would preach on and
prove that the world would end on a certain date in 1890, and that the saints
would then begin a thousand year reign with Christ. Perhaps the crowd increased a bit for this startling sermon, but it seems that most chose to wait
in other churches for the great day ahead.

Perhaps Burson's church was largely a grand monument to wounded pride,
but it did fill a place in the religious life of the town. In time it was used
as a meeting place for various other denominations, and was once used as
a school. It was still listed as a church in 1897 (three years after Burson's
death), and it is said that the building remained until well after 1900.

CENTRAL PRESBYTERIAN CHURCH

For a few years prior to 1874 there had been talk of establishing a
Presbyterian church on the Virginia side of Bristol. When First Presbyterian
became a little crowded, those who sought to form a new organization took
the opportunity to move forward with the plan. Valentine Keebler, a pioneer
merchant of Bristol-Goodson, and Victor Doriot were leaders in this movement. On December 20, 1874, First Presbyterian consented to the plan and
lettered out twenty-four members who desired to become members of the
new body. These were joined by four or five others from various churches.

On January 26, 1875, the Abingdon Presbytery met in the Episcopal Church
and there organized what was at first known as the Goodson Presbyterian
Church. But from the first it was popularly known as Second Presbyterian
Church. The first elders in this new organization were: E. B. McClanahan,
Professor J. H. Winston, Valentine Keebler and Victor Doriot. Dr. Charles
T. Pepper became the first deacon. Shortly, Dr. James Doak Tadlock became
the stated supply pastor and served twenty-six months. J. H. Winston became
the first Sunday School superintendent with Dr. Jere Bunting as his assistant.

In April 1875 the name was changed to Second Presbyterian Church. It
did not become Central Presbyterian until after 1900 (1902). From the first
there was full cooperation between the town's two Presbyterian churches.
Shortly after the new church was organized, there was a joint revival sponsored by the two bodies. The Second Presbyterian Church used the Episcopal
building for nearly three years, holding services early and vacating in time
for the service by the host church. And as it was with the Baptists and
Episcopalians in former years, there were those of both groups who attended
the two services. It is said that the Episcopalians were especially fond of
Rev. Tadlock, with very nearly the entire membership showing up for his
early sermons.

Shortly after the organization of the Second Presbyterian Church, a lot, situated on the northeast corner of Cumberland and Moore, was bought from the town of Goodson for three hundred dollars. By August 1877 a frame building was under construction. It was completed in the late summer that year and served until after 1903. Pastors who served this church during the period covered by this book were:

Dr. J. D. Tadlock	1875-77
Rev. James W. Rogan	1878-82
Rev. Benjamin Mebane	1882-85
Rev. James A. Wallace	
Rev. Samuel Rhea Preston	1890-91
Rev. Baldwin A. Pendleton	1892-93
Rev. Cochran Preston	1897-99

HOOD MEMORIAL A.M.E. CHURCH

A one-room frame schoolhouse for blacks once stood in a field beyond the end of present Alabama Street. It had been built by John G. King, upon whose land it stood. In October 1879 the Rev. Rufus Taylor, a descendant of a slave of George Washington, came and began Methodist services in this building. He soon organized what was to become the present Hood Memorial Church. Charter members were:

Jesse Rhea	Ellen Rhea
Stephen Beidleman	Nancy Washington
Ben Anderson	Rosa Beidleman
Burr Washington	Matilda Washington
Rebecca Anderson	Eliza Washington
Sallie Anderson	Ben Anderson
Lizzie Anderson	Hattie Brazelton
Nancy Carter	Emma Sims

It is known that Jesse Rhea of this list was the first chairman of the board of trustees. The second minister of this congregation was the Rev. George Brazelton. It was during his ministry that a lot in the King field was bought for $150.00, with the Rev. Brazelton paying the first one hundred dollars as a binder. A frame church was erected upon this lot soon after this purchase.

A Rev. I. D. Banks came to the church in 1886. The congregation at that time numbered some twenty people. It was during his ministry that the present lot on Fifth Street was bought and a new building erected thereon. The new building was soon damaged by fire, but was repaired and stood until it was completely destroyed by fire in 1910.

Rev. Rufus Taylor, descendant of a slave of
George Washington, founded the Hood Memorial
Methodist Church in 1879.

REYNOLDS MEMORIAL METHODIST CHURCH

It may almost be said that Santa Claus is the cause of the founding of what
is now known as the Reynolds Memorial Methodist Church. In 1879 Major
A. D. Reynolds played Santa Claus to a needy family living near the location of the present church. While presenting treats to the excited children
he asked them where they went to church and Sunday school. One of the
boys, said to have been a bright-eyed eight-year-old, sadly replied, "They
ain't no church for our kind around here." (He had likely heard his parents
say that.) Major Reynolds patted the boy on the head and told him to be good
and that Santa Claus just might bring him a church, even before next
Christmas. Within a few weeks Reynolds, J. W. Mort and another interested
party or two had started mission work in the neighborhood. At first meetings
were held in a small cottage that stood behind the present educational building.
Soon a store building was rented, and the work became known as the Bristol
City Mission. Services were held on Sunday afternoon by the Rev. M. L.
Clendenen.

On September 2, 1881, James C. and Susan V. Haynes sold the group
a building lot on Mary Street. Under the leadership of the Rev. J. O. Straley,

who came to the church in 1889, a substantial frame building was erected on the site of the present educational building. It was then that the work became known as the Mary Street Methodist Church. (It did not take the present name until 1929.) In 1894 the membership had grown to 294. The building was valued at five thousand dollars, there was no parsonage, and the pastor's salary was five hundred dollars per year. Major Reynolds provided a cottage for the use of the pastor, rent free.

In 1898 a parsonage was built on Goodson Street on a lot donated by Samuel McCrary. The Women's Missionary Society largely paid for the building and furnishing of this parsonage. Pastors who served the Reynolds Memorial Methodist Church from its founding through 1900 were:

M. L. Clendenen	1880	J. L. M. French	1891
T. S. Smythe	1882	Joseph Wampler	1891
E. E. Hoss	1883	J. B. Frazier	1892
D. H. Coman	1884	F. Y. Jackson	1893
B. W. Fielder	1885	A. B. Hunter	1894
M. L. Clendenen	1886	James Moore	1895
E. Blake	1887	W. W. Newberry	1896
Frank Siler, D.D.	1888	A. N. Jackson	1897
J. O. Straley	1889	J. W. Taylor	1898
J. W. Moore, D.D.	1890	G. W. Summer	1900

And what of the little boy whose sad statement had inspired the founding of this church? The writer was long ago told that when in his mid-teens he had moved with his family to Ft. Worth, Texas, and that he had become a very wealthy businessman there and had given heavily toward the building of a Methodist church in that city.

THE SALVATION ARMY

In the early 1880s the Salvation Army, then a young organization, sent a group of young and zealous English ladies, known as the "Hallelujah Lassies" to invade and conquer America. W. W. James, Jr., who had just set up a store in Bristol, was on an eastern buying trip when he encountered some of these lassies holding a street meeting. He introduced himself to the leader of the group and told her that Bristol, a wild, wooly, wide-open town at the time, needed that type of ministry. The leader was Captain Emma Westbrook. About two months later she, along with a helper simply known as the Quaker Lass and a trainee assistant called the Saved Newsboy, "marched upon Bristol." They actually came by train, arriving here during the night of March 10, 1888. Sadly, young W. W. James, Jr., who was responsible for bringing the Salvation Army to Bristol, had committed suicide just ten days prior to the arrival of Westbrook and her helpers. The group held three street meetings the next day, the first being on James Corner just across from the depot. Old Major Zack Burson, who happened to come upon the first meeting, took the three Salvation Soldiers into his home (at 342 Moore Street), where they were boarded free for several months. His Bristol Baptist Church had "played out" by that time, so he allowed the use of the church building for the Army meetings. It was soon being called Salvation Temple and it was in this church, located in the eight hundred block of Main (State) Street (Virginia side) that the work was first headquartered. And Burson was rewarded. Ever since he had erected this grand edifice in the early 1870s, he had longed to see it filled. For the first time he saw his dream become a reality. Almost nightly Captain Westbrook led a swelling procession down Main Street — the Newsboy beating the drum, the Quaker Lass trumpeting, and the captain preaching as they went. Saloons almost emptied behind them and even the notorious Pocahontas Hale, Madam of the largest brothel in town, and some of her "girls" sometimes followed the procession to Burson's Church (Salvation Temple) for the meetings. One of the great attractions of these meetings was the "time of testimony" when some of the formerly most "vile" characters in town told of their deliverance from the "powers of evil."

The workers here were soon joined by Captain L. O. Adams, who evangelized from before daylight to nightfall and beyond. One of his first converts was the old woodcutter, Lemuel Strait, who was considered the champion "cusser" of the town. Adams sought and found him in the woods in back of the Susong Cemetery. Near nightfall he came from the woods with a thoroughly converted Lemuel Strait, who gave a long and fervent testimony that night in the Salvation Temple. It was reported that old Zack Burson had his first shouting spell in seven years during that testimony and Major A. D. Reynolds, who was by then a frequent attendant of the Army meetings, remarked that it was amazing to hear old Lem say five words without uttering a dreadful oath.

These first Salvation Soldiers were constantly busy. As many as seven meetings might be held on a Sunday. Saturdays saw two public services — one at 3:00 P.M. and another in the evening. United meetings were held with other churches, and ministers of the town's various denominations sometimes spoke in the Salvation Temple. Many contacts were made with the social welfare program, as the needs of the poor were met. One of the first soldiers enrolled in Bristol was "Aunt" Betty Scott, who often received this writer into her humble Second High Street home back in the early 1950s. She finally became one of the oldest Salvation Soldiers (in years of service) in the world. She told many stories of the early work that limited space will not allow to be included in this book.

The work seems to have been carried on as more or less an outpost for several years. It was first entered in the Disposition of Forces in April 1897. At that time Captain and Mrs. Harper were appointed to the charge, being assisted by Lieutenants McDowell and Schultz. By that time the headquarters was located at Third and Main (State). In 1898 the officers included a Captain and Mrs. Clark, Captain Mills and the Lieutenants before named. It appears that the offices and meeting hall were then separated as additional property had been secured at Sixth and Shelby. Four captains were stationed here that year, Captains Mills and Bains and Captain and Mrs. Gassaway. By 1900 all the work was located at Sixth and Shelby. Captain and Mrs. Gassaway still remained and had then been joined by Captain and Mrs. Cumbie.

WOODLAWN BAPTIST CHURCH

As Bristol began to grow southward, there were those who thought that the churches should make arrangements to have a church near those living on the southern fringes of town. On December 5, 1887, the Goodson Baptist Church appointed W. S. Leak, H. W. McCarty, T. F. Wood, J. M. Trammel and John Brown to start a Bible study and prayer meeting in the Sparger Cotton Factory as an arm of the church. The effort was fruitful from the beginning.

On Thursday night, July 3, 1890, twenty-four members of the Bristol Baptist Church were granted letters of dismissal to form a new Baptist church of what had been known as the Sparger Mission. It should be noted here that the Goodson Baptist Church had officially changed its name to Bristol Baptist on January 2, 1888. By that time Burson's church, which had borne the same name, had "played out," thus the former felt it was wise to reassume its original name. On July 6, 1890,.the twenty-four former members of Bristol Baptist formally organized a new body and called it the South Bristol Baptist Church. The Rev. M. B. Upchurch, formerly of Bluff City, Tennessee, was called as the first pastor. This church was admitted into the Holston Baptist Association in August 1890. About 1895 this church obtained a lot at the corner of Southside Avenue and Cedar Street and a frame building was soon erected there. This author has no information as to when the name was changed to Woodlawn Baptist Church. Pastors who served before 1900 were M. B. Upchurch (1890-93), E. L. Smith (1894), J. A. Davis (1896), and W. C. Patton (1899).

ANDERSON STREET METHODIST

In the early 1890s Bristol began to expand westward. With this expansion came the need for churches to serve the newly settled borders of the town.

First Presbyterian Church, Fifth Street, Bristol, Tenn.

The erection in 1881 of a new and grand building by the First Presbyterian Church on Fifth Street signaled to the town that affluence had come to the churches of Bristol.

Among those who sensed this need to the point of being brought to action may be mentioned J. H. Swan and George P. Cannon, who along with other interested parties began a canvass of their neighborhood to see if there was sufficient support for a mission work. Finding enough interest, they organized a Methodist Sunday School in the old Cornfield Academy, an abandoned brick schoolhouse which stood on the northeast corner of Anderson and Tenth Streets. In 1894 Anderson Street Methodist Episcopal Church, South, was organized in this building with twenty-two charter members. The Rev. G. M. Moreland became the first pastor. Before Moreland, Captain L. O. Adams of the Salvation Army had filled the pulpit.

For the first four years or so of its existence the church continued to meet in the Cornfield Academy building. George P. Cannon served as Sunday School superintendent, while Walter Allen led the singing and served as church secretary. Mrs. C. J. White moved her pump organ from her home and served as church organist. Shortly the Women's Missionary Society bought a lot on the southeast corner of Anderson and Tenth, and plans were made to erect a new church building there.

In 1895 the Rev. Murray Mitchell came to the church and immediately began to promote the building program. In 1896 work started on the Victorian frame structure. Most of the work was done by the men of the church, with assistance by a master carpenter, Mr. Will Graham. The new building was occupied in 1898. The dedication service was conducted by the noted Rev. David Sullins. The trustees at that time were A. C. Harkleroad, C. J. White, J. W. Emmert, L. D. Mastin and J. H. Swan. Pastors who served from the beginning to 1900 include G. M. Moreland (1894-95), Murray Mitchell (1895-98) and R. K. Sutherland (1898-1900).

Other churches known to have been in existence before 1900 include Rice's Chapel at 1115 West Main Street, W. R. Hamilton, superintendent; Mt. Zion Mission Church (Baptist) at 30 Lynwood Street; Chalmers' Street Mission, corner of Chalmers and Rose Streets; and King's Chapel on Norfolk Avenue, Henry Dulaney, superintendent.

THE GLORY HOLE

Just below where Main (State) Street crossed Beaver Creek was a rounded pool of water, reached by a gentle sloping bank. This became the favorite baptizing place for those early Bristol churches that practiced immersion. It soon became known as the "glory hole." An early edition of the *Bristol News* tells of the Rev. J. T. Kincannon and B. G. Manard of the Baptist Church immersing twenty-five persons there on Sunday, February 24, 1872. Editor Fowler went on to say that it was the largest number to be baptized there to that time.

It was easy to tell when the black Baptist Church intended to have a meeting at the "glory hole." The entire congregation would gather at the church and then come singing through the streets toward the sacred spot on Beaver Creek. Those to be baptized would be dressed in white following just behind the preacher, who usually marched with open Bible in his hands. A large crowd gathered behind the marching singers. On one occasion a former Methodist preacher was one of three candidates for baptism. When he was raised from the water, the Rev. Parks shouted out, "Bless God, we captured one of the generals; we'll get the soldiers next!"

And there was once something other than religious excitement at the glory hole. A low tree stood at the edge of the pool. Young boys often climbed up into the branches of this tree for a better view. On one occasion a lad of thirteen or so years climbed far out on one of the limbs and was followed closely by a companion. About the time the preacher ended his ceremony, the companion gave the forward boy a shove, causing him to splash heavily into the water below. According to "Uncle" Ed Faidley, who told this long ago, the dunked boy jumped from the water shaking his fist at the companion above and proceeded to "give him a good cussing."

HOW BURSON QUELLED HIS HECKLERS

Soon after Major Z. L. Burson opened his church on lower Main Street, some of his enemies made plans to disrupt his sermons by sending young boys to heckle him. On the first occasion the major pretended not to notice, nor did he later file any charges of disturbing public worship, as he was expected to do. The next Sunday the hecklers came with greater courage than ever and in larger number. That Sunday Burson lingered until the crowd had assembled. Finally the major entered the left door as was his custom and bowing graciously to the congregation, mounted the steps to the pulpit. Strangely, this pulpit was located between the two front doors, with the pews in reverse fashion facing toward it. He looked long and steadily out over the crowd, noting that there were far more people in attendance than usual (some had come to see the expected excitement) and that scattered here and there were some of the worst ruffians of the town. Undaunted he slowly drew two enormous pistols from his coat, "mounted" one across the shoulder of the carved cherubim on his right and the other on the left. The effect was that of mounted cannons aimed toward an expected point of attack. Without saying a word he looked long and steadily at the very hushed crowd. That look was enough. The service then proceeded without the least semblance of disruption. The hecklers never returned.

THE DEVIL COMES TO THE CAMP MEETING

In the 1870s the Methodist Conference appointed a committee to select a camp-meeting ground "to be located near Bristol, Virginia." Before agreement was reached on a site, the local methodist and other churches decided to go ahead and have a summer meeting, hoping to have permanent grounds by the next year. A brush arbor was set up in Flat Hollow near the present intersection of Wood and Mary Streets. Great crowds attended both the morning and night services. Up near the present crossing of Buckner and Oakview Streets was a little pasture where John N. Bosang kept his large, but gentle, long-horned bull. One night some local boys, tired of the long meetings, decided they would have a little excitement at Bosang's bull lot. One carried along an old black slicker coat, which he tied to the animal's tail, as another boy petted the gentle bull. When the coat was securely in place, the boy gave it a slap or two around the bull's legs. The boys jumped back upon the fence hoping to watch a show that they thought would remain confined to the moon-bathed bull lot. But after a few rounds of bucking, snorting and pitching, the greatly frightened and agitated beast tore through the fence and headed straight toward the brush arbor meeting. Of course the arbor was poorly lighted and when old Tobe (the bull) came snorting, kicking and bellowing into the arbor, it was easy for the startled attendants, who could only glimpse long, crooked horns swinging around and something black waving in the air, to assume that Satan had arrived. According to old Daddy Thomas, who as a child witnessed this event, some woman screeched out, "Lord, it's the pure old Devil. Run, Children, Run!" But it was not only children who ran. The crowd fled en masse, almost knocking the arbor down in their panicky flight. This writer does not know if the arbor meeting ever resumed or where the bull finally ended his maddened dash, but it is certain that many Bristolians would never forget when the Devil came to the Flat Hollow camp meeting!

THE MUNSEY-MILLARD WAR

When the highly intellectual and eloquent Rev. W. E. Munsey was pastor of the early Methodist Church, he was challenged to a debate by the Rev. S. H. Millard on the question, "Is Immersion the Only Proper Mode of Baptism?" This three-night debate was well publicized in advance and drew large crowds from "the opening shot." By the second night the small Methodist building could not contain the audience. Many stood outside straining to hear every word through the open windows. And nightly the debate grew more heated. The ministers spent the days preparing arguments to refute the claims made the previous night by the opponent. On the third night Rev. Millard brought the local Baptist minister with him as an aide. When Munsey was asked if he objected to this additional ally, he replied that he did not and that he would gladly take on every "deep water preacher" in the country if any cared to come. On that third and supposedly closing night, it became clear that all the ground had not been covered, so it was announced that the debate would continue for at least another three nights. It was then that the Rev. G. A. Caldwell of the Presbyterian Church volunteered to assist Rev. Munsey in what was by then being called the Munsey-Millard War. And several area "deep-water" preachers volunteered to aid Rev. Millard.

It appears that most of the ministers, certainly the original debaters, remained gentlemen throughout the long debate. But it was not so with the audience. Heckling and shouted rebuttals and instructions from the crowd often reached the point that order had to be restored by the town constables. Several fights ensued in the yard, and one or two actually started in the church building. The legendary Rosetta Bachelor, a dyed-in-the-wool Presbyterian, is said to have "laid two sisters and a man in the floor." And before she was literally dragged from the church by constable John B. Keller, she had laid low another man who had called out to Keller to "arrest the old wench." Then once in the yard she had wrenched free and attacked the constable, calling him a vile, wretched ally of the Devil. It seems that the "battle" had started because Rosetta highly resented the rejoicing of the two sisters and the man when the opposition had scored a point. Old Daddy Thomas used to tell this and add that his father, an undefeated rebel, sometimes jokingly said that if the Confederates could have had Rosetta Bachelor as a soldier, the South would have won the war! And many bitter arguments and a few fights occurred on the streets during the day, as citizens discussed the debate of the night before. The Munsey-Millard "war" finally ended. Like today's debates, the winner was determined by the personal prejudice of whoever might be making the claim.

Take heed, you who would today debate doctrine, defend political concepts, or even clamor for the establishment of historical claims. One hundred and twenty summers have passed since the Munsey-Millard war and the Methodists still sprinkle and the Christian and Baptist churches still immerse — enough said!

Bibliography - Chapter Sixteen

Anderson, Joseph R. Notes, cir. 1880.

Anderson, Melinda King. As told to her granddaughter, Mrs. Herman Blackley.

Bachelor, Ann. Memoirs (unpublished), 1935-1937.

Bristol News, newspaper. Various issues, 1860-1889.

Daniel, Mrs. Thomas N. *Centennial History, Central Presbyterian Church.* 1975.

Harrison, Ann Strickland. *A Long Communion: History of First Presbyterian Church of Bristol, Tennessee-Virginia, 1820-1976.* Kingsport, Tenn.: Kingsport Press, 1979.

History of State Street Methodist Church, 1856-1976.

John Wesley United Methodist Church. (Paper supplied by Mrs. M. F. Redmon.)

Loving, Robert S. *Double Destiny; The Story of Bristol, Tennessee-Virginia.* Bristol, Tenn.: King Printing Company, 1955.

Paperville Presbyterian Church. Paperville, Tennessee. *Minutes,* 1850s.

Phillips, V. N. (Bud). Interviews with several Bristol citizens, 1953-1956 and 1986-1990.

Playl, Stephen, Rev. Notes regarding Woodlawn Avenue Baptist Church, 1990.

Preston, Thomas W. *History of Central Presbyterain Church.* 1950.

Sullivan County, Tennessee. Court and Deed Records, 1854-1900.

Sullivan County Historical Society. *Foundation of Faith in Sullivan.* 1986.

Taylor, Hattie King. Notes (unpublished).

WHCB Homecoming '86, Church Histories.

Washington County, Virginia. Court and Deed Records, 1854-1900.

Chapter Seventeen
EARLY BRISTOL SCHOOLS

THE LITTLE SCHOOL HOUSE WASN'T RED

It wasn't the proverbial little red school house that sheltered Bristol's first scholars and their stern master. No, the first school was of board and batten construction and was "well white washed" according to one who was a student there in 1855. This "little white school house" was erected in the spring of 1854 for the Rev. James King by early carpenter John Aiken. It was located at the northern edge of the Shelby graveyard, a little west of what was to become the southwest corner of Shelby and Fifth Streets. It was built to serve both as a school and a meeting place for the Presbyterian Church of Bristol. An early student of this school recalled that the grave of General Shelby was a short distance east of the school, that the children often played around the grave, and that she had often eaten her lunch sitting upon the iron slab that covered it. She also recalled how difficult it was to read in the poorly lighted building; it had only one small window to the side and one behind the master's seat.

In the summer of 1854 James B. Crabtree opened Bristol's first school term in this building with a very small group of scholars, many of whom came from the surrounding country. The Rev. James King paid Crabtree's salary, calling it his gift to the developing town. Professor Crabtree has been described as a stern master who always kept an ample supply of switches within hand's reach. For some reason he never removed his large, black, broad-brimmed hat. It was remembered that his bright, eagle-like eyes peered steadily out from beneath the ample shade of that hat as he watched over his scholars. He boarded with Joseph R. Anderson, whose home was within sight of the school. Often he brought four-year-old John C. Anderson (son of Joseph) with him and trotted the child on his knee as he taught the classes.

Professor Crabtree was replaced by Cyrus King, son of the Rev. James King. King lived on Waterloo farm about two miles down Beaver Creek. He rode daily to his school on a large white horse. It was remembered that he was a capable master who kept good discipline, though he was very kind to and understanding of his scholars. It was fondly recalled that he often played with the children under the giant oaks where he was so soon to sleep. (King died March 22, 1856.)

In the summer of 1855 Mrs. Angeline Lethridge, a young widow, taught school here. She has the distinction of having been Bristol's first female

In the center is Mrs. Angeline Lethridge, Bristol's first female school teacher. Her sister is seated at the right and her mother at the left.

teacher. She lived with a widowed sister (the two had married brothers) in a little cottage on Fourth Street that they rented from Joseph Anderson.

THE TWIN ELM SCHOOL

Just below where the old channel of Beaver Creek made a sharp bend to the south (very near the present intersection of Sycamore Street and Piedmont Avenue) once stood the massive triple elms. These ancient trees, standing on the west bank of the stream, grew from one sprawling stump. The triple elms were used as a landmark when the site of present Bristol was sold to Rev. James King in 1814. Near the elms there flowed a large spring, and it was by this spring that King erected a log wash house about 1820. An old slave of King's once recalled that one day as the washing was being done, a sudden and violent thunderstorm struck. During this storm a bolt of lightning made a direct hit on the middle elm, shattering it in a violent explosion. This frightened the wash maids so that they fled wildly back through the raging storm to the old King home on the hill above.

Thus the triple elms became the twin elms that stood until around 1885. In the spring of 1856 William L. Rice taught a short term of school in the old King wash house. It appears that he taught there again in the fall of that year. Ann Bachelor, one of the students, remembered that this was a morning school. Classes were held from about eight until noon and then dismissed for the day. Scholars coming from the town had to cross Beaver on a foot log that had no handrail. She remembered that if the creek were flooding there would be no school because of this dangerous method of crossing over high water. She also remembered that a boy once went early and soaped a portion of the log knowing that Professor Rice (whom he disliked) would be the first to arrive at the crossing. As expected, the school master lost his footing, dignity, and composure as he took a kicking, flaying, unexpected, sudden plunge from the log into the creek below, much to the mirth of the lad who had hidden in willow bushes near the foot log. The problem was discovered after early arriving students suffered a similar fate. Rice spared no effort to discover the culprit. The lad might have escaped detection had he not told several students of the mad fit which Rice displayed as he arose and waded from the water, especially the unholy oaths that had issued from one whose speech was usually pure and seasoned with grace. Among those students there was a "traitor." Before noon closing two seasoned switches had been worn out over the culprit's back. The boy never returned to school and, according to Ann, later went west and became a notorious outlaw. She also vividly recalled seeing some of the boys scooping up sand and rubbing the soapy spot from the log. The site of this second Bristol school would be near the present drive-in station of the Charter Federal Savings and Loan Association.

SPERRY'S SCHOOL

Operating a newspaper in early Bristol brought little financial reward. Thus, soon after J. Austin Sperry became editor of the *News* in late 1857, he turned to teaching to supplement his meager income. He was well educated, intelligent, and a lover of children and young folks; thus he easily fit into the professor's role. He set up his school in the newspaper office which was located on the east side of Fourth Street, about half way through the first block off Main (State) Street. Ann Bachelor, who became a student in this school in the spring of 1858, recalled that Sperry then had around fifteen students ranging in age from about six to fifteen years old. She wrote that later in the year, a young man of twenty-one years of age, who could not read or write, became a student in this school. Among the students was young John C. Anderson, son of Bristol's founder, Joseph Anderson. It was here that the noted future Bristol merchant, banker, and mayor first learned his letters.

For fifty cents per week per pupil, Sperry gave lessons twenty days per month. Young Ann Bachelor earned her tuition by helping fold the *News* and delivering the same over the town. (Was she Bristol's first newsboy—

nay—newsgirl?) When Sperry became involved in a morals scandal in late September 1858, he quickly closed his school, never to re-open. However, he continued as editor of the *News* for about four years.

BRISTOL INSTITUTE

Among the early Bristol settlers was LaFayette (called L. F.) Johnson. He was at first a commission merchant who in time became very successful. He arrived in 1857, and about one year later he and William Templin opened what became known as the Bristol Institute. (Some say it opened just after Sperry closed his school.) It was located first on the Virginia side of the town in a rented building that stood on Front Street (then called Fourth Street), but it was later moved to the old King home on Solar Hill. To head his school, Johnson brought from Lynchburg, Virginia, a Madam Henrique, a French lady who had long taught in that city. She brought with her Miss Martha Thom and Professors Bartlett and Greenleaf, who would make up the faculty of the Bristol Institute. Madam Henrique also had an adopted daughter whom she brought with her. This girl, Amalia Henrique (LeBlanc), was then sixteen and was one of the first to enroll in the new institute.

The institute, while not a college, was the first school in Bristol to offer advanced learning. There was a large enrollment from the town and surrounding area. Professor Greenleaf even offered courses in several foreign languages, but it is said that there were not many students for these classes.

Madam Henrique, described as a tall, bony, long-nosed woman, ruled the school with an iron hand. She alone determined who could or could not be enrolled in it, and expulsions were not infrequent. She was of almost Puritan persuasion and is known to have blocked the enrollment of one local girl whose morals were in question. It is also told that she was somewhat "prissy" and highly resented having to walk through the muddy streets of the little village to reach the school. (She boarded in the L. F. Johnson home on Third Street.) It is said that there were times when she commanded Professors Bartlett and Greenleaf to form a pack saddle of their hands and carry her over the muddiest portions of the streets.

Though Professor Bartlett, a widower, was almost twice the age of Amalia Henrique (LeBlanc), he soon fell madly in love with her. Apparently the feeling was mutual. Though courting a student was absolutely forbidden—both by school rules and ironclad custom—the two were able to marry without the benefit of extended courtship. Professor Bartlett simply sent the girl a note expressing his feelings and flatly asking for her hand in marriage. (The author once saw this note and remembers that it contained a lot of romantic and flowery language.) Madam Henrique consented to the match and planned and directed a high-toned public wedding. The ceremony was held in the

Christian Baptist Church. The couple lived in the Magnolia Hotel for the first few months of their marriage.

It appears that the onset of the Civil War closed the Bristol Institute. However, Mrs. L. F. Johnson (formerly Harriet Moorman) soon opened a small private school for young children in her home on Third Street. In 1953 a 96-year-old woman of Bristol, Tennessee, shared with this author her recollections of Mrs. Johnson and her school. This lady had apparently been the youngest student and was the teacher's pet. Just about every school day she became drowsy during classes. Mrs. Johnson would then lead her to another room, pull out a little trundle bed from under the big four poster, and tuck her in for a little nap. She clearly remembered Mrs. Johnson's many stories of her own childhood in Albermarle County, Virginia. It seems that the Moormans were neighbors of Thomas Jefferson. She fondly recalled being taken to Monticello for a visit and while there the aging ex-president trotted her on his knee and sang a merry little song for her. Nearly forty years later Mrs. Johnson told another little girl of her noted visit to Monticello, and that "girl" (now 99 years-old) recently shared with this author her memories of this pioneer Bristol teacher including the noted Jefferson knee ride story. Mrs. Johnson's school existed for about four years, and many a Bristol child learned the ABC's at her knee.

BRISTOL-GOODSON MALE ACADEMY

Joseph R. Anderson greatly desired to have an academy in town that would have a "Presbyterian flavor." In early 1860 he began a campaign among his friends to establish such an academy on the Virginia side of the town. Securing the promise of Thomas D. Walthall to head this proposed school, Anderson set forth to raise a subscription for the erection of a suitable building on a lot that he would give for the planned school. This lot fronted on Virginia Street and is now covered by a later addition of the First Baptist Church. Anderson's subscription list is dated May 12, 1860, and shows that the three heaviest donors to the project were the Rev. James King, who gave one hundred dollars and a building lot; Samuel E. Goodson, who gave a like gift (his gift lot was next to the Methodist Church); and Joseph R. Anderson, who gave the same. His lot was to be used for the building, and the others would be sold. Others on the subscription list were

James S. Clarenne	$25.00	J. T. Preston	$10.00
John B. Buchanan	5.00	W. A. Rader	5.00
John S. Mosby	10.00	W. K. Campbell	5.00
James King, Jr.	25.00	Valentine Beidleman	5.00
G. W. Blackley	5.00	John R. Delaney	10.00

J. H. Pepper	25.00	Henry Anderson	5.00
(in cash and labor)		James Witcher	5.00
H. T. Wilbar	5.00	W. J. Martin	5.00
John G. King	50.00	Thomas Johnson	100.00
(in wood-lumber?)		(in lumber; more if necessary)	
William Bushong	5.00	John Briscoe	25.00
Robert F. Bibb	15.00	(or $150.00 in brick work)	
Henry Harmeling	5.00	William L. Rice	20.00
A. C. Price	20.00	J. S. Shangle	10.00
J. W. Morgan	10.00	E. H. Seneker	10.00
Thomas W. Farley	10.00	G. H. Mattox	5.00
E. D. Rader (painting)	10.00	E. C. Stoffel	10.00
Henry Rosenheim	10.00	T. D. Walthall	40.00
John Keys	10.00	J. E. Pepper	25.00
		(in work)	

In addition to the names on this list, it is known that M. Womack, James Morgan, M. W. Hutchinson, J. W. Jones, and Dr. R. M. Coleman gave to the building fund.

The first trustees of the Bristol-Goodson Male Academy were T. D. Walthall, John G. King, L. F. Johnson, William L. Rice and James W. Morgan. Professor Walthall was guaranteed one hundred dollars to teach the first five month term at this school. Those who pledged to underwrite his salary were Joseph R. Anderson, James King, Sr., L. F. Johnson, Thomas Johnson and John G. King.

J. H. Pepper and Brothers took the contract to erect the two-story building and began work in mid-June 1860. It was finished in late August that year. This building contained one large room below and a large and smaller room above. Soon after the outbreak of the Civil War, this building was taken over by the Confederate government for use as a hospital. The War also interfered with the payment of pledges so that at the end of that conflict the builders still held mechanic's liens against the school. James Fields, an early builder who helped the Peppers in the construction of the building, had on February 6, 1871, traded his bill of $346.02 to L. F. Johnson for merchandise.

On November 30, 1865, Thomas D. Walthall, James W. Morgan, L. F. Johnson, William L. Rice and John G. King, trustees of the Bristol-Goodson Academy, sold the property (for the consideration of one thousand dollars) to the Masonic Fraternity of Shelby Lodge 162, the trustees of which were William S. Minor, John Keys and Dr. C. T. Pepper. The purpose of this sale was to pay the long overdue costs of building. Other than the bill of Fields (traded to L. F. Johnson), a debt of $374.00 was still due J. H. Pepper and Brothers. The plan was to pay these debts, and then what was left was to be distributed on a prorated basis to the original subscribers. At the final accounting it was determined that the amount remaining to be prorated among these subscribers would amount to about eighteen cents on the dollar. Most of the gentlemen signed a document relinquishing all interest in the remaining funds. Those who did not received amounts ranging from $7.20 to Thomas D. Walthall down to $.90 for W. L. Martin. The noted John S. Mosby received $1.80.

The Academy building had been damaged almost beyond use by the Confederates. It was necessary for the Shelby Lodge to expend around eight hundred dollars to make necessary repairs. Once repaired, the Lodge offered the use of the lower floor for school purposes. The old Bristol-Goodson Academy was revived and soon made the following announcement:

BRISTOL MALE ACADEMY

The next session of this school will commence in the Masonic Academy Hall on Monday, June 11, 1866, and continue five months. All the branches of an English and Classical education thoroughly taught. Tuition from $2.00 to $4.00 per month, payable monthly. Contingent fee 25 cents. A deduction of 25 percent will be made for the tuition of the session if paid in advance. A competent assistant will be employed in the Primary Department. Board can be procured in good families at reasonable rates.

THOMAS D. WALTHALL, A.M.
PRINCIPAL

The "competent assistant in the Primary Department" was Mrs. Angeline Lethridge, who had earlier taught in Bristol's first school. She was remembered as a very kind and patient teacher who, nevertheless, kept an abundant supply of seasoned switches, the liberal application of which kept good order in the school room.

In September 1872 Professor Walthall moved to Tazewell, Virginia, to take charge of a newly organized school there. The Academy continued under the leadership of Professor C. C. Minor, who was later assisted by his sister, Mrs. Henrietta Colbert. The school is known to have been in operation as late as 1882 and may have continued for some time after that date.

MRS. BAILEY'S SCHOOL

Mrs. Julia Ann (Womack) Bailey, a widow from Charlotte County, Virginia, arrived in Bristol shortly before the outbreak of the Civil War. Her son David F. Bailey, who was later a leading Bristol lawyer, early joined the Confederate forces. The widow and her two daughters continued to live in a cottage that stood on the south side of Shelby Street, a short distance west of the Fifth Street intersection. (The Elks Club later occupied the lot.) There was not much a widow could do in those days to earn a living and times became increasingly hard with the continuation of the war. Mrs. Bailey was well educated so proceeded to open a boarding school in her home. Locals also attended this school. One of the courses offered was music. A prized possession in the home was a rosewood piano upon which the students delighted to practice. But most classes had to cease after the Federals dragged this piano from the home, knocked the legs from under it, threw off the lid, and fed their horses in it.

Two known students of this school were Nancy B. and Mary M. Zimmerman, orphans of Dr. B. F. Zimmerman, Bristol's first physician. Receipts still exist that show certain costs billed to the Zimmerman estate for the schooling of these girls. One bill dated October 1, 1862, lists the following charges:

English and counting (arithmetic)	$16.00
Music and use of piano	15.50
Copy Book	1.25
French	2.00
1 piece music	.25
Total	$35.00

The above represents the cost of a five month term of school, beginning October 1, 1862, and ending March 1, 1863. This particular bill was for Mary Zimmerman, who later married Bruce Spurgeon. Other receipts show such items as a pencil for ten cents, a course in sacred history at $1.50, and a history book at $2.25. It must be remembered that these were war time prices and no doubt reflect a degree of inflation. Mrs. Bailey's private school was not only beneficial to the town, but it provided a living for her family.

CAPTAIN MANARD'S SCHOOL

Captain Bird G. Manard, a former Confederate officer, arrived in Bristol just after the close of the Civil War. He immediately perceived that there was room for another school in the town. The *Bristol News* of September 29, 1865, announced his intentions:

> The undersigned will open a school for a term of five months, commencing on the first Monday in October, in the Baptist Church, Goodson, Virginia. Tuition half payable at the end of ten weeks, remainder at the expiration of the session.
>
> | | |
> |---|---|
> | Elementary principles with Grammar, Geography, Declamation and Composition | $10.00 |
> | Algebra, Natural History and Philosophy, | |

Grammar, Declamation and Composition	12.50
First Lessons in Latin, Higher Mathematics, Moral and Mental Philosophy, Logic, Rhetoric, Declamation and Composition	15.00
Contingent Fee	1.00

B. G. MANARD

If the professor alone taught all the above, he indeed was a well learned and no doubt a very busy man. Editor John Slack commented elsewhere in the same paper that Professor Manard was a good scholar and no doubt would be thorough in his instructions. Known students of this school include John and Charles Palmer, sons of early lawyer Joseph B. Palmer; John Alf Brewer, son of the early merchant W. P. Brewer; and John H. Caldwell, who married a daughter of Bristol's founder, J. R. Anderson. Others were Jim Powers, John Jones, George Cocke, Jim Campbell, Zan Anderson, Charlie Minor, Sam Legard, George Robertson, Bob Burrow, Jim Trammell, and Jim Cowan. Manard's school existed side by side with the Bristol-Goodson Male Academy for several years. One requirement was that all Manard's students must attend prayer meeting at the Baptist church each Wednesday night.

NEAL-GALE SCHOOLS

Apparently a short time before the close of the Civil War, the Rev. W. W. Neal, a very learned and highly effective educator, set up a private school in the Temperance Hall at the southwest corner of Fifth and Shelby. Rev. Neal later moved to Kentucky. In the October 19, 1866, edition of the *Bristol News* appeared Mr. William B. Gale's announcement of his intention to continue the school:

> The undersigned intends to open a Female School in Rev. Mr. Neal's school room, on Tuesday, September 4. No pains will be spared to merit the patronage of the community. A music class will be formed of which Prof. Kehr of Abingdon will have charge. No males will be admitted. Tuition: $2.00 to $3.50 per month.
>
> Bristol, Aug. 30, 1866   Wm. B. Gale
>
> For further particulars apply at the school room on and after Monday, Sept. 3rd, or to Mr. Neal.

It is not known how long this school existed.

THE FREEDMAN'S SCHOOL

On February 26, 1868, Valentine Keebler, early Bristol merchant, sold one acre of ground to William Hill, Richard Campbell and Richard Watkins, Committee of Freedman's School of Goodson, Washington County, Virginia. This land is described as being the middle acre of a tract that had been purchased from William L. Rice and was bounded on the east by a lot that had been sold to R. T. Lancaster and on the southwest by the lot of W. D. Minor. The lot sold to the Freedman's School contained a cabin which had already been in use as a schoolhouse for the blacks of the town.

There is some indication that the school may have stood near and south of the intersection of Oak and Lindsey Streets. An old-timer once told this author that he remembered a path that led up from near Scott Street to a school for blacks that stood at the top of a steep hill behind the present Bristol Steel office building. He thought it was called the Freedman's School. He recalled that dirt steps had been cut into the steep hillside and fronted by pieces of railroad cross ties.

Professor Yardley, Superintendent of the Freedman's Schools west of the Allegheny Mountains, visited Bristol on March 18, 1873, and was interviewed by I. C. Fowler, Editor of the *Bristol News*. During that interview Prof. Yardley stated that he had founded the Freedman's School in Bristol in the late 1860s.

MRS. SMITH'S BAPTIST FEMALE SEMINARY

Soon after the Civil War (exact date has not been established), a Mrs. Smith opened a Baptist Female Seminary in a building that stood on Anderson Street between Sixth and Seventh Streets, the site of the later Baptist Female Institute or College. This institution operated for a few years then very abruptly moved to Glade Springs, Virginia. According to "Uncle" Ed Faidley and others, the cause of this sudden move was a falling window. It seems that Mrs. Smith had a male professor (whose name is unknown) in her school. According to Mr. Faidley, he was a former Confederate Captain and suffered from what might now be called intermittent shell shock. If suddenly startled, he was likely to jump and shout out his immediate thoughts. The school was having a public program of some sort, during which the nervous professor dozed. Near him was a raised window which suddenly fell with a loud, sharp crack, much like the sound of a rifle. The dozing professor leaped up and loudly called out, "Oh damn, I'm sure as hell shot!" One may imagine the impact of this unholy language upon a crowd that did not understand his acute case of war induced anxiety. The public gossip that Mrs. Smith harbored a professor who would "cuss" at the drop of a hat (in this case the drop of a window) caused the closing of the school and its resultant move to Glade Springs. It is claimed that this school was the forerunner of the present Virginia Intermont College.

BRISTOL FEMALE COLLEGE

Though the Bristol Female College (first called Bristol Female Institute) was not incorporated until 1872, it had existed for at least three years before that time. It may have been the continuation of the school that was set up by Bird G. Manard in the Baptist Church in 1865. There is indication that it had at one time had students of both sexes. It was reorganized in the late autumn or early winter of 1869 as a female only school. It was at that time that J. T. Kincannon relinquished the principal's office to Prof. W. J. Morrissett, a graduate of the Virginia Military Institute and also a graduate (A.M.) of William and Mary College. Elder Kincannon then became professor of moral science and history. Miss Jennie Lathiam was an assistant, and Mrs. M. E. Kincannon was matron and assistant. Evidently the school offered classes to all females from beginners (kindergarten) to college level. Tuition for the different departments varied from ten to eighteen dollars, with vocal music free. The school advertised (1869) that board with everything found (furnished) was available at twelve dollars per month. There was boarding room for sixteen students.

It appears that Elder J. T. Kincannon personally owned the building in which the school was housed. This was likely the building that had been so hastily vacated by Mrs. Smith and the "cussing professor." In 1870 Kincannon raised the frame building and had built beneath it a single story of brick. This doubled the size of his facilities.

On March 2, 1871, the Baptist Church of Bristol-Goodson voted to buy the property for $5,500. The trustees then appointed to manage the property were Major Z. L. (Zack) Burson, J. M. Robinson, A. T. M. Provence, W. B. Waldrop, R. B. Boatright, Elder J. T. Kincannon, W. P. Hulse, W. J. Morrissett, W. P. Hamilton, A. H. Burroughs and George Ambrose. Any five of this group could transact business.

In 1872 this school was incorporated as Bristol Female College by Elder John T. Kincannon, W. J. Morrissett, William Mullinix, B. A. Robertson, Noah J. Phillips, G. Cate, W. P. Hamilton, Jacob Hamilton, J. G. Nash, G. Cose, B. G. Manard and S. H. Smith.

The Bristol Female College, located on Anderson Street where now stands the Haven of Rest Mission, continued to operate into the 1880s. Apparently it had ceased operation by 1888, when the building was rented to the newly formed School Board of Bristol, Tennessee. In later years it was under the leadership of D. C. Wester.

PRESBYTERIAN FEMALE INSTITUTE

Soon after the founding of King College (then exclusively male), a move began among the Presbyterians of the town to set up a school of higher learning for young women. In 1872 the Rev. George A. Caldwell, Col. John G. English (a son-in-law of the Rev. James King) and Valentine Keebler founded the Presbyterian Female Institute. The old Temperance Hall that then stood on the southwest corner of Fifth and Shelby was bought from the Sons of Temperance for $600.00. Those of that organization who signed the deed were J. R. Anderson, G. B. Smith and Jay Spurrier. An additional adjoining lot was then bought from J. R. Anderson.

In early August 1872 a contract was let to John M. Crowell to erect a thirty by fifty two-story building on the property. The building was to be completed in November and was estimated to cost $2,300. The old Temperance Hall was rolled back on logs to the lot just south of the corner location. There it was remodeled into a residence and was long occupied by G. B. Smith and family.

But this school was holding classes "somewhere" (some say in the Presbyterian Church) by September 1872. The following notice appeared in the *Bristol News* dated August 13, 1872:

PRESBYTERIAN FEMALE SCHOOL

This school will commence the first Thursday in September, and will be under the control of a competent male teacher. Tuition rates will be about as other schools of the town. Persons from a distance wishing to send their daughters to this school will please inform one of the executive committee, and board in good families will be secured for them.

J. A. Templeton,
M. L. Blackley,
C. R. Vance,
Executive Committee

Though founded in 1872 this school was not incorporated until 1883. It is thought that it continued for several years after that date. The founders had planned that in time this school would become a college, but this hope was never realized. In 1874 Mrs. S. G. Crockett and Prof. E. Deichman were co-principals of this school. Mrs. Georgia Ripley, formerly of Georgia, was the teacher of the primary department. The wife of Prof. Deichman was in charge of the boarding house.

On January 10, 1872 the Rev. A. H. Burroughs was excluded from the Baptist Church for "siding" with Major Z. L. Burson. Presumably this ended his connection with the Baptist Female College (Institute). On August 13, 1872, the following notice appeared in the *Bristol News:*

BRISTOL HIGH SCHOOL
A. H. Burroughs, Principal
Rev. J. G. Talbert, Assistant

The next session of this school will begin on the first of September and will continue for five months.

Terms:

Primary	$7.50
Higher	10.00
Latin and Greek	12.50
Contingent fee	1.50

Virginia students will be entitled to the benefits of the public school fund.

Did Burroughs, like Burson, go out and start his own work once his connection was severed with the Baptist Church? It appears that he did. Evidently he was not able to live on the proceeds of the school. The same paper carried his ad for draying services. Apparently this school did not long exist.

ALABAMA CANE SCHOOL

About 1872 John G. King built a small board and batten school building on his land at the end of Alabama Street. This was meant for the black population of that end of town. He named the school for Alabama Cane, an orphaned daughter of former slaves who was being reared in his home. Thomas Balthis taught the first school there, probably beginning in the autumn of 1872. In March 1873 the *Bristol News* carried an announcement of a "rare entertainment" to be presented by this school. A dear friend of this author has told of her mother's attendance at this school, possibly in the mid-1880s. The late Revely Owen stated that her grandfather (John G. King) paid the teacher's salary, something like $12.00 per month.

MORRISSETT'S PRIVATE SCHOOL

Prof. W. J. Morrissett, who had early been connected with the Bristol Female College, set up a private school in the basement of the Presbyterian Church in 1874. This school existed for perhaps three years. No record of this early teacher has been found after the closing of this school.

CONWAY HALL SCHOOL

In the mid or late 1870s Professor Pendleton and the Rev. J. P. Doggett combined their two private schools to form what was called a free public school. This combined school was housed in Conway Hall, which stood on the south side of the first block of Fifth Street. How this school was financed is not known. During that period public funds were available for schooling in Virginia. Such may have been the case in Tennessee.

LONG ALLEY SCHOOL

In 1879 a one-fourth acre lot fronting on Long Alley was bought from John G. King for the purpose of erecting a black school for the town of Bristol, Tennessee. Trustees of this school were William Rhea, Jessie Rhea and Braxton Brewer. This was likely an outgrowth or continuation of the old Alabama Cane School. The Hood Memorial Methodist Church was organized in this school. How long the Long Alley School existed is not known by the author.

BRIGHT HALL SCHOOL

The original name of what is now the Weaver Funeral Home at Seventh and Locust was Bright Hall. It was built by D. J. Ensor around 1870, but has been extensively remodeled and added to since that time. In the September 6, 1881, edition of the *Bristol News,* there appeared an announcement of a new school:

> Mrs. D. J. Ensor has opened a select school for young ladies at her residence back of the Baptist College. She will take a limited number of boarders. Her special line is music, in that she excels. She already has a fine school.

Within a few years the Ensors moved to Meigs County, Tennessee, closing what had promised to be a very select school.

WOOD'S LAW SCHOOL

It was long a custom for those who wished to become lawyers to read (study) law under the tutorage of an older and well seasoned member of this profession. If a lawyer had an unusually fine reputation, he might have several studying with him. By the late 1880s Captain J. H. Wood had the name of being a "kingpin" (eloquent, very well learned and effective) lawyer, a reputation well known all over southwest Virginia and east Tennessee. As a result many young men aspiring to practice at the bar sought to "sit at his feet." The number became so great that he finally opened his own private law school. He used the parlor of his home for a classroom. His home, Pleasant Hill at 214 Johnson Street, still stands and is now the home of this author. The room in which he taught is immediately to the right of the front door as one enters the house. Here every weekday morning a dozen or so eager young men gathered to hear the old master expound the fine points of legal principles and practice. Often a mock trial was held with Capt. Wood acting as judge, and a portion of the students serving as the jury and witnesses.

Many of these students came from afar. For this reason Wood's wife, Laura L. James Wood (a daughter of the prince merchant W. W. James), built the old house that still stands at 223 Johnson as a boarding and rooming place for her husband's students.

There is no record of how many young men were taught by Capt. Wood. However, it is known that this teacher of law used to boast that of the many he had taught, not one had failed to be admitted to the bar. It is thought that this school operated until about 1895.

MISS ENGLISH'S SCHOOL

During the 1890s a private school was kept by Misses Fannie Lin and Maggie English, maiden daughters of Col. John and Margaret King English and granddaughters of the Rev. James King. Their school was in a rented building that stood on the south side of Shelby Street, between Fifth and Sixth Streets. This school was within a few feet of where once stood the little white schoolhouse that had been built for the town by Rev. King, grandfather of the English sisters.

The English School offered a broad scope of studies including "intellectual arithmetic," rhetoric, dictation and science, the latter being little taught in those days. Cost of tuition was $1.75 per month. Students had to maintain a grade point of sixty or above to remain in the school. This school operated in the 1890s, well after the beginning of public education in Bristol, Tennessee. At first public schools were not highly regarded by the elite of the town. "No daughter of mine will ever attend a public school," a statement made by a leading industrialist of Bristol, was typical of the attitude of many local residents at that time. Thus, it may be reasonably assumed that those who were taught by Misses Fannie Lin and Maggie English were from the homes of the town's elite.

SULLINS COLLEGE

One of the most awesome realities of life is that we do not know the potential of those who walk among us. Who would have thought that the anxious, insecure, sad and lonely widow who stepped down from a passenger coach, clutching the trusting hand of her fatherless daughter on that cold, snowy late afternoon in December 1867, would soon sow the seed that would lead to the establishment of a great Bristol college. No, if anyone looked it was with sympathy rather than hope or optimistic expectation. But so it often is with saviors of the world: they come forth from obscurity and, unheralded, press steadily along the pathway of dedicated service until their redemptive accomplishments are clear to all.

Like so many in those days, Mrs. Bettie Louisa Chapman Chanceaulme, widow of the Rev. E. W. Chanceaulme, came to the fast-growing town of Bristol seeking a means of livelihood. There was no systematic aid for widows in those days, so that such ladies must, through their own ingenuity, provide for themselves and their orphans. Many widows came here in like circumstances and for like purposes, but likely none of them had as far-reaching influence as did Mrs. Chanceaulme.

Soon after arriving here, Mrs. Chanceaulme turned to the only resource she had—her education. She had rented a small cottage that stood on the south side of Cumberland Street, immediately adjoining the present Emmanuel Episcopal Church property. Here she opened a private school for the younger children of the town.

This private school was an immediate success; so much so that it soon became necessary to seek a larger classroom. Mrs. Chanceaulme then rented a former store room in the Keller Block in downtown Bristol. Among the students in this location was a daughter and a son or two of W. W. James. Because of this, Mr. James recognized the unique ability of the widowed teacher and predicted that the town would long benefit because she settled in Bristol.

In 1868 soon after Mrs. Chanceaulme had moved her school to the Episcopal Church (again for more room), the Rev. David Sullins was appointed to the pastorate of the Bristol Methodist Church. He had been pastor of the church at Wytheville, Virginia, where he had been head of the Masonic Female Institute. Indeed, for several months after his new appointment, he spent only the weekends in Bristol, riding the Friday night train to care for his charge, and then taking the Sunday night train home to continue his school work. Some of those weekends were spent in the W. W. James home, and there the host learned much of his guest's varied abilities.

W. W. James, a quiet but solid and very influential member of the local Methodist Church, later admitted that while the learned and eloquent David Sullins delivered his messages, a little daydreaming was going on. Mr. James had quickly realized that the Rev. Mr. Sullins was not only a dedicated minister, but he was also a competent educator and effective administrator. James dreamed of what great benefit would result if Mrs. Chanceaulme's teaching zeal and qualifications were combined with the varied capabilities of Sullins. James envisioned a high school, a great academy, hopefully a college. The dream continued and became brighter.

After Sullins moved to Bristol, he began to assist Mrs. Chanceaulme from time to time in her school work. Then one Saturday afternoon when she went to the James store for her supply of butter and eggs (part of the James children's tuition), she found Sullins there. James took the two aside for a long conference. Later a committee probably formed by James, consulted with Mrs. Chanceaulme at the home of her brother-in-law, I.C. Fowler, who then lived at 417 Spencer Street. The result of these efforts is revealed in this ad that appeared in the *Bristol News* in early July 1869.

HIGH SCHOOL FOR YOUNG LADIES
Bristol-Goodson, Va.

This school formerly under the charge of Mrs. B. L. Chanceaulme will open at

"MOUNTAIN VIEW"

On the fourth Thursday in August in charge of the following teachers:

Rev. D. Sullins, A. M., Principal
Mrs. B. L. Chanceaulme
Miss Lucy B. Ruggles, assistant in the literary and
   ornamental departments
Miss L. Payne, teacher of music, instrumental and vocal

TERMS, PER SESSION OF FIVE MONTHS:

Primary Department	$10.00
Academic Department in two classes:	
1st Class	12.00
2nd Class	15.00
Collegiate Department including the Classics	18.00
Music or piano and guitar, each	20.00
Use of piano	5.00
Vocal music	5.00
Painting	10.00
Needlework and embroidery each	10.00
Modern languages, each	10.00
Board, wood and lights	60.00
Contingent fee	2.00

Boarding department in charge of Principal and his wife, but boarding can be had in private families near to the school buildings at the above rates if desired.

Young ladies furnish their own pillow cases, sheets and towels.

No deductions from bills unless in cases of protracted sickness.

For particulars, address the Principal at Bristol, Tennessee.

This institution, sometimes called Mountain View Academy or Mountain View High School, was located in the former home of the Rev. James King, which stood at what is now 54 King Street, Bristol, Virginia. The name of the estate was Mountain View, from which came the name for the school.

At that time the property was owned by Thomas C. Lancaster, who was forced to leave Bristol near the close of the Civil War because of his strong support of the Confederacy. At the time this school opened in his home, he was still in exile either at Jackson, Tennessee, or Holly Springs, Mississippi. (He seems to have spent time in both places.) W. W. James paid the first year's rent on the buildings.

For this first year, boarding students numbering perhaps twenty, were housed in the upper rooms and attic of the main house. The next spring much of the four acres surrounding the house was planted in vegetables for the boarding department. Young ladies might earn a part of their tuition by working in these gardens. Even before the first term of school began at Mountain View, W. W. James had a move afoot to buy land on which to erect a permanent building for this institution. He contacted Joseph Johnston of Philadelphia, who owned a choice piece of ground immediately to the southeast of the old King home. Mr. Johnston agreed to sell the site (containing approximately one acre, three rods and 27 poles) for $959.36. (Johnston had a strange propensity to add odd dollars and cents to his land prices.) James then sought aid from several close friends in raising the funds for the purchase of the Johnston property. The deed from Joseph Johnston was made on June 26, 1869, requiring three payments at six, twelve and eighteen months. However, most of the purchase price was still due as late as 1873.

On October 27, 1869, the land was conveyed to the trustees of the school. The signers of this deed are likely those who had joined James in pledges of the purchase price of the property. The signers include W. W. James and wife Mary J. James, Jacob and Susan Crumley, Jesse H. and Mary E. Pepper, Charles C. and L. L. Campbell, William and Elizabeth Dixon, Jesse A. and Eva T. Buckner, Isaac and Elizabeth (Wood) Nickels, David and Ann B. C. Sullins, and Edward G. F. Hughes and Dorcas M. Hughes. The trustees to whom this deed was made were W. W. James, Jacob Crumley, J. H. Pepper, Isaac Nickels, Edward G. F. Hughes, John G. King, L. F. Johnson, William B. Williams, C. C. Campbell, William Dixon, J. A. Buckner, David Sullins, W. P. Brewer, J. M. Robinson and U. L. York. Mr. York was a prominent local lawyer, and it is said that he handled all legal matters for the school at no cost. Although it is known that most of these trustees were members of the Methodist church, at least two of them, John G. King and W. P. Brewer, were staunch Presbyterians.

Soon after the making of this deed, a large, two-story brick building was erected on the lot. Evidence indicates that this building was finished in time for the opening of the fall 1870 school term. It is thought that John Crowell did the brick work on this building. The carpenter work was by James C. Haynes and cost $783.00. This original building contained a chapel, music

Early photo of the student body and professor of Sullins College.

rooms, two classrooms, dormitory and parlor. Some say that the former guest house and overseers' office across the road in the old King yard continued to be used as classrooms for several years.

About the same time as the building of the school, Rev. Sullins bought a large lot fronting on what is now James Street adjoining the school property. On this he built a large two-story house over an English basement. This was both his home and a boarding place for students. The home together with the dormitory on the second floor of the school building could accommodate about forty students.

One who was a student in those days remembered that meals for both places were served in the English basement at the Sullins home. Girls had to attend their own fires and carry in wood for that purpose from a large wood yard in back of the school building. The yard was supplied by the old woodcutter, Lemuel Strait. A fireplace was in every room of both buildings. This student remembered that during the very cold winter of 1873-74, a pitcher of water froze solid in her room in spite of a roaring fire which she kept all night in the fireplace. She remembered that to bring in wood or carry water from the old King spring at the foot of the hill (site of Boswell Insurance Agency), the girls were required to go in large groups. This, she said, was to protect "body and reputation."

During one of those earliest years of the school, Rev. W. B. Bays came to have a full week of chapel services. During the first service a "mighty revival broke out." Rev. Mr. Bays remained for over a month, during which every boarding student (about forty) professed religion.

It is a little known fact that the school in those days, and for years afterwards, included a department for young children. By January 31, 1872, the faculty had been enlarged to include Prof. E. Deichman, Ph.D. as teacher of mathematics and languages; Miss T. Cardwell as assistant to Mrs. Chanceaulme; and Prof. T. E. Hacker as the teacher of music, painting and drawing. Tuition remained the same, but room and board had increased to sixty-five dollars. Prof. Deichman was a German whose thick brogue made classes difficult for some of the students. He was very high tempered, and when he had a "flare up" he did his "cussing" in his native language—at least so it was rumored. In his classroom was a very deep wood box. The Professor was short so he had to step up on a wooden block to reach into the box for fuel for his classroom stove. On one occasion the box was nearly empty so he had to reach deep. He lost his footing and fell head first into the narrow, empty depth. The girls had to go for help to get him out. It is said that, once he was freed, he raved around the room "saying things in German!"

On April 1, 1873, Mountain View High School ceased to exist; the school then was incorporated as Sullins College. There had been considerable discussion as to what name the institution should carry. Many wanted it to be known as Chanceaulme College, while others proposed it be given the name of W. W. James. In the end the move to have it named for Rev. Sullins prevailed. The trustees under this incorporation were the same as those in 1869. It was required that vacancies on the board of trustees must be filled from the male membership of the Methodist Episcopal Church South in Bristol-Goodson. Another stipulation was that if the property failed to be used as a college for five years, it would revert to the original donors.

The college grew and prospered through the 1870s. Girls came from farther and farther away as the fame of this very effective institution steadily spread over the south. In spite of very strict rules regarding receiving visitors, writing letters and so on, some of the girls somehow managed to marry and remain. In March 1873 Mr. Joseph Hoge of Giles County, Virginia, brought a daughter Willie Hoge to be enrolled in the school. In time she became the bride of

John Alf Brewer and lived for years at 417 Pennsylvania Avenue. Another of Mr. Hoge's daughters was Senah, who had married Major A. D. Reynolds. Numerous other girls, who came to learn, also learned to love and became citizens of Bristol.

By October 1881 Rev. D. S. Hearon had become the second president. That year the boarding house was renovated and neatly furnished. Attendance was ever on the increase. The school advertised that a joyful surprise was in store for those who inquired of costs. The faculty at that time consisted of D. S. Hearon, president and professor of metaphysics and ethics; Mrs. Cleo Miles Hearon, modern languages and English literature; Mrs. Lou C. Couling, preceptress, Latin and mathematics; Miss Belle Blair, principal of academic department, and natural science; Miss Nannie Belle Fowler, assistant in music; and Miss Nep Tipton, drawing and painting. Mrs. Hearon also served as matron.

It was always the desire at Sullins to make an education available to all females who sought it. From the beginning, many students had a part or all of their tuition and board paid with produce from the family farm. Indeed, many girls labored through long summer days helping to grow that which would send them to school in the fall. The coming of farm wagons in late summer and early fall was a familiar and welcome sight. In them might be cornmeal, flour, sweet and Irish potatoes, sorghum molasses, honey, apples, dried peaches, salted or smoked pork, dried beans, peas in the hull, and a host of other articles. If eggs were brought (and they often were), they were stored in a deep, cool cellar behind the Sullins home. The same was true of butter, which was often kept until "its strength increased!"

Often benefit affairs were staged to help struggling students. In 1879 a meat supper, complete for twenty-five cents, was offered at the college. Hundreds must have attended, for it was later reported that this supper netted ninety dollars. By the early 1880s W. W. James had become one of the town's wealthiest citizens. Consequently, he decided to share some of that wealth with Sullins College. With a gift of $2,000.00, he set up what was known as the James Aid Fund. Interest was to be used for the promotion of female education, particularly that of worthy destitute girls between the ages of ten and sixteen, who lived within the limits of Bristol-Goodson and counties in which these towns were located. Aid was not to be rendered to any one girl for over three years. The trustees of this fund were A. S. McNeil, George C. Pile, Dr. M. M. Butler, G. B. Smith, Rives Walker (Walker married the daughter of Mrs. Chanceaulme), W. A. Sparger and S. R. Ferguson.

One provision of this fund was that if the state took over and provided free education, then the fund would be used to support the preaching of the gospel and as a charity fund. The fund was greatly added to by others and in 1885-86 a portion of it was used to erect a new building. The old building (adjoining the new) was then made into a chapel.

W. W. James had always been a noted financial friend of the college. In the very beginning when several notes were held against the struggling institution, he had taken these notes, sometimes at great loss to himself, to keep the school solvent.

By 1888 L. L. H. Carlock had become the third president. Mrs. Lou Chanceaulme was still living at that time, but it is not known if she was then connected to the school. It is known that she lived for a few years in Mississippi before returning to Bristol.

All through those early years the school prided itself on taking great care of its students. Actually being a student in those days was something between being in a convent and a prison, according to a former student. No one girl could go anywhere alone. When going to church or other activities, the girls marched in a group, with teachers marching with them. All dressed alike. Visitors could be received only under the watchcare of the matron and going out on dates was unheard of. Even the school physician was carefully selected. For years the saintly Dr. J. A. Templeton served in this capacity. According to a statement of a trustee, he was chosen "because it was thought that he was least likely to conduct undue examinations of the girls or to seek too familiar a closeness with them." Ironically, the local doctor who was most feared as one to seek "too familiar a closeness with females" (that was his reputation town-wide) early served on the board of trustees!

Soon after the first building was erected, a lean-to room had been added to the back. One rainy night as the girls were undressing for bed, a peeping-tom who had slipped up onto the lean-to roof lost his footing on the wet shingles and fell against a bedroom window. He quickly jumped from the roof and fled, but he was pursued by one of the professors who had been alarmed by the screams of the girls. The culprit and a companion (who had apparently not been on the roof) were caught at Beaver Creek trying to wash the make-up from their faces. (They had blackened themselves.) Mayor Fowler ordered 21 lashes at the whipping post, a spectacle which the girls as a body were allowed to watch. Soon afterwards both young men, sons of respectable parents, left town in shame. Dr. Sullins ordered heavy shutters for the rear windows of the building and sent out word that he had bought a good shotgun and would deal with future trespassers accordingly.

Perhaps diligent efforts to preserve the purity of the students were successful. This author has uncovered a lot of local scandals, but not one pertains to anyone connected to Sullins College, either students or faculty. It is evident that the leaders of this college watched over and cared for their wards with near-paternal affection. A girl from Russell County became ill soon after entering the school. She was lovingly cared for by the students and faculty until her death. The beloved Rev. Sullins, along with local undertaker H. A. Bickley, tenderly bore the remains home. Rev. Sullins conducted her burial service in the family cemetery and remained a few days trying to console the grieving survivors.

In 1890 the board of trustees consisted of W. W. James, president; A. D. Reynolds, vice-president; and Dr. Rives Walker, secretary and treasurer. Other board members were M. M. Butler, Samuel James, W. D. Haynes, W. A. Sparger, Dr. H. T. Berry, G. B. Smith, Rev. L. L. H. Carlock, E. D. Pendleton, S. R. Ferguson, G. C. Pile, R. H. Overstreet, and A. S. McNeil. All these trustees lived in either Bristol, Tennessee, or Bristol, Virginia, except Samuel James (son of W. W.), a resident of Philadelphia, Pennsylvania.

In the 1890s Rev. S. N. Barker became the fourth president. By then it was clear that the college had outgrown its space. In 1898-99 a fine, four-story brick building was erected. It was quite ornamental to the town, standing as it did high on the hill behind the present public library. The new building could accommodate over one hundred boarding students.

The faculty at the turn of the century included Miss Anna Hull, music; Miss Katherine Mitchell, Latin; Mr. F. J. Ziesberg, director of music; Miss Lacy Price, modern languages; Miss Sallie Mallicote, housekeeper; Mrs. J. C. Cowan, history; Miss Ada Barham, expression; Miss Sue Mitchell, chaperon; Mrs. S. A. Gillespie, matron; Miss A. Lou Neilson, art; Miss Laura King, assistant in mathematics and ccience; Miss Janie Muse, primary; Mr. Richard Harry Watkins, mathematics and science; Miss Florence Baird, vocal music; Miss Bessie C. Mallicotte, stenography and typewriting; Miss Katherine Jordan Bigham, English; and Miss Martha Pilcher, string instruments.

The board of trustees at that time included A. D. Reynolds, president; A. S. McNeil, vice-president; and W. B. Gillespie, secretary and treasurer. Other board members were Dr. M. M. Butler, William Burrow, A. C. Harkleroad, H. G. Peters, G. C. Pile, J. N. Huntsman, T. J. Newman, Dr. G. M. Peavler, Samuel McCrary, J. L. Kelly, and Joel Huntsman.

Mrs. Bettie Louisa Chapman-Chanceaulme, who laid the ground work for Sullins College, died in Bristol on January 31, 1894. (She was born October 31, 1821.) She is buried in the historic East Hill Cemetery. On her marker is the very fitting epitaph, "Let her own works praise her."

KING COLLEGE
One of the time honored and highly respected institutions of Bristol is King College. Indeed, it is the oldest educational institution in the city. This col-

lege had its origin in 1866, when the Holston Presbytery met at the Pleasant Grove Church near Bluff City. Among those attending that meeting were several who were very concerned about the fact that all three of the Presbyterian colleges located in east Tennessee had come under control of the northern branch of the Presbyterian Church. A committee consisting of the Rev. George A. Caldwell, Rev. James Doak Tadlock, Rev. John Rutledge King, Rev. S. B. Campbell, Dr. H. Walker and R. P. Rhea was appointed to study the feasibility of establising a new Presbyterian college. Evidently this committee found the proposal to be feasible, because during a subsequent meeting a committee on location was appointed, consisting of Rev. George Caldwell, Rev. J. W. Bachman and Elder R. P. Rhea. Both Bachman and Rhea favored Blountville as a site for the school, but a subsequent offer of a building and land in the new town of Bristol caused the latter town to be selected as a home for the new institution.

The building which was donated by Rev. James King for the new school had been built by Clifford D. Tyler in 1857 on lots at the southeast corner of Fifth and Olive Streets. Tyler had bought the lots from Joseph R. Anderson in 1855. On January 24, 1857, Mr. Tyler deeded two of the lots (numbers 59 and 77) to his wife, Ann Tyler. Very soon thereafter he had employed William Rodefer and James Fields to erect a handsome brick house. On November 19, 1857, James Fields filed a bill in chancery seeking payment of his bill. William Rodefer filed a similar bill on February 15, 1858. The house and lots were sold by court order on March 5, 1861. Joseph R. Anderson bought the property for the sum of $2,350.00. On May 26, 1863, Anderson sold the property to Thomas W. Farley for the sum of $3,500.00. A little later Farley sold out to Rev. James King. Sometime during those early years, a school known as Bristol High School was held in the house. This school ceased operation in 1862. Rev. James King gave the house and several surrounding acres to the Holston Presbytery for the proposed new college. His deed was made on July 14, 1866, to trustees William P. Brewer, Joseph R. Anderson and John G. King.

This original college building faced what is now Fifth Street, near its intersection with Olive (site of the present Beecham plant). At the very first the institution was known as Bristol High School. During that period the following gentlemen served as curators until "an institution of higher dignity and grade" could be chartered by the Tennessee legislature

Rev. James King	J. W. Deadrick
Rev. S. B. Campbell	E. B. McClanahan
Hon. John A. McKinney	Rev. J. W. Bachman
Hon. H. M. Barton	W. A. Phipps
Robert P. Rhea	J. H. Earnest

Joseph R. Anderson   Rev. George A. Caldwell
William P. Brewer   Dr. S. E. Lyon
Joseph Cloyd

Rev. James Doak Tadlock, a well educated minister and educator, was chosen as the first leader of the new school. There is some indication that he may have taught for a short time in the earlier school that had been conducted in the Tyler home. Rev. Mr. Tadlock was born in Greene County, Tennessee, in 1825. Much of his ministerial and educational activities had been centered in Jonesboro, Tennessee. One old record states that the school opened as King College (named for Rev. James King) on August 5, 1867. Apparently a term of high school had been taught prior to this time. That same year Tadlock built a home far out Fifth Street (then Bluff City or Union Road) across from the end of present College Avenue. This home stood until recent years.

The first term brought an enrollment of forty-eight students, mostly from Bristol and vicinity; but one came from as far away as the Indian Territory in what is now Oklahoma. A policy of the school was that no ministerial student would be charged, nor would tuition be required of a crippled or indigent Confederate veteran.

Finances were always close in those early years. Rev. G. A. Caldwell volunteered to solicit funds in the wealthy northeastern portion of the nation. Fearlessly, he went into the "yankee territory" of New York City and there enjoyed a surprising measure of success raising funds for this southern college. The pledges came in the form of legally binding notes. That the college took such notes seriously is shown by the fact that suits were filed in chancery seeking payment of past due pledges.

The first newspaper advertisement that the author has been able to find concerning King College is dated October 22, 1869. This advertisement states that the school had opened on August 5th that year and offered primary instruction at ten dollars for a five month term and college instruction at twenty dollars for the same period. Rooms were offered at $1.25 to $1.50 per week. It was stated that students might obtain room and board, including fuel, lighting and washing in private homes for $15.00 per month. The school then offered a catalog, which could be obtained by addressing Rev. G. A. Caldwell or J. D. Tadlock at Bristol, Tennessee. Professors at that time were Tadlock, J. H. Winston and Byrd (Bird) G. Manard. Caldwell was then president of the board of trustees.

One early practice which hampered the school for years was an unusual financial arrangement made with the president. The plant was turned over to him, along with the income from endowment, tuition and possible gifts. He was then to pay all expenses; and if any balance remained, it was to be his salary. And if there was an indebtedness, it became his sole responsibility. Several administrators found themselves deeply in debt because of this arrangement.

In early 1872 Hubbard and Fillinger, local builders, were employed to construct another building identical to the old Tyler house and to connect the two structures with a central hall over which would be an impressive tower. This construction was completed by June 7, 1872.

Early, King College became noted as a principal cultural center of the fast developing Bristol. Its programs and closing exercises were highlights of the year and noted speakers were often featured. King debates always drew a large and varied audience. One of the most memorable was the debate of J. H. Wood, Jr. and E. A. Tilley on whether or not animals have a future life. This debate, first held on February 12, 1881, had to be repeated several times, always to a standing room only crowd. The issue became heated and emotional; it was taken up by the local ministers and expounded from their pulpits. Local citizens carried on the argument for years. It was a favorite topic among the bench sitters on Main Street.

It seems that in spite of its many reverses, optimism for the college remained high through the passing decades. A newspaper article of June 23, 1873, states that the next term would open on the first Thursday in the following August. It went on to state that the location of the college was unsurpassed in the romance of surrounding scenery and salubrity of the climate and in the cheapness of living. It further stated that the faculty was determined to make the standard of scholarship second to no college in the south.

On June 6, 1875, Rev. John Rutledge King, one of the founders of the college, delivered the baccalaureate sermon, using the text, "A Light that Shineth in a Dark Place" (2 Peter 1:19). Editor Fowler noted that the crowd flowed into the yard and that King's address was both elegant and forceful. "King pointed out that the Bible was the true light to guide the young graduates through the dark places of life," Fowler reported, then pointed out that Rev. Mr. King was a noted example of his claims.

On June 17, 1879, editor Fowler mentioned that the closing exercises of King College had been held on the past Wednesday at 3:30 P.M. and that the town had closed up and turned out en masse for the program. Col. Bennett H. Young of Louisville, Kentucky, gave the literary address. His subject, "Is it true that every man has his price," had provoked much thought among the intellectuals of the town, Fowler stated. Several students had contended for the King Oratorical Medal. Among these were W. R. King who had spoken on "Labor is the price at which the gods sell the land," M. W. Doggett on "It still moves," J. A. Templeton, Jr. on "the Power of words," C. C. Sullins on "Joyous spring is cradled in the icy lap of winter," G. G.

Painter on "Self culture," L. Dixon on "There is a God," and W. B. Sullins who chose the rather cumbersome "Go tell Sextechins thou hast seen exile Marius sitting amid the ruins of Carthage." Judges of the speaking contest were Col. B. H. Young, Rev. S. B. Campbell and Major B. G. McDowell. M. W. Doggett and his "It still moves" won the medal. During the same program (it must have gone on for hours), R. E. Dixon spoke on "the Universality of law." C. C. Sullins delivered the salutatory address, and the valedictory address was given by George Painter. Before the program closed, J. W. Rogan was elected as president of the alumni association.

The King College faculty in 1881 consisted of Rev. J. D. Tadlock, D.D., president; H. W. Naff, A.M., professor of languages; Rev. J. Albert Wallace, A.M., professor of mental and moral philosophy; Dr. W. K. Vance, M.D., professor of chemistry; and Rev. Wallace, supply in the department of physics.

In 1885 Tadlock accepted a position with the Columbia Theological Seminary in South Carolina. He was succeeded by his son-in-law, the Rev. Jesse Albert Wallace. Wallace was a native of Soddy, Tennessee. As a young man he started walking to Virginia to enroll in a college somewhere in that state. When he stopped in Bristol, Tennessee, for the night, he was taken in by Charles Robertson Vance. Vance was on the board of King College and persuaded young Wallace to enroll at King College instead of journeying on to Virginia. After graduating in 1871 he attended Union Theological Seminary in Richmond, Virginia. He later returned to Bristol and became a professor in King College. The first and second presidents of King College are buried in the same lot in Bristol's East Hill Cemetery.

The college buildings were remodeled and enlarged in 1887, at a cost of around eight thousand dollars, a considerable sum in those days. To see that the college succeeded in its stated purpose, one has but to review the accomplishments of its early graduates. A little more than half of those graduates entered the Presbyterian ministry. Others became successful business and professional men. More than half the number later received honorary degrees from various institutions. Among them were five college presidents and five moderators of the General Assembly of the Presbyterian Church. Several were authors, producing some forty to fifty books. And no doubt among the lessor known were those who better served society because of the training received in Bristol's King College.

Those who served as president of King College during the period 1867-1900 were

Rev. James Doak Tadlock, D.D., L.L.D	1867-1885
Rev. Jesse Albert Wallace, D.D.	1885-1894
Harry W. Naff, Ph.D.	1894-1895

Rev. Jesse Albert Wallace, D.D.   1895-1899
Rev. Albert Gallatin Buckner, D.D.   1899-1902

VIRGINIA INTERMONT

There is some indication that Virginia Intermont College had its root origin in Mrs. Smith's Baptist Seminary, which was set up in Bristol soon after the Civil War. This school was moved to Glade Springs, Virginia in the very late 1860s or early 1870s.

About 1883 Rev. J. R. Harrison, D.D., a devout Baptist minister of Glade Springs, Virginia, conceived the idea to establish (perhaps reestablish or strengthen) an institution for the Christian education of young women. For months he rode his horse, John-the-Baptist, all over southwest Virginia and sometimes into West Virginia, Kentucky and Tennessee, soliciting funds for the proposed project. He endured much hardship while on this mission. (But do not all worthwhile achievements have within them a degree of painful self-sacrifice?) John-the-Baptist bore him through rain, sleet, snow and flood, as well as through balmy flower-scented days and grand arrays of autumn color as he went from church to church, home to home, and town to town on his holy mission.

The gifts ranged from a nickel given him by a little boy in a country store near Hillsville, Virginia, to five hundred dollars that an elderly maiden drew from behind a large picture that hung upon the wall of her humble log home near Pineville, Kentucky. She told Harrison that part of it had been left by "pa", and she had saved some of it herself; but since she felt she would be "going away" (dying) soon, she didn't suppose she would ever need it. She added, "When us gals were young there warn't any place to larn nuthing. Now I want to help out so gals today can know sumthin." The Rev. Mr. Harrison rode away more determined than ever that there would be a place "for gals to know sumthin." He never forgot this incident nor the words of the generous mountain woman. He often used this story in his fund raising sermons.

By the spring of 1884 Harrison had gathered perhaps ten thousand dollars. It was then that a plain wooden building was put under construction at Glade Springs. It was finished in time for the opening of the fall term in September 1884. There were thirteen boarding students, perhaps twice that many from the town and surrounding area, and three teachers for this first term of what was then called the Southwest Virginia Institute. Much of the tuition came in the form of barter along with a few promissory notes (Some of the latter were never paid.)

On the first board of trustees were several Bristolians among them Dr. James A. Dickey, Dr. J. F. Hicks, John R. Dickey (druggist), H. W. Powers (merchant), Horace G. Bramm (industrialist), and W. P. Hamilton (hotel keeper). These influential men of means were no doubt very helpful to the school, but their presence likely meant that it would not always remain in Glade Springs. From the beginning a move to Bristol was expected by those whose foresight was keen and realistic.

The school prospered from the start. Attendance and support far exceeded the expectations of its friends and founders. And Baptists in Bristol were not blind to the possibilities of a great educational institution emerging from so humble a start. About 1890, during the administration of President Samuel D. Jones, a move started to rename and move the institute to Bristol, Virginia. The board of trustees met in the home of John R. Dickey, that long stood on the parking lot in front of Bristol's First Baptist Church, and there voted to make the move and to change the name to Virginia Institute.

In looking about for a suitable location, it was learned that a sizeable lot on a high hill "north of town" could be purchased for $7,500.00. (This was a rather high price for land in that location at that time.) In 1891 the cornerstone of a commodious new building was laid. The building committee consisted of John R. Dickey, M. M. Morris, S. D. Jones, Thomas F. Wood and A. B. Echols. Before the time for fall opening in 1893, what might be termed the main building was ready for occupancy. At that time the town about ended at Mary Street. Large pastures were down the south slope in

Virginia Institute, Bristol, Va.

The first building of Virginia Intermont College was often called "Wood's Castle" because of the heavy financial support of Mr. Thomas F. Wood.

front of the new building. A student during that time recalled that the clanging of cowbells blended with the instructions of the professors.

The ornamental building, perched on its high location, somewhat resembled a castle. Because Thomas F. Wood, a local miller, banker and merchant had campaigned long for funds and poured much of his own wealth into the erection of this edifice, it was dubbed "Wood's Castle" and was often so called for several years. The school weathered hard times in the closing years of the century but came through to endure to this day. It was not renamed Virginia Intermont until well after the turn of the century.

PUBLIC EDUCATION

In the late winter of 1888, George C. Pyle (Pile) and E. W. King prepared a petition asking that a system of public education be established in Bristol, Tennessee. These prominent business leaders personally and persistently sought "influential signatures" for this petition. The completed petition, containing seventy-two names, was presented to the Mayor and Aldermen on April 10, 1888. The petition was favorably received, and an ordinance was then passed to establish a system of public education. Mayor at that time was J. W. Norvell, a local real estate developer. Aldermen were George B. Smith, photographer; John C. Anderson, banker and merchant; John H. Caldwell, lawyer, banker and businessman; and Dr. M. M. Butler, M.D. The first school board, elected the same month, included George C. Pyle (Pile), local businessman and noted inventor; E. W. King, prominent merchant; Dr. M. M. Butler; Marion L. Blackley, local lawyer; Col. N. M. Taylor, local lawyer; and Dr. James A. Dickey, M.D.

It was determined that county students could attend the public schools of Bristol, Tennessee, if the parents were willing to submit to the same rate of taxation as that imposed on town residents. The new public schools were to be segregated by the sexes. This was done in part to allay the fears of local citizens that once their children were schooled with the "commoners," gross immorality would occur. The old Baptist Female College building on Anderson Street was rented for $43.75 per quarter to house the girls' school, which was first taught by Prof. Rule. The boys' school was the old Cornfield Academy building at the northeast corner of Anderson and Tenth Streets. Prof. Cartwright was the teacher of the boys.

About a year later plans were made to erect a building on a large lot at the corner of Fifth and English (now Ash) Streets. For this choice property local clothing merchant A. S. Gump was paid $2,000.00. This substantial building was completed in the spring of 1893 at a cost of slightly under $18,000.00. Four or five years later enrollment was near six hundred students. By the year 1900 (where the scope of this book ends) the public school system had expanded to include a superintendent and thirteen teachers. The school budget had reached what some called "staggering proportions"—something over five thousand dollars. In comparison, one teacher today receives far more pay than the entire school system cost at the turn of the century!

PUBLIC SCHOOLS IN BRISTOL, VIRGINIA

Opposition to public education was a little stronger on the Virginia side of town, thus the start of such schools was delayed until 1891. Burson's famous old church in the 800 block of State Street (then Main) had the honor of housing the first public school in Bristol, Virginia. This school opened on September 15, 1891. A first day student there once informed this author that the huge old bell was used to call the students from play to study. This student also remembered that Prof. J. Ballard Young, who seems to have been the head of the school, always opened the day of study by standing in the grand old, hand-carved walnut pulpit to read a portion of scripture, after which he led the school in singing a hymn, sentimental ballad, or popular song of the time. One former student told of how a boy received a "thrashing" for sitting on the head of one of the carved cherubims that adorned Burson's fine pulpit.

Other teachers that opening year were Prof. Alson Hutton, Miss Alice Lelia Eaton and Miss Mary Coles Preston. The large church was divided by curtains which had been paid for by Major Z. L. Burson. Prof. Ballard taught near the front door of the church, Miss Eaton (later married to Robert Sheppe) taught in the next compartment, and Prof. Hutton taught "beyond the second veil" in the third compartment.

By the time of the opening of the school in Burson's church, a building was already under construction on Mary Street across from the head of Lee, though slightly to the west of that intersection. It was ready for occupancy sometime in 1892. This building was to house both the grade school and the newly formed high school. The author has been told that on September 5, 1892, the school met at Burson's church, then marched as a body to the Mary Street location. This march was done to the continuous ringing of the bell in the church and the answering bell in the new school building. The march was to symbolize that Bristol, Virginia, was taking a step forward in public education.

The first graduates of this high school were Arthur McNeil, a son of Capt. A. S. McNeil, local undertaker and furniture dealer (the family then lived at 322 Moore Street), and John T. DeHart. Young DeHart was a grandson of Major Z. L. Burson, who had allowed the first school to use his building rent free. This first graduate went on to become a noted lawyer of Bristol. His boyhood home still stands at 333 Moore Street.

In 1895 overcrowding of the Mary Street building made it necessary to rent a school house that had formerly been used by the Catholic church. This building stood near the north end of West Street, near the railroad. The classes of Mrs. George Wolfe were conducted in this building. A former student said that freight trains, coming through the cut and along Scott Street, usually were moving at a very slow pace. This proved to be a great temptation to two young boys who dared one another to ''hop the freight'' for a short ride. They had intended to jump off well within sight of the school. However, about the time the jump off had been planned, the train lurched forward and began moving faster. The fearful young ''hobos'' hung on for dear life until a stop was made near the present Valleydale Packing Company. With red faces they arrived back at the school long after the start of classes. Mrs. Wolfe dampened the ardor for train hopping by the liberal application of her hickory switch.

The first school trustees were appointed on June 5, 1890, over a year before the start of the first school term. These trustees were E. S. Kendrick, E. H. Seneker and Frank Collman. Later, Rives Walker and Capt. J. H. Wood were added to the group. Prof. Alson Hutton was the first superintendent of schools. The faculty numbered eight by 1895, and a few more teachers were added by the turn of the century.

Bibliography - Chapter Seventeen

Anderson, Joseph R. Manuscript, cir. 1880.

Anderson, Melinda King. As told to her granddaughter, Mrs. Herman Blackley.

Bachelor, Ann. Memoirs (unpublished), 1935-1937.

Barnes, Thelma Gray. *Adventures in Education, Sullivan County, 1773-1983.* [Tenn.]: Sullivan County Retired Teachers' Association, c1985.

Booth, Doris (Mrs. John). Paper, 1990.

Bristol News, newspaper. Various issues, 1857-1881.

Johnson, L. F. Notes, 1893.

Loving, Robert. *Double Destiny; The Story of Bristol, Tennessee-Virginia.* Bristol, Tenn.: King Printing Company, 1955.

Phillips, V. N. (Bud). Interviews with older Bristol citizens, 1953-1956.

Sullivan County, Tennessee. Deed Books, 1854-1900.

Washington County, Virginia. Court Records, 1854-1900.

Washington County, Virginia. Deed Books, 1854-1900.

Gideon Burkhart, Bristol's first lawyer, hailed from Paperville, Tennessee. His father's paper mill gave the town its name.

Chapter Eighteen
EARLY BRISTOL LAWYERS

Wherever there is a concentration of people there will be a need for lawyers. Evidently Bristol developed that need early, for before it could even be called a village, a lawyer had settled here. Gideon Burkhart, the first lawyer to practice in the new town of Bristol, was born in nearby Paperville, Tennessee, December 22, 1819. He was of the George Burkhart family that had moved to the area from Maryland. This family settled at Sinking Creek at Greenfield, a village established by a family of Willoughby. Soon after Mr. Burkhart set up his paper making operation the name of the village was changed to Paperville.

When young Gideon was about twelve years old, he went with his father to a court trial at Abingdon. There the lad was captivated by the eloquent pleading of a case by the noted lawyer Benjamin Estill. He always said in later years that it was while listening to this plea he became determined to become a lawyer. Later it was arranged for him to study law under Mr. Estill.

Just before starting his practice in Bristol, Gideon married Kitty E. _____. The couple lived in Paperville for a short time after his law practice opened. He would walk the three miles or so into town, usually arriving by daybreak and remaining until nearly nightfall. In later years because of these walking habits he was often called "the walking lawyer." After practicing a short time, he and Kitty moved to a small rent house that Samuel Goodson had erected on Washington Street in Goodsonville (popularly known as Bristol). After a short time there he rented a house in old Bristol, Virginia, and then on August 5, 1859, bought a Bristol, Tennessee, house from William Carmack. This was the only home he ever owned in Bristol, and one of its front rooms was used as his office. Up to that time he had been a "street" lawyer. This property is said to have adjoined the home of Joseph R. Anderson, but whether on Fourth or Main Street, the author does not know. It is known that the City Council of Bristol, Tennessee, often met in his office. Perhaps the reader may gain a more vivid picture of this first Bristol lawyer from a word portrait of the man and his works based on information from the memoirs of L. F. Johnson.

He was a striking figure; the embodiment of humble dignity and grace of movement. He moved with deliberate slowness. Ever placid, he never expressed alarm under the most fearful of circumstances. He seldom looked to the right or left except that he turned his entire body. He was always dressed in black - jet black, crowned by a tall silk hat.

His eyes were hawk-like and frightfully penetrating, causing some to tell the truth when the intention had been to cover it. But the most bizzare confessions never seemed to shock him.

He never held a grudge, nor did the sharpest of derogatory remarks freeze his kindness. Bitter words hurled at him one day were not remembered the next. He might ''law'' against you one day and ''law'' for you the next.

He was a familiar sight in the town. About any day he might be seen ambling along the muddy or dusty paths as then served as streets. Often he sat for long hours on his crude, stone bench — his office — under the giant elm tree back of Ensor's Drug Store (Fifth and State), or in winter behind the stove in Rosinheim's Store. There was always the long, gray note book under his arm. But wherever he took his seat, someone was likely to remark that ''court has set in Bristol.''

He never owned a horse or carriage. Wherever he went, he walked. And often the wherever included trips to Abingdon or Blountville. And even though at such times his steps were quickened they were still with deliberate measurement. His fees were low — often nothing. He never had wealth or seemed to desire it. His wealth was measured not in gold, but in accomplishment.

He was both loved and hated; respected and disparaged; admired and despised. None of this affected this noted barrister of long ago. Whether one shunned him or sought him, he still seemed to love and respect all. And whether sitting in private conference on his bench under the spreading elm, or in light conversation with a friend on the street, he carefully weighed each word, came straight to the point, and usually left his hearer the better for having listened to him.

As he moved along the streets, tall and straight as a poplar sapling, he had a kindly greeting for friend and foe alike. He invariably tipped his tall silk hat to the rare lady he might meet on the streets of the fast developing but wild and reckless town. Strangely though, when the occasion demanded that a gentleman remove his hat, he only held his a few inches above his head.

He was called lazy by some. But the leisure he loved was demanded and needed as a time to think, and his thoughts did more for the town than work could have ever done. His word was pure gospel to some and always doubted by others, but whatever he said it was plain that his words were flowers on a long stem of thought.

Gideon Burkhart became a legend in his own time and though more than a century has passed since he walked among us, his memory still lives.

Soon after the close of the Civil War, Burkhart, who was a personal friend of Andrew Johnson, was rewarded by this President with a job in Washington. He remained a few years in the capital and then returned for a brief stay in Bristol. Finding the town "crawling with lawyers," he decided to try farming. He bought a nice farm near Chuckey, Tennessee, and lived there until his death, which occurred November 6, 1882. Bristol's first lawyer is buried in the Ebenezer Church Cemetery near Chuckey, Tennessee.

SECOND LAWYER ARRIVES

Bristol's second lawyer arrived on foot in the new town September 3, 1855. Joseph B. Palmer, a native of Greensboro, North Carolina, had sojourned briefly in Danville, Virginia, after he married. For some reason he and his new bride then moved to Abingdon, Virginia. But that old town was full of seasoned lawyers, making the prospects for a beginner rather dim. He was advised by one of those older lawyers that prospects might be good in the new Town of Bristol. To "view the land," he walked here, arriving at dusk to find the town's two hotels full. But he secured lodging in the home of John H. Moore, an early merchant. That night, by a flickering candle, he penned the following notation in a pocket diary:

Bristol, Virginia.

Sept. the 3rd, '55 . . . The day has been very bright and mild, making the walk from Abingdon most pleasant but wearisome. This village thrives. The hotels are full — all looking toward the coming of the rails, hopefully next year. Tonite I abide in the cottage of John H. Moore in the midst of the village. This kindly merchant informs me that only one lawyer is in town, Gilbert (sic) Burkhart — I offer respects tomorrow. I feel I will dwell here and that life will be good. My candle flickers low — the bed beckons weary bones — Goodnight.

Palmer's feeling was right. He did indeed dwell here for a time and life was good. It is said that he quickly earned the love and respect of the town. Later entries in his diary reveal that he set up office on Front Street (then called Fourth) and that he first boarded in the Columbia Hotel, but later rented a house on Washington Street owned by Samuel Goodson. He wrote in his diary that his first case came in January 1856 and had to do with making a collection for the Joseph Anderson bank. For some reason this early lawyer seems to have moved in and out of Bristol several times over the next three decades. But he was here when his "candle of life" burned low and the eternal bed beckoned a weary traveler to rest. He died in 1891 and is buried in the East Hill Cemetery, where a large and handsome stone marks his final resting place.

JOHN S. MOSBY

John Singleton Mosby appears to have been the third lawyer to set up office here. He was born at Edgemont, Powhatan County, Virginia, on December 3, 1833. The family soon moved to a farm near Charlottesville, Virginia, where the future Bristol lawyer grew up and became a student at the University of Virginia. Becoming a lawyer in his early twenties, he practiced for about three years in Albermarle County. He then planned to move to Memphis, Tennessee, but for some unknown reason moved to Bristol-Goodson instead, arriving here in November 1858. Old Zimmerman estate papers reveal that he rented the former office of Dr. Zimmerman that stood near the northeast corner of present Lee and State Streets, and that he moved into this building in early December, 1858. It appears that the building also served the Mosbys as a home during their first months here. The Zimmerman papers show that the rent for this building was seventy-five dollars per year.

Mosby later rented an office located on the corner of Cumberland and Fourth Streets (Fourth later became Front Street). However, there is some indication that he may have moved back to the Zimmerman building before leaving Bristol. Apparently, Mosby never owned a home during his years here, but housed his family in various rented properties.

The wife of John S. Mosby was Pauline Clarke, whom he married in Nashville, Tennessee, on December 30, 1857. She was a daughter of Beverly L. Clarke, a prominent citizen of Franklin, Kentucky. Among the Mosbys' wedding gifts was Arron, a part Indian slave, given by the parents of the groom. It is said that he occupied the former cabin of Big Elbert, a Zimmerman slave, during the first months in Bristol. Mosby's practice was never large. Indeed, there is documented information that he continually had financial difficulties during his Bristol years. And though this statement must not be construed as to tarnish one who is now considered a hero, it is rather evident that he was not highly thought of by the local citizens. And when, after the war, he accepted an appointment from President Grant, he was all but hanged in effigy on the streets of Bristol. During the furor, I. C. Fowler, editor of the *Bristol News,* caustically commented that he hoped Mosby did better work for Grant than had been done when he presumed to do legal work for the citizens of Bristol.

In spite of his lack of financial success, Mosby must have had hopes of better days ahead. He once contracted to buy a tract of land close to where the Bristol Steel offices are now located on Piedmont Avenue. According to old-timers he had planned to build a fine home to be known as Mosby's Grove. No deed was ever issued for the tract. On some old records the area is referred to as the so-called Mosby land.

On April 20, 1860, a decree was issued by Judge Samuel V. Fulkerson in favor of several creditors of J. W. Morgan, and calling for the sale of several lots in Goodson, Virginia. Archimedes Davis, who was appointed a commissioner for that purpose, sold these lots on August 1, 1860. At that sale John S. Mosby bought lot 25 for the sum of $400.00, with W. J. Betterton as security. This lot, located on the southwest corner of Washington and Williams Streets, was the only real estate ever owned by Mosby in Bristol. In time, Betterton became half owner. This lot was not sold until a year or two after Mosby left Bristol.

As it became apparent that the Civil War was approaching, Mosby declared himself a Unionist, but later decided he could not fight against his mother state. In 1861 he enlisted in the Confederate Army and rode away from Bristol to become a famous guerrilla leader of the lamentable war. After the war he practiced law in Warrenton, Virginia, died there on May 30, 1916, and is buried in the Warrenton Cemetery near the Confederate monument.

CHARLES ROBERTSON VANCE

Charles R. Vance was the fourth lawyer to settle in this city and the second in Bristol, Tennessee. He was born in the valley of the Nolichucky River in Washington County, Tennessee, on August 22, 1835, a son of Dr. Joseph Harvey and Jane Sevier Vance. Jane Sevier was a daughter of Valentine Sevier, whose father, Robert, was a brother of Governor John Sevier. Robert Sevier was killed in the Battle of King's Mountain. Consequently, John Sevier took Robert's son, Valentine, to raise. A Dutchman lived nearby who had a bound girl named Kessiah Robertson. She ran away and came to the John Sevier place where she met and married the nephew, Valentine Sevier. And that is where lawyer Vance got his middle name, Robertson.

Charles R. Vance was educated at Rogersville and Rutherford academies. He studied law under Judge Thomas A. R. Nelson, and began his practice at Kingsport in 1858. While living there he met and married Margaret Jane Newland, a daughter of J. M. and Rebecca Anderson Newland. She was a niece of Joseph R. Anderson, founder of Bristol.

Shortly before this marriage, Joseph R. Anderson had persuaded the young Charles Vance to begin a practice in Bristol, Tennessee. The day after this marriage, the bride and groom rode double horseback to Bristol, and lived for a few weeks in the Anderson home. Later they moved to a home on Main

Street in which he maintained an office. They were living in that location at the outbreak of the Civil War.

Lawyer Vance joined the Confederate Army, Company K, 19th Tennessee Regiment soon after the beginning of the Civil War. While sleeping in the trenches in Murfreesboro, Tennessee, he became ill with typhoid fever and was never able to return to active service. He had been scheduled to take charge of the regiment.

Later he collected arms for the Confederacy. He is said to have been very successful in this endeavor, even though working in east Tennessee where Union sympathies were very strong. But because of this he had to leave Bristol soon after the war. He moved to Estillville (now Gate City), Virginia, where he successfully engaged in the mercantile business for a few years. Later he returned to Bristol, Tennessee, where he and J. H. Wood formed a law

Charles Robertson Vance (1835-1911) the second lawyer in Bristol, Tennessee, was a partner of Capt. J.H. Wood, in the firm of Vance and Wood. His old home still stands at 412 Sixth Street, Bristol, Tennessee.

partnership known as Vance and Wood. This partnership existed until 1885.

Mr. Vance became a very highly respected citizen and a noted civic and church leader of Bristol. He served for twenty years as president of the King College Board of Trustees. He was an elder in the First Presbyterian Church for thirty-five years, and also served as church clerk. He was a leader in the local and state temperance movement, and was once a candidate for congress on the Prohibitionist ticket.

Two of his sons, Rev. James I. Vance and Rev. Joseph A. Vance, became outstanding Presbyterian ministers. One headed the Northern branch of the Presbyterian Church at the same time the other headed the Southern branch. Such a situation has never before or since occurred in that denomination.

In the early 1870s Charles R. Vance bought half of the four hundred block of Sixth Street (then called King Street). This included a house that had been built for Nannie J. Robertson. In the 1890s he remodeled and added to the existing home. This fine house still stands at 412 Sixth Street and is now occupied by the Troutdale Restaurant.

This fine Victorian house located at 412 Sixth Street was the home of Charles Robertson Vance, one of the first lawyers in Bristol, Tennessee. It is now occupied by the Troutdale Restaurant.

Lawyer W.W. Langhorne was practicing his profession in Bristol by 1860. His family built the first Virginia House Hotel of Bristol, Virginia, in 1855.

Some years prior to his death he suffered a stroke that ended his law career. He died November 12, 1911, and is buried in Glenwood Cemetery, Bristol, Tennessee. He was first buried in East Hill Cemetery, but was removed to Glenwood in October 1943.

LANGHORNE AND CARNER

W. W. Langhorne and Sam Carner (or Carmen) were here in this early period but nothing further is known of them. Langhorne was of that family who built the original Virginia House Hotel.

LAWYERS AFTER THE CIVIL WAR

The smoke had hardly cleared after the Civil War when several lawyers came to Bristol, which was slowly resuming the noble pursuits of peace. Some of them, indeed most of them, spent the remainder of their lives in Bristol enjoying varying degrees of success.

COL. NATHANIEL M. TAYLOR

Among the post-war arrivals was Col. N. M. Taylor, who was born in Carter County, Tennessee, in 1826. His father's name is unknown by this author, but his mother was Betsy Taylor, who died in March 1879 of pneumonia, at the age of seventy years. She was a half sister of W. P. Brewer, an early Bristol merchant. It is known that he was of that distinguished Taylor family of Carter County, from whence came the noted brothers, Bob and Alf Taylor, who served in the governorship of Tennessee.

Lawyer Taylor was here by September 1865. From Joseph Anderson he bought a lot located on Third Street, built a house, and lived there for the remainder of his life. It can be said that he enjoyed a great degree of success, being especially good in straightening out entangled land titles. Taylor Street was named for him. Col. Taylor died at his Third Street home on April 17, 1898. He is buried in East Hill Cemetery, where a handsome monument marks his gravesite.

JAMES V. DEADRICK — A DESCENDANT OF GENERAL SHELBY

Jonesboro, like Abingdon, was a little overcrowded with lawyers. That is why young James V. Deadrick hung out his shingle in growing Bristol. He at first boarded with the James King, III family and there met the prosperous, man-of-affairs, John G. King, brother of his host. The latter took a liking to the personable young lawyer and gave him much employment.

In about 1870, John G. King gave Deadrick a building site that is now numbered 332 Sixth Street. The deed states that the lot was given in consideration of respect and admiration of young lawyer Deadrick, and further that he is a descendant of General Evan Shelby. The lot was near the site of Evan Shelby's fort.

But young Deadrick never built on the lot. In a year or two he sold it to Isaac A. Nickels. About 1874, Nickels sold it to Dr. John Givens Pepper, who soon commenced the erection of the oldest portion of the house that is now the office of Dr. J. L. McCord. Deadrick left Bristol soon after the sale of his gift lot.

YORK AND FULKERSON

One of the most prestigious law firms of early Bristol was that of York and Fulkerson, composed of U. L. York and Col. Abram Fulkerson. These were two former Confederate officers who had served in the war together. They were practicing law together in Bristol by November of 1866. U. L. York of this firm was born in Warren County, Tennessee, January 4, 1835, a son of G. W. York. During the Civil War he served as Adjutant of the 63rd Tennessee Regiment that was commanded by his future law partner, Col. Abram Fulkerson.

York married Miss Mary Deadrick, a daughter of Dr. William Deadrick of Athens, Tennessee. It is thought that this marriage occurred before the start of the Civil War. As did his partner, York came to this city without funds or property, but in the brief period of fifteen years here he amassed a considerable fortune by the standards of the time. Along with his fortune came the love and respect of the town. It is said that within a few years he had the largest law practice in this area.

York had the unique ability to make even his enemies love and respect him. Some of those he had "lawed against" became his best friends. He also had the peculiar ability of weaving good advice and sound counsel into his interrogations. York was a "schooled lawyer," having been educated at the University of Virginia. Most lawyers in those days had simply studied under older lawyers and then taken the standard examination. His fine schooling may account, at least in part, for his great success.

After forming the partnership with Fulkerson, offices were set up in the Lancaster Building on Front Street in the second block north of Main Street. By 1876 the firm was known as Deadrick, York, and Fulkerson. The third partner is probably W. V. Deadrick, known to have practiced in Bristol for some time. By 1881 the offices were located on Cumberland Street, which was then rivaling Main as the chief business street of the city.

When only forty-five years of age and at the height of his success, U. L. York became chronically ill, enduring much suffering for several months. At times during those months, he was able to go to his office and even tried a few court cases, even though at great, sometimes almost heroic, physical effort. And all the while he was trying desperately to wind up his affairs. This author has his original will which was penned during those months of suffering. The *Bristol News* of May 24, 1881, reported that York was much improved and had been to his farm the day before. But the improvement was of short duration. He finally succumbed at 6:00 A.M. on July 28, 1881, at his home on Virginia Hill. He was buried in the East Hill Cemetery near what was then called the new gate (between the old gate and what is now the main gate).

Col. Abram Fulkerson, of the York and Fulkerson firm, was born May 13, 1834. His birthplace is unknown by this author, but was likely in either Scott or Washington County, Virginia. It is said that he first studied law under the noted Benjamin Estill. Later he attended Virginia Military Institute at Lexington, Virginia, where he studied under Stonewall Jackson, and graduated in the class of 1857.

Col. Fulkerson had an imposing figure and keen intellect, and was a very accomplished orator. One old gentleman, yet living when this author arrived in Bristol in 1953, told of how his father often took him to court just to hear Col. Abe speak. He further stated that others of the town often did likewise. Like his partner, Col. Fulkerson earned the admiration of the town and area. He was ten years in the State House of Delegates and Senate, and then served in the 47th Congress. Over the years Col. Fulkerson amassed a considerable fortune. Late in life he erected a fine brick home on the southwest corner of Russell and Spencer Streets. It was clearly of Victorian style, but about 1913, E. Gouge, a local brewer, added Grecian columns on three sides and thus somewhat changed its appearance. It burned sometime in the 1980s.

Col. Fulkerson died at this home on December 17, 1902. He is buried in East Hill Cemetery at the first left hand corner after one enters the main gate. A fine monument marks the site, and includes much data of his life and work. And the legacy of York and Fulkerson lives on. A short time ago a trunk full of old papers from their law firm was presented to this author. In it were priceless papers, dating back to the very beginning of Bristol. And many of them can be used in the effort to establish a true history of the Virginia side of the city.

DAVID F. BAILEY

Another lawyer who began practicing in Bristol soon after the close of the Civil War was David F. Bailey. Over the years he became eminently successful and truly a legend in his own time. For years he was associated with W. D. McCroskey, another early lawyer. Finally he became the senior partner in the firm of Bailey and Byars (Byars was his son-in-law). Young Bailey was married on February 29, 1872, to Sarah Ellen Preston at the home of her father, John F. Preston, (Locust Glen) near Abingdon, Virginia. For years the Baileys lived in an old brick house at 27 East State Street. This house, which stood directly across the street from the present Salvation Army office, was demolished in 1973. They later lived on the west end of the same block.

Nothing better could be written of him than that which was written by his charming and lovely granddaughter, Mrs. Virginia Caldwell of Blountville, Tennessee. With inexpressible gratitude to her it is presented here.

Portrait of My Grandfather
by Virginia Byars Coontz Caldwell
(Mrs. Joseph Anderson Caldwell)

A talk delivered before the Washington County Historical Society by Virginia Byars Coontz Caldwell (Mrs. Joseph Anderson Caldwell), July 24, 1944. This same sketch was requested as a "repeat-performance" for the Historical Society's Meeting of November 20, 1945, and is herewith presented.

My subject is one whom many of you knew better than I did — my Grandfather, David Flournoy Bailey.

He was born at "Buck Mountain," the residence of his Grandfather, Andrew Bailey, in Charlotte County, Virginia, January 23, 1845, the son of Joseph R. and Julia Ann (Womack) Bailey.

His Father, a native of Charlotte County, Virginia, and a lawyer, served in the Mexican War and died several years later from wounds received in battle.

David came to Goodson after his Father's death, worked as a printer's devil on the *Bristol News*. He met W. L. Rice on the railroad tracks above town and he gave him the job.

When asked why he was walking in, my grandfather told Mr. Rice that he had had money enough to pay his fare all the way by stage but that the stage had broken down and he had to spend the night at Dublin, Va. He had walked from there as he had no more money. In after years he became the Editor of that paper.

Later, he brought his Mother and two sisters out to Goodson. They lived where the Elks Club now stands, on Shelby Street. There his Mother and Sisters taught a school — the first in this section of the country. He learned all he knew in early life at his Mother's tutoring.

They were gifted musicians and linguists but impoverished by the War between the states. When Federal soldiers came through here they fed their horses in her piano. Dragged it out and dumped oats in it.

My Grandfather was almost sixteen when he went to war. His Mother prayed all night and the next morning cut him a raincoat or slicker from the oil-cloth on the kitchen table, and sent him off to fight for his beloved Southland. He was thrice wounded. After being mustered out, he attended Cumberland Law School at Lebanon, Tennessee. Graduated in 1869 and that same year started practicing law in Washington County, Virginia, and continued in the practice for more than half a century.

He married Sarah Eleanor Preston of "Locust Glen," near Abingdon, Virginia, 1872. She was his sweetheart and wife, whom he loved and adored above all else till his dying day. And she, in turn, was as the Earth is to the Sun — even unto the end.

They had seven children. Three grew to womanhood. The three Bailey Gals as they were known — Jane, Julia and Martha or Mattie. Jane and Joseph Cloyd Byars are my parents.

Grandpa Bailey went into the Republican party in the days of the Funders and Re-adjusters. He was a rampant Republican, a Slemp man, a political power, the Old War Horse of The Fighting Ninth. A Legislator, a State Senator, a criminal lawyer of great ability.

He had an Eastern Virginia drawl. He said "Cyar," "gyrl," 'gyarden,'' mixed with the vernacular of the mountaineer, whom he came to know and to love so well. I recall his singing mountain songs, "Old Dan Tucker," "Sour Wood Mountain," and "Fare Ye Well, Old Joe Clark," and "the Little Brown Jug," — though I expect he was more fond of the contents of the jug than of the song.

He loves his mint Julep and taught me to make them. "Crush the mint leaves and the sugar, th'ow in your ice, and pour a dram o'licker on, and drink her frosty white."

His subsequent history should be familiar to most of the older members of this Society. "With a big body and a big brain and a big heart, and a good deal of every-day human nature, he has gone in and out with the people of this section; loving his friends and ignoring his enemies; diligent in business and energetic in politics." No lawyer had a larger or more widely scattered clientage — for he began back yonder when the lawyers rode a circuit. As a forceful pleader at the bar he was a power in jury cases.

He used to walk with his hands clasped behind him, and rehearse his cases at night. "Your Honor" and "Gentlemen of the Jury" were early phrases I learned, in the wee small hours of the night, as he shuffled about in his old "Cyarpet slippers;" out to the dining room, where he would whittle on the ham on the side-board and munch a beaten-biscuit and some of Sary-Ellen's watermelon preserves. He loved hawg jowl and turnip sallet, and corn pone and pot-licer. And Sorghum lasses (or black-strap), were his favorite sweetenin'.

I remember he wore a black broadcloth, swallow-tailed coat when he dressed up. Often an old rusty black alpaca. His breeches hung loosely always needed pressing, held up by galluses (often only one gallus). A wing collar and string tie (Grandma made these) and Congress gaiters.

He was a horse-trader — always leading or riding an old sway-back nag home, with fet locks or a blind eye. Always got stung, never believed it and never learned.

Some of his bosom companions were of a lower social strata than that in which his wife and family moved. This annoyed them at times, I am sure, but I too, loved the company of Pat Ryan and Tom Crusenberry, the harness mender; so we often visited them or sat with Pat Ryan while he swapped watches.

Grandpa could sway a jury — cry or laugh at will and make them and the whole court room do likewise. He was very emotional, a born actor, would sniff, wipe his nose on the back of this hand and dry his eyes with the tail of his old black coat. He would get excited and jerk off his tie and flip it at the jury, then tear off his collar and throw it; pull off his coat and toss it aside. I guess his was the first strip tease act. It was said of him that "For every tear that rolled down his cheek a dollar rolled into his pocket."

Grandpa chawed tobaccy. He would gage his distance, walk around the old brass spittoon in the court-room and eye it several times, all the time accumulating juice, and get the rapt attention of the spectators and jury alike. Then, with amazing accuracy he would cut loose from a great distance and hit that spittoon every time with a resounding ring. The Court room would heave a sign of relief, the jury recross their legs or slap a thigh in admiration and the case would go on. I have seen him lean over with stiffened knees, and hit the floor with the back of his hand, as he bellowed out a point, for emphasis.

He was eloquent or vulgar, tender or brutal, a dual personality.

His stories and stories about him are famous but do not bear repeating here!

He was one of the outstanding characters around Bristol — old Colonel Baily, or Uncle Dave, as he was affectionately called. He was quick witted and rapier-tongued with a keen sense of humor and delightful repartee.

"The biggest and best thing about him was his big heart — tender and loving." He was poetic in his nature — cared little for money and the material things. He loved human beings. He loved history and fine sentiment. He loved oratory — good sermons and good songs and he tapped his foot to the fiddler's tune. He loved all out of doors. He loved the country, the mountains and valleys of East Tennessee and Southwest Virginia. He loved to drink from every pure flowing spring. He had much, as we now look back on his seventy-eight years of life, to love and admire and cherish.

He was a precious jewel — a diamond in the rough, set in a heart of gold. A mixture of Eastern Virginia Chesterfield and Southwest Virginia Mountaineer — My Grandfather.

W. N. "BIG BILL" CLARKSON

W. N. "Big Bill" Clarkson arrived in Bristol in the late 1860s. The late Frances Hinds remembered him as being tall, very handsome, of dark complexion and having very black hair. She also remembered that he had very sharp, piercing eyes, which he often used to great advantage in the courtroom. For a time he boarded at the Nickels House Hotel near the depot. And for the most of his stay in Bristol he maintained an office in the west end (basement) of that building. He was a capable lawyer and became very successful, but always maintained a notable humility. He was feared in the courtroom, and it is rumored that he was also feared by certain fathers and husbands, whose daughters and wives found Clarkson to be extremely charming.

After boarding for a year or so, he moved his wife and family to Bristol. But he soon faded from the picture and nothing further is known of him.

W.N. (Big Bill) Clarkson, one of Bristol's early lawyers.

Capt. James Harvey Wood, 1842-1917, was an early lawyer in Bristol-Goodson, Virginia. He built his home, Pleasant Hill, at 214 Johnson (Johnston) Street in 1872. It is now the home of the author of this book.

CAPTAIN JAMES HARVEY WOOD

One of the most successful lawyers of early Bristol was Capt. James Harvey Wood. He was born at old Pleasant Hill, the estate of his father, near what is now Gate City, Virginia, on February 22, 1842, a son of James O. and Elizabeth Godsey Wood. He was a grandson of Henry Wood who was an early sheriff of Scott County, Virginia. His great grandfather, Jonathan Wood, was a Revolutionary War soldier and claimed to have fired the shot that killed General Ferguson during the Battle of King's Mountain.

He was educated at Virginia Military Institute at Lexington, Virginia, and from there began his Civil War service, serving in the 37th Virginia Regiment. During the last year of the war he was held prisoner at Point Lookout, Maryland, and finally at Ft. Delaware, Delaware. During this period he began the study of law under a fellow prisoner, a lawyer from Savannah, Georgia, later joined by another lawyer from Nashville, Tennessee.

He was released from prison on July 13, 1865. His health had been virtually ruined by prison life, so much so that his father had to go for him, taking a horse named Prince for the son to ride home. Old Prince was used in the famous Johnston Land Sale in Bristol, July 4 and 5, 1871. The famous horse died in 1887 and was buried on the ridge beyond the railroad cut and Scott Street near the beginning point of present Prince Street.

Soon after returning home, young Wood was licensed to practice law. In the late 1860s he opened an office in Bristol with Charles R. Vance. He quickly became a highly respected and much sought after lawyer, not only in Bristol but all over the area, finally becoming one of the most conspicuous figures in southwestern Virginia and east Tennessee.

Wood's first Bristol law office was in the west end of the Nickels House Hotel (raised basement). During his short bachelorhood in Bristol he roomed and boarded in the same hotel, in room 3, second floor. Anglewise across Main and Fourth Streets which crossed at this hotel was a large mercantile establishment of W. W. James. James had a young daughter, Laura Lucretia James, who helped in the millinery department of her father's store. Of course no respectable bachelor would venture into that sacred domain of women, but he could seat himself on a bench outside the store; and it seemed that on those warm spring days of 1868, young Laura James often found excuses to come out and sit near him. About that time Lawyer Wood decided to find a church and for some reason he chose what is now State Street Methodist. Perhaps it was coincidental that this was the church attended by the James family. Soon a budding friendship turned into full-fledged courting. W. W. James encouraged this courtship and gave it his full blessing and approval. He was ever attuned to the pursuit of prestige and prosperity and he sensed that J. H. Wood was on the way upward.

J. H. Wood and Laura Lucretia James were married on July 15, 1868, by the Rev. David Sullins for whom Sullins College was later named. The wedding took place in the James home, located by his store on Front Street and facing the depot. After a honeymoon spent at Holston Springs the couple moved into the Virginia House Hotel where they boarded for several months. Old receipts show that room and board for the two came to $22.50 per month. Later they moved to a house owned by the new bride.

Soon after the Johnston Land Sale, Capt. Wood bought lot 32, which had first been sold to a Mr. Moore. In 1872 he contracted with Uncle Will Smith to build a brick house on the lot. His home was finished in April of 1873, and the family soon moved in. Here this early Bristol lawyer reared his family, and here two children and his wife died. After the death of his first wife, he married Mrs. Virginia Holmes of Winchester, Virginia. Their only child died as a baby, and this second wife died within a few years.

In 1901 J. H. Wood left Bristol and moved to Washington, D.C., where he founded the J. H. Wood Corporation, which served as legal counsel for

PLEASANT HILL, 214 Johnson Street, Bristol, Virginia, was built by Capt. J.H. Wood in 1872-73. Capt. Wood was one of the early lawyers of this town. This is now home to V.N. (Bud) Phillips, author of this book.

two railroads and numerous businesses. He also became president and principal director of the Blackenship Law and Corporation Company with offices at 14th and "G" Streets.

In 1909 Wood moved to New York City and became associated with the New York Urban Real Estate Company, of which his son, J. H. Wood, Jr., was president. While living in New York he wrote his memoirs of the Civil War. Today this book is priceless to those who cherish such first-hand recollections of the war. Capt. J. H. Wood died of high blood pressure November 12, 1917, at the home of his daughter, Gertrude Wood Dillard, who also lived in New York. He was returned by train to Bristol and kept overnight at the home of a sister, Miss Sallie Wood, who then lived on Anderson Street at the site of the present Haven of Rest Mission. After funeral services in the First Presbyterian Church, he was buried in East Hill Cemetery.

Capt. Wood raised four children to maturity. They were J. H. Wood, Jr., who lived in New York and died before his father; Gertrude Wood Dillard, who also settled in New York City; Mary Wood, who married Samuel G. Harris and built and lived in the house still standing at 203 Johnson Street,

Bristol, Virginia, but later moved to Lynchburg, Virginia; and William Scott Wood, of whom nothing further is known. On Valentine's Day, 1889, these children of J. H. Wood penciled their names and the date on a mortar joint of the old Wood home at 214 Johnson Street, Bristol, Virginia. After the passage of a century, this writing can clearly be seen today. The Wood home, Pleasant Hill, was still standing in 1990, much as Wood had left it eighty-nine years earlier, still proudly looking out over the town where its builder reached fame and fortune. It is now the home of this author.

MARION L. BLACKLEY

One of the more colorful lawyers of early Bristol was Marion L. Blackley, who began his work here in 1869. He was born at Scottsboro Ferry, Albermarle County, Virginia, a son of George and Margaret Hoag Blackley. Through his mother's line he was related to George Washington. Blackley's first office was in the west end of the Nickel's House Hotel. The first floor of this hotel was high off the ground at that end and several offices and one store room had been built underneath. When Blackley started his practice his rent was seven dollars per month.

Early in life he married Miss Sallie Thomas of the Holston Valley area. She was a lady of marked refinement and dignity and was a great help to him for the remainder of his life. M. L. Blackley was well-known for his unusual ability in successfully conducting chancery cases. It is said that he spent much time reading the files of past cases in this realm. Evidently this gave him great insight as to how to conduct his own chancery suits.

For years the Blackleys lived at 930 Fifth Street in Bristol, Tennessee. It is likely that part of this house was there when it was purchased by the Blackleys, but was later added onto by them. It was demolished in December 1988. The children of Marion L. and Sallie Thomas Blackley were Erskine, who never married; Hoge; Marion, daughter who married Walter Fortune; Reba; Jacob (Jake); and Herman, who married Allie Linn Anderson, granddaughter of Joseph R. Anderson, founder of Bristol.

In December 1905 Marion L. Blackley was on the porch of his home when an acquaintance passing along the street paused to talk with him. After a short conversation the friend started to pass on. Blackley paused at the door to call out a Merry Christmas to his departing friend. The friend said Blackley then reached for the door and instantly fell dead. His wife lived until December 1920. The Blackleys are buried in East Hill Cemetery.

GEORGE I. BLACKLEY

George Ignatius Blackley, a brother of Marion L. Blackley, briefly practiced law in the early 1870s. For some time he was a partner in the firm of Blackley, Robertson and Blackley. It is known that this partnership operated under that name in 1874, and perhaps later. George Blackley was a highly intelligent and effective man at the bar.

As a young man he married a daughter of the legendary Major Z. L. Burson. They soon moved to Greenville, Texas, where he set up a new practice. An item in the *Bristol News* mentioned that Blackley was a rising star in the legal profession in that thriving town. But his young wife soon became ill and died in the new climate. Blackley was devastated. Shortly he returned to his family home (122 East State Street) and remained there the rest of his life. As far as can be determined he did not resume his law practice, but lived a sad and tragic life until his death. Old-timers used to tell of how he would sometimes suddenly burst into tears and quickly retire to his bedroom, where he might remain for hours. His spirit had died in Greenville, Texas, but his body lingered on in Bristol for years.

"HELL" JOHN BURSON

In September of 1871, John E. Burson began his Bristol practice. He was a son of the first family of Major Zachariah L. Burson. The old major gave his son a fine education including the benefit of a first class law school. John E. Burson was remembered as being very brilliant, a man of much wit and common sense, a notably shrewd and effective lawyer. One of his legendary tactics, which probably wouldn't be allowed in any court today, was putting the "holy fear" in his more religious witnesses. And this tactic gave him his nickname of Hell John. Here is a typical example, taken from an actual deposition being made for a Bristol divorce case. (The witness was testifying against the defendant.)

MR. BURSON: Now Mrs. Hinner, you say you saw the defendant, Mrs. Lacey, going into a cornfield with Duke Faidley, on a moonlight nite and they didn't come out for two hours?

MRS. HINNER: Yes sir, I did, I sure did!

MR. BURSON: Now isn't it true that you are on the outs with Mrs. Lacey, and that you have told around that you would do her damage anyway you could?

MRS. HINNER: Why, no sir.

MR. BURSON: Now Mrs. Hinner, do you know where folks go who tell lies?

MRS. HINNER: Well, I reckon I do.

MR. BURSON: Now you know that all liars go straight to the fires of hell. Mrs. Hinner it is my solemn duty to tell you that you may be sealing your doom, sitting right here before me. You may die before you get home today — you could drop dead in the streets like Tom Jent did yesterday, and if you're lying to me you'd be scorching in the fires of the damned before you quit kicking. Tell me the truth or go straight to hell when you die. You'll go there as sure as you are born, if you tell me a lie! Now, didn't you just make up that moonlight, cornfield tale?

MRS. HINNER: O Lordy yes, and I hope there's some forgiveness for me. I sure don't want to go to hell.

And further the deponeth sayeth not.

And "Hell" John Burson won that case, as he did many others by the same tactics.

After the death of his father (September 1894), John Burson bought the old family home, The Oak, at 342 Moore Street, from his widowed step-mother Nannie J. Baker-Burson. After a few years he had the old house demolished, and then erected on the site a very nice brick home, said to have then been the finest in Bristol. Alas, he did not long enjoy it. Through a series of financial reverses, he came to the sad day when his fine mansion was sold at the courthouse door to a neighbor, Mr. J. O. Susong. Burson continued to practice law in Bristol but never fully recovered financially. He died at an unknown date. His widow, the former Patty Hines, who hailed from the Buffalo Pond area near Wallace, Virginia, and whom he married at Blountville, Tennessee, in 1881, survived him by several years.

THOMAS CURTIN

By the early 1870s "lawing" had becme quite lucrative in Bristol. Young Tom Curtin, formerly of Bluff City (then called Union), Tennessee, was then operating a grocery store here. As he pondered his situation he came to the realization that he could make more money at the bar than he could at the grocery counter. In May 1873 he sold his store to a brother, P. J. Curtin, and enrolled in Georgetown College. After completing his studies he set up practice in Bristol, where he became a noted trial lawyer. By 1893 he was in the prestigious firm of Curtin and Haynes, and had offices on the second floor of the Anderson Building at 410 State Street, Rooms 7 and 8. The two law partners had put together what was considered the finest law library in the area. But the tornado of June 1893, tore the roof from the Anderson building, and the torrential downpour that followed all but ruined this fine collection of books.

The Thomas Curtin family lived for years in what is now the Burwill Construction building on Locust Street in Bristol, Tennessee. Descendants still live in Bristol.

BRISTOL LAWYERS, 1875-1900

JOHN H. CALDWELL

Records indicate that John H. Caldwell was practicing law in Bristol by 1875. He was born July 8, 1856, a son of the Rev. George A. and Margaret E. Brooks Caldwell. His father was a great believer in education and saw to it that his son received the best instruction then available. Young Caldwell was early married to Margaret Anderson, the only daughter of Joseph R. Anderson, who founded Bristol, Virginia-Tennessee in 1852.

Though Caldwell did indeed practice law, his consuming interest seems to have been in the promotion of business enterprises and city development, at which pursuits he was quite successful. Craig H. Caldwell, Sr. and his son Craig H. Caldwell, Jr. represent the third and fourth generation of this family line to practice law in Bristol.

John H. Caldwell lived on the southeast corner of Locust and Seventh Streets in what is now the Weaver Funeral Home. He did extensive remodeling of

Early lawyer John H. Caldwell is pictured here with his mother, grandmother, and son. Caldwell also engaged in numerous business pursuits.

The grand mansion pictured above was long the home of John H. Caldwell, early Bristol lawyer and son-in-law of Joseph R. Anderson, the town's founder. Located on the southeast corner of Locust and Seventh Streets, it now houses the Weaver Funeral Home.

this house shortly after it was bought from David Ensor, an early Bristol druggist. Caldwell died June 25, 1936, and is buried in the Caldwell family addition to the Glenwood Cemetery.

WILLIAM F. RHEA

On June 28, 1879, Law Court was organized in Bristol, Tennessee. The first act of that court was to license William F. Rhea to practice law. Just how far he would go in the pursuit of his profession that court could not then know. By August 1881 Rhea had become a member of the prestigious firm of York and Fulkerson. A little later he was associated with "Hell" John Burson in Burson and Rhea. Around 1890 he became a partner with H. G. Peters. And he was ever moving upward in prestige and gaining favor with the citizens of Bristol and the surrounding area. In 1898 he defeated General James A. Walker in a race for Congress, and served until 1902. This author has no information as to the final years of Rhea, nor when he died or where he is buried. His old home still stands at 804 Cumberland Street, Bristol, Virginia.

BUTLER AND McDOWELL

Judge R. R. Butler and Bryon G. McDowell formed a law partnership on May 27, 1879. The services of these well learned and successful partners were eagerly sought by clients from near and far. By 1896 McDowell had become a partner in the firm of McDowell, Blackley, and King. This latter firm maintained offices in the 400 block of Main Street, Tennessee side. He was a favorite of Major A. D. Reynolds, who saw to it that a street was named for this much trusted attorney. In the 1890s McDowell built his home at 412 Pennsylvania Avenue. It still stands. A few years later he built his last home, the house that yet stands at 622 Ash Street. Judge R. R. Butler is said to have been the very epitome of the old breed of effective lawyers. He possessed a bearing and grace of movement that commanded respect anywhere he might be. It is said that if he were hoeing his garden (which he often did) he still maintained the aura of the judge and lawyer that he was.

On July 5, 1881, Judge Butler went into the woods where some men were cutting timber for him. While there he was caught in a violent storm. The strong winds blew down a huge tree that killed the horse on which he was mounted, injuring the judge, though not seriously. But tales of such things have a way of quickly growing big and distorted. Word soon reached Bristol that the judge had been killed by the falling tree. Late in the afternoon of the next day, a local lady was coming down East Main (State) Street carrying a basket that contained several dozen eggs. Hearing a horseman passing by she glanced up to see the "dead judge" riding into town. The somewhat superstitious lady, supposing she was surely seeing a ghost (if it were but an injured lawyer and a borrowed horse), immediately fainted and fell backward, swinging the egg basket upside down over her head. Eggs showered down upon the fainting woman, which along with other products of extreme fright created quite a mess.

Though Judge Butler seems to have practiced in Bristol only a short while, many received help from him.

BLANCHARD AND MILES

A. H. Blanchard, who became a very prominent Bristol lawyer, arrived by 1881. His work soon became very extensive and he reached a marked degree of prosperity. Blanchard long lived at 909 Cumberland Street. At one time he was associated with A. F. Miles. Miles was not only a laywer, but for years served as a notary public. His name appears frequently on official papers of the era.

Blanchard, who was born June 20, 1850, died December 2, 1921, and is buried in East Hill Cemetery. His wife was Bessie Wallace.

SAMUEL V. FULKERSON

Samuel V. Fulkerson, a son of Col. Abram Fulkerson, was born October 22, 1863. As a youth he was sent to Virginia Military Institute (1881), where he graduated at the head of his mathematics class. He also received much of his education at Emory and Henry College at Emory, Virginia. After being licensed to practice law he associated himself with his father in Bristol, Virginia. He was very successful from the start of his law career.

Fulkerson married at an early age, but was not destined for long-enduring marital bliss. This part of his life ended in a tragic set of circumstances. Ever after he was a sad man, yet this darkness in his personal life did not affect his climb to the zenith of professional success. He lived in his father's old home on the southwest corner of Spencer and Russell Streets. Passers-by in the wee hours might glimpse him pacing back and forth along the wrap-around porch of this old home. Whether practicing for a case or trying to relieve his emotional agony, no one ever knew.

Fulkerson maintained offices at 476 Cumberland Street. He died July 2, 1926, and is buried near his father in East Hill Cemetery.

HERBERT G. PETERS

Another lawyer who became highly respected in the legal circles of Bristol was Herbert Greyson Peters. He was born in Henry County, Virginia, September 10, 1859, a son of Dr. Henry D. and Mary Frances Gravely Peters. His law studies were done at the University of Virginia. In 1889 he was elected to the Senate of Virginia. While serving, he met William F. Rhea of Bristol, who persuaded him to come and open a law practice in the city. The firm of Rhea and Peters was set up in 1890. In 1894 he married Electra Smith of Martinsville, Virginia. Mr. Peters became a very prominent lawyer. He died in Bristol, August 2, 1925. Herbert G. Peters, III, is his grandson and the third of the name to practice in this area.

JUDGE JOHN W. PRICE

As far as can be determined, John W. Price was the only lawyer who was also a medical doctor. He was born in Washington County, Virginia, in 1869, and was educated at Emory and Henry College, graduating in medicine from Southern Medical College, Atlanta, Georgia. After practicing medicine in Atlanta for two years, he took up the study of law at Atlanta Law School. He came to Bristol, Virginia, in 1895, and soon married a daughter of the noted lawyer, Col. D. F. Bailey. In the late 1890s he was in the firm of Bailey, Byars, and Price. In 1899 he was elected to the State Legislature, and later was a Bristol judge.

JUDGE HAL H. HAYNES

Hal H. Haynes, who clearly left his mark on Bristol, was born at Blount-ville, Tennessee, August 26, 1862, a son of Matthew T. and Kate Elizabeth Snapp Haynes. He was a grandson of "King" David Haynes and his wife Rhoda Taylor. Through this grandmother, he was related to the noted Taylor family of Carter County, Tennessee. Haynes was married October 1, 1883, to Laura Dulaney. His second marriage was to Kate Wallace.

Hal H. Haynes opened practice in Bristol when still a young man. By 1893 he was practicing with Thomas Curtin, and the two had offices in the Anderson Building at 410 Main (now State) Street. His rise toward eminent success never faltered. In time he branched out into various business pursuits that added much to his prosperity. Haynes worked on for decades after 1900, and beyond the scope of this book. He died August 14, 1947. The Haynesfield section of Bristol, Tennessee, was named for him.

THE GRAY LINE

Robert Gray, Sr., a prominent lawyer of Rockingham County, Virginia, had two sons and a son-in-law who were practicing in Bristol at about the same time. Preston Lewis Gray had offices in the Wood Building on Lee Street during his brief stay. He married Mary Stuart Bingham, daughter of Col. William Bingham, who operated a school at Mebane, North Carolina. Young Gray and his wife moved there to help operate the school. After Col. Bingham died, Gray and his wife sold the school and moved to Los Angeles, California, where they remained for the rest of their lives.

H. Peyton Gray also practiced law in Bristol. He had offices at 483 Cumberland Street, and lived at 410 Spencer. His wife was Bessie Massie. Nothing further is known of him.

Rockingham Paul, named for the county of his nativity, married Susan B. Gray, a sister of the Gray brothers. He pursued the profession of law for a few years in Bristol. He lived at 401 Moore and his mother-in-law, Mrs. Robert Gray, Sr., also made her home there. The house still stands. After a few yars here the Pauls moved to Roanoke, Virginia, where Mr. Paul's success and prominence continued.

OTHER BRISTOL LAWYERS 1875-1900

JOHN H. WINSTON, JR. Known as Jack Winston, he was a son of Prof. J. H. Winston. He served as mayor of Bristol, Virginia.

J. CLOYD BYARS He was of the prominent Byars family of Brook Hall estate at Glade Springs, Virginia. He was a son-in-law of the promi-nent lawyer, D. F. Bailey, and long practiced with him as Bailey & Byars. His home still stands at 422 Lee Street, Bristol, Virginia. He is buried in East Hill Cemetery.

J. WINSTON READ He was a son of Charlotte Winston Read-West, and grandson of Prof. J. H. Winston. He was of the firm Taylor, Winston, and Read with offices at 6 Fifth Street. He lived with his mother at 228 Johnson Street.

JAMES H. WOOD, JR. He was a son of old Capt. J. H. Wood. Young Wood lived at 210 Johnson Street. The house still stands, now the offices of lawyer B. S. Via. J. H. Wood, Jr. later moved to New York where he became president of the New York Urban Real Estate Company. He died in New York before 1917.

J. S. ASHWORTH J. S. Ashworth began his Bristol practice several years before the turn of the century. He was a well known and highly successful lawyer. By 1896 he was living at 202 Johnson Street. His home burned and he later built the house which is presently home to Woody's House of Portraits.

W. S. STUART In 1897 this young lawyer was boarding at the St. Lawrence Hotel and had offices at 505 Main. He later built a home on the southwest corner of Lee and Edmond Streets. This house still stands.

HENRY W. SUTHERLAND His name appears on several old court papers. It is known that he once boarded at the Hamilton House Hotel, and had offices at 505 Main Street.

GEORGE E. BOREN In 1896 he and his wife, Ida F. Boren, were living in the Hamilton House Hotel. He was associated with Holston National Bank and Loan Company.

H. S. GOOKIN Gookin was also a J. P. and sometimes served as coroner. In the 1890s he had offices in what was called the Law Building (Lee Street) and advertised that he was a collecting agent.

A. M. DICKENSEN Nothing further is known of him.

_____ ROWAN Mentioned in old papers, but nothing further known.

L. N. BUFORD He was a lawyer in Bristol in the late 1800s. May have been a son of James Buford, who built Oak Grove on present Buford Street.

GEORGE M. WARD Old papers indicate that he once practiced in Bristol. Nothing further known.

MARCELLUS SHEPHERD It is known that he had offices at 5 Fourth Street. At one time he was boarding at 621 Broad Street. One old timer remembered that he was called "crooked nose" by some of the town residents, and that one was in for a fight if the nickname were used in his presence.

ALFRED DEADRICK It is assumed that he was related to the other lawyers of that name who once practiced here. Nothing further known.

JUDGE HENRY FLOURNOY He practiced briefly here then became Secretary of the Commonwealth of Virginia.

JUDGE CHARLES ST. JOHN Charles St. John came to Bristol from Blountville. His home was at 300 Eighth Street. A man who commanded much respect among local citizens, he spent many years in the legal profession.

GENERAL JOHN FAIN He was of the Blountville Fains. He had offices at 600 Main (State) Street, and lived at 952 Anderson.

W. S. HAMILTON He was once in the firm of Hamilton and Miles (A. F. Miles). His practice was very successful and extended over several years. He was once in the firm of Hamilton and Grumpecker. Hamilton lived at 919 Cumberland Street.

G. W. GRUMPECKER Little is known of this Bristol lawyer. In the late 1890s he was in the firm of Hamilton and Grumpecker with offices at 20 Lee Street.

ALFRED PARLETTE Though a lawyer, he mainly engaged in business pursuits. For years he maintained offices at 416 Main Street. His old home yet stands at 728 Georgia Avenue, Bristol, Tennessee.

A. B. WHITEAKER Alexander B. Whiteaker (known as "Bo") had offices in the Bristol Bank and Trust Company Building at 224-226 Main (State) Street in 1896. His old home, recently restored, still stands at 1002 Anderson Street.

A. C. KEEBLER He long practiced in the firm of Keebler and Martin, with offices in the Pile Building at 600 Main (State) Street. His old home still stands at 1112 Anderson Street.

T. R. MARTIN Partner of A. C. Keebler. Nothing further is known of him.

W. V. VANCE His office was at 642 Main (State) Street in 1896. Nothing further is known of him.

J. P. RADER Mr. Rader was a "jack of all trades," among them a lawyer though not to a marked degree. He one time served Bristol, Tennessee, as lamplighter. His office was at 7 Fifth Street, and his home was at 623 Shelby.

JOHN A. FAW In April 1892 Mr. Faw had a law office in the National Bank Building. By 1896 he had established, along with a Mr. Underwood, *the Daily Times.* He lived at 544 Alabama Street.

THE BURROWS James Arnold Burrow, born October 16, 1823, came to Bristol from Carter County, Tennessee. His wife was Ann Elizabeth Carty, who was born June 14, 1823. He served Bristol, Tennessee, as Recorder and City Judge. His wife died February 20, 1893, and he then took up residence with a son, William Burrow, a printer and publisher, who lived in the old home that yet stands at 902 Windsor Avenue. James Arnold Burrow died there February 11, 1894. Both he and his wife are buried in the East Hill Cemetery. In the late 1890s three of his lawyer sons, Joseph H., Thomas J., and Robert had offices at 512 Main Street, Bristol, Tennessee. Robert became known as Judge Burrow. About 1904 he built the grand house that now stands at 711 Holston Avenue, Bristol, Tennessee.

W. A. RADER He was of an old and prominent family of the Bristol area, and was practicing law here by 1879. He later served as mayor of Goodson and Bristol, Virginia.

Bibliography - Chapter Eighteen

Bachelor, Ann. Memoirs (unpublished), 1935-1937.

Bristol Herald Courier. Special edition, 1917.

Bristol News, newspapers. Various issues, 1857-1881.

Bristol, Virginia-Tennessee. *City Directory,* 1896-1897.

Fulkerson, Abram, Col. Notes, 1881.

Loving, Robert S. *Double Destiny; The Story of Bristol, Tennessee-Virginia.* Bristol, Tenn.: King Printing Company, 1955.

Palmer, Joseph B. Diary (unpublished), 1855-1876.

Phillips, V. N. (Bud). Interviews and information supplied by many older Bristol citizens, 1953-1956.

Sullivan County, Tennessee. Court and Chancery Records, 1854-1900.

U. S. *Census,* 1860-1880.

Washington County, Virginia. Court and Chancery Records, 1854-1900.

Wood, J. H. Paper (unpublished), 1892.

Chapter Nineteen
THE HEALERS

THE DOCTORS OF EARLY BRISTOL

Perhaps a month before Joseph Anderson moved to Bristol from Blountville he made a trip to Abingdon, Virginia, in an effort to induce a young doctor, whom he casually knew, to settle in the new town of Bristol, Virginia-Tennessee. In Abingdon he found this willing healer ready to relocate. It seems that the medical field was a little overcrowded in the old county seat, making practice rather slow for a newcomer, so young Dr. B. F. Zimmerman immediately saddled his horse and rode with Anderson to the new town site. Before sunset he had selected lots 153 and 154 for his future home and office. These lots covered about half the 400 block of Main Street (State), Virginia side, and ran northward from the northeast corner of present State and Lee Streets. These were the second lots sold in Bristol, Virginia. The Signet Bank now occupies a portion of the former Zimmerman property.

Dr. Benjamin Frederick Zimmerman was born in Washington County, Virginia, in 1821, a son of Abram and Mary Montgomery Zimmerman. He received his medical education in Baltimore, Maryland. Family stories tell of his going to and from that city by stagecoach and once on horseback. Upon completion of his education he opened an office in Abingdon. Old tax records show that his property in Abingdon was located one half mile southwest of the courthouse. Records further show that he had property on Wolf Creek near Abingdon and a large acreage on Steele Creek near Bristol.

On May 12, 1847, about a year after he had opened practice in Abingdon, Virginia, B. F. Zimmerman was married to Martha R. Buchanan of near present Bristol. She was a favorite neighbor of the Rev. James King, who married the couple in the grand parlor of his mansion that stood at what is now 54 King Street. This marriage took place in the same room and before the same mantel where Joseph R. Anderson and Melinda King had been married about two years prior to the Zimmerman wedding. It is said that near the end of the ceremony a great windstorm struck followed by copious and incessant rainfall. This prevented their riding back to Abingdon as had been planned. The Kings graciously allowed them to spend their wedding night in the estate guest house. This house, a one room over one room structure, stood at about the northeast corner of the Margaret Mitchell yard at 54 King Street.

Once being persuaded to settle in Bristol, and having bought lots, Dr. Zimmerman immediately contracted with Fields and Rodefer to commence the erection of his home and office. These were the first two buildings to be finished in Bristol, Virginia. (This was before that side of town became Goodson). At this time the store and home of John H. Moore were under construction in the eastern portion of the 500 block of Main (State) Street.

For some reason Dr. Zimmerman chose to erect his home near mid-block, instead of the often preferred corner location. This home stood just above the present Signet Bank. The corner lot (now corner of Lee and State) was the garden site. His office, consisting of two contiguous rooms of near equal size, stood near the southeastern corner of the garden. Behind the garden, about where is now located the drive-in window of the Signet Bank, stood the slave cabin of "Big Elbert." (This slave was farmed out after the death of Zimmerman in order to help support the widow and children.) Behind the main house was a detached kitchen. The office, house, and kitchen were of brick construction, while Big Elbert's cabin was built of board and batten and whitewashed. The Zimmermans' slave cook and housekeeper, Louthia (called Tish), lived in an attic room over the kitchen.

Dr. Zimmerman and family moved into the new homestead in June 1854, but he was not long to enjoy his home and growing practice. He died five months later, November 11, 1854, at the age of thirty-three. His former office was later rented for various purposes. In 1858 it became the first home and office of John S. Mosby, an early Bristol lawyer. The Zimmerman estate papers show that Mosby's rent was $75.00 per year. It also served as the second location of the post office when it was briefly moved into Virginia. The widow of Dr. Zimmerman later married John Keys. She died in 1900, aged seventy-four years, and is buried in East Hill Cemetery.

BRISTOL'S SECOND DOCTOR

When Lewis Bachelor (originally Bauceler) arrived in early 1855, he found the town proper without a doctor. (Drs. Hammer and Willoughby then lived in the old King mansion, but that was not within the limits of Bristol, Virginia.) Prior to his move, Mr. Bachelor had become acquainted with Richard M. Coleman, a recent graduate of the Jefferson Medical University of Philadelphia, Pennsylvania. It was this early Bristol pioneer who persuaded the young doctor to settle in Bristol.

Dr. Richard M. Coleman was born in 1828 at Amherst Court House, Virginia, and there grew to manhood. He received his medical education at the University of Virginia and Jefferson University. He and his wife, Mary B. Coleman, and two-year-old daughter, Annie Walton Coleman, arrived in Bristol by stagecoach in the late spring of 1855. For their first stay the

Dr. Richard M. Coleman, the second physician to practice in Bristol, opened and operated the town's first drug store.

family lived in a rented house belonging to Col. S. E. Goodson. The house stood on Washington Street in Goodsonville. However, the doctor had an office in a small room behind the John H. Moore store on the northwest corner of present Lee and State (then Main and Eighth). He later moved his office into a small brick building that stood on the southeast corner of what is now State and Fifth, and owned by Joseph Anderson. Here, in late 1855, he opened Bristol's first drugstore which he operated along with his medical practice.

About 1859 the Colemans moved to west Tennessee. All that is known of their location there is that it was on the Forked Deer River. But by 1861 they were back in Bristol. Dr. Coleman, who had long been an agnostic (considered by some to have been an atheist), joined the Baptist Church in 1861. He was a faithful financial supporter of this church for the remainder of his life. This change in the doctor's spiritual perception had a far-reaching consequence in the life of another Bristolian, as the author may be able to reveal in time.

Apparently Dr. Coleman prospered in his second stay. On January 11, 1864, he was able to buy property from R. T. Lancaster, for which he paid ten thousand dollars in cash. This was the same property that Mr. Lancaster had bought from Joseph and Mary Johnston of Philadelphia, Pennsylvania, on May 2, 1863, and consisted of lots 211, 212, and 213 in the plan of Goodson, and fronted on the west side of Moore Street in the first block north of Scott. This was the homesite of Dr. Coleman and was later erroneously called the Mosby House. On February 10, 1866, the Colemans bought ten acres in northwest Bristol from William L. and Sarah Rice, for which was paid $355.00. Then on February 15, 1856, this tract of land was deeded to their daughter Annie Walton Coleman, probably in anticipation of her marriage. In the winter of 1869 Annie became engaged to Alden Legard. On April 20, 1869, Dr. Coleman contracted with Henry T. Wilbar of Bristol, Tennessee, to build a house for this daughter and her future husband. The engagement was long and, alas, before the wedding Annie became ill and died. Her death occurred September 20, 1870. She was seventeen. Three weeks and one day later (October 12, 1870), Dr. Coleman died. Both are buried in the old section of East Hill Cemetery. His obituary paints a splendid word portrait of him:

As a physician he combined all the skills of his profession, and with a comprehensiveness and accuracy of judgement second to none. As to the technicalities of Physics as well as the great theories underlying this science, he was regarded by the medical fraternity as occupying a high standard. He was devoted to his profession; and such was the exalted estimate that he placed upon it that he had contempt for those who were not conversant with the great principles of this science, and yet claimed its honors and emoluments [there were many such "quack doctors" in his day.] He was a man of marked eccentricities; they were however, peculiar to himself, and their origin more in his habit of abstract thinking and theorizing than in his heart. He lived much within himself but was communicative with those who were congenial. He reveled in the great theories of medicine, and those touching upon the moral and physical world... He was confined to his room for several months before his death by that most flattering of disease, consumption. During this time he was patient and resigned.

The widow, Mary B. Coleman, later married David E. Head and moved to Hancock County, Illinois.

BRISTOL'S THIRD DOCTOR

Little is known of Dr. Flavius Hartman, Bristol's third physician. He came to Bristol about 1856 and for a while lived in a house located in the 400 block of Main Street rented from Joseph Anderson. By July 1857 he was serving the town as alderman. During that month he was designated to get up a subscription to fill up the pond above the railroad tracks. (This pond would now be in the middle of State Street and between the tracks and the Bristol welcome sign.) On December 31, 1858, he resigned as alderman. Since no further mention of him has been found, he may have left town at that time.

OTHER BRISTOL DOCTORS OF THE 1850s

Dr. William Hammer moved into Bristol, Tennessee, soon after the arrival of Dr. Falvius Hartman. His home and office stood on Main Street about where now stands the Interstate Hardware building. He was of the prominent Hammer family of Sullivan County, Tennessee, and was highly respected by the local citizenry.

About 1858 a large family of Peppers moved to Bristol from Mt. Airy, Virginia (now Rural Retreat). Among them were Drs. James R., William H., C. T., J. H., and John Givens Pepper. The oldest was Dr. Jesse H. Pepper, who was born in 1822. Dr. James R. Pepper, who was born May 23, 1831, and who died in Bristol, Tennessee, January 11, 1860, was one of the first to be buried in East Hill Cemetery. The wife of Dr. J. H. Pepper was a direct descendant of Sir Francis Drake. She spent years trying to gain a portion of his estate, which even in the 1800s amounted to several million dollars.

It was a common practice in those days for doctors to own and operate drugstores. Among the early Bristol drugstores was that of the Pepper Brothers (Drs. C. T. and J. G. Pepper). This store was located in the 500 block of State Street (then Main) about where now stands Ball Brothers Furniture. Their sign was that of the red mortar. At one time the firm was known as Bunting & Pepper. Dr. William H. Pepper was in the firm at that time.

The Peppers made their mark in Bristol, but not one of that name now resides in the city. In later years a member of this family concocted the well known and popular Dr. Pepper soft drink. It is thought that this was a descendant from Dr. C. T. Pepper, who moved back to Mt. Airy, Virginia, in August 1879.

BRISTOL DOCTORS OF THE 1860s

Dr. R. M. Coleman, Dr. William Hammer and the Peppers of the medical profession practiced in Bristol during the war years (1861- 1865). These doctors spent much of their time aiding in the treatment of sick and wounded Confederate soldiers after hospitals were set up in Bristol. It is said that a Dr. C. T. McGee came here for that purpose. Apparently, he remained a few years after the war. His professional card appears in a post-war newspaper or two.

Dr. Michael Carriger of Carter County, Tennessee, settled in Bristol at about the time of the close of the war. Ann Bachelor described him as being an ex-Confederate soldier, extremely handsome, and of a rather worldly inclination, but a devoted and very competent physician. From Joseph Anderson he bought lots near present Anderson Park and may have built one of the earliest houses in that section.

Dr. John H. Morton arrived in Bristol in 1866. He advertised himself as a physician and surgeon, with offices in the Campbell and Thomas Drugstore. His card gives further notice that he was boarding at Mrs. Moore's and that he might be reached there when not in his office.

Dr. William N. (Nick) Vance came to Bristol from Kingsport, Tennessee, in late 1865 or early 1866. Dr. Vance, born November 12, 1814, was a grandson of the noted Dr. Patrick Vance, who had perfected a method of saving victims of Indian scalpings. His first office in Bristol was one door east of the Campbell and Thomas Drugstore. This would have placed him at the site where Bunting's Drugstore was later located. By December of 1869 he had moved his office to the King Block on Front Street, "upstairs, first door on the right." In 1879 he moved back to the Tennessee side with offices over King and Hill's Book Store. This store was one door east of what later became Bunting's Drugstore, 400 block of present State Street. By 1878 Dr. Vance was living in the fine home he had built on Fifth Street. This home was near what was later numbered 317 Fifth Street.

The first wife of Dr. Vance was Sarah Anne Netherland. She was of the noted Netherland family of Kingsport, Tennessee, and was a sister of Mrs. Lizzie Rhea Netherland Brewer, wife of W. P. Brewer who also settled in Bristol, and Mrs. Harriett Netherland King, wife of John G. King, whose father had owned the land on which Bristol, Virginia-Tennessee, was located. Sarah Anne died February 13, 1868. Some time later when the doctor was about sixty years old, he made a trip to Ireland and there met Helena McIlwaine, a beautiful girl of 19 summers, whom he later married. Descendants of both marriages still live in Bristol. Dr. Vance died February 12, 1895. He is buried between his two wives in East Hill Cemetery.

Dr. Sanders was practicing in Bristol by 1867. He seems to have emained in Bristol only a short time. In the late 1860s Dr. James A. Templeton began his practice in Bristol. He is often referred to as the "saintly" J. A. Templeton because of his strong Presbyterian faith which he mixed with his medical practice, often praying with his patients as often as giving them medical advice or dosing out medicines. L. F. Johnson described him as being of a pious, almost saintly, nature, and easily fitting in with the elite, refined, and educated of the town. His very kind and religious nature caused him to become the victim of many who wanted medical help but had no intention of ever paying the bill. Yet, there were those who needed help and honestly could not pay. They received as much attention as those who were well able to meet their financial obligations. Dr. Templeton often went far beyond the call of duty by spending long and attentive hours with the severely sick and dying, even staying to help with funeral arrangements for the deceased, and occasionally paying the funeral bills for the indigent. But in spite of his marked generosity, he soon was able to take his place among the wealthy of Bristol. By April 1, 1871, he had set up offices in the King Block on Front Street, and remained there for several years. There was not a more beloved and respected citizen during his stay in Bristol.

Dr. John M. Hoffman, who began his practice in Bristol around 1868, was a forerunner of those many Bristol physicians who would later mix medical practice with the pursuit of business enterprises. Dr. Hoffman was reared on his family farm located two or three miles up Beaver Creek above Bristol. (The Hoffmans owned a part of the former John Goodson land.) Hoffman Mills was located on this land, of which the doctor was part owner when he moved down to Bristol. This was a flour and lumber mill, supplying much of the building materials for the new town. Though a young man when settling in Bristol, he already possessed considerable means. Within a year or two he set up Bristol's first commercial drug manufacturing plant. The "plant" was a small frame building occupying the southwest corner of present Lee Street and Winston's Alley. (The structure was later demolished to make way for the new *Bristol News* building.) There the enterprising young medic brewed up Dr. Hoffman's Liver Invigorator, which some local users said was too vigorous in its action. It was made of herbs, roots, and barks, all grown and gathered on the Hoffman farm. He also promoted Dr. Hoffman's Nerve Tonic, which had a pronounced high alcoholic content but was a very popular seller. And there was a tonic recommended for the "peculiar female diseases."

Dr. Hoffman lived for years in the former A. K. Moore home at the northwest corner of Cumberland and Moore Streets. Near this house was one of the better springs of downtown Bristol (Goodson). The Hoffmans built a nice cut stone springhouse over this water source. Much of the family provisions were kept there, and weekly washings were done there. One night Mrs. Hoffman, intending to start a large washing the next morning, carried two or three baskets of soiled laundry and placed them in the springhouse. This lot included most of the family clothes and linens. Thieves broke in that night and not only took much of the food stored there but the baskets of laundry as well. A few days later on Main Street, Mrs. Hoffman met one of the town deadbeats wearing her husband's best shirt. Her fiery Irish temper and strong physique combined to down the man and take the shirt from his back. Alas, insult was added to injury, for the fleeing man was not only arrested for burglary but was further charged with indecent exposure (as being shirtless was considered in those days). There are court papers in Abingdon, Virginia, which charge the man with burglary at the homestead of Dr. J. M. Hoffman and for being "indecently exposed in a vulgar manner before the public gaze." Dr. Hoffman later moved his office and medicine plant to the family farm on Beaver Creek.

Like Dr. Hoffman, Dr. H. T. Berry, who arrived in Bristol around 1869, mixed business with medicine. At one time he was a partner with Major Z. L. Burson in Burson and Berry Mercantile Company. At a later date he and J. A. Burrow formed Berry and Burrow, another mercantile enterprise. Dr. Berry lived at 45 Third Street. He was an extremely well learned and competent medical practitioner, much sought after in difficult cases. He may have been so far ahead of his time that he was then considered unorthodox. He often prescribed rest, fresh air, exercise and diet as better cures than medicine. He also frequently advised young people what to do to avoid many of the health problems that plague the aged. L. F. Johnson remembered that Berry had once prescribed honey dissolved in hot milk for nervousness and insomnia.

Apparently Dr. Berry had some belief in mind over matter. John N. Bosang once developed a severe and prolonged case of hiccoughs. After spending a sleepless night, he finally called Dr. Berry. The good doctor dutifully doled out some kind of powder, told Mrs. Bosang to give him a large dose, and if that didn't work to repeat it within an hour (all said and done with serious professionalism). In about a half hour Berry—on sweating steed and seemingly in a great state of excitement—reigned up before the Bosang gate. "Have you given John that medicine?" he excitedly called out before dismounting. The wife replied that she had. With a frightened groan, he called back, "then, he's sure as sin a dead man, for I left the wrong stuff. It was a powerful poison and he'll be gone in minutes." All this was said loud enough for John to hear every word. Of course he was greatly frightened and ran out onto the porch yelling, "Do something, doctor, save me!" The doctor pretended to be searching in his bag while the victim ran back and forth across the yard.

Dr. John Rutledge Keys, M.D., D.D.S., was the first to practice dentistry in the new Town of Bristol. He later moved to the State of Alabama.

After a few minutes Dr. Berry asked what had happened to the hiccoughs, then began loudly laughing. The deception and great fright had cured them. Even though Bosang's hiccoughs were cured, he was never very friendly toward Dr. Berry after that incident. He evidently did not appreciate the mind over matter treatment. Dr. Berry had many friends and many enemies, but the town would never forget him.

Dr. John Keys, who was both a medical doctor and a dentist, offered his services to the town in October 1867. His office was in the old stand of Dr. William N. Vance, next door to Ensor's Drugstore. Among the many Civil War veterans who settled in Bristol during the first five years after the end of that conflict was young Dr. Alfred M. Carter. He was born in Carter County, Tennessee, in 1842, a son of David and Elizabeth Carter and a direct descendant of Governor John Sevier. During the war Carter received a severe leg wound. The army surgeon had recommended that the leg be amputated, but young Carter did not want this to be done and asked his brother to prevent it if he could. It is said that the brother finally stopped the surgeon from

Dr. Alfred M. Carter long served in the medical profession in early Bristol. His second wife was a daughter of the town's first physician.

his purpose at gun point. However, it was necessary to remove a small portion of bone. This piece of bone was kept through three generations of the family and has recently been given to a museum.

When Dr. Carter announced his plans to settle in Bristol, his father bought him a fine new buggy and an extra nice horse. Years later the grateful son told how he drove this buggy to his chosen town through the grandest display of autumn color that he had ever seen (fall of 1868). He used this buggy for years in his Bristol practice.

Soon after settling in Bristol he won the heart and hand of young Charlotte (Chassie) King. She was a daughter of Cyrus King, and granddaughter of the Rev. James King, who once owned the land on which much of the new Bristol was located. She is said to have been a favorite granddaughter of Rev. King. He willed her much personal property and his last home. The home, an English cottage, stood near the northeast corner of present State and Moore Streets. Here the young couple lived for the first few years of their marriage. Later Chassie developed tuberculosis. Dr. Carter, knowing that the dampness of their location was not good for her condition, rented what was later the Bunting house in the 300 block of Moore Street. It was there that Chassie died. Her death was a hard blow for the young physician. Their first two children had died shortly before his wife's death. He was left alone with little Maude. (She was later Mrs. Maude Crymble, mother of the late A. Carter Crymble.) He hired Nannie Zimmerman, orphan of Dr. B. F. Zimmerman, to look after little Maude while he carried on his extensive medical practice. He shortly married this girl, and they moved back to the house at Moore and Main (State). Later he bought the A. Pickens house that still stands at 409 Fifth Street. It was then (1886) a new house, having been built by A. Pickens in 1881.

About 1888 Dr. Carter erected the building that now stands at State and Moore (former site of the King home) and houses Ryland's Jewelry and the Merry-Go-Round. He maintained an office in the building for several years. In 1915 Dr. and Mrs. Carter went to Florida to spend part of the winter. One day while they were fishing from a low bridge that spanned a small stream, Mrs. Carter had need of a pocket knife which she requested from her husband. As he handed it to her, he fell dead at her feet. He was returned to Bristol and buried in the Zimmerman lot in East Hill Cemetery. His widow lived on for several years in the Fifth Street home. Toward the end she spent only summers there, taking up residence in the Bristol Hotel during the winter months. She died in 1937 and is buried by her husband.

A Dr. Stallard, who came here from Yokum Station in Lee County, Virginia, had a brief Bristol practice, beginning in 1869. In about one year he returned to his former home.

BRISTOL DOCTORS, 1870-1900

One of the better known and highly respected doctors of Bristol was John J. Ensor. Dr. Ensor, a son of Thomas Ensor, was born in 1829. He was educated at Washington College and later studied medicine under Dr. A. Jobe at Elizabethton, Tennessee. It is thought that he married Dr. Jobe's daughter, Amanda. Dr. Ensor began his practice in Jonesboro, Tennessee in 1848, at the age of 19 (then said to be the youngest doctor in Tennessee). A year later he moved to Blountville, where he practiced for a little over twenty years. At first spurned because of his youthfulness, he later built a wide and successful practice. During the Civil War he served as a surgeon in the Confederate Army, and for the remainder of his practice his specialty was surgery.

Around 1870 many Blountville residents moved to Bristol. Among them was Dr. John J. Ensor, who arrived April 1, 1870. He and his family first lived on Virginia Hill in the former home of William Powell. Dr. Ensor had not been in Bristol long when he bought a choice home site from John G. King, who had recently inherited a large tract of land from his father, the Rev. James King. This site is located at the southeast corner of Seventh and

This lovely old home at the southeast corner of Cherry and Seventh Streets, Bristol, Tennessee, was built in 1871 for Dr. John J. Ensor, beloved Bristol physician. It now houses Sesco. The columned porch was added in recent years.

Cherry Streets. In the spring of 1871, Dr. Ensor contracted with William H. Smith to build a nice house on the site. This solid brick house was nearing completion in late July of that year. It still stands at 934 Cherry Street and is now headquarters for Sesco. Though Ensor's specialty was surgery, he enjoyed an extensive general practice. He often traveled to distant points of the surrounding area, sometimes spending an entire day and night with a seriously ill patient. A newspaper item of the early 1870s tells of his delivering an 18 pound baby near Bristol. The editor mentioned that this was within two pounds of the nation's record. Old-timers have told this writer that the giant baby grew up to be a very small person! For two or three years in the early 1870s, Dr. Ensor was associated with Dr. H. Q. A. Boyer, who operated Bristol's first civilian hospital in the former Thomas House Hotel.

There were times when Dr. Ensor boarded patients in his home. Often they were patients upon whom he had performed surgery. It is said that his dining table often served as an operating place. It has further been said that during summer months he often performed operations on his side porch because daylight enabled him to see better. A letter is extant from his brother,

David J. Ensor, seeking help for his wife, who apparently had advanced breast cancer. Perhaps it is typical of several letters received by this well-known Bristol surgeon. It is given here:

Ten Mile Stand
Meigs County, Tenn.
September 4, 1884

Dear Brother,

Yours rec'd today. John, I am not willing to risk the life of my wife in the hands of strange physicians. It is a case of highest magnitude to me to place her in hands of those we know nothing about. So you say the treatment previous to the operation and after the operation is very important, and the distance that you would be from her renders it impossible for you to undertake the case. Now the next thing is for her to come to Bristol as I do not intend to risk her life in the hands of strange Drs.

Now what will you be willing to board her for and perform the operation. If you cannot board her, please see Mrs. Shelton and see what she would charge. Please attend to this at once, as a delay would be hazardous. Please get up that money—$100.00—as soon as you can. We had to borrow money to get here. And we have no money yet. Mary teaches Mr. Peak's little ones as they are here yet. And Mr. Peak is making her up a music class, but she will even have to give that up until she is better. Last night in stooping down she struck her breast on the edge of the Piano, and she fainted from the pain, and is extremely weak today. The nipple is drawn under and partly eaten off, and it exudes a little all the time. If you were to see it you might lance it probably for the matter is so thick around the nipple, does not run, only exudes and is very offensive.

Dr. Scruggs, Sweetwater, had a patient and accompanied her to Philadelphia twice—she finally died—so I do not think he would come, besides he is 15 miles off and has a fine large Drug Store to attend to. Would prefer you coming to her going there, but as you could not stay long to attend her after the operation it may be better for her to come there. We will be dependent on that $100.00 to pay our way there and our board in Bristol. So if you cannot raise it all send what you can get in a registered letter as no P.O. for orders at this place.

John, Mary is wilting down rapidly under such suffering. She must have relief; she is wasting away. If she don't get relief soon she will be forced to use morphine to get sleep. So you see how demands are increasing. You would be sorry to see her, and yet she bears it all like a philosopher. This is my language not hers. I want you to know but I need not delineate. You witnessed the suffering of Mandy's mother [Dr. Ensor's mother-in-law]. So please attend to all that you see in this letter at once.

Your brother,
David

P.S. I forgot to mention about my farm, as Mary's suffering reaches so deeply into all the calculating I made about my farming Interest. Yet I am delighted with the prospects before me. In a few years we will be out of debt and independent. Would have been glad if you could have visited us under the circumstances and brought Mandy so you could see that we have a good thing of it. It looks like no end to our misfortunes.

All through this letter there runs the piteous, distressed, even anguished plea of a very devoted husband, to a loved and trusted brother. The ailing woman was brought here, was operated on, but survived only a short while. This writer has been told that she died in the east, upstairs bedroom. (This was the sick room, where boarding patients were kept.)

Rebecca Holmes Wright was still living when this writer arrived in Bristol in 1953. She used to tell a beautiful story of her experience with Dr. Ensor. When she was five years old (1889), she stepped on a broken fruit jar, receiving a severe cut on her right toe. In a day or two the wound developed into a frightful condition. After she had spent a fitful night of terrible suffering, her father went at daybreak for Dr. Ensor. (He lived only three or so blocks away.) She remembered the doctor coming and, after a quick examination, holding a quietly spoken conference with her parents, then returning to her bedside. "Becky," he kindly said, "we have ripe strawberries at our house, and you shall have some with sweet milk today. Your father and mother are going to bring you up and I'll tell Mandy [his wife] to pick some nice ones for you." She remembered that her father carried her to the Ensor home. Sure enough, Mandy was in the garden picking the ripe, luscious berries. The doctor came out with the prettiest little handkerchief all printed with pink flowers. (She remembered the color vividly after sixty-four years.) "Becky, I want you to smell these flowers," he had told her. Then he covered her face and nose with the handkerchief. There was no odor of flowers, but the cloth was saturated with that which sent Becky to slumberland in seconds. And while the little girl dreamed of strawberries and cream, the gangrenous toe was removed. After she awoke the kind doctor held her in his lap and fed her the promised treat. No doubt, his quick action had saved her life.

Ensor's most famous patient was ex-President Andrew Johnson. In 1874 Johnson spent two days with the surgeon, during which time a growth of

Rebecca Holmes, the little girl who dreamed of strawberries and cream as Dr. John J. Ensor amputated her gangrenous toe.

some sort was removed from his back. In order that his well-known patient might have complete rest, Dr. Ensor sent his buggy to Union (Bluff City) and transported Johnson here in the darkness of night. Most of the ex-President's time in Bristol was spent secluded in the sick room (east upstairs bedroom). Two well-known Bristolians were admitted to this room by Johnson's request: Major Z. L. Burson and Charles R. Vance. Both kept their secret well. Dr. John J. Ensor died at his Cherry Street home in 1909.

Coming to Bristol at about the same time as Dr. Ensor was Dr. Matthew Moore Butler. Dr. Butler was born March 2, 1838, a son of William and Elizabeth Gaines Butler (called Uncle Billy and Aunt Betsey by their neighbors). When he was still a young man, his father bought a lot in the 500 block of Main Street in Bristol, Tennessee, and there erected the Famous

Hotel (later Thomas House). The Butler family resided in the hotel, and young Matthew helped in its operation. While so doing he met Dr. R. M. Coleman, who lived nearby. Dr. Coleman, seeing the young Butler's leaning toward medicine, encouraged him to pursue that profession. In 1860 Dr. M. M. Butler began his practice in Bristol. But the Civil War came, and the promising young physician became a surgeon in McDowell's 37th Regiment of Virginia Volunteers of the Confederate States of America. Dr. Butler's moment with fate came after the Battle of Chancellorsville, Virginia, in which the legendary Stonewall Jackson was mistakenly wounded by one of his own men on May 2, 1863. Dr. Butler was called upon to assist in the removal of Jackson's arm. He kept some of the instruments that were used in that operation for as long as he lived.

After the war Butler returned to Bristol, practiced a short time, then moved to Verona, Kentucky, to practice with a doctor with whom he had served in Confederate service. His prosperity there was great, but deep in his heart he knew he would have to return to his beloved Bristol. It was during that time he began sending money to his father to have a fine brick home erected at the corner of Ninth and Anderson Streets.

Dr. Butler returned in 1870 but for some reason did not live in his new home for the first year or so. Instead he lived on the homeplace of his father on Steele Creek, not far from the present Beech Grove Methodist Church. The home was the site of the old Butler mill and tannery, which had been built by the doctor's father, William Fields Butler. After about one year on the old homestead, he moved to Butler Hill, the Anderson Street house (848 Anderson), and remained there the rest of his life. For years he had an office at 7 Fifth Street. Early in life Dr. Butler married Mary T. Dulaney, who was born March 7, 1843. A daughter of this marriage, Lorena Butler, married John I. Cox, who served as Governor of Tennessee, 1905-1907. A son, Joseph Owen, who died April 15, 1879, at the age of twenty months, was the source of the doctor's perpetual grief (see chapter entitled Mortality). Another son was Dr. Charles St. John Butler (1875-1944). Dr. M. M. Butler died August 12, 1913, followed by his wife who died January 9, 1914. Both are buried in the East Hill Cemetery. Their home, Butler Hill, was demolished to make way for the Volunteer Parkway.

Dr. H. V. Gray, a very personable and distinguished physician, came here from Richmond, Virginia, in 1871. He was in some way related to the Martin brothers, early Bristol merchants, and may have been persuaded by them to make this move. He first boarded with Capt. W. L. Martin on Main Street while maintaining an office in Dr. Bunting's Drugstore nearby. In 1872 he moved his family from Richmond, at first renting a house from W. D. Minor on Virginia Hill. In his short time in Bristol, he easily won the respect and

Dr. H.Q.A. Boyer operated Bristol's first civilian hospital, which was located in the Thomas House Hotel in the early 1870s.

confidence of the town, so much so that after moving back to Richmond he long did medical consultations by mail. His move back to his former home was occasioned by failing health. He and his family left Bristol by train in March 1873. Old-timers have said that a great host of his friends followed him to the depot for a mournful parting. He later placed a notice in the paper stating that he would return if his health improved and expressing regrets that he was not able to bid farewell to all his friends and former patients when leaving town. There is no indication that he returned.

DR. BOYER AND BRISTOL'S FIRST HOSPITAL

In early 1873 Dr. H. Q. A. Boyer came to Bristol. He was from Wytheville, Virginia, where he had reached high esteem and success in his profession. He owned considerable property in Wytheville and Mt. Airy (Rural Retreat), Virginia. Soon after moving he advertised that he was permanently settled in Bristol and that he would trade a three-story building in Wytheville and a brick hotel and store house located across from the Mt. Airy depot for Bristol property.

After the death of J. Wheeler Thomas, Boyer leased the Thomas House Hotel, formerly operated by Mr. Thomas, and there in May 1873 opened

Bristol's first civilian hospital. Dr. Boyer advertised himself as one with twelve years experience—a specialist in the diseases of females and children. He assured prospective patients that while they were in his hospital, his wife would see to their comfort and supervise their well regulated diets and that capable nurses would be on duty around the clock. He urged those living at a distance to come and board at the Thomas House while taking treatments, even though not sick enough to require hospitalization, stating that this would be cheaper than having doctors visit them in their homes. He also reserved two or three rooms for hotel guests. But it is not thought that this phase of his business did too well, for no one wanted to take shelter in a building full of sick women and children.

Dr. John J. Ensor assisted Dr. Boyer in the operation of this hospital. He possessed great surgical skills and was often needed for that purpose among Boyer's patients. For some reason, these operations were performed in a small building that stood in back of the hospital. Elizabeth Pelley, whose mother operated the hospital laundry, remembered seeing a woman being carried on a stretcher through deep snow to the operating room. She remembered that the woman was "taking on" in apprehension of what was to follow.

An indication of how busy that hospital was is shown by the need for daily laundering. The widow Pelley presided in the laundry shed that stood at the side of the little building where the surgical operations were performed. The widow was assisted by her little daughter and an older son. The son was almost constantly drawing water from a large but shallow well nearby, while the daughter stirred the boiling pots. (Most laundry was boiled in those days.) Seventy-nine years later Elizabeth remembered that winter or summer, laundering was virtually a daily task and that she was horrified by the blood-stained sheets that often were sent from the operating room. She further remembered that the sheets, though laundered, usually retained brownish blood stains. Thus, the next patient had to lie down upon salient reminders of past surgical "horrors." But Dr. Boyer did not long remain in Bristol. In the mid-1870s James Thomas, son of J. Wheeler Thomas, resumed operation of the Thomas House Hotel, and the doctor moved on to another town.

OTHER DOCTORS ARRIVE

By May 1873 Dr. J. K. Simmon had set up a treatment center on what is now Anderson Street, across from the Haven of Rest Mission. (The Baptist Female Institute then occupied the site of the mission.) His set up was similar to that of Dr. Boyer, though on a much smaller scale. He, too, advertised as a specialist in the diseases of females. But he also had a department for men "who were afflicted with social diseases." (Sometimes he called them private diseases.) With the rampant immorality in the town, the latter department was ever busy. Though apparently successful, his stay in Bristol was brief.

But the stay of Dr. Simmon was not as brief or perhaps eventful as that of a certain Dr. Mitchell, who arrived in 1874. He also claimed to be a specialist in female diseases and rented the entire upper story of a building belonging to Lewis and Rosetta Bachelor located in the 700 block of Main (State) Street, Virginia side. He quickly gained fame as being the physician who cured the sleeping beauty of Virginia Hill. A certain woman living on Russell Street could hardly stay awake, or so it seemed. Awaking only for food, she would often sleep for forty-eight hours at a stretch. But the apparently very observant doctor made a new diagnosis of her "illness" and the cure thereof. His second trip there he called for a pot of boiling water. When it was ready he announced in a loud voice that the only known cure for such a malady was to dash boiling water onto the face and arms of a person thus afflicted. The pot rattled loudly in his hand. But the patient experienced a sudden and dramatic cure before the remedy was applied. She sprang up and was through and far beyond the back door before the doctor had taken one step toward her bed. After all, she was not the first person who ever sought to evade dreaded responsibility by taking to a bed.

It seems that Dr. Mitchell claimed to be very effective in the treatment of infertility. As strange as it may seem in those days of twelve children for twenty years of marriage, there were still childless couples who desired to have children. Indeed, a childless marriage was then considered to be almost disgraceful. Rumor soon circulated that the doctor was offering an unorthodox remedy in such cases, especially when it was suspected that the husband was at fault. After all, he had fathered ten children in thirteen years of marriage. Alas, the understanding and helpful doctor soon had to quickly flee town, a few jumps ahead of an irate husband who preferred his wife to remain childless than to submit to the remedy recommended by Dr. Mitchell. And the old gentleman who told this to the author over thirty years ago avowed that a line of a yet prominent Bristol family owes its existence to the unorthodox treatment administered by this early, but more or less transient, physician.

Also practicing during the 1870s were Dr. J. A. Murphy, Dr. J. W. Haller, and Dr. William Whitten. Dr. Murphy was noted for his ability to remove skin cancers, with patients coming from near and far seeking his services. It is thought that Dr. Haller lived on Solar Street and maintained an office in his home. Dr. Whitten may have also lived in that vicinity. Dr. A. C. Emhert may have also practiced during the 1870s. Dr. Whitten was noted for his willingness to ride great distances to see the sick. There is record of his having gone some twenty miles to lower Smith Creek and while there discovering a case of smallpox. Upon his return to Bristol, he warned the town fathers to watch the roads and make sure that no one from that area entered the town.

During the first week in July 1875, Bristol welcomed Dr. James Franklin Hicks, who would make a high mark in the medical circles of the city. Dr. Hicks was born January 3, 1827, a son of William Hicks. It is the opinion of this author that the Hickses were from west Tennessee, possibly near Memphis. Dr. Hicks had a brother who owned a large department store in that city. The doctor had long been a visitor to Bristol before he made the move of July 1875. He and his family boarded with Capt. Howe in July of 1874. Perhaps this family, as did so many, fled from the yellow fever scourge of west Tennessee to refuge in Bristol. And apparently he was here briefly in June 1875. On June 15th that year, he bought from J. R. Anderson what the *Bristol News* declared was a grand site for a residence. This lot was sixty feet by two hundred sixty feet and reached from Fifth to Fourth Streets, north of the alley in the first block south of Main (State) Street. (This had been the site of the Anderson barn and truck patch or garden area.) The editor of the *News* commented in usual candid manner that the old barn and stable would have to go, much to the betterment of the town. The price of the choice building site was thirteen hundred and nine dollars.

In the early spring of 1876 Hicks had a Knoxville architect design his new residence. It was constructed of brick, was of the Italianate style, and stood where later was (about 1928) constructed the building of the Tennessee Fire Department, 18 Fourth Street, Bristol, Tennessee. At the same time of the building of his home, Hicks built his office at the opposite end of the lot to front on Fifth Street. He built his carriage house midway between the two and opening on the alley. Between the home and the office was a beautiful flower garden. In it was perhaps the grandest collection of roses in the town. The garden is said to have been the undisputed showplace of downtown Bristol. An old-timer remembered that on one occasion Dr. Hicks had a very nervous and agitated middle-aged female patient. After talking to her a while he opened the back door of his office and told her to go sit in the rose garden for awhile, adding that it would do her more good than all the medicine he could prescribe. One might say that the first tranquilizer in the Town of Bristol was thus administered.

By September 1875 Dr. J. Wister Walke, Jr. was practicing with Dr. Hicks. Nothing further is known of him. On March 23, 1878, Dr. J. F. Hicks paid twelve hundred dollars for the drugstore of D. J. Ensor. The store was on the southeast corner of present State and Fifth Streets and adjoined the Hicks property. It was then that his office was moved to the back of the drugstore. After a long and successful practice here, Dr. Hicks died April 21, 1920, and is buried in East Hill Cemetery.

Dr. Nat T. Dulaney, Sr., formerly of Blountville, Tennessee, was practicing in Bristol by the mid-1870s. He was of a line of distinguished doctors who early settled in and near Blountville. Dr. Nat, as he was affectionately called, had a noted humanitarian disposition and quickly endeared himself to the Bristolians of his time. His home stood in the 500 block of Shelby Street. For years he maintained an office in a room of this home, but later he rented a two-room setup on Fourth Street for that purpose. In January 1875 he was joined in his practice by his brother, Dr. Joseph Dulaney, who lived briefly in Texas but decided to return to his native county. His brother moved into a cottage that stood in behind the Methodist church near the northeast corner of Scott and Lee Streets.

Dr. Dulaney had a son, Nat T. Dulaney, Jr., who also became a doctor and settled in Bristol. For years he maintained an office in an "ancient" building that long stood on the southwest corner of Fourth and Shelby Streets. He was of marked intelligence, having a remarkable insight into human nature. He possessed talent along literary lines, producing some very fascinating manuscripts. One of his books, **Speaking of Accidents,** is still much sought by lovers of common-sense philosophy. Dr. Nat kept no records and sent no bills. His belief was that those who intended to pay would pay. In spite of his laxity in the collections department, he reached a comfortable degree of prosperity. He was married to Lillian, daughter of the noted merchant, H. P. King.

Dr. James A. Dickey came to Bristol from Peach Bottom, Grayson County, Virginia, around 1875. For years he maintained an office at 526 Main (State) Street. His extensive and successful practice was considered especially good in obstetrics. There are a few citizens still living in Bristol who were delivered by Dr. Dickey. Sometimes he admitted his limitations and advised prayer in the place of medicine. When the late A. C. Crymble was a small child, he swallowed a large horsefly, becoming violently ill within minutes. Dr. Dickey, who had delivered the child four years earlier, was called. He soon admitted that he had done all he could do and advised the mother and others to pray. A. C. Crymble lived to the age of ninety-two.

On April 10, 1882, Dr. Dickey bought a lot at 421 Fifth Street (then called College Avenue) from N. B. and Ritter Hays, for which he paid four hundred dollars. He soon built a fine home there that still stands, though much remodeled and added to. Both he and his wife, Kate W. Dickey, died in the home. He did much for Bristol, both as a competent physician and civic leader, once serving as mayor of Bristol, Tennessee.

Dr. W. K. Vance, a son of Dr. William N. Vance, was born May 27, 1852, and by 1879 had commenced his practice with his father. He married Marie Doriot, a daughter of Victor Doriot, and lived at 222 Fourth Street. After a long and successful medical career, he died December 28, 1928, and is buried in the East Hill Cemetery. Dr. Vance made most of his local calls on foot, saying that the exercise was good for him. Some called him "the walking doctor." Dr. F. C. Miles was in Bristol sometime in the 1870s. Nothing further is known of him at this time.

There were physicians here and there across the nation in the 1870s known as "electric doctors," because part of their therapy consisted of treatment by electric current. At least one practiced for a time in Bristol. He was Dr. Thomas Hicks. The editor of the *Bristol News* noted that Dr. Hicks had attended the Electric Medical Institute in Cincinnati, Ohio, and was ready to practice the new art in Bristol. He added that the electrics had shown that they possessed many means of cure that were new. Old-timers told of how Dr. Hicks generated his electricity by turning a crank on a strange looking machine. One of his early patients fainted during the treatment, causing tales to circulate that the machine was dangerous and almost ruining the young doctor's practice here. Nothing further is known of this "electric doctor."

Dr. Joseph Bachman married Hattie, daughter of W. P. Brewer, and lived in the unique and beautiful late Victorian home at 940 Anderson Street, after having lived for some time at 525 Shelby. His office was long located at 13 Lee Street. During the same period came Dr. G. M. Peavler. He was from the old and prominent Sullivan County family of that name. His first office was at 11 Lee Street. He later set up an eye, ear and nose clinic at the northeast corner of Sixth and Shelby Streets, which was patronized by patients from near and far. He built the huge home that still stands at 912 Anderson Street. And across town at 220 East Main lived the only known black doctor at that time, Dr. W. R. Seattle (pronounced Settle), who had an office at 9 Fifth Street.

Anderson Street seems to have been a favorite residential area for doctors. At 932 Anderson lived Dr. Thomas Fain, of the old Sullivan County family of that name. Not too far away at 1203 West Main Street lived Dr. William T. Delaney and his son, Dr. J. A. Delaney. The father and son team long maintained offices at 6 Fifth Street. Not far from the Delaney office was that of Dr. M. M. Pearson at 14 Fifth Street. This block of Fifth seems to have been somewhat of a medical row. Dr. Pearson's old home still stands at 423 Pennsylvania Avenue.

Dr. Robert Edmond Dixon, son of William and Elizabeth Charles Lucas Dixon, born December 26, 1861, in Greenville County, Virginia, practiced briefly in Bristol in the 1890s. He married Victorine Doriot, and the couple lived a while with her parents on Scott Street (site of the present Utilities Board Office). The Bristol medical field was rather crowded at the time, causing Dr. Dixon to move to Handford, California, where he prospered and became a highly respected and beloved citizen. He died there in early 1932.

Dr. W. B. St. John long practiced in the city. He lived at 918 Windsor Avenue and once had offices at 508 Main Street. Old citizens have told this author that St. John strongly believed in the healthful benefits of fresh air, and his office windows would be wide open, even if it were freezing cold outside. Some called him the "overcoat" doctor because one going to him should take a heavy overcoat in order to endure the rigors of an ice cold waiting room. His brother, Dr. Matt St. John, also practiced in Bristol.

Other Bristol doctors were Dr. Thomas Halley and Dr. A. S. Kilby. Henry Wood, who long lived at 112 Solar Street, had an M.D. degree but never practiced. Dr. Hardin Reynolds practiced briefly, then became a leading businessman. And Dr. J. G. Berheike practiced a short time around 1893. While in Bristol he rented a house from Mrs. John C. Anderson. And living well after 1900 was the early Bristol doctor, Nathan H. Reeve, who was born February 20, 1847, and died in 1924. There likely were other Bristol doctors of the period covered, but the author has no record of them.

BRISTOL ACADEMY OF MEDICINE

In 1875 most of the Bristol physicians were organized into what was at first called the Bristol Academy of Medicine. By 1893 the name had been changed to the Bristol Medical Society. Doctors whose names appear in the records of this group include Dr. W. N. Vance (the first president), J. S. Bachman, Nat T. and Joe Dulaney, W. T. Delaney, M. M. Butler, J. F. Hicks, J. A. Templeton, J. J. Ensor, J. W. Haller, W. B. St. John, A. C. Emhert, C. T. Pepper, M. M. Pearson, G. M. Peavler, N. H. Reeve, J. A. Murphy and perhaps others.

The Society met monthly either in a member's home or office. The principal object was "the advancement of knowledge upon all subjects connected with the healing arts." Other objects were "the elevation of the character and interests of those engaged in the practice of medicine, and the regulations of fees charged for services." At each session a member was assigned an essay to be read at the next meeting. If he failed to deliver, he was fined $2.00. Dr. N. T. Dulaney once spoke on "Blood Letting as a Remedial Agent." Later, Dr. J. J. Ensor spoke on "Electricity." (This was when the "electric doctors" were becoming popular.)

In the matter of interests of the profession the Society once prepared a list of "deadbeats"—described as local residents who could but would not pay their bills. It further seems that the Society was somewhat of a lobbying group. It succeeded in having the city release doctors from taxation "due to their large amount of pauper practice." When the telephone company refused to lower residential rates for the doctors, their home phones were removed (1893). Later the phones were put back in at the rate of $15.00 per year. And the Society went "claw, tooth, and nail" after a Dr. Herben of Chicago who set up at the Nickels House and advertised a sure cure for cancer without pain or the knife. One of the doctors, posing as a sick patient, received a positive cancer diagnosis of a simple corn on his foot. He was promised certain cure for only ten dollars. But before the Society could decide upon a course of action, the "doctor" suddenly packed up and left town. It was thought that he had learned of the "trap".

At a meeting of the Society held in the office of Dr. J. A. Templeton on July 5, 1879, Dr. M. M. Butler was elected president with W. T. Delaney as vice president. Dr. Templeton became secretary, with Dr. C. T. Pepper as treasurer. Dr. W. N. (Nick) Vance was chosen as the critic. The annual address that year was by Dr. Vance, and Dr. N. T. Dulaney was to speak at the next annual meeting. It appears that the Bristol Medical Society disbanded about 1894. One of its last acts was to set the fee for the amputation of an arm at fifty dollars. Dr. Joseph Bachman was the last survivor of the Society.

EARLY MEDICAL COSTS

As compared to today, medical costs to early Bristolians were extremely low. A few old account books survive, recording such low charges for professional services as to be almost shocking. In 1856 Dr. R. M. Coleman charged W. W. James one dollar for a visit and lancing of a boil. A year later he charged a patient simply listed as "old man Moon" five dollars for childbirth (presumed for Moon's wife). He allowed Mr. Moon a credit of one dollar for a half bushel of peaches. Another patient was charged thirty cents for extraction of a tooth. But by the Civil War period the charge for that service had reached fifty cents! In late 1870 Dr. John J. Ensor billed William H. Smith two dollars and fifty cents for a visit to three of his children and medicine for them. At about the same time he charged Smith three dollars for setting a broken arm, "and supplying splint for the same." At the same time, Dr. Ensor charged only ten dollars for making a house call for Joel Kaylor who lived near Mendota, Virginia, noting that it was an all night visit. By 1875 Ensor had raised his baby delivery fee from five to ten dollars, and office visits from one to two dollars. During the same period one might see Dr. J. A. Templeton in his office for one dollar, but a house call was two dollars, and a night house call was four dollars. Dr. Templeton was then the official doctor for Sullins College (perhaps because of his reputed saintliness); and a call there, day or night, was only one dollar.

It is apparent that some doctors charged according to ability to pay. One doctor showed a charge of four dollars for a night visit to an affluent citizen of the town; three nights later he charged only one dollar for a visit and medicine for a sick child in a poor section of town. On January 14, 1871, James Appling, a wealthy citizen of Bristol, was charged ten dollars by Dr. W. N. Vance for delivering Mrs. Appling of a male child. A month or so later, a birth in a poor family was four dollars.

As low as medical charges were then, a large part of the pay was often in barter. Dr. Ensor's account book shows that Joel Kaylor of Mendota, Virginia once became indebted to him in the amount of one hundred and thirty-eight dollars. Probably by choice (Kaylor was rather wealthy) sixty-six dollars of this debt was paid in pork. Dr. Coleman once allowed a debtor a credit of one dollar for four chickens. Dr. M. M. Butler was owed ten dollars; he credited the account with two dollars for a sheep, five dollars for one hundred pounds of flour, and three dollars worth of lumber. And Dr. C. T. Pepper once credited a three dollar account with fifty cents worth of blackberries. It is hoped that he enjoyed his blackberry cobbler, for the rest of the account was never paid!

In spite of these low charges, barter payments, and unpaid accounts, most early Bristol physicians enjoyed a good measure of wealth. And most of them possessed the greater riches of the love and respect of a grateful town.

COMPETITION

There was a time, beginning in the summer of 1879, when Bristol doctors had some rather stiff competition. This was not from supposedly superior doctors in nearby towns but from a "faith healer" of sorts who lived in the gap between Kingsport, Tennessee, and Gate City, Virginia. A Bristol couple had gone by buggy to visit the wife's relatives at Gate City (Estillville). When they returned, a portion of the road gave way, causing the buggy to turn over into the rocky creek bed that closely skirted the roadway. The wife received a very painful shoulder injury. A passerby, who came to the aid of the couple, advised that the husband take her to "Dr." Miller who lived within sight of the accident. The couple found "Dr." John Miller in his very humble roadside home. But there was no medicine or surgical tools. Miller simply looked long and intently at the injured shoulder. The woman declared that all the pain and sign of injury faded away. Reaching Bristol, the couple spread the news of the "miracle" all over town. There was soon a "stampede" of the sick and injured, heading for Miller's home. Among the first to go was John N. Bosang, who was feeble and suffering from several ailments. Miller's reputation was greatly enhanced when this well-known old Bristol citizen came home literally turning hand springs in the streets, claiming he was young again and looking for a new wife in case the one he had didn't "last from here on out" as he put it. But he took his wife, who was sick with consumption, to the healer and she came back claiming to be cured.

I. C. Fowler of the *Bristol News* then began to publicize the "cures." It is apparent that he was impressed by the evidence of the power of the strange healer. He wrote of Old George Stoffle, who had long been unable to walk except by the aid of crutches, coming back to town walking briskly with his crutches on his shoulder. And Mrs. Jones, an upright older Bristol citizen, was reported as being free from the rheumatism that had long afflicted her. Fowler reported that Esq. George DeVault was completely cured, though his ailment is not named. Even cancer had been cured for a Mr. Massey, as reported by Fowler. But the case that perhaps touched the town most of all was that of a little daughter of John M. Crowell, who once had been a bright-eyed, cheerful little girl, healthy, robust, and full of play, a darling of the town. Then she had become so afflicted with rheumatism that she could not walk or wear shoes. Her suffering was so intense that she had "faded away" and was thought to be near death. The Crowells placed her on a feather bed in back of a buggy and drove to "Dr." Miller's. Awe and overwhelming joy flooded Bristol when the Crowells came driving back up Main Street, the little girl skipping along and playing with the family dog behind the buggy. She was bright and happy again, and wore blue and white shoes that had been given her by a merchant of Gate City, who had been "completely overcome" by the incident. "There was not a dry eye along Main Street," Fowler stated. "Strong men wept openly."

After this the sick of the town went almost en masse to "Miller the Healer," as he was then being called. Fowler reported that several carriage loads were leaving town early every morning for Miller's at McMullen's Mill. He went on to say that Miller was a poor man, who made no charges for his services, but who would accept small sums as a person chose to give. He further reported that the healer, whom he judged to be about fifty years old, claimed no supernatural powers and that his method of healing was to simply look quietly and intently at the afflicted person. Several of the cured said that they did not know how it happened but knew it *had* happened.

The small sums must have added up. In 1880 Fowler noted that Miller the Healer had removed to Big Lick (Roanoke), where he had built a new home, "being able to pay cash for it," and he practiced his art there. A few local residents traveled by train to his new location, but most returned to the services of the local doctors. And alas, Bosang's restored youth was not perpetual. He died March 31, 1883, an old and feeble man.

CITY OF REFUGE

On at least three occasions during the 1870s, Bristol became a city of refuge for many who fled the yellow fever epidemics of Memphis. Even when Chattanooga, Tennessee, was forbidding eastbound trains to stop in that city, Bristol was welcoming the refugees with open arms. A news item of the period mentioned that at least one hundred refugees were registered in local hotels, and more had to go farther east because there was no more lodging available. A Memphis merchant sought the safety of Bristol in 1879. Near the end of summer he became bored and returned home. But he was too early; within a week he had contracted the fever and died. Though there is no record of any of these patients bringing the fever to Bristol, the local doctors enjoyed increased patronage while the numerous guests were here. Most of them were of the wealthier class and were health conscious, thus making good and frequent patients. But there were times when the health refuge was not so hospitable. When there was smallpox at Benhams (1870s), the local doctors advised the city officials to place guards on the roads leading from that village to Bristol to see that no one from that area entered the town. There were similar actions when epidemics threatened in other nearby areas.

THE HEALERS - PART TWO

DENTISTS - DRUGGISTS

During Bristol's first forty-eight years (1852-1900), there were but a few dentists. Perhaps one reason for this was that virtually all medical doctors pulled teeth, which was then the principal work of dentistry. Few people bothered to have fillings or other repair work done, and the occasional set of dentures made did not provide sufficient income for the full-time practice of dentistry. Consequently, two or more of Bristol's earliest dentists were also regular physicians.

The first known Bristol dentist was Dr. John Keys, M.D., D.D.S., who was practicing by 1860 and perhaps a little earlier. Though a regular M.D., he confined his practice to dentistry. His first Bristol office may have been one formerly occupied by Dr. B. F. Zimmerman, located near the present northeast corner of State and Lee Streets. By 1869 he had moved directly across the street and next door to Ensor's Drugstore. Dr. Keys was born in Virginia, cir. 1829, as was his wife, Mary J. Keys. His wife and several children are buried in East Hill Cemetery.

The second dentist to open an office in Bristol was Dr. L. M. Hall, who was practicing by 1862. It appears he did not remain long though he was still in Bristol as late as September 1865.

In 1866 Dr. H. M. Grant, M.D., D.D.S. of Abingdon, Virginia, advertised that he would practice dentistry in Bristol on Tuesday and Wednesday of each week. His local office was next to Ensor's Drugstore (400 block of present State Street—Tennessee side). A little later he moved his office to the 500 block of Main (State), Virginia side. Dr. Grant, a former professor in the Baltimore Dental College, operated a dental school in Abingdon, Virginia, where he also maintained a laboratory. In his solicitation of students for the school he cautioned that all applicants must give proof of moral habits and general character. When the Southern Dental Association met in Richmond, Virginia, on August 2, 1872, Dr. Grant was elected president of this group. Dr. Grant practiced in Bristol as late as 1881.

By the late 1860s Dr. A. J. Dunn had opened practice in this city. He advertised that he was a resident dentist and could be found in his office on Thursday, Friday, Saturday and other days when not visiting nearby towns. In 1879 Dr. Dunn sold his practice to his son, Dr. James W. Dunn. The latter long practiced in an office upstairs over King and Hills Book Store, 400 block of Main (State), Tennessee side.

In January 1873 Dr. J. H. Scales, D.D.S. opened offices over the Bunting and Pepper Drugstore, Main Street, Bristol, Tennessee. Old-timers remembered him as a kind, patient, easy-going practitioner who seemed to dread to inflict pain upon his patients. He often went to the homes of the patients after their visits to see how they were doing. On one such occasion he spent the night in the home of a patient who was bleeding badly from an extraction done a few hours before.

By September 7, 1875, Drs. Wilbar and Atkins had opened offices in Bosang's Block, over Yarbrough and Wood's Store. They guaranteed satisfaction to their patients and solicited those who had "suffered fearful experiences" with other dentists. It is thought that such fearful experiences were common in those days. Dr. Wilbar was of the family of that name who very early settled in Bristol.

About 1878 Dr. Samuel W. Rhea opened his dental practice in Bristol. His first office was on Main (State) Street, the first door west of J. W. Rogan and Company. A little later (1879) he moved to the 500 block of Main Street, Tennessee side, next to the J. P. Farris store. During those early years he served Blountville, Tennessee on the first and third Monday of each month. An elderly lady living in Bristol in 1954 told this writer of a time when Dr. Rhea had a strange and unwelcome visitor in his office. By that time (about 1885), he had moved his office upstairs over a store that stood about where Ball Brothers is now located (500 block of State Street). A wide and gently rising stairway led up from the street level to his office, which was on the left, and a photography studio on the right. This lady, then a girl of ten or so, was in the doctor's chair having a tooth pulled (she called it "drawn") when the strange visitor arrived. A horse was loosely tied below at the hitching rail. A prankster, perhaps having looked for an unattended and loosely tied animal for days, threw "high life" on the, until then, docile horse. (High life is a very potent, fiery chemical.) Likely the prankster expected to see a bucking and kicking race down Main Street. But when the chemical took effect—some say it is like a coal of fire burning into the flesh—the horse broke loose, lunged forward, plunged through the stairway doors and raced upward with a tremendous jarring, crashing noise. At the head of the stairs, the frenzied beast chose to visit a dentist rather than a photographer, for he turned left and lunged into Dr. Rhea's outer office, just "snorting, and kicking a circle, and spreading a sight of filth," as the elderly lady expressed it long ago.

This little girl had opened wide, and the tooth was about half pulled when she was suddenly yanked from the chair, and both she and the dentist landed on the porch roof beyond an open window. Her mother, who was in the outer office, took refuge in a closet. The maddened horse had about wrecked the office before the potent chemical lost its sting. Then it took a dozen or so men to get the horse back down to the street. Dr. Rhea finished the job on a bench in the hall of the building.

Within a short time he set up a new office at 418 Main Street, where he remained for several years. In 1897 he was still at that location and was then residing at 325 Sixth Street. The doctor was of the distinguished Rhea family who settled in Sullivan County, Tennessee, in the latter part of the 1700s.

In 1881 Dr. George E. Wiley, D.D.S. was practicing with Dr. H. M. Grant. Dr. J. M. King had opened his practice of dentistry by 1881. He was a son of the noted Rev. John R. King, for whom the Kingtown area of Bristol was named. His mother was Elizabeth Thomas of the Cold Spring area of Sullivan County, Tennessee. At first Dr. King practiced in Bristol the first nine days of each month, then he set up at Union (Bluff City, Tennessee) from the tenth through the sixteenth. The remainder of the month was spent in Johnson City. His Bristol office was at 600 Main Street. In time he built a fine home at 534 Alabama Street, which stood until recent years. Dr. King was twice married and still has descendants living in Bristol.

In May 1889 Dr. Frank Sproles, then twenty-six years old, arrived from Radford, Virginia, where he had practiced briefly before coming to Bristol. All that is known of his family is that his wife was a sister of John Pettyjohn. By 1897 Dr. Edward T. Jones offered his dental services to the city. He was then boarding at 308 Moore Street. Nothing further is known of him.

EARLY DENTAL COSTS

Fifty cents for pulling a tooth seems to have been the standard price among the early medical doctors of Bristol. And for several years dentists stayed in line with this charge. A receipt is extant where Dr. H. M. Grant charged fifty-one cents for the pulling of a tooth for Hannah, servant of G. W. Blackley. Why the odd cent was placed on this bill defies explanation. There are old records showing that extractions were done for as little as twenty-five cents, but this seems to have been done in consideration of the very poor.

In the 1870s a set of dentures went for five to seven dollars. By the 1890s the price had gone up to a staggering $10.50; a little more was charged if one wanted the front teeth to be gold covered or outlined. Just before 1900 the Modern Dental Parlors, located on the second floor of the Bower Building that stood on Sixth near Main (State), published the following price list:

Silver fillings	$ .50
Gold fillings	1.00 and up
Gold crowns, 22k	4.00
Bridge work	4.00
Porcelain crown	3.50
Painless extraction	.25
First class dentures	10.50 and up

As with medical doctors, dentists were sometimes compelled to receive payment in barter. On December 10, 1874, Dr. A. J. Dunn noted that Mrs. Sicily Solomon, James Street, had paid her denture bill of $7.00 with a feather bed and blanket. Perhaps he envisioned a very cold winter ahead! The same amount and for the same purpose was credited to John Dailey for painting Dunn's carriage house. And Daddy Thomas once told this writer that around 1882 he had carried a hen under each arm when he went to Dr. Rhea to have a tooth pulled. The hens were valued at twenty-five cents each and fully paid the fifty cent fee for extraction. One wonders where Dr. Rhea parked the chickens until time to go home!

DENTAL SATISFACTION

Not all patients were fully satisfied with dental work, especially with the "operation of dentures." One man complained that his wife's new set of "false teeth" fit so poorly and were so painful that she could only endure them for church services, when visiting or receiving visitors, and when she sat for the photographer (surely not very often); and she had to take them out in order to eat! A local politician may have complained, too, after his were "blown out" and went sailing through the crowd during a fiery oration. Editor Fowler reported that this caused considerable mirth in the audience and was a welcome relief from the speakers' "loud but senseless harangue." A few years later Fowler wrote of a Mr. Oney who had received a large filling at the hands of a local dentist. But the filling had been lost during the first meal—swallowed it was supposed—and it was wondered what might result from swallowing such a large bit of metal.

John Bosang once told of having such a bout with pain after an extraction that he had to arise from his bed and go through cold and snow to a neighbor's for a quart of liquor, most of which had been consumed over the next two days, and yet much pain remained. On the other hand there was the testimony of the legendary Rosetta Bachelor, given in support of the services of Dr. George E. Wiley (1882), that with her new dentures she could again chew her much loved peanuts and that she no longer had to cut apples into small bites as she had formerly had to do with an earlier set of "false teeth." And George Harmeling stated that a filling put in by Dr. J. M. King was far less painful than one put in earlier by an unnamed local dentist.

EARLY BRISTOL DRUGGISTS

Dr. R. M. Coleman opened Bristol's first drugstore in late 1855 in a small brick building that stood on the southeast corner of present Fifth and State Streets. The building was owned by Joseph R. Anderson. About 1860 David J. Ensor took over the operation of the drugstore and thus became the second druggist in the new town. David Ensor came from Blountville, Tennessee. He was a brother of the noted physician and surgeon, Dr. John J. Ensor. In 1862 Ensor purchased the location of his drugstore from Anderson. He continued to operate his business until the mid-1870s, when he sold it to Dr. J. F. Hicks.

Meanwhile, around 1870 he had built his home near the southeast corner of present Locust and Seventh Streets on lots purchased from John G. King. The house, a large two-over-two with ell structure, now forms the oldest portion of the present Weaver Funeral Home. Around 1880 Ensor suffered severe financial reverses. He later moved to Meigs County, Tennessee—he was there by 1884—where he engaged in farming.

The firm of Thomas and Campbell operated an early Bristol drugstore, but the author has no further information concerning this business. In the late 1850s the "medical family" of Pepper (virtually all of them were in the medical professions) arrived here from Wythe County, Virginia. By October 19, 1866, and possibly long before that date, Drs. C. T. and J. G. Pepper had bought out Thomas and Campbell and were operating a drug business on Main Street in Bristol, Tennessee. It appears that this Pepper Brothers Drugstore was located about where the western portion of Ball Brothers Furniture now stands. The firm operated until 1875.

Dr. Jeremiah Bunting came from eastern Virginia to Bristol in 1869. He had been in charge of the drug department of the Confederate States of America during the Civil War. He opened a small drugstore in a building that stood on Front Street and was owned by W. W. James. A few years later he was associated with Drs. William H. and C. T. Pepper in the firm of Bunting and Pepper, Druggists. By 1881 Bunting had associated himself with John R. Dickey in the firm of Bunting and Dickey. This store was located at No. 6, James Block. By October 24, 1885, Dr. Bunting had associated himself with a Dr. Wallace in the firm of Bunting and Wallace. At a later date Bunting's enterprise had become Bunting and Son. Later in the century the store was moved to the 400 block of Main (State) Street, in Bristol, Tennessee, where it remained until the building was demolished in 1983.

After the death of Dr. J. G. Pepper in 1875, his administrator, J. R. Hill, sold his stock to John R. Dickey and a Mr. Wester of Grayson County, Virginia. By March 23, 1876, the firm of Dickey and Wester, Druggists,

This much remodeled house at 332 Sixth Street was built about 1875 for Dr. John Givens Pepper, who died before it was finished. It was long the home of Uncle Billy Wood, last survivor of the youth cadets who fought in the Battle of New Market. It is now the office of Dr. J. L. McCord.

was operating at the sign of the golden eagle, Main Street, Bristol, Tennessee. But this partnership was short lived; by September the firm had become Dickey and Wright. John R. Dickey continued in the drug business for several years, finally manufacturing various medical preparations. Among the most famous of these was Dickey's Old Reliable Eye Wash, which he began making and selling in the late 1870s. Dickey was once associated with Dr. J. F. Hicks, from whom he procured the formula for his famous product. It remained on the market for a century or more.

John R. Dickey was twice married. His first wife was Sarah James, daughter of the prince merchant W. W. James. He married the Bristol belle on April 5, 1881. Not long afterwards he built a fine home on Main (State) Street, between Washington and Virginia Streets, Bristol, Virginia, on the lot where Bristol's first hotel had stood. It is said that the Dickey home had the second bathroom in the city. (The first was at the Fairmount Hotel.) After the death of his first wife, he married Julia Hoffman, a music teacher at Virginia Intermont College.

Dr. Dickey died in October 1923 after a long and successful career as a druggist, drug manufacturer, real estate developer, and church and civic leader. He is buried in the East Hill Cemetery. He was a loyal native Virginian. When his grave was dug, it was discovered by a family member that the opening was being made in Tennessee. The workmen were instructed to move over a few feet and begin anew. "Daddy would never rest on Tennessee soil," they were told.

In the mid-1870s Dr. J. F. Hicks bought David J. Ensor's Drugstore. The store, located on the southeast corner of present State and Fifth Streets, adjoined the home and office property of Dr. Hicks. For a time John R. Dickey was associated with Hicks in this operation, under the name of Hicks-Dickey and Company, Druggist. It is not known how long Dr. Hicks continued operation of this drugstore. By 1881 the City Drugstore had opened under the ownership of Dr. James A. Dickey. Dr. Dickey, a brother of John R. Dickey, hailed from Peach Bottom, Grayson County, Virginia.

In 1889 a Bristol drugstore was founded that is still in operation today. C. C. Minor opened the business on the old drugstore corner (southeast corner of State and Fifth). At first the firm was known as Williamson and Minor. Later the store was moved to the present site of Pendleton's Jewelry (525 State Street). Later it was moved to the southwest corner of Sixth and State, and then to its present location at 8 Sixth Street, Bristol, Tennessee. It is not known when C. C. Minor and J. L. Williamson dissolved their partnership. Late in the century Rives Walker opened a drugstore under his name at 507 Main (State) Street. He built his home at 208 Johnson Street in the mid-1890s. The house still stands and is now occupied by the Odell family.

Benjamin C. Cochran, Druggist, located his firm at 537 Main (State) Street around 1895. For several years he rented the old Wood home (Pleasant Hill) at 214 Johnson Street, Bristol, Virginia.

In 1897 Dr. Samuel Evan Massengill began the manufacture of drugs in Bristol. For a time his brother Norman Massengill was associated with him in the business. Within a half century Massengill's company had become one of the largest drug manufacturing firms in the United States. It long was housed in a sprawling plant along the east side of the 500 block of Fifth Street (old campus of King College) and continued in business until recent years.

VARIED STOCK

It is a common misconception that early drugstores sold only medicines. In early Bristol, as now, those establishments tended to be variety stores. In October 1866 Pepper Brothers, Druggists, advertised that in addition to medicines, drugs, chemicals and patent medicines, they carried paints, oils, dyes, varnishes, varnish brushes, paint articles, coal oil, coal oil lamps, lamp chimneys, lamp fixtures, cigars, tobacco, stationery and numerous other articles. The trend continued through the remainder of the century, with even a wider variety of goods being offered in the 1870s, '80s and '90s. Indeed, it seems that the early drugstores were, and long remained, the principal suppliers of paint, window glass and other building materials. One drugstore is known to have offered a limited stock of clothing (Hicks, 1878). As a special for May 10, 1881, Dickey's Drugstore offered Dandrufuge, a preparation to clean the scalp and prevent hair loss. It sold for twelve cents per bottle. In 1874 Dr. J. G. Pepper sold Atmospheric Odorator that seemed to be very much like modern deodorant sprays. He recommended it for use on trunks, wardrobes, parlors or even on self! The latter use was likely very much needed in those days before showers or bath tubs! The price was fifty cents. Another popular item was hair dyes.

Most of the early druggists announced to the public that they would fill prescriptions at any hour of the night and would deliver if necessary. Sometimes doctors who owned drugstores would ride back for more or stronger drugs, if they felt it to be necessary. The late Amy Wisdom told of being eleven years old and walking through deep snow on a very cold night to the home of Dr. J. G. Pepper on Main Street to secure needed drugs for her sick widowed mother. The Wisdoms lived far out on Fifth Street, making a long and tiring walk for a child of such tender years. But she didn't have to walk home. The kind Dr. Pepper saddled a horse and delivered both the child and the medicine to the Wisdom home. And Aunt Amy used to smile and say that it must have been good medicine, for her mother fully recovered and lived to be one hundred and one years old!

Bibliography - Chapter Nineteen

Anderson, Melinda King. As told to her granddaughter, Mrs. Herman Blackley, 1890-1908.

Anderson, Rhea. Notes.

Bachelor, Ann. Memoirs (unpublished), 1855-1870.

Bristol News. Various issues, 1857-1881.

Bristol, Virginia-Tennessee. *City Directory,* 1896-1897.

Crymble, A. Carter. Data supplied to author. (Kingsport, Tennessee)

Dulaney, Dr. Nat, Data supplied to Hattie King Taylor.

Johnson, L. F. Memoirs (unpublished), cir. 1893.

Palmer, Joseph B. Diary (unpublished), 1855-1876.

Phillips, V. N. (Bud). Numerous interviews.with Bristol citizens, 1953-1956 and 1986-1990.

Sullivan County, Tennessee. Census Records, 1860 and later.

Washington County, Virginia. Census Records, 1860 and later.

Washington County, Virginia. Chancery Records, 1853-1900.

Chapter Twenty
MORTALITY/CEMETERIES

The Bristol pioneers were mortal. Then, as now, death was an ever present, irresistible, and inevitable reality and was no respecter of persons. Young or old, rich or poor, known or unknown, mortality triumphed and they are no more. Some, like the last roses of summer, lingered on and on, even well into this century; but one by one the Bristol pioneers fell away until none remained. There are a few elderly Bristolians who have faint memories of the pioneers who lingered longest; and strangely, two or three children of a pioneer still live. But they, too, shall pass; and that first generation will be known only by what is written of them.

The first death to occur in the new Town of Bristol was unexpected, devastating, and of far-reaching consequences. Dr. Benjamin Frederick Zimmerman had just completed a fine new home and detached office in the 400 block of Main (State) Street in Bristol, Virginia (before that side of town became Goodson). He had a bright future and was expected to be an asset to the developing town. The doctor, then thirty-three years old, rode through a cold rain to see a patient at Paperville. Before his return the rain turned into sleet and snow, and the ride home chilled him to the bone. Reaching home late at night, weary and becoming ill, he went to bed and never arose. Gradually becoming worse, he died at dawn, November 11, 1854. He was first buried in the old Oak Grove (commonly called Shelby) Cemetery near the present intersection of Fifth and Shelby Streets, but in 1871 he was moved to East Hill Cemetery. Thus he, who had come to the town to resist the grim reaper, was himself cut down at a young and promising age.

The next known death in Bristol occurred in late January 1856. A free black man had rented a small house (described as a shack by Ann Bachelor) from Col. Samuel Goodson. The house was located at the north end of Washington Street. The wife of the man went into labor on a bitterly cold and snowy night. (Ann Bachelor described the weather as being near blizzard condition.) Rosetta Bachelor, a newcomer to the town and a noted midwife, was called. She braved the blowing snow and cold to assist in the birth. Ann Bachelor stated that she and her foster father, Lewis Bachelor, went with Rosetta to make sure that the journey was made in safety. A male child was born shortly after midnight. Rosetta sat up the rest of the night holding the baby before a blazing fire to keep the newborn infant from freezing to death. But the baby suffered from critical health problems and died about daybreak.

The bereaved parents were new in town and had no friends. Lewis Bachelor and the father dug a shallow grave in the frozen earth under a huge walnut tree that stood near the present northwest corner of Mary and Goodson Streets. Rosetta placed the body in a small trunk, the only thing available for a coffin, and bore the substitute coffin on her shoulder through yet swirling snow and bitterly cold winds to the burial site. For years afterwards she often lamented the fact that the baby had been buried without a song or a prayer. The baby buried so long ago without the benefit of religious rite now has many hymns and prayers over his grave every Sunday, for the Lee Street Baptist Church has arisen like a shrine over his long lost burial place. And now Rosetta Bachelor's long lament may end.

The third known death in Bristol was that of Mastin J. Ayers, who early moved here from Bedford County, Virginia. On September 1, 1856, Mr. Ayers had contracted with Joseph R. Anderson for lot 161 in the plan of the original Town of Bristol, Virginia (Goodson at the time of the contract). He built a dwelling and other improvements on the lot. All seemed to be going well for this man and his young family until May 9, 1857, when he came down with what Dr. Flavius Hartman diagnosed as cramp colic but which was likely appendicitis. His condition worsened through the night, ending in death near sunset on May 10, 1857. Mastin J. Ayers left his widow, Susan L. Ayers, and seven children. The children were all under the age of eighteen. It is thought that the widow lived on for a time in their Bristol home, located just east of the present Ryland's Jewelry, but later took her family and went back to Bedford County. Mr. Ayers was first buried in the Oak Grove (Shelby) Cemetery but was later moved to the City Cemetery (now East Hill).

Not many weeks after the death of Mastin J. Ayers, a railroad workman was murdered just above the old depot. Thus, the town's fourth death was by the worst of violence. (See the chapter entitled Law and Order.)

An early infant death in Bristol was of the same family in which the first had occurred. B. F. Zimmerman, Jr. was born May 29, 1855, something over six months after the death of his father, Dr. B. F. Zimmerman. He was a bright-eyed, handsome little boy, called Benny by his family and friends. He became ill in May 1858 and died the day after his third birthday (May 30, 1858). L. F. Johnson wrote of carrying the small coffin on his shoulder from the Zimmerman home to the nearby Oak Grove Cemetery for burial. The body was moved in 1871 to the East Hill Cemetery (then called City Cemetery).

So before Bristol was scarcely more than an oversized village, the grim reaper had asserted his relentless and supreme reign over its inhabitants and so continues today.

SO SWIFT THE REAPER

While there were often long lingering illnesses before the triumph of the grim reaper, on occasion the dread sickle swung with unusual swiftness. It was so with Mrs. Elizabeth Wood Nickels, wife of I. A. Nickels of the Nickels House, and a sister of the five noted Wood brothers. Her death on April 24, 1873, was totally unexpected and a great shock to the town. The *Bristol News* of April 29, 1873, tells the grim story:

A few minutes before her death she stepped into her chamber and was met by the maid who was passing out, and who observed nothing wrong with her. In a few minutes she called to her sister in a manner which gave alarm, and sank back upon the bed saying, "I am gone, try and save me." Drs. Vance and Pepper were immediately summoned, but every effort to resuscitate her was fruitless.

The death rate among infants and children of early Bristolians was very high. These two little sisters, daughters of John G. King, died within a few days of one another in 1857.

Mrs. Nickels is buried very near the highest point in the East Hill Cemetery.

Col. Samuel E. Goodson, who figures prominently in early Bristol history and the history of this area, spent the last four years of his life in the home of Joseph W. Owen, who then lived on Mary Street near the railroad overpass. He was then old, weary and failing. But almost daily, when the weather permitted, he walked down through an area of old Goodsonville to sit on a stone wall near the present John Wesley United Methodist Church (Scott and Lee Streets). There he often remained for hours, just looking out over the town or gladly visiting with anyone who might pass by. January 30, 1870, was an unusually mild day for mid-winter. Goodson took advantage of the pleasant day to walk again to his favorite sitting and visiting place. He had seemed unusually well the previous several days, and four days earlier he walked all the way to G. B. Smith studio on Main Street and had his only known photograph made. Philip Rohr, who lived nearby, came to sit on the wall with him. While in the midst of a cheerful conversation, Goodson suddenly gave a low sigh and sank backward. Others were summoned and someone provided a quilt from which to fashion an improvised stretcher to bear the stricken man to the Owens home. A nearby resident, John E. Burson, assisted in this task. As the man was being carried across the intersection of Lee and Edmond Streets, he apparently suffered another, much more severe, stroke. John E. Burson told that Goodson had been able to speak a few words up to that point, but when stricken the second time he became totally unconscious, never speaking another word. He died at 1:00 A.M. the following morning, Monday, January 31, 1870. The grim reaper had so swiftly swept away a beloved citizen that many in the town knew nothing of his sudden illness. Bristol business came to a standstill for his funeral and burial. The rich and poor followed him to his final resting place in East Hill Cemetery.

Ann James, a maiden sister of the prince merchant, W. W. James, sitting and talking with him on a bench in front of his store, complained that she had suddenly been stricken with an excruciating headache. In moments she was gone.

Though discretion will not permit the mention of his name, a very prominent businessman and scion of one of the elite pioneer families of Bristol dropped dead in a room of a locally notorious house of ill fame on May 7, 1884. Then as now, the dread sickle often swung where and when least expected.

DEATH BY ACCIDENT

Accidental death was by no means unknown during the formative years of Bristol. Indeed, it was by this means that the dread sickle often swung in its most unexpected, sudden, and tragic forms. The first known accidental death to occur was in mid-October 1859. On a bright but windy autumn day, Mr. Bibb, father of Thomas Bibb (one of the first settlers), took a basket and strolled up to what is now the northwest corner of Goodson and Mary Streets where a giant and heavily laden walnut tree stood. This was the tree under which the newborn had been buried as mentioned earlier in this chapter. While he was busily engaged in picking up the fallen nuts, a large limb fell from the tree, striking Mr. Bibb in the back of his head. A family member found him about sundown. He was lying face down, the heavy limb still across the back of his head, evidently having died almost instantly. He is buried in an unmarked grave in East Hill Cemetery.

On August 31, 1873, a heavy thunderstorm struck the Virginia Hill section of Bristol, where the Trammels lived on Russell Street. Miss Dolly Trammel, daughter of Jack Trammel, hastened to a side porch to place a metal downspout into a water barrel, the common means of catching extra water in those days. Just as she took hold of the metal spout, a fearful bolt of lightning struck, killing her instantly. The editor of the *Bristol News* interjected into his story of this incident the admonition never to do this dangerous thing. Perhaps his warning saved other lives.

On a crisp December morning in 1880, hog killing was being done at Campbell's Grove, where the Athens Steak House now stands. A child fell backward into a pot of scalding water. As word spread, virtually every doctor in town went of his own accord to see what could be done for the dreadfully suffering child, but to no avail. Mercifully, death came in mid-afternoon.

In 1875 Uncle Will Smith was building a brick home for Dr. J. G. Pepper at what is now 332 Sixth Street. By late January the second story joists had been laid but no flooring had been put down. Late one afternoon, Dr. Pepper closed his drugstore, located where Ball Brothers Furniture Company now stands, and walked the short distance up to the construction site. While there he climbed up to the second floor for a closer inspection. Standing on the joists, he lost his balance and fell. He was severely injured by this fall and was carried to his home, which stood at the west side of his drugstore. Dr. Pepper lingered a few days, enduring much suffering. He breathed his last at 12:40 P.M. on Sunday, February 7, 1875. He was buried on Tuesday, February 9th, in East Hill Cemetery, after services at the First Presbyterian Church, of which he had long been a faithful member. In East Hill Cemetery there is a stone, still clearly legible after more than one hundred years of winter's blast and summer's heat and storms. It reads:

John Givens Pepper
Oct. 18, 1828   Feb. 7, 1875

But those who pass by know not of the tragic accident that caused such future promise and cherished hope to be buried there. Mrs. Pepper would never live in the new home; in a short time it was sold to others. It is now the office of Dr. James L. McCord.

An accidental death did not spare the family of the town's founder. On August 10, 1861, a beautiful baby boy was born to Joseph R. and Melinda King Anderson. He became the pride and joy and pet of the family. For some reason he always wanted and was given red shoes. For this reason he was called "Red Shoes" as a pet name. January 3, 1863, was a gloomy day with intermittent rain that became heavy and steady toward late afternoon. But in spite of the inclement weather, relatives of the Anderson family had arrived from Blountville. As visiting was going on in the parlor, little Red Shoes wandered away from the group, through the kitchen at the end of the ell, and onto a side porch. After a while he was missed and a frantic search ensued. Old Mariah Gammon, an ex-slave and longtime cook for the Anderson family, found him. Looking along the back porch, she saw a pair of red shoes protruding up from a full rain barrel. The child had fallen headfirst into the barrel and drowned. He is buried in the Anderson lot in East Hill Cemetery.

The railroad (and particularly the railroad yard) was always feared as a place of sudden, accidental death. From a newspaper account (probably late 1870s) comes the news of such an accident:

> We regret to report the tragic death of young Warwick Appling. He was knocked down and run over by the yard switch engine, at a moment when his attention was drawn elsewhere. Warwick was the son of James A. Appling, and grandson of L. F. Johnson. He was aged 17, and was doing brave work toward support of his father's family. He was taken out from beneath the engine entirely dead.

And through the years there were many deaths connected to railroad operations in this area.

SO SLOWLY SWINGS THE SICKLE

But local deaths did not always come quickly, neither by accident or sudden sickness. Some were doomed to linger and suffer long. On March 22, 1881, the *Bristol News* reported that Mrs. Katherine Echols had died at her home on Virginia Hill, after a long and dreadful bout with cancer of the lower jaw. Ironically, Mrs. Echols had devoted her life to nursing the sick. The *Bristol News* of February 9, 1875, carried the obituary of Mrs. Elizabeth Feldburg, who had died at her home after "a long and protracted illness, at the age of 46 years." Mrs. Feldburg was a native of England, yet while in a town named for an English city, she suffered, far away from the land of her nativity and from family and early friends, but kindly ministered to by golden-hearted Bristolians. And the baby of Mr. and Mrs. R. F. Betterton won the hearts of the town as it bravely battled for six weeks against a disease that usually was fatal to children within three days. Newspapers of the period (1880s) carried weekly reports of this unusual survival and later commented that more people than usually follow the great and well-known made up the solemn procession that followed the baby to the East Hill Cemetery.

J. Wheeler Thomas, longtime proprietor of the famous Thomas House Hotel, suffered for years from a cancer that formed near the inner corner of the right eye and which eventually entirely destroyed that organ. He traveled far seeking relief from this condition. He finally died at Healing Springs, Bath County, Virginia, while taking treatments for his horrible condition. His death, which occurred on February 6, 1873, was due to a severe hemorrhage, which was caused by the cancerous condition and began at 4:00 A.M. on the morning of his death. The body of Mr. Thomas arrived in Bristol by train on Sunday, February 9, 1873; and it is thought that he is buried in East Hill Cemetery.

Not always did the town's well-known escape a slow, lingering death. Capt. U. L. York began his law practice in Bristol shortly after the close of the Civil War. During the next sixteen years he became one of the best known, highly respected, most loved, and wealthiest citizens of the area. The *Bristol News* of August 2, 1881, carried this somber item: "After an illness of more than fifteen months, he breathed his last on July 28th, at 6 o'clock P.M." Capt. York was forty-six years old. He was buried in the East Hill Cemetery, near what was then the main entrance, located between the west gate and the present principal entry.

DEATH BY CHOICE

But there were some Bristolians to whom death was a choice over life. When life became so fearful or trouble-ridden that it could no longer be faced or endured, they purposely sought the sickle of the grim reaper.

In 1874 a lady living on Fifth Street just beyond King College (now site of Beecham Laboratories) sat one night before her fireside sewing. She asked her daughter, who sat nearby reading, to bring a larger pair of scissors. The daughter complied, then returned to her book. In moments the mother stabbed herself in the throat with the larger pair of scissors. Dr. W. N. (Nick) Vance, who lived only a few blocks away toward town on Fifth, was quickly summoned. Upon arrival he found the lady bleeding profusely and struggling for breath. But she had so injured her vocal cords that she could not speak or reveal why she had so suddenly and unexpectedly chosen death over life. She died soon after the doctor's arrival.

W. W. James, Jr., namesake of his father, the prince merchant W. W. James, was a promising young Bristol merchant when pressing financial problems began to sorely oppress him. His father had set him up in a nice new store building on old James row on Main Street. Things went well for a few years. During those good years, he met Miss M. Jennie Fulton, whom he married on April 26, 1881, at Glade Springs, Virginia, at the home of Mrs. Alex Robinson. Soon after this marriage he built a nice high Victorian cottage on Johnson (Johnston) Street, near Cumberland. Three children were born to the happy young couple, though only one survived.

As did most early Bristol merchants, young James made two trips per year to Baltimore, Philadelphia, or New York to purchase stocks of goods for his store. Perhaps he overextended himself creditwise, or maybe business was slack for a season or two. Whatever happened, creditors began to close in on him in late 1887 and early 1888. On March 1, 1888, after spending a restless night, he arose very early, dressed, and started toward his store. On the way he met a well-known local lawyer, who represented one of his creditors. The two talked long, then James proceeded on toward Main Street. After a few steps he suddenly stopped, turned and quickly walked back to his home on Solar Hill where his wife and child were still sleeping. He spent a little time writing, using his wife's spinet desk, then entered an unoccupied bedroom and closed the door.

On March 12, 1888, a still-grieving father penned the following letter to the creditors of his late son:

> Bristol, Virginia
> March 12, 1888
>
> Gentlemen:
>
> Mr. W. W. James, Jr., executed a Deed of Trust or assignment to me for the benefit of his creditors, preferring his borrowed money debts, and then providing for the other debts, which was duly executed and recorded in the Clerk's Office at Abingdon, Virginia.
>
> It is hoped that his effects may pay his debts, but it will require some considerable time to sell his goods and close up his business—but I expect to do the best I can for all concerned, as soon as I can—I regret to say that on the 1st instant, he committed suicide by shooting himself at his home.
>
> Yours truly,
> W. W. James, Sr.

The writing that young James had done on his wife's desk was not the usual farewell note, but was a calmly written obituary of himself, which was used by the local papers and read at his funeral. He is buried near his father in the East Hill Cemetery.

It is well known that there used to be an over-street bridge leading from the depot across to the Virginia House Hotel. One misty, foggy morning in late September 1877, a railroad conductor, walking to the depot from his boarding place on Virginia Hill, was the first to discover the body of a young lady hanging from this bridge. There were no street lights then, and the conductor actually bumped his head on her feet before making the ghastly discovery. It seems that the young woman had a former sweetheart who was then boarding in the Virginia House. The young man had withdrawn his affections and found another, causing the distraught maiden to end her emotional turmoil within sight of his bedroom window.

In June of 1892 a couple living on Goodson Street lost a darling little girl to diphtheria. She was buried in the old section of the East Hill Cemetery. On a warm moonlit night, a short time after this tragic bereavement, the young husband awoke to find his wife missing from the home. A search ensued, but it was not until well after daylight the next morning that the mother was found lying dead across her child's grave. Her husband's pistol was still in her hand.

And why did the young son of a wealthy and well-known Bristol family go to the new Palace Hotel about midnight on August 23, 1889, and rent one of the attic pauper's rooms (twenty-five cents per night)? The clerk, who knew the young man well, was puzzled, but asked no questions. The following morning the mystery was solved. His room was at the back, and from its lofty height he had jumped to his death. His broken, mangled, lifeless body was discovered by a cook coming to work in the hotel kitchen. She still lived in Bristol in 1954. This author will never forget her relating this incident and how she ended with, "Law, honey, when I see'd that man a layin' there all twisted and bloody, I lit out fer the house, and I was plum there afore I knowed what I was a doin'." (The house was over a mile up East State Street!)

BIZARRE DEATHS

The Yerby Cline family lived in a rented house near the end of Railroad Street (later Spencer, now Randall Expressway). The youngest child of this family, a boy named Glenn, was born in 1887. From birth he had violent temper tantrums. When about two years old, something provoked him into one of these marked temper "fits." By then the family paid little attention to him, so they were not much concerned by his screams as he kicked and rolled in the kitchen of their home. But they did become concerned when his screaming and thrashing ended so quickly as to be alarming. Rushing to him, they found him dead. His anger had brought on sudden death at such a tender age. No doubt this strange death caused many a grown person to guard against temper fits in the years ahead.

Bristolians talked for years of the strange death of old Major Z. L. Burson. Major Burson was a very wealthy citizen of Bristol, who was very active in real estate and business ventures for the several decades that he lived in the town. He was almost as well-known for his eccentric nature as he was for his great success in business. He lived in a fine old home at 342 Moore, which was replaced by the brick home of his son, "Hell" John Burson.

As the major began to fail in health he thought much of a brother, then living in California, whom he had not seen for around forty years. Finally he sent this brother a railway ticket asking him to come to Bristol for what he predicted to be their final visit. The brother arrived in Bristol about 4:00 P.M. on September 11, 1894. A son also came home that day. The two received a grand reception at the Burson home. Over the next several hours they enjoyed a great reunion with Major Burson, including a fine supper, prepared and served by Dessie Page, the family cook for many years. At bedtime, Major Burson bade each family member a fond farewell, especially "making over" his little daughter, seeming very reluctant to free her from his tender embrace. Finally he glanced at the clock and stated that when it struck the hour of eleven, he would be gone. He retired to his bed and peacefully died just before the striking of the clock. He is buried in the old cemetery at Jonesborough, Tennessee. His grave is marked by a large and beautiful monument, befitting his high station in life.

Similar to the death of Major Burson was that of Thomas Franklin, who in the autumn of 1877 strolled into town from his Virginia Street home to bid his friends farewell. He stopped at many business houses where he was known, thanking his acquaintances for their great friendship and stating that he would die sometime that day. He spent several hours stopping at such places and also meeting and talking with friends on the street. At mid-afternoon he started home. As he crossed the railroad tracks, he suddenly dropped dead, falling between the rails. He rests in an unmarked grave in East Hill Cemetery.

Perhaps the most bizarre death in all Bristol's existence occurred in late 1883. There was to be a twenty-fifth wedding anniversary supper at the Mary Street home of a well-known Bristol citizen. A husband and wife living on upper Russell Street were invited to the grand affair. The aged father of the husband, who made his home with this couple, was also invited but chose not to go. It was a fatal choice. Before the son and wife left for the supper (scheduled for 9:00 P.M.) the father retired to his bed. The bed was in a little one story side room, over which there was a metal roof, with no ceiling or attic space beneath it. The partying and feasting went on until well after midnight. When the couple returned to their home, they assumed the father was quietly sleeping so did not look in upon him. But next morning he did not arise early, as was his custom. Still, the daughter-in-law had breakfast almost ready when the son, who had become somewhat alarmed by the situation, went to investigate. Opening the door, he discovered one of the most horrifying and bizarre tragedies ever known to have happened in Bristol. There was a gaping hole in the metal roof directly over the bed; there was a large, well-defined hole in the middle of the bed, and one through the floor beneath it. And the man's body had been all but severed by the bullet-like passage of the meteorite as it crashed through his room. Fired like a celestial cannonball from the blue, its target became the back room of that little home on upper Russell Street. Later the floor was removed and excavation revealed that the meteorite had buried five feet into the ground, being stopped by a large boulder. The victim was buried in the Sharrett Cemetery and the meteorite was placed at the foot of his grave, where it remained until it was stolen by a morbid souvenir hunter. And it is said that folks on Russell Street, and likely elsewhere over Bristol, were a little nervous about going to bed for a long time after the incident.

The news of the meteorite was carried by newspapers at various locations over the country. Though the author cannot locate a Bristol paper for the date, a north Florida paper published a rerun of an earlier story twenty years after the tragedy. This paper was picked up in an antique book shop by a Florida friend and has been seen by the author.

A "heavenly" cannonball of about the same size (said to be about the size of a basketball) once plummeted to earth about four feet behind the author's grandfather, as he was plowing in a Johnson County, Arkansas, field. It remains in the family to this day.

The following incident may not belong in a section on bizarre deaths, nevertheless it was indeed a bizarre happening. In May 1883 an early morning thunderstorm became rather violent, especially over the Solar Hill section of town. As a grandmother tried to close a back window, a bolt of lightning struck a large tree only a few feet away. The grandmother fell back on the floor, apparently killed by the close strike. Even Dr. Kilby, who lived only a few blocks away and quickly arrived on the scene, pronounced her dead. After the storm cleared a neighbor was sent to Bickley's shop for a coffin, and other men went up to East Hill to start the digging of the grave. A few hours later the coffin was in her room, ready to receive the body. Neighbor ladies were giving the "corpse" a final bath, and the burial clothes were laid out. In the midst of all of this, the "corpse" suddenly sat up and in puzzlement asked what was going on. In moments, what was going out might have been a more fitting question. The poor grandmother was quickly left alone to complete her dazed recovery. She lived a little over another decade in her Solar Hill home.

OBITUARIES

For decades, editors seemed to reach their height of eloquence when writing obituaries. Those were the days of lengthy and detailed accounts of the dead person's life, accomplishments, and even personal reviews of the final sickness and dying moments. Most obituaries had a rather maudlin slant and usually carried much religious sentiment. Not to have a ''tearjerker'' write-up of a deceased relative was almost considered an insult.

Too, some local editors had a tendency to write what this author calls ''pre-death notices.'' Items such as the following were not at all uncommon in those days:

> John Rencher [the town's first barber] is laying quite low at his home on Main Street. It is not likely nor expected that he will live through this day.

Virtually the same thing was said about Thomas C. Lancaster when he lay very ill in the late summer of 1875. As the end neared for U. L. York, a very prominent Bristol lawyer, a local editor dwelt on the fact that it appeared that the illness that had long afflicted Mr. York was about to triumph over him. ''Doctors hold no hope for his recovery,'' or ''she is not expected to live,'' were very common phrases in local papers of the time. Occasionally the editor might be wrong. Thus a recovered citizen might read the portent of his own death.

It is fitting to record here an obituary of the Rev. James King, who once owned the land upon which downtown Bristol is located. This author has not been able to find a local paper containing such an obituary but did find one that had been clipped from the *Christian Observer* under the date, July 25, 1867. Rev. King left Bristol by train on Monday, July 8, 1867, to visit his daughter and son-in-law, Mr. and Mrs. John G. English, who lived in Egypt, Mississippi. On Sunday morning, July 14, 1867, he died suddenly while preparing to attend church. The *Christian Observer* said this of the passing of Rev. King:

> The Abingdon ''Virginian'' brings the painful intelligence of the sudden death of the Rev. James King of Bristol, Tennessee [he actually lived in Goodson, Virginia, northeast corner of Moore and State], one of the oldest ministers in our church, and one of the noblest, purest,

and best of men. He left his home on Monday, the 8th instant, in company with his grandchildren, to visit his daughter in Mississippi, where he died, of course suddenly, though not unprepared; and his remains reached his late home on Tuesday evening the 16th instant.

Typical of the super-religious type of obituary is that of Mittie Jane Burson Campbell, who died at the home of her father, Major Z. L. Burson, 342 Moore Street, Bristol, Virginia, at 1:00 A.M., September 2, 1873, at the age of twenty-five. She had been the wife of Joseph S. Campbell for around nine months. Mrs. Campbell is buried in the old cemetery at Jonesborough, Tennessee. David Sullins wrote of her:

For some month or two before her death she had a conviction that she would die very soon, and not long before, she told her father that in a trance she had seen Jesus, angels, and her mother and brother Willie, and that her mother said to her ''be of good cheer Mittie.'' Mittie was not afraid to die. She loved her Bible and her church. I find noted in her Bible that she had finished reading the blessed book through three times, ending the last reading just two' months before her death. She has left a kind husband in tears, and her father and family heart sore, under the twelfth death in the household. May Heaven grant them all a place at last, in the house not made with hands, eternal in the heavens.

A little more restrained, but still in the religious-sentimental vein, was the obituary of Mrs. Susan K. Tadlock, wife of the Rev. J. D. Tadlock, who died at her home of Fifth Street, on the morning of September 27, 1875:

She was the mother of eight children, all of whom together with her husband, stood by her dying bed, overwhelmed by the providence which extinguished the light of home. Her health had not been good for some weeks, but it was not until a few days of her death that the family had reason to apprehend any serious danger to her life. Indeed she seemed unconscious herself as to how far the work of death had gone. But once knowing the end was nigh, she gathered up her faith in God and His truth, and calmly resigned all into His hands. Calling her family to her bedside, she addressed a few short, well chosen words to each. She sweetly fell asleep in Jesus, after a loving, trusting life of more than forty years.

Obituaries in those days tended to be very personal, giving intimate details that would now be considered in bad taste. Consider the obituary of J. A. Smith who died July 6, 1879, at the age of thirty-two:

Though in bad health for some time past, his death was unexpected.

His last moments were spent in conversation with his wife. He expressed his gratitude for her unwavering attention and tender devotion during his long illness.... He arose and went to the bed where his children were sleeping, looked sadly and thoughtfully in each face. "My darlings," said he, "some day you will know how much I love you." He again took his place on the bed, talked very rapidly for a few moments, then suddenly he ceased and began to quiver like a reed in water. Then followed a low moan, a few short breaths, then all was over. On Tuesday the 8th, instant, with tears and sadness, kind and devoted friends laid him in the grave, there to await the sounding of the last trumpet.

As did many obituaries of the time, Mr. Smith's contained a poem:

> Then let the last trumpet sound
> And bid our kindred rise;
> Awake ye nations underground,
> Ye saints ascend the skies.

The choice of poetry was perhaps at bit more discriminating for Mrs. Elizabeth Feldburg, mentioned earlier in this chapter:

> I know you have gone to the home of the blest;
> Then why should my soul be so sad,
> I know you have gone where the weary ones rest,
> And the mourner looks up and is glad.
> Where love hath put off in the land of its birth
> The stain it had gathered in this,
> And hope, the sweet singer that gladdened the earth,
> Lies asleep on the bosom of bliss.

Occasionally, and perhaps when the deceased was not overly devout, sentimentality gave way to secular praise. It was so when J. Wheeler Thomas, of the famous Wheeler House Hotel, died on February 6, 1873:

> Mr. Thomas has for many years been one of our most esteemed and useful citizens. As a hotel keeper he had few equals and perhaps no superior in the country. As a citizen he was remarkable for his integrity, high sense of honor, and generous impulses. There was perhaps no one gentleman in Bristol who was more nearly universally respected. The death of such a man is a common misfortune.

Local editors seemed to have a propensity for "pulling out all the stops" when it came to the death of children. And in Bristol they had much opportunity to exercise their talent at sentimentality, for infant and child mortality was appallingly high during that era. Over and over the sad story was repeated in Bristol newspapers; little so and so died yesterday, or last night, or this morning of diphtheria, whooping cough, congestive croup, or perhaps complications of measles. The numerous little stones in East Hill Cemetery stand as salient reminders of the grim outlook for children of a century ago. Often the stones reveal that two or three in the same family died within a few days of one another. The obituary of little Mary Williamson Wood is typical of those written at the death of Bristol children. She was the only child born to M. B. Wood, one of the five well-known Wood brothers who moved from Scott County, Virginia, and his second wife, Mary Williamson of Winston-Salem, North Carolina. The Woods then (1890s) lived at 124 Solar Street, in the house now occupied by Mr. and Mrs. Eddie Canter. And many Bristolians wept as they read their Monday morning paper:

> She is dead. Her young life has gone out. Though not quite twenty-two months old, her little life was a sermon of faith, patience and love to those who knew her. She was the only child of Judge Wood and his present wife. She had a perfect and beautiful form and face, clear penetrating brown eyes, and a steady, frank expression that was at once observed by all who came in contact with her. She had the spirit of a heroine which the world was not permitted to know but angel tutelage will develop around the great white throne. She had cholera infantum followed by flux, finally developing into typhoid fever which lasted for more than three weeks before nature succumbed. The last words she said were, "Good-night, Papa," and in the morning angels answered, "Good morning, Mary." Mother tenderly nursed her on a pillow to rest her weary little body. Death came Sunday morning at 6:30.... It is an inscrutable dispensation of Providence that even little innocent children must go to heaven through pain, suffering, and affliction, but God gave and hath taken away, blessed be the name of the Lord.

The funeral for little Mary Wood was held in the home on Tuesday, following her death on Sunday. She was buried in East Hill Cemetery.

UNDERTAKERS

Bristol's first undertaker was G. H. Mattox, who was practicing his profession by May 1857. Mr. Mattox first had a set-up near the present First Baptist Church. He had a furniture shop where he not only made fine furnishings for the town's homes but also made most of the coffins used to bury the town's dead. (In those days coffins were often called burial cases.) He also offered a line of metal caskets, but they had to be ordered from Lynchburg, Virginia. At first his machinery was powered by horses on a tread wheel. Later he installed steam-powered machinery. By the 1880s he was turning out fine trim for Bristol homes, but was still offering undertaking services. He was a kind, honest, and competent practitioner, but he was more successful in his furniture works than in his undertaking endeavors.

The second undertaker was the legendary and unforgettable Hiriam A. Bickley, who arrived here from Wise County, Virginia, near the close of the Civil War. He secured property on Railroad Street (later called Spencer Street) just north of the present First Christian Church. Soon it became clear that he meant for Bristol to have an undertaking service second to none. Mr. Bickley had a fine black brass-trimmed hearse sent from Baltimore to Bristol. Somewhere he secured three perfectly-matched gray horses and a little pony of the same color.

A few of the older residents still living in Bristol a number of years ago described the grand funeral processions put on by Bickley. He stood six feet two inches tall, and, wearing a black scissor-tail coat, a white lace-front shirt, and a black bow tie, always walked ahead of his horse-drawn hearse. Over his heart he held his black silk top hat. Standing straight as a poker, he never flinched at the rain, snow, or broiling sun, through which, hatless, he sometimes had to go. Behind the hearse came the third horse, riderless, trained to walk with head very low as if bowed in sorrow for the rider he would never again bear upon his back. And the always meticulous Mr. Bickley made sure the saddle was correct: a side saddle for a deceased lady and a regular saddle for a man. If the deceased were a child or youth, the gray pony served the same purpose, always correctly saddled. And he did not forget to have a proper mourning display for babies. In such cases, his wife, who was tall, came with ever so much a sorrowful stance, pushing an empty baby carriage behind the hearse. She was impressive, but the sight of Bickley strutting grandly, followed by the very impressive horses, hearse and whatever else was appropriate, winding through town and up the slope to the East Hill Cemetery, was something rarely forgotten by the town's residents.

And when at last it came time for Hiriam A. Bickley to make his final journey to East Hill Cemetery, A. S. McNeil, at the request of Bickley's family, preceded the hearse in the same manner as had the deceased, holding the old familiar tall silk hat over his heart. Bickley is buried in the large cemetery he helped to fill. His grave is marked by a small and simple stone. But something remains: that old silk hat which so often covered his heart is now a treasured relic in the home of the author.

Captain Augustus S. McNeil, who came to Bristol from Tazewell, Virginia, in the mid-1870s, also served the town as an undertaker. This business was conducted along with a fine furniture store that he operated at 532-34 State

Street (then Main Street). At first he operated in a building rented from W. W. James that stood in the 700 block of Main (State), but prosperity was quickly his, so in 1889 he was able to erect the building that still stands at the before-mentioned address. It is now home to William King Clothiers and Goodman's Jewelry Store. Capt. McNeil served long and well. His family residence still stands at 328 Moore Street. His undertaking establishment was the forerunner of the present Weaver Funeral Home.

While most early Bristol funerals were held in local churches, a considerable number were held in the homes of the deceased. In those days the custom was to hold funerals in the morning (some as early as 9:00 A.M.), although a few preferred the now-common early afternoon services.

Funeral by invitation only was not unheard of in Bristol as late as 1890. And it was not uncommon at all for funeral notices to end with an invitation to all relatives and friends to be present for the final rites.

It was almost a universal practice that the bell of the church to which the deceased belonged or attended toll out the death news. At such times town folk made diligent efforts to ascertain who had died and when and where the services were to be held. If the deceased had no church home, then the bell in Burson's Bristol Baptist Church usually pealed out the sad tidings. There must have been a lot of unchurched people in the city, for Walter Ross, the toller at Burson's church, once said that in twenty-five years he had tolled for over three hundred persons. Too, it was a custom to toll the bell as a body was carried into a church for the service, as well as when the body was carried out.

If the deceased were a prominent, well-respected citizen, the town turned out very near en masse for the service. And even a service for someone insignificant or unknown was usually well-attended. There were some in the town who seldom missed a funeral, whether friend or relative, known or unknown. Among these was "Uncle" Will Smith, who often left a construction job and, still in his work clothes, would slip in and sit near the back of whatever church held the funeral, listening to the proceedings in respectful silence. Isaac A. Nickels of the Nickels House Hotel and the Silver Plate Saloon was another citizen who seldom missed the funeral of the known or unknown. And the beloved Mrs. L. F. (Harriett) Johnson claimed to have attended every funeral in the town from 1857 until three years before her death. (She died in 1916 at the age of 98.)

If the deceased were the operator of a local business, many business firms would close for the service. It is said that virtually the entire town closed for the funeral of Joseph R. Anderson, the town's founder. As a symbol of mourning, W. W. James draped an entire bolt of black cloth across and around the porch posts of his store. The draping was left in place for a week after

Anderson's funeral. And instead of the customary white flowers that now adorn the doorways of the dead, a black ribbon then served the same purpose.

Then as now, certain ministers in the town were most in demand as funeral speakers. By far the most popular of these were Rev. David Sullins and Rev. George A. Caldwell. Both ministers were often called upon to conduct the final rites of people they did not know, but whose families were aware of the ability of both these venerable ministers to give expression to the deepest sentiments of the mourners. Both were adept at saying the appropriate and inspiring thing, even over the remains of some of the town's most corrupt characters.

It fell the lot of Rev. Caldwell to conduct the funeral of the notorious Pocahontas Hale, who had long operated the town's largest brothel. The funeral was held in Burson's church before a capacity crowd, and Rev. Caldwell waxed eloquent on the text, "Woman, where are thine accusers?" At least one person still living in Bristol until a few years ago had not forgotten that sermon, and could quote long passages from it.

A few other funeral texts are known. The funeral of J. Wheeler Thomas, of the famous Thomas House Hotel, was preached at the Main Street Methodist Church (later State Street) on Monday, February 9, 1873. The largest known funeral crowd to that time heard Dr. David Sullins "reach a sublime height" as he expounded the text, "There shall be no night there." His words must have moved them, because a local editor commented that "some of the town's most astute and dignified businessmen were weeping unashamedly before the minister closed his profound message." Dr. Sullins also spoke at the funeral of Jesse Aydlotte, an early town builder and a founder of the State Street Methodist Church, on the text, "And he fell asleep and was gathered to his fathers." Aydlotte's funeral was held on August 31, 1875, in the church he helped to found.

Perhaps the funeral text used for Dr. John G. Pepper's service was especially fitting. It may be remembered that his death had been caused by a fall. Dr. Caldwell did a masterful job on the passage, "Know ye not that there is a Prince, a great man fallen in Israel." The Pepper funeral was held at the First Presbyterian Church, Tuesday, February 9, 1875. The text was engraved on Pepper's monument and is clearly legible today.

It is likely that the largest funeral ever held in Bristol prior to 1900 was that of Joseph R. Anderson, held in the First Presbyterian Church on May 20, 1888. Folks arrived at the church at least three hours before the service, hoping to get a choice seat. An hour before the scheduled service, the church was full; and folks were trying to take positions on the outside near the windows so that they might hear what they expected to be the crowning effort of Dr. Caldwell's funeral orations. They were not disappointed. No more appropriate text could he have chosen for the town's founder than "He hath built for us a city." It is said that a shortened version of this was given at the cemetery, where many who could not gain entry to the church had gone and awaited the final rites.

Other local ministers who were much sought for funeral services included Rev. J. D. Tadlock and Rev. J. A. Wallace. Occasionally Major Z. L. Burson was called upon for the same purpose. Burson was often asked to preside over the services for the town's lowly and always came through with something fitting. Rev. Kincannon of the First Baptist Church was also a gifted minister who would "well deliver beauty for ashes."

But what may be said of all of them is that they did not preach by the clock. No fifteen minute funerals in those days! There were always several hymns, often previously requested by the deceased, long prayers, and then a sermon which seldom lasted less than an hour. In 1953 an old gentleman showed me an "ancient" watch by which he said his father had timed the funeral sermon for J. Wheeler Thomas. It had taken Dr. Sullins an hour and thirty-two minutes to fully describe the joys of the nightless abode.

THE MOURNERS

Grief was just as real to the early Bristol pioneers as it is to the citizens of today, perhaps more so. Grief and mourning certainly received greater public display in those days, and newspapers often commented on the matter. Those in mourning dressed in black, sometimes for a year or longer, and guarded closely against any display of levity. They would not attend parties and such and often kept themselves more or less homebound. A bereaved spouse dared not remarry until at least a year had passed, preferably two or three, although occassionally some did.

L. F. Johnson, a pioneer merchant and leader, died in 1904. His widow, the beloved and highly respected Harriett Johnson, went into perpetual mourning. She lived twelve years longer, but always wore her mourning clothes, including a long black veil. And she was careful to observe all other unwritten rules. In the early 1990s there were two or three persons still living who could recall seeing her on the porch of her home at 203 Solar, or slowly walking on the street nearby, or perhaps making a somber call on a friend. She was always dressed in black.

James P. Lewis was a master bricklayer who also served as an officer of the law on the Tennessee side of town. He lived north of what is now called the pink house, east of Anderson Park. He had a precious little golden-haired girl (his only daughter), who was the light and joy of his life. She was constantly at his side, wanting to be with him so much that she sometimes cried and begged to go wherever he was working. He frequently gave in and took her, and once there she would play contentedly for hours. When she was not with him, she was always waiting for his return. He once told a friend that his spirit lifted when he saw little Becky running to meet him.

Rebecca Jane Lewis died October 4, 1879, aged five years, eight months, and twelve days. Not long after her funeral, the *Bristol News* reported that Mr. Lewis was so sick with grief that he had taken to his bed. This grief never left him.

For eleven more years he labored in the building trade, but his sorrow remained heavy and his depression almost unbearable. His grief manifested itself in many ways; for example, two years after he lost Becky he took a contract to do the brickwork on the Pickens house next door. At night, unable to sleep, he would arise and lay brick by moonlight. He died March 2, 1891, and those who knew him best had no doubt that he died of a broken heart.

The well-known and respected Dr. Matthew Moore Butler spent the last thirty-four years of his life in perpetual grief over the death of his twenty-month-old son, whom he believed he could have saved had he been present. The doctor had gone to a fraternal convention in Nashville, Tennessee; and as he returned home a friend had persuaded him to stop in Chattanooga for two or three days. During that period his son became desperately ill, but since his family did not know where to reach him, they could not send the doctor a message. Fowler noted in the *Bristol News* that he arrived home only in time to see the baby die.

Dr. Butler always blamed himself for this tragedy, and apparently he never saw a light moment from that day forward. Sadness and depression were his constant companions. Every Sunday afternoon, rain or shine, he walked from his home on Anderson Street to the East Hill Cemetery to visit the grave of his son. Those who knew him well said that he always had a "hard time of it" when he was called upon to attend sick children. He died in 1913 and was buried beside the child he mourned for so many years.

In May 1871 a well-dressed, affluent family named Beasley registered at the Virginia House Hotel. A doctor, Beasley had come by train from Fayette County, Georgia, with his wife and daughter on a sad but special mission, which would soon become clear.

The next morning Dr. Beasley asked for directions to the City Cemetery (now East Hill). Mrs. J. G. Wood, whose husband operated the Virginia House, offered to accompany the family to show them the way. Once there, Dr. Beasley produced a diagram of the cemetery and began a search of the rows of Confederate soldiers. After a while he stopped at a certain grave and said, in a low voice, "Here he is." Whereupon the three locked arms about one another and (according to Mrs. Wood) wept, wailed, and lamented for several minutes. Mrs. Wood later said she never forgot this incident, and was troubled for years by recurring dreams about it.

Before Dr. Beasley left town, he had W. A. Ray, a local monument seller, place a marker at his son's grave. Alhough its inscription is barely legible, with persistence one can still read:

JAMES BEASLEY
Born in Fayette County, Ga., June 8, 1842
Died in Bristol, Tennessee, April 5, 1863
"Oh, my son, my son!"
2nd Samuel 15:33

Not all the bereaved of Bristol went into mourning, however. A woman on Spencer Street, who was constantly battling with her second husband, certainly did not regret his passing. Evidently some bitterness, if not outright hatred, existed between the two, and when the husband died his wife did not attend the funeral. Then, as Mr. Bickley's hearse passed their home on the way to East Hill Cemetery, she remarked to a neighbor, "The old devil is dead and gone and won't be back here any more. Glory be!"

In an 1899 incident, two sons-in-law did not appear to be in mourning as they attended the graveside rites of their mother-in-law in East Hill Cemetery. Evidently they were both concerned about an estate that was yet to be settled, because a fistfight broke out between them, ending only when one pushed the other into the open grave, where he landed flat atop the casket of the deceased!

THE LOW COST OF DYING

Compared to today's funeral costs, early Bristolians could be buried cheaply. The oldest available records on this matter concern the funeral of Mastin J. Ayers, who died on May 10, 1857. G. H. Mattox, the new undertaker in town, charged $12.50 for Mastin's coffin; burial clothes were bought from Henry Rosenheim for $5.50. The same Mr. Mattox charged $18.00 for a coffin for Campbell Galliher in 1870.

When Jackson Worley died in 1875, his coffin, bought from H. A. Bickley, cost $15.00. His burial clothes, bought from J. R. Anderson & Company, came to $7.75.

There is the record of a man buried in 1883 whose clothes cost more than his casket. The casket was sold by McNeil for $17.50; the burial clothes were bought from J. M. Barker and Company for $19.25.

There are records of local carpenters having made full-size coffins for as little as $2.00. The big hearted H. A. Bickley often set his price according to one's ability to pay. One of the most touching entries in his account book is, "Walnut coffin and brass name plate for little Flora Davis, aged three, $2.50.''

Mrs. L. M. Rhea had something of a status funeral. She was buried in a satin-lined metal casket, and A. S. McNeil's receipt for it, dated January 15, 1889, shows that the total charge was all of $35.00! Another McNeil receipt shows that a complete funeral, including coffin, clothes, and the use of a hearse came to a total of only $25.00.

Costs had increased somewhat by the closing years of the century, but even then a fine funeral cost around $40.00.

BRISTOL CEMETERIES

When the Town of Bristol was laid out in 1852, there was only one small cemetery within its limits. About 1784 a pioneer traveler, said to have been a young man, died at Ft. Shelby. His family, along with General Shelby, chose as a burial site a gently rolling knoll located to the northeast, within sight of the fort. This knoll was shaded by several giant oaks, and the cemetery that subsequently developed around this pioneer burial was first called Oak Grove. Then by popular usage it became known as the Shelby Cemetery.

Apparently the stately oaks served as more than pleasant shade, for many of its early burials were without the benefit of coffins. Instead, the bodies were covered by a thick layer of fallen oak leaves, then topped off with dirt. General Shelby, whose death occurred about ten years after the beginning of Oak Grove Cemetery, was buried there in this manner.

This first Bristol cemetery was located directly across what later became Fifth Street, just south of its intersection with Shelby; a small portion of its grounds extended westward onto the lot later occupied by the Redeemer Lutheran Church, now the lot of the U. S. Post Office. From the days of Shelby until the founding of Bristol in 1852, the old oak-shaded cemetery lay unkept and unused. Then when the Rev. James King sold the land to his son-in-law for a town site, he reserved the cemetery lot. At about the time Anderson started building on his land, King cleaned it off and fenced in the old burying ground, probably anticipating its use by citizens of the new town. And several people who died in Bristol at the beginning were in fact buried there, including some of the King family. However, the lot was small with no room for expansion, and many people realized that it could not long meet the needs of the local population. After land was set aside for a cemetery on Round Hill (now East Hill), most town burials were done elsewhere.

By 1871 the town was expanding rapidly, pushing hard against the old Oak Grove Cemetery. At that time several of the town's developers envisioned a grand avenue leading from downtown to King College, which was then located on the present site of Beecham Laboratories. Indeed, some developers had plans to erect fine homes along this avenue, and the cemetery lay directly in the path of this "progress." Consequently, town officials proposed moving the bodies to other locations. L. F. Johnson, an alderman, began correspondence with Shelby descendants concerning the plan, and Mayor E. B. McClanahan began negotiations with both the trustees of the Presbyterian Church and members of the King family. Joseph R. Anderson, a King in-law, vehemently opposed the removal of the cemetery, so he sought and won a temporary court injunction against it, granted by Chancellor Smith. During the time of this bitter dispute, the town became sharply divided on the issue; at the height of the controversy, I. C. Fowler, the ever frank and witty editor of the *Bristol News,* offered a suggestion, perhaps facetiously, for the settlement of the affair:

> We have a suggestion to make to our Bristol Town Council. It will help them out of the Fifth Street difficulty. It is a bright idea and we cannot withhold it. Let the Anderson injunction stand, and let General Shelby lie — lie till the crack of doom. Fifth Street we have heretofore called Third, and Third we believe it is, but out of deference to the Council we call it Fifth. It must be graded and there could be nothing nicer than a tunnel under the sleeping Shelby. Leave the unoffending hero where he lies — leave him high in the air. A proper grade of the street would pass far beneath his coffin. To prevent his falling let the tunnel be arched. (March 24, 1871)

The cemetery feud dragged on for over a year, and the city finally proceeded with its plan to remove the bodies. Anderson remained embittered for years over it and spared no words in condemning the mayor and council for what he called the "desecration of a hallowed place." (The mayor at the time was E. B. McClanahan, and the Councilmen were John M. Crowell, Dr. J. G. Pepper, Isaac A. Nickels, and L. F. Johnson.)

By late summer 1871, bodies were being removed. The *Bristol News* of September 1, 1871, gave a morbid but informative account of the process:

> Messrs. J. W. Owen and Dr. Carter on Saturday last removed from the Shelby burying ground the bodies of Cyrus King, his two wives and child. They had been resting there for about 12, 15, and 18 or 20 years. The first wife and the child of the second one were within a brick vault and both coffins were in shape, though only that of the child was strong enough to bear removal. Its remains were yet but little decayed, while the coffin of the mother crumbled at the least touch. The clothing of Cyrus King were yet strong enough to aid materially in removing

the remains. It was buried in a separate brick vault. The second wife was buried in the ordinary way and in this case decay had done its work completely. The bodies were removed to the cemetery [East Hill]. The child had been within the vault for some 18 years.

On Friday, February 22, 1872, Tobias Wade and Nathan Stepp, hired by the Council of Bristol, Tennessee, shoveled up the bones of General Evan Shelby from interment of seventy-seven years. I. C. Fowler, the ever-watchful local editor, lamented the fact that this was done in such a mundane way, without fitting ceremony. Perhaps wisely, the Council had not let out news of when the disinterment was to be carried out. The bones were put into a goods box and locked up in the jail that then stood on Fifth Street.

That afternoon Fowler was admitted to the jail by John Crowell, Town Sergeant. His purpose was to view and measure Shelby's bones. He later commented that the skull did not look to be that of an intelligent man, noting that the forehead seemed very low and retreated greatly. Fowler also noted that Shelby's leg bones together measured slightly over thirty-one inches.

Early on Saturday morning, February 23, 1872, Tobias Wade, Nathan Stepp and John Crowell removed the box of bones from the jail and started toward East Hill Cemetery. An aged daughter of Nathan Stepp, still living in Bristol a number of years ago, always delighted in relating an incident that occurred just before the trio reached the cemetery. Tobias Wade had the box on his shoulder and was walking a little ahead of Crowell and Stepp. Wade, the daughter said, was already a little "juberous" about his burden, so when a bird suddenly alighted on the box and began pecking at the lid, Wade must have thought Shelby was knocking to get out. With a wild yell, he threw the box backward, scattering bones at the feet of his companions and "took out over the ridge toward Beaver Creek like a jack rabbit." It remained for Crowell and Stepp to gather up the remains and make the interment.

The first Shelby burial site in East Hill Cemetery (then called City Cemetery) was just inside and to the right of the western-most gate. Again I.C. Fowler lamented that the old hero had not been given a fitting burial, and he kept the matter before the public over the next three months.

Wednesday, May 20, 1872, was set for decoration day for the City Cemetery, and that decoration had something of an added and unforgettable feature. General Evan Shelby was finally going to be given a public, ceremonious burial; and on Monday, May 18, 1872, his bones were again shoveled up by H. A. Bickley and an assistant. They were taken to Bickley's establishment over by the First Christian Church, where they were "laid in order" in a fine $14.00 walnut casket. Then, on decoration day, Bickley hauled the coffin to the First Presbyterian Church where, within a few feet of the very spot where the old hero had rested for seventy-seven years, Charles

R. Vance and George B. Smith delivered eloquent orations over the long deceased. Following this, Bickley again put on his grand procession to the cemetery, followed by virtually the entire population of the town. Some said that it was difficult for many people to get within hearing distance of the graveside rites. Rev. G. A. Caldwell gave the final prayer over the wreath-covered coffin; and at 11:45 A.M., May 20, 1872, Shelby was lowered to his final resting place.

Even before the last rites were spoken over his remains, work pushing Fifth Street across the old cemetery was progressing. All but one of the great oaks were felled at that time; the lone remaining tree (spared because it stood a little to the west of the street right-of-way) lived until August 6, 1874, when it was sawed down by the same Tobias Wade and Nathan Stepp who had shoveled up the bones of Shelby. The usually "hard as granite" I. C. Fowler admitted that he wept when the last of the Shelby oaks crashed to the ground.

SHELBY'S SLAVE CEMETERY

Another old burial ground that no longer exists was Shelby's slave cemetery, referred to as the "Grove Cemetery" in a few old writings or (in one instance) "the cemetery in the grove." This little plot of land lay just outside the southern wall of the fort, at the present south corner of Rose and Seventh Streets (now a vacant lot). Several slaves were buried there, and it is said that the cemetery also contained the bodies of two friendly Indians and an Indian child. After Rev. James King moved to a place later called English Grove on Beaver (within sight of this cemetery), he buried two or three slaves there, including old Nancy, who was the King household cook for several decades.

In 1871 John G. King, who inherited the land that included the old cemetery, laid off the area in lots and streets and sold the lots at auction. Col. Snapp of Blountville bought the lot on which the slave cemetery was located; and a few days after the sale, the *Bristol News* reported that the bodies were being taken out of "the cemetery in the beautiful grove." It is thought that they were moved to what is known as the Tennessee Colored Cemetery just off Weaver Pike in Bristol, Tennessee.

ORDWAY CEMETERY

Ordway is one of the oldest cemeteries within the limits of Bristol, Tennessee. It began on December 21, 1806, with the burial of Sarah Goodson King, wife of Col. James King and mother of the Rev. James King. (Rev. King once owned the land where much of the core of present Bristol is located.) During the remainder of the life of Col. King and for years thereafter, Ordway was sometimes referred to as the cemetery at Holly Bend (the name of the King plantation) or as the Orchard Hill Cemetery. After the death and burial of Col. King in 1825, it became known as the King Cemetery.

Several years later the land was bought and occupied by the Trigg family, and by popular usage it became known as the Trigg Cemetery. It took its present name around the turn of the century, when the Ordway Manufacturing Company built a plant on the former Holly Bend plantation.

FLAT HOLLOW CEMETERY

In the mid-1830s a slave cemetery was started in a place then known as Flat Hollow, which is now the northeast corner of Oakview and Buckner Streets. The Rev. James King had an elderly slave who had been relieved of field service but who was still able to carry water from the big spring at the foot of the hill below the King mansion (at the back of what is now the Boswell Insurance Agency). This woman habitually put down her water pails and paused to rest under a huge poplar tree that stood about halfway between the spring and the King mansion. One day she did not return and was found sitting there, leaning back against the massive tree. For some reason a site up by the old stage road was chosen for her burial, and it was the beginning of Flat Hollow Cemetery. Slaves from both the King and Susong families were buried there.

After the Civil War this cemetery became the burying ground for the black population of the Virginia side of Bristol. Finally the Colored Cemetery Association was formed to have oversight of the Flat Hollow Cemetery. In 1891 the trustees of this association were J. W. Davis, David Jefferson, Robert Morrison, and Jesse Green. On June 10, 1891, J. W. Owen and his wife (a King descendant) sold the land upon which the cemetery was located to the Bristol Land Company. But of course this company could not legally build on the cemetery proper and consequently offered five acres of land at the end of Piedmont in exchange for the one and thirteen hundredth acre burial plot. This offer was accepted by the trustees, and in time all the bodies were moved from Flat Hollow to what is now known as the Citizen's Cemetery.

SUSONG CEMETERY

Susong Cemetery in Bristol, Virginia, began on Christmas day, 1818, with the burial of Margaret Baggs Susong, the forty-seven year old wife of Jacob Susong. Bristol old-timers have told tales about how it was a "strange day," with alternating sunshine, snow showers, and thunder and lightning; many of the more superstitious professed grave concern about the "unusual manifestation of the elements."

The Susong family arrived in the area in 1794, on the day that General Evan Shelby was buried. They set up homestead on Baker's Creek, locating their "mansion house" about where Eckerd's Drug Store now stands in the Little Creek Shopping Mall. (The old homestead spring now forms pools of water near the main entry of the mall parking lot.)

Jacob Susong had chosen a site on the ridge behind his home for a family cemetery, and that is where he buried his wife that strange Christmas day. Other members of the family were later buried there, and it finally became a public cemetery.

SHARETT CEMETERY

On a long Sunday afternoon in late April, 1837, Nathan Worley and his wife, Susannah, took a stroll around their farm to choose a place for a family graveyard. In the course of the afternoon they settled on a site located on a rounded hill above the Beaver Creek valley. At that time several wild cherry trees crowned the top of the hill. The Worleys could not have known that one week from that day a promising son, Nathan Worley, Jr., would be buried there. However, that is what happened. The lad grew ill and sickened toward the end of the week, then he died and was buried the following Sunday. Some old land deeds refer to the burying ground as the Cherry Hill Cemetery, but later it is called Worley Cemetery. A Sharett family eventually bought the adjoining property, and the present name was taken. It was slow in expansion, but is now a sizeable graveyard.

RUTHERFORD FAMILY CEMETERY

A few sunken graves with no markers and the remnants of a picket fence, all lying under a thick growth of briars, brush and weeds, are all that is left of the Rutherford family cemetery. The site is located a few yards northeast of the stop light where Georgia Avenue and Williams Street join East State Street, just to the south of the abandoned concrete water tank that is still there. Leona Street runs by immediately to the east of this cemetery. The old Rutherford family early owned much of the land in that area, and it is thought that their homesite was nearby. There are a few graves just to the southwest of the Rutherford plot, two or three of which are marked. No date has been established for the beginning of the Rutherford burying ground, but it was likely in use long before the Civil War. A member of the Rutherford family who is long dead once recalled that as a youth he had plowed corn in the eastern half of what is now the East Hill Cemetery.

ST. ANNE'S CATHOLIC CEMETERY

St. Anne's Catholic Cemetery dates from 1883. When it was established it was considered to be far out of town. It was reached by a rough, narrow, rocky road that led up from Flat Hollow to its present back edge. The earliest burials in this cemetery were members of the Flannery, Byrne, Harmeling, Burke, Long, Shea, Powers, and Burns families.

OTHER BURIAL SITES

The story of a black infant who was buried on the lot where the Lee Street Baptist Church now stands is related at the beginning of this chapter. This grave was never marked. The child's parents left Bristol soon after he died, and the grave was soon lost. Within a few years a house which still stood until several years ago was erected on the site. Later the aforementioned church was built there.

During the Civil War a mother and her child, a boy four or five years old, lived in a little house that stood on the southwest corner of Eighth and Main (State) Streets. The husband was serving in the Confederate Army. In the late winter or early spring of 1863, the child sickened and died, and the distraught mother buried him at the edge of the garden behind her home. The father fell at Gettysburg, and shortly thereafter the mother returned to her family in Wytheville. With the passing years the grave faded out and became overgrown, and eventually a commercial building was erected on the lot. The grave now lies under (or immediately behind) the First Tennessee Bank.

It is said that there is a Whittaker family graveyard somewhere in the Fairmount section of Bristol, Tennessee, but no sign remains of it. Development has doubtless spread over it. A few years ago a descendant of this family came here, searching for it.

Although the Mountain View Cemetery largely developed after 1900 and its history is beyond the scope of this book, there is, at its extreme lower side, a small family lot with a few burials made in the 1880s and '90s. The family name is Dunlap, and it is likely that the lot is a part of the Dunlap home farm.

THE EAST HILL CEMETERY

The prominence on which the oldest part of this cemetery developed was long known as Round Hill. In the earliest days of Bristol and Bristol-Goodsonville, certain men of both towns sometimes gathered there, in a heavily wooded area, to fight gamecocks. Thus, by popular usage, the knob became known as Rooster Hill. However, this name was not dignified enough for a graveyard, so after burials began the area again became known as Round Hill. The cemetery kept this name until well after the war years.

BEGINNING OF EAST HILL CEMETERY

According to information passed down through the Owen, King, and Anderson families, this cemetery began with the burial of a child named Nellie

East Hill Cemetery began in 1857 with the burial of little Nellie Gaines, aged five years. The site was recently marked by the Bristol Preservation Society.

Gaines in late February of 1857. As the story goes, Col. Samuel E. Goodson had a tenant farmer named Gaines living on his upper farm. The Gaineses had three or four children, among them a five-year-old named Nellie. The family planned to move to Texas; and just before their journey began, little Nellie sickened and died. The parents could hardly bear the thought of burying her on the farm where they lived, knowing that in time the grave would be neglected and lost. Col. Goodson heard of their fears. He suggested that burial be made at a site that he was planning to set aside as a burying ground for Bristol-Goodson. He believed that in the years ahead the planned cemetery would grow and be cared for by the local citizens. The parents agreed and gratefully accepted his offer.

As the solemn procession climbed the knob from the Williams Street side, the wagon driver cut a poplar stick to use as a horse prodder. Then when the burial was completed, he stuck this stick in the ground as a marker at the head of the child's grave. A warm, wet spring soon enveloped the land that year, causing the stick to sprout. Over time it became a giant tree and stood until October 1, 1977, when it was blown down in a windstorm.

On April 30, 1860, Col. Goodson sold a tract of land that covered most of the west side of Round Hill. In the deed he reserved a two-acre tract for a cemetery; but somehow he never deeded it to the town, as was his apparent intention. Over the next few years, several local gentlemen talked of buying the tract, but nothing was done until May 22, 1868, when L. F. Johnson paid Col. Goodson one hundred dollars and received the cemetery deed. This document, recorded in Deed Book 27, Page 332, was notarized by Valentine Keebler, a local merchant and civic leader. The next day, May 23, 1868, Johnson deeded the two-acre tract in trust to the Ladies Memorial Association of Bristol ''in consideration of respect for our Southern dead, and for the accommodation of the citizens of Bristol-Goodson.'' The Memorial Association, apparently already then operating, was made up of the following pioneer women of Bristol:

> Melinda King Anderson, wife of Bristol's Founder, J. R. Anderson
> Jane A. Wilbar
> Carrie E. Stover
> Marietta Moore
> Bettie M. Robinson
> Mary B. Coleman, wife of Bristol's first druggist, Dr. R. M. Coleman
> Anne E. Johnston
> Margaret Rohr, wife of Philip Rohr, early civic leader
> Elizabeth Moore
> Keziah Fowler, wife of I. C. Fowler, local newspaper editor
> Isabella Pepper
> Levicy Campbell
> Mary D. York, wife of local attorney, U. L. York
> Harriett E. Johnson, wife of L. F. Johnson, who bought the tract

These women were to keep the cemetery enclosed and the soldiers' graves in good condition, and they had the privilege of selling eighteen-by-twenty-foot lots for burial purposes but nothing else. The money received from such sales was to be used to keep the cemetery in good repair, enclosed, and beautiful. The price was then $20.00 per lot.

L. F. Johnson, his wife, and many of the women of that association now rest in this cemetery. From the first interment in 1857 until Johnson's gift, many were buried in original Round Hill area, including soldiers of the Civil War who had died in local Confederate hospitals. Within a short time the cemetery had grown beyond the original two-acre tract; and when Col. Goodson died in early 1870, he was interred far down the eastern slope, well beyond the limits of the original site. Others near him were buried about the same time. By 1890 the eastern boundary had reached the present driveway leading in from East State Street.

To the north the cemetery crept down the jungle-like hillside toward

Williams Street; some of that section may have been taken by possession or usage rather than by deed. A Potter's Field was set aside in this area, for in a growing town like Bristol, with its many homeless drifters, one was needed.

The principal gate moved with the expansion of the cemetery. The first main gate was from Main (State) Street, at the extreme western edge of the old cemetery. Then around 1870 this gate was moved to a point over a little rise, about even with the Joseph Anderson lot. The main entry was fixed at its current location well after 1900.

MOVING IN - MOVING OUT

In some respects the East Hill Cemetery has had an unusual number of move-ins and move-outs, including General Shelby's two reburials mentioned earlier. A careful observer will note that several of the gravestones mark deaths which occurred before the area became a burial ground in 1857. These are people who were first interred in other cemeteries and then moved to East Hill, marker and all.

Such is the case with Dr. B. F. Zimmerman, the town's first physician, and his son, as well as Cyrus King, his two wives and one child. Sarah Ann Anderson, the daughter of Joseph and Melinda King Anderson, died at Blountville on May 6, 1853, and about twenty-five years later she, too, was moved to the Anderson lot in the City Cemetery.

James O. Wood, father of the five prominent Wood brothers of Bristol, was buried at Estillville (now Gate City), Virginia, in 1874; then he was moved to the City Cemetery in 1878. Capt. George Davidson, who is said to have fired the first Confederate gun at the first Battle of Manassas, died in early March of 1881 and was also buried at Estillville; however, his son, who lived at Blountville, had him taken up and moved to the East Hill Cemetery a few days after his original interment. An item in the January 21, 1873, *Bristol News* says that the remains of Mr. John T. Wilbar had been reinterred in the town cemetery; the place of his first burial was not given.

Most move-outs occurred after 1900, but two notable removals come within the time frame of this volume. About 1896 a lad of fifteen ran away from home in Ashe County, North Carolina, and came to Bristol. His reason for leaving and why he chose Bristol as his destination is not known.

He was sick when he arrived and was taken in by the Ed Faidley family. Although he was questioned repeatedly, he would not reveal any information concerning his family or his origins and died within a week. He was buried in the Hines family lot in East Hill Cemetery (Mrs. Faidley was a

Hines and could not bear the thought of someone so young being buried in the Potter's Field.)

About a week later the boy's widowed mother and his two older brothers arrived in Bristol searching for him. Upon learning that he was dead and buried, they had him exhumed, loaded him into their wagon, and hauled him back to the family graveyard near her home.

A few years ago your author was privileged to read the history of the dead boy's family. It told of their long journey back to Ashe County and described how fires were lit at campsites along the trail in order to frighten wild animals and keep them away from the coffin.

Because another mother could not bear the thought of leaving her child's remains at Bristol, another unusual removal occurred. "Daddy" Thomas thought the family name was Yelton and that the event took place about 1877. Whatever the exact date, it is a moving story. It seems that a little girl died and was buried in East Hill Cemetery a few months before the family made a decision to move to southern Missouri. However, the mother would not leave Bristol without taking the remains of the little girl. Consequently, the body was exhumed, sealed in a metal casket by H.A. Bickley, loaded into a wagon, and taken along. ("Daddy" Thomas thought they settled in Bakersfield, Missouri, which is likely, since there is a place by that name in Ozark County.)

BEAUTIFICATION AND UPKEEP

Some folks living in Bristol as recently as 1953 could remember when East Hill Cemetery was filled with flowers and shrubs. Roses ran everywhere, peonies abounded, jonquils outlined many a lot, and flowering shrubs, such as snowball, forsythia, and wedding wreath, spread wider and grew taller. A spring rarely passed that dozens of new plants were not added to the grand display of perennial beauty.

For years the custom was for the townsfolk to gather at the cemetery on a Saturday in early May to clean off the grounds and make ready for the annual memorial service. On the designated day there was usually a great turnout of citizens, young and old, rich and poor, who for long hours cut brush and grass, straightened stones, and repaired lot fences. The late Minnie Faidley Bridgemon once told of seeing the very aristocratic Mrs. Harriett Johnson pulling tall weeds from her family lot and of the beloved Melinda King Anderson, aided by a servant, planting roses at the graves of her two young children.

Some local businessmen not only worked faithfully at cemetery clean-ups; they even hired others to aid in the task. W. W. James is known to have allowed some of his debtors to earn credit on their accounts in this manner.

Aunt Minnie recalled that lunches were taken by the workers and eaten in the shade of a giant cherry tree that stood just south of the John G. King family lot.

Some have recalled that the cemetery was then full of trees, most of them set to shade family lots. In 1892 J. H. Wood brought a maple sprout from Washington Spring, Virginia, and planted it in his family lot to shade the graves of his wife and children. It is now a large, beautiful tree. (Your author and and several others were most thankful for its shade when the town founder's monument plaque was dedicated on July 10, 1988. The sun that day was bright, and the temperature was nearly 100 degrees!) When Mr. Wood returned on visits after he moved to Washington, D.C., he would often go and sit for hours under that tree.

During long summers the cemetery grew over again, and autumn usually found it so overgrown that the local newspaper called its condition disgraceful. Editor Fowler often commented on its sad condition, once noting that a part of the fence was down and that hogs and cattle were running loose all over the "sacred soil." Hogs, he said, were rooting around and weakening the bases of the monuments, and cattle had pushed down several lot fences. And if that were not enough, he added, vandals had done much damage, folks were stealing flowers from the graves, and lewd persons were slipping in for immoral purposes. (The good editor was probably right. Great improvements were then many years away.)

MEMORIAL SERVICES

For years it was the custom to conduct an annual memorial service for the town's dead. A crowd would assemble at the First Baptist Church and, laden with wreaths and bouquets, march up the hill to the cemetery. This service was usually held in late May or very early June; the date seems to have been set year by year. At the cemetery they assembled under the giant cherry tree near the King Lot and heard mournful sermons by the town's clergy or (sometimes) an eloquent address by a local orator, often a lawyer. In 1875 editor Fowler, urging the townsfolk to attend the annual decoration, closed his preachment with a bit of poetry:

Their spirits wrap the dusky mountains,
Their memory sparkles in each fountain.
The meanest rills, the mightiest river,
Rolls mingling with their fame forever.

And your author asks you, his reader: Could Bristol not have such memorial observances again?

MYSTERY CEMETERIES

In one of her writings on early Bristol history, Mrs. Wirt Carrington Johnson tells of an old Buchanan Cemetery that contained the bodies of Revolutionary soldiers and was located within sight of downtown Bristol. Her comments have given rise to much speculation among local historians. In all honesty it must be said that there are some aspects of the matter that do not harmonize with other information, and for that reason this writer will let the matter rest. Perhaps in time the mystery will be unraveled.

Remains of the oldest cemetery of all were unearthed in the early 1870s as the foundation was being dug for Temperance Hall, which once stood near the southwest corner of Fifth and Shelby. Evidence of an old Indian burial ground was uncovered at that time, so the young man resting under the giant oaks in 1784 was not alone after all.

MONUMENTS

The first grave marker placed in what later became the town of Bristol was most likely the iron slab placed over the grave of General Evan Shelby. It is said that this marker was made at the King iron works at Holly Bend plantation. Soon after the beginning of Bristol, Thomas W. Farley, one of the town's earliest settlers, became the local agent for the Caddess Monument Company of Lynchburg, Virginia, and placed some of the earliest markers in the East Hill Cemetery. He is known to have hauled the heavier ones from the depot to this cemetery in a two-wheeled cart pulled by a single oxen named Buck. Some of the very small and light ones were carried there on his shoulder. There was also a marble shop in Abingdon during the 1850s that may have supplied some of the early grave stones for several local cemeteries.

About 1860 A. T. M. Provence set up Bristol's first monument works. His business was located on at the southeast corner of Main (State) and Second Streets, on property rented from Joseph R. Anderson. Provence closed during the war years but reopened at the same location in 1866. Business must have been slow or money scarce, for a year or two later he was advertising that he would cheerfully accept farm produce as payment for grave markers. A story handed down through the Parrott family tells of a marker bought from Provence and paid for with a calf and a pig. It may truly be said that he ate up the profits!

Provence was followed closely by W. A. Ray, who eventually had a thriving marble works on a lot across Main from the First Baptist Church. Mr. Ray operated there for several decades and within the memory of some people who are yet living. In those days it was a common practice for monument makers to inscribe their names in discreet, small letters near the bottom of

**After helping build the town, Uncle Will Smith built his own
monument, which stands near the old gate in East Hill Cemetery.**

the stone, as a subtle form of advertising. Both the names of Provence and
Ray, as well as the earlier Caddess Monument Company of Lynchburg, may
be seen on stones in East Hill Cemetery. The earliest monuments were usually
small, thin, and almost exclusively of white marble. Monuments became increasingly taller, heavier, and more elaborately carved through the 1870s
and '80s, reaching the height of grandeur in the 1890s. Those were the years
of much ornamentation and statuary work, and some prime examples of the
period still stand in this old Bristol cemetery. The soaring obelisk style of
monument also became popular during that period. The graves of several
early and prominent local citizens are marked by this type of monument,
including J. R. Anderson, John Crowell, James P. Lewis, Isaac A. Nickels,
W. S. Minor, Cyrus King, and others.

There are a few examples of the unique hollow bronze monument in East Hill Cemetery. Among those who chose this type of monument, which even then was very expensive, were W. W. James, Ben L. Dulaney and Hal H. Haynes. The hollow bronze monument had to be ordered from Baltimore and took some time for delivery.

In the very earliest days a decent marker could be had for $12.50. Very small ones sometimes sold for as little as $6.00. Long after the Civil War was over, a very fine stone could be bought for $25.00; $50.00 would designate the affluent of the town. There were some who chose to go even further and put an ornamental iron fence around their burial plots. Many such fences were made and erected by the Dixon and Smith Foundry, located on Fourth Street at the present site of the S. P. Rutherford Company. Others settled for the less expensive picket fences, but not a one of either kind remains today.

Some went even further in honoring their dead. Around 1880 the father of little Nellie Gaines returned to Bristol from Texas to erect a small house over his daughter's grave. He told the carpenter whom he hired that he and his wife, by then an invalid, had wanted to cover the grave ever since they had left. After the little house was completed, Mr. Gaines surrounded it with a picket fence and hired G. B. Smith to make a photograph of the finished work, so that his wife might be able to see what had been done. Many persons still living remember both the house and fence, but time has done its work; today not a trace remains of either.

Bibliography - Chapter Twenty

Anderson, Joseph R. Paper, circa 1880.

Bachelor, Ann. Memoirs (unpublished), 1935-1937.

Blackley, Mrs. Herman. Notes.

Bristol News. Various issues, 1857-1900.

Faidley, Ed. As told to a daughter, Mrs. Minnie Bridgeman.

Johnson, L. F. Notes (unpublished), 1893.

Owen, Revely. Notes, containing much information given to her father by Col. Samuel E. Goodson.

Phillips, V. N. (Bud). Interviews with older Bristol citizens, 1953-1956.

Taylor, Hattie King. Paper. (Later owned by Rhea Anderson.)

Washington County, Virginia. Chancery Records, 1854-1900.

Washington County, Virginia. Deed Books, 1854-1900.

Mrs. Joseph R. Anderson, called the pioneer mother of Bristol, still lived in 1900 and lingered on until 1908.

EPILOGUE

From open meadow and rutted cow trails to busy streets and thriving businesses; from near-silence to the buzz and hum of a busy town; from the creak and rattle of the lurching stage coach to the roar of the rushing train; so it was with Bristol in the brief forty-eight year span from 1852 to 1900. A place that had been known to so few such a short time ago now had fame that reached across the nation. Where once only the feet of plowmen, herdsmen, and playing children had trod, throngs now hurried along busy streets. By 1900 Bristol had indeed become a magnet that drew its sons and daughters from both near and far; many came by choice while others came out of circumstance and necessity; but whatever their reasons for coming, most loved the place of their abode. To her nearly ten-thousand inhabitants, Bristol was no longer just a name; it was the hallowed name of home.

And among those thousands who then crowded the meadow and surrounding hills still dwelled some of the pioneer settlers of the town. Although most of their fellow pioneers had already made that final journey up to the East Hill Cemetery, some still lingered as do the last blossoms of a long summer, even more loved and appreciated because they, too, would soon be laid low by the wintry blasts of age and infirmity. Yet a few of them would survive for another decade or more, living to tell their great grandchildren how a vast, green, flourishing meadow had been covered by a city. Sadly, some who remembered the pure tranquil breezes that once blew over that budding village even realized they had lived to inhale the polluted air of progress: the smoke that poured from the chimneys of numerous thriving industries.

What, in 1852, had been only the dream of a young Blountville merchant became a reality in greater measure, perhaps, than he or anyone else could have imagined. Yet in 1900 there were those dreaming of an even greater Bristol to come. As the new century dawned, the surveyors' stakes had already been driven and streets already laid out across adjoining fields and woods, marking the growth of a city that could no longer be contained within its original boundaries. More than ninety years later, many of those dreams, too, have been realized. Places then far out in the country are now inside the city, and expansion still pushes relentlessly against current boundries, on toward ever more distant fields and denser woods. Dreamers live and die, but the dream lives on.